PIMLICO

573

EDWIN LUTYENS

Jane Ridley is Lutyens's great-granddaughter, and this biography was authorised by his last surviving daughter, Mary, who died in 1999. Jane Ridley has read over 5,000 letters between Ned Lutyens and his wife Emily, and she travelled to New Delhi and Washington to research this lively book, which paints a devastating yet entertaining picture of Edwardian society.

Jane Ridley is an historian at Buckingham University where she teaches a course on biography. Her previous books include *The Letters of Edwin Lutyens* (co-edited with Clayre Percy), *The Letters of Arthur Balfour and Lady Elcho* (co-edited with Clayre Percy) and *The Young Disraeli* described by Andrew Marr in the *Independent* as 'a rich and thoughtful biography which may . . . become the definitive one', and by John Grigg in the *Sunday Telegraph* as 'a major new biography . . . it is difficult to see her work being superseded'.

Praise for *Edwin Lutyens*

'This biography is written by his descendant, but Jane Ridley's understanding of her great-grandfather determinedly avoids bias, dispassionately stating Lutyens's ruthless ambition alongside his remarkable achievements . . . Jane Ridley is particularly good at bringing Lutyens's houses alive to the layman . . . uncompromising.' Simon Blow, *Independent on Sunday*

'It is a story which his great-granddaughter, Jane Ridley, now tells with spirit and humour.' Peter Lewis, *Daily Mail*

'A densely researched book . . . Captivating.' Brian Case, *Time Out*

'Illuminated and made compelling by often unexpected flashes of wit and insight.' Andrew Lycett, *Literary Review*

'The value of this impressive double biography is that, while recording the near lunatic irresponsibility of her great-grandmother, Ridley still conveys her loveable qualities and growing feminist self-confidence. In the same even-handed manner, she exposes her great-grandfather as a ruthlessly ambitious workaholic and eccentric while writing persuasively, even seductively, about the inspired individuality of his houses.' Timothy Mowl, *Times Literary Supplement*

'Endlessly fascinating and well told.' Hugh Pearman, *Sunday Times*

'Enormously enjoyable as well as informative.' Philip Ziegler, *Daily Telegraph*

'This fine and even-handed book is trenchantly written in crisp, short sentences.' Andrew Saint, *Guardian*

'In a pacy, punchy narrative, she puts together an unforgettable portrait of 'Ned', a complex, inarticulate man who never really grew up.' Hugh Massingberd, *Mail on Sunday*

'Jane Ridley is Lutyens's great-granddaughter, and her ease and familiarity with her subject add greatly to this extraordinary story. She is excellent too, at depicting Lutyens's work . . . Perhaps her finest achievement is in making these two grotesque characters not only believable but in the end almost sympathetic.' Selina Hastings, *Sunday Telegraph*

EDWIN LUTYENS

His Life, His Wife, His Work

JANE RIDLEY

PIMLICO

Published by Pimlico 2003

2 4 6 8 10 9 7 5 3 1

Copyright © Jane Ridley 2002

Jane Ridley has asserted her right under the Copyright, Designs and Patents Act 1988 to be identified as the author of this work

This book is sold subject to the condition that it shall not, by way of trade or otherwise, be lent, resold, hired out, or otherwise circulated without the publisher's prior consent in any form of binding or cover other than that in which it is published and without a similar condition including this condition being imposed on the subsequent purchaser

First published as *The Architect and His Wife: A Life of Edwin Lutyens* in Great Britain by Chatto & Windus 2002

Pimlico edition 2003

Pimlico
Random House, 20 Vauxhall Bridge Road,
London SW1V 2SA

Random House Australia (Pty) Limited
20 Alfred Street, Milsons Point, Sydney,
New South Wales 2061, Australia

Random House New Zealand Limited
18 Poland Road, Glenfield,
Auckland 10, New Zealand

Random House (Pty) Limited
Endulini, 5A Jubilee Road, Parktown 2193, South Africa

The Random House Group Limited Reg. No. 954009
www.randomhouse.co.uk

A CIP catalogue record for this book
is available from the British Library

ISBN 0-7126-6822-5

Papers used by Random House are natural, recyclable products made from wood grown in sustainable forests; the manufacturing processes conform to the environmental regulations of the country of origin

Printed and bound in Great Britain by
Mackays of Chatham plc, Chatham, Kent

Contents

List of Illustrations	vii
Author's Foreword	xi
Chapter 1: 16 Onslow Square 1869–1876	1
Chapter 2: Surrey 1876–1887	21
Chapter 3: Ernest George versus Gertrude Jekyll 1887–1892	43
Chapter 4: Munstead Wood and Barbara Webb 1892–1896	61
Chapter 5: Emily and the Lyttons 1896	79
Chapter 6: Engagement 1896–1897	99
Chapter 7: 29 Bloomsbury Square 1897–1900	117
Chapter 8: *Country Life* 1901–1905	135
Chapter 9: The Turn to Classicism 1906–1910	161
Chapter 10: 'The Shoreless Sea' 1910–1911	187
Chapter 11: India 1912–1913	209
Chapter 12: East and West 1913–1919	233
Chapter 13: 31 Bedford Square 1914–1916	249
Chapter 14: MacSack 1916–1920	273
Chapter 15: The Dolls' House 1920–1924	299
Chapter 16: Emily's Great Adventure 1924–1925	325
Chapter 17: The Elemental Mode 1926–1931	345
Chapter 18: The Torch of Humanism 1931–1937	373
Chapter 19: Lord Cough of Cough 1937–1944	399
Notes	420
Author's Acknowledgements	463
Index	465

For my Mother

List of Illustrations

Colour section

Ned as boy, about twelve. Painted by his father Charles. *On loan to the National Trust at Lindisfarne from Conrad Clarke.*

Sketch of The Hut inscribed 'Abandoned Oct 9th / 1892 / Restored to favour July 16th 93'. *From the Munstead Wood Sketchbook. Pen, pencil and watercolour. Copyright © RIBA.*

Sketch of Plazzoh, the fantasy house that Ned drew for Miss Jekyll in 1893. *From the Munstead Wood Sketchbook. Pen and watercolour. Copyright © RIBA.*

Barbara Webb. *Bourne and Shepherd Photographers.*

Design for the entrance to an imaginary palace called 'Château d'Ease, en Air, sur Fleuve des Rêves'. *From the Castles in the Air Sketchbook. Pencil and watercolour. Copyright © RIBA.*

Le Bois des Moutiers, Varengeville. *Gavin Stamp.*

Tigbourne Court. *Gavin Stamp.*

Deanery Garden. *Gavin Stamp.*

Orchards. *Gavin Stamp.*

Lindisfarne Castle. *Photograph © Colin Dixon, 1995/Arcaid.co.uk.*

Folly Farm. *Gavin Stamp.*

Castle Drogo. *Gavin Stamp.*

Marsh Court. *Lucinda Lambton/Arcaid.co.uk.*

Cartoon bust of 'Lut', made by the staff of his Delhi office (1917). *RIBA, British Architectural Library, Drawings Collection.*

Viceroy's House. View from the gates with the Jaipur Column in the foreground. *Gavin Stamp.*

Viceroy's House. Front portico and dome surrounded by Buddhist *stupa. Bridgeman Art Library, London.*

Garden front of Viceroy's House showing the butterfly garden as it is today. *Pavan Mahatta, New Delhi.*

Indian motifs disciplined by western geometry in the *chujjah* or projecting cornice of Viceroy's House. *Caroline Dawnay.*

Portrait of Lutyens as Master of the Art Workers Guild in 1933, by Meredith Frampton. *Art Workers Guild Collection/Bridgeman Art Library.*

LIST OF ILLUSTRATIONS

First section of black and white photographs
Charles Lutyens, Ned's father. *Candia Lutyens.*
'Three Racehorses' by Charles Lutyens, 1869. Oil. *Lord Palmer.*
Ned's mother, Mary, aged about seventeen. *Charles Lutyens.*
Mary Lutyens as Ned knew her. *Charles Lutyens.*
Miss Jekyll wearing a feathered hat. *From F. Jekyll, Gertrude Jekyll (1934).*
Emily Lytton in Paris, aged about seventeen. *Jane Ridley.*
Design for the Little White House which Ned made for Emily and stored in the casket he gave her as an engagement present. *Private collection.*
Ned with hair plastered down, about 1897. *Candia Lutyens.*
The classical terrace at Homewood, which Ned designed for his mother-in-law, Edith Lytton. *Candia Lutyens.*
Lady Constance Lytton, Emily's suffragette sister. Drawing by Neville Lytton, 1911. *By courtesy of the National Portrait Gallery, London.*
Two interiors which Ned designed for Hudson: at Deanery Garden and Lindisfarne Castle. *Country Life Picture Library.*
Nitya and Krishna at Adyar, after the 'First Initiation' in 1910. *Adam Pallant.*
Mrs Besant arriving at Charing Cross station with Nitya and Krishna in 1911. *Adam Pallant.*

Second section of black and white photographs
Lutyens in 1920. *National Portrait Gallery.*
Emily in 1915. *Adam Pallant.*
Heathcote House, Ilkley. *Country Life Picture Library.*
Summer 1916. Emily with Barbie and Robert at Folly Farm. *Candia Lutyens.*
Emily with Robert at Varengeville. *Candia Lutyens.*
Betty, Ursula and Mary in 1915. *Adam Pallant.*
Lady Sackville, dining al fresco at White Lodge. *Nigel Nicolson.*
Queen Mary's Dolls' House. *Country Life Picture Library.*
Interior of 13 Mansfield Street. *Candia Lutyens.*
Krishnamurti at Pergine in 1924. *Adam Pallant.*
The Midland Bank in Piccadilly. *Gavin Stamp.*
Lutyens at the temporary Cenotaph in 1919. *Jane Ridley.*
Herbert Baker in India, 1913. *Michael Baker.*
Lord Hardinge, Viceroy of India, and eight dead tigers. *Lord Hardinge of Penshurst.*

LIST OF ILLUSTRATIONS

The Delhi Town Planning Committee, surveying from the back of an elephant. *Adam Pallant.*
Garden front of Viceroy's House, 1931. *Jane Ridley/Public Works Department Archive, New Delhi.*
Stone pergola at Viceroy's House. *Jane Ridley/Public Works Department Archive, New Delhi.*
Ned snapped by Ursy at the Parthenon. *Jane Ridley.*
Ned loved entertaining children. *Candia Lutyens.*
Emily on her 80th birthday, with her five children: Ursula, Robert, Barbie, Betty and Mary. *Adam Pallant.*

Drawings in the text
Unless otherwise stated, the illustrations in the text are drawings, sketches, doodles, designs and architectural plans by Edwin Lutyens or the staff in his office. Copyright © RIBA.
Chapter 1: *Survey of London*, vol. 41. Chapter 8: *Mr E.L. Lutyens exhorting his young men.* Caricature by Paul Phipps, 1906. *We are all getting very fat, as there is now so much cake for us to eat at tea.* Illustrated letter from Paul Phipps, sent to Barbie for her birthday from *Your affectionate uncles in the office.* Both copyright © RIBA. Chapter 11: Delhi and its environs; Chapter 12: Plan for New Delhi. Both from Christopher Hussey: *The Life of Sir Edwin Lutyens.* Chapter 19: Menu of a dinner given at the Café Royal in honour of Sir Edwin Lutyens, President of the Royal Academy, dated 24/2/1939. Copyright © RIBA. Menu by Munnings for a dinner in honour of Lutyens at the Arts Club, 30 January 1939, courtesy of Mrs Richard Chester-Master.

Every effort has been made by the publishers to trace the holders of copyrights. Any inadvertent omissions of acknowledgement or permission can be rectified in future editions.

Author's Foreword

Mary Lutyens, who was the youngest daughter of Edwin Lutyens, asked me to write this book. I owe her a very great debt. Thanks to her, I have shared my life for over six years with two remarkable people.

Ned and Emily Lutyens were my great-grandparents.

Great-grandparents, I have learned, are ideal subjects to write about. I knew neither of them. Ned Lutyens died before I was born; and, though I overlapped with Emily, I have no memory of her. I have no axes to grind or grievances to air, at least none that I am conscious of. Nor have I suffered from the problem of 'widow and heirs' – from family members who censor the biography which they authorise.

None of the children of Ned Lutyens is still living: Mary, who was the last surviving child, died in 1999. She gave me several interviews before she died. Mary was nearly ninety, but her memory was needle-sharp, her human curiosity strong as ever. We would sit at a tea table in her house in Maida Vale. I scribbled in the notebook on my lap as she recalled her parents, speaking softly and sometimes stretching thin fingers over her face. Listening to her, it was as if Ned and Emily were alive; she was still caught up in the immediacy of their concerns. I miss our conversations.

Pockets of material kept turning up by serendipity. My grandmother, Ursula Ridley, was another of the daughters of Lutyens, and her letters, stored in 1960s box files in a stable loft, turned out to chronicle her father's wartime years, decline and death: a discovery of the kind which biographers dream about – even though it did mean crashing through yet another deadline with my long-suffering publisher.

Ned and Emily Lutyens wrote more than 5,000 letters to each other over forty-seven years of marriage. Most of these letters now belong to the RIBA. Reading my way chronologically through thirty-odd card-board document boxes bulging with files of letters brought a strange kind of intimacy. As I filled notebook after notebook, transcribing snatches of a lifetime's 'conversation', between husband and wife, I could hear Ned and Emily speak. On my desk I kept a rusting Victorian photograph of Barbara Webb, perhaps Ned's most important friend.

I have enjoyed researching this book more than any book I have written. No one could complain about a project which brought long summer days exploring magical Lutyens houses buried in hidden corners of Surrey and Berkshire. The quest for Lutyens has taken me to wild and exotic places. I have been to Lambay, washed in its waters on an island off the coast of Dublin and, for my money, his most romantic house. In Rome I lectured about Lutyens in the British School, which he designed. This was fairly terrifying, but nothing like as frightening as the lecture that I gave at Lutyens's impressive British Embassy in Washington.

Viceroy's House (now Rashtrapati Bhavan), New Delhi made me proud (yes, I admit it) to be his descendant. I could never have negotiated the perils of Indian travel without the help of my intrepid agent Caroline Dawnay. Nor will I forget the excitement when I realised that deep in the basement of New Delhi's Public Works Department we had stumbled upon an archive of 8,500 Lutyens and Baker drawings which had remained intact since the 1930s.

Ned Lutyens doodled, sketched and designed wherever he was – in taxis, in the bath (he used a child's slate), on menus or tablecloths, on the backs of Emily's letters. He was prodigiously prolific: he designed his first house at nineteen, and the catalogue of his work contains over 600 items. The built material – the work – is overwhelming.

This book does not pretend to be a definitive study of the work. I am not an architect but a historian, and what I have tried to do is to use the work to tell the story of the life.

I soon found that I couldn't write Lutyens's life without writing Emily's too. Her life is even more fully documented in letters than Ned's. From the age of thirteen, when she began an intimate correspondence with a seventy-one-year old clergyman, Emily lived through letters. Some of these she published; others, such as her letters to Judith Blunt and Krishnamurti, have disappeared. As well as thousands of letters to Ned, she wrote daily to her grown-up daughter Ursula.

The story of the marriage of Ned and Emily was first told by Mary Lutyens in the memoir she wrote in 1980. Mary always said that she meant in her book to put her mother's point of view, and she was surprised and a little dismayed when readers sympathised with Ned. Two generations on, the wounds have healed. In this book I have not tried to put one side or the other; I have simply attempted to show how it really was between the Architect and his Wife.

Jane Ridley, London
February, 2002.

Chapter One
16 Onslow Square
1869–1876

Onslow Square, south side: the house where Edwin Lutyens was born.

Dr Merriman arrived punctually, driven up to the stuccoed porch of Number 16 Onslow Square by a coachman with gold braid round his hat. Mary Lutyens gave birth every fifteen months or so, producing babies with such calm assurance that she knew from the progress of her labour pains exactly when to summon the doctor. Now thirty-six, she was experiencing her eleventh confinement.

So far, she had produced nine boys (one of whom was stillborn) and only one daughter. The arrival of a tenth son was a mild disappointment. But Mary Lutyens didn't complain. She adored all her babies. The name of the new one was carefully added to the long list of children inscribed in the leather-bound family Bible with its strange old German script: 'Their eleventh child born March 29th 1869 Edwin Landseer at 16 Onslow Square.'[1]

Captain Charles Lutyens, the child's father, paid Dr Merriman with one of his paintings. He entered his occupation on the baptismal certificate as 'Gentleman', but this revealed little. With his strange German name which no one was quite sure how to pronounce (the first syllable should rhyme with hut), he was a foreign, rather puzzling figure, isolated and eccentric. Now forty, tall, bearded and exceptionally long-legged, he had the athletic bearing of a soldier, but his coloured neckcloth, short jacket and tight checked trousers revealed him as an artist. His paintings, though, fetched stubbornly low prices and his earnings grew far slower than his family. But Charles Lutyens had inherited wealth, and he welcomed the addition of another son in frilly white petticoats to the crowded nursery at Onslow Square.

Edwin Landseer, the most famous painter of the day, was patron, master and teacher of Charles Lutyens, and by giving the baby Landseer's name Charles paid him a compliment, discreetly hinting at sponsorship or support. Landseer was not, as is sometimes said, this baby's godfather.* Edwin's godparents are recorded in the Bible as Mr and Mrs Berniers and Captain E. H. Verney RN, and it was they who accompanied the three-month-old child to the new church, built of startling yellow stone at the end of the square, where Mary Lutyens's

---

*Landseer was godfather to Mary Lutyens's next son, William, born in 1872.

friend, the vicar Capel Molyneux, performed the baptism. But the grizzled, thickset Landseer loomed large over his infant namesake. He believed he was his godfather, and he hovered round the cradle of Edwin Landseer Lutyens like a bad fairy and threatened to abduct him. Aged sixty-six, fogged by alcohol and just recovering from a bout of madness, he offered to adopt the child, although he had already fathered a brood by the Duchess of Bedford. Mary Lutyens refused; she had ten surviving children, and couldn't spare any of them, she said. 'I am like the old woman who lived in a shoe, I have so many children I don't know what to do . . . One more won't make any difference.'[2]

Number 16 Onslow Square was a new house, built in the Italianate style of the 1850s as part of the Victorian development of South Kensington. A tall terraced house on the south side of the square, it was four storeys high, six if you counted the garret and basement, and two bays wide. Tall steps led to the front door through the high, stuccoed porch, flanked by Doric pillars. A grey brick box, iced like a cake with gleaming white stucco and adorned with a crinoline-patterned balcony, the house was too high for its width, giving a top-heavy, claustrophobic feel. It did little to educate Edwin Lutyens's architect's eye; if anything, it was a lesson in what to avoid.

Inside, the house was crowded and untidy. Clutter was swept under beds and chair covers and behind sofas, and Charles's vast canvases were stacked against the walls. 'There's always room,' Mary would say in her soothing Irish way, and somehow there always was. Mary was oblivious to the chaos, but her son Edwin reacted neurotically against it. Loose covers, valances and patterned wallpaper upset his nerves, and the interiors he was to create would be bare and white, sparsely furnished with tightly upholstered chairs.

Upstairs in the nursery, Priscilla the Nannie and Alla the red-haired nursery maid had covered the walls from floor to ceiling with pictures cut out from magazines which they stuck on and varnished, and the children played 'that's you, that's me' pointing to their favourites. The children lived at the top of the house, and all day long they clattered up and down the single staircase. On wet days they rode the rocking horse down the stairs. Most days they played in the garden of the square; it was shadowed by gaunt elm trees, the survivors of an avenue planted in the days when Brompton was a semi-rural suburb, but now the square was fenced round with iron railings, locked with a gate to which each householder had a key. When Nannie lost the key it was a disaster, marked by praying. Sometimes the children walked in a straggling crocodile to the South Kensington museums. Once Nannie thought Edwin was lost, and she ran desperately looking for him up and down Queen's Gate and Exhibition Road, but he was holding her hand all the time. She thought he was one of the others; even Nannie sometimes didn't know which boy was which.[3]

Mary Lutyens gave birth to fourteen children altogether. After Edwin came her second girl, Aileen, then William, and finally Margaret, the baby, born in 1876. Edwin grew up to love the shape of a pregnant woman's figure.

Mary's life revolved round the barn-like church at the end of the square. St Paul's, which had only been consecrated a few years before, was strongly Evangelical, especially after Hanmer Webb-Peploe became vicar in 1876. Mary was Webb-Peploe's devoted acolyte. Wearing the shawl she always wore, fastened in a manner known only to Priscilla the Nannie, she dispensed charity and collected for evangelical causes, earning the contempt of snobbish neighbours including Margaret Warren of Number 67, who wrote in her diary: 'The inhabitants of Onslow Square are very neighbourly and send each other small bits of food and old newspapers. They are all very poor.'[4]

Unlike the rich families on the posh side of the square the Lutyenses had no butler or footman. (One embarrassing time when the children went to one of the smart houses to collect money for the church's Bird's Nest home they confused the butler with Lord So-and-So, he seemed so grand.) Each morning the younger children sat on Mary's bed and read a chapter of the Bible. On Sundays they went twice to church and also to Bible class. The evangelical Hymn Book was imprinted deep in Edwin's consciousness: punning on hymns was second nature to him. *How sweet the name of genius sounds / In the reporter's ear.* The stories of Edwin's childhood were about children who promise to be good, but somehow they forget, and they do all sorts of naughty things, and they repent and are forgiven. 'Then mother knelt down on the floor, just as she does when we are sorry, and she held out her arms, and she loved Tony till he felt much better.'[5]

Edwin Lutyens's early memories of his mother were all about church. After she died he remembered her with a wave of 'ronge' or nostalgia: 'Sunday church (of all places), darling Mother praying – and myself.' (She was always 'darling' mother.) Years later in Gibraltar, listening to the garrison at early service singing 'From Greenland's icy mountains', he was moved almost to tears. 'All that Mother believed, felt and taught flooded back – the mysteries of the child's conception brain waved again.'⁶

Edwin Lutyens, known as Ned, was to win early fame by building houses that were lyrical celebrations of Englishness, but he had only one English grandparent. None of his grandparents was living when he was born, and he had only the vaguest sense of his family history. He thought the Lutyenses came to England from Holland at the time of Charles I or Charles II.⁷ In fact they came a century later, and they were Germans from Hamburg.

Ned's father Charles Lutyens was the fourth generation of his family to live in England, but he spoke English with a German accent. He seemed an outsider, a rather odd, solitary and naive character. Over four generations, the Lutyens family had failed to become fully assimilated. They were immigrants, who kept themselves to themselves.

The family sprang from an island, now sunk, at the mouth of the Elbe. Charles's great-grandfather Bartold Lutkens was a Hamburg merchant who settled in London and was naturalized a British subject in 1739, anglicizing his name to Bartholomew and declaring that he had 'constantly professed the True Protestant Religion'. He had a son named Nicholas, who prospered as a West Indian merchant, married Mary Messman, daughter of Daniel Messman, a rich Huguenot silk weaver of Spitalfields, and had ten children. Nicholas and Mary can be glimpsed moving in a tight-knit, closed community of immigrant cousins, Huguenot Messmans and Lutyenses with German names such as Englebert or Salomy. Nicholas was a friend of the anti-slavery agitator Thomas Clarkson and he supported the campaign against slavery in spite of his West Indian interests. He made enough money to move his family out of London, and bought a house at Broxbourne near Watford in Hertfordshire.

Nicholas had eight sons. Three of them followed him into the City, becoming bill brokers in the firm of Lutyens & Ripley, Old Broad Street. The portrait of the eldest son, also called Nicholas, shows a plump, alert gentleman with bright eyes, pointed nose and curling dark hair, rather resembling a prosperous vole, soberly and expensively dressed in black. He had made money during the Napoleonic wars, when Lutyens & Ripley helped feed the government's unquenchable thirst for credit. He and his bachelor brothers lived at Broxbourne with their spinster sister Martha, carefully hoarding their bonds and counting their silver spoons. Five of the brothers joined the army, and three brothers fought together at the Battle of La Coruña.[8]

Ned's only remotely distinguished relation was his great-uncle Englebert Lutyens who was orderly officer to Napoleon on St Helena. His duty was to report to Sir Hudson Lowe, the Governor of the island, on events at Longwood, Napoleon's residence. When Bonaparte was dying, Englebert refused to obey orders to spy on him through a hole in the shutter. Bonaparte rewarded him with a pair of pistols, but Englebert was forced to resign his post as orderly officer for accepting presents, though he was later reinstated. Years later, Ned would thrill his children with a story that 'Englebert was on duty the night after the post-mortem on Napoleon, guarding his remains, when waking from a doze he was just in time to stop a rat from making off with Napoleon's heart'.[9]

Englebert's brother Charles was Ned's grandfather. Charles Lutyens was a general in the army commissariat, which meant that he was a Treasury servant though he wore uniform. He seems to have been more German than English. His first wife, Charlotte de Wangenheim, was the daughter of a Hanoverian general, whose portrait, showing a stout, happy-looking gentleman in a white wig and scarlet coat with ruffles pointing to a burning city in the distance, hung in the dining room of Ned's home when Ned was a child. 'That is our great-uncle watching the burning of Sodom and Gomorrah,' explained the children.

When Charlotte de Wangenheim married Charles Lutyens in Hamelin, Hanover, in 1795, she brought with her her leather-bound German Bible, printed in 1770 and stamped 'Ch. de W'. Inside she entered in Frenchified English the names of their two sons: Henry de Wangenheim, born at Camberwell in 1798, and Augustus Wilhelm, born at Hamelin, Charlotte's home town, in 1800. A daughter, Anna, was born in 1803.

This entire German family was wiped out. First Charlotte died in 1813, on a passage to Lisbon. Next Henry the eldest son died aged twenty-two in Jamaica of fever. Anna died aged twenty. Augustus died aged twenty-eight fighting in the Greek War of Independence. Charles Lutyens married a second wife, but she died too. Undaunted, Charles married again. His third wife, whom he married in May 1824 when he was fifty-one, was a woman named Frances Jane Fludger.

'The Fludger' was Ned's only English grandparent. She was a woman of mystery. Her portrait showed a handsome, rather fashionable woman. Her family were lesser Berkshire gentry, owners of an estate known as Sherwoods in Mackney, which she eventually inherited.

Ned's son Robert was to speculate that the family's artistic talent derived from the Fludger seed, the Lutyens *métier* being 'entirely pedestrian'. This was an exaggeration. The Lutyenses were remarkable in their way: immigrants who quietly carved out comfortable livings in the military-fiscal state of eighteenth-century England. They were careful, shrewd, calculating bourgeoisie and mercenary soldiers; if the Lutyenses showed no interest in art, there is no reason to believe that the Fludgers did either.

Ned's father, Charles Henry Augustus, was born in 1829. His first name was his father's; his two other names were those of his two dead half-brothers. By then the family was living near Reading in a large rented house named Southcote Manor. Ned's grandfather was a wealthy man. The administrative offices of the army were notoriously venal and, though in his war diaries he grumbled about dishonesty and graft, it seems unlikely that the shrewd and worldly Charles Lutyens, as commissary-general, neglected altogether the chance of enriching himself.

Southcote Manor (now demolished) had been a Roundhead stronghold during the Civil War. It was a barracks of a house: the stables held one hundred and fifty horses, the house had forty bedrooms and three hundred and sixty-five windows. Southcote was said to be haunted by a lady on a white horse who crossed the moat each night at 12 o'clock. As children Mary and Louisa, Ned's aunts, were petrified by ghosts who, they maintained, seized the bedclothes on their beds and threw them to the other side of the room. Old Charles Lutyens kept open house, thronging the oak-panelled rooms with guests. They dined at 4 in the afternoon, and 'a page boy would come in to unloose the neck cloths of those who had slipped below the table. At nine o'clock the man servants came in and in laying supper would wake up the assembled company and snuff the dying stinking candles.' Then the little girls were fetched down to play duets in the drawing room while old Charles, a 'well-seasoned vessel' who had himself cupped twice a year, snored on.[10]

Young Charles had a neglected childhood. Bizarrely, he attended a day school in Hammersmith. According to his son Frank, whose love for a good story sometimes got the better of the facts, Charles travelled to Hammersmith each day by coach from Reading, arriving on winter mornings hungry and chilled to the bone. Vigorous whipping warmed him up. His studies terminated when he threw a slate at his drawing master. Like his father, the boy was an enthusiastic fox-hunter: a passion for hunting was the family's only English trait.

In December 1848 old Charles Lutyens died, aged seventy-five. In his will he left everything to his wife. 'The Fludger' died little more than a year later. Her property at Mackney she left to Charles, as her eldest son; the rest of her property she divided equally between all her children.

Young Charles Lutyens joined the Lancashire Fusiliers and left England with his regiment for Canada. He was briefly Master of the Montreal Hunt, making friends among fox-hunting officers such as Lord Mark Kerr and Major Hay-Boyd. And he showed talent as an artist, painting watercolours of the Niagara Falls and the St Lawrence River. Several of his pictures hung in the Club House at Montreal. He already seemed different from his rather dull sisters, one of whom, Mary, reminded Ned of a large sheep, 'without any idea but a bleat when she smiles. How one stockpot could have produced Father and his sister Mary I can't think – she is like Father too. Shave Father and put silver bandeaux for hair and very pale blue eyes – you have Aunt Mary and of course dress him as a woman (and dress him badly).'[11]

In Canada Charles Lutyens met Mary Gallwey, a nineteen-year-old Irish girl, staying with her older brother, Major Thomas Gallwey of the Royal Engineers, then serving in Montreal. Like Charles she was an orphan.

Mary, Ned's mother, was the daughter of General John Gallwey (1781–1845) of the Royal Irish Constabulary; her family came from Killarney in Kerry. Her uncle Christopher was agent to the Earl of Kenmare; another uncle, Thomas, was a naval captain who served as Consul at Naples and married a daughter of the painter Hoppner. The Kerry branch of the Gallwey family were Catholics; they traced their pedigree back to John de Bourge Gallwey, knighted after the Battle of Balls Bridge, Limerick, in 1361; hence their coat of arms, a bridge. Mary's mother was Bridget (Biddy) Blood, daughter of Neptune Blood of County Clare and a famous beauty. Biddy Blood's portrait miniature stood on the Lutyenses' mantelpiece; she gazed out, wide-eyed and artlessly pretty in ringlets and bare shoulders.

Next to Biddy's portrait stood a photograph of Mary aged about seventeen. There were the same large eyes and small mouth as her mother, but a very different expression – heavy, dark-ringed, downcast eyes, hair disfigured by tight corkscrew curls, shiny black satin tied tight to her chin. Mary was the survivor of a terrible childhood. The seventh child in a family of five boys (one died in infancy) and three girls, Mary was born in 1833. Her mother died when she was three; her father when she was twelve. Then came the Famine, when death was everywhere in the remote west of Ireland. Little wonder that Mary grew up devoutly religious. She was educated at a convent, apparently intending to become a nun. Her cousin Peter Gallwey was a distinguished Jesuit priest at Farm Street, the best preacher of his generation after Cardinal Manning. But Mary didn't follow him into the Catholic Church. According to the story Ned told his children, the girls in the convent were encouraged to write notes for the Virgin which they placed upon the altar, and one night Mary peeped and discovered that the notes were removed not by the Virgin but by the nuns. This so shook Mary that she left the Catholic Church and became an Evangelical, though still fiercely religious.

Mary was dark-haired and lovely when young; constant childbearing later made her fat. Ned cherished her small, perfect wrists and hands, and her nails which, he said, fitted over her fingers like the skin of an almond. When someone remarked that Ned's daughter Mary looked like his mother Mary, Ned retorted, 'Oh *no*, Mother was *beautiful*!' (This rankled.) Her beauty was as much spiritual as physical. She always wore the marriage ring of the Claddah Tribe which the poet Tom Moore had given her – a crude gold ring showing two hands grasping a phallus. The ring was supposed to descend to the favourite child.*

There was something of the Celt about Mary. She was mystical and musical, and her gentleness gave her a kind of strength. After she died, her husband Charles said that 'he was glad to think he had never said an unkind word to her and that no word of his could ever have troubled her'. Only a saint elicits behaviour of that kind, but like a saint she was unreachable. Her children worshipped her, but she didn't allow them to come close to her. Scarred by her childhood, 'darling mother' escaped into a world of godliness and goodness, keeping reality at a safe distance.[12]

Charles and Mary were married in Montreal in November 1852. Charles was only twenty-three, but he had already inherited a fortune.

---

*My father, Nicholas Ridley, Ned's grandson, inherited the Claddah ring and, relishing his role as Lear, he would tell me and my two sisters the story about the favourite child. Knowing that the favourite wasn't me, I felt that this was monstrously unfair. In the end none of us got it.

Neither bride nor groom had any parents to restrain them. Six months later, they returned with the regiment to England. Southcote House had by now been given up, and their first child was born at Rose Hill Cottage, Winchester, in December 1853. When the Crimean War broke out in 1854, Charles's regiment was ordered abroad, but Charles for some reason was detained in Malta. He missed the Battle of Inkerman (5 November 1854) when the XXth charged the Russians with bayonets, uttering the regiment's unearthly 'Minden Yell'. Perhaps it was just as well that he never saw action, as he was tender-hearted. He reached the Crimea in September 1855 when the fighting was over, and spent his time painting watercolours of Balaklava and Sebastopol. In the Crimea, Charles advanced from ensign to captain, and in 1856, after training at the newly established School of Musketry at Hythe, he was appointed Inspector of Musketry to his regiment. At Aldershot one day he was instructing his regiment wearing full uniform, when the hunt came by and, according to the regimental story, Charles jumped on his horse and galloped after hounds. Charles invented a rangefinder for judging distances known as the stadiometer, which was used for forty years, though he grumbled that he obtained neither credit nor reward.

In 1857 Charles left the army, narrowly avoiding being sent with his regiment to help put down the Indian Mutiny. Aged twenty-eight, he wanted to become a painter. His experiments in ballistics imply a mathematical mind, of the kind that is often linked to artistic talent; the type of mind that his son Ned inherited. Charles's younger brother Englebert, a shadowy bachelor who disappeared from the family record, was also an artist.[13] Charles was sweet-natured, devoutly Protestant, happily uxorious and a devoted father. But his nature was perhaps too simple, his faith too pure, his marriage too happy for him to have the makings of greatness. Perhaps he inherited too much money when too young. He lacked the urge and the angst which drives the Romantic artist, yet he was too naive, eccentric and undisciplined to succeed as a jobbing professional painter.

He was untrained too. In *Trilby* (1894), George du Maurier's novel set in Paris in the late 1850s, there is a character named the Laird, who rather resembles Charles: a Crimean veteran, splendid-looking and athletic with Dundreary whiskers, who trains in Paris. Charles was not as adventurous nor as ambitious. His painting grew out of his early watercolour drawing. The army taught perspective and accurate drawing in pencil as preparation for military reconnaissance. The drawings Charles made in Canada and the Crimea, in monochrome wash heightened with white and accented with local colour, are the work of an accomplished amateur. The one art historian to make a study of Charles's work considered that he had 'a more than average talent. Of genius or originality – those indefinables – none: but of talent a quite remarkable degree: and a talent which, under whatever guidance, for whatever purpose, with whatever encouragement, he had understood how to exercise.' Charles's weakness was his lack of training, his ignorance of 'formal drawing with its combination of observation and analysis and its deeper references', which he might have learned in a painter's studio or the Academy Schools.[14]

'A painter ought not to be married,' Burne-Jones once said, 'children and pictures are too precious to be produced by one man.' Charles certainly had no trouble in producing children. When he left the army in 1857 his family consisted of three sons. A stillbirth and three more boys followed between 1858 and 1863, each birth carefully recorded in the Wangenheim family Bible. The Lutyenses were now living in Kensington, at Palace Gardens Terrace, a new house of sparkling white stucco built in the mid-1850s, backing on to Kensington Church Street and within easy reach of Kensington Gardens. Charles's painting career can be tracked from the names of his sons' godparents. All the children born after 1860 were sponsored by his patrons.

In 1863 Charles and Mary and their six sons moved into the house where Ned was to be born, Number 16 Onslow Square, South Kensington. In the 1860s Onslow Square was prosperous and respectable. Houses cost at least £2,000 and most families employed at least four servants.* Thackeray was a neighbour at Number 36 (admittedly he thought it 'a shabby genteel house', but he was a snob).[15] At Number 34 lived the French-Italian sculptor Baron Carlo Marochetti. An émigré from the 1848 Revolution, Marochetti was Queen Victoria's favourite sculptor. A handsome courtier, resented as a flashy, tricksy foreigner who owed his commissions to his friendship with Prince Albert, he was renowned for his equestrian statues. *Richard Coeur de Lion*, which he made for the Great Exhibition of 1851, still prances on his charger outside the House of Lords. Vast bronzes were cast in the foundry at the back of his house in Sydney Mews.

Marochetti made a painted plaster statue of Henry Lionel, Charles's

---

*The 1881 Census shows the Lutyens family employing six servants: Priscilla the Nannie, a nursery maid, a lady's maid, a cook and two housemaids.

third son, known as Daisy and apparently so beautiful that he converted a Jew to Christianity (why this should be so history does not relate), who died at the age of eight in 1865. It was in Marochetti's studio that Charles learned to model in clay. When Charles painted horses he first made clay models of the animals – his studio was littered with discarded casts of equine torsos. Starting from clay models, which he draped, Charles could paint muscular, lifelike horses and riders, even when the landscape he set them in was leaden. He began to be known as a painter of horses and hunting scenes, gaining commissions from the fox-hunting officers he had known in the army.

Since 1859 Landseer had been at work in Marochetti's studio on a much-publicized government commission: the four lions at the foot of Nelson's column in Trafalgar Square. (The column itself was designed by the architect William Railton, who also lived in Onslow Square.) The studio walls were hung with life-size crayon and oil sketches of lions, made by Landseer in London Zoo, and on the floor Landseer, with beetle brows and a face like a bulldog, struggled with colossal clay models of couchant lions, which Marochetti cast in his foundry. Irascible and unsteady, hypochondriacal and insomniac, Landseer had violent moods and bouts of depression from which he escaped by means of drugs and alcohol. Yet his paintings commanded fabulous prices.

Landseer's success was beyond Charles Lutyens's wildest dreams. In 1862 he exhibited his first painting at the Royal Academy, a *Portrait of a Lady*. At the same time he began to keep a little red book, listing his paintings and their prices. In 1864 he exhibited one painting of *The Children of Robert Hay with a Pony*, which sold for £100, and another of the Marquis of Ailsa, looking rather like Karl Marx in his spectacles and beard, mounted on his favourite horse 'Farmer' (£70). Paintings sold from the walls of the Royal Academy averaged around £50; but year after year Charles's paintings were 'skyed', or hung too high to see. As a schoolboy Ned wrote in an essay: 'There is a large place in London called the Academy to which artists send their pictures, and then if people like them they by [sic] them. The very best are hung on the line, that is on level with your eye. There have been some great painters in the world and are now – such as my father and Milly [sic].' Paintings by Millais, G. F. Watts and Landseer, which stole the show at the Summer Exhibitions of the 1860s, were sold for thousands of pounds.

Charles's prices were low partly because he didn't really need the money. In 1865 his bachelor uncle Sam died, the last of the careful, calculating bill-broking brothers of Lutyens & Ripley whose only recorded utterance was 'Never marry a woman who plays the piano'. Charles was now the oldest surviving male of the Lutyens family, and he inherited £12,000 and the house at Broxbourne.[16]

As the house in Onslow Square filled with boys – Lionel was born in 1864, Arthur in 1866 – Charles found no room to paint. In 1866 he rented a stable behind his house in Cranley Mews, which he used as a studio. Four years later Charles Freake, the developer, built a central arched passage linking the two facing rows of stables in Cranley Mews, to form a colony of fifteen artists' ateliers. Sydney Mews, or Avenue Studios as it became known, was a tunnel-like white passage lit from above by round holes pierced through the vaulting, and lined by black doors and gas lamps; a very masculine Victorian space.

Charles recorded his sporting world in a vast canvas which hangs today in the basement of a country house in Berwickshire. It began as an exhibition piece of a finish between three racehorses which was exhibited at the Royal Academy in 1872 under the title *Blue Wins*. It was slated by the critics. 'The horses don't move,' wrote the sporting paper *Baily's Magazine*, 'and the riders are of the wooden order. Both quadrupeds and bipeds are taking it uncommonly easy, and there is not the least go or fire in either.' William Miller, who lived at Manderston in Berwickshire, spotted the canvas standing forlorn and unsold in Charles's studio and, wishing to help, offered to buy it if Charles would fill the background with portraits of his sporting Borders friends – Lord Hume, Lady Tennant, Rufus Hay, Major L'Amy, Mr Milne Hume and Lord Mark Kerr, all of whom were clients of Charles. Mingled with the sporting gentry are portraits of Charles's wife Mary and his friend the sculptor Joseph Boehm, who lived nearby in Onslow Square.

By the early 1870s Charles Lutyens was established as a horse painter. He painted endless pictures of racehorses, standing broadside on, unnaturally still, in palatial stables. These were boring to paint, and Charles attempted to vary the formula but without success. 'In his anxious endeavours to avoid the errors of conventionalism,' commented *Baily's Magazine* in 1875, Mr Lutyens has 'rushed into the opposite extreme of offence against realism in his attempts to inaugurate a new style of equine portraiture'.

Charles's hunting pictures were far better. In the curious autobiographical novel he wrote in his sixties, he recalled the painting visits he made to hunting clients. He would travel by train to a country station with a pair of battered hunting boots in his luggage, dine in a stately mansion in a room hung with old masters, and hunt next morning if he was lucky. Dressed in a shabby old ulster, his artist's beard flowing in the wind, he would sidle off on his own, only to astonish his hosts by reappearing jumping fences at the front of the hunt, knowing better than anyone which way the fox had gone. He was an artist on horseback. 'If that fellow could paint as well as he can ride he would be P. R. A. [President of the Royal Academy].'[17]

Charles's love of sport was reflected in his work. 'The painter, evidently a hunting man, has caught all the minutiae of the sport he illustrates,' enthused *Baily's*. In 1875 *Baily's* picked out Charles's painting of *The Covert Side* as the best hunting picture of the year at the Academy. 'Man and horse, boots and breeches are perfection. The elderly dandy . . . sits his horse like a workman, and the whole thing looks like business. Mr Lutyens must be congratulated.' Charles excelled at the presentation portrait, paid for by subscription, typically a large stiff canvas of a Master of Fox Hounds astride his favourite horse. His painting of the Hon. Francis Scott was praised by *Baily's* as 'best picture of the class they had ever seen'. As for the paintings of Burton Persse with the Galway Blazers and Mr Hargreves with the South Berks, both ought to be engraved and the likeness was 'simply marvellous'. Giant presentation pictures commanded high prices – £380 for Francis Scott, £577 for a 'wonderful' painting of Major Browne and the Northumberland Hounds crossing the River Coquet. Charles's earnings grew steadily. In 1863 he made only £450 from painting, but by 1874 his income had climbed to £1,040 and in 1876 he made £1,720. He may have made more by selling the copyright on presentation pictures; painters reckoned to double their earnings from the sale of copyright for engravings.

But no sooner had he achieved success than Charles became discontented. Each time he returned from visits to paint clients' horses his studio seemed grimy and poor, the canvases he was working on less true to nature than when he left them. More and more he was drawn to the painting of landscape, increasingly the fashion in the 1870s. He wanted to move to the country, to live in a cottage and paint nature.

Ned's earliest surviving letter was written in a careful copperplate, at about the age of eight, while he was staying with his mother's brother, General Thomas Gallwey.

Darling Mother,

I am quite well and so happy. I have had three rides on the pretty pony and I drive with my Cousins to drill, which I like very much. Thank you and Mary for your kind letters I was so pleased with the book mark which I shall keep in my Bible. My love to all I wish you could be here you would like it every one is so kind. Many kisses from your loving child Ned.

My braces are too small.

Lutyens, who already signed himself Ned (he disliked the name Edwin), was no infant prodigy. He was dutiful and affectionate, anxious to please his mother by reading his Bible and, like his brothers, fond of riding.

The Lutyens children were born over a period of twenty-three years, and they really formed two families.* First came 'the boys'. There were seven older surviving children, starting with Charlie, who was sixteen when Ned was born, down to Arthur, born in 1866. One after another they left home for school. Charlie, who was educated at Winchester, left England at seventeen to make his fortune in Ceylon, growing coffee with his father's friend and patron Sir Graeme Elphinstone. John, the next brother, was educated at Woolwich and joined the Royal Engineers at nineteen. Next came Frederick, who went to Westminster and afterwards to Trinity College, Cambridge. Francis followed Fred to Westminster. Lionel left home for Cheltenham College in 1878, and he was joined there the following year by Arthur.[18]

The birth of a girl, Mary, known as Molly, marked a natural break. The second family comprised Molly, Ned, Aileen, William and Margaret. Molly was a year older than Ned, and his particular friend among the brothers and sisters. In term time, when the bigger boys went back to school, the younger children, including Ned, had lessons with a governess; Ned's childhood was dominated by women – mother, sisters, Nannie – whom he got on with better than with his boisterous, athletic elder brothers.

Establishing an individuality in a family as large as this was not easy. Ned's elder brothers stand out not as individuals but as a group – 'the boys', curly-haired and precociously long-legged: their shins were so long that when they crossed their legs both feet could be planted comfortably on the floor. They spoke a private language, played rowdy

---

*The children were: Charles (born 1853), John (born 1855), Henry Lionel (Daisy) (born 1857, died 1863), Frederick (born 1860), Graeme (born 1861, died 1876), Francis (born 1863), Lionel (born 1864), Arthur (born 1866), Mary (born 1868), Edwin (Ned) (born 1869), Aileen (born 1871), William (born 1872), Margaret (born 1876).

games of cricket and sang together as an orchestra, mimicking the instruments. They were easily moved to tears. At school in Wimbledon Charlie was called the WWWW, meaning the Wonderful Wimbledon Water Works. (Ned's tears were always very near the surface.)[19] The boys were not without talent. Frederick became a painter, producing pictures which are sometimes impossible to distinguish from his father's. Charlie painted watercolours in Ceylon, and Francis, who was witty but lazy, drew accomplished cartoons of hunting scenes in the manner of Randolph Caldecott. None had sufficient talent to make a career in the arts; or if the talent was there, the drive was not. Why Ned, alone of his brothers and sisters, succeeded as an artist is a question which is not easy to answer.

Ned himself attributed his success to childhood illness. Years later he told Osbert Sitwell: 'Any talent I may have had was due to a long illness as a boy, which afforded me time to think, and to subsequent ill-health, because I was not allowed to play games, and so had to teach myself, for my own enjoyment, to use my eyes instead of my feet. My brothers hadn't the same advantage.'[20]

Childhood illness had another, even more important effect. It brought Ned close to his mother, establishing him in a privileged position as Mary's favoured child and giving him the confidence his brothers lacked. The illness was rheumatic fever, an alarming condition at the time. Ned was about eight when he went down with a high fever and swollen, intensely painful joints. 'The patient lies helpless in bed,' wrote the doctors' manual, 'restless, but afraid to move or be touched, and unable to bear even the weight of the bed-clothes.' The precise cause was then unknown. In the days before penicillin there was no treatment but rest. Ned lay in bed, his joints wrapped in flannel cloths soaked in a solution of washing soda and laudanum. He never forgot the pain and awful weakness.[21] Just as alarming as the disease itself were the complications: inflammation of the membranes of the heart, or organic heart disease. Again, rest was the only prescription, condemning Ned to week after week in bed and to the sheltered, cosseted regime of a sickly child, forbidden to run about, buttoned up in woolly combinations, not allowed out of doors in wet weather.

A year or so before Ned fell ill, while his mother Mary was pregnant with her youngest child, fifteen-year-old Graeme had suddenly died on holiday by the sea. According to the doctor his death was caused by going out in hot weather without his head covered. Graeme's death shadowed the Lutyens nursery. As Molly remembered, 'mother was sad, and Nannie cries when Alla [the nursery maid] says, "Do you remember?"' Having lost two of her boys, Mary was terrified when Ned got rheumatic fever. Death, which had left indelible scars on her own childhood, now seemed to be closing in on her children. Fear jolted her out of her other-worldly saintliness and she drew especially close to Ned. After her death he remembered with a wave of misery 'my rheumatic fever and all Mother was to me in those days'.[22]

Thirty years later, Molly wrote a children's book about her childhood. 'Peter', who is Ned, 'is old for his age because he has been ill'. Peter buys a bottle of cheap scent, and 'he went to mother's room and he opened the door ever so gently, and went up to her bed and said, "Why should lovely woman suffer? I have brought you some eau de clore"; that's what Peter calls it, and he poured it over mother's head, and mother said it made her well. It didn't smell very nice.' Peter is anxious too. Once in the schoolroom at teatime a spider appears, and 'Peter had a dreadful fit of nervousness, and he shook his hands about like I don't know what'. Peter is frightened of horses. 'Peter had a real nervous fit because his pony moved its ears.' Highly strung and sensitive, he makes up for any deficiency in animal spirits with imagination. Out riding with Molly

> we pretended we were in London, and we bowed to pretence people who were really fir trees, but Peter didn't take off his hat; it was safer not. So he said –
> 'Excuse me, my horse is so frisky.' And the people said –
> 'Aren't you nervous?' and Peter said –
> 'Oh no!'

Then there was the time Aileen's canary died, 'so we had to have a funeral'.

> Peter rang the back door bell, and it sounded just like a funeral, and the garden boy came, because he thought it was rung for him, and Peter said –
> 'Woe unto us, woe unto us, the canary is dead,' and Tober laughed, which he oughtn't to have done.
> Then we put on our nightdresses over our other clothes, and we walked to the cemetery.
> Mother doesn't like us to have real services, so we didn't.
> Peter made up the words, and they sounded all right. Then we made a tombstone.[23]

Mary longed for her favourite son to become a priest. This Ned was unable to do. He never challenged Christian belief but he mocked it, imitating Webb-Peploe in the pulpit and composing scurrilous puns on Mary's evangelical hymns. He shocked and disappointed Mary, forfeiting his place as favourite son.

For the rest of his life Edwin Lutyens tried to recapture the paradise that he had enjoyed as his mother's favourite, pleasing countless older women with beautiful houses as he had once pleased Mary with 'eau de clore'. When his mother died, Ned wanted only one thing: the favourite's Claddah ring.[24]

Chapter Two

Surrey
1876–1887

Dec 31 = 1877
Cottage Thursley.

Dearest Mother,

we are very happy with my dear old Bicy, this morning, I took it to the kitchen yard and polished it and oiled; But! — never had I got in such a dirty muck in my whole life dear dear me I smelt of sweet oil and polish, just think how I looked with one of Nan's aprons = as —

Letter written by Ned aged ten to his mother.

In 1876 Charles Lutyens rented a house in the village of Thursley in Surrey. It was called The Cottage, and Mary Lutyens fell in love with it at once. 'How delicious,' she would sigh as she sat on the lawn. Charles sold the Berkshire estate he had inherited from his mother, breaking his last link with family tradition.[1] At first, Charles and Mary and their brood divided their time between Onslow Square and Thursley. Later, Ned came to prefer Thursley to London and a myth grew up about the importance of Surrey during his childhood: his first major biographer, Christopher Hussey,* thought his entire childhood had been spent there.

Ned's new home was not a cottage at all, but one of the biggest houses in the village, a pretty Regency house with little of the Surrey vernacular about it. Built in 1827, the stuccoed Cottage was well-proportioned and well-mannered in the fashion of the period, with wide sash windows, low hipped roof and a curved front staircase almost made for Elizabeth Bennet to descend. To one side of the hall opened the dining room, a small room hardly designed to accommodate the Lutyens family of twelve or so at meals. The Cottage had only six bedrooms, and in holiday time every available space was packed with boys. A handsome front door opened almost on to the village street, and the garden was surrounded by a high wall. Many of the houses Ned Lutyens was to build were not grand mansions but village houses with street doors like The Cottage, hiding secret gardens behind tall brick walls.

Not so long ago Thursley had been a wild and lonely spot on the high road between Portsmouth and London, the haunt of highwaymen and smugglers working the route to France. In Ned's day, the road and hedges were white with dust in summer, and a man sat by the roadside cracking stones to patch the potholes.[2] When the railway came in 1859, bringing nearby Godalming within an hour's journey of Waterloo, the invasion of Londoners began. Witley, a straggling village of tumble-down, picturesque houses, was colonized by artists. By the time the

---

*Christopher Hussey's biography of Lutyens was published in 1950, six years after Lutyens's death.

painter Helen Allingham came there in 1881, the church was regularly surrounded by half a dozen white umbrellas, under which were aspiring artists all painting the same stiffly composed subject from the same point of view.[3] Thursley, which had a population of over 800, was a village of painters too, as Ned wrote in a schoolroom essay: 'The beautiful village of Thursley has had many artists . . . most ladies, one of the name of Miss Rose Barton the other Miss Emily Smith, they both paint very well.'

Not all artists fell for Surrey. Randolph Caldecott came to Frensham, a couple of miles from Thursley, when Ned was twelve, and began to sketch bits of buildings in landscape to illustrate his children's books – *Bye Baby Bunting* and *The Fox Jumps Over the Parson's Gate*. He grumbled that 'when the wind is in a cold quarter all the chimneys smoke . . . the front door requires a Hercules to shut it . . . the cold blast pierces the wall of the dining room; the rats scuttle noisily under the drawing room'. Burne-Jones visited George Eliot, who had bought a house at Witley; he complained that Surrey was 'a soft land, too soft. I wanted some desolate bits, a woeful tale or two . . . everybody smiled fat smiles at the big green carpet . . . I like to see Hell in a landscape. All that is like a silly Heaven.'[4] But for Charles Lutyens, who was tired of studio portraits, and anxious, like many of his contemporaries, to paint landscape, Surrey gave the chance to join the artists in their picturesque cottages and paint *en plein air*.

In some senses, the boy Ned Lutyens never really grew up. The man who built children's gardens and crawling windows for children to peep down into goldfish ponds, who designed round nurseries on the principle that no child should ever be put to stand in a corner, still possessed into adulthood a child's view of life. Children roared at his puns, his nonsense, his picture letters and his transparencies – deftly sketched in crayon, often slightly rude as two fingers poked through a torn flap to reveal a pair of untrousered legs.

Artists who empathize with children are themselves often the victims of unhappy childhoods. Two of the greatest children's writers of Lutyens's generation, J. M. Barrie (b. 1860) and Rudyard Kipling (b. 1865), were emotionally maimed by childhood trauma. But no Freudian trauma seems to have scarred Ned's childhood. In his sister Molly's account, their life at Thursley was serene, an idyllic, sunlit paradise. Her books are free of the cruelty which marks so many children's books; there are no frightening figures in Molly's world.

Behind the high brick wall there grew 'roses and potatoes and cabbages and daisies and sweet sultans and parsley and carrots and turnips and strawberries and apple trees and pear trees and plum trees and a roller, and lots more things'. Molly and Ned jumped the paths, held grasshoppers until they grew too tickly and played Mad Bulls – roaring and stamping and butting one another as they foamed sherbet from their mouths.

But their childhood Garden of Eden was threatened by 'the boys'. Molly remembered her brothers coming home for the holidays, little specks in the distance walking up the hill from Witley station to spare the old pony which pulled the trap, an equine cripple Charles had rescued from the gypsies. This was a day Ned dreaded. The boys ran races, played cricket and got into scrapes. Ned was left out. All the children pooled their money to buy a badminton set, but not Ned. Not allowed to run about, he bought a fishing rod instead. He and Molly went fishing on their own.[5]

When Ned first met his future wife she thought he was the only son of a widow, he talked so much about his mother. He was assured a place in Heaven, he said, because his mother, being so good, could have no other destination, and it would not be Heaven to her without him.[6] There was an element of forbidden pleasure in his relations with his mother, as if he were stealing her from the others and writing 'the boys' out of the story. 'We must have our Mother to ourselves sometimes,' said the children when visitors came, and Ned needed her most of all, especially in the school holidays when he resented the attention she paid to his elder brothers.

When 'the boys' went back to school, and Charles and Mary returned to Onslow Square, Ned and his sisters stayed at The Cottage. They played paperchases with the village children and went rabbiting. 'Don't be frighted [sic] for it *is not* with a gun,' the nine-year-old Ned told his mother.[7] Ned was still at home having lessons with the girls when he was ten. He wrote to his mother from Thursley:

> Dearest Mother,
>   Thanks much for your charming letter. Remind Mary to send me the drawing book she promised as soon as possible. The ice has melted away. We will all be very glad when we are in London . . . I have not a particle of news to tell you . . . I am making paper houses such a lark.

Clearly Thursley was not yet home. Ned longed to return to the cosy, warm untidiness of Onslow Square. He wrote again a few days later:

Dearest Mother,

I am very happy with my dear old *Bicy*; this morning I took it to the kitchen yard and polished it and I oiled; But! – never had I got in such a dirty mess in my whole life dear dear me I smelt of sweet oil and polish; just think how I looked with one of Nan's aprons . . . my hands were black from the greasy wheels . . . We are very happy here with Miss Kent [governess]. But everyone is anxious to go to London. It is very cold and damp in the evenings after tea, but do not be alarmed for we are not allowed to go out after tea we are always out till 3pm or half past 2pm for the rest of the afternoon we do lessons.[8]

To his children Charles Lutyens was a distant figure, smelling of oil paint and fenced in by canvases stacked against the walls. Not that he was a cruel or stern father. Once 'the boys' (not Ned) shot a hole through one of his pictures with an arrow, especially dangerous because they might have shot each other. Charles went upstairs with a whip. It was bedtime, and he found three of his sons kneeling by their beds in their nightgowns, saying their prayers. 'Then father was moved with compassion,' wrote Molly, 'and he didn't whip them, but he went out and he bought them a piece of sugar-cane and some beautiful peaches . . . That is the only time father was going to punish them seriously.'[9]

Nearing fifty, Charles was growing restless. Still in demand as a horse painter, he spent a fortnight with Percy Wyndham at Wilbury in Wiltshire in 1878, painting two canvases of fifteen horses. The Wyndhams were friends of Burne-Jones, and Charles, too, knew Burne-Jones, with his 'seductively captivating voice'. Another friend was E. W. Godwin, the architect and designer, whose sketchbook contains a drawing of a young girl, probably one of Charles's daughters, inscribed 'At Lutyens / Mar 1879'. Godwin in 1877 designed the startlingly modern White House in Tite Street, Chelsea, for the painter J. M. Whistler; if Whistler was the leader of the Aesthetic movement, Godwin was its most daring architect. Charles disliked the new style. He disliked light, bright paintings almost as much as he despised studio-painted subject paintings of imaginary nature. His own pictures, he thought, were as good as most others of the day; but he no longer felt he was on the right road. He lacked conviction.[10]

'What odd chaps you painters are!' wrote Oscar Wilde. 'You do anything in the world to gain a reputation. As soon as you have one you want to throw it away.' In 1879 Charles's earnings dipped sharply to £625, less than half that of the year before (£1,458). In 1880 he quit the studio behind Onslow Square – the lease was taken over by Boehm – and though keeping on the house in Onslow Square, settled himself and his painting at Thursley.

Charles Lutyens was only really happy when he was hunting. Surrey was a poor hunting county, much despised by Jorrocks, and Thursley was in the worst part of it. Charles hunted with the Chiddingfold, a recently formed pack, which had its kennels at Milford, a couple of miles from Thursley. Of all the Surrey hunts, it was the scruffiest, but it was strikingly picturesque, a country of woods and heaths, 'the home of the artist and the man of letters'. Even the very timber was 'a thing of actual beauty' wrote one keen-eyed observer, noting five-bar gates fastened with upright handles easily opened by a man on a horse and oak stiles burnished from the friction of the labourers' corduroys.[11] Charles collected broken-down horses, nappy or vicious, lame ponies, sad donkeys – anything to mount himself and his numerous sons. '*Charles!*' Mary would say in her 'clergyman' voice, when men came to the door bringing yet another addition to the stable. His son Francis remembered a day with the Chiddingfold in 1880 when Charles was riding a five-year-old thoroughbred mare turned out of the Islington Ring for violence. 'He had bought her at Tattersall's for £40 and had ridden her down to Thursley, in his trousered legs, to the vast delight of his offspring.' Francis, who was then about fifteen, was riding his mother's driving pony, and he and Charles were standing beside a wood near Aldershot. 'Father, we've lost the hounds,' said Francis. Charles pointed a wise finger at a single hound a quarter of a mile away. A whipper-in arrived. 'Go and see what that hound is doing,' said Charles. 'I think it is our fox.' It was. The whip rode to a hill a mile away and raised his cap, and Charles cheered on the rest of the hounds – the first time Francis had ever heard him holloa. 'I had heard him say "Shut, shut the door!" That was nothing. "Huick, Holloah, Buick!!" All the hounds stopped singing to listen. Every rabbit sought its burrow.'[12] This was a side of his father which Ned, who was nervous of hunting, never saw.

Contrary to legend, Ned was not too delicate to be sent to school. Two letters have survived written by him aged twelve to his mother from a boarding school named Sutherland House on Inner Park Road, Wandsworth, near Wimbledon Common. One of many such establishments with pseudo-aristocratic names like Blenheim House, Hamilton House or Apsley House, Sutherland House was a small private school.

Ned's brothers had gone there before him. The 1881 Census shows Sutherland House having fourteen boarders, including Ned, and two masters, the Head, aptly named Mr Birch, and his twenty-eight-year-old partner, Charles Penrose.[13] 'Tell Father not to expect me to see him on Thursday because I don't think Mr Penrose likes me to be always running up to see him. I am very sorry,' Ned wrote to his mother, 'but he has not mentioned it yet but I can see he does not care for it. I am very sorry indeed. It does not matter in the slightest on Saturday being a holiday but, I can't help it', signing himself formally and forlornly, 'I remain, your ever loving son, E. L. Lutyens.'[14] Even his handwriting has been disciplined from its natural unruly sprawl into a regimented copperplate.

Though artistically talented, Ned was woefully ignorant of Latin and knew no Greek. Mr Penrose filled him with terror. Public-school men all his life made him feel threatened and inadequate. He compensated by playing the fool. Buffoonery, jokes, a never-ending flow of puns formed a kind of smokescreen, an elaborate diversionary tactic. Being fearful at school also left him with ambivalent feelings about authority. At first, as a young man, he attempted to charm it; as he grew older, he embraced it. Classical architecture, with its rules and proportions, provided him with both a discipline and a grammar – a language for the expression of power.

After a year or so at Sutherland House, Ned was back at Thursley. He was considered too delicate for public school, but the decision to educate him at home was partly dictated by economy. Money was short. There was a family story about the dead Graeme's trousers, which were made to serve for each of the younger boys in turn until they reached Ned, whom they fitted so lamentably that he was sent home from school because he was thought to be deformed.[15] Charlie, the oldest brother, had triggered a crisis in the family finances.

Charlie had lived in Ceylon since Ned was a baby, the first of the brothers to feel the lure of the East. Ned barely knew him, but he figured as putative head of the family. 'Send for Charlie to say goodbye,' wailed the eight-year-old Ned when he pricked his finger and blew on it and waited to die. Charlie had joined the rush into coffee in 1870, when coffee was the principal crop of Ceylon. He married a woman named Beatrice Airey who was killed in a pony cart accident, and their baby daughter Beatrice was shipped back to England to be brought up by Mary at Thursley. Charlie remained in Ceylon. In 1882–3 the coffee crop was devastated by disease, which stripped the leaves from the bushes; the principal bank of Ceylon crashed and the planters faced bankruptcy. Small wonder that the planters of Ceylon were notoriously heavy drinkers.

Charlie hastened back to England for talks with his father. Charles took the opportunity to paint his eldest son full length, a splendid mustachioed figure in gaiters. He also put Charlie back in business, buying a new plantation, named Mornington, on behalf of 'Graeme Elphinstone and Captain Charles Lutyens and his heirs'. It was an investment which old Charles could ill afford. To raise the capital, he advanced money destined for his younger sons as well as much of his own. Profits were very slow to come. Charlie at first planted cinchona – the tree whose bark provided quinine which many planters cultivated after the collapse of coffee. The market was soon glutted, cinchona prices collapsed, and Charlie replanted in tea, then a relatively new crop in Ceylon. Four decades later, Mornington yielded Charles Lutyens's estate a steady income, but meanwhile the family fortunes were buried in tea. No family money was available for the younger sons. Only Charlie and John, the two eldest, received capital from Charles when they came of age.[16] Both went East. India, with its tightly bonded male world of good fellowship and sport, exercised a magnetic pull on the more extrovert of the Lutyens brothers.

John joined the Royal Engineers after Woolwich and arrived in India in 1882. An instinctive horseman, he flourished in the sweat and dust of the polo ground or late at night in the officers' mess, and stories of his wild exploits followed in the wake of his postings around India and Burma. At Lahore where he was stationed in 1884, John met Kipling, then a precocious cub reporter who thirsted for the company of officers; John befriended him and invited him to the mess. Perhaps John was the young subaltern (he was not promoted captain until 1886) who held a moonlight picnic with Kipling in the fairy-tale rose gardens of Shalimar; and surely John played hero and fool at the fortnightly pony races for gentlemen riders, earning loud guffaws for his antics in such events as the cheroot and umbrella race. Kipling later paid tribute to John in *The Maltese Cat*, the story of an old, flea-bitten polo pony who is a supreme player of the game and so clever that it wins the cup when its master is injured. The rider's name is Lutyens.*

---

*I can vividly remember how Kipling's stirring account of Lutyens's bravery after his fall brought a lump of pride to my throat as a child.

'What's the damage?' said Powell, his arm round Lutyens.

'Collar-bone, of course,' said Lutyens between his teeth. It was the third time he had broken it in two years, and it hurt him.

Powell and the others whistled. 'Game's up,' said Hughes.

'Hold on. We've five good minutes yet, and it isn't my right hand,' said Lutyens. 'We'll stick it out.'

'I say,' said the captain of the Archangels, trotting up. 'Are you hurt, Lutyens? We'll wait if you care to put in a substitute. I wish – I mean – the fact is, you fellows deserve this game if any team does. Wish we could give you a man or some of the ponies – or something.'

'You're awfully good, but we'll play it to a finish, I think.'

The captain of the Archangels stared for a little. 'That's not half bad,' he said . . .

Back home at Thursley the family's finances were seriously strained. Nevertheless, Ned's brothers were sent to public school, even the youngest, assisted by a legacy from Landseer's sister Jessie, who died in 1880, leaving £500 to 'My dear friends Mr and Mrs Lutyens . . . for educational purposes'.[17] The brothers nearest to Ned in age were conspicuously successful at public school. Arthur, three years older, triumphed at Cheltenham (1879–87), where he was captain of the First XV for Rugby, captain of the First XI for Cricket and Senior Prefect or head of the school. William (Bill), three years younger than Ned, was an exceptionally fast runner who became Head of House at Sherborne (1887–91).

Fred came down from Trinity College, Cambridge, in 1882 with a degree in classics. No money was available to set him up in a profession, so Fred, who was modestly talented and a dedicated fox-hunter, stayed at home, hunting as often as he could and learning to paint from Charles.

Ned was removed from Sutherland House and Fred acted as his tutor. Ned welcomed the opportunity to leave school. Thirty years later, he recalled 'how I loathed the two years I was at school and the dullness of them and the blind apathetic injustice and the dead levels (for the masters' convenience – then I was at *very* bad schools) of the layered classes – and the pupils are mere salmon as they are in a Canadian river that are caught to be canned for the catchers' benefit'.[18] He wrote to his mother about this time: 'Fred returned to London yesterday, so there are only your chicks at the Cottage and I think that's their proper place – don't you?'

Loss of fortune wore down Charles Lutyens's spirit, and during the

1880s he and Mary retreated into inner worlds of their own. A quarter of a century later, when Ned read Edmund Gosse's *Father and Son*, he recalled those years of disintegration :

> Gosse's story is so like my own – the home part. Darling Mother's evangelicalism and Father's Venetian Secret. It is thrillingly interesting. If I had been Father's only son! But then I don't think Father would have taken things to heart as he always loved good fellowship and horses and with loss of money and hard times friends left him.[19]

The Venetian Secret was the obsession of Charles's late middle age, the holy grail which led him to end his career in tragicomedy and isolation. The exact nature of the secret is somewhat obscure. Charles told no one except his artist son Fred, and the secret died with Fred. According to some, it was a formula for obtaining a deep, luminous Venetian red; in another version it was 'a system of tonal perspective obtained by means of underpaintings'. Charles actually wrote an autobiographical novel entitled *The Venetian Secret* (1893), the story of a hunting painter who stumbles across the Venetian Secret in a bundle of manuscripts brought back by his father from the Peninsular War. The secret turns out to be a mathematical formula which Titian had rediscovered from the Greeks. 'I have always been told that the Venetian secret was a varnish and not a mathematical secret as this seems to be,' reflects the painter, realizing that mistranslation of the Greek has caused confusion. Using the formula, he produces a brilliant portrait in only a few brushstrokes, but no one – neither the critics nor the Royal Academy – believes his claim to have rediscovered the secret known to Titian and Joshua Reynolds. His discovery is dismissed as the work of an obscure unknown, his painting condemned as too dark, like the old paintings in the National Gallery.[20]

Charles did indeed offer the Venetian Secret to the Royal Academy and was bitterly hurt when it was rejected. He became paranoid, accusing the Royal Academy of persecuting him and suppressing his discovery. Ever since his army days, when he had invented the instrument for judging distance, Charles had been fascinated by secret geometrical formulae. Perspective was an obsession. 'My father made an instrument which is made of wire which gives you the perfect perspective,' wrote the schoolboy Ned. Like many autodidacts, Charles believed in secret rules and formulae – an obsession he shared with his son Ned, also largely self-taught, for whom architecture was to become a matter of secret angles and mathematical ratios.

At Thursley, Charles presided over a household which was eccentric, unswept but God-fearing. Devoutly Protestant, he stalked into Thursley church with his family, and while they knelt in prayer stood erect and 'smelt' his tall hat. At breakfast each morning he said the Lord's Prayer, always stretching for the porridge before he reached the end.[21] Mary, now growing plump, was more and more absorbed in her religion: church twice on Sundays, Bible reading each night, good works, and over all a gentle, absent vagueness which enabled her to overlook such worldly matters as holes in sheets or children's clothes out at the knee.

A portrait of Ned aged about twelve by his father shows a rather grave little boy with a pointed nose, sharp chin and large, dark-ringed eyes, looking little different from his brothers in his collar and tie. Reading a packet of 'awful little letters of mine' twenty years later, Ned Lutyens was vividly reminded of those days of neediness and want.[22] Above all he remembered his Thursley years as a time of boredom, when there was no school, no one to direct him and nothing to do. 'I should have done better if my mind had been disciplined – I should have had more moral courage, and my mind is dreadfully apt to run about.'[23]

Ned always claimed that he received no formal training in painting or drawing from his father.

The three years he spent in Surrey (1882–5), from the age of thirteen to fifteen, were critical in shaping his future. Instead of attending a 'boy farm', he rambled alone on the heaths of West Surrey and explored hidden villages on his bicycle. In a saffron bag he carried a pane of glass in a wooden frame. The pockets of his too-short trousers bulged with pieces of yellow soap, sharpened to a fine point. When he came to something that interested him, he would prop the glass on a stile or gate and sketch rapidly in soap.

What he saw with sharp eyes was a land of open purple heath – Thursley Common alone was well over one thousand acres; a land of woods which in spring yielded basketfuls of primroses, wood anemones and violets; a land peopled by a silent, sullen peasantry, a race apart – of dumbstruck children who followed old pagan customs, presenting flowers on sticks at May Day, and women in straw bonnets and print gowns, and labourers wearing linen smocks over their corduroys. Ned was hardly likely to realize how fast the peasantry were disappearing, their way of life destroyed by the invasion of suburbia and middle-class Londoners like himself. But he looked for hours at curious shapes such as the baroque curve of a beech tree's roots lining the shady twisting smugglers' roads cut deep into the sand. He saw parish churches, low, dark, damp and squat, crouched and higgledy-piggledy. Cottages fascinated him; timber-framed and casement-windowed, projecting upper storeys hung with tiles, their tile roofs swept down, overhanging the upper windows, and forming curves and angles which he drew with his sharpened soap.

Although Ned later claimed that he educated himself, wandering alone like a vagabond child through the Surrey lanes, the pane of glass has every mark of being Charles's invention. Ned's brother Fred apparently learned to draw the same way.

Only when Ned was older did he think of architecture. 'I got the architectural idea about fifteen or so, and then I was fired and went off at work and never went to bed!!'[24]

The fifteen-year-old Ned was a pathetic figure. 'I don't think you would have looked at me then,' he later told his wife, 'dressed in a brother's clothes, pale, peaky and big-eyed, and in a state of perpetual pencil dust. I am sure the whole two-penny worth of pencil must have gone onto my nose, cheeks and ears – and yet what prodigious designs I essayed. Town halls and Cathedrals ad lib.'[25] A competition design he made about this time survives. Entitled 'Twin-screw Engine for Torpedo Boats and Launches' and carefully inked in red on a large piece of card, punctured deeply with the compass point, its intersecting circles and straight lines anticipate the gardens of his adult designs.

Years later, Ned used to say that it was Randolph Caldecott who had turned his thoughts towards architecture. Probably Caldecott met Charles out hunting but, though a keen rider, Caldecott was no hearty hunting johnnie. Delicate beneath his straggly beard, he was cursed by ill health (he died aged forty in 1886); Walter Crane recalled 'his quiet manner, low voice and gentle but rather serious and earnest way of speaking [which] did not suggest the extraordinary vivacity and humour of his drawings'. His picture books evoked a vanishing English countryside, a Georgian past of half-timbered vernacular buildings, Regency decoration and red-coated squires. He perfected a style of free, loose line drawing in pen-and-ink which he evolved from the tight cross-hatching of Victorian illustrators such as John Leech. Lutyens thought Caldecott 'found a new simplicity of expression in the buildings he so wittily portrayed', though he also claimed that Caldecott cheated by oversimplifying. Caldecott's letters are alive with small, rapidly executed figures, a kind of visual shorthand very similar to the sketches which fill Ned Lutyens's letters.[26]

That Caldecott steered Ned towards architecture rather than painting was a sign of the times. A generation before, in 1856, Rossetti had persuaded the young William Morris to abandon his training in the architect's office of G. E. Street and take up painting, saying that 'if any man had poetry in him, he should paint it, that the course of poetry had almost been run, but painting was still an unknown art in England, and that the next Keats ought to be a painter.' Few architects of the middle decades of the nineteenth century had much poetry about them. Gilbert Scott (1811–78) and William Butterfield (1814–1900) were stern, hard-working professionals, respectful of their clients, grimly Anglican and respectable. Butterfield has been memorably portrayed by his biographer: 'A tall, thin figure, grey-haired by the seventies, with long side-whiskers and round steel spectacles, he invariably dressed in a black frock-coat, white linen shirt, high collar, loosely tied black bow, grey trousers and immaculately polished black capless shoes.' Each day for thirty years Butterfield worked alone in his study, starting in the early morning, lunching in his rooms, walking out to visit his club in mid-afternoon, and returning to his study where, as dusk fell, his servant brought in his shaded reading lamp.[27]

In the 1860s and 1870s, as painting boomed, it was artists, not architects, who made large fortunes, commissioning lavish studio houses from designers such as Norman Shaw. In the 1880s, however, as Shaw's biographer Andrew Saint wrote, 'a whole generation of artists fledged among the cottages, found their passion in architecture, rather than the gradually dying picturesque school of painting. In architecture alone was the rural, romantic tradition really alive at the turn of the century, when literature had turned elsewhere and English painting was uncertain of its course.'[28] One of these cottage fledglings was Ned Lutyens.

Ned later despised architects who sketched, claiming that he could memorize the buildings he needed to know, but as a fifteen-year-old he sketched compulsively. In a letter to his mother, undated but probably written early in 1886, he wrote, 'I hope to go on with sketching excursions harder than ever, and I hope to benefit by the experience obtained last summer.'

It was an endangered Surrey that he drew. Helen Allingham, living at Witley, painted the Surrey vernacular with the eagerness of a woman driven by a mission, desperate to record an English picturesque in imminent danger of disappearance or redevelopment. Of the cottages shown in her 1886 exhibition, six had already been vandalized by landlords who, in the name of modernization, had straightened uneven tile roofs, replaced lattice windows, eliminated thatch and cleared moss, ivy and vine. Never mind that the cottages were previously damp and unhealthy hovels. In her studio stood a pair of diamond lattice windows, which she painted into her sketches, and she freely added picturesque details such as thatch.[29]

In 1877 William Morris formed the Society for the Protection of Ancient Buildings; and ancient weather-beaten parish churches, so vulnerable to the blundering zeal of Anglican restorers, at length received a limited protection, especially necessary in Surrey, whose churches suffered worst of all from the Victorians. Helen Allingham was an ardent supporter, but the SPAB was an unpopular body in the 1880s, disliked on account of its leaders' interfering busybody manner and offensive superiority.

Lord Derby, one of the principal landowners at Thursley, agreed in 1883 not to enclose the land near Hindhead, promising that he 'intended to do all he could to keep the beauty of these places unspoilt'. But in the same year the architect J. W. Penfold began a savage restoration of Thursley church, ripping apart the Saxon fabric and tearing down the ancient ceiling and wooden gallery that flanked the ship-like Tudor timber frame planted in the centre of the nave. Penfold encased the timber frame in a cold, hard stone structure and packed the interior with straight lines of dark-stained sticky-varnished pews. This was precisely the kind of mauling the Society for the Protection of Ancient Buildings was dedicated to prevent. At fifteen Lutyens was too young to protest, but he took a keen interest in Penfold's work, preparing his own drawings and making careful sketches of the old timbering.

Ned Lutyens remembered spending hours in the carpenter's shop in Thursley. At Milford nearby he befriended the carpenter George Tickner. Often taciturn, gruff and uneducated, men like Tickner were the heirs to centuries of ancient wisdom and skill, transmitted not by words but by apprenticeship and example. Only by spending long back-breaking, arm-wrenching hours, coated in sweat and sawdust, in a sawpit pushing a two-man saw, could a man learn how to saw one-inch planks from oak timber. Only experience could teach a man how to choose his timber as it grew, avoiding for instance the oak grown on one particular clay hollow of Alice Holt, where Charles hunted, which had a trick of going 'foxy-hearted' or pithy in the core. In the 1880s these skills were still alive, though threatened increasingly by machinery. George Sturt, who took over his father's wheelwright's shop in nearby Farnham in 1884, considered that his craft was more art than science: 'Our two-foot rules took us no nearer to exactness than the sixteenth of an inch ... very soon a stage was reached when eye and hand were left to their own cleverness, with no guide to help them.'[30]

When, later, Lutyens worked as an architect, his buildings owed much of their effect to traditional craftsmanship, but they never grew solely out of the master-craftsman's skill. He created buildings which evoked vernacular design, but he achieved this by the application of mathematical proportions and geometry. This was not something a boy could absorb by loitering in builders' yards or sketching old churches; it was an exact science which had to be taught.

Shortly before his sixteenth birthday, Ned enrolled as a fee-paying student at the South Kensington School of Art. He probably went on the recommendation of Randolph Caldecott, whose friend Thomas Armstrong was Director of Art at the School.

The South Kensington School was a ten-minute walk from Onslow Square, occupying an L-shaped block on the South Kensington Museum site. Through the Science Gate – a tall arch bearing a terracotta inscription which reads, 'Science and Art Department/Schools Museum 1852' – stands the art school: a bleak block of nondescript smoke-blackened brick. Built in 1864 by Captain Francis Fowke, architect to Henry Cole's South Kensington, it was designed expressly for the school's needs, with large windows and no interior walls but partitioned by screens. By the time Lutyens arrived the school had outgrown Fowke's building, which was crammed with decaying plaster casts and poorly lit. Male and female students used separate entrances and were taught in separate classes; teachers complained that the men students played noisily instead of working and the women chattered.[31]

The syllabus had been drawn up over thirty years before, and under Thomas Armstrong, who became Director of Art in 1881, the school still taught industrial design or applied arts. Armstrong appointed Walter Crane to lecture on the crafts allied to decorative design, such as gesso, plaster relief-work, stencilling and embroidery design. Crane's appointment, a year after Ned enrolled, marks the beginning of Arts and Crafts influence at South Kensington. A successful illustrator,

Crane was also a socialist, a follower of William Morris in the Socialist League and a founder member in 1884 of the Art Workers' Guild.

Crane taught that design derived, not from copying old historical forms, but from the study of natural forms – the square, the circle and the human body. This view of design derived from William Morris and also from Ruskin, who insisted that beauty in architecture was only achieved when it imitated nature. Ned probably absorbed little of Ruskin's message at South Kensington. Later, he was consistently critical of Ruskin, whom he scorned for attempting to describe art in words. His own work, claimed Ned, could never be approached nor understood through literature: true art began where words left off.

Meanwhile, Ruskin was not much on Ned's mind as he walked each morning from Onslow Square, gazing at such sights as a pair of lovers quarrelling on the corner of Exhibition Road. 'The lesson,' he told his sister Molly, 'is that you must *not* elope with any young m–n and I with any l–d–.' He continued: 'I have to pass examination in Perspective in about fortnight's time, ought to pass easily does not matter if I don't.'

Ned spent most of his time in the architectural atelier, following the national architectural course. This consisted of four elements. First came the classical orders. Candidates were required to give the proportions of the parts of an order, and to draw it out, an exercise testing a sense of proportion. Gothic architecture was also studied. To a question in the 1885 examination – *Draw in plan and elevation the door to a Gothic church. Sketch in profile the mouldings, and sketch the carving, if any. State approximately what the date of such a doorway as you select would be* – answers, commented the examiner, were only superficially correct: having obtained his knowledge from books rather than sketching for himself, the student all too often had 'no real idea of the mouldings he was attempting to employ, or the forms he was dealing with, still less of the mode in which the stones, of which his doorway was constructed, would be put together'.[32]

The second element of the course was a paper on architectural construction, including a question on building with iron – a topic which, according to Professor Roger Smith, the school's examiner in Ned's time, was usually poorly taught. The third paper was architectural ornament; the fourth, the most important of all, architectural design. Here too Roger Smith was critical of Ned's class: there was not enough careful study of architectural details and forms, he noted, 'less skill in the application of them than in former years and not such good draughtsmanship'.[33]

South Kensington scored badly in the national architectural course and its students won few medals. It was profoundly resistant to change. Throughout the 1880s, numbers fell: when Ned joined in 1885 the school had 656 students, falling by over thirty each year. Bound in knots of Victorian red tape – neither a flower nor a piece of drapery for an art class could be obtained without a proper form, duly signed and countersigned – South Kensington was paralysed by bureaucratic inertia.

The teacher of architecture at South Kensington in Lutyens's time was Mr Hagreen. A good teacher, but old-fashioned, Mr Hagreen taught his students to indicate shadow on their drawings by tinting, and to paint-in local colour.[34] Ned's South Kensington drawings, which have survived, are stiff, flat and careful, edged by hard lines ruled in Indian ink, which students were taught to use because, unlike pencil, black ink could be reproduced by the technique of photo-lithography. Each stone is laboriously inked in, each window-pane coloured in black-green ink, each shadow tinted. Most of the designs contain half-timbering, and they are strongly influenced by Norman Shaw, then at the height of his fame.

In 1886 Ned submitted a design for a villa residence to the *Building News*. Commending 'Simplex et Prudens' (as Ned called himself) for his familiarity with 'the red-brick houses of Queen's Gate and Cadogan Square', that is, the Queen Anne style of Norman Shaw, the judge commented, 'Had his drawings been better he would have been placed much higher in our list.'[35]

More indebted to Norman Shaw is Ned's competition design for a country house, drawn when he was eighteen. Mounted on large boards of card, the seven careful drawings depict a massive ship-like structure: half-timbered with a Tudor prow, a gothic hall and tracery windows. Strongly influenced by Shaw's Pierrepoint and Merrist Wood, both of which Ned must have seen in Surrey, the design won a National Bronze Medal in 1888, though this was not especially distinguished: in 1887 fee-paying South Kensington students won one gold, five silver and ten bronze medals.

We can glimpse Ned's life at South Kensington from a long letter he wrote to his mother from Onslow Square at this time:

My darling Mother,
  You are going to get a letter at last.
  On Sunday I went to Great St Bartholomew Smithfield a most beautiful old church full of interest . . . The interior is beautiful!! Norman with a

Norman apse (has lately been very well restored by Aston Webb)* there is also a remainder of a Norman arcade down the church 3 or 4 piers still remaining with their semi circular arch and Norman triforium the clerestory is of later work there is also a trace of Early English evidently built at the same time as gateway additions in perpendicular ... Take away the gas and you can imagine yourself in a country church ...

Father would admire St Bartholomew's very much I mean to take him there ... I am going to sketch there as soon as I get my competition drawings done, over which I have had a run of bad luck and so will not be able to make a good show which is very disappointing.

Read the following extract to Father, it is from the Surrey Archaeological Society's paper. Speaking of Sutton Place Guildford 'The whole house is built of brick and terracotta *no* stone whatever being used in its construction or ornamentation.'†

When I came home from my first excursion from Sutton I told Father that it was built of terracotta and brick which he flatly contradicted and said that it was impossible terracotta being used for building purposes then and that it was a fine sandstone.

Not that I bring any accusation against Father but only to show him what a small amount of confidence I have in the little I know, to allow myself to be convicted of a thing which I knew was wrong and that it only shows how necessary it is for me to concentrate my whole attention, energy and time on possessing that confidence and also to obtain that great amount of knowledge required to help make a 'successful architect' and an architect without that success (not financial necessarily) is, well I can't describe it ...

I doubt very much if my competition things will win anything. So be ready for a blow when my failure is announced.

I heard today that a fellow called Mayhew who has been working at S K Museum has gone violently mad it took 6 men to take him to an asylum, he was 19 years old. They say it was from overwork but that's all bosh ...

... met Mr Peploe‡ he asked me where I had been to church. I told him where I had been to but could not answer any of his questions as to who was the vicar etc, and then I told him that I went for sake of the architecture, he looked shocked and asked me whether I brought back a good word I said O yes!! Did he mean an architecture tip? Next Sunday he will bring in his sermon, My – de-ar – brethren – Last – Sunday – I met a lad – who went to the house – of God (here looks round his crooked eye fixed on me) for the architecture etc etc. Now I feel much better disposed

---

*Aston Webb's restoration is less well regarded today by Pevsner and the heirs of the SPAB.
†According to the journal of the Surrey Archaeological Society (1886): 'The whole house is built of brick and terra-cotta, no stone whatever having been used in the construction or ornamentation.'
‡Webb-Peploe was the Evangelical vicar of Onslow Square.

towards man and beast and feel (holier?) when in a beautiful church with good music, and after all you get the lessons, prayers etc wherever you go and the sermon is at best a bad translation of the bible . . . I hope you won't think me a heretic I admire Mr Peploe as much as I ever did . . .

Does Arthur come up next Sunday we will have to share our top hat again. I have not one I use Arthur's ask him if he remembers when we changed hats in the street much to the amusement of the cabby. My billycock, handed down from Frank, has a hole in the top, it was there when I had it . . .

Yr very loving son, E L Lutyens

PS I hope Father's big picture is getting on alright. Frank says it is beautiful. It sounds good . . .

12 p.m. I will get through another hour's work yet.

I am still charged with the complaint of singing in the early hours of the morning at hours I can prove that I was in bed (and asleep). Perhaps I dream of Palaces etc and trumpet in my joy or rather sleep. A dreamless sleep is a joy.

At sixteen, Ned lived, breathed and dreamed architecture. Already he knew how to 'read' St Bartholomew's as the examiners at South Kensington required. Crouched under the gaslight late at night in his upstairs bedroom at Onslow Square he laboriously inked in his competition designs, absorbed in a fantasy world of palaces where he could escape the neediness, the shared top hats, the handed-down trousers and joshing of brotherly life. Towards his father Ned is respectful and anxious to impress, but it is Mary whom he wants to please through his success; Mary to whom he opens his thoughts, frightening her with the story of the boy who went mad through overwork. Rewarded with her encouragement, the result, as he foresaw, would be an 'astonishing confidence'.

Back in Surrey the following summer Ned made measured drawings of more early churches: Compton with its dog-toothed Norman arches and rare two-storey chancel, and Dunsfold, an architect's building designed and built entirely in the year 1270. His growing confidence can be seen from the designs he made for the Earl of Home, a client of his father, who generously invited him to design an extension to the Hirsel in Berwickshire. 'It is one of the most interesting [problems] I have ever had,' wrote the seventeen-year-old architect, nothing if not cocksure, and he submitted a grandiose proposal for transforming the house's Georgian windows into Tudor bays, raising the roof and opening up the saloon.[36]

In a lecture on 'Mistakes in Architecture', Professor Roger Smith of South Kensington remarked that one of the worst mistakes a student could make was not to go to the Continent. Ned did not reach Italy until he was forty. But in 1887 as an eighteen-year-old he visited Normandy, following the architectural trail trodden by the 'Victorian Goths': Ruskin, G. E. Street, Gilbert Scott, William Morris and Edward Burne-Jones.

The only evidence of the visit is a set of four large battered boards of competition drawings now in the Royal Institute of British Architects (RIBA) which came to light in 1973. Labelled 'Set of Architectural Sketches in Normandy', they are mounted with fifty-four drawings cut from a sketchbook and dated 'Aug 24th – Aug 28th'.

Reginald Blomfield, Lutyens's later colleague, who travelled through France and Spain in 1883, lamented that 'owing to the disastrous misconception of architecture spread abroad by Ruskin', students were taught to waste their time sketching unimportant details of architectural ornament rather than analysing the structure of buildings. Not knowing what to look for, Blomfield packed his own notebooks with useless sketches, and learned little of plan, composition and proportion.[37]

Did Ned know what he was looking for? The sketches suggest a young architect in search of the picturesque, his eye educated by Surrey, early churches and the Arts and Crafts enthusiasm for the vernacular. At Rouen he ignored the great cathedral which fired the Gothic revivalists and later the Impressionists, and instead sketched timber-framed houses and the simple fifteenth-century Hôtel de Bourgtheroulde. After taking the train to Bernay, he sketched a fourteenth-century church; a few miles further on, at Lisieux, he sketched timber houses and, at Caen, an eleventh-century church. At Coutances, he skirted the soaring gothic cathedral of Notre Dame and drew a fifteenth-century church.

But it was Mont-Saint-Michel that seems to have impressed him most. A pointed cone of granite sticking out of the sea, the island could be reached only at low tide, by crossing the sands in a ramshackle canvas-covered open omnibus. The single narrow street swarmed with tourists, most of them English, sitting on their portmanteaux as they queued for a bed in one of the two inns.[38] Ned was fascinated by the gothic verticals perched on a granite point; memories of Mont-Saint-Michel surely informed the massing he achieved on the granite rock of Lindisfarne nearly twenty years later. At Mont-Saint-Michel he found a simple, elemental gothic which he could absorb, and he filled his sketchbook with high-pitched roofs, battered walls and buttresses; with details such as the simple tracery in the windows of the parish church and a massive stone chimneypiece in the Salle des Chevaliers.

Detmar Blow, a fellow architectural student at South Kensington, won the Architectural Association travelling scholarship in 1888, and embarked on a sketching tour of northern France. In Abbeville, as Blow prepared to sketch the ornate cathedral much praised by Ruskin, he and his friend Sidney Cockerell ran into the great man himself. Nearing seventy, Ruskin was erect and fierce as ever, blue-eyed beneath the mane of Viking hair. Invigorated by the admiration of the young men, Ruskin played the lion. Cockerell reverently carried his umbrella and wrote down every word he said, while Ruskin organized daily expeditions at 8 a.m., climbed church steeples and gave away his sketches. Alone with Blow – dear Detmar, as he fondly called him – Ruskin journeyed across France, through Italy and Switzerland. Detmar, wrote Ruskin, was 'exactly the companion I wanted – eagerly enjoying everything – absolutely obedient – and an entirely skilful measurer and surveyor – with the *taste* of a painter which I am fast developing in him'. But Detmar's intercourse with the light soon became a descent into nightmare. On the journey home Ruskin sank into deep depression, and the nineteen-year-old Blow found himself chaperoning a sick man across Europe.

Ruskin never recovered but lingered on until 1900, drivelling into his long blond beard, a pathetic victim of dementia. Lutyens, who must have heard this story, always thought of Ruskin as mad. But Blow's adventure brought him a celebrity which Ned must have envied. 'Cockerell never liked me and he used to be very rude,' he wrote later. 'I think Blow – he was a friend of his – upset him towards me.'[39] Young Ned Lutyens was unknown, he had no patron, and very little money; nothing but ambition and 'that confidence' which he knew an architect must have.

Chapter Three

Ernest George versus Gertrude Jekyll 1887–1892

Sketches by Ned of Gertrude Jekyll. *Above:* With a sunflower. *Below:* Her apotheosis.

Late in 1887 Ned Lutyens left South Kensington and entered the architect's office of Ernest George. Becoming an articled pupil was the usual course for a Victorian architect in the days before professional training schools existed. Articles lasted usually three, sometimes five years; but Ned, who started younger than most, stayed only a year and a half. Later, he claimed that he learned nothing in this short time. The claim was untrue, but even by the haphazard standards of that date his professional training was minimal. Ned despised his master Ernest George partly because he was not Norman Shaw. As a boy Ned had dreamed of joining Shaw's office, and when he was eighteen he met the great man.

Forster Arbuthnot, a hunting neighbour of Charles Lutyens, had come across the Lutyens family living like gypsies on the wildest part of Surrey's heathland.* 'A shock-headed boy [Ned] and a lovely girl [Molly] appeared when they perceived strangers approaching. Father was summoned to speak with us. There was no mistaking the man's vocation; artist was written in every line of his face, and a certain inspiration glowed in his eyes.' Arbuthnot took pity on the old bohemian and commissioned him to paint first his horse and then his dog. He enjoyed Charles's conversation in mangled English interlarded with idiomatic French and German. Believing that Charles was an exile from Alsace-Lorraine, he sensed that here was 'a case of frustration, a soul sundered from its true anchorage, adrift in a wide ocean of unfamiliar currents', and he determined to help the family by finding a husband for the daughter and a profession for the son.

Arbuthnot had married a wealthy widow, Elinor Guthrie, who lived nearby at Shamley Green. Norman Shaw had twice enlarged her house, and in 1887 she engaged Shaw to make still more additions. Arbuthnot showed Ned the plans, and encouraged him to suggest improvements. Shaw was annoyed. 'Whom in the world have you been consulting?' he asked. Arbuthnot told him about the eighteen-year-old who built

---

*Violet Guthrie (later Stuart-Wortley), Forster Arbuthnot's stepdaughter, told the story in her memoirs sixty-five years later.

wattle-and-daub cowsheds for the local farmers. 'Send him to me,' said Shaw. 'That lad is worth training; he has ideas! Still, it was pretty good cheek . . .'

Next time Shaw came down to Shamley Green, Ned was summoned. Violet Guthrie remembered how the hobbledehoy tidied himself for the meeting. His hair was anointed and plastered down with streaks of grease, he wore a borrowed suit of ill-fitting clothes and the vicar's boots, which made him limp. Shaw, then in his mid-fifties, was a professional Scot with a steely glint in his eye; well over six foot tall, broad-shouldered and thin, he was precisely spoken and wryly humorous. Soon Ned was telling him about his experiments in farm buildings. Mud-encased on wooden piles, roofed with heather, resistant to wind and weather, warm in winter, cool in summer, they conformed to what he gravely called 'my fixed principles', namely that anything built by man should harmonize with Nature. 'Very interesting, my boy,' said Shaw with a smile, 'but not always feasible. All right for cowsheds but . . . if you had my experience you would find that the newly-rich, who after all are the patrons of today, demand replicas of something they have seen in other countries they have visited.'

As soon as Shaw had gone, Ned gave a boisterous imitation of him. Violet remembered laughing at his parody of Queen Victoria: he puffed out his cheeks, wore an antimacassar on his head and spoke in a strong German accent. As for his imitation of the local vicar hurrying through the Athanasian creed, that was 'convulsively comic'.[1]

Ned's 'fixed principles' of building in local materials were the basis of Arts and Crafts style, and his wattle-and-daub garden sheds and farm buildings are still being identified by architectural historians today. But Shaw did not take Lutyens as his pupil. Perhaps the bumptious *wunderkind*, ingratiating yet pushy, annoyed him. Perhaps he had no places. As the fame of his office grew, its waiting list lengthened; eighty names queued for pupillages.[2]

Ned's failure rankled. Ten years later he was still having anxiety dreams about meeting Shaw.[3]

But the office of Ernest George was not in any way a backwater. Sometimes called the Eton of architects' offices, it was smart and fashionable, but it stood to one side of what might be called the Great Tradition of Victorian architecture. By contrast with Norman Shaw, who could claim descent from the apostolic succession of Scott and Street, Ernest George was an outsider who had never touched the holy flame.

1887–1892

If one draws a family tree of Victorian architects, tracing them back to the offices where they were trained, the founder of the dynasty emerges as Sir George Gilbert Scott, who designed more than five hundred churches. He ran the largest office in England, with thirty assistants and draughtsmen. Much of his time was spent steaming around the country by train. Like Mr Pecksniff in Dickens's *Martin Chuzzlewit*, Scott took credit for designs that were actually made by his pupils, though in Scott's case the reason was not guile but overwork. Each morning three or four young men stood waiting with their drawings outside his door. The door flew open and out he came. 'No time today!' The cab was outside and he was whisked away.

Run on a loose rein, such architects' offices were fertile with talent. Pupils there had the chance to design, rather than merely copy drawings.* Scott's haphazard methods cost him control over his designs, but his office produced such talents as T. A. Jackson, the architect of an Oxford expanding in response to mid-Victorian university reform, and G. F. Bodley, most meticulous of the gothic revivalists.

Most successful of all Scott's pupils was George Edmund Street. For him there was only one style of architecture, and that was gothic, early French especially, Chartres and Amiens. Gothic for Street was a crusade, and he wore himself out in the cause; no job was too small, no church too distant. In his office, the rattle of his T-square was grimly incessant. 'Mr Street works by drawings,' said Gilbert Scott, 'I by influence.' Street was an autocrat. He controlled every detail and his pupils were not allowed to design so much as a keyhole. Stout and bearded, with large feet and a vigorous walk, he drove himself to death over the Law Courts, a flawed and impractical attempt to realize the gothic ideal. The young architect Reginald Blomfield, who encountered Street at the Royal Academy, thought him faintly absurd; an elderly doctrinaire, stubborn and intolerant, trapped in a doomed attempt to realize a historically inaccurate theory.[4] Ned would no doubt have agreed. A generation before, however, Street's reputation as leader of the gothic revival had attracted a galaxy of talent: Philip Webb, William Morris and Norman Shaw, all were pupils of G. E. Street. Norman Shaw was the most prolific, and his career encapsulates the shift from ecclesiastical gothic to metropolitan classical via Old English

---

*Copying drawings was the kind of tedious, mechanical work that drove the young Thomas Hardy to leave the office of the church architect Arthur Blomfield.

47

and Queen Anne; nor is it surprising, given his gothic training, that some of his country houses seem like churches.

If Ned Lutyens had become Shaw's pupil, he would have joined a fizzing and rumbustious office at 29 Bloomsbury Square. Shaw was a father figure to his pupils, allowing them freedom to collaborate on designs. Five men to whom Shaw was especially close formed a tight-knit group known as the 'family'. Ernest Newton, William Lethaby, Gerald Horsley, Edward Prior and Mervyn Macartney were all about ten years older than Lutyens; all, except Lethaby, were public-school or university men. In 1883 they formed the St George's Art Society, a group dedicated to the discussion of Architecture and Art with a capital A. Neither bohemians nor limp-wristed aesthetes, they were muscular and earnest; the heirs to the Victorian ecclesiologists, they sought moral meaning in architecture; armed with sketchbooks, they tramped the countryside in search of Englishness.

Architecture, for the five of the St George's Art Society, was an art not a profession, and they resented the Royal Institute of British Architects, which threatened to make architecture a profession like law or surveying, straitjacketing it with professional examinations and regulations. Encouraged by Shaw, the five endeavoured to bring architecture closer to art, canvassing artists and designers such as Walter Crane and the bookbinder Cobden-Sanderson to join a new society which they called the Art Workers' Guild (1884).

Reginald Blomfield recalled the fortnightly meetings of the guild, held initially in a room in St James's and after 1887 at Barnard's Inn, Holborn. They met at 8 p.m. The guild's officers wore specially designed robes. No women attended.* Someone read a paper on his craft, illustrated by demonstrations. Everyone smoked, and the meeting adjourned for whiskies-and-soda, followed by discussion. Often they talked about practical things, the understanding being that no one kept back his secrets; but sometimes the arguments became heated, as when someone dared to pour scorn on Raphael. Blomfield believed that the guild helped rescue the arts from the paralysing conventions of Victorianism and liberated architecture from 'the slow death of revivalism'.[5]

Ernest George was a small balding man with slightly protuberant blue eyes and a wispy blond beard. A pupil of the obscure Samuel Hewitt, he had been influenced by G. E. Street, but by the time Ned Lutyens

---

*Even today, when women members are admitted, the guild persists in calling them brethren.

joined the office George, then nearing fifty, had long shaken off gothic and emerged as leader of a hybrid style of Flemish and Queen Anne. His practice was largely domestic, and he was known for two types of building: big country houses in historic styles, such as the Mitfords' Batsford Park; and London houses in the style Osbert Lancaster was to dub Pont Street Dutch.

Norman Shaw was said to have a printed card which alleged that he was 'too busy to oblige Lord —'. He would cross out 'Lord' and insert 'Mr', and his pupils would add, 'but advises clients that Mr Ernest George's office is at 18 Maddox Street'.[6] This was unkind. The office of Ernest George and his partner Harold Peto was one of the busiest in London. Number 18 was a bright red-brick office building with shops below and three floors of offices above. George's office was on the first floor, up a steep, dark, narrow flight of stairs to the side of the building. The front door was operated by a wire which saved the office boy running up and down the stairs. The landing at the head of the stairs was unexpectedly wide and hung with gold-framed architectural drawings of George's elephantine country houses. There was a waiting room, a room for George and one for Harold Peto and a drawing office where Ned Lutyens worked.

George's own room was oak-panelled in the Dutch style. George loved beautiful things, and antique dealers called regularly at the office with Persian rugs, Delft plates and Japanese china. He furnished the windows with Flemish shutters and patterned them with panes of Dutch and German stained glass which reflected pools of coloured light on to the brightly polished bare oak boards of the floor. Sweet-smelling logs smouldered in the open fire. Above it hung a sombre Italian oil and the room was scattered with Italian dishes; and in the midst of this ostentatious good taste, down the centre of the room, ran the drawing board where George worked. Secretly admiring, Ned fitted out his upstairs room at Onslow Square with Dutch shutters and an 'oversized and over-hanging fireplace'.[7]

In the drawing office where Ned worked there were six articled pupils and two assistants. The desks were inscribed with initials, carved with a penknife and filled in with red sealing-wax. EGD, AM, HR, HB – E. Guy Dawber, Arnold Mitchell, Herbert Read, Herbert Baker. Lutyens soon added his own ELL.[8]

The chief assistant was Herbert Baker. Tall, idealistic and priggish, Baker had been captain of cricket and football at Tonbridge. He was seven years older than Ned, but he became his friend.

Ernest George was essentially a pictorial architect. An exceptional watercolourist, he would start by producing a watercolour perspective of a house, where other men began with a plan or section. Not that George's houses were poorly planned. Quite the contrary, he was an able and meticulous planner. Two of the country-house plans which he revived, the Elizabethan H (Batsford, 1887–93) and the medieval quadrangle (Rousdon, 1874–82), were adapted and developed by Ned Lutyens. As Darcy Braddell, one of his pupils, pointed out, however, George's pictorial approach meant that he never conceived a building as an organic whole. He did not think in three dimensions.[9]

Diving apologetically into his sketchbooks, offering his clients a choice of styles – Gothic? Queen Anne? Jacobean? – George was an irresistible figure of fun to Ned, who was an accomplished mimic. His burlesques of his master set off gales of laughter when the drawing-office door was closed. Herbert Baker remembered him joking through his short pupillage; however wearisome the jokes were to seem in middle age, Lutyens at eighteen was endearingly and outrageously funny. Yet Baker noted how quickly Lutyens absorbed all that was worth learning. 'He puzzled us at first, but we soon found that he seemed to know by intuition some great truths of our art which were not to be learnt there.'[10]

George had made his reputation building flamboyant South Kensington houses in a style which grafted Flemish motifs on to Queen Anne, exactly expressing the reaction of the mid-Victorian upper-middle class against the formal Italianate stucco of such terraces as Onslow Square. George's gabled, decorated houses were the high point of Victorian architectural individualism; each one was different, though in fact they formed an organized speculative development. By the time Lutyens joined the office, George was finishing work on Harrington Gardens and Collingham Gardens, his showcase project – a small Dutch town – where he produced a series of 'wildly picturesque Flemish burghers' houses, inflated to suitably Victorian size, injected with a certain amount of Jacobean and Renaissance detailing, and carried out ... in the fashionable material of the moment, yellow terracotta'.[11]

George's formula was immensely successful and widely copied, but Lutyens was later to condemn him as

> an architect who took each year a three weeks' holiday abroad and returned with overflowing sketchbooks. When called on for a project he would look through these and choose some picturesque turret or gable from Holland, France or Spain and round it weave his new design.

Location mattered little and no provincial formation influenced him, for at that time terra cotta was the last word in building. All honour to Philip Webb and Norman Shaw (in his later period) for their gallant attempt to bring England back to craftsmanship and tradition.[12]

Neither Norman Shaw nor Philip Webb would touch terracotta, which was the rage of the 1870s, shiny and man-made. But Lutyens's attack on Ernest George's sketchbook school of architecture misleads, deliberately or not. He implies that he himself never sketched, but as a young architect he sketched all the time. In 1887 he had barely heard of Philip Webb. Nor was he as dismissive of George as he implies. When Lutyens married, George sent him a watercolour of a French village ('quite nice and good') and wrote 'such a kind letter ... saying he always looks upon me as one of his pupils'.[13] Later Lutyens became ashamed of it, but George meant much to him at the time.

In 1887 Lutyens's drawing was stiff and immature. George taught him to draw designs in soft perspective, washed in brownish sepia ink, often taken from a 'worm's eye view', looking upwards from below ground level.[14] George, like Street, designed almost everything himself. He made plans, elevations and details, and he drew full-size mouldings. Lutyens and the pupils in the drawing office then elaborated the plans of roofs, the direction of flues, the exact spacing of stairs and, as George explained, the 'innumerable details (many of them not interesting) but on which the comfort of the house so largely depends'.[15] Lutyens learned to draw plans to a scale of one-eighth of an inch, using ink produced in the drawing office by laboriously grinding a stick of Chinese ink round and round in a pool of water, and Whatman drawing paper which had first to be strained on a board.

Furnishings and ironwork George would also design himself, making full-size drawings with sections showing the precise planes of each object. He would lie full-length on the floor, rapidly and accurately sketching. The drawings were handed over to skilled craftsmen whom he summoned to his room: men such as the metalworker Starkie Gardner who executed George's elaborate designs for locks, hinges and firedogs.

Lutyens, too, was to make full-size drawings for ironwork and he, too, was to employ Starkie Gardner. He was to organize his office in the same way as George, designing everything himself. Above all, he learned from George a sense of history. George's strength lay in his ability to assimilate historic styles and motifs, Dutch in London, Elizabethan in his country houses. Old towers, outbuildings, outside stairs, unconcealed roof timbers and most of all the medieval hall: these were typical of Ernest George. He was a romantic architect, 'a northern Romantic who has never been tempted by Italian brilliance and rhythm'.[16]

Lutyens absorbed far more from George than he cared to admit.

When he was fifty-one Lutyens told the Architectural Association:

> I was sent at first to an architect whose name I forget and was set to draw circles on oily paper. After two days I ran away. At least I refused to go back. My father wanted me to work with a builder, but I didn't see that that had anything to do with architecture. Of course I see now. [Laughter and applause.] Then I got a house to build at nineteen, and I've been building them ever since. That's all. It was great fun that first house. *I advise everyone to build a house at nineteen*. It's such good practice.[17]

In fact Lutyens had spent not two days but well over a year in the office of Ernest George. And though it must have seemed crazy at the time, leaving George's office in London and setting up practice on his own in Surrey turned out to be the making of his career.

At nineteen, his training had barely begun. He had neither completed his articles, nor worked as assistant in an architect's office. He had no experience of supervising a site. He had barely travelled. Though he attended evening classes of the Architectural Association, he had not enrolled at the Royal Academy architectural school, the classes to which Shaw and George entered their pupils after a year or so in an office. English architectural education was woefully inadequate by contrast with the rigorous classical training provided by the Ecole des Beaux Arts in France; architects were trained to look 'rather with the eye of the scene-painter than with that of the scholar'. The Royal Academy was England's leading architectural school in the 1880s, but Lutyens never gained his 'bone', the ivory disc students received on admission: nor does his name appear on the school's register.[18]

The house that Lutyens was commissioned to design at the age of nineteen was Crooksbury in Surrey, but little is known about how he got the job except that it was through local connections. The romantic narrative of Lutyens's life ascribes a key role during these years to his relationship with Barbara Webb. More than twenty years older than Lutyens, she was the wife of Robert Webb, the local squire. Cultured, charming and an insider in the great world of London society, Barbara Webb is credited with taking up the young Ned Lutyens, adopting him as her protégé, and introducing him to the gentry of West Surrey, who opened their doors to him and commissioned him.

Like the stories that he was brought up totally in Surrey and never went to school, this is only half true. It rests partly on Lutyens's subsequent denial of the role of his family, partly on the romantic myth of the Surrey *wunderkind*. At this point, Ned still lived at home, dividing his time between Thursley and Onslow Square. Barbara Webb was certainly a figure in his life, but her importance came later. The truth is that the years following Lutyens's time in George's office are a blur. Very little evidence has survived but the record of the designs he made, which is almost certainly incomplete. Lutyens remembered these as years of work. 'For five or six years I went to no parties; I knew no one and worked till 12 or 2 in the morning. I bicycled a lot and walked a good deal, but no sport and relaxation, just work.'[19] He made it a habit to draw something new each day, usually between 12 and 2 at night, but he had not yet found a voice or style of his own, and many of the houses he designed are strongly influenced by Ernest George.

His first documented work was a cottage called The Corner in Thursley, across the village green from his family house, The Cottage. The drawings, made while he was still a pupil in George's office, are exquisite; more like an illuminated manuscript than builders' designs, the plans, sketch and elevations are inked and washed in miniature on a single piece of brown paper. But though he could draw like an angel, as an architect Ned was still immature. The brief was to add a sitting-room extension at the back of two tiny cottages which had been knocked together. A sweetshop specializing in enormous bull's-eyes, The Corner was owned by the village builder, Mr Fosberry, who carried out the work; perhaps he was the builder with whom Charles wanted Ned to go into business. Lutyens's design, with its tile-hung gables, tall chimney and ingle, was stolen from a cottage at Harpenden which Ernest George was building at the time; today, it seems rather pert and overwrought.[20]

Crooksbury, too, pays passing homage to George. The client who commissioned the nineteen-year-old architect to build a holiday house was Arthur Chapman, who had known Ned since he was a schoolboy, when Charles Lutyens had painted his mother. 'I think Mrs Chapman's portrait will be very good,' the twelve-year-old Ned told his mother from school.[21] Chapman, now thirty-seven, was a partner in Piggott & Chapman, jute merchants of Calcutta. His wife was Agnes Mangles, a cousin of Elinor Arbuthnot of Upper House, and he had bought a plot of land on Crooksbury Hill, close to Agnes's brother Harry Mangles who lived near Seale. Crooksbury was a family connection, and not, as has been suggested, a result of the patronage of Barbara Webb.

Mary Lutyens was probably the link between Ned and the families of the Chapmans and Mangles. Although her evangelicalism meant that she thought going into society was wrong, Mary liked Agnes Chapman, a serious-minded woman who was not only devoutly religious but an enlightened housekeeper who kept a strict system of accounts. The Chapmans had kept a benevolent eye on Ned since his days at South Kensington. 'Chapmans . . . have a jolly house in Hereford Square awfully kind dine there every Sat,' Ned told his sister.[22]

Experts on Ernest George have detected quotations from him in Lutyens's L-shaped, timber-framed design.[23] But something else is at work here too. At Crooksbury the horizontals of the long, low house are punctuated and balanced by tall brick chimneys. The massive inglenook chimney in the hall, elaborately angled in brick, is copied from an old cottage at Shere nearby. This is possibly the first example of Lutyens deliberately incorporating traditional Surrey motifs into his work. It also happens to be a feature illustrated in a book published the same year by the architect and Surrey antiquary Ralph Nevill.

Nevill pioneered the rediscovery of traditional Surrey building. He wrote up old churches and contributed an influential series of drawings of old Surrey houses in the *Builder*, later published as a book, *Old Cottage and Domestic Architecture in South-West Surrey* (1889). Lutyens knew of Nevill's work; as a boy of sixteen he was already reading about Nevill's researches in the journal of the Surrey Archaeological Society. By comparing features such as the Crooksbury chimney with Nevill's drawings it becomes possible to document Lutyens's sources. Crooksbury is a breakthrough, however, because it goes beyond mere historical imitation. Traditional features are used to create something new, the first hint of a 'new' Surrey style. On the garden front at Crooksbury, for the first time, 'the numbers of the combination lock click together'.*

Lutyens was so nervous about Crooksbury that he would visit it on

---

*The architectural historian Ian Nairn, writing in the Surrey volume of *Pevsner*, thought the garden front of Crooksbury one of the best things Lutyens ever did. 'The effect here of space flowing uniformly in all directions is a true equivalent to Frank Lloyd Wright. The inside of this part, with intimate space flowing freely from room to passage to staircase, all on different levels, is as experimental and fresh as anything Wright was doing in 1890.'

his bicycle at night, after the builders had gone. The plans he signed with a flourish: E. *Landseer* Lutyens. The inglenook chimney smoked dreadfully and Lutyens and Chapman tried everything to correct it, which they eventually succeeded in doing by boring holes.

Later, Lutyens refused to visit Crooksbury. He said it held too many memories.* The house is a kind of potted biography, as Lutyens added another wing to it in 1898–9 which he then reluctantly altered (and ruined) to please new clients in 1914.

But perhaps Crooksbury also brought back memories of his mother. A quarter of a century later, standing in the churchyard at Thursley beside Mary Lutyens's freshly dug grave, which was heaped high with dead and dying flowers, Ned looked north, towards the village; he could clearly see the garden at The Cottage which she had so loved and beyond that the beautiful view towards Crooksbury. 'It was last night wondrous pathetic and heartbreaking,' he wrote. 'All that country is so much wrapt up with Mother and my first work.'[24]

Next door to Crooksbury at Littleworth lived Agnes Chapman's bachelor brother Harry Mangles, 'a dear kind man' who had bought a twenty-acre plot of sandy soil of 'little worth' in 1878. Here he built a Norman Shaw-like half-timbered house and planted a jungle of rhododendrons. Harry Mangles and his brother James, who died prematurely, were both breeders of hybrid rhododendrons, which flourished on Littleworth's sandy soils, and Harry Mangles named the flowers he bred after the women he knew. Harry's Agneses, Hildas and Lillians still scatter their petals in the Littleworth jungle, like the ghosts of pretty women of the 1890s – blousy, décolleté and a little overblown in mauves and pinks and whites. (Lillian, beautiful stepdaughter of the painter G. F. Watts, disliked her eponymous rhododendron: 'I bet it was ugly, he hated me.') Lutyens may have been as young as sixteen when he first came to Littleworth and made crude drawings for seats and gazebos to put in the clearings. In the summer of 1889 he designed a fowl house, a simple barge-boarded hut, hung with tiles, thatched with heather and standing on stone supports. Perched on top was a dovecot in Ernest George's medieval style. That summer he also designed a gardener's cottage at Littleworth, half-timbered and tall-chimneyed, also influenced by George.[25]

The design for the gardener's cottage is dated 17 May 1889, and at

---

*One memory, Ian Nairn was to remark, was the ghost of Lutyens's artistic integrity.

the time that Lutyens was working on the plans Harry Mangles invited him to Littleworth to meet his gardening friend Gertrude Jekyll. At the tea table over the silver kettle, the talk was of rhododendrons. Ned Lutyens observed a stout, plain, abruptly spoken spinster of forty-six wearing steel-rimmed spectacles with pebble lenses and a black felt hat springing with alert black cock's tail feathers above the 'bunch of cloaked propriety' he later knew as her 'Go-to-Meeting Frock'. She addressed not a word to him at tea, but as she left, one foot on the pony-cart step, she invited him to her home at Munstead the next Saturday.

'I was there on the tick of four,' he remembered. Tearing along the Surrey lanes on his 'bone-shaker', untamed hair streaming backwards in the wind, Lutyens arrived to find a very different Miss Jekyll, genial and even skittish. She wore a short blue skirt well above the ankle, a pair of thick-soled, lovingly dubbined men's boots, size eight, a blue linen apron, its ample marsupial pouch bulging with horticultural instruments, and a blue-striped, box-pleated linen blouse cut like a Norfolk jacket.[26]

Women who met Gertrude Jekyll (pronounced to rhyme with treacle) always noticed her plainness. 'She is very fat and stumpy, dresses rather like a man, little tiny eyes, very nearly blind and big spectacles,' wrote Emily Lytton a few years later.[27] But Jekyll's plainness was in reality her liberation. Her father called the tomboy with a face like a squinting currant bun his 'curiosity'. 'More of a boy than a girl', she was never expected to do the things other women of her class did, to flirt, marry and rear children. Exempt from the male gaze, Jekyll could do what she pleased. She attended South Kensington School of Art, mixed with feminists, including Barbara Bodichon, and painted Turneresque oils. She wore clumpy men's boots. She excelled at embroidery, metalwork, silverwork, gilding, carving, wild flowers, music, shell pictures . . . In short, she was a one-woman Arts and Crafts movement. How do you manage to do so much work, asked an admiring neighbour. 'By not going to tea parties,' responded Jekyll. 'I don't go to tea parties,' said the neighbour. 'Ah, but you are married, and that is one person's occupation.'[28]

In 1878 Jekyll and her widowed mother bought a plot of land at Munstead outside Godalming where they built a house. Jekyll laid out the garden, following the advice of William Robinson, editor of the *Garden* magazine, who decreed that every garden should grow out of its local habitat. In her forties her eyesight deteriorated alarmingly and painfully. Doctors diagnosed acute myopia, and Jekyll must have feared that she was going blind.* Desperate to record what she saw while she still could, she taught herself photography. 'Keep the camera level. Expose less. More pyro. Less bromide,' she scrawled on her prints. As the world closed in about her, she photographed the things she cared about: mainly flowers, but also trees, landscapes and old Surrey cottages together with the gnarled, weather-beaten peasants who lived in them, stiffly posed in smocks and bonnets. The old Surrey she recorded was itself disappearing almost as fast as her eyesight was failing. Driven by the disciplined energy of an obsessive, between 1885 and 1888 she shot and developed an archive of photographs that was to supply the basic material for the books she began to produce fifteen years later.[29]

Exactly what Jekyll taught Lutyens has always been a matter of speculation.† Lutyens's impact on Jekyll, however, is fleetingly documented in the pages of her photograph album. Pasted into the album for 1889–90, abruptly interrupting her studies of spring plantings, are photographs of four Surrey houses Lutyens designed in 1889–90: Crooksbury; a barber's shop in the village street at Shere; Hoe Farm at Hascombe, where he designed a spectacular chimney; and a pair of lodges at Park Hatch. Some of these are juxtaposed against prints of old cottages. How to read these photographs is the puzzle: who is teaching whom? Was Jekyll recording the work of the twenty-year-old prodigy, or did she help inspire these early essays, providing vernacular examples for him to replicate? Whatever the relationship, it is clear that here is the tentative beginning of the Surrey style of Ned Lutyens, a style which Gertrude Jekyll was the first to promote.[30]

Jekyll took Lutyens on voyages of discovery through Surrey and Sussex, 'within a range possible to Bessy and the pony cart she drew'. Jekyll's short-sightedness made her a frightening driver, and the jolting pony cart was exceedingly uncomfortable: the ring through which the reins passed, dividing the seat into two, had been shifted several inches to one side, allowing room for the ample Jekyll but squashing Lutyens

---

*Even today, no one seems certain what exactly was wrong with her eyes.
†Gertrude Jekyll kept careful diaries, but the volumes for these years are missing. In 1940 her nephew and biographer Francis (Timmy) Jekyll gave Gertrude Jekyll's papers, which he had used for his biography, to the Royal Horticultural Society's Red Cross sale. Her planting plans and photographs somehow found their way to America, where they were bought by Barbara Farrand for the library of her Reef Point school of landscape design, now housed at the University of California at Berkeley. A great deal 'disappeared', allegedly burned or lost.

into a cramped corner. 'Old houses, farms and cottages were searched for,' Lutyens recalled, 'their modest methods of construction discussed, their inmates and the industries that supported them.'[31]

What the two of them saw can be reconstructed precisely from the photos in Jekyll's albums, many of which she published fifteen years later in *Old West Surrey* (1904). How closely they peered at old cottages, noting the oak frame filled with brick-noggin, sometimes lime-washed below and tile-hung above, sometimes coated with roughcast. Chimneys, they observed, should be built of thin two-inch bricks rather than the standard two-and-a-half, thus giving the ornament formed by the projecting courses an added delicacy. Plain rooftiles might be varied with slabs of Horsham stone, or tiles rounded in the shape of a fish-scale. The honey-coloured Bargate stone, dug from quarries around Godalming, bricklayers sometimes studded at the mortar-joint with small pieces of black ironstone, a practice known as galleting.

'I have a passion (though an ignorant one) for matters concerning domestic architecture that almost equals my interest in plants and trees,' wrote Jekyll.[32] Lutyens perhaps understood better than she did how to make a house stand up – he had learned that from Ernest George – but she taught him how to read and absorb an architectural vernacular, how to use traditional craftsmanship and local materials; in short, she made him an Arts and Crafts architect.

In September 1890 Lutyens went on a walking tour through Shropshire, North Wales and Cheshire with Herbert Baker, his friend from Ernest George's office. They climbed the Wrekin and Ned ate too many blackberries, was sick and declared that the red fluid was his blood. Baker filled a book with careful pencil sketches, but Lutyens stubbornly refused to draw, storing his impressions in his memory instead. They saw Stokesay Castle, widely famed for its sixteenth-century timberwork. Lutyens later said that much of his timberwork derived from it.* Lutyens admired Much Wenlock, 'a most beautiful old house', where he spotted a stone fireplace, which Baker sketched; and at Rug church, with its Jacobean painted ceiling (also sketched by Baker), he saw a 'delicious' old chandelier, 'all made of wood and painted green'.[33] Perhaps Lutyens was self-conscious about his drawing. He didn't illustrate his own

---

*The Hansel and Gretel-like half-timbering at the Institute on the village green at Tilford, Surrey, which he designed that year, is influenced by Stokesay.

perspectives when he published them in the *Builder*; it was Baker who drew the lodges Lutyens designed at Park Hatch for Joseph Godman.³⁴

Despite his precocious talent, there was still much Lutyens didn't know. He recalled: 'It must have been in 1891 that I first saw an example of Philip Webb's work, and I remember exclaiming, "That's good; I wonder who the young man is?" His name was unknown to me then* . . . The freshness and originality which he maintained in all his work I, in my ignorance, attributed to youth.' Only when he learned that Webb was already sixty did he realize that it was 'the eternal youth of genius'.³⁵ Philip Webb, the guru architect of Arts and Crafts, who wore a hairy brown suit and belonged to the 'gruffly understated homo-erotic faction of the Arts and Crafts movement', was a socialist and a disciple of the simple life; he shunned publicity. He built few houses but his influence was then at its height, and his houses were architectural prodigies, the 1890s equivalent of Le Corbusier's Villa Savoye.

Jekyll introduced Lutyens to Philip Webb's work. Pasted into her album next to a photograph of an early Lutyens cottage is a photograph of Great Tangley Manor, an old half-timbered Surrey house added to by Webb. Jekyll had taken a photograph there in 1887; she admired the way Webb had built a new wing that looked old without imitating or competing with the old house. This effect, using traditional materials to create something new, was the essence of the Surrey style. Lutyens derived much of the language of his garden designs from Great Tangley: tile-capped walls of Bargate stone and oak pergolas.³⁶ The owner of Great Tangley was Wickham Flower, but it was really his wife who restored it, as Lutyens was quick to realize. Mrs Wickham Flower he thought 'such a dear clever women with real taste, most forbidding in manner with little black eyes without whites or pupils . . . Her house is quite beautiful and her husband a brute to her.'³⁷

---

*In 1891 Sydney Cockerell attended the annual general meeting of the Society for the Protection of Ancient Buildings where, he recorded in his diary, he met Lutyens; Philip Webb was in the chair.

Chapter Four
Munstead Wood and Barbara Webb
1892–1896

Ned's sketches of himself, the humble architect, paying homage to Gertrude Jekyll.

Lutyens lived at his parents' house, Number 16 Onslow Square, until he was twenty-eight. Until 1894 Onslow Square was his office too, and he signed off his plans from that address. The story goes that the house was crowded with adult sons, but in fact most of Ned's brothers had already married and left home. Fred the painter married in 1890: Ned designed a studio for him in Wetherby Place which wasn't built.[1] Lionel, who was an estate agent, married soon after and so did Arthur, who went to make his fortune in Malaya as a coffee planter. Ned's closest friend among his brothers and sisters was Molly, and she married George Wemyss in 1890. So Ned lived at Onslow Square amidst unswept clutter with his bachelor brother Frank, who was six years older, a humorous man who worked in the City.

Lutyens seems to have belonged to a circle which included Detmar Blow, Arthur Collie, a Bond Street art dealer, and the sculptor John Tweed. They would meet on Saturdays at an inn named The Cricketers near Thursley, and occasionally Ned went with them to a meeting of the Art Workers' Guild, the élite club of Arts and Crafts architects, though he wasn't a member and (he later recalled) 'no one knew me and those few that did patronised or snubbed me'.[2] Almost all his work was in Surrey*, but he spent less and less time at Thursley, where his parents lived with their younger daughters, Aileen and Margaret.

At Thursley the household was sliding into muddle, eccentricity and squalor as the family's income dwindled to a trickle. Charles's earnings from his painting had dropped from £800 or £900 a year to little more than £300 to £400 a year after 1883. Having sold all his property in Berkshire, invested heavily in Charlie's tea venture in Ceylon and educated seven sons, he seems to have exhausted his capital reserves. And so far as his painting was concerned, Charles's move to Surrey was disastrous. His list of clients in the 1870s reads like a directory of fashionable aristocratic society: dukes, marquesses and earls – names such as Yarborough, Londonderry, Portland, Coventry, Westminster and Bradford – reappear year after year, and he would be invited to send sketches to society charities such as Lady Knightley's Ladies'

---

*He gave Detmar Blow's younger brother Sydney a job on one of his Surrey buildings, mixing mortar for twelve shillings and two pence a week.

Guild. From the mid-1880s, however, the carefully inked list dwindles to a few lines in a pencilled scrawl. After 1890 it ceases altogether. Old clients fell away. His last major commission was two large paintings for the Duke of Westminster commemorating his service as Master of the Horse. Outside the Royal Mews stands the duke's carriage, drawn by clumping horses, a subject (according to *Baily's*) which was not worthy of the painter's brush: 'Fat Hanoverian cream-coloured horses, grooms in scarlet, and the dull surroundings of the Buckingham Palace stables, are difficult to invest with anything beyond the commonplace.'[3]

Charles no longer painted the bright, crisp portraits of hunting men on thoroughbred horses which had made his name in the 1870s. Occasionally neighbours sat for portraits of themselves, with a dog or a horse, and he would charge £20 or so. But Charles's chief preoccupation at Thursley was landscape. His landscapes are depressingly dark and dull, dominated by dirty greens and blacks; the brushwork is coarse, the detail crude and the paintings have an unfinished look. His painting was driven by his obsession with the Venetian Secret which, he believed, it was his mission to reveal to the world. He had invented an instrument for measuring tone and colour, but the pictures he painted with the help of this secret aid were unimpressive. He thought them masterpieces, but those who saw his Venetian experiments dismissed him as cracked.[4] As old friends left him and fellow painters cut him he became paranoid, scenting a conspiracy to silence him and clinging pathetically to the belief that one day his theories would be vindicated.

At Thursley his studio filled with large, dark canvases, overpainted on earlier efforts, gloomy after the crispness of his earlier work, mostly unfinished and all unsaleable. He painted queer subjects too: naked men riding horses in the sea, and his daughter Aileen fondling a large naked boy. In his sixties Charles's sight began to fail, and his landscapes grew even darker as he lost his sense of colour. Desperate to develop tonal contrast, he added stronger and stronger quantities of black and white, making the colour cruder than ever. He could no longer see to paint. Those dark, dirty greens and blacks really did shut out the light. Perhaps he suffered from cataracts, like Manet, whose sense of colour was painfully distorted.* Charles's sight became so dim

---

*'Red appeared to me muddy, pinks insipid and the intermediate or lower tones escaped me,' wrote Manet. 'What I painted was more and more dark, more like an "old picture" . . . and when I compared it to my former works, I would be seized by a frantic rage, and slash all my canvases with my penknife.'

that he would dictate the colours he saw in his mind to his daughter Aileen, who forlornly attempted to transcribe them on to canvas.

Charles still hunted. Riding an unclipped pony, he would arrive at the meet with his legs dangling almost to the ground, looking like Leonardo da Vinci with his flowing beard and long white curly hair beneath a soft cowboy hat.[5] Fred, the artist son, wrote a hunting story entitled *Mr Spinks and his Hounds* (1890). Illustrated by Charles, it is the story of an old but brilliant huntsman dismissed by a flash confidence trickster whom he sabotages. Fred's tale of neglected and misunderstood genius is inspired by Charles's misfortunes as an artist and the consolation he found in hunting. 'How often the humility of true genius has shrunk from the lash of the ignorant and merciless critic!' wrote Fred. 'Who can tell of the happiness wrecked, of the homes make desolate, of the life crushed slowly from sad hearts by the witty word of a clique, or the thoughtless creature of a fashion!'

At home, Charles introduced bizarre economies. Meat was banned, and the family lived on cabbage cooked in oil. Charles burned no fires, mended his own shoes and used newspapers as tablecloths. Having lost his teeth, he would soak his chip potatoes in tea to make them soft enough to eat, dunking bread sauce and gravy in the tea as well. His dress became eccentric. He stamped about in spurs and 'variegated costume', but the more ragged his clothes, the more splendidly princely he looked.[6]

Ned observed all this with shame and horror. He resented what he saw as his father's intolerance and he complained that his family was bigoted, sentimental and emotional.[7] His own art education and the lessons he had learned from Gertrude Jekyll about colour theory must have taught him how hopelessly cranky Charles's Venetian Secret was. No longer respecting his father's work, he came to loathe his obsessions. At family meals he would toss provocative remarks into the conversation and watch them being torn apart like a bone thrown to a pack of hounds.

Mary was still beautiful, with a soft and gentle face and voice, but she was retreating further into her private world. Resigning herself to the will of God, which meant resigning herself to life with Charles, she shut her eyes to the squalor around them and left the household to be run somehow by Priscilla the Nannie. Mary read the Bible each night and became more and more saintly and reclusive. 'Though she talks religion quite freely,' noted Ned's future wife Emily Lytton, 'not a word jars upon one, and she has not one touch of cant or hypocrisy, and her creed seems an unbounded love for all human beings.'[8]

Unable to follow Mary in her religious devotions, Ned revenged himself by wickedly mocking parsons, until his sarcasm jarred on Mary's simple nature. And his position as Mary's favourite son was now threatened by his younger brother William (Billy). Billy was a success story. He achieved fame at Cambridge as a champion runner. He won the mile against Oxford in four successive years and later set a British record for the 1,000 yards (2 minutes 14 seconds) which lasted for thirty-one years. As if this were not enough, he realized Mary's dreams by entering the church. He was ordained in 1895. Ned, who was jealous, teased Mary and 'her Billy' mercilessly.[9]*

Meanwhile, Ned tried to write his embarrassing father out of his life. But Charles's slide into eccentricity was to leave Ned with a lifelong fear of blindness, poverty and professional failure.

Ned Lutyens was rescued from the squalor and social humiliation of Thursley by Gertrude Jekyll. His name first appears in the visitors' book at Munstead House in January 1892, and soon weekending at Munstead became a habit.[10]

Lack of evidence makes it impossible to reconstruct their relationship precisely, but it is clear that they 'figuratively fell into each other's arms', becoming intimate in a way that must have surprised Jekyll's family. Gertrude Jekyll was usually indifferent to the charms of bumptious young people like Ned Lutyens. Silliness irritated her, and her snubs could be devastating. Her nephews and nieces feared her as a threatening deity, and dreaded her anger which was terrifying.[11] Ned's daughter Mary knew Jekyll as a gruff and frightening old woman, and she found Jekyll's warmth towards her father hard to understand.

Shortly before Lutyens first stayed at Munstead House, Jekyll had consulted an eye specialist, Pagenstecher of Wiesbaden, who ordered her to give up painting and embroidery. This was the catalyst that spurred her in her late forties to build a career as a garden designer. If she couldn't see to paint, at least she could make pictures with flowers.

---

*Perhaps William *was* a little strange. He was a close friend of John Cowper Powys, with whom he had shared a study at Sherborne. He officiated at Cowper Powys's wedding in 1896; perhaps he shared Cowper Powys's horror of sex and twisted, phobia-ridden view of women. He had a woman friend who died of a heart attack in his arms after six hours of agony ('I hope she has left a lump to him and not merely her Bible,' commented Ned). He then became a Cowley father and swore a vow of celibacy, but he was surrounded by adoring women; he emerged at the age of seventy to marry a woman who (apparently) looked exactly like a man.

Following the principles of colour harmony that she had absorbed at South Kensington, she began to mass drifts of colour like brushstrokes in the Impressionist pictures she had once tried to paint. Spurning the formal bedding-out of the mid-Victorians, who planted scarlet geraniums, blue lobelias and yellow calceolaria in soldier-like patterns, she used flowers to create colour 'rooms' – a blue/lilac garden or a red/yellow garden, or a riot of carefully choreographed colour in a herbaceous border. She had already created a garden on the fifteen-acre plot she bought in 1883 across the road from Munstead House, the Other Side, where she meant to live when her mother died. Little by little she had reclaimed the poor, scrubby soil – she planted a nut walk in 1887, then a primrose garden and woodland gardens. Here she planned to build her house, for which she had left a hole.

Lutyens knew little of gardening and confessed himself bored by flower picking. (Once he picked a flower of Miss Jekyll's which she had marked for seed. 'Such was the effect on me of her distress that I have never picked a flower since.'[12]) But he was the architect Jekyll needed to realize her dreams; she also discovered that he had the ability to make her laugh – he was both young and unafraid of her. 'The business of building became a witty and exciting sport, with full disputations and discussions,' he recalled. Soon they were talking a private language and giving each other pet names – she called him Nedi and he christened her Bumps, the Mother of Bulbs, and Mab (Queen of the Fairies). Perhaps he glimpsed her at work one day in early summer, deftly dividing with a sharp knife the bulbs for replanting in her primrose garden. Here she was truly queen, a primitive goddess seated on her low stool, plagued by midges, and attended by slaves. 'A boy feeds me with armfuls of newly-dug-up plants, two men are digging in the cooling cow-dung at the farther end and another carries away the divided plants tray by tray, and carefully replants them.' Outwardly stern, with thin greying hair scraped back into a bun, Bumps had an earthy motherliness to which Lutyens intuitively responded.*

Bumps set him to work in her workshop. This was the room where she felt most at home. Linked to her bedroom by a spiral stair, the room was lined with cupboards and drawers stacked with the rare woods and shells, horn, ivory and mother-of-pearl intended for inlay work or shell pictures. Presiding over the comfortable mess was Pigot, the divinity of

---

*Years later, Lutyens brought Lady Sackville to visit Bumps at Munstead Wood. Lady Sackville wrote: 'She loves him, and follows him about with such loving eyes and treats him like a child.'

the workshop, a small, penguin-like mascot Jekyll had constructed with ermine waistcoat and mother-of-pearl eyes who, like his mistress, was 'capable of flashes of scornful indignation when bad work is done or the glue-pot boils over'. 'All my best friends know Pigot,' she wrote, 'and never fail, on entering the workshop, to offer him a respectful salutation.'[13] Soon Lutyens was among them.

Jekyll wanted her new house, she told him, to have the restfulness of Tudor and Jacobean building: she would like a little of the feeling of a convent. In an account written later of how the house was built, she refers to a false start.[14] This early design can be seen in a pocket-size sketchbook (measuring five inches by seven) of 1892 which survived through a lucky chance, rescued by a removal man from the rubbish thrown out when Lutyens moved his office at 5 Eaton Place in 1939.

Lutyens's pen and watercolour sketches are charming, but the house he proposed for Jekyll was not. Palazzoh-Pergola or Plazzoh, as they called it, was a large, rambling tile and roughcast country villa in the manner of Ernest George (even George's characteristic dog-legged drainpipe is here). The Tudor hall is a cold and gloomy room of stone and oak. Tacked on to the back is a strange octagonal tower and oblong loggia surmounted by a pergola and approached by steps from the garden. Here Lutyens sketched Jekyll standing as she gave orders to her gardeners cowering deferentially below. In the sketchbook Lutyens scrawled 'Bad' over the tower and loggia.

One can see why this version of Plazzoh was never built; Lutyens still had some way to go before he could produce the kind of house that Jekyll wanted. On the final page of the sketchbook he drew a woodland view and wrote 'to the Egress': he was being shown the way out. But all was not lost. On the next page of the sketchbook after Plazzoh is a drawing of a vernacular cottage inscribed The Hut. This was derived from a Surrey cottage at Eashing, with a deep hipped roof which Jekyll had photographed; Lutyens added an oversized chimney rather like the one he built at Hoe Farm, Hascombe. The drawing of The Hut is inscribed by Lutyens, 'Abandoned Oct. 9th 1892' and 'Returned to favour – July 16th 93'.

The Hut was built at Munstead Wood in 1894. With two rooms upstairs and two below it was like a child's playhouse, where Jekyll could play at living the simple life. At first she installed a village woman, Mrs Cannon, who spoke the purest local dialect and dressed in peasant costume, obligingly posing for Jekyll to photograph her like a doll peeping out of her white linen cap outside her new/old house. In

1894 Lutyens built a tiny half-timbered gardener's cottage, a replica of an ancient manor house.

None of this brought Lutyens any money, but his connection with Jekyll brought a lot of work. Miss Jekyll's backing reassured Surrey neighbours, who commissioned Lutyens to build houses for which Jekyll advised on the site, integrating the house with the garden, which she designed.* None of these Surrey houses had the classical Italianate gardens that were to make the Jekyll–Lutyens partnership famous. The first formal garden they collaborated on was Woodside (1893), near Chenies in Buckinghamshire, for Adeline, newly widowed Duchess of Bedford. Its timing is significant; the previous year the architect Reginald Blomfield had written a polemic challenging the control of garden design by landscape gardeners like William Robinson, and claiming the garden as architect's territory which should be designed as an extension to the house. The garden at Woodside is sited on a north-facing slope. A strip of formal terracing links the house at the top with the river garden at the foot; the central feature is a round pond enclosed by Tuscan stone columns crowned by heavy oak lintels to form an octagonal pergola. Walburga Paget, who visited Woodside in 1905, admired 'the pretty terraced gardens in which blue lobelias and azure salvias and delphiniums predominate right down to the flat-banked river where the lazy waters flow between borders of large yellow musk'. Being an early essay in classical design, Woodside was carefully photographed and written up by Lutyens's later biographers, who disliked the vernacular picturesque of the Surrey houses, which they largely ignored.[15]

Between 1892 and 1896 Lutyens executed twenty or so† documented jobs; and at least twelve of these were either collaborations with Jekyll or due to her influence or patronage. In January 1894 he began to lease his own office at Number 6 Gray's Inn Square, helped by a loan of £100 from Bumps and £100 left to him by Miss Landseer, in the mistaken belief that he was her brother's godson.[16]

His biggest commission was a house on a hillside at Wonersh almost within sight of Munstead: Chinthurst Hill. This was his first country house. The client was Maggie Guthrie, a daughter of Elinor Arbuthnot

---

*After Crooksbury, where they worked together, came Red House at Effingham (1891) for Jekyll's friend Susan Muir Mackenzie; Wood End, Witley (1892), for Lady Stewart; Winkworth Farm at Hascombe (1893); Ruckmans (1894) for Miss Lyell; Lascombe, Puttenham (1895), for Colonel Spencer; and Munstead Corner (1895) for C. D. Heatley.
†Historians are still adding to the list of Lutyens's buildings from this early period.

who had arranged Lutyens's meeting with Norman Shaw, and a cousin of Harry Mangles. She was unmarried, in her mid-thirties, and studying in London to become a doctor. She seems to have taken very little interest either in the plans or the cost, and the house was built, as the architect-critic Goodhart-Rendel wrote (and he knew better than anyone, as he spent his childhood there), with 'a recklessness of economy and convenience'.[17] Lutyens planned a bold experiment on the sloping south-facing site. Entering a dark porch on the north front at ground level, you pass through the house to find yourself surveying a panoramic south-facing view from a second-floor window. Many of the Munstead sketchbook features are here. Chinthurst has an overpowering stone hall which is a cross between a church and a Victorian railway station, with a massive fireplace, stone arches and gothic windows. Built of Bargate stone, with buttresses and little towers, it rambles rather like a doctoral thesis; it has little sense of form. Chinthurst is a house in need of an editor. The elements are all in place – the carefully designed door furniture and ironwork, the oak stair and red painted woodwork; each fireplace is different and the firebacks are sixteenth-century – but somehow the pudding doesn't rise.

An inscription carved on the loggia testifies to the pride of Chinthurst's creators: *This House was built by / Aemilia Margaret Guthrie / October 1893 – March 1895 / James Simpson. Builder / William Herbert. Mason / Edwin Lutyens. Architect.* But Maggie Guthrie hated it. Returning from abroad, she found (so her sister, Violet Stuart-Wortley, wrote) a house with its back turned on the view and the principal rooms looking glumly to the north up a hill. According to Violet, who always exaggerated, Maggie paid off the architect and then set about turning the house round, moving the plumbing and kitchen. Lady Sackville heard a different version many years later from the metalworker Starkie Gardner. 'He told me how L was so disappointed with his first house, and yet did not prosecute the Lady or ask for any money from her, which started him with a good reputation, as Miss Jekyll then took him up and helped him tremendously.'[18] Whether or not Maggie Guthrie paid Lutyens, she evidently made plain her displeasure and Lutyens was mortified. He never revisited the house, but dropped it into oblivion – a bitter memory.*

---

*Maggie Guthrie sold the house soon afterwards, and it was bought by Lord Rendel of Hatchlands for his widowed daughter Rose Goodhart and her son Hal Goodhart-Rendel. Goodhart-Rendel's Chinthurst childhood was an architectural education which left him with a lifelong admiration for Lutyens's work: he was one of the few architectural critics to defend Lutyens's reputation after his death in 1944.

To her credit, Bumps stood by Ned over the Chinthurst fiasco. She did more. She took a risk and commissioned him to build her a house – a new version of the Plazzoh idea.

Julia Jekyll, Miss Jekyll's eighty-two-year-old mother, died suddenly in July 1895. Miss Jekyll's brother Herbert Jekyll inherited Munstead House and brought his family to live there; Miss Jekyll inherited money. At last she could afford to build. She commissioned Lutyens to design a tombstone for her mother in Busbridge churchyard. Meanwhile, she moved into The Hut. Here Lutyens came with his plans, and the sketchbook design was transformed.

In her account of 'How the House was Built' Jekyll mentions one occasion when 'fur flew'. Arguing over a point of detail that would have added greatly to the expense for the sake of external appearance, Bumps expostulated: 'My house is to be built for me to live in and to love; it is not to be built as an exposition of architectonic inutility!' She learned, she wrote, 'from the architect's crushed and somewhat frightened demeanour, that long words certainly have their use'.[19] The contrast between Chinthurst Hill, recklessly experimental and boldly extravagant, and Munstead Wood, where the innovations are severely disciplined, is a measure of Gertrude Jekyll's influence on Lutyens.

Jekyll described her house as a mixture of old and new. It felt as if it had stood for two hundred years, but there was nothing sham-old about it. It was not a copy of an old building, but was built in the 'honest spirit of the good work of old days'. The sources for Munstead Wood were documented with scholarly precision in Jekyll's book *Old West Surrey*. Almost every detail was derived from the Surrey vernacular. The oak mullions, flush with the outer wall allowing broad oak window boards on the inside, were (Jekyll explained) in the manner of the best old buildings of the country.* The Bargate stone was dressed in the local way so that it seemed to grow naturally out of the ground. Jekyll had known the oak beams that stretched across the ceiling of the hall and supported the bedrooms above: they were trees which she had ridden past as a child. They were treated with hot lime to give a greyish powdery effect: nearly forty years later, when Ned's daughter Mary stayed there, the house still smelled pungently of new wood. Exposed oak joists expressed the morality of the house as no bad work was hidden behind dishonest plaster. Nothing was bought from the manufacturer's pattern book. Doors of bare oak were fitted with

---

*Visitors complained that the high windows let in very little light, but Bumps insisted that she needed dark interiors to rest her eyes.

wooden latches, individually designed by Lutyens, and no two door or window fittings were the same. But the composition is unlike any traditional Surrey house. Lutyens raked the steep tile roof down to the tops of the ground-floor windows and bisected the tall gables with casement windows which formed modernistic horizontals.

The plan is an unequal H. One leg was the kitchen and servants' wing, the other was Bumps's workroom, and the waist of the H was a long central hall, the main living room. Above the hall was a gallery, wide and low, its massive oak beams barely above head height. Here Bumps kept her church vestments, her tear-bottles, ostrich eggs and Surrey horse brasses. It gave the house a feeling of great spaciousness. Lutyens played a trick to achieve this. The hall was 20 feet wide, but the bedrooms above were 15 feet and the gallery 12 feet; he gained an additional 6 feet by hanging the gallery over the hall, so that outside it formed a covered terrace or loggia, thus at once integrating the house with the garden court that filled the waist of the H.*

Jekyll insisted that she needed an architect to design the house because only an architect possessed an understanding of 'the qualities that belong to the higher knowledge' which, she believed, gave the house its convent-like feel of 'reposeful simplicity'.[20] By 'higher knowledge' she may have meant something very specific: the ratios and proportions governing classical architecture. Munstead Wood is more balanced and controlled than earlier houses like Chinthurst partly because the design is governed by geometry and proportion. A 1999 research project measuring the 'footprints' or outside outlines of forty Lutyens houses and the dimensions of the principal rooms yielded an unexpected result: in Munstead Wood the plan 'footprint' as well as the dimensions of the main rooms conform to simple mathematical ratios. The ratio 4:3 recurs in the plan. 'It is the first house to present a repetition of similar shapes and with the final composition approximating a square footprint there emerges a series of simple whole number divisions in its massing (the 1:1, 2:1, 4:3, 3:2 and 8:5) interlocked in a highly controlled manner.' These were among the ratios that Palladio had proposed for the design of principal rooms (1:1, 2:1, 4:3, 5:3, 3:2), and the inference is that Lutyens was beginning to experiment with the classical geometry which later became an obsession. It seems likely that it was Bumps who encouraged her protégé to apply this 'higher knowledge'. Certainly, her South Kensington training had taught her

---

*Pevsner called this a 'foretaste of later naughtiness'; in 1902 it was necessary to insert a tension rod to support the ceiling of the hall below.

about proportion and compositional structure, and she designed her embroidery by blocking in patterns on one-eighth-inch squared paper.[21]

Bumps was obsessive about privacy. Her house had a hidden entrance, which was approached by a footpath from a quiet shady lane and entered by a close-paled locked hand-gate that could only be opened by the few who knew of the secret nail where the secret key hung. She wanted the entrance to be 'as quiet and modest as possible . . . and to tell its own story as the way in to a small dwelling standing in wooded ground'. In her journalism, however, she brilliantly publicized the house and garden, and Munstead's growing fame brought flocks of visitors whom she desperately tried to deter from entering her secret compound. She used her eyesight as an excuse. 'The extra strain on my unfortunate eyes brings on the painful headaches that often lose me the whole use of the next day,' she would write, putting off hopeful visitors.[22] Obesity, too, was a problem. Soon journeys became impossible, and Bumps rarely ventured forth from Munstead Wood.

Lutyens had so much work in Surrey in 1895–6 that he spent most of his time there. He avoided staying at Thursley, but travelled down to Godalming station from Waterloo, bringing his bicycle, which he called Angelina. After Bumps moved into The Hut and her brother Herbert into Munstead House, he often stayed with Bob and Barbara Webb at Milford. Bumps was designing the garden at Milford for the Webbs, and Bob Webb commissioned Lutyens to rebuild a house at Warren Lodge, near Thursley.

Milford House was built of pink brick in about 1730 in the manner of Wren. Sybilla Holland, Barbara Webb's sister, admired its 'lofty rooms, large high windows, thick walls, polished doors shutting off passages and staircases . . . excellent temperature and solid quiet ancestral portraits. A great yew hedge and long sunny wall enclosing a garden full of fruit and flowers; plenty of books, old and new.' Lutyens dismissed the architecture as only 'half and half', but staying at Milford was his first exposure to life in a large country house and he learned the house by heart, quoting it as a reference point when he saw other houses.[23]

Bob Webb was stolid and ponderous, with a dry sense of humour; a large kindly man who took his squire's duties seriously. His wife, born Barbara Lyall, was a sister of the Indian administrator Alfred Lyall. She had married aged forty in 1885, and no one could quite understand why the sophisticated and intelligent Barbara should have chosen such a pedestrian husband.[24]

The Webbs had no children, and soon Ned became Barbara's protégé. 'He is the only one of his family we know at all well,' she wrote in 1896. 'For the past year or more we have seen him constantly, he comes and goes between this house and G. Jekyll's – a familiar and very dear young friend; I have the highest opinion of his "moral character" and he is extraordinarily clever and ingenious and with a merry sweet temper, very engaging.'

Barbara was fun to be with. Ned made her laugh by telling her stories about his crushes on the local girls. She tried to teach him how to avoid giving a 'silly' flippant impression, and she lectured him on the dreadful hand-me-down clothes he wore. She pampered him with Milford's 'excellentissimo' cooking (though anything would have been better than Thursley's cabbage) and she began to take him about with her in London. Perhaps she influenced him at a deeper level, too. Barbara was a niece of the great Victorian cleric Dean Lyall, but she followed her brother Alfred into unbelief. 'I am constantly shocked,' she told Alfred, 'to find how far you and I have drifted from the faith of most of our friends. Sometimes I have nights of anguish.' She may have sensed the lack of faith that charged Ned's comic imitations of vicars – a knot of unresolved tension, distancing him from his beloved mother.[25]

It was *Pygmalion* in reverse, Ned playing Eliza Doolittle to Barbara's Professor Higgins. She taught him how to behave, tutoring him in the voice, manners, eating habits and conversation of the upper classes. He was a willing pupil. He had never before encountered this kind of worldly, seductive charm. Naturally, he fell in love with her. But though he was besotted and obsessed, though he flirted outrageously with her, there was little that was sexual about their relationship. A variation on the theme of mother and son, it was strictly platonic – almost unhealthily so. Ned was frightened of sex. True to his Victorian evangelical upbringing, he was proud of remaining a virgin until he married. He was disturbed to learn, much later, how sexy Barbara had been when she was young in India. 'How everyone proposed to her, and how she ran away from them. And what she looked like – her lovely figure – pale colourless face of lovely contour, glorious eyes, flashing teeth and masses of dark wavy hair. A good deal of this is new to me and a new picture difficult to see,' he wrote, preferring to think of her as the older woman he had loved as a mother figure.[26] But that younger Barbara Webb, the romantic sex goddess of India, was soon to plunge him into a series of emotional tangles that were to shape his destiny.

The building of Munstead Wood was Lutyens's chief occupation in 1896. Across the field in The Hut, Gertrude Jekyll was in raptures. She and Ned between them supervised the masons, carpenters and bricklayers: it was part of Bumps's Arts and Crafts philosophy that no clerk of works was needed to oversee the craftsmen. Bumps wrote lyrically about the chop and rush of the trowel, the moist slither of the mortar, the neat sliding and slapping of the brick. Rarely has building been described in such sensuous language. For Bumps the process of building her house was a kind of aesthetic orgasm, and she worshipped the leather-gaitered, leather-aproned builders with their long beards, horny hands and strong, deft fingers. Living close to nature at The Hut, she wallowed in physical sensation, rejoicing each morning as her bare feet met the brick floor of her downstairs bedroom. Ned was constantly in attendance, and together they pored over plans, surrounded by Bumps's six or seven cats who also lived at The Hut – the chewed corner of one drawing is labelled 'Pussy's work'. The silky head of Bumps's favourite Tittlebat was always in reach of her hand, in her workroom and at her writing table. After dark on summer evenings, alone at The Hut, she gathered rose petals for pot-pourri, plunging hands and face into the deliciously scented mixture with pagan abandon.

Lutyens took no commission on Munstead Wood, which cost £4,000 to build, but Bumps had earlier lent him, or rather given him, a much-needed £100, and he was too timid, or too tactful, to broach the matter of a commission which at 5 per cent would have earned him £200.[27] After all, she brought him so many jobs. The following year they collaborated on Red House at Charterhouse for the Reverend W. H. Evans, a retired schoolmaster in poor health who had bought a sloping site which plunged steeply down the wooded escarpment outside Godalming.[28]* Here Lutyens made even more dramatic use of the gradient than he had at Chinthurst. The low, discreet brick street front gives on to an astonishing Tudor keep, four floors of lantern windows jutting below a battlemented parapet. Inside, the rooms are hung from

---

*The precise date of Red House is uncertain. It may have been as early as 1896, but most authorities place it in 1897 or later.

a central, top-lit staircase: there are no regular floors; you move from room to room by means of gently sloping stairs.

With asymmetrical windows and lantern windows wrapped around corners, Red House is daringly modern.* It was one of his most inventive and original designs, though it was perhaps a bad joke for Lutyens to inflict upon an invalid a tower spiralling around stairs, and in winter the staircase was a chimney of icy howling draughts. Until very recently, no one much liked living there, and it became a shabby tea-room where Charterhouse boys ate buns beside Lutyens's battered fantastical baroque fireplaces.

Lutyens's inventiveness at Red House documents his restless mood. His relationship with Barbara Webb deepened when she became ill with cancer. He wrote her stories of 'how she would come to a valley full of daisies, framing a merry rippling river, rolling in happiness to the sea and that the Baa Lamb would be so happy and all should be sunny and beautiful trees should throw soft shadows over her, as blessings, when she paused her gambols, midst the daisied meadows'. How much easier he found it to write to Barbara as though he were still a child rather 'than as something of this world 28 years old'.

He filled a sketchbook for 'Baa Lamb' with watercolour drawings of a fantasy palace, the *Chateau d'Ease, en Air, sur Fleuve des Rêves*.† Rather than express his feelings in words, he wrote to her in the language he knew best, the language of classicism. The sketchbook is an architectural love poem.[29] One sketch in the book shows a woman's profile: Barbara resting in bed. When she grew weaker he designed her a bed, a grand fourposter, decorated with hearts and baa lambs and bearing the inscription, 'As Faith wills / So Fate fulfils'.

On her good days Barbara took him about with her in London. One evening in the early summer of 1896 he accompanied her to the Blumenthals, musical friends of Gertrude Jekyll, who lived at Hyde Park Gardens. Here in the upstairs music room, decorated with stencilling by Bumps in her William Morris phase, listening to piano playing which bored him, he spotted a girl across the room. She was

---

*Like Chinthurst, Red House was edited out of Lutyens's official record. Admirers of Lutyens's classical work suppressed his early flirtations with modernism, which they found embarrassing and distasteful.
†A Renaissance–Byzantine fantasy with elements of French chateau and baroque but surprisingly little from Wren, the *Chateau d'Ease* contains the germ of ideas that surfaced many years later in his work, especially at Delhi. It shows that he was already dreaming of classical palaces at a time when most of his work was in the very different language of the Surrey vernacular.

tall, very fair and rather overweight; not exactly pretty – her features were too irregular, her nose too long – and she looked cross and unhappy.[30]

Emily Lytton *was* cross and unhappy. Her life had come to a full stop. She had just emerged from a semi-scandalous infatuation with Wilfrid Scawen Blunt, her father's oldest friend.

Chapter Five
Emily and the Lyttons
1896

Ned and Emily bicycling back from Warren Lodge in the moonlight.

'The cartoon for the week is doubtless the stern spirit of Architecture swearing at me for going – whither I would follow.'

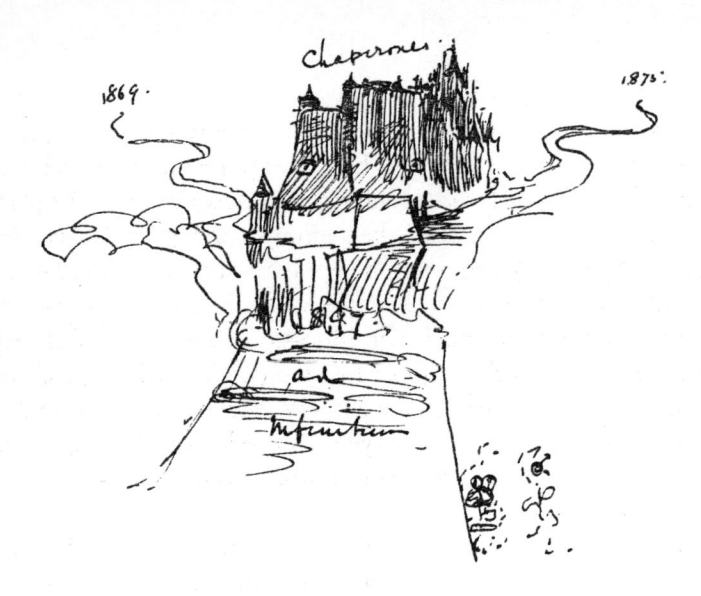

Ned to Emily: 'We are running oh so closely now, but stern fortress walls of Chateau chaperone do separate us but a few more bends and then over a weir of happiness we splash each to the other into one broad stream of great contentment.'

Ned as knight in armour about to conquer the world.

For ten years, from 1886 until 1896, Ned Lutyens himself is silent. None of his letters survive. Biographers have had to reconstruct his life during this time from scraps of evidence, from the houses he built, the plans and sketchbooks he drew, and from the memories of Ned and others. Neither Gertrude Jekyll nor Barbara Webb kept his letters. When Ned met Emily Lytton all this changed. Emily had been brought up to pour her thoughts out on paper every morning; her education consisted of little else but letter-writing and novel-reading.* Every phase in her life was chronicled in her letters, and she kept all the letters she received from Lutyens.

In his letters to Emily, Ned Lutyens can be heard speaking in his own voice; at last it becomes possible to unlock his inner life.

Born in 1874, Emily was the third daughter of Robert, Earl of Lytton. Being a Lytton was a source of pride to Emily, but the tribal values of her family enslaved her in a way that Ned, who was deeply ashamed of most of his relations, must have found hard to understand.

Emily spent most of her childhood at Knebworth, in Hertfordshire, where she lived in a fairy-tale world of knightly romance. Knebworth was the creation of Emily's grandfather, the writer Bulwer Lytton. It was he who encased the remains of an Elizabethan quadrangle house in stucco, creating a sham gothic castle that bristled with turrets and griffins. Perhaps Knebworth was Bulwer's most enduring work of fiction. Looking back with eyes educated by Ned, Emily realized that nothing at Knebworth was as it seemed. The oak staircase was papier mâché; a full-length portrait of 'Sir Rowland de Lytton' was a copy of Velázquez' *Charles V*. To Emily as a child, however, Knebworth was an enchanted castle. Curled up in the library she devoured the historical novels of Bulwer, whom she worshipped. 'I had a tremendous sense of noblesse oblige, and felt myself to be an aristocrat to my finger-tips – and very proud of it.'[1]†

---

*Emily later published a book of the letters she wrote before she met Lutyens. *A Blessed Girl* (1953) was a minor best-seller.
† In fact the Lytton family tree that Emily so treasured was, like the pedigree of most families claiming direct descent in the male line from Elizabethan ancestors, crooked, gappy and criss-crossed by female lines. 'I wish one did not know that the real name of the Lyttons is Widgett,' wrote the waspish Augustus Hare.

Bulwer Lytton died in 1873, the year before Emily was born. Thickly rouged, his hair elaborately curled over a high narrow forehead, he was a dandy to the end, smoking opium in a hookah and telling stories of 'Dis-ra-eel-I' as his pale blue snake's eyes flickered evilly about him.[2] His marriage to the Irish Rosina Wheeler was acrimonious. After a violent separation in 1834, Rosina refused to go quietly. Emily was brought up to believe that her grandmother Rosina, whom she never knew, was a drink-sodden madwoman who had neglected her two children and tormented Bulwer unreasonably. In fact she was a deeply wronged woman, persecuted and destroyed by Bulwer who sent spies after her, ostracized her, robbed her of her children, condemned her to a life spent wandering from lodging house to lodging house and committed her to a madhouse – all in order to obtain the one thing she was determined he shouldn't have: a divorce.

Rosina's fierce anger had its roots in her west of Ireland childhood at Ballywire, County Limerick, a straggling pile of tumbledown grey buildings lashed by the spray of the Atlantic ocean. She remembered the barracks-like dining room with its acres of claret-stained mahogany, the battleground of her ill-matched parents, Francis Wheeler and his wife Anna. Rosina's alcoholic father's hands would shake in the mornings while her mother, neglecting her children, lay on a sofa absorbed in the writings of Mary Wollstonecraft. Anna Wheeler left Francis and became a feminist virago – feminism seems to have been almost encoded into the Lytton genes: Emily herself flirted with the women's movement and her sister Constance became a suffragette martyr.

Emily's father Robert was by profession a diplomat who wrote poetry under the name of Owen Meredith. People laughed at his foreign way of kissing women's hands, but Robert Lytton was a Byronic figure adored by women. Emily was terrified of him. She was sixteen when he died, but he cast long shadows. In a curious way, her emotional life was a working-out of her father's romantic entanglements.

Robert Lytton had survived a childhood that was privileged but lonely, turbulent and loveless, even by the harsh standards of the Victorians. His parents separated when he was five, and he saw little of Bulwer who removed him from Rosina's custody at the age of eight and entrusted him to the care of a strict, joyless woman called Miss Greene. His sister Emily died of neglect from typhoid in a London lodging house. According to one psycho-historical study, Robert was an 'affectionateless character', displaying a 'marked lack of guilt, an inability to abide by rules or to obey superiors, and a notable incapacity for forming lasting relationships'.[3] He was subject to periods of what he described as 'almost intolerable hysterical depression'. Like Bulwer, Robert used opium, and he chain-smoked cigarettes. 'In moments of excitement or depression,' he wrote, 'I almost unconsciously put a cigarette into my mouth, as a drunkard would unstop the dram bottle.' Rejecting his mother, whom he referred to coldly as 'the Dowager', he was father-fixated; rejected in turn by Bulwer, he sought to outdo him, becoming alternately bullying or craven towards authority. He could not bear to hear Bulwer's work criticized. He copied his father's bell-bottomed trousers and square-tipped shoes. The artist Leslie Ward, who caricatured him for *Spy*, noticed that Robert even walked like Bulwer, taking short steps and stooping from the neck.[4]

Robert was thin and handsome with intensely blue eyes. As a twenty-year-old attaché in Florence, he was befriended by Elizabeth Browning. He wrote love poems sitting at her feet, and fell hopelessly in love with a married woman, Mrs Fleetwood Wilson, who had romantic links with the Risorgimento. His poems are filled with violet eyes and lost romances: 'Whom first we love, you know, we seldom wed,' he sighed. Robert himself was loved unrequitedly by a novelist nearly twice his age named Isa Blagden. Bulwer was jealous. 'I fear,' he told his son, 'that being born with fortune's spoon in your mouth, which I was not, and being so popular and good-looking, you fall at last into the literary dilettante, writing only what pleases yourself. If I did that, I should do nothing but scribble verses that no one would read.'[5]

Looking back on his life, Robert perceived a divided self; the poet self, whom Bulwer had done his best to crush, and the public, diplomat self. 'All the successful and known side of my life,' he wrote, 'is a suppression ... of the natural self. I feel like a wild bird in a poultry yard, and if now and then the cramped wings flutter under the coop, they are subdued at once by a perception of the unseemliness of such flutterings of a diseased personality. Of this side of my life, whether I look forward or backward, an immense despair always comes over me.'[6]

Robert's poetry was, as Lytton Strachey wrote, like beautiful pebbles wet and glowing from the brook; moving and eloquent when he declaimed it, in print it turned to dull and common stones. One poem, gloomily entitled 'Last Words of a Sensitive Second-Rate Poet', was Robert's poetical testament. 'Think! That I might have been ... what? / Almost, I fancy at times, what I meant to have been and am not.'

Swinburne wrote a parody, entitled 'Last Words of a Seventh-Rate Poet': 'Tis a dark-purple sort of a moonlighted kind of a midnight, I know / You remember those verses I wrote on Irene, from Edgar A. Poe?'[7]

Robert married in 1864. Edith Villiers, who was taller than he, was beautiful and sweet-natured, and she gave him the domestic security he had never known. But she was uneducated and unintellectual and knew nothing of poetry. The Lyttons thought she was stupid. To Robert's poet self, Edith could not speak.

In the summer of 1865 Edith sailed back to England to have her first child, leaving Robert in Portugal, where he had recently been posted. Robert's attaché was the twenty-four-year-old Wilfrid Blunt, who stayed with him in his house at Sintra. At first Robert was irritated by the handsome, casual Blunt, who slept on his floor and treated everything of Robert's as though it were his own – 'my tobacco, my wine, my beer, and even my money, observing with the utmost seriousness that agreeable intercourse in life is quite incompatible with the doctrines of meum and tuum'.

'What a queer chap Blunt must be,' Edith tartly commented. 'I don't approve of young Mr Blunt helping himself to all that belongs to you in that cool way either!'[8] Edith never changed her mind about Blunt, but Robert was soon won over. He spent a dreamlike summer with Blunt in the shimmering heat of the Portuguese hills. Late at night Robert would declaim his poems in his musical voice, and the two men became close.[9]

In 1876 Robert was appointed Viceroy of India by his father's old friend Disraeli. No one was more surprised than he, but Robert was an unexpectedly successful and charismatic Viceroy. At the Delhi Durbar of 1877 he looked splendid seated on the viceregal throne – even if his piles were so painful that he was obliged to sit sideways, and he offended the Anglo-Indians by interrupting a levee in order to smoke a cigarette. Lord Salisbury the Indian Secretary criticised 'the gaudy and theatrical ambition which is the Viceroy's leading passion', but Disraeli was delighted. 'We wanted,' he said, 'a man of ambition, imagination, some vanity and much will – and we have got him.'[10]

Robert wore prune-coloured quilted satin jackets and looked much younger than his age. He was openly affectionate to men and flirtatious with women. He seemed foreign, exotic and sexy.* In India Robert

---

*Robert's valet used to steal his nightshirts, hoping that they would bring him luck with his sex life.

complained that he missed the 'pleasant scamps and scampesses of pleasant France', but he found plenty of women to flirt with. Tongues wagged when he danced with the pretty, fast Mrs Plowden.* Lady Strachey, wife of the Indian administrator Richard Strachey, was bewitched by him. She treasured those Indian nights, when they sat talking until 2 a.m., Robert resplendent in a blue satin dressing gown. Robert was godfather to her son Lytton, who was named after him and rumoured (probably wrongly) to be his son.[11] Another of Robert's woman friends was the beautiful Barbara Lyall; and this romantic friendship was the link that was to lead Emily Lytton to Ned Lutyens.

Robert's undoing was Afghanistan. He disobeyed orders from London not to invade. He resigned in disgrace; his contemporaries thought he had gone mad. Lord Derby certainly thought so: 'with a mother insane and father eccentric, he has every right to be in that way: & he used like his father to use opium'.[12] Robert was made an earl but complained that he couldn't afford it. Always careless with money – maids picked it off the floor and out of the wastepaper basket – he returned to find that extravagance, coupled with neglect of his depressed Knebworth estate, had reduced his income from a princely £11,000 to a mere £2,600.

At Knebworth he made no economies. Emily remembered peeping into the hall where the servants ate their meat in complete silence; when pudding came, the upper servants took their plates and marched solemnly into the housekeeper's room, enabling the underlings at last to speak. Only the very rich could afford such hierarchies, so Robert was not exactly a pauper earl, as he claimed.

Emily looked back on her childhood as a time of unhappiness. 'I had a sense of being a prisoner, caught in a long tunnel of childhood which would never end.'[13] Her father ignored her, her mother did too, and she hated the people who looked after her. She was a lonely child. She had no friends in her family though she came in the middle, her sisters Betty and Con being older than she, and her brothers Victor and Neville younger.

When Emily was fourteen, her father was appointed ambassador in Paris. 'She is still fat, and stoops her head terribly,' wrote her mother Edith, 'but I am going to make her take dancing lessons. She is wilful and often very cross.'[14] After Knebworth, where Emily had run wild,

---

*Mrs Plowden's daughter, the even prettier Pamela, grew up to marry Robert's son Victor.

living in an imaginary world fired by her reading of Scott's novels, Paris was incarceration. The slow, repetitive daily walks in the Bois, the polite conversation with patronizing grown-ups, the smart, tight clothes; all were torture. Edith had no time for her, pushing her away and telling her not to be a nuisance, and Emily would run to her room in tears. Edith did not believe in educating girls. 'Charm, and a power of adapting themselves to their husbands' she considered far more essential than study, 'which might only ruin their healths'.

Robert was a success in Paris. He was popular with the French, who were delighted by his habits such as stopping the embassy carriage outside a pissoir if he happened to need it. 'I devoted my life to India,' he said, 'and everybody abused me. I come here, do nothing, and am praised to the skies.' Yet happiness eluded him. He was tired, depressed and often ill, eating his way like a dyspeptic caterpillar through long and wearisome dinners. Racked by bronchitis, and persecuted by an affliction of the tongue, he deadened the pain with cocaine and laudanum. 'Lytton is now said to have gone heavily into opium-eating or smoking,' wrote Lord Derby.[15]

Emily would pray for courage before entering his room. She dreaded his sarcasm; and when he read his long narrative poems aloud in his beautiful voice in the evenings, she grew so bored she had to pinch herself to stay awake. Robert's ill health increased the distance between them. In 1889 he was operated on for a malignant tumour inside his nose, and – not helped by the surgeons leaving behind a wad of lint – he never really recovered.

Emily began to correspond with a seventy-one-year-old clergyman, Whitwell Elwin. Once editor of the *Quarterly Review*, he lived at Booton in Norfolk and in old age he amused himself by conducting sentimental correspondences with 'blessed girls', as he called them. Betty, Emily's much prettier older sister, had been one of his girls and, after Betty married, Emily began to write to him. In long letters to 'My Darling Rev' she poured out everything she was too lonely or shy to say – 'I just put down what my mind is most full of,' she told him. In summer she visited him at Booton, holding his hand after tea as he sat in his favourite green velvet armchair. Mrs Elwin sat sewing at the other side of the room muttering, 'May God forgive you,' when Elwin uttered anything especially indiscreet.

Emily's pen raced across the paper, blurting out her sins and indiscretions and anxieties. His Rev, as she called him, gave her advice and comfort, teaching her to become Wordsworth's Phantom of

Delight: 'A perfect Woman, nobly planned / To warn, to comfort, and command.' Emily wore Elwin's Victorian ideal of womanhood like a tight-fitting dress. Overweight and awkward, she was uncomfortable in her new ideas. Priggish and prudish, she disapproved fiercely of the Parisian women with their acknowledged lovers, and she refused to be impressed by Oscar Wilde. When Wilde visited the embassy, Emily found him 'very amusing and not so odious as we expected, though he is evidently fearfully conceited'.[16]

Emily disapproved of her father's poetry too. She especially hated the decadent *Marah* poems, which Robert wrote in 1890–1, depicting an adult world of weary, sated disillusion. 'If I read *Marah*,' Emily told Elwin, 'and believed there was no love, no truth, no reality in anything, I should kill myself at once.' For Robert life had become a meaningless succession of appetite-numbing cigarettes and adulterous affairs. 'O I could weep, weep, weep away this weight / Of tearless, time-worn inarticulate pain,' he wailed.[17]

By October 1891 Robert was suffering agonies of pain from an inflammation of the bladder. For six weeks he was dosed with morphine and brandy. His illness made it harder than ever for Emily to reach him. The last thing he said to her, as she left to go to church, was, 'How happy for you that you like it!' A day or so later he was dead, killed softly and swiftly by a stroke as he sat in bed working on a poem to his mistress, the American actress Mary Anderson.

> ... the newness of our own desires
> That would not suffer joy to be at ease,
> And thoughts that, as along electric wires,
> Flash'd none but brief and broken messages
> Because the stint of costly time forbade
> Love's longed-for luxury of full utterance ...

Robert wrote a letter to Edith to be opened after he died. He admitted that he had loved 'M. A. [Mary Anderson] deeply and too much', but told of his 'unspeakable love' for Edith, his 'heart of hearts'. Edith could choose to believe which version she wished.[18]

Robert's death brought the family face to face with the money problems he had evaded for too long. Knebworth had been let since 1890, and there was no question of returning to live there. Instead they borrowed houses from Edith's relations, and in 1893 went to live at

The Danes, in the village of Little Berkhamsted. Walburga Paget, who had known them in their grand days, described it as 'a little cottage with paper walls and no special attraction', a smell of mutton constantly pervading its tiny rooms.*

Widowhood was hard for Edith. In spite of his philandering, she missed Robert dreadfully. Lord Rowton brought her a packet of Robert's letters, which a servant let fall into a slop-pail. 'She took it terribly to heart, poor dear,' wrote Walburga.[19] Family life was very dull. Edith, who loved walking, dragooned her children to trudge the lanes each day, berating the sulky Emily for holding herself badly. At mealtimes they all argued, and Edith scolded Emily for being too positive and outspoken in her opinions. In the evenings Edith read aloud in a bored voice, and none of the family listened. Victor went to sleep, while Neville kept asking hopefully whether it was the end of the chapter.

When the boys were away at school at Eton, Emily was left at home with her sister Con. Con was different somehow. She had none of the Lytton family pride. She disliked Knebworth and despised Bulwer, resolving to seek out and rescue his many illegitimate children. She was not the favourite of either of her parents, and, unlike Betty and Emily, she was never one of Elwin's 'blessed girls'. As a child she had suffered from rheumatic fever which left her with a weak heart. Outwardly submissive, she possessed a steely independence, fired by the purest motives. Con worshipped Tolstoy and always made a point of dancing with the saddest young man in the room. She was a talented pianist, and she longed to go to Vienna to train, but when Betty married and left home, Con was needed at the embassy in Paris. She obeyed, though she hated the rich and titled world of Paris.

Each day she played the piano with passionate intensity for hours or exercised her fingers on a dumb keyboard. In 1892 she visited the Cape with Edith, and fell in love with Arthur Ponsonby, who was ADC to her uncle Lord Loch, the High Commissioner. Edith forbade marriage on grounds of money, and Con remained semi-engaged to Ponsonby for fourteen years – though, as her brother Neville remarked, lack of money never hampered true lovers. 'Pon' had no roof to his mouth, which made him hard to understand but endeared him all the more to Con. He angered Emily because he seemed to appreciate Con so little, and never raised a finger to make their marriage a possibility. Emily longed to kick him.[20]

---

*In 1999 the asking price for The Danes, which has ten bedrooms, was £1.25 million.

Perhaps Con did not want to marry. Her family pitied her as a failure, condemned to a lifetime of dreary spinsterhood, but Con had made a choice. Not marrying meant that she could take control of her own life. She was gently feeling her way towards the feminism of her great-grandmother Anna Wheeler, though unlike Anna she was no virago, far from it. She lived at home, meekly obedient to Edith. But she began to write, reviewing novels and contributing a column for a woman's paper which earned her £4 4s. a week. The very idea of working for money made even Emily furious. 'To think she has come to this!' she raged.[21]

Emily had no wish to emulate the bluestocking Con. Escape from the boredom of home came through her other sister, Betty. Betty was eight years older, beautiful and intelligent and married to Gerald Balfour, politician nephew of Lord Salisbury. She had adored her father, and after he died she became emotionally dependent on Barbara Webb, who was like an older sister to her. 'Bets darling, now do make old Rothschild devoted to you,' Barbara wrote. 'You don't make enough of your opportunities and your peculiar charm. C. Lyttelton might labour for years and couldn't get the sort of influence over people, that you could, with ease.'

Betty's friends were the Souls, clever, smart and social. Their sophisticated worldliness, intellectual conversation and cruel after-dinner games frightened Emily, perhaps because they reminded her of her father. 'If Souls could but have their thin coat of paint scraped off, what poor wooden blocks they would be,' she wrote. Even Betty was corrupted when she was with her Soul friends, thought Emily. The trouble with the Souls was that they made Emily so shy and tongue-tied. When they bothered to speak to her, her hostility easily melted. 'I was quite prepared to detest Mrs Horner,' she wrote from Mells, where she was staying, 'and I have ended by loving her.'[22]

How did it happen that eighteen-year-old Emily, priggish, virginal pupil of the Reverend Whitwell Elwin, fell for the charms of Wilfred Blunt, a fifty-three-year-old married philanderer? Years later, Emily blamed Blunt. 'He drew me out, flattered me, encouraged me in playful chaff, leading me on until I unconsciously found myself deeply in love with him,' she wrote. Blunt was a villain. But Emily was willing; she made the first moves.

Emily had become friends with Judith Blunt, only child of Wilfrid Blunt and his wife Anne. Judith was tall, strong and athletic. At sixteen her chief delight was wrestling her friends, and she shot and played tennis like a champion. Emily and Judith formed a gang named the Pawsoff and Rude Club, the rules of which were that you were direct and ill-mannered and never shook hands. In the summer of 1892 Emily went to stay at Crabbet, the house created by Blunt to live the ideal English country life. Blunt was still striking, especially when dressed as an Arab chieftain. Emily thought him the handsomest man she had ever met. That autumn she began a correspondence with him. She teased that when he tired of flattery and wanted truth he must come to her. He replied that he was in need of serious spiritual advice. He came to stay with Betty in London. She told him that the dogs devoured everything he wrote.* One day in May 1893, in Betty's house, Blunt suddenly kissed her hands. Emily turned pale and ran upstairs.

In August, she stayed again at Crabbet. She went for a walk with Blunt, and he teased her about the novel she was writing with Judith. He took her hand in those long thin hands of his: 'Won't you let the villain love you, the villain does love you, and will you love the villain!' He kissed her hand, and told her he had loved her for two years: 'Are you angry with me for loving you?' Did she love him, Blunt asked. Emily said very simply, yes. 'It was all very sweet and delightful,' wrote Blunt, 'but it must not go much further.'

It did, of course. A few days later Blunt caught her alone before dinner, and after a very hot embrace asked if he could come to her room. Emily was alarmed. She said no, and she blamed herself for encouraging him. Next day she attempted to explain. 'I have been brought up differently from most girls, in a much freer way, and I have let you do things to me which other girls might not have allowed, or if they had you would have misunderstood them, and you have probably misunderstood me, but I want you to understand that I care for you only as my friend, and I ask you as a favour to me not to kiss me.' Blunt was undeterred. That evening he and Emily both wore Arab dress. Alone before dinner, he gave her a ring and made her his Mohammedan wife. 'With this ring I thee wed, with my body I thee worship.'[23]

The day after she left Crabbet Emily wrote to Blunt, whom she called 'My dear Thing': 'I wear your ring and it is lovely. Whenever I see it or feel it I think of you, and as there are little sharp points on it which stick into my fingers when I press them together, I have to think of you very often.'[24]

---

*'I call that flirtation,' said Gerald Balfour, Betty's husband, gravely shocked.

She also wrote to Elwin, telling him in intimate detail of everything that had passed between her and Blunt. The result was that furious letters from Booton rained down, warning of the awful dangers of a woman's physical passion. Emily must be saved from losing her virginity to a philanderer. Many of these letters Emily tore up, but in the end she capitulated. She had been a fool, she now saw, to trust so base a villain. She was overcome with self-loathing. Pushed by Elwin she wrote obediently to break off with Blunt: 'the love you said you felt for me is a love which you should have been ashamed to offer, and which I should die rather than accept or return'.[25]

Like the heroine of a Victorian novel, Emily had been rescued from disgrace worse than death and saved from the baseness of her own sexuality. All the lessons Elwin had taught her about the Phantom of Delight were put to the test by Blunt's advances. But part of her did not want to be saved. By pretending to be Blunt's spiritual adviser she had mocked Elwin's values. She railed against the double standards which blamed a woman for sinning, once and for love, yet overlooked the repeated sins of a man driven by lust.

The truth was that she was obsessed by Blunt. She could think of no one else. And yet she realized that his fascination for her was the reason above all others why she should avoid him. It was agony; but agony of an exquisitely exciting kind.

Back home at The Danes, Emily was bored and frustrated. That summer the family finances plumbed new depths with the crash of Read, the man to whom Robert had entrusted his savings for investment. Edith's income shrank to £1,900. She struggled to economize. There was talk of Emily becoming a maid of honour at court, to which she responded unhelpfully and untruthfully that she was a republican.

The crash relieved Emily from the trials of London society. She never came out. Instead she was presented to the tiny, dignified Queen privately at Windsor. The crash was hardest for Edith. Putting her hair up herself when she dressed in the morning was out of the question. Emily ridiculed her mother for caring so much about small things like having servants, and being able to afford dresses by Worth. Edith became a lady-in-waiting at court.

Emily was loud and outspoken; she was so flirtatious that Edith considered it impossible to engage a tutor for the boys' holidays. Men hate a great strong, chaffing girl like you, she told her daughter. Emily must soften down if she was ever to attract a husband.[26] Mealtimes at

The Danes became a succession of rows. Emily was openly contemptuous of her mother for being stupid and conventional.

Meanwhile, Emily lived mainly in her dreams, and her dreams were about Blunt. She was a character in a novel: should she let the villain love her, the villain did love her, should she love the villain . . . Not that in reality she saw much of Blunt. In October 1893, after her letter breaking off the relationship, she stayed at Crabbet again, and felt in a 'perpetual internal tremble'. Blunt reproached her for her 'horrible' letter, but she found him all the more fascinating because he pretended to be indifferent.

Soon afterwards Blunt left to spend his usual winter in Egypt, but Emily stayed close by reason of her friendship with Judith. As her sister Con wrote, 'I can't help thinking that *some* of the charm (if only a little) she has for you is due, not to her being *Judith*, but because she is the daughter of Blunt, lives near him, looks at his face every day, speaks to him of you and to you of him.'

Judith never saw this, and she became intensely involved with Emily, who probably meant more to her than any man. Both Blunt and Emily, in a way, enjoyed the drama and the heartbreak. But Judith's emotions were genuine, and she was being 'used'. Of the two girls, it was Judith who was vulnerable, not Emily.[27]

Through Judith, Emily kept alive her love for Blunt. When he returned from Egypt she was drawn into his life, and the old game of temptation and resistance began again. Elwin became almost hysterical. 'In a minute or two,' he warned, 'a woman may be plunged into unutterable wretchedness for life . . . the ruin is instantaneous and it is complete.'[28]

Unsurprisingly, Emily's letters to Elwin dried up. Meanwhile, in Egypt the next winter Emily was far from Blunt's thoughts. He was in the throes of a grand passion for a married woman, Mary Elcho. She was the mistress of his enemy, the passionless Conservative politician Arthur Balfour, and Blunt was enjoying the sweet revenge of seducing her. He made her his Bedouin wife and, after a desert honeymoon, she became pregnant.

In August 1895, a month before the birth of Mary Elcho's baby, Emily and Judith stayed together at Cromer with the Locker-Lampsons. Emily wrote to Blunt and asked him to come too. They spent a happy day together by the sea, and Emily remembered holding his hand under the table as they played the letter game. In bed that night she heard someone trying her door, which she had locked. Later, she charged him with this. But why did she lock her bedroom door? Blunt was a philanderer, but he surely wouldn't have come to her at night without prior encouragement. He left that morning, and she wrote him a letter brimming with love. 'I was sad to wake and know you had gone. But it is good to know you are fond of me, and you know I am your affec. Emily Lytton.'[29]

When Blunt set off on his travels that autumn, Emily showered him with love letters. 'Dear thing,' she wrote. 'I think I had better come and be a hermitess with you on Mount Sinai.' She meant it. Father and lover rolled into one, Blunt was all she wished for. Detesting house parties because she was always cold, shy and bored, Emily would retreat to her bedroom to write to him. In long gossipy letters she told him about the Souls: about getting lost on a bicycle ride, when 'Lady Cowper smoked cigarettes and said "Damn" very frequently . . . Ettie Grenfell and Mrs Horner proceeded to divest themselves of their skirts by putting them over their heads and their silhouettes in the twilight were anything but beautiful.'[30]

Emily did not, in her letters, treat Blunt as a confessor, like Elwin. But Judith, nevertheless, grew resentful of her father. Meanwhile, Emily drew closer to Judith. Each morning Judith would wake her; they were as close as friends could be. Emily told Blunt that 'all the jealousy which she [Judith] used to feel for Mr Bootles [Elwin] she now feels for you.'

Of course the two girls talked. Emily told Judith how she planned to elope with Blunt to Paris and how they would live together on Mount Sinai. Shocked and horribly stung, Judith responded by telling Emily that Blunt was in love with Mary Elcho.* Soon the whole story tumbled out.

Emily was very angry. Blunt's unfaithfulness meant far more to her than all Elwin's warnings of hellfire. She ceased to answer Blunt's letters, nor was she at the station, as she usually was, to welcome him on his return to London in April 1896. So far as she was concerned, that was the end.

Little suspecting what had happened, Blunt expected to hear that Emily had become engaged to some young man, ruefully admitting that 'there is no one elsc in England that I shall care to see'.[31] When he learned the truth, he was furious with Judith. Terrible scenes ensued. Blunt insisted that he had done nothing wrong in trying to make Emily

---

* Blunt had misguidedly confided in his daughter, and had even sent Judith to see the baby.

happy. Oh yes, responded Judith, what about the bedroom door at Cromer? Blunt, who apparently had not realized that Emily had heard him, was speechless, stammering something about seduction making Emily permanently happy. He told Judith that 'it would have done Emily all the good in the world – she wasn't pretty enough to get much of a husband and wasn't likely to get such a chance again'.

When Emily met him that summer he thought she looked pale and frightened, especially when Judith was near. 'I do not yet understand the influence [Judith] has exercised and is exercising over the child,' wrote Blunt, 'but it has all the appearance of being mesmeric.'[32]

A few weeks after she broke with Blunt Emily met Ned Lutyens at the Blumenthals'. 'Do you dance till you are dishevelled?' he asked, when she said she was going to a ball. 'I do.'

They met often at dances that summer. At Mrs Lyulph Stanley's, Lutyens told her to dance as if he were the only crowned head in Europe and she the only queen, 'and we made little bows to each other all the time. I thought you mad but so nice,' wrote Emily. 'And then you said something about being at your office next morning and I thought you were a clerk of some kind and thought how you would fidget on an office stool!'[33]

Ned admired her from a distance. He wasn't sure when he fell in love with her, but he remembered that he always looked for her and was disappointed when he couldn't see her. Not allowed to sit beside her or talk to her, he thought she looked 'so fair and good and altogether something holy'.[34]

Emily remembered Ned as a wildly eccentric and energetic dancer, but no more than that. After three years' infatuation with Blunt and already twenty-one, she felt that she was on the shelf and was determined to make up for lost time. Her mother knew nothing of the Blunt affair; to Blunt's unspeakable relief, Judith had not told her, and nor had anyone else. Edith scolded Emily for not being nice enough to young men and worried lest she was fast. Staying in Ireland where Gerald Balfour was Chief Secretary, Emily flirted with one of the aides-de-camp who was engaged to someone else. She invited a young Frenchman who had admired her in Paris to stay at The Danes, but Edith despaired when he left 'without the least hint of proposing. No Frenchman would think of marrying without money and all Emily would have would be £5,000 . . .'[35]

Emily set her sights on Gerald Duckworth. She had first met him with

Judith, back in the days of the Pawsoff and Rude Club. Gerald's mother, who was married to Leslie Stephen and supposed to be beautiful, Emily found 'languid and sugary' and Stella his sister 'like a ruminating cow'. Gerald, however, was refreshingly direct. 'I hear you are frightfully rude,' he said, and after that there was no stiffness between them.[36]

In September 1896, when Edith Lytton went to wait on the Queen at Balmoral, Emily spent a month at Milford with Barbara Webb. She wanted to be near Gerald Duckworth and the Stephen family, who had rented a house at Hindhead that summer. On the first Sunday she bicycled over and spent the day with 'Mr Gerald'. Only a month before at Hindhead Stella Duckworth had become engaged to Jack Hills, who rode up each day on his bicycle: Virginia Stephen remembered 'a black and silver night of mysterious voices'. For Emily, Gerald Duckworth brought no such magic. At lunch Leslie Stephen groaned and grunted and sighed heavily (is he an idiot? wondered Emily) and afterwards the young people raced around the garden on bicycles with their feet up, Vanessa Stephen coming a cropper with the bicycle on top of her. 'Mr Gerald rode back with me,' Emily told her mother, 'and was very nice.'[37]

Not nice enough. If Gerald Duckworth had proposed, Emily would doubtless have accepted, and for the rest of her life she rather regretted not marrying him.* She returned to Milford, tired and disappointed, to find that 'Mr Lutyens' had arrived and was waiting impatiently for her.

When Barbara Webb told Ned that Emily was coming to Milford, he had begged her to invite him, telling her 'I should make War!! It was life and death!!!'[38] He lost no time. After dinner that Sunday he proposed a 'housebreaking' expedition with Emily by moonlight to Warren Lodge, the house he was building for Bob Webb in the village of Thursley. They broke in through a window and wandered about.

Then something happened in the dark, half-built house. A moment of intimacy, a flash of recognition – nothing was said, but it was enough to make Ned, who was sentimental, feel a wave of *ronge* whenever he passed Warren Lodge in later, harsher times. Now Ned sketched them both pedalling into the moonlight holding hands.

Their midnight escapade raised eyebrows. An elderly guest named Madame Vitelleschi complained to Barbara, who pretended to be

---

*Though if Virginia Woolf's allegations of sexual abuse by Gerald Duckworth were true, Emily should perhaps have been thankful to have escaped.

shocked while secretly encouraging them – she was enjoying her role as matchmaker.

Next day Ned took Emily to Munstead to meet Bumps. Emily thought Miss Jekyll enchanting, and her cottage, The Hut, the most fascinating she ever saw. Ned and Emily gave Bumps a surprise dinner, arriving at The Hut with mutton chops and eggs and almonds and cake (in her agitation Emily dropped the eggs). After 'the best dinner I ever ate', they drank Bumps's hot elderberry wine sitting in the inglenook.[39]

Ned left for London a few days later, downcast by Emily's coldness and refusal to encourage him. He said goodbye to Barbara as she sat in her carriage. He told her: 'I had made all the little war I could and that it was all over. Barbara said, Yes, she supposed it was "all over", and I said, "But it can't be – how can I go on?" And she laughed and said I must take my chance and that it was probably all over.'[40]

Emily who knew perfectly well how Ned felt (had Barbara told her?) was enjoying herself. 'I just loved to have you on the verge and then laugh and see you shrink back.' Next time Ned came, a few days later, she played the guitar to a cousin of Barbara's called Julian Spicer, which made Ned miserable. 'I watched you the whole time with the corner of my eye, and felt oh! so tempted to throw the guitar at him and throw my arms round your neck.'[41]

Ned flitted back and forth between London and Milford, taking Emily on bicycle rides to see his houses. One wet Saturday in Godalming the rain made the green dye of her straw hat run down her nose, and in a shop window Ned spied a red lacquer cabinet for 'our house', he told her. They talked about the house one evening at The Hut, drinking elderberry wine, and Ned promised to design her a casket for her birthday.

On Ned's last day at Milford Emily frightened him by announcing that she was engaged to Gerald Duckworth.[42] He was so agitated that on the way to the station he ran his bicycle into a wall and cut his hand. Bumps had insisted, much against his will, that he keep his appointment with Mrs Horner of Mells.* Bumps was right. Frances Horner was to become a lifelong friend and client. But as Lutyens steamed down to Frome, miserably watching from a coupé at the back of the train 'the receding landscape which seems to draw with quick perspective my very hope', he bitterly regretted his lost opportunity.[43]

---

*Frances Horner, whom Emily knew through her sister Betty, was the sister of Aggie Jekyll, who was married to Bumps's brother Herbert Jekyll.

'My dear Lady Emily,' he began, writing in pencil, 'how I regret – Bumps or no Bumps – that I did not have the courage to play truant to my work and stay by you . . . I would have told you how I love you. Would you have laughed? Except my love I have nothing to offer you. I am poor, unknown and little altogether.' In the very next breath he contradicted himself. 'My life's work would be yours. One word from you would turn my world to one great sphere of happiness and I would become a man. Give me some chance to prove it.'[44]

It was the beginning of a strange romance. To Christopher Hussey, biographer of Lutyens, it read as if 'J. M. Barrie and Charlotte Yonge had collaborated to invent it after reading William Morris, then got Randolph Caldecott to draw the pictures'.[45] Certainly this was true of Lutyens's love letters, but the emotional realities were darker and deeper. Emily Lytton was on the rebound from Wilfrid Blunt. She had nothing in common with Ned Lutyens at all. Lutyens was caught up in a painful emotional entanglement with Barbara Webb, who was dying of cancer. It was Barbara Webb who brought them together, pushed by Ned to arrange a meeting; but even she began to take fright when she realized that things were getting serious. She warned Emily not to encourage Lutyens, 'as he is inclined to be bumptious'. And she cautioned Ned to be absolutely sure and true in his love, which was code for saying that the odds – especially social – were heavily stacked against him. But the more Barbara tried to warn him, the more determined Ned became to prove that his 'love' was higher, purer, better, stronger . . .

Miss Jekyll also tried to put Emily off. Refusing to believe that Emily, who had a 'handle' to her name, could possibly be in earnest about her homegrown protégé, Bumps warned her not to be a frivolous influence in his life: his work was too important for that. For Emily, Ned drew the cartoon for the week: the stern spirit of Architecture, a female goddess brandishing a T-square, swearing at a small figure on a bicycle for going whither he would follow – in pursuit of Emily on a bicycle. By the next letter the stern figure has become Bumps, at whose feet Ned humbly kneels.[46]

But the more Emily learned about Ned's 'genius', the more attracted she was. Emily was a worshipper. Lutyens was no father-figure, but his work gave her the mission that she needed.

Chapter Six

Engagement
1896–1897

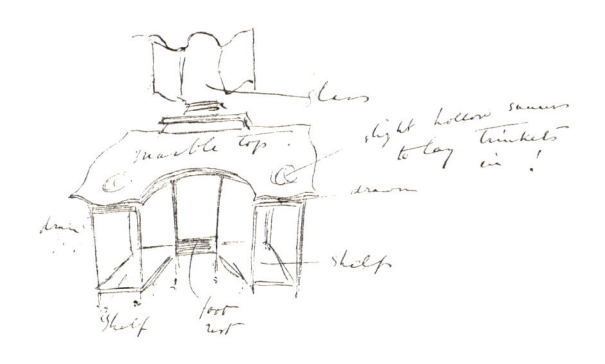

Ned's sketches of the furniture he designed for their bedroom.
(All these pieces were made.)

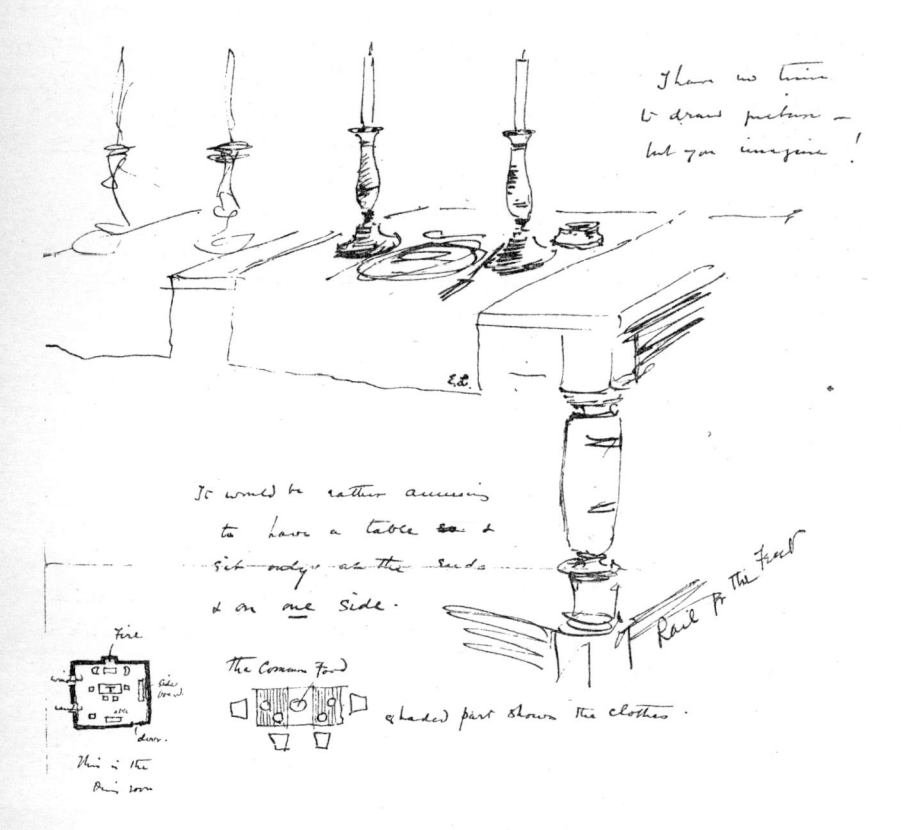

The dinner table: Ned even designed the place settings.

'I stand as on some dear little hill alone and desert round me,' Ned told Emily. 'The lovely valley seems to rise and give me warmth and you. Then I wax strong and great and worthy of you.' But then he woke, and though the valley was still beautiful it was too distant, and he was cold and alone.

If the imagery of Ned's dream is sexual, it is curiously impersonal, as if he were an architect surveying a site. Harping on his own littleness and deficiencies was typical of Lutyens, yet he was always to be tempted to put his work before Emily.[1]

Ned Lutyens retreated to his office at 6 Gray's Inn Square, an architects' enclave in the lawyers' district of London. Number 6 was a handsome, dark brick, double-fronted building, built in the time of Wren. Inside hung a white board inscribed with a list of names in black lettering. High up the square wooden staircase with its bulging banisters were his two white-panelled rooms, their old windows looking out over Gray's Inn garden, where the rooks cawed and the roar of London traffic seemed miles away. In one room Lutyens stood to draw at his high board. Next door were one or two paying pupils, a clerk without a roof to his mouth and his first assistant, pious, simple 'Billee' Barlow, who arrived at sites to measure buildings wearing gaiters, an ink bottle strapped to his buttonhole and an especially solemn expression.

At the same time as Ned was flirting with Emily at Milford, he was wooing work from young Mrs Streatfeild, who planned to build at Fulbrook, which was nearby, a few minutes' ride on a bicycle. 'I have been working at your sketches,' he told Mrs Streatfeild, a few days after his first love letter to Emily. 'They have not quite "arrived" yet . . . I am awfully keen.' Mrs Streatfeild was the daughter of Richard Combe, who twenty years before had commissioned Norman Shaw to build Pierrepoint, a house which Ned knew and admired. Combe was a brewer and a friend of Barbara Webb; '*very* rich', according to Ned, and 'big in the county of Surrey – Jockey Club man etc'.[2] Fulbrook was expensive: the site alone cost over £2,000 and the lowest tenders came in at £6,800. At Fulbrook Lutyens's inventiveness ran wild. Perhaps his excitement about Emily went to his head, and his designs for the house were spoiled by new ideas which were not fully resolved, though it did contain his first classical interior.³*

Lutyens's other major job was a house for Lord Battersea near Cromer. Cromer was a Surrey by the sea, a fashionable resort for the cultured rich. Emily had been there to stay with the Locker-Lampsons, and also with her mother for seaside holidays, staying at a guest house with hideous coffee-chrysanthemum-embossed wallpaper and red plush furniture. Once, before she really knew him, Ned had called on Emily there. She thought little of him then, but she remembered him cycling down the hill with his coat streaming behind him.⁴ He had been visiting Overstrand, the site of The Pleasaunce, the house he was working on for Lord Battersea.

Cyril Flower, Lord Battersea, was a rich, extravagant dilettante, a narcissist who adored beautiful things. He married Constance de Rothschild, was briefly a Liberal MP and retired early from politics to build himself a house at Overstrand. Constance Battersea hated Overstrand, which she thought 'cold, draughty, windy, bitter, bleak', but her husband thrived on seaside life, prancing along the beach, admired by all, 'clad in white samite [silk], as mystic and wonderful as he can be, with a bath towel round his neck, or a camera slung on his back'. At Overstrand he bought two plain red-brick villas, and hired Lutyens to encase and enlarge them, creating more room for his throngs of visitors. 'We are *never alone*,' groaned his wife. Lutyens, she wrote, 'entered fully into my husband's views', which was code for saying that he did exactly what Lord Battersea told him to do. The result was eccentric, to say the least.† One 'nightmarish' elevation contained eight different architectural elements, dropping 'backwards and forwards and up and down in a seemingly endless array of twists and turns'.⁵ Lutyens later regretted The Pleasaunce, and he panicked when Lord Battersea was tarnished by a homosexual scandal. 'I do wish the Battersea house was better and not so spoiled by him. I suppose people realize this,' he wrote, worrying that it would harm his

---

*Writing in 1950, Christopher Hussey thought Fulbrook the worst design Lutyens ever made. However, as Roderick Gradidge, who admired it, pointed out: 'Those who find Lutyens at his most exciting when he is at his blandest – shall we say at Gledstone – will find little to praise at Fulbrook.'
†The Pleasaunce divides Lutyens's critics. Writing in 1913, Lawrence Wheeler described it as 'markedly lacking in definite form'. More recently, the reputation of The Pleasaunce has revived as critics such as Roderick Gradidge have recognized it as an instance of Lutyens's youthful art nouveau.

reputation. 'He so murders and alters everything I design whilst it is being built that there is no credit and people who know must hate the work.'⁶

Back at The Danes, Emily was embroiled in domestic diplomacy. She had hooked her fish, but not yet landed him: she needed to persuade her family. Ned's pencilled letter declaring his love was a serious document of intent, and the first thing she did was consult her mother. Edith Lytton, who considered herself a pauper and her daughters penniless, promptly asked Barbara Webb about his expectations. Barbara's reply to her letter of inquiry was not satisfactory.

> I don't think that there is a *chance* of the father being able to do anything: in fact I feel sure of this. They are very poor, and a very large family. If only darling Em hadn't rather set her heart that way, I should say, not much harm done. For N.L. *is* a flirt; and this is the first time I believe, he has ever been seriously hit, and it will do him more good than harm. But never mind him. What does pain me is any worry to you and Emily.⁷

Annoyed that Emily was involved with someone unsuitable yet again, Edith Lytton ordered her to write to Ned breaking it off.

Emily obeyed the letter of her mother's instructions, but made no attempt to hide her feelings. She told Ned he must go forth like a knight of old and conquer a name for himself, and she signed herself 'Yours? (I cannot write "sincerely")'. Soaking herself in her father's love poetry, she selected a motto for the casket which Ned had promised to design for her. 'Man cannot make, but may ennoble, fate, / By nobly bearing it.' Robert Lytton had continued: 'So let us trust / Not to ourselves but God, and calmly wait / Love's orient', but when the casket was made Ned added a more defiant coda, the same couplet that he had inscribed on his design for Barbara Webb's deathbed: 'Yet as Faith wills / So Fate fulfils'.

'Would it comfort you,' wrote Emily, 'to know I could have loved you, oh, so well! which means I suppose that I love you now.' This letter from Emily turned the ill-cleaned Onslow Square to a heaven of burnished gold. Ned's world, once so flat, became quite round; but it was flattened again by a frosty letter from Lady Lytton.

'I cannot remember having been introduced to you,' she began, which was Victorian code for saying that he wasn't someone whom she *could* know socially. Lutyens told her that he earned £1,000 a year.

This, for a self-made man of twenty-seven, was impressive and he knew it. But he had no capital, and that was the sticking-point. 'I must now go back to my shadow,' Ned told Emily, and there he remained.[8]

Terrified of offending Lady Lytton, paralysed by the fear of losing Emily, he dared not write. Each morning Emily came down longing for a letter, or some mention of his name, and there was nothing. His life in the two white rooms in Gray's Inn was 'black darkness' to her, and she began to despair.

She consulted Elwin. Anxious that the flirtatious Emily should be married off, His Rev reassured her that 'the immense majority of weddings take place under circumstances less promising . . . Mr Lutyens has both income and prospects.' Far from being penniless, Emily had £5,000 of her own on marriage; a substantial sum, the price of one of Ned's houses. If Ned could insure his life for the same amount or more, her mother's objections would be met.

Emily departed for Dublin, to stay with her sister Betty Balfour. Betty also wanted Emily married, and she did her best to convert their mother. Barbara Webb had convinced her that Lutyens was 'exceptionally pure-minded and honourable'. His defect was 'a sort of frivolousness of talk which, attractive in its way, seemed to indicate a sort of absence of seriousness'.[9]

Acting on the advice of Barbara Webb and Betty Balfour, Ned asked for an interview with Emily's uncle, Lord Loch, ex-South African High Commissioner, and family adviser on money matters. Loch had expected a request to intervene with the Duke of Westminster, who only a few weeks before had commissioned Lutyens to design a garden temple, and he was 'somewhat surprised' to discover it was about 'dear Emily'. But he was impressed by the balance sheet Lutyens brought, which showed his income almost doubling from £700 in 1894-5 to £1,300 in 1896-7. Surely, urged Loch, Lutyens could afford to insure his life for, say, £12,000, paying an annual premium of £240, which would still leave a clear income of £1,000.

Edith was not convinced. The professional income of Mr Lutyens was too uncertain; he had no savings, and he could not guarantee to pay the insurance premium out of income. Emily wrote to her mother: 'He can prove himself by his work, and I by my patience, and we both trust to your kindness for the rest. God help us all.' But Edith refused to meet Ned. He tried to charm her by his letters. 'I *want* to comply with your every wish, so that I may always have your confidence.' When Edith told him not to send the casket 'for the present', he replied with a pun. 'I hope the Present will not reach too far into the future! All my happiness lies in your hands.'¹⁰

Ned had another interview with Loch, and proposed insurance of £10,000. This, said Loch, was not enough; but he hinted that if Ned was prepared to insure his life for a larger sum, say £15,000, then Edith would probably relent. Edith by now was convinced the thing must be settled, the sooner the better. Accordingly, Loch summoned Ned again, and Ned agreed to insure his life for £13,000.

Loch thought the conditions 'very moderate', but Ned had really been forced to mortgage his income to buy his wife. His father contributed a lump sum of £1000, but Ned engaged to pay a hefty annual premium of £190. Lord Loch had acted as broker, putting a price on the gulf which separated the earl's daughter from the horse painter's son. At times, the gulf seemed unbridgeable; when Bumps laughed because Emily had a 'handle' to her name, Ned had broken down and cried 'like a little boy'.¹¹ Besotted by Emily and ashamed of his own tattered family, he meekly complied with the conditions the peer dictated.

When Lord Loch wired that the insurance was settled, Edith instantly summoned Ned to The Danes. Arriving home at midnight on 28 January 1897 to find her letter, he scribbled to Emily at 3 a.m.: 'You will be wife to me? It is too much for me to dare ask I feel so unworthy of you and so small beside you.' 'Only think,' responded Emily, 'how much happier we shall be now for all that miserable time.'

Ned arrived at Cole Green station two days later, clutching the casket and wearing new patent-leather boots. He had hoped that Emily would be there to meet him, but instead he found her mother. They walked through the snow from the station to the house. Ned was shy and nervous. When Edith admired his boots and fretted lest he ruin them in the snow, he worried he was wrongly dressed; and when she asked him about a house she wanted him to build at Knebworth (and which he did build a few years later), he dared not say anything, 'lest it should be wrong'.

Back at The Danes, 'she questioned me and I was terrified, and in every question and answer I thought I was undone, and all Emy did was to wink'. Alone together, Ned and Emily kissed properly for the first time. 'I just kissed my Emy and Emy me,' Ned wrote, and he sketched the combs tumbling from her hair. Between kisses they became engaged.¹²

Edith's mood turned from storms to sunshine in one of those 'fascinating' changes for which she was notorious. Barbara Webb, whom Edith had blamed for troublemaking, was amazed to receive a letter 'warmly thanking me for bringing about this match!!! My brain whirls,' she wrote. With his blue eyes and cigarette-smoking, Ned reminded Edith of her husband Robert. Ned's fear soon melted, and he marvelled, somewhat insincerely perhaps, at Edith's 'sweet tenderness and woman-like grace. Her quickness too without ever moving a muscle.'

Nothing could be announced until Edith had told the Queen, which she did at Osborne the following week. In a cartoon for Mrs Streatfeild, Ned imagined Victoria purring, 'It gives me great pleashurr.' In fact, Victoria merely asked whether they had enough income and remarked that Edith was unselfish to rejoice. The only good thing about it, she thought, was that they were in no hurry. 'She does not care for girls marrying I am told,' commented Edith, who was cheered by a letter from Lady Salisbury, saying how interesting for Emily to marry a rising man, 'at least she had found it so'.[13]

Becoming engaged was a licence, almost a command, to write love letters. Twice or thrice a day they wrote, and the more often they wrote, the more unreal their letters became. How absurd it was, wrote Emily; 'you are quite a stranger to me, and I really don't know anything about you – and yet I have given myself to you for ever, and there is nothing mine that is not yours, and we are going to live together alone to the end of our lives!'

At Onslow Square she met the family with whom Ned still lived in boisterous, disorganized squalor. Ned's mother, so gentle and unworldly, talked at tea about 'Willie and missionaries and acting and the end of the world and a little about my Ned'. There was never enough to eat, and Emily worried that food was bought especially for her. She was shocked when Ned's brother Frank played his guitar and sang 'I am a woman' in a high falsetto voice.[14]

A weekend visit to Hascombe in Surrey to stay with Ned's eldest brother Charlie ended in disaster, when Emily developed a fever of 103°. She worried about the 'awful impropriety' of Ned's 'close nursing': he had spent most of the weekend in her bedroom. Ned was ashamed at the miserliness of his brother and his puritan wife. 'How I hate sanctimonious prayers and cant in a dirty ugly house – if they go on their knees let them scrub first.' The social tensions were palpable, and Ned was easily bruised.

Ned's sense of social inferiority left him with a grudge. Anyone with money to spare he saw as fair game. 'Ha! hee!! What can we get out of her?' he asked when Emily described a rich widow to him. Of the owner of the *Garden* magazine, William Robinson, he wrote, 'Don't smoke before him until we have got out of him everything we can get. Oh what a little villain I am!' Ned's little-boy charm did not conceal his lack of breeding. Even Emily could not resist telling him that her cousin Adela Villiers thought him 'a little vulgar!!'[15]

None of this mattered one jot to Emily, who by now was head over ears in love. 'You have a beautiful brow and eyes, and a very nice nose, and a beautiful mouth and the only falling away is in your chin,' she told him. She had little else to do all day but think of Ned, write to Ned and hem sheets for their home together, sewing initials in small crosses once Ned had approved the colour of the thread, he having first consulted Bumps. How she longed to throw her arms around his neck and interrupt his work – to rumple his hair, which began the day so horribly smooth, black and plastered down and became so deliciously rough and curly at night.[16]

Gerald Duckworth told Edith that Lutyens was a rising architect who had more work than most men twice his age, but when he met Emily in Piccadilly he merely said how do you do and passed on. 'Thank God I have you and not him,' Emily told Ned. But Gerald gave her fifty-one volumes of Balzac as a wedding present, which suggests that he really did care for her. As for Wilfrid Blunt, whom Ned hated, fearing that he meant to be vicious, 'He cannot hurt me, he has no power,' said Emily.[17]

Emily's pride and ambition all centred on Ned's work. Unable, or so she believed, to achieve greatness herself, she longed for vicarious greatness as the wife of a great man. Ned's 'genius' validated her love for him. She had fallen in love with his talent, not with Ned himself. She pictured the days when people would visit his two rooms in Gray's Inn, 'and tell each other what a big genius worked there and what great things he did ... But they will not know that he had a little Emy who knew all about it when he was still quite a little boy, and who sat and chortled with pride because that little boy was all her own.' Her only worry was that Ned would compromise his art to make money for her. 'I want you to be able at the end of your life to look back upon your work, and know in your own mind that all of it has been very good.' Of course, this imposed a burden on Ned. Would you still love me, he asked, 'if I fail in this world's greatness?'[18] When Emily's Aunt T,

Teresa Earle, suggested that she might become jealous of Ned's work, she was indignant.

Aunt T, Edith's sister, had an annoying habit of being right. Emily in fact had grasped very little about Ned's work. When someone asked her if he built Queen Anne houses, she replied that she knew nothing about styles, only that Ned built beautiful houses. The best way to learn, as Elwin advised, was for Ned to teach her. But Ned was so sure of his own judgement, so dismissive even of Emily's embroidered linen bedcover, that rather than learn she first deferred and then gave up. How could she compete with a man who itched to design even the shape of a joint of meat in its dish? A palace of art – an equal partnership of love and art – was not what Emily wanted. Her ideal was one of close companionship, of being alone together in the evenings, talking in the firelight. 'Nedi shall tell me beautiful stories, and build for me delicious castles in the air and we will talk together over everything in our lives.' You are locked into my heart, she told him: 'Such bars and chains of love keep you in – you can never escape from your prison any more.' There was just one escape: 'to break the little heart that holds you. But you will not do it, will you?'[19]

Ned ached for bars and chains but not for companionship. He doodled sketch after sketch of Emily as a queen, frigid and passive, himself crouched before her, a tiny figure with a T-square. Queens are worshipped from afar. No one lives in cosy companionship with a queen on her throne.

He knew exactly how he wanted their life together to be. It was a vision of bareness and whiteness so perfect and clearly focused that reality could only fall short of it. 'Our house,' wrote Emily, 'is to be all white and everything in it of the simplest kind and yet all beautiful. Ned likes nothing that is not simple.' An oak dining table featured in his fantasy, blue cloths, white china, brass candlesticks, coloured Delft ware and green-handled knives. If the dining room, with its lavender and pot-pourri and crisply curling bacon, was redolent of Bumps, the parlour, as he called it, was arty and modern. No portraits – Ned dreaded being given full-lengths such as Charles painted: 'so bourgeois too!' he wrote, damning his father and brother Fred. Guthrie of the modern Glasgow school must paint the walls: 'I almost prefer his painting in this sort of decoration to E. Burne-Jones,' whispered Ned. The pictures must be 'small, Italian in feeling, gorgeous in colour and in exquisite frames, Madonnas and St Georges to inspire our respective selves'. A few flowers, simply arranged:

'Japanese methods I love, but they must not rush at one shouting vive Japonaise!'[20]

Ned's passion for simplicity and uncluttered space led him to Glasgow and art nouveau via Japan but also Holland. 'Remember Holland! de Hoogue [sic] interiors!' De Hooch, an artist of the seventeenth century, painted calm, ordered interiors with bare floors, casement windows and Delft-tiled fireplaces which evoke early *Country Life* photographs of Lutyens houses. A woman nurses a baby while a maid sweeps a spotless floor. Perhaps this was how Ned saw Emily, as a Madonna rolled into Bumps. 'Emy to her accounts shall go,' he wrote, 'and write in her nut-brown ledgers the moneys of the day. Peerless mistress, with apron and a bunch of keys that chime of home and honey in the store and to the kitchen, where pots and range glisten in the light.'[21]

It was not a picture that Emily shared. For the Edwardian art of homemaking she had neither talent nor interest. Her Aunt T published the fruit of a lifetime's domestic husbandry in the best-selling *Pot-Pourri from a Surrey Garden* (1897), which she wrote with the help of Emily's sister Con. But Emily, who burned with idealism, thought there was more to marriage than pot-pourri.

Ned believed that if Emily had refused him Barbara's illness would have broken him. He went to Milford immediately after he became engaged. Barbara was much weaker, though she was still finding work for him. It was she who had encouraged the Streatfeilds to commission Fulbrook, and she persuaded the millionaire Whitaker Wright who owned land at Whitley to give him a small job – a bathing pavilion for £20. By now she was suffering acute pain, and Ned felt powerless to help. X-ray treatment brought a brief respite, but she was soon too ill to see him. Ned began to lose hope. 'I love BW so much,' he told Emily, 'to you, my darling, I can tell this and I know you will love me the more for it. BW I look upon as a mother to the two – E and I.'[22]

But it wasn't as simple as that. He had loved Barbara more deeply than he admitted even to himself, let alone to Emily. 'I used to love Barbara better almost than anyone.' Now his love for Emily made him feel a traitor to Barbara, 'yet I do not love her one whit less'. Naturally Emily was jealous. 'I felt she had a share in your life and I had none.' Ned himself felt the need to apologize to Emily when he visited Barbara – 'You don't mind my seeing Barbara who is ill' – but Barbara's suffering made him ache all over.[23]

ENGAGEMENT

Bumps too made him feel a bit of a traitor. She sent him a poem, entitled 'The Lament of the Neglected':

> The Architect's wanted galore, galore,
> The work's at a standstill for ever more;
> The bricklayers playing – they've nothing to do,
> The carpenters smoking – they're idle too –
> The plumbers carousing till all is blue.
> Oh Plazzoh go hang, old Bumps is a bore
> For Nedi's gone courting, galore, galore!

If Ned neglected Plazzoh or Munstead, it was not because of Emily; quite the contrary, he worked harder and faster than ever before in those early months of 1897. Driven by the desperate need to earn enough for marriage, he set to like a man possessed, obsessively scribbling running totals of the year's earnings as he added each client's tally. Night after night he stayed late at Gray's Inn, working until 1 or 2 a.m. and then crossing London to sleep a dreamless sleep at Onslow Square. He worked on over twenty jobs in 1897 (in 1896 he had only three or four) and as the list swelled, he seemed magically fluent – the designs came effortlessly. 'A furore of work is on me,' he wrote. One day in April he worked or wrote letters on a total of nine different jobs. 'Oh Emy, it is splendid having YOU to work for. It *must* make me do good work,' he wrote. 'I seem to have developed a wonderful capacity for loving, and this must develop my capacity for work.'[24] Emotional excitement released creative energies that he hardly knew he possessed.

The key to his creativity was squirrelled away in the casket of green-tooled leather which he gave Emily as an engagement present. The casket was divided into compartments containing sentimental objects – a Bible, a pipe-stopper, a heart, an anchor. In the most secret part of all was a miniature roll of plans for the house 'such as we talked of and like to where we sat, drinking the elder vintage' with Bumps at Munstead. This, with its plan formed from the interlocking of their two initials – EL and EL – was the little white house where they were to live.* The casket house has a Mogul-style garden of central diagonals laid on a rectangle and flagged paths flush with the

---

*In fact they never did live in it, but Lutyens built the house all right. At Marshcourt (1901) the miniature plans were translated into the massive reality of an Elizabethan E-shaped house built entirely of chalk.

lawn.* Even the proportions of the little white house are significant, being the first instance where Lutyens uses the simple ratio 2:1 in the principal rooms – another nod towards classicism.²⁵ The casket design is a blueprint in miniature, a time capsule of design.

Meanwhile, Lutyens formed another friendship with a woman, this time Princess Louise, Queen Victoria's youngest daughter, who was a sculptress. Louise's childless marriage to the eccentric Lord Lorne, heir to the Duke of Argyll, was an empty shell and, according to her niece, Princess Alice of Athlone, she ran after everything in trousers. She was skittish, fickle, manipulative and very good company. One moment she would appear in the bedroom of a lady-in-waiting, dance reels beautifully in her knickers, and fly out of the room with a military salute and a kick-up behind; the next she was busily intriguing at court, telling 'more lies in ten minutes than most people do in ten years'. She was a pupil of the sculptor Boehm, who had collapsed and died in her arms, though probably not while making love to her.²⁶†

In 1896 Louise commissioned Lutyens to design a large extension to the Ferry Inn, Rosneath, near Glasgow. Her tenderness towards him raised eyebrows at court, though some said she sought sons not lovers (Louise was twenty years older than Ned). Her relationship was flirtatious, and Ned's engagement to Emily made him even more interesting. She used him as a pawn to make trouble with her own husband, Lorne, and his relations. Her brother-in-law, Eustace Balfour, was an architect, but Louise thought Eustace was 'cumbrous and heavy and impossible to do with his extraordinary ideas'. Since Emily's sister Betty was the wife of Gerald Balfour, one of Eustace's brothers, this gave Louise an excuse to push Lutyens's claims to be the 'family' architect in place of Eustace.

When Lorne's brother-in-law Carr Glynn, Bishop of Peterborough, wanted alterations to his Bishop's Palace, Louise intrigued to get Ned the job, outwitting her husband, who wanted to give the work to Eustace. Lutyens rather liked Eustace Balfour ('a very curious mixture of geniality and pomposity'), but he was ruthless about jockeying him out of the job. 'I must shove on,' he told Emily, 'and get beyond these little breakers to a big position ... Think three years ago what I was doing and what I am doing now! Eustace Balfour complains he has no

---

*Quite unlike any garden he had designed before, this was realized at Hestercombe (1904), where the garden has a 'Great Plat' of central diagonals.
†Boehm died in the studio in Avenue Road where Ned Lutyens's father Charles had once painted. Charles and Boehm were friends.

work!!' But Eustace Balfour was a pitiful alcoholic with an empty office, a reluctant architect who far preferred soldiering with the volunteers. 'The whole thing,' said Ned, 'is rather like a European question and allies are chucked at crucial crises.'[27]

Ned's appointment angered Eustace's wife, the flame-haired Lady Frances Balfour, far more than mild, morose Eustace who, said Emily, was 'too kind to have nasty feelings'. When Emily called on Frances and greeted her with a kiss, 'she repressed me with a firm hand'. '*What a dull month!*' Frances snapped, when Emily said she planned to marry in September. Frances told the Bishop that Ned could build only 'cottagey' houses without bathrooms. Emily thought her 'not worth considering, she is half mad and abuses everyone without exception', but Frances bullied the Bishop and persuaded him to drop Ned. Not that the Bishop needed persuading. Ned wrote letters that were so humble and unbusinesslike that the Bishop was made to feel that he was bestowing a favour, which added to his qualms. Eustace was an architect to the Duke of Westminster, and Emily scolded Ned by saying Eustace 'is never even offered a chair or expects it. And that is what men expect of you – to draw the line . . . between business and friendliness. With women it is different because they are not naturally businesslike, and they like mixing business up with other things.'[28]

Ned never learned to draw that line; he never learned to separate the spheres of business and friendliness. Nor was this a weakness, as Emily supposed. Ned knew very well it was an asset, and he refused to take 'your darling lecture on business relations' very seriously. Instead of writing businesslike letters, Ned relied on Princess Louise, who blew up the Bishop, with the result that Ned got the job after all.

The Princess brought other benefits too. Her commission at Rosneath took Ned to Glasgow, where he saw Miss Cranston's Buchanan Street Tearooms newly decorated with art nouveau wall stencils by Charles Rennie Mackintosh; 'all very elaborately simple on very new school High Art Lines', he wrote. 'The result gorgeous! and a wee bit vulgar! . . . It is all quite good, all just a little outré, a thing we must avoid, and shall too.'[29] Ned admired the new school and even borrowed from it. At Rosneath, he experimented with eccentric modern features such as elongated corner oriel windows.*

---

*The critic Goodhart-Rendel, writing in 1945, considered that in Lutyens's work at Rosneath 'we first feel there is magic in the air'. Because of its art nouveau influences, Rosneath was censored from Lutyens's official record by the *Country Life* school of architectural critics. Lawrence Weaver ignored it, and Christopher Hussey dismissed it as a 'half-hearted' adaptation of Surrey picturesque to Scottish baronial.

At Rosneath Ned was Louise's willing slave, chopping down trees with her – don't tell Lorne, she warned him, he wouldn't like other people to cut them. Ned asked her permission to marry in August and she roared with laughter and said of course, what had she to do with it? When he was in London frequent telegrams summoned him to Kensington Palace, often on the flimsiest of pretexts – to arrange a mantelpiece, to discuss a plan – and Louise's project to buy a house in Surrey provided countless excuses for meeting.

Naturally Ned was flattered. How could he fail to preen when the Princess disparaged Emily's grand relations? 'Lord what a lot of cousins you will have,' she said, and advised him to 'keep clear of 'em'. She even claimed that Edith owed her position at court to her intervention.[30] Everything the Princess said Ned passed on to Emily; he couldn't resist crowing, even though it showed him shamelessly social-climbing.

Edith worried that Ned was 'fascinated' and warned him not to become too intimate with Princess Louise. Emily became alarmed. 'Thank God I have no cause to be jealous!' she wrote (which meant she *was* jealous). 'I hate that people should think you run after her, and I hate that she should feel you are her slave.'

'O Emy,' wrote Ned, 'I did play just one little bit but your remarks about the Princess hurt ever so much worse.' The thought of the Princess 'fascinating' him made him squirm. Real friendship was impossible with a princess. 'One makes believe and has jokes innumerable.' Ned was contrite, and promised never to play again, but the jokes continued nonetheless. Louise swooped him off on a semi-official visit to Guildford, which Ned persuaded himself was good for work, as it gave him credit with local authorities, pot-bellied and snub-nosed but 'essential for interest where public buildings are to be built'. Louise, who enjoyed flouting court rules, travelled without a lady-in-waiting, so they hid from a Queen's Messenger, and at Uxbridge station when Lady Curzon appeared 'made panic like Greeks from Larissa to the astonishment of a cabby into whose cab we were getting', buying lunch of buns and ginger beer in a shop. 'What fun you have!' was all that Emily could say.[31]

At the end of May Bumps summoned Ned urgently to Munstead for a 'galorious' mystery. Sitting in the garden, 'cheek by jowl' on the tomb-like stone seat named the Cenotaph to Sigismunda 'on account of its monumental simplicity', Bumps told him a story.

William Chance, a philanthropic barrister whose money came from a family firm of Midlands glass manufacturers, and his wife Julia, sculptress and cousin of Lytton Strachey, had bought a plot of building land less than a mile away from Munstead Wood. Passing down a sandy lane one day, they spotted a portly figure on a ladder top giving directions to workmen. This was Bumps. The Chances were entranced by her new house, but they had already commissioned the architect Halsey Ricardo. Ricardo was connected by marriage to the Stracheys, and he was architect to the Strachey–Rendel tribe, encrusting their houses with blue de Morgan tiles and William Morris papers: his masterpiece was the gleaming glazed house in Addison Road, Kensington, built for the shop owner Ernest Debenham. But the Chances preferred the craftsmanship of Lutyens's Surrey style, and they were subtly encouraged by Bumps, who said 'they could not possibly chuck Ricardo on any account and that Nedi would not oust Ricardo on any account, and they became all the more strenuous to get hold of Emy's Ned'.[32]

Perhaps the brilliance of the result owed something to the fact that Lutyens was ousting a rival. He was hopeful too that the Chances would tell their friends, 'and so another rippled ring will be made by my splash in the surface of the world'. Orchards was designed at a time of hectic rush when clients complained that he neglected them. Lord Loch, for whom Ned designed additions to Stoke College in Suffolk, grumbled that Ned took a month to produce the design and it would take another six months to build. Emily Lawless, the Irish poetess for whom he built a house at Burrow's Cross, near Shere, moaned that Lutyens could only build cottages and never allowed more than one WC. Ned retorted that her house had two WCs, while the Streatfeilds had seven and Lord Battersea ten or eleven, and Bob Webb 'gave a snort and said she was an impossible woman and it was far too small a job for you to have undertaken'.[33]

Ned liked the Chances, whom he described as 'nice quiet commonplace people with right feelings etc'. As for their house, it was 'a nice job of the sort I like – good simple building without bombastic pretension – and such that will bring me credit and emblazonment'.

The site was spectacular, on a steep hilltop above Godalming, a district which was becoming as thickly studded by Lutyens as Vincenza is by Palladio. The design was swift and intuitive. As Ned explained, 'When I get excited and rather hurried I do the best work, isn't that funny?' The basic idea of an arched entrance with stables projecting at right angles along the drive Ned had proposed at Fulbrook, where it was rejected as too expensive. He sketched the plan in a letter to Emily: the courtyard, entered from the north, has kitchen and pantry on the west, the main house and its entrance on the south, and cloisters on the east. 'Don't all this bore you?' he scrawled, having asked her to watch him sketch; but perhaps Orchards owed some of its magic to the fact that Emily claimed a share in his success as she had never done before.[34]

The builder at Orchards was Thomas Underwood, who built Munstead Wood. The building is beautifully crafted in Bargate stone, dressed with thick-mortared red rooftiles. But Orchards is more than good building, it is the realization of an idea; as architectural historian Ian Nairn wrote in 1962, Lutyens was here obsessed by a spatial idea, as Soane was obsessed with top lighting or Michelangelo with the Pietà. 'The idea is that of an immensely sophisticated entrance approach, deliberately calculated from the moment one turns into the drive, and an inner kernel of space, a courtyard or quadrangle, using the same motifs and sophisticated balance for the benefit of a static observer as the entrance does for a moving one.'

Orchards (Ian Nairn again) was 'part of the miraculous and short-lived flowering between immaturity and the fatal reversion to classicism'.[35] It was also almost the last design he made as a bachelor. While he was working on it he visited the Bishop of Peterborough with his plans. After a dinner of suffocating clerical small talk, followed by full evening service which was rattled through in ten minutes, Ned escaped for a late-night smoke in the ruined cloister. He told Emily that he heard an organ and 'lo! the ancient cloister grew restored in all its early loveliness. The southern door did open and there came through with mournful paces a throng of holy white robed monks chaunting to glorious music.' They carried a coffin high aloft, and Ned interpreted it to Emily as a dream: a shrouded figure touched his shoulder and, behold, he saw the funeral of his bachelorhood.[36]

Emily's letters thumped through Ned's letter box once or twice a day, and he kept them close to his heart in a pocket, which he gently stroked when business bored him. But her letters became repetitive and dutiful. Ned found that his ideas came so fast as he wrote to her that without a slippy stylo pen he could not keep pace, but Emily had less and less to say.

Ned burned, he told her, 'with great romping flames'. Not so Emily. True, she longed to wake next to him and, of course, women were not supposed to burn. But she was occupied with someone else – Judith Blunt. Before Ned, Judith had been the most important person in Emily's life, and Judith wanted to stay that way. She tried to join the marriage.

When Judith met Ned's parents, Charles thought her so strange that she must have been bought in an Eastern market, while Mary loved her out of sheer pity because she was a Catholic – a burning brand to be rescued. Judith wrote to Ned without telling Emily and he wrote back ('Naughty boy to write to Judith!!' said Emily). Judith dreamed about Ned (and repeated the dream to Emily).[37] But Ned's jokes never quite succeeded with Judith, there were misunderstandings and awkwardnesses. Instead of growing close to Ned, Judith pursued Emily's brother Victor. 'Falling in love' with Victor was another way of staying close to Emily.

In July Emily stayed at Milford while Barbara Webb was dying. Bob Webb and Barbara's brother Alfred Lyall sobbed uncontrollably as Barbara groaned with pain and doctors came and went. 'I have no panic of Death,' wrote Emily, 'I have seen Death and seen my Father dead, and I have no fear . . . when once you have seen Death in a beautiful way it takes away all that panic and leaves a sense of unutterable Peace.'

Barbara asked for Ned, and Emily begged him to come. 'In the sadness of the presence of death I have no knowledge,' he wrote. 'The sadness has a terror – indescribable – for it is not want of faith in God – and Goodness – only the mystery and that sweet Barbara should be drawing so near to the great dividing curtain fills me with terror.'[38] In spite of his love for her and in spite of all that she had done for him, he refused to come. Always frightened by pain, he couldn't bring himself to say goodbye.

Barbara was miserably disappointed. 'It is so sad,' she said, 'and yet they are all so happy, and it is all just as I wished it to be.'

Emily sat by Barbara's bed, watching her slip in and out of consciousness, a glorious look of peace on her face as all the horror and pain passed away and she murmured again and again, 'It is much nearer now, but it is all right.'

Barbara worried that Ned did not appreciate Emily's love. There was more than a hint of reproach in her dying message to him: 'she says everything in your life depends upon what you do now. She keeps saying, "He must be good to her, tell him to be good to her and to take such care of her."'[39]

Charles Lutyens, Ned's father, shortly after he decided to become an artist.

'Three Racehorses' by Charles Lutyens (60.5 ins x 95 ins). Charles's original painting of the 1869 Derby finish was bought by William Miller, who then commisioned him to add at least thirty portraits in the background. Mary Lutyens is above the head of the leading racehorse. Boehm, the sculptor, stands next to her.

Ned's mother Mary as a girl, shortly after she left her convent.

Mary Lutyens as Ned knew her.

Miss Jekyll looking formidable and wearing her 'go-to-meetings' feathered hat.

Emily Lytton in Paris, aged about seventeen.

(*Left*) 'The Vice Empress', 1876. *Spy* cartoon of Robert Lytton at the time of his appointment as Viceroy. The artist noticed that Robert walked with a stoop just like his father Bulwer Lytton and wore similar flared trousers.

(*Right*) Edward Hudson, the founder-owner of *Country Life*, at Lindisfarne. Hudson, who was Ned's most important patron, reminded Lytton Strachey of 'a fish gazing up adoringly through his own element'.

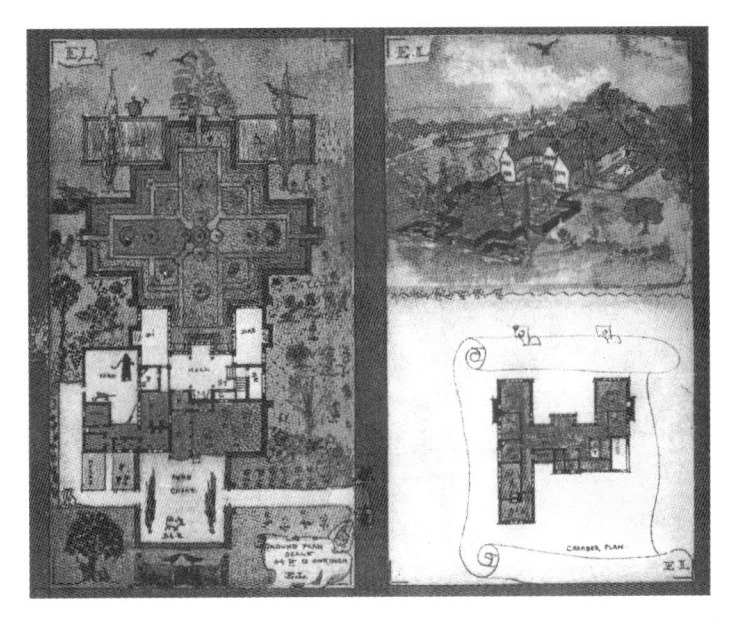

Design for the Little White House which Ned made for Emily and stored in the casket he gave her as an engagement present. He never built a little white house for Emily, but the design reappeared at Marsh Court.

Ned studiously avoiding the camera (about 1897). His dark curly hair is plastered down.

The classical terrace at Homewood, which Ned designed for his mother-in-law, Edith Lytton (left).

Drawing of Constance Lytton, Emily's suffragette sister, by their brother Neville, 1911.

TWO INTERIORS WHICH NED DESIGNED FOR HUDSON (*Above and facing page*)

The hall at Deanery Garden, photographed for *Country Life*. Ned's bare oak and whitewash was sparsely furnished with Hudson's corkscrew-legged Jacobean furniture and Persian carpets.

Ned's oldest child, Barbie, at Lindisfarne Castle. The pewter dishes and the curtains hung on metal rods are characteristic of Ned's spartan style. The cage belonged to a pet raven.

Nitya (left) and Krishna at Adyar, after the 'First Initiation' in 1910.

Mrs Besant arriving at Charing Cross station with Nitya and Krishna in 1911. George Arundale next to Krishna.

Chapter Seven
29 Bloomsbury Square
1897–1900

The honeymoon. Illustrated letter written by Ned to his mother-in-law, Lady Lytton, showing him and Emily sitting side by side on the beach at Scheveningen.

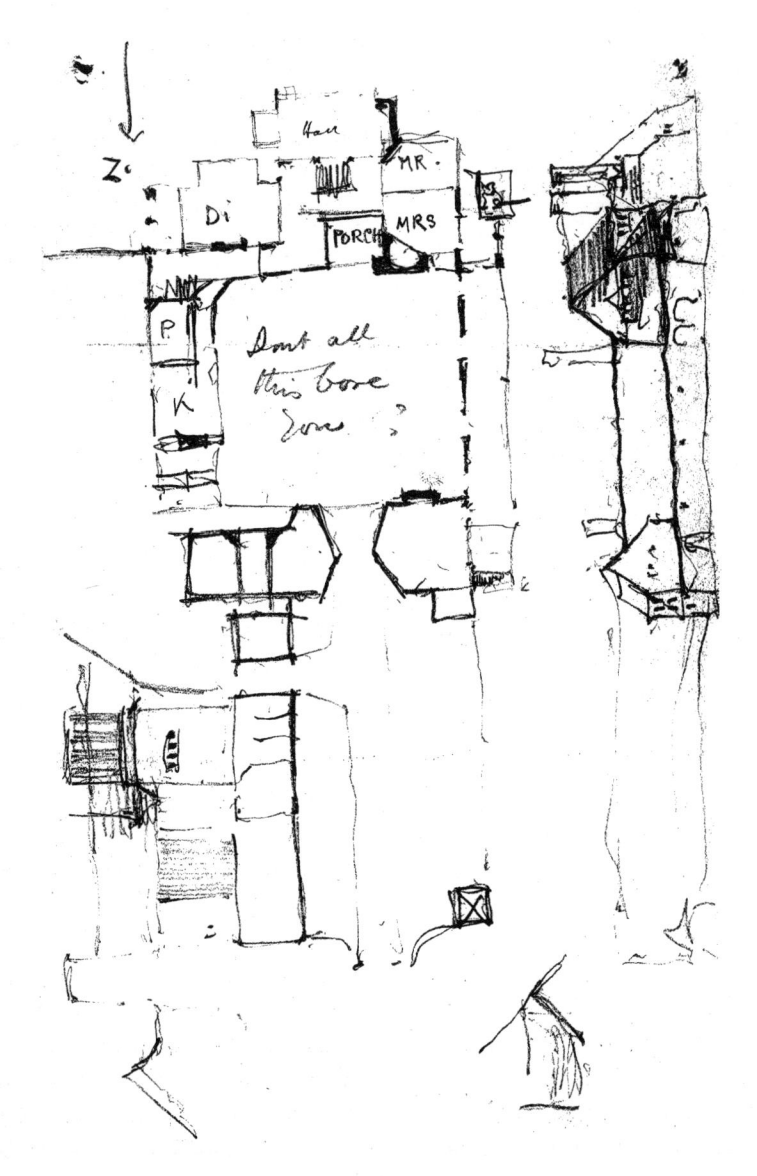

Sketch plan of Orchards for Emily: 'Don't all this bore you?'

Ned depicted the future with Emily in a letter he wrote to her two days before their marriage:

> The years shall roll away in volumes bound in happiness and tooled with golden sorrows ... and strangers shall see us as a quiet couple. She – beautiful with calm Madonna face so dear so gentle yet with a great lamp of truth flaming from her face. He – no trace of boy except when quite alone with his beloved wife when he can bubble lovingness into her soft and lenient ear. A quiet man, earnest and by high purpose taught, apt pupil of his darling Ems.[1]

It didn't turn out like that; Ned never lost his boyishness nor became earnest and quiet, and Emily's lamp of truth beamed with unforgiving candour on her husband's failings.

They were married at Knebworth on 4 August 1897. Emily was disappointed that His Rev couldn't marry them, but Blunt was there. Ned's clergyman brother Bill officiated, and his brother Frank was best man. Emily, who was given away by her brother Victor, wore white satin and a veil of Brussels lace. Knebworth house was still let, so lunch was held in a tent in the park, later used for the festivities surrounding Victor's coming of age.

Emily changed into a pale grey dress and red straw hat with black plumes, and they drove away for the first part of their honeymoon to Warren Lodge, the house which Bob Webb had lent them, where Ned had taken Emily on that fateful housebreaking expedition the summer before.

Emily was 'seedy', as she called having the curse, so consummation was delayed. Ned, she told her mother, was 'mother and nurse and maid, as well as husband to me, and such a darling'. Two weeks later they set sail for Holland. Ned believed (wrongly) that his family had originated there, but Rotterdam and its architecture did not impress. Fleeing the canals with their smells of bad fish and manure, they travelled to The Hague, which Emily liked better because it was more French than Dutch and very like Paris. Staying at the best hotel, they gorged on sole and sweet omelettes and Ned smoked 'cigars and cigarettes ad lib'. Most days they spent on the beach three miles away at Scheveningen, an expensive resort much favoured by the aristocracy, according to *Murray's Guide*. Here they sat in high basket chairs which looked like bisected beehives, and watched the grey foam-flecked sea and prancing bathers. Ned drew a picture of the beach with rows of beehive chairs, looking like 'a sort of prolific Stonehenge – mostly in couples!'[2]

It is tempting to see the scene on the beach as symbolizing their marriage. One can imagine them, as did Lutyens's first biographer, Hussey, sitting serenely, close together but back to back, looking in opposite directions, Ned, who hated the sea, craning at the land, while the sea-loving Emily gazed out at the waves. Real life was not so romantic. They sat side by side, staring out to sea and huddled into their basket chairs, sheltering from the high wind which blew from the land, numbed by a disappointment which neither of them dared mention. The honeymoon had been a disaster.

Emily never forgot it. Ned was a virgin and proud of it, but his lovemaking was inadequate and painful. In spite of Wilfrid Blunt's hot embraces, Emily knew little of what to expect, beyond the chilling advice from her mother never to refuse her husband and always to keep a pot of cold cream beside the bed. Her memory of Scheveningen was of dragging herself round the beach feeling so sore that she could barely walk.

Losing one's virginity is not always wonderful; the wonder is not that it was a fiasco, but that Emily cared so much, raking again and again over those first awful nights together. A note of desperation crept into her letters. She disliked hotels, complained about the smell and thought the art galleries boring; she longed for news and couldn't wait to get home. Ned escaped into fantasy, imagining himself a famous architect giving celebrity lectures. In search of distraction, they set out in pursuit of Emily's cousin, Lionel Earle, who was staying with some grand Dutch friends, even though he hadn't answered their letters. Being alone together was not a success. Emily was still rooted deeply in her family, and Ned fretted without his work.

They never took a holiday together again.

Back in London Emily was disappointed to find herself 'seedy' once more. There was to be no honeymoon baby. Betty Balfour lent them her house, 24 Addison Road, and Emily busied herself unpacking wedding presents – those fifty-one volumes of Balzac from Gerald Duckworth – while Ned returned to work.

They stayed at Addison Road until December. Emily wanted a baby, but she accused Ned of hurting her. 'I am so unhappy to think that my selfishness may have been causing you pain,' Ned wrote. 'Teach me to pray,' he begged, 'even as my mother used to teach me, teach me to have control.' The combination of sex, prayer and guilt unsettled him. Instead of dreaming of volumes bound with gold, he now had nightmares. He dreamed that he went to a smart party wearing the wrong clothes; then he was bitten by hyenas and Emily vanished in the crowd and he wondered whether he could ever get away when Norman Shaw came and rescued him, and they went on a tour of jobs together . . .[3]

It is no wonder Ned dreamed of Norman Shaw. The house he had chosen for them to live in was once Shaw's office: 29 Bloomsbury Square. Ned had found the house in July, a few weeks before his wedding and a few days after Barbara Webb died. 'Now darling if I were a Duke,' he wrote, 'I should love to take my Emy to live in 29 Bloomsbury Square.' Large, square and grim on the outside, inside it was a paradise, he thought. Above the offices were a drawing room and dining room and two floors of bedrooms. 'It is like a country house,' he wrote, 'like Milford House, but the architecture is good, so good, instead of being half and half.'[4] He longed for Barbara to be there so he could tell her – 'how her darling laugh would thrill me'.

The house belonged to the decorator Aldham Heaton, who had worked for Norman Shaw. He was an old man, he had had a stroke and one arm was bound up: 'He discourses on art and truth and beauty whilst his upper teeth insecurely fixed clap applause.' Lutyens told Heaton that he would furnish the house himself: 'I was afraid he would not approve of all our ideas – of bareness and whiteness – simplicity – how I had to furnish out of income.'[5]

One reason for 'bareness and whiteness' was that it was cheap. Bloomsbury Square was a recklessly ambitious and extravagant house to have chosen. The rent was £200 and this alone was more than Ned's overstretched finances could afford. He had unpaid debts and no capital reserves. Bloomsbury Square coupled with the insurance premium drove him to fight for work with the ruthlessness of a desperate man.

Panicking about money, he was anxious to move his office immediately; he got flu and fretted even more, and the week before Christmas hired an expensive coupé and they moved in. Ned immediately went to arrange the office downstairs. Emily went upstairs. There was not a stick of furniture, no carpets nor curtains and the unheated house was icy cold. Kind Mr Heaton, who lived round the corner, sent in a temporary bed and some matting for the bedroom floor. The smell of the matting made Emily feel sick. She was already pregnant.

Years later Emily returned to this incident; the bare house became part of her litany of grievances. This was not altogether reasonable. Ned after all was working frantically hard to pay for his large house and expensive wife. The strange part is that Emily apparently expected to walk into a house that had been completely furnished by Ned. Perhaps she really did believe that her social superiority entitled her to be cosseted and cherished like a Chinese woman with bound feet. Or perhaps she felt that the house was Ned's sphere; he had been so dogmatic about how it should look that she may have lost confidence in her own judgement. Ned hadn't the nerve to tell her that the house was not finished. He was too frightened to confess the full extent of his debts.

The first months of her marriage Emily spent resting – sex apparently necessitated hours of rest, and pregnancy was a permanently horizontal state. She visited her family and friends. Sometimes she sewed.

The white rooms were cheerless and empty, and bare painted boards made it very cold. They had few possessions, and there was little furniture, except the pieces Ned had designed. In the bedroom stood the great oak four-poster with its baroque posts in wrought iron: a case of suffering for art, as its beautifully sharp mouldings proved a source of considerable pain. Over the bedroom fireplace stood the casket. Electricity wires were laid, but never used. The house was spartan. Soon after their marriage Emily stopped eating meat; the French-sounding *rôtis* and *salmis* which the cook produced for Ned were actually cold shoulder of mutton and gravy soup.

Ned's real home was not upstairs but in his office downstairs, where the cornices, architraves and chimney pieces stood bare and unpainted and the rooms were lit by electricity. Beneath the glare of electroliers, Ned stood at his board in the front room, once the morning room. The old dining room next door was the drawing office. Here he had six clerks and a shorthand man named Dalton, who came cheap at 25 shillings a week with a first-class character from Colonel Spencer, for whom Ned had built Lascombe: Dalton had accompanied the colonel all through the Berber campaign in the Camel Corps. Lutyens rarely entered the drawing office himself. Too shy to talk to his clerks, he gave orders in the morning to the chief clerk and prowled the drawing office late at night, covering the drawings with little notes.[6]

When Emily told His Rev that Ned employed six clerks, he was astounded and thought she must often feel very anxious. He was reassured to hear that Ned had a partnership with 'a moneyed man': 'as then at any time if ready money failed you – you could use the partner!' The moneyed man was E. Baynes Badcock, who owned a share in the building firm of Badcock & Maxey. He acted as business manager on the understanding he could take work on his own account. It was a risky arrangement. At Fulbrook, Lutyens invited Badcock to quote and advised Mrs Streatfeild to accept Badcock's tender – 'Badcock and Maxey are good, sound and straight people!' – without apparently telling her that he was a partner. When Badcock exceeded his estimates to the tune of £1,838 (on a total of £9,391) Mrs Streatfeild complained. Lutyens found himself in the difficult position of 'blowing up' Badcock, pretending to check through the extras item by item and forgoing his own 5 per cent on the extras. Badcock & Maxey, he reported, have 'lost £1,100 on this job and are in rather an impossible temper to deal with'.[7]

At Bloomsbury Square, Badcock occupied a small room at the back of the ground floor, near the lavatories. Badcock, who was a Cambridge blue, liked to talk, and when he was in the office he expected to call on Emily. His bumptious habit of butting in irritated her. Sometimes guilty conscience told her he was in the office but she pretended not to know and didn't ask him for a meal.[8]

The presence of Badcock threatened to break down the invisible partition between the office downstairs and Emily's territory upstairs, which was so important to both Ned and Emily though neither realized it. When Emily was away Ned lived on easy terms with Badcock, who stayed with his attractive, artistic wife, despite Emily's neurotic anxieties about an infant Badcock being conceived in her marriage bed.

When Emily was at home Ned placed her on a pedestal; she became 'Her Eminence' as Bumps tartly remarked, and she lived in lonely splendour in the tall, bare rooms. Neither Ned nor Emily could exist in an easy, untidy muddle of work and family, and Ned's life after his marriage became strictly compartmentalized.

He was busier than ever. He worked on at least twenty-five houses in 1897–8. Envious colleagues carped at his 'good' marriage which, they thought, brought influence and work. But the female influence behind Lutyens's early work was not petticoats but hobnailed boots: for every one commission due to Emily ten can be traced to Bumps. Robert

Lorimer the Scottish architect admired the new-old style of Munstead Wood ('you feel people might have been making love, and living and dying here and dear little children running about for the last – I was going to say 1,000 years – anyway 600') and wrote of Lutyens:

> I've always heard him derided by the Schultz school as a 'society' architect. Miss J has pretty well run him and now he's doing a roaring trade and has just married a daughter of Lord Lytton, he's evidently right in with the right lot of people – Princess Louise – Lord Battersea etc. etc. . . .[9]

But the houses Lutyens designed for Princess Louise, Lord Battersea and Archibald Grove were different from the Surrey houses like Munstead. Experimental and boldly inventive, with more than a nod towards art nouveau, these are his 'dream houses' in which Lutyens seems to be moving away from Jekyll's cautious, scholarly, English Arts and Crafts style to the eccentric modernism associated with Mackintosh and the Glasgow school.[10] The dream houses were designed far away from Bumps's puritanical gaze,* commissioned by a clique of rich, arty friends who admired Rodin, Whistler and Degas. They wanted not country houses but villas, with asymmetrical windows, chunky shapes, steep sweeping roofs, strong horizontals and oriel lights hung like hinges on corners.

Lutyens himself was never really comfortable with art nouveau. Emily and her relations thought it was vulgar, foreign and decadent; perhaps even indecent. Later, Lutyens became ashamed of it and tried to write it out of the record. Like his embarrassing family, he managed to drop his art nouveau period gently into oblivion.†

In 1898 he gained a key commission which deflected his interest from art nouveau. Like so many jobs, he owed it to Bumps. Colonel Herbert

---

*Nevertheless, Lutyens owed his introduction to this group to Bumps, who knew Princess Louise.
†Lutyens's early biographers censored the dream houses. Lawrence Weaver, who compiled *Houses and Gardens by E. L. Lutyens* in 1913, suppressed most of the houses in this group. He belonged to the school of critics, published and promoted by *Country Life*, who interpreted Lutyens's career as a linear progression from Surrey Arts and Crafts vernacular to grand formal classicism. This view was to some extent encouraged by Lutyens himself, who helped Weaver with his book. Christopher Hussey, who wrote the official biography of Lutyens in 1950, also chose to ignore the dream houses. Hussey's biography is part polemic against modernism, and it was not convenient to his purpose to admit that Lutyens, whom he portrayed as the last of the humanists, had flirted with art nouveau in his youth. The dream houses were anathema to the neo-Georgians who admired Lutyens in the 1950s. Lutyens's art nouveau work was rediscovered by Roderick Gradidge, who in 1980 published *Dream Houses*, an important piece of architectural revisionism. The result is not shock horror; on the contrary, Lutyens emerges as a more complex and interesting artist.

Jekyll, Bumps's brother, was Commissioner for the British Section of the International Exhibition to be held in Paris in 1900, and he invited Ned to design the British Pavilion. 'It is a house in which the Prince of Wales will entertain whilst in Paris!!!' Ned wrote excitedly. 'An Elizabethan house!!'[11] No matter that it was to stand for six months only and that it was to be a replica which gave 'no scope for originality in design': it brought him closer to great work, to the world of government and politics.

Country-house Englishness, Ned learned, made the governing class feel safe. Encouraged by Emily's cousin Lionel Earle, a civil servant at the Office of Works who was Secretary to the Committee, Lutyens designed a Jacobean house using Kingston House, Bradford-upon-Avon, as a template. He checked Knole and measured Blickling. 'O to do, to have the chance of doing, big work,' he had written a year before, thinking of Blickling and great houses which 'bear on their dear faces the stamp of quiet repose. Impossible now with all the rush of competition, steam and chiming clocks.'[12] The Pavilion was an education: it taught him that it was possible to replicate those 'dear faces', to reinvent that sense of quiet repose by designing in the style of the seventeenth century.

Ned crossed to Paris in May 1898 on Pavilion business. He stayed with Emily's brother Neville who was an art student. Ned thought the architecture of Paris was '*rot*', but he had a good meeting with a new client, Guillaume Mallet, who wanted to build in Normandy – 'getting there about 11.30 and did not get away until 5.30! or so'. Ned owed the job to Emily's Aunt T. Her great friend, to whom she dedicated *Pot-Pourri*, was an Alsatian woman, Marie Grunelius, an enthusiast of vegetarianism and the rhythm method of birth control, who converted Aunt T to vegetarianism: Aunt T then converted Emily. The Gruneliuses were a family of Protestant bankers, and Marie Grunelius's cousin Marie-Adelaide had married the Protestant banker Guillaume Mallet, an Anglophile with a love of gardening and beautiful things. He had bought a large, plain *bourgeois* house at Varengeville near Dieppe, where he wanted to create a garden of camellias, rhododendrons, anemones and hydrangeas reaching down to the sea.[13]

This house Lutyens transformed into Le Bois des Moutiers, a fairy tale in washed pink, perhaps the most magical of the dream houses, with its art nouveau lantern windows wrapped round corners, its asymmetrical porch, oddly grouped windows and extraordinary Mannerist elevation. It could hardly have been more different from the formal house of 1620 which he designed for the Exhibition. Perhaps Lutyens felt he could relax in Normandy after the stiff formality of Paris, but Le Bois des Moutiers also drew energy from *fin de siècle* Paris.

Lutyens was often in Paris that summer, and the eroticism of Parisian decadence both attracted and repelled him. He dined on frogs' legs in the Quartier Latin and went to the Moulin Rouge. Asked what he thought, he could only say, 'Well yes, but I cannot help trying to realize my mother's face were she here.' The walls and ceiling were decorated with 'indecencies', and he saw a cabaret 'by a lady who vocalized with organs not intended for the purpose, and I marvelled at the Mercy of God'.[14]

Emily missed him. 'How I would like to have my arms round your neck and my cheek next to yours,' she wrote. When she had been away, Ned had written her jokey letters from his lonely dinner table at Bloomsbury Square. 'Fish!! Whiting with their tails in their mouths – naughty! Household wants Wmywyfish . . . Roti – cold shoulder! And oh it is a cold shoulder not to be jostling against my wife!' Something of the excitement and sexual energy of that first year of their marriage was transposed into his work at Le Bois des Moutiers. 'Such a day of it yesterday,' he wrote from Varengeville in August 1898. 'Seven French builders, the different trades . . . Whenever excitement reached its highest we all went on our knees and drew pictures on the floor . . . Oh Emy it is so lovely here, so quiet and delicious, gloriously fine, yet quite cool and pleasant and the smells are all so good.'[15]

'Great crises going on here – cabs upon cabs all day,' Ned wrote to Mrs Streatfeild on 7 August 1898. 'I think you are right to cut out the East wall and summer house and so save money.' He was pretending to work downstairs in his office. Upstairs, Emily was in labour. Emily had wanted Ned to be beside her when she suffered, but when the pains came on, her mother took over. A daughter was born at 4.15 the following morning. 'I enclose receipt,' wrote Ned to Mrs Streatfeild, 'not for the daughter but for your cheque!'[16]

The birth of Barbara – she was named after Barbara Webb – completed the circle of Emily's happiness. She drifted into a sensuous world of milk and sleep, nursing the baby, resting, lying next to Ned. A nanny named Sleath was engaged, and the baby was trained to feed and sleep with enviable regularity, delivered each morning to her room punctually at 5 and again at 7.30.

But Emily was restless. When Barbara was only a few weeks old she was already on the move, to her mother at The Danes, to His Rev at Booton. She complained to Ned that his lovemaking made her 'somewhat sore'. But Ned couldn't help himself.

> I feel so brutal, yet I knew at the time I would be no better and just as begging and impassioned of my most precious beastie ... So all that I can do is to give myself entirely to you, at your feet and at your service humbly and you must hold me and chide me and guide me and teach me to obey your wishes for love I am yours even as you wish and I am yours so willingly, and it makes me so happy, after, to think I can not do something I want, for your sweet sake.[17]

His syntax is ominously complex and involved. Sex was already becoming an issue fraught with tension.

Emily and Ned stayed with Edith Lytton, where they met Wilfrid Blunt, who thought Ned 'a rather inferior little young man, good natured and anxious to oblige, and naively uxorious, even to the extent of hugging his mother-in-law and singing to the baby'.[18]

Accompanied by two-month-old Barbie and Nannie Sleath, Emily visited Archibald and Mrs Grove at Berrydown, the wildly eccentric dream house that Ned had built for them in Hampshire. On the garden front, zany M-shaped tile-hung gables swept down to the first-floor windows; the central M was flanked by a chaos of steep roofs like orange quarters, bold truncated blocks and slabs of chimney. Its eccentricity matched its owners. Mrs Grove, who had had an unhappy first marriage, was large and bosomy, a free spirit and a friend of J. M. Barrie. She burned foul-smelling carbolic all over the house and ran outside in the evening wearing thin shoes and a tea-gown without stays which, thought Emily, made her look funny.

The Groves loved their house; they could talk of nothing else, reported Emily, but Nedi and his genius. When Ned came and drew chalk murals of Barbara in the hall, they thought them quite divine, though he was ashamed of them. 'I feel I am looked upon as a rare bit of furniture – another proof of your good taste!' wrote Emily. This was high praise, as the ex-Liberal MP Archie Grove was a financier and property speculator who specialized in spotting architectural talent. He had commissioned the young Voysey to build art nouveau houses in Hans Place, and after quarrelling with Voyscy, he hired another trendy Arts and Crafts architect, A. Mackmurdo.[19] Pleasing a client who knew as much as Grove did about modern architecture was a real achievement.

Soon after Barbara's birth, Judith became engaged to Emily's brother Neville. But Judith was in love with Victor; or perhaps she was really in love with Emily and married Neville, who worshipped her, in revenge when she realized that Victor would never care for her. It was not an auspicious match. Judith was twenty-seven to Neville's nineteen. Ned thought she was heartless, selfish and cruel; a spoiled only child who had 'every indulgence and no battle to fight with school, parents, brothers and the world'. But Judith's apparent heartlessness, her lack of a sixth sense of kindness as Ned called it, masked an instability that was already worrying. A nurse who had been treating her remarked darkly that she was worse 'at certain times' than any case she knew.[20]

Emily and Ned envied Judith's money: she and Neville received £1,400 a year from Blunt, out of his wife's fortune. But Neville, who thought he was marrying a solid, maternal figure, was ill-equipped to cope with Judith's difficult moods. His self-portraits show a curly-haired Greek god. 'Very flattering,' said Emily; but Neville's narcissism was perhaps his undoing.[21] Cursed by the fatal Lytton discontent, he became snobbish and waspish, carping at Ned, whose apparent easy success he envied.

'Money matters seem all right,' wrote Ned, 'but now it is my work. It ain't good enough and I don't work hard enough and think enough – o dear!' Commissions flooded in as Lutyens rode the wave of the country-house building boom. The partnership with Bumps was still very much alive, partly perhaps because she made a point of getting on with Emily, in spite of the condescending remarks Aunt T had written about her in *Pot-Pourri*: 'She has gone through the stage, so common to all ambitious and enthusiastic amateurs, of trying to grow everything, and of often wasting much precious room in growing inferior plants.'

'Oh what a darling baby,' exclaimed Bumps when Emily showed her Barbara, who smiled at her thick spectacles and gazed happily at the cats produced by Bumps, to the horror of the cat-fearing Nannie Sleath.[22] Emily had expected Bumps to dislike the baby, but Bumps was determined to retain Emily's friendship, if only because it allowed her to continue her collaboration with Ned.

Bumps collaborated with Ned on Goddards, near Abinger, a rest home for ladies of small means. The client was Frederick Mirrielees, whose wife was a shipping heiress, due to inherit a million and so, thought Ned, 'worth business while to "cultivate". This sounds beastly and is, specially as they are really wondrous kind and easy to get on with.' From the village street Goddards was unspectacular enough: two roughcast gables and an off-centre door hiding behind a high yew hedge – Bumps was always obsessed with privacy. The house turned a gruff front to the outside world and looked inward to the sunlit garden. The garden front was U-shaped: two splayed wings pivoted from the central block which contained the ladies' common room. Bumps's contribution was instantly visible. If Goddards had a subtext, it was the book Bumps was working on, a scholarly study of the vernacular of *Old West Surrey*. The roof had plain tiles above and rough Horsham stone slabs below in traditional Surrey fashion, and the garden well was filled with water collected from the roof. Pure *Old West Surrey* were the details: larder ventilators, oak pegs supporting timber work in the hall and the curious iron contraptions and hooks which decorated the building. But Goddards is not mere archaeology. On the contrary, the tension between Bumps's *Old West Surrey* and the subtle angles and repeated curves of Ned's splayed geometrical plan gives the house a peculiar ambiguous charm.[23]*

Munstead Wood or Plazzoh continued to work its magic, bringing with Miss Jekyll's encouragement a steady stream of new commissions for Lutyens. Some of these came from Emily's friends. 'DD' Lyttelton, wife of the sportsman politician Alfred Lyttelton and a friend of Betty Balfour's, wanted to build a house on the golf course near North Berwick. This was poaching on Eustace Balfour's territory (it was close to Arthur Balfour's house at Whittingehame), but (Emily told Ned) nothing would induce DD to employ Eustace. 'Alfred has seen your work in Surrey and greatly admires it and raves of Bumps's house'; though DD insisted that she wanted big windows, as 'she thought your little windows did not give enough light'. You must be businesslike and stick to your estimates, warned Emily: mind your Ps and Qs, don't sit in DD's pocket or smoke your pipe in her face: 'Their approval might be a very good thing for you and their blame do you a great deal of harm, and your reputation is rather that of being extravagant and not exact about money.' In spite of his reputation for extravagance, Lutyens got the job, and duly built Grey Walls (1901) for the LyttELTONs. Another crucial convert was Edward Hudson, owner of the new magazine *Country Life*, who thought 'Plazzoh the most perfect house he had ever seen'.[24]

*Lutyens enlarged Goddards and converted it into a house for Mirrielees's son in 1910. The 1898 house had no bathrooms, as it was only used in summer.

In August 1899 Emily stayed in Cromer with the Locker-Lampsons, and Lutyens sent her feverish instructions to promote his work. Lord Battersea was as much of an embarrassment as ever. He commissioned a nonconformist chapel at Overstrand, which Ned was ashamed of. 'It is no use looking at the Overstrand chapel,' he told Emily. 'It cost 2½d and is not Dutch or anything at all just a brick wall and a skylight, and a door and a stove. The inside spoilt, as its main salvation was simplicity, by a d—d moulding and horrid furniture and e-light fittings.'* Emily went to a bazaar at The Pleasaunce. Lord Battersea welcomed his guests with open arms, and read the first verse of a hymn, which everyone proceeded to sing out of tune. 'Dear Lady Battersea did not know the price of anything – and had not the heart to ask more than sixpence for her rubbish.' Ned cringed with embarrassment when Emily told him she had met his friend the sculptor John Tweed, whom she showed round the house. 'I am not at all proud of the Pleasaunce,' he wrote.[25]

He was far prouder of another house near Cromer: Overstrand Hall, which he built for Lord Hillingdon, a partner in Glyn Mills bank. Ned estimated Hillingdon's income at £80,000 and found him a 'very satisfactory person to deal with. Never fusses and knows what he wants.' He visited the Hillingdons at Overstrand in September 1899 and found his client clever and amusing with a keen insight into matters of art and men, 'practical, economical and not unduly mean'. Lady Hillingdon puzzled him, as she seemed so inane and vague: 'I wonder if she has any influence and if so what?'[26] Overstrand Hall created a stir and brought talk of a commission from Hillingdon's neighbour, the solicitor Sir George Lewis.

Grasping work was all that counted. Ned had distanced himself more than ever from his own family. Old Charles thought of little but his Venetian Secret; 'it is all such pathetic delusion,' wrote Emily, 'and nothing can come of it but more disappointment and worry.' Emily stayed at Thursley; but Ned always excused himself on grounds of work, which caused terrible disappointment and hurt. 'Mother' wore a huge hat and babbled about 'Dreyfoo', adamant that all partisans of Dreyfus were really Protestants. 'They are ... so *bigoted*!! how it bores people,' wrote Ned. Emily implored him to visit: 'Don't tease Mother

---

* According to Gavin Stamp, however, Overstrand Chapel is 'a fascinating and eccentric little building, with the clerestory supported on cross beams which appear on the exterior'.

and her Billy,' she wrote. 'You are out of it now, and can afford to smile with love.' Lady Emily, the peer's daughter, was far less snobbish and neurotic about the Lutyens family than Ned, who disowned them. He hated the suffering of his mother and the recurrent money crises, but worried obsessively that the pigginess and poverty of Thursley would reflect on him and lose him work. When Emily stayed there he instructed her: 'I should strike at going about and seeing 1st people who won't build, 2nd people who bore you, 3rd people you don't want to know. How badly they always manage things in muddled Thursley.'[27]

At the other end of the scale, Ned and Emily stayed together in a grand house party with Gay Windsor, daughter of Walburga Paget, at Hewell Grange, the new country house built by the architect Thomas Garner for the Earl of Plymouth. Emily, who was a veteran of country-house parties, hated it, as she always did. She escaped to her room whenever she could, worried about getting in the way, came down to breakfast at the wrong time and felt self-conscious about her clothes, which were old-fashioned, dowdy and inappropriate. Ned was no help. She complained that he 'is very shy himself, and furious because I am. Doesn't think it a bit funny or terrible – only indignant because I don't shine – yet if I did he would be very uncomfortable and feel left out.'[28] Ned wanted more work, and he wanted Emily's grand connections to provide it, though he was still ill at ease in this new world. This particular weekend's torture brought only one small and very distant commission.

In spite of the pressure, or perhaps because of it, Lutyens was working better than ever. That winter he designed a house in Surrey which some critics claim is his best building: Tigbourne Court. The client was Sir Edgar Horne, chairman of the Prudential Insurance Company and MP for Guildford; a dear old man, Emily thought. To old Mrs Horne, Ned was unblushingly manipulative: 'I made *desperate* love, quite desperate,' he wrote.[29]

Tigbourne's entrance front is outrageously pretty – a gem-like evocation of a seventeenth-century manor house. Unlike many Lutyens houses, the front is friendly and inviting. But the expectation this sets up is immediately frustrated. Instead of forming the prelude to a grand axial entrance, the vestibule opens playfully on to a blank wall, forcing visitors to turn sharp right to find the hall. The plan is circular. At its core is the staircase; to move through the house you are constantly deflected, and all the classical rooms are entered at corners. This is the architecture of paradox. Every time an expectation of climax is set up, it is immediately baffled and contradicted; architecture becomes a kind of teasing foreplay. Is this an architecture born of sexual longing and disappointment?*

Tigbourne was expensive to build. The Bargate stonework is galleted (the mortar joints are studded with black ironstone) and patterned with ribbons of herringbone tiles and tile voussoirs. Bob Webb thought it was 'very extravagant', but Lutyens knew it was good. Like Munstead it became a show house, and he used it to advertise his work. Gerald Balfour, for example, who was hesitating about throwing over his own brother Eustace and hiring his brother-in-law Ned instead, was finally persuaded by a visit to Tigbourne in February 1900. 'Gerald was very appreciative and nice and Betty ventured up a ladder,' wrote Lutyens, noting that Gerald found Munstead 'fascinating'.[30]

'Why are we for ever on the move?' wailed Ned. Preparations for the opening of the Exhibition took him often to Paris in the New Year of 1900. He had nightmares of suddenly losing his sight there, struck blind as he walked along the Paris streets, groping his way round and waking to black darkness in his hotel room.[31] Blindness had destroyed his father's career, and Lutyens constantly dreaded that it would destroy his too.

The Exhibition was a success. Chauvinists grumbled that the British Pavilion was too small and overshadowed by the huge pavilions of Belgium and Hungary, but the architect was lauded. Ned's attention to detail – his thoroughness at driving and chivvying; the frequent visits to attend to colouring the building and to picture hanging (it was hung with Reynoldses and Gainsboroughs) – paid off. He received a gold medal. He was photographed, which made him nervous – he told Emily that being photographed was like going to the dentist. He was interviewed by journalists, one of whom was so overcome by his bons mots that he begged to take them down: 'had they been published before at all – not all said I'. Ernest George, who later wrote a report, praised him as an able architect, but regretted the red-brick chimneys of the Pavilion – 'he's wrong!' wrote Ned.[32]

Ned's standing, Bumps told Emily, was 'wonderfully different' since their marriage three years before. He was admired by architects such as

---

*In 1963 Ian Nairn raved over Tigbourne, which he thought Lutyens's best building. 'For once he was really and unselfconsciously gay, witty instead of facetious. The crispness and panache is like nothing else he built. It could only have been done by a young man – Lutyens was thirty – and perhaps it could only have been done once in a lifetime.'

Baker and Schultz, who 'spoke of the wonderful position you had already acquired and said you had started a school of your own – and were turning men out of your office who did quite good work'.[33]*

At Cromer again in the summer of 1900, staying at Newhaven Court with the Locker-Lampsons, Emily tried to capitalize on his success. Lutyens wrote her frantic instructions, urging her to take the Liberal MP Henry Fowler (who was staying at Newhaven) to Lord Hillingdon's Overstrand Hall and impress him, as 'if this government goes out he may be useful! . . . Do all this in a very casual way, love – and have an answer ready for every criticism, and if you fail – say Lord Hillingdon asked for that!' Emily did her best, taking not Fowler but the Groves, who were talking of building again. 'The courtyard they greatly admired – as I do – and loved the dining room. All agreed that the windows were splendid and the house quite beautifully light.'[34]

Emily disliked her visit to Newhaven Court. The Locker-Lampsons were Quakers, and Jane Locker-Lampson was teetotal, very religious and apt to disapprove; she needed irreverence, thought Ned, 'as frogs do tadpoles'. Ned found her intensely irritating, and Emily, who thought she was 'next door to an idiot', was a critical and subversive guest. She formed an alliance with a Miss Clarke, who drank half a glass of champagne at dinner on her first night, thinking she had escaped Mrs Locker's vigilant eye; after that her wine glass was removed each evening. Emily disliked wine, but she was vegetarian, which annoyed Mrs Locker, who gave her nothing but potatoes to eat. 'I feel an element of hostility behind her kindness,' said Emily.[35]

Emily begged Ned to come to Cromer, reproaching him for avoiding her. 'You always wait till I have gone to come and look after jobs.' She stayed with his family in Surrey too, but there also he avoided her. 'You simply *must* come here,' she wrote. 'They would die of disappointment if you did not . . . Poor old people you have not been near them for so long and they are all counting on this visit.' Ned's brief, jerky letters, scribbled in trains or at the dinner table, brought little comfort. 'You of course can't leave Barbie, darling and Barbie can't summer in London and it would be bad for you too, and yet I must run about everywhere. I hate the summer.'

Too many musts and can'ts, too many unexamined imperatives fenced them in. Ned insisted that he *had* to work, as he anxiously totted

---

*When Emily ventured down for once to the office – or the 'mens', as she called it – and took tea with the clerks, she thought their work was 'rather a feeble imitation' of Ned's.

up 5 per cent commissions and balanced debts against income. He *must* do the little jobs if he was ever to get the big work he wanted, and in the end they would be rich with a country house of their own. But the truth was that work had become an end in itself. Late at night at Bloomsbury Square, or jolting across the country by train, he could escape into a closed, tidy, smoke-filled world of geometry and design. A day spent writing letters or doing business without drawing or designing was for him a day wasted.[36]

Chapter Eight
Country Life
1901–1905

Barbie.

Sketches by Paul Phipps, c. 1902

Above: 'Mr E. L. Lutyens exhorting his young men.' From left: Lutyens, S. H. Evans, Oswald Milne, Paul Phipps, Wallich, A. J. Thomas, I P (Infant Prodigy) Huddart, G. Alwyn. *Below*: Illustrated letter witten by Paul Phipps to Barbie: 'We are all getting very fat, as there is now so much cake for us to eat at tea because you and Robert have gone away.'

In April 1901 Ned Lutyens decorated his house at Bloomsbury Square. At a time when Charles Rennie Mackintosh was decorating his Glasgow flat in pale grey art shades studded with gem-like shapes, and Baillie Scott was impressing *The Studio* with designs for airy light-blue and white painted rooms, Ned chose a style that was bold and masculine. He wanted to make a stir. Away went 'bareness and whiteness'. The dining-room walls were painted red and the floor green; strong colours matched not with art nouveau but with simple seventeenth-century English oak furniture. Ned designed a massive oak refectory table which (said Hussey) was 'striking', especially to the knee of guests encountering its frame. The drawing-room walls were painted dull glossy black.* He repeatedly adjusted the furniture, breaking up space with screens and bookcases, punctuating the black with gilded frames and a red lacquer Dutch chest.

The only picture in the drawing room was a portrait by Burne-Jones of Edith Lytton, painted as a girl. Ned refused to hang any of his father's paintings – 'we can't hang a father picture, they are so funny'. The choice of the Burne-Jones portrait caused bitter hurt to old Charles, who sent his wife to see the room but refused to come himself. Emily's artist brother Neville, jealous of Ned's success, thought the room typified Ned's style. 'Ned's aims,' he said, 'are perfect, only in carrying them out I think he wants thoroughness and chasteness.' Rather than gild the frames in the Sienese style, rubbing gold leaf over red bole, Ned had had them gilded in the modern way over white. 'Of course he is not to blame for not knowing how the gilding should be done, but I think he ought to have known that the result of his idea as carried out by a modern gilder was not the right thing.'[1]

With the redecoration of Bloomsbury Square, the centre of Ned's practice moved from Surrey to London, and he used the house as a showroom as he had earlier used Munstead Wood or Tigbourne. Clients were invited to admire the black walls.

---

*Lutyens's use of bold colours – black, red and green – may have been influenced by Miss Cranston's Tearooms in Buchanan Street, Glasgow, designed by George Walton and decorated by Mackintosh. When he visited in 1898 he admired the decoration: 'Green, golds, blues, white rooms with black furniture, black rooms with white furniture.'

Meanwhile, downstairs in the gaunt office rooms, Lutyens and Badcock were barely on speaking terms. Badcock's habit of coming in at 11 and leaving at 4.30, arriving at odd times to half-do odd things, putting his head around the door and chattering endlessly, Ned found intensely irritating. The row came to a head in 1901 when Badcock was discovered to have gone fishing when he should have been on a job. Ned seized the chance to fire him. Emily was unforgiving. 'He has put himself entirely in the wrong – first by his shameful neglect of work – secondly by leaving you like this. You would be a *fool* if you had anything more to do with him . . . He is not nearly conscientious enough or hard working or businesslike in any way. He is a chattering conceited cad.'[2] A tombstone was made in the office:

>   In Memory of E B B
> For 3 Years Sleeping Partner at 29 B S
> Died of Talking and from Doing no Work

Ned listed his jobs: 'those with a cross he has given a belated assistance in, those not marked I have had to do everything'.[3]

Sonning [Deanery Garden for Edward Hudson]	I alone
Fisher's Hill [for Gerald Balfour]	×
Woolverstone [St Peter's Home for Lord Berners]	×
Rake [for Mrs Cavan Irving]	I alone
Tigbourne [for Edgar Horne]	× awful mess*
Varengeville [for Guillaume Mallet]	× late
Paris [British Pavilion]	I alone
Great College Street [for Alfred Lyttelton]	× mess
Lyttelton [Grey Walls]	I alone
Rossall [New Town, not built]	
Hillingdon [Overstrand]	
Mirrielees [Goddards]	
Watson	EBB mess
Abbotswood [for Mark Fenwick]	
Marsh Court [for Herbert Johnson]	
Hoare [Daneshill, Basing]	×

Badcock had become a liability, but the list of country-house jobs was now so long that Ned could safely afford to buy him out. One of Badcock's complaints was that Lutyens refused to introduce him

---

*'Mr Horne is very cross about Tigbourne,' Ned wrote in August 1901. 'He says he has had trouble with the house all round everywhere.'

(Lutyens grumbled that when he did introduce Badcock he behaved like a cad) but this meant that Badcock took no work with him when he left – 'he can't have much influence with the right people,' said Emily. The only client who remained loyal to Badcock was Princess Louise at Cowes (Mrs Badcock was her lady-in-waiting).

A few months later Dalton, the ex-Camel Corps office secretary, bolted with £400, with the result, Lutyens complained, that 'I have had an extra amount thrown on my shoulders'.[4]

In 1901 Ned was working on three country houses for Emily's relations and their friends: High Walls (now Grey Walls) for Alfred Lyttelton, Fishers Hill for Gerald Balfour and Homewood at Knebworth for Emily's mother. None of these was a conventional country house on an estate. High Walls was a holiday house for a politician addicted to the Edwardian craze for golf, planted almost on the first tee at Muirfield golf course in East Lothian. Fishers Hill was a suburban villa in Woking also within shot of a golf course. Homewood was a dower house.

DD Lyttelton wanted a holiday house where her husband Alfred Lyttelton could both entertain and exercise his passion for golf; a house suited to golfers in wet tweeds and nailed boots at tea-time who transformed into dinner-party guests in white ties at 8.30. The plot she bought on Muirfield golf course overlooked the flat wheat prairies of Scotland's east coast, cradle of golf and playground of Edwardian Britain's ruling group of Balfours and Asquiths. DD wanted fifteen bedrooms and very few other rooms, all for £4,000. This, said Ned, was too small a sum; and 'if you have a lot of bedrooms you must carry the house up high to get the rooms – which would be a pity'. At first the estimates came out at £6,400, but this was inflated by Badcock's incompetence, and Lutyens managed to revise it down to an acceptable £5,500.

DD Lyttelton wanted a house with large windows; she also wanted something solid that looked as if it could withstand a siege. To which Ned replied, with sketches illustrating the point, 'Mrs Lyttelton can't have large windows and a fortress too.'[5]

Mrs Lyttelton *did* get large windows and a fortress too. Ned's solution was to surround the house with high, curved grey screen walls recalling seventeenth-century fortifications by Vauban or perhaps the baroque fortifications at Berwick-upon-Tweed. He made a formal entrance off the road which created an expectation of a grand axial approach, then deflected visitors sharp left up a diagonal drive, and gave the house an extraordinary curving front sliced between screen walls. Visitors couldn't enter the garden without going through the house. The garden, divided into courts with grey stone walls capped with Dutch grey pantiles ('the Lytteltons *love* the grey tiles,' wrote Ned), was really a series of rooms, and the climax of the design was not the house but the astonishing view over the dunes to the North Sea. Ned succeeded brilliantly in funnelling people through the house, but DD Lyttelton found the constant stream of visitors overwhelming and the lack of privacy unbearable. Exhausted by her six weeks' holiday she sold the house in 1906.*

DD Lyttelton's baby son Anthony died suddenly of croup while Ned was working on the house. He wrote her a letter which gives a chilling glimpse of his architect's values. 'I see it,' he wrote, 'as when the spire at Chichester fell – falling without warning – with a crash and clouds of blinding dust – which when dispersed disclosed a blue sky over a great hole where the spire once stood.'[6] DD Lyttelton's reply to this absurd piece of consolation has not survived.

The house Ned built for his brother-in-law Gerald Balfour, also a golf-playing politician, was really two houses. Ned designed a long, low, rambling gabled brick house for servants and children, recalling Surrey houses such as Fulbrook; and this he loosely linked to something quite different: a chunky square brick tower, banded by two projecting bay windows reaching up three floors, a foretaste of later twentieth-century blocks of flats.

In spite of Aunt T, who could not resist interfering – 'she is very naughty,' complained Ned, 'and wants to put everyone into her own jerry-built Woodlands'† – Ned succeeded in pleasing the cool and frightening Gerald, who was 'in a fearful state of excitement' about it. Even Neville Lytton liked it, though he objected to Ned's signature of filling up the holes left by the scaffolding poles with little initials which Neville thought 'sweet and nice (in the bad sense)'. Strangely modern for a classically educated patron such as Gerald Balfour, Fishers Hill was ignored by later critics, who saw it as an aberration, but the house exactly suited its owners' needs. As Emily wrote: 'This is a delicious comfy warm light house – and they do love it so.'[7]

---

*Alfred Lyttelton remained loyal to Lutyens, whom he commissioned to remodel his new house, Wittersham in Kent (1907). DD Lyttelton made no mention of Lutyens in the *Memoir* she wrote of her husband in 1917, an omission which says something about the status of architects at the time. Today, Alfred Lyttelton is perhaps remembered more as a patron of Lutyens then as a politician.

†Woodland was Aunt T's house near Cobham in Surrey.

Betty Balfour was unworldly and helpless in practical matters. She shocked Ned by travelling in dirty third-class carriages with her children, none of whom 'looked as if any care, thought or trouble was taken with their appearance, either clothes or body'. For a family of intelligent, tomboyish and rather neglected girls, Fishers Hill was paradise; it had a high loggia projecting from the house, ideally suited to games and outdoor theatricals. Betty's grandchild Anne Balfour remembered it as a magical house, with the feel of Kipling and *Puck of Pook's Hill*.

Gerald Balfour dabbled in psychical research, conducting seances in the drawing room in a lifelong but futile attempt to prove the existence of the afterlife. The house became home to the Society for Psychical Research. Even today owners complain that the house has a creepy, haunted feel, so saturated was it in ectoplasm. There, too, Gerald Balfour could engage in the flirtations with adoring sisters-in-law which seem to have been an integral part of Balfour/Lytton family life. Frances Balfour was passionately in love with him and 'ready to go all lengths but he was not'. Emily's sister Con Lytton loved him too, which was perhaps why her relationship with John Ponsonby lingered on so inconclusively.[8]

Ned planned Homewood with Con. She wanted a square, boxy house which, Ned told her, would need 'such a deal of setting – outbuildings, walls, canals, avenues' as well as 'v thick walls and great spaces between windows'. A square boxy house was what she got: Ned imagined it as a dolls' house where the architect would suddenly remove the front and reveal at each end two women employed after their own hearts.

Ned gave the entrance front three barge-boarded gables with sweeping low tiled roofs. But the weatherboarded, cottagey shell enclosed a classical core. On the garden front he dramatically sliced away the timber gables to reveal a white-painted classical villa in the high Ionic order. Ned worked best when his houses were about an idea, and his idea at Homewood was about the villa's decay and nature's growth; about a classical villa swamped by the 'metaphorical overgrowth' of a vernacular farmhouse.*

Ned played jokes at Homewood too. He pierced the north-facing entrance front with an arched classical door, which has its tympanum

---

*Homewood is brilliantly paradoxical. As the architect Peter Inskip wrote in 1979: 'A large brightly lit staircase is discovered within the centre of a rather low, dark villa, a classical villa surprisingly within a cottage and a vernacular cottage within formal terraces.'

– the semicircular space between lintel and pediment – simply left open. This is architectural wit, playing games with the language of classicism. But Edith and Con Lytton suffered sorely on account of Ned's humour. The door opened on to a long interior tunnel – the Freudian significance of tunnels in Lutyens's work is undeniable, and the entrance tunnel at Homewood was like a vagina, opening on to a womb-like house: but in winter it acted as a wind tunnel, funnelling an icy blast into the house. Edith Lytton's room on the west corner with its two outside walls was known as Vladivostock. The chimneys smoked, and in winter the long pointed noses of the Lyttons glistened with permanent drips as they ate congealed food in the freezing dining room.

Homewood was a skewed cube in plan, and Ned gave it three different fronts. The result was chaos at roof level, as ridges running from triple gables and double gables intersected, causing chronic maintenance problems. The Lytton estate was, as ever, short of money, necessitating reductions to the plan. Ned protested that these 'were all face value affairs (except hot water) which Vic and I settled to reduce cost'. But the builders from the Knebworth estate had none of the skills of Ned's Surrey craftsmen, and corner-cutting to save costs meant that Homewood lost the texturing of the Surrey houses. Beneath their white paint, the bricks were standard size; the elm boarding was not properly seasoned and liable to buckle; the tiles on the roof were shoddily hung; the white-painted doors were second-hand, with beech panels tacked on to old pine frames.

In summer, though, the house was 'delicious', Emily thought – 'all except the drawing room which I consider a dull dark room always'. Nothing much grew in the garden, as the builders' rubble which had been dumped was never properly removed.

Con was unhappy there. John Ponsonby, her indecisive hare-lipped lover, nerved himself to end their nine-year quasi-engagement, and her health collapsed. She sat in the barren garden, even in summer miserably swathed in furs and shawls.[9]

Edward Hudson was the founder of *Country Life Illustrated*, a paper he started in 1897, for which Gertrude Jekyll wrote gardening pieces. Hudson was a bachelor. Tall and plain with a large head, bulging eyes and scrubby moustache, he reminded Lytton Strachey of a fish, gazing up adoringly through his own element; a 'kind of bourgeois gentilhomme' as well. He lived in London in a gloomy mansion north of the park with his invalid brother Henry, and two stiff, spinster sisters who looked like old-fashioned dolls waiting to be wound up. From his father he inherited a printing business and an unlikely passion for beautiful things. Uneducated like Lutyens – Hudson had started work in a solicitor's office at the age of fifteen – he was inarticulate and shy, jerky and intuitive. The idea for *Country Life* struck him, he said, while playing golf with the solicitor George Riddell at Walton Heath: an illustrated paper that would not only feed the townsman's appetite for country houses, so many of which Hudson had glimpsed on motor-car tours with his brother Henry, but also attract advertising revenue from the estate agents Knight, Frank & Rutley which would keep the magazine afloat.

After seeing Munstead Wood, Hudson determined to commission a Lutyens house of his own. Deanery Garden was an old orchard enclosed by a sixteenth-century brick wall in the Thames-side village of Sonning, near Reading. Here Ned designed a weekend house of old red brick, with a double-height timber-framed hall and a tall Elizabethan oriel window. 'Hudson came and took away the drawings – he says he can't say how much he likes it but is afraid of the cost,' wrote Ned.[10]

Ned linked the house to the garden by means of a geometry of mesmerizing sophistication. The house was placed against the north wall, and the old garden divided into a series of spaces. Each of the three fronts of the house related to a different terrace, which was really an extension of the house.* Perhaps he thought of Deanery Garden as a fortified site, treating the house as a metaphorical castle. The thread of water in the iris rill that ran the length of the lower garden symbolized a moat. As Peter Inskip wrote 'The water contained in the narrow channel is treated as something very precious to be stored in tanks and raised by elaborate hand pumps, almost in anticipation of a siege.' The planting was by Bumps. 'Bumps very appreciative and kind and admired Sonning,' wrote Ned.[11]

Deanery Garden convinced Hudson of Ned Lutyens's genius, and soon he was illustrating Lutyens's work in *Country Life*. The first Lutyens house to appear there was Crooksbury (September 1900),

---

*The terraces of the garden imply a 'hidden frame' which is essentially symmetrical, a Euclidean abstract superimposed upon the ancient vernacular of Berkshire brick wall and orchard, as Robert Williams wrote. 'But because this layout was deliberately superimposed on a walled enclosure unfitted to receive it, and which interferes with the margins of the layout, the visitor is inevitably disorientated, since by turns he is encouraged and then discouraged from believing that there is a unifying principle of organization. On the ground one senses formal balance, yet the key to it remains elusive.'

followed by Munstead Wood: before long they were regular features, appearing at the rate of two or three a year. 'I saw those *beautiful* Country Life photos of Orchards which will come out in C Life soon and Bumps is writing the description,' wrote Ned. He preferred to publish new work in *Country Life,* which was more widely seen than the building journals. Hudson's knowledge of photography impressed him.

Country Life's photographer was called Charles Latham. He worked from photographic notes made by Hudson, who drew plans on squared paper with arrows showing what he wanted to be photographed. Using glass plates and long exposures, Latham produced images of spotless aristocratic lawns, crisp roof angles and bold shadows. Often photographing houses from an eye level only two feet above the ground, he would accentuate their scale in the same way as Ned's worm's-eye drawings. Hudson checked the prints, correcting them as though they were watercolours. 'Tone down water a *little* and lighten cows a *little*,' he would tell the printer.[12]

Hudson collected antique furniture, and his ideas about interior decoration were very close to Ned's. *Country Life* photographs of Deanery Garden show the hall sparsely furnished with Jacobean corkscrew-leg chairs, gate-legged tables, pewter plates and runners of Persian carpet. It is an image as austere and ordered as the Dutch paintings Ned so admired. When *Country Life* photographed a house, Hudson would prowl the rooms noting the furniture, suggesting how it should be moved and what should be excluded from a picture. Victorian clutter was banished, creating the kind of bareness Ned understood.

Ned became curiously dependent on Hudson. Over the quarrel with Badcock, it was to Hudson that he turned. Encouraged by Emily ('Hudson is a dear angel,' she wrote, 'I am so glad he likes me – I love to be liked by *your* friends'), he told Hudson everything, even confessing his financial problems. ('You have so much work in hand, there is no loss of credit to say you are short of money temporarily,' urged Emily.) Hudson took him to his solicitor George Riddell, with whom the details of the separation between Lutyens and Badcock were arranged.* Lutyens paid Badcock compensation, but 'Hudson will back me up (I think) money-rarily'.[13]

Soon Hudson came to play the role once played by Bumps: agent,

---

*Riddell too became a client.

confidant, patron, financial adviser and above all partisan and publicist. Like Bumps, 'Huddy' was devoted to Lutyens and utterly convinced of his genius. For Lutyens he provided a lifeline, ensuring that he did not remain stranded, as so many architects did, during the 1900s, when the Arts and Crafts movement began to change direction and art nouveau lost its way.

Hudson tried to help Ned find a new class of work, urging him to prepare drawings for the Savoy Hotel and compete for the Queen Victoria Memorial outside Buckingham Palace. Neither of these attempts to move into bigger, London work came to anything. The Victoria Memorial competition was won by Aston Webb, an architect whose moustache grew so bushy that he needed to drink from a special cup and whom Ned thought 'absolutely futile – worse, vulgar!'

Ned was depressed by his failure. 'I do wish I could get on,' he told Emily. 'I have done nothing yet that would give me the slightest claim to be remembered as an architect of my time.'[14] Emily brushed aside his worries. 'You are still very young,' she purred, 'and have already made a great mark in your profession.'

He was busier than ever. In 1901 he was altering Abbotswood, near Stow-on-the-Wold, for Mark Fenwick, whose wife Molly Clayton was a member of the Northumbrian banking family who had commissioned Norman Shaw to build Chesters. Ned admired Chesters for its butterfly plan – 'an enormous house and the details left go lucky beyond a point. Yet the planning of it all is a masterpiece.'[15] For Walter Hoare, also banking money, he built a cottage in the brickfields at Old Basing, and then a fortress-like house at Daneshill, made from Hoare's own bricks. Walter Hoare took him fishing, and together they scoured seventeenth-century sites, to source the narrow (2½-inch) brick, which Hoare made in his brickworks at Old Basing. 'What a real good chap he is,' wrote Lutyens. He liked his pregnant wife – 'Mrs Hoare very energetic and unweary! I don't know how near she is but she must be imminent! from her size.'[16] At Ammerdown in Somerset he designed an Italian garden for Lord Hylton: 'rather troublesome and fussy, and I found him in a great state, but have left him alright, but I had to tell him not to be silly'.[17]

Marsh Court, an astonishingly confident exercise in Tudor style, came through *Country Life*. The client, Herbert Johnson, was the kind of exuberant outdoor man Ned instinctively warmed to: a forty-five-year-old self-made bachelor stockjobber who, having made half a million, wanted a country life. 'Tiger, tiger!' Ned wrote after a visit to Johnson in March 1901, fishing on the Test, most famous of trout rivers, and lunching late on beer, port and strong meats. 'Going to start Johnson drawings at once, and he wants me to furnish and do the whole thing, garden and all,' he told Emily. 'So that I shall do a complete scheme and fishing the while makes it very happy.'

'I do like Johnson,' wrote Ned in August. Fishing on the evening rise, dining at 10, and looking over plans till past midnight ('Johnson . . . seems awfully pleased with them') was followed by early morning gallops on the Downs astride a seventeen-hand hunter – the first time he had ridden since his marriage. 'Yes, I loved Marsh Court – how I envy the possession of it – in a nice way of course.'[18]

Something of this physical exuberance found its way into Ned's design. Perhaps a deeper emotion, too. The entrance front of the white chalk house with its red-brown tile roof comes as close as anything he built to the designs for the little white house, detailed in the engagement casket he gave Emily. But Ned's simple entrance, with its long, low horizontals, was no preparation for the drama of the garden front he designed at Marsh Court, where bold verticals and Elizabethan oriels plunged steeply to a dramatically sunken pool, contained within an elaborate composition of steps, terraces and balustrades.* Inside, the opulence was almost overwhelming, with heavy swags of plasterwork and a dining room constructed entirely of walnut, like a box of Havana cigars: as Christopher Hussey remarked, 'our stomachs, weaker than the Edwardians', may not be able to take such rich fare'.

Ned built the house of 'clunch' or hewn chalk, which he decorated with squares of flint, mischievously suggesting the ruin of an older building buried beneath. The chalk was quarried from nearby, then slung from ash poles and carried by horses to the site. Even the billiard table was built of solid chalk.†

Ned's output in 1901 is staggering. In spite of his dissatisfaction with country-house work, he poured out an amazing range of designs with astonishing speed, versatility and fluency. He complained that he had

---

*Goodhart-Rendel observed in an obituary of Lutyens in 1944: 'at Marsh Court is one of those complicated gardens full of architecture and water which photograph very well but do not perhaps add very greatly to the pleasure of life'.
†Clunch is rarely used as building material, and Marsh Court vividly illustrates the reasons why. It is easily stained and porous, absorbing water like a sponge. The lead hoppers act as bottlenecks, and in a downpour water is spilled back over the chalk, which rots.

made no mark on the architecture of his time, but many of these houses were to become classics of art history. Most were produced in collaboration with Bumps, who wrote the planting for the gardens. Her gardens softened and blurred the hard lines of Ned's geometry. Her drifts of flowers added a dimension of colour, as well as feminine curves which complemented the harsh, austere masculinity of Ned's garden architecture.

In spite of Bumps's painful eyesight and deteriorating health, their partnership was more than ever in demand. She told Betty Balfour that the difference between working with Lutyens and the Scottish architect Robert Lorimer was as between quicksilver and suet. When Ned stayed at Munstead, they played 'like little children, and her eyes got well and she got a headache from drinking beer and I helped her to wash Russian cucumbers, and she was good old Bumps, stern and revelling in every petty naughtiness'.[19]*

A Lutyens house and a Jekyll garden became an Edwardian status symbol. Perhaps it was also a metaphor for Edwardian marriage, a reworking of the old Victorian idea of separate spheres. Lutyens controlled the interior decoration of his houses, banishing the stuffy fussiness and chintzy clutter brought to the private sphere by the Victorian angel of the home. When Ned visited Mrs Willie James at West Dean he rearranged the hall: 'I managed with about three men to get rid of an enormous palm, two screens, a large white stuffed bear and an old sedan chair – and then there was enormously too much in the room.'[20]

Working with a team of men – the upholsterer Muntzer, the ironworker Starkie Gardner and the antique dealer Collie – he created austere masculine interiors with plain black or bare white walls, green or yellow painted floors and bleached seventeenth-century oak furniture. His houses were notorious for their lack of comfort. The fires smoked, the pokey casement windows made the rooms dark and the chairs were hard and uncomfortable.

The woman's sphere was not eliminated, but moved. It was redefined to be outside the house, in the garden. Ned's gardens were themselves a series of rooms and, as his houses became increasingly classical in form, the climax of his designs shifted subtly from the house to the

---

*Bumps had an earthy, lavatorial sense of humour. 'She left the room this morning,' wrote Ned from Munstead Wood in August 1901, 'for obvious reasons, and as she returned quite soon, I said – "ug! It was only a petite vitesse" – and she laughed and laughed!! wasn't it naughty . . . Just before lunch, I kissed her hand, and she said, "Well now I must wash," wasn't it rude! but she delighted in the saying of it.'

garden terrace. Here he was content to design the architecture, leaving the planting, the colours and texturing to Bumps.

There was no room for Emily in the Lutyens–Jekyll programme, but she was crucial to his productivity. Her role was just to *be* there, to be worshipped and adored, to be the reason for his work, the still centre of his frantic, driven life. For the time being she was content with that. She was achingly, obsessively in love with him.

Their second child, Robert, was born in April 1901. Emily spent the summer at a seaside lodging house in Devon: 2 Marine Villas, Paignton. Breastfeeding Robert with only Nannie and Barbie for company she worked herself into an agony of longing for Ned. 'The very thought of seeing you makes me throb and quiver with joy,' she wrote. 'I am quite sick with longing for you. I want you in *every* way.'[21]

Emily wanted 'to make love all day long', but Ned stayed for only one night. He never darkened the door of Marine Villas again, not even when Emily suffered a sharp attack of mastitis. Of course he was frantically busy. But somehow his work always came first, no matter how small the job.

At first Emily accepted the role Ned had written for her. Never had she loved him as she did now. 'I love you so so so much that sometimes I wonder if it is too much. You are just the whole meaning and centre of my life, its aim and object, its beginning, middle and end . . .' Success made him glow for her. She loved him, too, for what he wasn't: not a public-school authoritarian, not an imperialist like the proconsul Frederick Lugard ('how I should hate Robert to grow up with that code of morals and honour. It seems to me just bestial,' she wrote). Already a vegetarian, Emily had been taught by Con to think as a feminist. Barbie, she wrote, is 'not to be idle and ignorant as I am, living on her husband's charity'. Emily suggested to Ned that she should earn money herself, perhaps writing articles for *Country Life*. 'I feel on literary subjects that I know so much more than you do that I don't feel afraid of your opinion,' she wrote. When she proposed, half-seriously, to work part-time cataloguing old books, Ned was indignant. 'Certainly NOT are you to think of undertaking any job.'[22]

'I do so *hate* asking you for money every week,' wrote Emily. Unfulfilled but not really knowing why, she scolded. 'You are so extravagant over the champagne and never think it must be paid for. It is too silly for a man in your position to give champagne as you do.' Ned's pipe-smoking was also a constant cause of complaint, but perhaps the real trouble was that he was a clumsily inadequate lover. Almost childlike in his innocence and purity, his lovemaking was always over too quickly for her. Loving babies as he did, he thought that all Emily wanted was to have babies too: according to Mary, he always left Emily frustrated and dissatisfied.[23] Women to Ned were mother figures, pregnant perhaps or standing on pedestals chastely robed as in his engagement sketches of Emily.

On the last day of 1901, Ned stayed at Orchards with William and Julia Chance. Julia Chance's eighty-year-old father, blind Colonel Strachey, a Gurkha officer who had built barracks in India, explained that he had designed two buildings in his head, a cathedral and an opera house. Ned offered to draw out the cathedral, which was rectangular. They started after dinner, Ned drawing on squared paper to the colonel's dictation. They were still at it at 2 a.m. when the colonel's wife came down in her dressing gown to tell him to go to bed. Looking over Ned's shoulder she said, ' "Oh! But it's beautiful!" and the old man's blind face lit up as though all sorrow was of the past.'[24] Ned could sympathize with Colonel Strachey's blindness given his own anxiety about his sight.

Next day he was in Scotland, staying with Alfred Lyttelton at Gosford to supervise Grey Walls, which was nearly finished. Gosford, an Adam house belonging to Lord Wemyss, did not impress ('good in conception but oh so many technical mistakes').[25] Then Hudson wired to say he had bought Lindisfarne castle, and would Ned inspect the site.

Ned found an island off the Northumbrian coast reached by horse and cart across the sands at low tide. A ruined Tudor castle, once a strategic fort in the wars against the Scots, gripped a grim, craggy rock. Ned's task was to create a house within the castle shell. Avoiding the pedantic historicism of the Victorians, he fused Arts and Crafts detail – herringbone cobble paths and brick floors – with a kind of abstract medievalism: pillars that look but aren't Norman, gothic tracery contained within round arches. There was no need to imply fortification here; Lindisfarne *is* fortified. (To stress the castle's isolation Ned sited the garden, a small stone-walled enclosure, a field away from the house.) Ned's idea at Lindisfarne was about *moving*: moving through dark, constricted spaces on to light, airy platforms; moving up the winding stone ramp, through narrow, dark passages and stairs and cramped, cave-like rooms on to windswept ramparts and stone batteries, rather like decks on a ship.

Lytton Strachey, who stayed in 1918, described it as 'all timid Lutyens – very dark, with nowhere to sit, and nothing but stone under, over and round you, which produces a distressing effect'.[26] It was one of Ned's more uncomfortable houses. There was only one bathroom, and Emily complained about the cramped kitchen. Firewood to heat the cold stone rooms had to be carried on a man's back up the steep winding ramp; Ned designed a special log-carrying wooden backpack which looks like a medieval instrument of torture.*

Twenty-one-year-old Oswald Milne joined Lutyens's office as a draughtsman in 1902. He was paid only £2 a week. ('Didn't you hate me?' Lutyens asked him later.) Milne worked in the back room with three other draughtsmen and three pupils, each of whom paid a yearly fee of £100. The office manager was eighteen-year-old A. J. Thomas, a short, stocky red-headed Welshman who joined the same year. They were all very young and sang a lot; the atmosphere was light-hearted, the humour schoolboyish.† Nicholas (Beau) Hannen, who also joined in 1902, once lobbed a pat of butter at Evans, who ducked, so it hit Lutyens's door hard. Lutyens opened his door and looked out, but all he said was 'Steady'.

Milne remembered 'Lut' as a great worker. 'If not visiting a job, he stood working at his drawing-board in the front office – I do not remember him ever sitting down – legs apart and usually smoking a pipe. He spoke somewhat incoherently; he never explained himself; his wonderful fund of ideas and invention were expressed not in speech but at the end of his pencil.' Lutyens worked in the office all day until dinner time, and returned to his drawing board after dinner, with Emily sometimes sitting at his side. Often his assistants would work for weeks on end until 10 p.m.[27]

When Milne joined the office, Lutyens was working on Marsh Court and also on Little Thakeham for Ernest Blackburn. Like Orchards, Little Thakeham was poached from another architect; but this time the rival went public.

Ernest Blackburn was a schoolmaster with five children. He inherited

---

*Lindisfarne's record-breaking statistics as a National Trust property show that it has achieved its purpose as a historical dream machine, a series of dramatic architectural spaces which visitors experience as they circulate.

†Paul Phipps (father of Joyce Grenfell) who was also a pupil, remembered reciting nonsense in unison in the 'refained' accent of an unctious curate: 'Once when I was travelling in South Africa with a very dear friend of mine (he's dead now poor fellow and we all mourned his loss), I was called to the bedside of a poor dying child and, as she looked up into my sweet face, she said: "Oh Mr Clark – Mr Clark – I die happy, oh *so* happy."'

a fortune and decided to retire early and devote himself to gardening. He appointed an architect named Hatchard Smith, who began to build on a lovely Sussex plot. As the brick walls began to rise, Blackburn became increasingly dismayed, realizing that he had commissioned a 'blot on a beautiful landscape' – a red-brick villa fit only for Wimbledon or Putney.

Blackburn first tried to limit the damage by commissioning Lutyens to design interiors. When Hatchard Smith objected, Blackburn fired him. A week later, on 2 May 1902, Ned visited the site. On his return to London he handed Oswald Milne two sheets of squared paper with his design worked out completely in sketch form with all the plans, sections and elevations. He had designed the house entirely on the train.* Hatchard Smith complained, and Lutyens wrote him a letter in reply: 'it is not intended to alter any of your design but to replace it with a new house and move the site, using such of the well-built walls at one end that would work in'. Ned insisted that Blackburn pull down Hatchard Smith's walls, which already stood 10 feet high.

By August, Ned's house was rising – a house not of brick but of the local marble-like brownish-buff stone. Hatchard Smith paid a visit, preliminary to writing a long letter to the *Building News* (8 August 1902). 'This will form amusing reading,' wrote Ned; but when he learned that Hatchard Smith accused him of breach of professional etiquette, he was dismayed. 'I shall never get a church to build now!!!' The *Building News* carried a six-column editorial, condemning him for unprofessional conduct. Of course, said the *Building News*, an architect should give a second opinion if invited, but no architect should ever make the first approach to a client; and this, hinted the editor, was precisely what Lutyens had done. 'There was no intriguing,' Ned insisted. Emily was in a 'choking fury', and Blackburn so angry that he concocted a letter, protesting the client's right to choose his architect and exonerating Lutyens. 'The position of Mr E. L. Lutyens is too well assured for your words to do him much harm, or mine to do him much good'; but 'there was no professional intriguing ... all the advances were on my side'.[28]

Lutyens took the case to Belcher, Vice-President of the RIBA. Hatchard Smith refused to withdraw: he wrote to *Country Life*, and Hudson came to the rescue, telling Hatchard Smith that if his letter was

---

*This story may be apocryphal. Drawings surviving in the RIBA show that Lutyens did not reach the final design so easily. Milne's story does show, however, that by this date Lutyens was using squared paper as a matter of course.

published the editor would feel bound to take Lutyens's side. Perhaps Lutyens went too far in his efforts to vindicate himself; certainly his friend Schultz reported that architects rather sniffed at Ned for overreacting, as they thought Hatchard Smith 'an awful cad, and the editor of the B news was known to be one'. Lutyens was cleared by the RIBA of Hatchard Smith's charge of misconduct, but the affair left a nasty taste, adding to Lutyens's reputation as a predatory adventurer.

In spite of the row, or perhaps because of it, Ned achieved greatness at Little Thakeham; he himself thought it was 'the best of the bunch'. He organized the plan of the Elizabethan manor house around the hall, which forms the climax of the design.[29]* He gave the hall an eighteenth-century stone doorway, a completely unexpected fragment of baroque architecture within the Tudor shell. Here he brought exterior architecture into the inside, and the effect is extraordinary, disturbing and unforgettable.†

The night before the coronation of Edward VII (8 August 1902), Ned dined with William Nicholson the painter, having kept the office working until dinner time. After dinner, he took Nicholson to see George Dance's Newgate prison, shortly to be demolished, a building admired by Bumps. Newgate, with its 'stone upon stone – its grim severity and grace withal', was perfect, thought Ned, for Nicholson's woodblock-cutting methods. It may also have influenced Ned's own work in the hall at Little Thakeham, where he too placed stone upon stone with grim severity. Back at Bloomsbury Square, he worked until 2 a.m., finishing off the drawings of Monkton, near Goodwood, for a new client, Willie James, heir to an American railway fortune, and 'for a very rich man, sitting in Hoheit's [Royalty's] lap, delightful'.‡

---

*One way of achieving this effect was to give an above-average ratio of space to hall and corridors. At Little Thakeham, as at Deanery Garden, the hall, stairs and corridors account for over half the floor space (21:19), in contrast to the normal country-house ratio of roughly one-third (6:15).

†Ian Nairn, writing in the Sussex volume of *Pevsner* in 1965, described the hall as a 'Piranesian fragment, something left over from an abandoned Gonzaga Palace ... This is a complete understanding of classical design rather as Hawksmoor understood it, and something very different from applying styles.' He added the usual sting in the tail, anticipating Lutyens's mid-life crisis: 'Perhaps it was impossible to expect Lutyens to stay at this pitch of creative interpretation for long. What a brilliant young man he was, and how thoroughly and wilfully he burned himself out.'

‡Mrs James, who reminded Ned of a barmaid, was rumoured to be the King's mistress; in fact the closely guarded secret was that she was his daughter. Monkton was a summer house on the Downs near Goodwood, where the Jameses could escape from the oppressive grandeur of their house at West Dean, enlarged (badly, Ned thought) by Ernest George. Monkton was 'about the size of Homewood, but there will be additions of cloisters etc and a more generous layout to a gorgeous south view'.

Next morning Ned sallied forth in tailcoat to watch the coronation from Mrs Beaumont's house in Piccadilly. He was not impressed. The crowds were few and seemed dejected. The King and Queen arrived in 'a real fairy story gilt coach looking absurdly large and ginger bready swaying like a ship at sea'.

> I cannot help feeling the cheap mockery of the great spirits that moved the men of old to pageantry now but a husk that shelters little aught but sheer vulgarity. But it moved dissolute majesty – dissolving in age so near its dissolution. (Others said how well he looked.) His bow so lame and overpowered by a crown whose shape I could not read . . . So slowly rocked the gilded coach past out of view. The little knot of colonials on their dowdy bay ponies – in khaki 'mongst the Household Brigade Bands – choked me as much as anything. There was a feeling of simple reality about them that all else seemed to want.[30]

Lutyens was no imperialist, and his response was as much aesthetic as political, for theatre was on his mind. He was designing the stage sets for J. M. Barrie's *Quality Street*, which opened the following month. 'Simple reality' was the theme of his sets, which showed a plain domestic interior. Ned had met Barrie through the Groves back in 1897. They shared a sense of whimsy; and Emily liked Barrie because she enjoyed his books. She held theatrical tea parties for him (Ned didn't come) and believed she was the inspiration for Phoebe Throssal, the heroine of *Quality Street*. Ned drove round London in a coupé, buying furniture for the play. Afterwards he wrote Barrie a letter, which shows him still in stilted awe of the famous writer. 'My youth save the march (of time?) convinces me that the more real a scene is, the better it must be in effect and that scenic conventions are a fraud.'

In 1904 Lutyens designed the sets for *Peter Pan* (Nicholson designed the costumes). Mary Lutyens believed that Ned invented Nana, the dog-nurse in *Peter Pan*. 'It was through our night-nursery window at Bloomsbury Square that the Darling children flew to the Never Land.' Barrie's children's world held a strong appeal for Ned; like Barrie he found adult emotions hard to deal with, preferring to escape into fantasy and theatre.[31]*

*

---

*Writing in *Apollo* in 1992, Alan Powers suggested that *Peter Pan* is the text which best explains the mentality of James Pryde and the Edwardian generation of artists, who never made the conceptual breakthrough to modernism. (Pryde was William Nicholson's brother-in-law.) Preferring nostalgia and fantasy, they failed to achieve creative maturity. Lutyens was the exception. 'Is it justifiable,' asks Powers, 'to construct around Lutyens and Pryde a missing modernity of the Edwardian period?'

Emily spent the summers of 1902 and 1903 with Barbie and Robert in Felixstowe. In 1903 she brought servants, warning Ned that 'I am giving them all plenty to eat, but I expect it will cost rather a lot, with many cakes and tea and extra milk'. Ned's client, Mrs Berners, sent her yacht over to Felixstowe, and after lunching on hock and salmon they admired St Peter's Home, which Ned had built. 'The windows are the only fault,' reported Emily, 'being much too high.' Her mother Edith, she added, 'raved of you and your genius to Mrs Berners', which was tactful, as Ned worried that the socialite Mrs Berners disliked St Peter's. 'She is one of those people,' he wrote, 'who don't understand a blank wall – and sees in it no difference from a factory wall. Nor does she understand the absence of bay windows and porches etc, but that is her fault not mine.'[32]*

Ned shuddered at the very thought of the Felixstowe lodging house. 'Cold water how I hate it! . . . those second-rate ladies how they make me squirm.' Working in London, he was so frantically busy that there was no need even to make excuses. 'O Emy what more can I do – I have worked so late and so hard these last three days,' he wrote. The beautiful Lady Helen Vincent commissioned him to restore Esher Place and design a garden. Her thickly painted face made Ned uneasy. 'I don't believe any of these smart lovely society women are really happy or really well,' he wrote. 'She is sponge cake or lovely Easter egg with nothing inside, terribly dilettante and altogether superficial. I feel cross with her and long at times to contrive that an elephant should give her a baby!'[33]

Two days later he was near Taunton at Hestercombe with the Portmans, clients recommended by Hudson. They wanted a garden and an orangery for their house, a Victorian pile which Lutyens thought '*very* bad architecturally', though it was 'a typical self-satisfied comfortable English sporting-squire of a house and place'. Mr Portman (a vast eater and 'a real good sort (not mine a bit!)') was rich but reluctant to spend more than £1,000. Ned's tumbling architectural gardens needed £10,000, and the key was Mrs Portman, lady bountiful and, surrounded by refractory puppies, bazaar opener to the county. At first Ned was frostily received, until he discovered that Mrs Portman was 'one of the many very bored by Bill', his clergyman brother. 'Hudson told me,' said Ned. 'Very funny, isn't it.' Once that problem was removed, Ned got his way.

*Ned did not enjoy his visits to the wealthy Berners family at Woolverstone Park. He was made to feel that 'the younger lot of purse prouds look down on professional architects'.

For the Hestercombe garden Ned conceived a complex sequence of terraces and steps, of paths, platforms, water channels and pools which cascaded down from the Victorian balustraded terrace in front of the house via a rose garden to the lowest level, the Great Plat, a rectangle bisected by a diagonal cross bordered by a pergola. All this he supported by massive buttressed retaining walls of rubble which push against the great rectangle to stop it collapsing under its own weight.*

Ned had first hinted at the design of the Great Plat, with its diagonals laid within a rectangle, seven years before in the casket drawings of the garden for the Little White House. With Hestercombe's massive tumbling gardens and the giant chalk Marsh Court, the programme encapsulated in the miniature roll of plans he drew for Emily's casket was finally realized.[34]

The day after his visit to Hestercombe found him working on a church at Dorking ('sanctuary ... in chalk and tiles like Sonning with a domed ceiling or roof in chalk etc'). Designing the wood gilt altar, he wrote to Emily: 'I want to make love to you ... I just burn in your worship. I do so want to do great work, for your sweet sake ...' But the long-anticipated night he spent with her at Felixstowe was the usual disappointment. Half hoping for another baby, Emily began to think that her only chance of conceiving was through Christian Science, by '*thought* influence – and no other means. So don't be shocked if I tell you I am in for one!'[35] Ned was uncomfortable, depressed by the lodging house and critical of everything; Emily was sharp-tongued, cross and tearful.

On holiday with her feminist friend Mrs Webbe, known as Pussy, wife of the cricketer A. J. Webbe, Emily pondered modern marriage. Her own marriage was a 'true' one, based on love and total faithfulness; but the sexual double standard, which allowed men to make love not only to their wives on demand but also to other women, preoccupied her. Its consequence was 'the social evil' – the spread of syphilis, especially among wives and prostitutes, innocent victims of diseased male lust. Emily devoured books and pamphlets on venereal disease, throwing herself into the movement for 'moral education'. Ned

---

*Hestercombe is the culmination of Lutyens's partnership with Jekyll and probably the greatest flowering of their work together. It is possible to detect a hidden geometry behind the design, a series of perfect squares enclosing the square formed by linking the Great Plat with the old terrace. But Lutyens does not allow art to dominate nature; the formal garden merges easily into the landscape, proving that art *can* become one with nature.

had grave doubts: 'I did not like you to do it but would not stand in your way of doing work so full of mercy.'

Safely back in London, Ned was once more gloriously busy, telling Emily, 'I am I think working keenly and with some confidence and definitiveness . . . I do want to do really really really well. So well that you will be covered in wreaths and flowers as Nedi's wife and be justified in the pride your very dear love prompts you to.'[36]

Ned's quest for Emily's favour put him under constant pressure to succeed. It was as if he felt that her love for him was conditional on his success, as his mother's love for him perhaps had been. His mother now counted for nothing. She had been ill, but he could barely bring himself to spend ten minutes writing to her, let alone to visit her. All the attention and approval-seeking once directed at her and then at Barbara Webb was now focused on Emily. Barbara Webb's illness and death he now saw almost as 'an ordained sacrifice to seal our happiness'. But he seemed to know that his weakness, his timid nature and lack of moral courage, were destined ultimately to lose him Emily's love; for these were qualities that counted far more to her than artistic creativeness or success. In a moment of self-knowledge, Ned confessed his fears:

> It seems wrong that I should want you so awfully. I am not good enough or strong enough for you darling . . . I feel so depressed about myself and have a feeling that I shall some day lose your love. I deserve your great love so little. Oh Ems don't let this happen. You are so good love that I have no fear really – only I wish I had confidence that by my own merit I could keep and deserve your heart. I feel dependent on your loving kind heart.[37]

Ned's brother Arthur died suddenly in 1903 at the age of thirty-six. If Ned, too, had died at thirty-six, he would already have earned a small place in the art books. The German architect Herman Muthesius, who published a survey of *Das Englisch Haus* in 1904, hailed him as a young man 'who may soon become the accepted leader among English builders of houses, like Norman Shaw in the past'. By 1903 his income (after office expenses) was £2,572, rising to £2,884 in 1904, more than double what it had been when he married.[38]

Wary of his colleagues' rivalry, Ned had so few architect friends that Emily often scolded him for being jealous. Apart from Hudson, his closest male friend was Herbert Baker, his old colleague from Ernest George's office. Baker was now safely out of competition, working as architect first to Cecil Rhodes and then to Milner in South Africa. Though seven years older than Ned, he was oddly deferential towards him. He sent photographs of his South African work, which Ned criticized mercilessly. One Sunday morning in 1903 with Barbie and Robert playing round his feet – he never saw his children, except on Sundays – Ned wrote Baker a letter. 'In architecture,' he declared, 'Palladio is the game!'

> It is so big – few appreciate it now, and it requires training to value and realize it. The way Wren handled it was marvellous. [Norman] Shaw has the gift. To the average man it is dry bones, but under the hand of a Wren it glows and stiff materials become as plastic clay . . . It is a game that never deceives, dodges never disguise. It means hard thought all through – if it is laboured it fails. There is no fluke that helps it – the very what one might call machinery of it makes it impossible except in the hands of a Jones or a Wren. So it is a big game, a high game . . .[39]

The letter reads like a manifesto for classicism, but there was little sign of Palladio and the high game in his work in 1904. At Nashdom, Taplow, he designed a riviera villa for weekend entertaining for Princess Dolgorouki. The Scottish heiress wife of a Russian émigré, she was born plain Miss Wilson. ('She is no one,' said Mrs Willie James dismissively, 'vulgar, but kind and very fond of entertaining . . . Style her HH and she will take any amount of it.') Princess Dolgorouki demanded a red-carpeted staircase with a red plush handrail, grand rooms opening off each other en suite and a fountain on the dining-room table, and she was willing to spend no more than £6,000. Anything further removed from Lutyens's bareness and whiteness or his subtle circulating plans would be hard to imagine.

Asked by Ned why she came to him, she replied that 'she came against everyone's advice, as they told her that I build houses of my own type – a type not at all suited to her. But she said she couldn't get a clever man without a type of his own and she would rather deal with and get what she wanted from a clever man than from an ordinary man who did what she wanted and let her in for mistakes.' At first he despaired, but soon he was kissing her hand and teasing her for surrounding herself with 'unmannish men' or 'its' as he called homosexuals; and she agreed to spend £15,000 and put the staircase between walls with no handrail at all. 'I can scarce credit it,' he wrote, 'but we have actually arrived at a scheme in which we *both* have pleasure!'[40]

Nashdom was one of Ned's most contradictory, paradoxical designs. He gave Princess Dolgorouki a house where nothing is quite as it seems, repeatedly undercutting and deflating her opulent ideas with his subversive architectural wit. He set up grand ideas by axial planning only to contradict them by putting a main entrance to one side or designing a peripheral route. His grandiose five-storey entrance front concealed a steeply sloping site, and the house was smaller than it looked, with only three storeys on the garden front. The Princess had pretentious French furniture which Ned mocked with his austere detailing; he questioned her wide Italian stair by designing a low ceiling height at its head.

Ned could not be so high-handed with the millionaire Ivor Guest, who commissioned him to restore and add to Ashby St Ledgers; 'a dear old fifteenth century house added largely to but in such a way as not to hurt it'. The Paying Guest, as Ivor Guest was known, was a plutocrat with a William Morris sensibility.* Ashby St Ledgers turned out to be a lifetime's work: a matter of a rich man adding cumulatively to an old house. With Guest, Ned played his 'town game', imagining a town out of *News from Nowhere* with canals, white horses on the tow path, wooden docks and trades such as tapestry, wrought iron, barge building, boot-making and weaving. Ned's approach to restoration, equally, was reliant on imagination rather than detailed research. Ashby St Ledgers was the old home of the Catesby family, who were implicated in the Gunpowder Plot, and Ned convinced himself that he saw ghostly footprints of immense length in the thick dust leading to a haunted room.[41] Stories of haunted country houses ran deep in the Edwardian imagination, and Ned's ghostly footprints were a way of absorbing the atmosphere of the place in order to replicate it. His gift of intuitive insight was crucial to his work.

In spite of his growing obsession with Palladio's 'high game', Ned as yet had no fixed style in architecture. He told Herbert Baker in a letter written on Boxing Day 1904 that he admired Norman Shaw especially for his versatility: his 'attitude (I wish it was not apparently so flippant) ... of doing what comes to hand without effort without thought of the morrow – more like a linen draper selling reels of cotton over his counter than that terror the yellow-tied self-centred artist modern production [sic] often called an architect.' No arty yellow ties for Ned, who was indifferent to clothes. He wore suits and waistcoats of grey serge and tweed even in the hottest summer, provoking complaints from Emily that his crumpled, stuffy garments smelled. Despairing of

---

*In London he lived at Arlington Street, next to the Ritz, which once asked if his house was for sale: 'No,' said Guest, 'is the Ritz for sale?'

important public work ever coming his way, he depended on rich clients who always filled him with 'a feeling of antipathy and depression – yet they are so important to me'.[42]

In the summer of 1904 Lutyens went fishing in Norway with Victor Lytton, leaving Emily, who was pregnant once more, at home. Victor and Ned shared a cabin for the long, slow sea voyage, which was spent chugging round the jagged coast of Norway in 'horrible smelly shaky old humanity ridden boats'. In Horstad, in the remote northern fjords, the waters boiled with trout and salmon. Ned fished each night till past midnight, returning to a hot wood fire. He wrote to Emily at 1.30 a.m., sketching himself with his feet in a bucket of hot water – 'by his tonsure ye shall know him': he was already balding. He derived a horrible satisfaction from catching more than anyone else, fishing with determination, pipe firmly clamped in his mouth. Victor had political ambitions, envying Winston Churchill his success. On the train to Hull, where they had caught the boat, he had written a letter to *The Times* on the fiscal crisis. Ned observed him closely. Victor, he saw, was kindly and courteous but cold and though ambitious 'has not stamina and real application'.

Ursula was born on 31 October 1904. Their third child, she was a sickly baby with webbed feet, and her illness triggered the first crisis in the marriage. Emily felt that Ned gave her insufficient support, and she scolded him for running away. She tried to explain her feelings:

> I get so afraid lest we drift further apart, instead of growing closer. I don't think you feel it quite as I do, for your work is so much to you, and you see so many people, and I don't think you have a complicated nature ... The deep things of life – God, religion in any form – mean so much to me, and you only scoff, till I have shut all these thoughts away from you ... All I know of your work is its worries. I see so little of you and when we do meet you are absorbed in your paper or a book, and often you never look up or listen when I speak ... I want more of you, not your body, but your soul and intellect, something big to take hold of and share, and when I am in a mood of longing for sympathy and all you give me is criticism and jokes, then I feel as if I bleed inwardly ...[43]

Already Emily was tiring of the role Ned wanted her to play. The casualty of his manic work was not his talent but his marriage; he didn't burn himself out, but he and Emily were already growing apart.

Chapter Nine
The Turn to Classicism 1906–1910

Heathcote (1906). Detail of entrance front.

September 1906. At Thursley Ned's mother Mary Lutyens lay dying. Since January, when she had suffered a stroke, she had slipped in and out of consciousness, barely recognizing her family. At first she was troubled by a nightmare of ceaselessly, wearily travelling, but when she reached the peace of Thursley she became calm and radiant: 'Isn't it a wonderful beautiful world just like fairyland?' she kept saying.

Ned was cruising the Baltic on a luxurious yacht with Herbert and Aggie Jekyll when she died. Too late for the funeral, he hastened down to Thursley. He found her grave high up in the churchyard covered deep with decaying flowers looking out over the garden she loved and on towards Crooksbury, where he built his first house. At Thursley, the woebegone Priscilla, Nannie for fifty years, could talk of nothing else but Mary and how each of the fifteen babies had been born. Old Charles, broken and lonely but self-deceiving as ever, insisted that he had said or done nothing to hurt her, forgetting the long years of poverty, eccentricity and disappointment when he had threatened to move into the kitchen and live on potatoes.

Mary left Ned the Claddah ring, the phallic Irish fertility symbol that was supposed to pass to the favourite child. In a way her death released him. Already he had turned his back on Surrey. The death at Thursley broke his last links. Ned designed a simple white cross for her grave; a slab or lid to a brick box he thought 'so dreadfully cold and unthoughtful looking'.[1]

Ever since Mary's stroke Ned had been working on designs for a house in the Leeds suburb of Ilkley that was the antithesis of his Surrey style. The client John Thomas Hemingway was a wealthy wool merchant and Heathcote, as the house was called, was a startling essay in Italian classicism.

It cost Ned enormous amounts of time and work, and he dreaded the estimates coming out too high. To his relief Hemingway accepted and signed a contract for £17,500; he turned out to be even richer than Ned thought, with an income of £20,000 out of which he spent a mere £3,000. 'He didn't know how to spend his money until he met me,' quipped Ned.

Classicism was the typical style of the nouveau riche, and Hemingway was undoubtedly that. Ned described with snobbish horror how he ate a 'coursed' breakfast in slippers, and afterwards put on his boots in the sitting room with its painted dado, frieze of flying sparrows, garish electric lighting and shiny doors painted blue, brown and gold. From 'weird' people like Hemingway, Ned thought, Emily must at all costs be protected. But Hemingway, about whom he was at first so dismissive, soon won his affection. 'Such a child in all matters which interest me. Yet with a child's sound judgement and sense of justice.'

Ned treated him like a child too.

'I don't want a black marble staircase,' Hemingway told him. 'I want an oak staircase.' 'What a pity,' said Lutyens.

Later, on seeing the black marble staircase which dominated his hall, Hemingway said, 'I told you I didn't want a black marble staircase.' Lutyens: 'I know, and I said "What a pity" didn't I?'

Hemingway nonetheless gave Lutyens a free hand to decorate the house, running a brilliant green carpet up the black marble treads.[2]

Ned wrote a letter to his friend Herbert Baker about Heathcote in 1911. 'I have been scolded for not being Yorkshire in Yorkshire,' he explained, but his idea had been to create 'something persisting and dominating, with horizontal lines, to stratify the diarhetic [i.e. diarrhoea-like] conditions produced by the promiscuous villadom: in fact an architectural bismuth.' The 'bismuth' was the crystal cited by Ruskin in the 'Lamp of Beauty' as an example of a form so rare in nature that the architect should not attempt to imitate it; rather he should attempt to replicate what was already there. Ned used a style that was deliberately intended to set Heathcote apart from the surrounding 'villadom'. Instead of composing a 'pot-pourri of Yorkeological details' he proposed 'hard labour, hard thinking over every line in all three dimensions and in every joint'. Not that he merely copied classicism. 'You can't copy it,' he told Baker. 'To be right, you have to take it and design it.'[3]

Heathcote is often seen as a turning point: the house that marks Lutyens's turn to classicism. It is a defining moment in English architecture.

His contemporary Voysey, who rated Lutyens the ablest architect of his generation, thought his turn to the Renaissance was a disaster: 'if Lutyens had not defected to the Classical Camp, England might have developed a sound modern architecture of her own'.[4]

*

As a self-taught child of the villages, Ned had never received a rigorous classical training, and he had much to learn. His principal teacher was Christopher Wren. The opportunity to replicate his hero came with an invitation to enter the competition to design County Hall for the London County Council. Encouraged by both Emily and Hudson ('you are undoubtedly the cleverest architect in England!'), Ned decided to make a dash for fame in the autumn of 1906.

Seven architects were invited to compete for the huge South Bank site adjoining Westminster Bridge. Led on by the fat commission of £38,000, which brought the prospect of buying his own country house within reach once again, Ned threw himself into the project. Externally, his plan was not very different from the other entries. It consisted of three giant blocks joined by two cupolas which were modelled on Wren's cupolas at Greenwich Hospital. With its pedimented first-floor windows, mansard roof and tall chimneys, his design was in the style which he punningly called his Wrennaissance.[5]*

Busy with the mass of internal planning involved in the building, for nine months Ned shut himself up, working through the night. 'Time seems to go so quick, and there is such an immense never ending list of rooms,' he wrote in March 1907. Next day he reported, 'At half-past midnight I decided to begin all over again.' By August he had finished the planning, but the drawings were still to be made, and all the heating and ventilation fitted in. Soon he was wondering whether his plan would do at all – 'I suppose a way out of it will come' – and the drawings expanded all over the house while Emily and the children were away. 'The outside of the LCC is coming on alright, but the inside is such an enormous puzzle.'[6]

Lutyens submitted preliminary drawings in August 1907. The final drawings together with a report followed in December.

'Glad to get back to my LCC. What shall I do without it!' he told Emily in September. Emily felt excluded. 'You seem far away where I cannot come . . . She is a mistress of as many moods as your wife!' Ned again: 'I wish I didn't keep on wanting to win the LCC. My chief feeling is a wish to get back to that office again and the excitement of the big work.'

A few weeks later he learned that the assessors, Norman Shaw, Aston Webb and W. E. Riley, had chosen a young unknown architect named

---

*The one thing that spoiled the design, thought the *Builder*, was the 'up and down skyline made by the high roofs. It may be "truthful" to show the roofs in this way, but it forms a line quite at variance with the monumental character and horizontal lines of the substructure.'

Ralph Knott as winner. Knott was employed as an assistant in the office of Aston Webb, and his victory led to a change in competition rules under which he would have been disqualified. This was no consolation to Lutyens, who was bruised and snubbed, having expected both Shaw and Riley to support him. He had wasted nine months' work; he told Herbert Baker that he had lost because of his intricate detailed drawings working out the impossible conditions laid down by the assessors. 'What they chose was a corridor 700 feet long, 8 feet wide, shocking detail, without any architectural quality. I feel mine was all quality! only to be appreciated as a building *built*.'[7]

Cruelly protracted and time-wasting architectural competitions like this were much criticized, but the aim was not so much to choose a design as a man for the job. Ralph Knott's design was drastically modified, the budget was pruned and his precocious prize ended by being the grave of his career. Emily was sure that, had Ned won, 'it would have been a curse – and no good for your reputation', but Ned found it hard to pick up the pieces after the disappointment. Perhaps he was beginning even then to shut his eyes, to become out of touch and aloof from everyday reality. Immersing himself in the truths of pure geometry, he retreated into the late-night world of pipe smoke and pencil dust, just as he had done twenty years ago at Onslow Square.

'Oh to win this competition and live "happy ever after",' Ned wrote at the time of the LCC. The happy ever after of perpetual pregnancy and country life was just what Emily didn't want, and she was secretly relieved by Ned's failure at County Hall. She didn't want a country house at all, she confessed; she feared that Ned would park her there with the children while he stayed in London, and she worried that 'you would have grown away from me had you become so *very* celebrated'.[8]

Ned was already growing away. He told Emily that he had only his work to write about, and he doubted he could ever put it into words. His design, he wrote, 'just comes because I want it to, and if it don't I have to grip inside and make or force it and there is no speech that can describe it'. Struggling to 'find a language to describe building and my aspirations in my work to you', he wrote Emily a long letter describing the Elizabethan architecture of Chipping Camden, which (though a wonderful letter) didn't really help. 'I am terribly conscious,' she explained, 'of having *no* artistic perception whatever. When I love and admire what you do I still feel it is no real test because I don't *know* . . . All the same deep down in my heart I am *tremendously*, *desperately* proud of you, and I am dreadfully jealous of people whom I think can help you when I can't – Pamela [Lytton] and Mrs Horner.'

Ned never taught Emily to understand his work, and her attempt to persuade him to speak *her* language, the literary language that she was brought up with, failed too. Reading aloud was a Lytton family craze; Emily knew almost by instinct which parts to cut, and she could put expression into *Tristram Shandy* while knitting a sock with four needles in the dentist's waiting room. But when she tried to make Ned read *Puck of Pook's Hill* for fifteen minutes each evening before dinner, he complained that she didn't listen, and she retorted that he had given it up because he was too busy. After dinner Ned retreated to his drawing board ('I *must* work at night') and Emily, who was an early riser, yawned over a book. At bedtimes they were 'as buckets in a well'.[9]

When they were together they squabbled. Emily resented Ned's habit of sitting silently for hours playing patience and smoking. 'Books, patience do help when I can't work and can't think so have nothing to say,' he explained. Once he wrote her a sermon on beauty, about Inigo Jones and Wren. This was not Emily's kind of beauty. 'The doors of my soul open to the north and yours to the south,' she wrote. Her kind of beauty was moral beauty; the beauty that Ned cared for 'I can't see'. Her trouble, she wrote, was a Puritan conscience. But Ned was a Puritan too. He detested luxury, and his spartan aesthetic of bare oak and pewter was about as protestant as one could get. Reared on the gold plate and fake Tudor of Knebworth, Emily was not so much puritan as indifferent. 'Things', pretty stuffs and furniture, bored her more than ever. As for cooking, she was incapable of making even an omelette – the one time she tried on the cook's night out she forgot the whites of egg.[10]

The massive four-poster bed that Ned designed became a kind of metaphor for their marriage: hard, uncomfortable, unyielding. Not so much a marriage bed as an architectural monument, it was cold and painful, with 'lacerating mouldings, even sharper steel ballusters and the folding wooden tracks on which it was negotiated with difficulty away from the wall like a piece of old-fashioned ordnance'.[11] Together, Emily and Ned read Edward Carpenter's 'beautiful book', *Love's Coming of Age*, which sought to elevate 'the sex passion', liberating it from the prostitute's stuffy dens of dirty upholstery. Carpenter's Appendix explained the rhythm method of contraception, which Ned and Emily used. But Ned's fumbling, over-hasty love-making fell far short of the ecstasies described by Carpenter, and Emily was dissatisfied, the more so as she now believed that sex was crucial to the perfect marriage she hungered for.

That women could, indeed should, enjoy sex, and that sex didn't necessarily mean pregnancy was part of the 'modern' idea of marriage which Emily learned from Mrs Webbe. Pussy Webbe was an activist in the women's movement, and Emily was a willing recruit. With Pussy she visited the Lock Hospital for Venereal Disease and read aloud to the sick prostitutes: defenceless victims of the sexual double standard, they at least appreciated her reading even if Ned didn't. Soon Emily was campaigning for the Moral Education League, going to conferences with Lady Battersea and organizing women's meetings at Bloomsbury Square. Eminent doctors lectured on sex and family planning to a room packed with women and crackling with suppressed sexual anger. When one woman from the audience declared that the appalling sensuality of the day was due to the fact that men did not respect their wives' bodies during pregnancy, the eminent doctor could only reply that it was a very complicated question and not suitable for discussion.

Small wonder Ned felt uneasy. Emily was fighting the sex war in his own drawing room, and he resented Mrs Webbe for interfering in his marriage. He was frankly jealous, but as Emily tartly pointed out, he had no right to be: Pussy had helped to educate her and fill her life with new interests 'as no one else has done since I married'.[12]

Ned's jealousy turned to panic when Pussy began a gossip campaign over a society scandal – the de Vesci marriage. Lady de Vesci had been ostracized for leaving her husband, but Emily, led on by Mrs Webbe, took her side, claiming she was a wronged woman. De Vesci was apparently subject to attacks of 'mania' and the doctors pronounced him unfit for marriage, but when the marriage failed it was his wife, not he, whom society blamed, even though her life was ruined. Fired perhaps by memories of her grandmother Rosina, Emily waxed indignant in Lady de Vesci's defence, dismissing Ned's pleas for a 'George Eliot tolerance'. Emily's feminism was all very well, but it threatened to destroy Ned's interests. Lord de Vesci was the son of Mrs Portman, for whom Ned designed spectacular gardens at Hestercombe. Desperate not to alienate Mrs Portman, Ned implored Emily not to be carried away by theories, 'for Emy if moved moves so very deliberately and with no equivocation, and equivocation is a cousin germaine of tact'.[13]

In the summer of 1907 Emily and Mrs Webbe and the children took the usual 'squalid' lodgings on the Sussex coast at Rustington. Bumps came to stay, laden with peculiar luggage packed in baskets and spotted handkerchiefs. Emily drank beer with her and begged Ned not to apologize constantly for the food – 'It is really such bad taste – quite unworthy of you.'

Nearby at Littlehampton was the Green Lady Hostel, where the wealthy suffragette Mrs Pethick Lawrence brought the young women members of her North London working girls' club, the Esperance Club. She was a friend of Mrs Webbe, and she sent her motor over to collect Emily for tea. Mrs Pethick Lawrence personally funded the militant suffragette Women's Social and Political Union, and Emily was just the kind of discontented upper-middle-class woman she wanted to recruit. Emily fell into her lap like a ripe plum, and joined the WSPU. Ned was dismayed, worrying once more that his clients would be put off. The Clutterbucks, who were flirting with the idea of building, cancelled, apparently because of Emily's feminism. Ned had built a house for Mrs Pethick Lawrence (the Dutch House at Holmwood, 1901–4), and he told Emily that she was 'oh so common – you should see her house – the newest of new art'.[14]

Accompanying Emily to the Pethick Lawrence tea was the newly-widowed Arthur Chapman, known as Chippy, Ned's first client. 'You are a bold man to come into such a nest of suffragettes,' said Mrs Pethick Lawrence, but Chippy felt quite at home. A Liberal MP, he sympathized with the women's movement, the more so because it brought him close to Emily. Ned was commissioned to design a grave for Chippy's pious wife Agnes, but he somehow couldn't bring himself to do it. 'I have drawn so many,' he wrote, but none would do. It was as if he didn't want to kill her off and admit that Chippy was a free man, which he very much was. Chippy was godfather to Emily's fourth child, born in July 1906, named Agnes Elizabeth after his wife but always known as Betty, and he stayed most holidays with Emily. 'I miss Mr Chip Chap so,' wrote Emily pointedly to Ned in 1907, 'which makes me realize what a great pleasure in life is doing things in company and having interests in common. If only we had something we *both* liked.'

Not even the children filled this role. Ned saw so very little of them; Emily insisted that they were her department, and Ned never tried to interfere. She was a determinedly progressive mother. When Robert, aged seven, looked like a guttersnipe eating a bacon sandwich she was delighted: 'I am glad to think that there is no trace of played-out aristocracy about Robert or indeed any of the children – Ursula the most.'[15]

Barbie, now ten, and Robert, who was seven, were too young to understand their mother's theories. Robert later wrote that the children lacked 'an essential background'. There was nowhere they really wanted to be. At Bloomsbury Square, Ned's office ('the men's') was strictly out of bounds and they were confined to the nursery. Ned decorated the nursery with a green paint made by mixing Antwerp blue and yellow chrome, but he never visited; Emily came in after tea and read aloud for hours; but the most important person in their lives was Nannie. For two or three months each summer they stayed by the sea, where Emily took a house. Fading Kodaks show them bathing or posed in floppy hats and big-buttoned coats – small and rather lonely figures rarely smiling.

Robert, the only boy, resented his upbringing. When he was only eight Emily worried that he would turn into an idler, adored by women. Barbie was a serious little girl who had the gift of concentration. Emily thought she would become a schoolmistress (she couldn't have been more wrong) and predicted, more accurately, that her life would always be full of care. Emily's hatred of public school meant that she failed to educate Robert, who was sent to a girls' day school and encouraged to paint sunsets in oils before breakfast, wearing woollen gloves to keep his hands clean, with predictably discouraging results. Ursula (four) was the prettiest and sweetest, an incorrigible flirt who lived on her nerves. She 'will always be a butterfly and marry a rich man who will adore and pamper her and bore her at the same time – and she will be brutal and a tyrant but always fascinating'. Ursula was the child Ned found easiest, though the other children thought her a show-off. At tea one day, Robert said, 'Mummy, do you simply adore Father?' Before she could answer, Ursula piped up, 'I do.'[16]

If Ned spent more time than Emily liked with other women, it was because of his work, of course; but Emily was jealous of women who had 'taste' and could talk to him about houses and furniture: a subject to which she was so stubbornly and neurotically indifferent.

At Knebworth, where Ned had established himself as architect to the estate, blocking other architects and scattering the village with cottages and a golf club, there was Pamela. Pamela was the daughter of Mrs Plowden, who had flirted with Robert Lytton in India. Her marriage to Emily's brother Victor caused a permanent rift with Judith, Neville's wife, who had married Neville to be close to Victor, whom she still pined for. Pamela was smart and charming with very round eyes of startling sapphire blue; and she loved men. She had decided to marry Victor in preference to Winston Churchill because his political prospects seemed brighter, and already she was regretting her choice. When Ned spotted her with the Duke of Westminster, whose car stood outside her London house all afternoon, she blushed. Sexy women made Ned uneasy, but Pamela was unhappy; Victor was moody and irritable, and Ned had the power to cheer her with plans for redecorating Knebworth. Together they transformed the place, banishing Victorian clutter, dirty tapestries and stuffed upholstered chairs. They bleached varnished oak, painted dark walls white and removed tons of stone tracery from the windows to let in the light. They simplified the garden, too, ripping out the overgrown, densely planted Victorian shrubs.

Even Emily liked the result, accepting the need for 'an architectural waste paper basket', though she regretted the passing of the Victorian fantasy of her lonely, neglected childhood. She worried about Ned's closeness to Pamela, especially when Pamela confided in Ned a pregnancy, which she ascribed to the magical powers of the Claddah ring that Ned had lent her. 'Who is the father?' Emily asked Ned. 'Not you I hope.'[17]

Cecil Baring was a banker and a classicist, spare and dry with a chiselled face, a John Buchan hero who ran off with Maude Lorillard, the American wife of his New York business partner, causing a scandalous divorce. In 1904 he bought Lambay, a remote island off the Dublin coast, as a haven from the disapproval of the great world. Combining 'the Homeric simplicity of Ogygia with the almost untouched ecological condition of the Galapagos', the island had a tumbledown keep which Cecil wanted to restore.

Ned first visited Lambay in 1905, making the perilous three-mile crossing in Fargie the ferryman's brown-sailed mailboat, the *Shamrock*. As he sat in the sitting room with Cecil, Maude walked in and out, pretending to make tea, emptying hot water out of the window and sizing him up as she passed; eventually she joined the conversation, having made up her mind that he would do. Ned thought her a curious creature. 'She can be very reserved and stand offish,' he wrote, 'but she is more like a girl and childlike in many ways. She is very American, very dark. She describes herself as a squaw.' He liked her earthiness and warmth. She told him how, when pregnant with her daughter Calypso, she had rolled down the hills, she was so big; one could hardly imagine

Pamela or Emily doing that.[18] Ned was invited back to draw plans in 1907, and work started in 1908.

The old castle at Lambay was almost Scottish in character, with crowsteps up the gables. Four little vaulted rooms built at the corners of a central block had canted sides, which interested him, built for the purposes of 'a mild defence', so no one could come round a corner without being seen and shot at. Lutyens made the castle's splayed sides the key to the geometry of his plan. In spite of Cecil's love of Homer, he avoided classical motifs. (Not until many years later, in 1925, did Lutyens build a Catholic chapel in the form of a Greek temple for Cecil.) Lutyens rebuilt the old castle and projected its walls forward around a forecourt; behind he added a new wing, which he sunk deep into the rising ground to avoid dominating the original castle.

In a speech to the Architectural Association made in 1908, which, though brief, cost him much agony, Lutyens argued that 'Every wall, path, stone and flower bed has its similar problem and relative value to the central idea. A garden scheme should have a backbone, a central idea beautifully phrased.'[19] This was certainly true of Lambay, where Ned's central idea is the contrast between wildness and civilization, between nature and design. Lambay is a poem, written in landscape. Around the castle, Ned threw a massive circular wall, creating an island within an island, surrounded by a sea of grass. He pierced the wall with an entrance gate which is gridded like a portcullis, set between two primitive bastions. Within this refuge he set the approach to the house: a lawn path edged by flagstones, then a screen between classical piers, taming the wildness of the island with formal devices which mark the transition to civilization.[20]

The joy of Lambay is its total isolation: as Ned wrote, 'it is such a delicious aloof place alone in the wash of its waters'. Cecil Baring banned Dublin pleasure-steamer day-trippers from the island, which could only be reached by Fargie's boat once or twice a week when the tides and wind were right. Cecil ruled the island like an eccentric monarch. He mapped the island's unspoilt fauna and flora, collected earthworms and imported exotic animals – moufflons, chamois and rheas. He composed Latin inscriptions, and banned Victorian round-legged furniture, filling the house with square-legged pieces from Heal's. Maude lived the simple life. She churned butter, and herself planted the walled vegetable garden, wearing a leather jerkin and motoring veil for protection from the roaring winds. She stopped the islanders' teeth and, when they died, it was Maude who laid them out.

But she was no earth mother. Arcadian bliss was clouded for her by migraine and depression ('think of leaving the island' occurs often in her diary), and she never lost her rich-girl habit as she undressed of leaving pools of clothes on the floor wherever she happened to step out of them. She dressed her children in white lace sewn by nuns from Paris which was exquisitely laundered and goffered each day by a woman who did nothing else.[21]

Lambay was a lifelong commission. As with Ashby St Ledgers or Knebworth, Ned returned again and again over the next thirty years or so. Cecil Baring was important in other ways too. He gave Ned financial advice, lent him money and introduced him to a new world of rich banking clients.

Ned needed Cecil Baring's help all the more because the demand for country houses was drying up as prices fell on the Stock Exchange. Mr Broadmead, who wanted to build at Enmore Castle in Somerset, cancelled the job in August 1907 because he had lost £10,000 in depreciation in stocks and shares in a fortnight. Perhaps it was just as well: Ned considered him '*very* second-rate – coarse, fat, shortsighted and full of self-importance'. He was obstinate too, and refused to do what Ned wanted, insisting instead on a pillbox ornamented with mock battlements. 'Blow the Battle of Hastings says I!'[22]

'No one has any money now,' complained Ned. Consols were down to 81, playing old Harry with the settled well-to-do, who were in no mood to build. Fortunes were being made in Lancashire, where exports boomed and Lutyens heard that the return on capital was 60 per cent, but few with new industrial fortunes came to him. Those that did got short shrift. The crippled Mr Hobson of Sheffield was 'a good type of manufacturer', but his house was 'a regular villa ornée and everything about it vulgar except the simple straightforwardness of the occupants'. (Ned designed a garden for him.) Mr Buckley, the heir to a £300,000 Manchester fortune, Ned thought 'common and vulgar – motors and a launch on the river – leading a life of absolute idleness punctuated with bridge and racing'. (Buckley didn't build.)[23]

Loyal patrons, however, commissioned work in London. Queen Anne's Gate became a Lutyens enclave, beginning with Hudson's house, Number 15, an old red-brick corner house with a pitched roof and a statue of Queen Anne, 'a dear little house', which Hudson had always wanted, ever since he peeped through the window as a boy. Over the road, Ned did up Number 32 for Lady Allendale and Number

28 for Haldane, the Liberal politician, whose solicitor brother had the temerity to write 'a rude common letter' complaining about his fees.[24]

In London or the country, the syntax was the same: small grey bricks with red quoins and window heads, small-paned sashes, a sparing use of stone, tiled roof, towering chimneys. This was the formula Ned used at Great Maytham (1909) in Kent for H. J. Tennant, a conventional great house. At Wittersham (1906), the Kentish house he restored for Alfred Lyttelton, there is a Doric portico, but at Middlefield (1908) near Cambridge for Dr Bond, a Cambridge don, he resisted the temptation to introduce the orders, and the house is bold, simple and severe. It frightened the owner, though Ned thought he had 'for a little house, got an extraordinary amount of dignity into it'.* The severity of the design was tempered by delicate brickwork, often using specially small bricks made in Walter Hoare's Basing brickworks.

Wren was everywhere in the work of Lutyens. The golf club houses he built at Knebworth (1908) and Walton Heath (1906) were square brick boxes with pitched roofs and tall chimneys, nodding homage to the lodges at Wren's Chelsea hospital. In London, the *Country Life* building for Hudson (1904), Lutyens's first major London building, was a slice of Wren's Hampton Court Palace. But Lutyens's 'Wrennaissance' implied a social conservatism which was sharply tested by his encounter with Edwardian progressivism, in the shape of the formidable Henrietta Barnett, wife of Canon Samuel Barnett of Toynbee Hall, the founder of Hampstead Garden Suburb.

'There is a boom coming for Garden Cities,' Lutyens told Herbert Baker. With little new work coming in, he watched carefully as the Liberal government proposed Town Planning bills. Ned responded eagerly to overtures from Alfred Lyttelton about work at Hampstead. 'The Hampstead Garden City solicitor came today to consult me! And their architect came afterwards, rather perturbed I think,' he told Emily in August 1907.[25] Lyttelton, for whom Ned was then designing the impressively conservative Great Wittersham, was chairman of the Hampstead Co-Partnership Tenants.

When the Hampstead tube came to Golders Green, Henrietta Barnett had formed the Garden Suburb Trust to buy land on Hampstead Heath

---

*James Lees-Milne stayed at Middlefield in 1948 and recorded in his diary: 'Lutyens evidently played a joke on the bachelor for whom he built this house. The staircase is supported by one stout twisted column, so fashioned to reproduce the outlines of the female bosom and buttocks, always there as you move around the newel post, either ascending or descending.'

and plan its development as a garden city, preventing building developers from defacing Hampstead's fields with jerry-built villas and cheap terraces. To push through so large a project on the basis of private philanthropy and a joint-stock company rather than public funding required extraordinary energy and organizing ability, qualities which the childless Mrs Barnett possessed in abundance. As town planner she appointed the Fabian socialist Raymond Unwin, creator of Letchworth (1903), where he pioneered the garden city, the Edwardian utopia which became the prototype for twentieth-century suburban sprawl. Unwin gave Hampstead wide and winding tree-lined roads which were designed to catch a series of street pictures rather than focusing on central axial views; existing landscape features such as woods and fields were carefully preserved within the plan. He dreamed of subsidizing cheap working-class housing from the rents on middle-class houses, thus creating an ideal community.

Lutyens's brief was to prepare designs for Hampstead's central hilltop square, with two churches (St Jude's and a Free Church), an Institute and houses. The longed-for church that had eluded him for so long was within his reach at last, and he threw himself into the Hampstead plans in the early months of 1908, soon after his failure at County Hall. After staying up all night ('almost an LCC night'), and in spite of feeling 'very slack' and finding it hard to work, he presented Mrs Barnett with his plans on 14 April. She liked the brick Queen Anne houses which he designed for Central Square, but had doubts about his church. She wanted a gothic church, and 'I have designed a Romantic-Byzantine cum Nedi'. Ned gave St Jude's a tall pointed spire, sweeping barn-like roofs and an early Italian domed crossing. The aisles were especially 'Nedi like', as Bumps would say; a brick and timber medieval structure that in fact quoted his own design for the skittle alley at Goddards. (Quoting himself was soon to become a Lutyens subtext.)

Encouraged by Mrs Barnett saying that she sat at his feet ('to which I never know what to say'), Ned worked on at the church, which needed to be approved by the Bishop of London. 'I cannot, at least have not, arrived at a church, which is depressing,' he wrote to Emily from Lindisfarne, where he went with Hudson to receive the Prince of Wales in July, scribbling designs for St Jude's on the back of Emily's letters. 'How goes the Hampstead Church?' wrote Emily. 'I care so much that you should build that.'[26]

Pleasing the Bishop was only half the battle. Mrs Barnett soon began to realize that her architect's conception of her brainchild differed radically from her own. 'A nice woman,' as Ned scathingly wrote, 'she is proud of being a philistine, has no idea much beyond a window box full of geraniums, calceolarias and lobelias, over which you can see a goose on a green.' If Henrietta Barnett imagined Hampstead as a progressive, villagey William Morris community, this was not at all what Lutyens had in mind; but she got her 'green', which became the climax of his design.

Balked by Mrs Barnett, Lutyens enlisted the sympathy of Alfred Lyttelton, who used his politician's skills to push through Lutyens's design against Mrs Barnett's opposition. 'Mrs Barnett was vanquished, and the church reduced, is agreed to, but Oh I do want more money for *my* church,' Lutyens reported in October 1909.

Ned wanted his church to dominate, and to achieve that he needed to give it height. 'I want a certain height of building in a certain place for the general effect,' wrote Ned. 'Mrs B is dead against this certain height on the ground of the other houses near being overshadowed.'[27] To please her, he repeatedly revised his plans, bringing the sweeping eaves of St Jude's down to the level of the cornices of the surrounding houses. But the spire of St Jude's juts high into the London skyline, creating dramatic vistas along the axial chinks that Unwin cut into his winding roads.

Ned's eye at Hampstead was fixed on the skyline. Approaching Central Square from Erskine Hill, the spire is first glimpsed behind the dome of the Free Church and then disappears, only to reappear once more through the window of the Free Church. Part of the experience of Hampstead is the constant realignment of the three pivotal points, the Free Church dome, the spire of St Jude's and the Institute cupola, as you circulate around the square.

Ned enclosed Central Square with houses, blocking out the view on to London or Hampstead Heath. In the centre of the square he designed a large rectangle of green, bisected by thin canals; an island of country within a sea of city. Perhaps he was playing with the idea of *rus in urbis*, the country in the city, divorcing the square from the surrounding garden city.* Mrs Barnett's progressive mixed community was hidden away behind Ned's tidy symmetry of design. He made the houses intended for working-class tenants look bigger than they were by

---

*Ironically perhaps, Hampstead's winding roads today are lined with millionaire villas, many of which derive from the template of Lutyens's 'tudorbethan' country houses.

concealing doors at the corners, or using one entrance for two houses. The Free Church manse, which balances the vicarage, is in fact two houses concealed behind the façade of one (the Free Church minister was far poorer than the vicar, who received a handsome stipend of £3,000 a year).

Lutyens was no progressive. He had no interest in using architecture to change the way people lived, to eliminate servants or smooth social divisions. Art nouveau he came to dismiss as 'common' and lacking in intellect. He disliked the bossiness of social reformers such as Mrs Barnett. Ugly, squalid towns such as Manchester depressed him, but he didn't see town planning as a motor for change. All he wanted was to build beautiful buildings: 'Loveliness alone is akin to godliness and whilst [ugliness] is countenanced and excused Hell is possible.'

An outsider to the architectural profession, he was suspicious of his colleagues, from whom he learned little. When the Architectural Association visited Marsh Court in 1906 he didn't preen, but complained that 'the chaps make criticisms and then anything that may be good they adopt'. Social acceptance mattered far more to him than professional recognition. In 1907 he was elected to the Athenaeum Club, his card signed by seventy-eight people, and he felt very grand though rather alarmed by the company of 'a lot of old men very much at home'.[28] Too soon he was to become one of them, his buildings celebrating the values of the governing élite.

Yet Lutyens's classical 'higher game', seemingly so conservative, was in fact subtly subversive. He was no mere 'historicist' as his modernist critics claimed, slavishly replicating the styles of the past. He immersed himself in the language of classicism, as he had earlier learned the vernacular of Surrey, but once he set up its rules he softly broke them. Having established an idea in the design of a house, he then contradicted it, in what is sometimes called the architecture of paradox. He used the language of classicism to make jokes as the Italian Mannerists had done, leaving void the semicircular space above a door, or designing a capital without a pilaster. He knew very well what he was doing. 'There is that in art which transcends all rules, it is the divine,' he wrote.

> Then with inspiration rules are forgotten, and some great immeasurable cycle of law is followed, unconsciously by some unaccounted impulse – in my own kind of work and with the moderns. There is I. Jones breaking through all rules when it suits him. He does it softly and is hard to find

out. Wren flagrantly defied them and he applied his ingenious intellect – he had more an intellectual than an artistic gift – yet with rules broken there was the great result, as you say there is with Carlyle in his work.[29]

Even when his classicism was at its grandest and most academic, as at Heathcote, or conventional and pompous, as at Great Maytham (1907–9), he undercut it. At Heathcote he created an expectation of a classical axial plan which he promptly baffled by designing a grand entrance that leads nowhere; visitors are deflected sharply to the right, ultimately reaching the grand marble hall in a plan which resembles a series of Chinese boxes set within each other. Great Maytham, which he built for H. J. Tennant, has a conventional symmetrical plan which is sometimes criticized as dull, but Hudson, who understood Lutyens houses better than most, was 'awfully pleased' with it. Perhaps he realized that the house itself was intended to be read as part of a grand axial route, which climaxes in the garden beyond; except it doesn't because the garden when you reach it is open-ended, itself an anticlimax.[30]

Classicism for Lutyens was not a matter of absolute values, but a set of rules. Revealingly, he always wrote of it as a game, with rules which existed to be broken. 'I hope the Clutterbucks will build,' he wrote, 'but she wants an Elizabethan house and my sympathies are not at all with that period at present. I want to go for the higher game, at least what I hold to be higher.' By now Elizabethan houses frankly bored him.[31]*

Ned was in the throes of furnishing Heathcote – 'curtains, carpets, gardeners, electricians, door handles, carvers' – when Emily gave birth to her fifth and last child, Edith Penelope Mary, known as Mary and born on 31 July 1908.

Mary's birth coincided with the summer holiday, and that summer Emily rented a house at Storrington, near Little Thakeham. Here she came with a monthly nurse, five servants and five children. As usual, the servants were miserable at leaving London; Emily could never

---

*'I don't like the Botley house very much,' he wrote of the massive Elizabethan brick pile he designed for Mrs Franklyn to house her Jacobean Bristol merchant's interiors. New Place, Botley (1906), was indeed a flop, arguably one of the most depressing houses he ever designed, which was unfortunate as he had gone to great lengths to 'hook' the client, Mrs Franklyn. She had come to Lutyens having read an article in the *Magazine of Art* on 'The Difficulty of Choosing an Architect'. She told him she wanted an architect young enough to take an interest in the work, which Lutyens was not. He replied that the claim that 'I am "so busy" as I have often heard repeated may do me harm and end my business', but uninspired piles like New Place would certainly have done him harm.

understand why they so disliked 'holidays' by the seaside. The cook gave notice when Emily asked her to clean the front doorsteps, and the departure of the monthly nurse reduced Emily to tears. 'It is such a desolate feeling, being deserted when one has been cared for and protected from all worries for so long.' She spent much of the time in bed with the baby and Betty (now two) and Ursula (five), both of whom were fiercely jealous of each other and of the new arrival. One night Betty was in bed and apparently asleep, Emily was holding the baby and Ursula talking to her, when Betty popped up: 'That baby is *mine*.' Ursula: 'Don't you think Betty would feel much better if she didn't talk?' Already emerging were family patterns that would take a lifetime to work out. When Hudson arrived in his grand motor and showered Ursula with expensive toys, she remarked: 'I am going to ask Mr Hudson to give me a baby like Mummy's.'[32]

Ned spent a week or so at Storrington, sandwiched between visits to Heathcote. Never before had he spent longer than one night in a seaside lodging-house single bed, cooped up with his family on summer holiday. Now he did a lot of work, slept a great deal and enjoyed himself. He began to think seriously about setting up in partnership with Herbert Baker, who was tiring of South Africa, of enlarging the office at Bloomsbury Square and of moving the family to Hampstead or perhaps Knebworth. His pipe dreams were dispelled by Emily, who as usual had other ideas. When Victor offered a house on the estate at Knebworth, she refused it. Far more important to her than a little white country house was the 'freedom' to escape.

Ned escaped too. With Hudson and Barbie, he prepared Lindisfarne for a visit from the Prince and Princess of Wales. His first encounter with the future George V was not especially auspicious. The Prince was alarmed at the steep gangway up the battery and wanted a wall built ('I told him we had pulled one down and that if he really thought it unsafe we would put nets out. He thought that very funny'). The Princess couldn't bear the cobbles, they hurt her feet. 'I told her we were very proud of them! The only thing she specially admired were some fleur-de-lis on a fireback.'

Lindisfarne brought more work in Northumberland: Whalton Manor for the rich widow Mrs Eustace Smith, a conversion of four eighteenth-century houses in a village street. Ned gave it a monumental staircase and a grand processional route, creating an impression of opulent space which forms a bold contrast with the old village houses.[33]

He stayed too at Renishaw, where he made the first of many wild goose chases at the behest of the whimsical Sir George Sitwell, whom he found 'rather difficult to persuade and make see – he has travelled so much in Italy that unless he sees an Italian picture he knows in a suggestion, he demurs'. Ned befriended Lady Ida Sitwell ('a darling'), who was distraught because 'Sir George has got the hump and is going over to the Liberal party', which Lutyens tried to dissuade him from doing, as 'if he don't turn Liberal he will build a house in Sicily *at once!* as he can spend the money he would otherwise have to subscribe to the Lib party'. But Sir George's talk of employing Lutyens to redecorate the whole of Renishaw came to very little; the only job he did was the ballroom. After flattering Lutyens and picking his brains, Sir George liked to save money by employing local builders.

In October Ned was staying with Princess Dolgorouki in a house party at Mar Lodge, Braemar, near Balmoral. Puns flowed. Where did Mar Lodge? In Fife's Arms. One evening there was a fancy-dress contest and Ned wore the costume of a baby, for which he won first prize. After dinner he gave a toast: 'To the happiest days of my life / Which I spent in the arms of another man's wife / My Mother.' How shocked you would have been, he told Emily, when someone had a bilious attack and he told the piper at dinner to play the Blue Pills of Scotland. Ned was fun. No wonder the Princess hid his luggage when he wanted to leave.[34]

Back in London, Ned found the Lytton family plunged into crisis. Con had converted publicly and very dramatically to the suffragette movement. Emily claimed the credit for introducing Con to Mrs Pethick Lawrence in August 1908, but Con's transformation from gentle semi-invalid into militant tigress came as a shock. On 12 October, when suffragette leaders were arrested for inciting to violence, Con was asked by Mrs Pethick Lawrence to petition Herbert Gladstone, the Home Secretary, to treat them as political offenders rather than common criminals. That evening Con visited Mrs Pankhurst, who was held prisoner in a bare, verminous cell at Bow Street. Appalled, Con brought round blankets. This was reported in the *Daily Mail*, which devastated Edith Lytton, who made herself ill with worry at the disgrace that Con had brought on her family name. 'I am truly sorry for her,' wrote Emily, 'but I feel more sorry for Con that at her age she may not follow her own principles.'

Con waded deeper and deeper into the suffragette movement,

campaigning fanatically for better treatment for women prisoners. She was manic and utterly fearless, driven by the blind passion of a religious martyr. Her brother Vic supported her, throwing away his eloquence and political career, his colleagues thought, on a cranky cause, but Vic's wife Pamela, like Edith, was mortified. When Con addressed a letter to Pamela's baby daughter as 'the new woman of Knebworth' Pamela took it to mean suffragette and was most upset, fearing, as Emily wrote, that her daughters should take after Vic's sisters.[35]

Late one night in February 1909 Con walked into 29 Bloomsbury Square. 'Are you arrested?' asked Emily as a joke. 'Yes,' said Con, who had joined a WSPU deputation to the Prime Minister. She was in a state of exhausted collapse with a racking headache, but Emily revived her with hot-water bottles and Betty (who was staying the night) rubbed her, 'and we were so happy we could be together'. Next day Con went to Bow Street, where she was sentenced to a month's imprisonment in Holloway. She made a short speech in court, saying it was the proudest day of her life.

Edith was heartbroken by this new adventure, and even Emily, who sympathized with the women's movement, disliked Con's militancy. 'We cannot disguise from ourselves,' she wrote, 'that our old Con has gone for ever.' She had ceased to have private affections, thought Emily, and become an impersonal being, a fanatic. How could one sympathize with this new Con who claimed that Holloway was 'the greatest, most wonderful experience of her life'.[36]

The women's movement shadowed Emily's seaside holiday at Southwold, where Mrs Webbe and Arthur Chapman, who disliked each other cordially, argued so bitterly about the suffragettes that Emily had to ban the subject. Mrs Webbe persuaded Emily and the children to tramp the beach, selling the Pethick Lawrences' *Votes for Women*. They sold all thirty of their copies – 'I feel we have thoroughly established ourselves as Suffragettes,' wrote Emily. As usual, the servants grumbled; Sewell the cook was cross and the nursery maid gave notice. Emily complained that Chippy and Mrs Webbe forced her to do too much 'hard reading' – *Esoteric Christianity* in the morning, *Jane Eyre* after lunch and George Meredith in the evening. Pussy was like a Japanese pug; she sniffed where other dogs would never sniff and didn't know where to stop. Chippy, on the other hand, was tolerant and good-humoured and cuddled the babies. He all too obviously worshipped Emily, and Nannie worried that they were growing too intimate. 'I have made a great point of locking my door to satisfy

Nannie's scruples,' Emily told Ned. 'He would be very clever if he found room between Barbie and Betty!'[37]

This tease hurt, especially as Emily now played her usual game of pretending to have no room for Ned. He stayed with Bumps: 'oh! her life now' – in spite of the stifling August heat, she breakfasted on sausages, bacon and eggs, drank beef tea at 11, and lunched on beefsteak pudding and beer.

Ned bombarded Emily with irritable letters, growling angrily about politics, the Liberal government, democracy and Lloyd George. The political scene in the summer of 1909 was unusually fraught as the parties quarrelled over Lloyd George's People's Budget, but Ned had never shown much interest in the subject before, and his tirades had not a little to do with the fact that Emily sympathized strongly with Chippy's Liberal politics. Ned was growing into 'a crabbed old Tory'; soon, he told Emily, he would become 'a sort of rogue elephant deserted and shunned by his tribe'.[38]

Aged forty, Lutyens's mild, agnostic liberalism was hardening into a pro-feudal toryism, in an evolution that paralleled his stylistic shift from art nouveau to classicism. Emily talked a different language. 'I am afraid you may not have noticed that I sound more sympathetic,' she wrote – too true, he hadn't; 'but somehow I feel I understand your point of view of life better than I have done before'.[39] Exactly how this new understanding had come about she didn't explain.

The truth was that Emily needed Chippy. Carelessly wealthy and generous, he lent or gave her money, where Ned was mean and difficult. He paid for holidays. He helped in politics, too. As Emily became more involved in the suffrage movement, she came to value Chippy's Liberal contacts.

Emily's disapproval of Con's militancy was tinged with jealousy. She envied Con, who had found leaders she could blindly follow and a cause she could lose herself in. Emily too longed for a calling, but she knew the women's movement wasn't it. In September 1909 she reluctantly resigned from the WSPU, claiming that they meant murder.

On 8 October 1909 Con was arrested at Newcastle for throwing a stone at Lloyd George in his motor car. She was locked into a filthy flea-ridden prison cell where she went on hunger strike, but when the doctors found heart disease she was freed. She returned to London in an extraordinary state of emotional excitement: she knew for a fact that she had received preferential treatment on account of her name and she was determined to expose the double standard. Emily heard her speak at the Queen's Hall where she was so inspired that she made her audience weep.[40]

'My whole soul is filled with the suffrage question and the horror and pity of it all,' wrote Emily. She felt that she was betraying Con by leaving the movement. 'I know I am right, and yet it seems so contemptible to stand aside and criticize when these other women are giving their lives.' Edith by now was so upset that she wanted Con to change her name: 'Con doesn't mind as she says she will then be treated like any other woman and no one of her family shall know what name she takes'.

Ned bolted for Italy. 'I start for ROME tonight,' he wired Emily on 15 October. He had little sympathy with Con. He disliked militancy, hated notoriety and shrank from pain. His instinct was always to flee, as he confessed to Emily: 'it does express one's feeling – to run away and hide is a very natural if not a very valiant instinct.' But Emily certainly didn't think he should have stayed. 'I am glad you went,' she wrote, 'as you needed rest and change, only you must work up the Hampstead affair and not let grass grow under your feet, or Mrs Barnett will put you in the wrong again.'

The Italian job came through Vic, who was chairman of a Royal Commission responsible for mounting exhibitions in Brussels, Rome and Turin to celebrate Italy's fiftieth anniversary, to which he appointed Ned consulting architect.[41]

Ned's first destination was Turin, where the Italians were holding an industrial exhibition. He advised Rennell Rodd, the British Ambassador, that the exhibition buildings being erected by the Italian government at Turin could not be accepted by Britain because of the risks of fire or collapse. The interminable discussions that followed in language he didn't understand he enlivened by drawing cartoons of the Italians with and without their clothes on. Travelling on to Rome, he snatched a few hours' sightseeing in Genoa, where he found few buildings that he didn't already know from books. 'The lavish space given away in staircases makes me sick with envy,' he wrote, noting how small an area of window was required to light a room brilliantly well. But the streets were too narrow for the palaces, the churches decorated with 'dreadful Rococo muck', and the architecture was dirty and poorly finished ('which would make me wild if it were mine').

'I do wish I could have come with Wren,' he wrote. Rome was full of old friends – buildings which he recognized from their backs or from doorways and staircases, though he had never seen them. 'There is so much here in little ways of things I thought I had invented! No wonder people think I must have been in Italy. Perhaps I have but it was not Rome.' He felt no 'internal *ronge*' or emotion, partly perhaps because he was suffering torture from piles and sharing a hotel with Vic and Pamela, who quarrelled constantly. Pamela was pregnant again, but the child was not Victor's, and their unhappiness made Ned's spirits sink. While Vic went to the office, Ned and Pamela went sightseeing, but so much of Rome seemed tawdry and vulgar; even the dome of St Peter's was a disappointing pimple. Over the city hung a great cloak of decay, as if, he told Emily, his wife was always dirty and every thought she had was vulgar and pretentious.[42]

If Ned's visit to Italy was a pilgrimage to the source of his classicism, it was strangely disappointing.* But the Rome trip did at least produce work. On his return, he was commissioned to design the British entry at the Italian exhibition, which was to be a replica of the upper storey of the west front of St Paul's Cathedral. To the civil servants at the Board of Trade, Ned's design looked very like the original, but as he explained to Herbert Baker it wasn't a bit, 'which is where the fun came in for me. The whole order had to be altered, and I think it takes more architectural technique to do this, and make every other part fit in, with the design of an undoubted master like Wren. The cornice, columns, etc were altered, the portico and pediment etc; and a great labour it was but very interesting.'[43] This time the joke was so private that only the men in his office could share it.

One evening in January 1910 Emily was dining with Mrs Webbe in Eaton Square when Ned telephoned from Knebworth to say that Con was in prison in Liverpool under an assumed name. She had got herself arrested for throwing a stone in a suffragette demonstration. Emily immediately telephoned Chippy, who discovered from the Home Office that Jane Warton, as Con had called herself, was due to be released the following morning as she couldn't tolerate forcible feeding.

Emily hastened home to pack a bag and caught the midnight sleeper to Liverpool. She arrived at 6.30 a.m., and found Con at Walton Gaol; she had cut her hair short and bleached it (which suited her) and she wore spectacles and a prison-like green serge coat. Emily couldn't help

---

*When, however, he was asked at a meeting of the Architectural Association in 1920 whether Greek and Roman should be learnt in architectural schools, Ned replied: 'Study the Roman rather than the Greek. The Greeks were too subtle, the Romans simpler and more human.'

giggling, especially when the prison doctor described Con's nose, never her best feature, as 'Wellingtonian', but Con had lost two stone and was in a state of near-collapse. After four days in which she had refused to eat, the prison officers had forcibly fed her without first examining her heart. Strong wardresses pinned her to her bed on the cell floor, while a doctor forced her mouth wide open with a steel gag and then stuck a large rubber tube down her throat. 'I felt as though I were being killed – absolute suffocation is the feeling,' she wrote. It was an anorexic's nightmare. When food was poured down the tube, Con choked and writhed and vomited; she vomited so much that the tube was at last removed. This torture was performed eight times, and Con was left, staggering and retching, to clean up her cell.

Con's nightmare ordeal proved her point. Forcible feeding of suffragettes was publicly discredited, but her heart disease worsened. She was never really well again. Edith became ill too. She took pills for her nerves that did no good, her deafness got worse, and she became hysterical whenever Con was in the house. Homewood was a prison. Con escaped, taking a post as organizer to the WSPU on a salary of £2 a week, which allowed her to rent a small flat near Euston.

Ned watched anxiously as Emily tended her sister. 'Don't get too suffragey and woman crazy. Please,' he begged. 'Your children give you more than you can do – and then do let me have some small claim on your time.'[44]

Chapter Ten
'The Shoreless Sea'
1910–1911

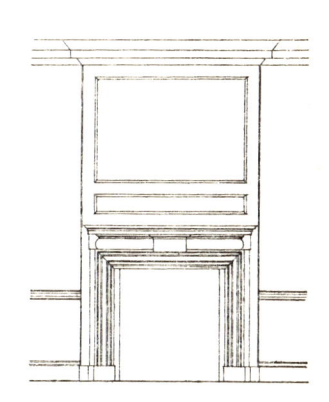

FIREPLACE DETAILS

Three fireplaces for 15 Queen Anne's Gate, Hudson's London house which was next door to Ned's office.

'I am seriously thinking of writing my autobiography,' wrote Emily in 1911. 'It would be thrilling but too improper for publication.' Emily had embarked upon a journey that was to take her far, far away from the humdrum routines of architect's wife and mother. She recorded her journey across the 'shoreless sea' of theosophy with clear-eyed candour in *Candles in the Sun*, the autobiography she wrote over forty years later. 'I did not find in my marriage the companionship I had hoped for,' she began, 'nor a release for my energies.'[1]

The mischief started with Ned's clients, the Mallets, for whom he had built Le Bois des Moutiers, at Varengeville near Dieppe. Guillaume Mallet wanted him to convert a farmhouse, Le Clos du Dans, nearby. When Ned complained about rich patrons who insisted on asking him to build conversions rather than the dream house he carried in his head, Mallet replied, 'Well, build it!'*

Ned's wish was granted, but it came at a price. He discovered that the Mallets had embraced a strange cult called theosophy.

Emily was intrigued when Ned told her of secret books which the Mallets kept in a locked cupboard in the music room. An eminently sane banker with a taste for English Arts and Crafts – he bought beds by Heal, chairs by Morris, a library table by Lethaby – Guillaume Mallet was hardly a man to be associated with occult religion. His serious-minded wife Marie read holy books wearing a black tulle dress designed by Worth. Her fierce fussiness frightened Ned, who worried that when she stayed at Bloomsbury Square she could smell leaves in the water supply.[2]

At Christmas 1909 Madame Mallet sent Emily Annie Besant's 1907 *London Lectures* on theosophy. It is hard today to penetrate the dense, clotted prose, but Emily read with mounting excitement. She shouted with delight as she learned of a new religion which combined the psychic and the spiritual, which was not fenced round by theology or priests, which preached reincarnation and, most exciting of all,

---

*Les Communes, built on a Y-shaped butterfly plan, is indeed a dream house. Like Goddards, it turns a windowless blank face to the outside world, opening on to a garden which is really another room.

promised a second coming of the World Teacher. Mrs Besant wrote thrillingly of the god-figures of the Masters, Morya and Koot Hoomi, who lived on a ravine in Tibet, together with the Count, who had a castle in Hungary.*

Emily was captivated. In the spring of 1910 she visited Varengeville. In the gloom of Ned's church-like music room, with its art nouveau oriel window and dark Burne-Jones tapestry depicting *The Adoration of the Magi*, Madame Mallet opened Pandora's box: the locked cupboard of theosophy books. Back in London, Emily hastened to the Bond Street headquarters of the Theosophical Society. Convinced that she had known the secretary Miss Sharpe in a previous incarnation, possibly as a mouse, Emily enrolled. The reading room, with its air of muffled dinginess, now became the centre of her life. It was lined with cheap editions of the works of Annie Besant and the *Bhagavad Gita*. Madame Blavatsky, the cult's founder, stared from large photographs on the walls, an obese, squatting icon with snub Slav features and round, psychic eyes.

Emily's piety was rewarded when she heard Mrs Besant lecture. A short, stout figure with flowing white robes worn meringue-like over several layers of voluminous white petticoats, Annie Besant was a charismatic lecturer. She spoke standing motionless without notes, in a low, measured, rather beautiful voice. Emily was mesmerized. 'While she was speaking, I was completely carried away, and felt myself face to face with something immeasurably greater than anything I had ever known.'

One day in June Mrs Besant came to lunch. Pussy Webbe came too, seeking comfort for her obsessive worries about cancer. 'Don't *you* live in constant dread of dying of cancer?' she asked. 'Certainly not. I should not be so stupid,' replied Annie briskly. Annie joked with Ned, but her tiger-brown eyes were fixed on Emily, seeming (Emily thought) to look right through her and to penetrate her inmost thoughts.[3]

Annie Besant was sixty-three, and she had already lived through at least four lives. Born plain Annie Wood into a poor branch of a wealthy City family, she endured a fatherless childhood which left her with a lifelong need for male leaders. At twenty-seven she walked out of her marriage to the unpleasant, bullying Reverend Besant and declared herself an

---

*The Masters, who took pupils on probation, preparing them for initiation, were discovered by Madame Blavatsky (1831–91) and Colonel Olcott, who founded theosophy in New York in 1875, and moved their headquarters to Adyar, near Madras, in 1882.

atheist. Journalism and social work led her into the London world of threadbare socialist hacks. With the atheist Charles Bradlaugh she campaigned for contraception, achieving notoriety but loosing custody of her children, who were clawed back by her vengeful husband. She became intimate with Frederick Aveling, the sadist whose cruelty later drove his wife Eleanor Marx to suicide, and she was unrequitedly in love with Bernard Shaw. At forty-two her life changed again when she was dramatically converted to theosophy by the charismatic Madame Blavatsky. To Shaw she seemed to embrace life as a series of roles into which she threw herself unreservedly; unlike a great actress, however, she identified so entirely with her roles that she became incapable of any kind of detachment.

As the granddaughter of Bulwer Lytton, Emily instantly attracted Mrs Besant. Bulwer's occult novels *Zanoni* (1842) and *A Strange Story* (1862), which Emily had devoured as a child, were key texts for Blavatsky's theosophy. In their exploration of esoteric religion, dreams and the occult, and the idea of a secret doctrine uniting all religions, Bulwer's works, so Mrs Besant assured Emily, were not works of fancy but described his real-life experiences as a disciple of the great lodge. Emily remembered stories of her grandfather eating fern seeds and declaring himself invisible; esoteric religion seemed second nature to her whose mind (she now believed) had 'always meandered in the realms of metaphysics'.[4]

Theosophy pulsed with excitement in 1910. There was talk of a second coming, of a World Teacher, a Lord Maitreya who was to occupy the body of a young Indian boy whom Mrs Besant had already discovered. Miss Sharpe, the society's mouse-like secretary, showed Emily a secret photo of a bony-featured Indian boy with shoulder-length black hair parted in the centre in the fashion of Christ or the Buddha. Emily knew at once that this was the World Teacher. During 1910 the *Theosophist* magazine carried a series of articles on the Lives of Alcyone, as the boy was called (his real name was Krishnamurti), describing his nightly audiences with the Master Koot Hoomi across the Tibetan ravine when he revisited his many past lives. The features in the magazine became a kind of theosophical *Debrett*. 'Are you in the *Lives*?' theosophists anxiously asked; and Emily was delighted to discover that not only she but also Robert and Barbie were mentioned.

She never asked herself how a backward fifteen-year-old South Indian boy who spoke little English and had never ventured beyond Madras could conceivably have encountered her and her children on the astral plane or written their names down afterwards. Nor did she dream of questioning the story of Krishnamurti's discovery, which had already become theosophical legend. Krishna's father Narianiah was a poor South Indian clerk whose wife had died young. Being a theosophist, he obtained work at the theosophical compound in Adyar, which enabled him to bring up his four sons. One evening, as the boys bathed in the sea, they were spotted by Mrs Besant's colleague, the clairvoyant C. W. Leadbeater, who saw at once that Krishna had a remarkable aura. Convinced that the boy was the vehicle for the Lord Maitreya, he removed him from school and from his father, brought him into the compound and began training him, investigating his past lives in nightly seances.

Annie Besant warmed instantly to Krishna and his brother Nitya. She legally adopted them as her sons in March 1910, and they became substitutes for her own long-lost children. She must have known she was taking an extraordinary risk in endorsing Leadbeater's choice of Krishna as Lord Maitreya. A bearded, leonine ex-clergyman, C. W. Leadbeater was a misogynist and charlatan, though he undoubtedly possessed psychic powers. He rocked the Theosophical Society with scandal in 1906, when he admitted teaching adolescent boys entrusted to his care to masturbate. Proof of his guilt was a cypher letter discovered in a waste-paper basket, which read: 'Glad sensation is so pleasant. Thousand kisses darling.'

Today he would be disgraced as a pederast, but Annie Besant needed him. He was to her as Bradlaugh had been: collaborator, teacher and leader. He was also indispensable to her theosophical credibility. Together, they made nightly visits in their astral bodies to the Masters; visits which, according to theosophical teaching, could only be made by initiates who had achieved total human purity. If Leadbeater was impure these visits could not have taken place, yet Annie knew only too well that his psychic powers were far superior to her own. Her career on the astral plane – the communications with the Masters which gave her such authority in the society – was totally bound up with Leadbeater. Naturally, she rehabilitated him when she became president of the society in 1907.[5]

Leadbeater's discovery of Krishna seemed to vindicate Annie's judgement, for the boy was hardly a paedophile's dream. He was slow at school and undernourished; his ribs jutted, he smelled unpleasantly of oil and he wore his hair in the brahmin style, shaved in front and growing long down his back. But ugly rumours spread when

Leadbeater insisted on total control of the boy, personally supervising his diet and sleeping habits, and insisting that he washed in the Western fashion between his legs.

None of this was known to Emily, who could think of little else but her new-found beliefs. The children were forgotten as she took lessons in public speaking, overcoming her shyness to give lectures in dingy halls, socializing afterwards over Marmite sandwiches. Arthur Chapman meant little to her now. She no longer needed his political connections, and he was hurt when she lost interest in Liberal politics, whilst his attempts to plod after her on to the astral plane were merely comical. Mrs Webbe screamed with unkind laughter at Chippy's puzzled face when Emily read aloud from books about theosophy, and Robert and Barbie composed teasing verses.

> At croquet and at letters too
> Chippy is noted for cheating you
> So my advice is to you all
> Not to play with Chippy at all.

In the summer of 1910 Emily stayed again at Varengeville, revisiting the locked cupboard. She was at a loss to understand why Guillaume Mallet became so irritable when she talked theosophy with his wife.[6]

At first, Ned was thrilled by theosophy. Its lack of dogma appealed to him,[*] while it seemed also to bring Emily closer to him. 'It seems a new and wider lease of love,' he wrote.

But not for long. Theosophy left little space for marriage; perhaps that was one reason why it appealed so strongly to suffragettes. Bloomsbury Square was more cheerless than ever. Never a meat-eater, Emily became a doctrinaire vegetarian, subsisting on nut cutlets disguised as lamb with a piece of macaroni wrapped in a paper frill instead of a bone.[†] The children were brought up as strict vegetarians too, but Ned was an unregenerate meat-eater, so two sets of dishes appeared in the dining room at meals.[7]

Ned moved his office out of Bloomsbury Square to 17 Queen Anne's

---

[*] As Emily noted, the universality of theosophy probably influenced Ned's designs for the Cenotaph.
[†] Mrs Earle gave the recipe: Take two ounces rice, boil till soft in milk, pound in a mortar till quite soft like paste. Put 2 oz almonds or any other sort of nuts through the nut mill, pound in a mortar, add them to the rice, make them into small cutlets, brush over with white of egg, and fry a nice brown.

Gate. The extra space provided by the three bare and gutted floors allowed him to take on more pupils who, at 200 guineas a year, generated sufficient income to pay the rent. Bloomsbury Square was redecorated, and Ned bought twin tables for the office he now shared with Emily. 'I do want to be with you more and cherish you,' he wrote, 'for you want taking care of and I don't know how to do it.' Too true he didn't – how could he? – and instead of spending whole days at Bloomsbury Square as he had intended, Queen Anne's Gate became a surrogate home. The caretaker Paget filled his small pipes each morning, and Mrs Paget cooked his lunchtime chop, providing the nursery comfort that he missed at home. Next door at Number 15 there was Hudson, with whom he dined or stayed when Emily was away.

'I seem to have no friends,' Ned wrote gloomily, 'just the people I build for. I never see them again. I wonder if I am managing my life very badly. And it is awful not being more with you.'[8] He was living his life vicariously, pouring imagination and emotion into other people's houses, which left his marriage empty and impoverished. But it wasn't true that he had no friends; many of his clients became friends for life.

Cecil and Maude Baring were among these friends. Ned stayed with them in Devon at Mothecombe, the home of Alfred Mildmay, a Baring cousin. Maude Baring, who was pregnant once more, made a scene, so socialistic did she feel about the big house with its troops of servants. Emily sympathized. 'I long to clasp hands with her over her little temper and hatred of the big house,' she wrote, remembering how oppressively artificial her Knebworth childhood had been. Ned disagreed. 'I look at the big house from the other and best point of view. A centre for all that charity that should begin at home and cover, hen-wise, with wings of love all those near about her that are dependent, weaker and smaller. A house with the soul of a Wilton gives me a choke of veneration and its unending possibilities of giving and receiving love.'

Ned wanted to build a great house like Wilton, but he was baffled by his new client Julius Drewe. Having made his fortune from Home & Colonial Stores, Drewe had retired at the age of thirty-three. He commissioned Ned to build not a country house but a castle on the edge of Dartmoor at Drewsteignton which, said the genealogists, was the lair of his ancestor the Norman Count Drogo de Teign.

> Mr Drewe writes a nice and exciting letter to go on with drawings not more than £50,000 though and £10,000 for the garden. I suppose £60,000 sounds a lot to you but I don't know what it means. If I look at Westminster Abbey it is an absurd, trivial amount. If I look at a dear little

old world two roomed cottage it merely looks a vast and unmanageable amount. Only I do wish he didn't want a castle but just a delicious loveable house with plenty of good large rooms in it.⁹

£50,000 was three times the cost of Heathcote (£17,500), which had been thought expensive; but Lutyens didn't really know what Drewe wanted for his money.

Until now, the houses Ned had built had not, strictly speaking, been country houses, but villas: houses in the country, compactly planned, with very little land, which were essentially dependent upon the life of the city. Drogo was no villa, but nor was it a conventional great house. Lack of certainty about the programme meant that it became a house where 'only visual requirements were left to predominate and the house could only depend on ideas about massing and movement through a sequence of spaces'.¹⁰

Lutyens's early sketches, made in August 1910, show a great house with pitched roofs and tall chimneys built around a symmetrical courtyard. He had already decided how to pre-empt the nouveau riche decoration he so disliked. Invited to stay a night on Sir Frederick Mirrielees's (Goddards) steamship, the *Balmoral Castle*, Lutyens was fascinated by the ship's engineering but found the decoration 'so vulgar and silly'. Where there was no decoration, but just building, 'a feeling of veneration, at least respect, was given' – exactly the feeling he wanted to convey at Drogo. Drogo's vaulted stone corridors and Piranesi-like staircase defy mere decoration. Tongue in cheek, Lutyens gave Drewe a free-standing Tuscan pillar in his bathroom, an object lesson in taste for him to contemplate in the bath.

In September 1910 he visited the site, a rocky promontory commanding dramatic sweeping views over Dartmoor. He lined up the new road, Mrs Drewe pulled a mangle to mark the drive, and he staked out the castle, arranged around a symmetrical courtyard. Hot and sweaty from a glorious walk across the rocky stream, Ned ate a picnic lunch with the Drewes. Drewe was a small man, a moth-eaten dandy with a drooping moustache, but he was in his own way a romantic, driven by an ambition to commemorate his ancestor. 'Drewe told me of his dream of a Commemorative tower or Keep and this we planned and plotted and he was mighty pleased and proud.'¹¹ An idea for the house was beginning to emerge. Ned spent the evening talking castle with Drewe, and the early sketches were revised. The new drawings, enlivened with sketches of knights in armour, showed an asymmetrical courtyard design, with a long projecting stable wing like Orchards, and a Norman tower.

Ned's courtyard plan evolved through several stages over the next two years. As it became symmetrical once more, it ballooned, with rooms growing ever larger to fill the needs of a U-shaped courtyard (Ned balanced the billiard room with a vast brushing room: no one could have so many boots). In November 1911 the courtyard plan was splayed, in a giant version of Les Communes or Goddards. The design evolved from the crudely eclectic drawings of 1910 into a Tudor style, where sharply chiselled walls cut by mullion windows recalled earlier work at Buckhurst Park (1902–3), Red House at Godalming (1897–8) and Chinthurst Hill (1893).

Then in 1912 Julius Drewe blew the whistle. Realizing that the castle had grown far bigger than he needed or could afford he ordered that only one side of the splayed plan be built. Pedantically, he insisted that the castle be constructed in medieval fashion of solid granite with walls six feet thick, quashing Lutyens's plans to cut costs by building six-feet walls with two-foot cavities. This doubled the cost. Lutyens did, however, succeed in persuading Drewe to build in smooth, dressed granite, which was vital to the razor-sharp edges and chiselled angles of the walls of his design. But then Drewe ordered more cuts. In 1913 he eliminated the gatehouse, stubbornly maintaining his point despite Lutyens's attempt to dissuade him by building a full-scale timber mock-up. Lutyens eventually made do with thick yew hedges to suggest the lines of the original design: a sort of virtual castle.

Castle Drogo was a compromise, a conversion of the kind Lutyens was always anxious to avoid. Today it stands truncated, gaunt and visually disturbing. Drewe's mutilations played havoc with the south-orientated courtyard plan; but Lutyens's initial uncertainty had allowed the plan to balloon into unreal giantism. Inside, however, Drogo contains some of Lutyens's most dramatic spaces: a vaulted granite staircase lit by an impossibly tall oriel window, and a vast basement kitchen top-lit by a dome which resembles a vault in John Soane's Bank of England.

Drogo took twenty years to build, and by 1930 the social and economic change brought by the Great War had made the house obsolete. Drewe's eldest son was killed at the Battle of Ypres in 1917, and for Drewe the heart went out of the house; it became a mausoleum, bereft of its dynastic purpose. Nikolaus Pevsner, writing in 1951, saw Drogo (which was originally intended to be three times the size) as an elephantine folly, confirming his view of Lutyens as the greatest folly builder the folly-building English had ever produced. 'Castle Drogo beats Fonthill, the Drum Inn at Cockington beats Blaise Castle and Viceroy's House at Delhi beats any other folly in the world.' For Lutyens's admirer Christopher Hussey, on the other hand, 'The ultimate justification of Drogo is that it does not pretend to be a castle. It *is* a castle, as a castle is built, of granite, on a mountain, in the twentieth century.'

Folly or not, Drogo is surely one of the most extraordinary buildings of the twentieth century. It brilliantly dramatizes the idea of a castle, translating it into an abstract architecture that relies for effect on angles and wall planes rather than historical quotation or gothic medievalism.[12]* With its astonishing skyline and its truncated massing tensely crouched over the moorland, Drogo is superb cinema.

Building a colossal granite folly to commemorate one's family history was one way of disposing of Edwardian surplus wealth. Another was to buy modern art: swagger portraits by Sargent or Mancini, heavily impastoed full-lengths of women in shimmering white tulle with powdered faces gashed by violent red lips. Lutyens's introduction to this flash and self-regarding world came through the Irish impresario and dealer Hugh Lane. A nephew of Yeats's patron, Lady Gregory, and six years younger than Ned, the homosexual Lane was a dandy, a hypochondriac and a gifted connoisseur. He could spot an old master through several layers of dirt and varnish in a junk-shop window. Beginning as a penniless apprentice with Colnaghi's, at the age of twenty-three and with no capital he set up on his own as a dealer and speedily made a fortune. The money he made from selling old masters he used to buy pictures by living painters, becoming a patron to Orpen, Mancini and Wilson Steer.

At thirty-four he was knighted, and later bought Lindsey House, a distinguished old house in Cheyne Walk. Lane saw that Lutyens's light, well-mannered classicism was exactly appropriate to the paintings he wanted to hang by Sargent, Tonks and Augustus John; accomplished, unsubversive and slick. No disturbing post-Impressionist awkwardness for him. Lane commissioned Lutyens to put a marble floor in the hall and panelling on the walls. Lutyens designed the garden too, adding a

---

*Drogo's unusual building methods have made it expensive to maintain. Drewe's solid granite walls are porous, the flat roof leaks and the steel beams which Lutyens used to support his concrete floors are rotting.

classical screen, making a round pond beneath the ancient mulberry tree and punching statue alcoves into the old brick garden wall.

Lane shared Lutyens's love of Wren, and sought his advice on restoring the ruined Kirby Hall, Northamptonshire, a project which Ned estimated at £200,000.[13] That hare-brained scheme did not come off – the perilously speculative nature of Lane's business meant that he lived on a financial roller-coaster. Nonetheless Lane brought Ned important introductions. Networking was his joy, and like Ned, he excelled at persuading people to spend their money. It was probably through Lane that Ned met Arthur Grenfell, a City speculator to whom Lane sold a collection of old masters, including Titian's *Portrait of a Man in a Red Cap*, which Grenfell bought for £25,000 in 1909. Having made a fortune out of Canadian land shares and married a second wife, Grenfell commissioned Lutyens to make additions to Roehampton House, Putney. It was a rushed job, employing 200 men by day and night. Grenfell thought it 'one of the nicest and most beautiful places near London', but his lavish summer balls and fireworks already seemed boringly old-fashioned to the weary, jaundiced eye of younger men such as the prime minister's son Raymond Asquith.[14]

Lane also brought Lutyens work in South Africa. His contact was Mrs Lionel Phillips, wife of the South African diamond magnate, whom he advised about buying pictures for the art gallery she proposed to create in Johannesburg. Lane advised her to buy modern art, not old masters, and when she failed to find a South African architect, Lane telegraphed Lutyens.

'Impossible abandon work here immediately consult Baker partnership,' Ned telegraphed in reply, but Mrs Phillips's invitation and consultancy fee of £1,000 proved too good to refuse. South Africa, with its buoyant architectural opportunities, had excited him ever since 1897, when he angled for the Cape Town Cathedral project (which Baker built); and the creation of the Union of South Africa in 1910 offered handsome opportunities for government building.

But South Africa was Herbert Baker's territory, and before sailing Lutyens consulted Baker. Baker replied telling him not to come as there was no work. The letter was opened by Emily; by the time it arrived Lutyens was steaming towards the Cape.

Before leaving London on 17 November 1910 he went through a list of sixty jobs ('Isn't it a lot?') with A. J. Thomas, now his head man. On board the SS *Saxon* with his assistant Hall he played the game of pretending to be at Queen Anne's Gate, asking each morning for a list of the day's appointments and winding up by asking Hall to call a taxi. By Madeira he had cleared his desk ready to work on Castle Drogo. Distracted by the wash and roar of the water and the ship's persistent creaking, he designed a castle whose multi-levelled plan resembled the many decks of an ocean liner, powered by great coal boilers that roared and purred in the far-distant basement. Each morning as he lay in his bath he calculated the ship's pitch from the angle of the water level.[15]

Baker came to Cape Town to meet him. Unaware that Baker had tried to stop him, Ned was effusive and affectionate, playing Brer Ned to Brer Baker, as they called each other. Baker showed him the work he had done since coming over as Cecil Rhodes's architect in 1891. Ned saw at once the magic of the veldt. 'No wonder the Boers fought for their country,' he wrote, secretly envying Baker's success. Baker's Union Buildings in Pretoria, which resembled Ned's London County Hall design with hemicircle and Wren cupolas, were already going up. Ned must have felt bitter about the failure of his County Hall designs. Later, he criticized Baker for the 'colossal errors' he made in Pretoria, 'for which he said he was sorry', but at the time he tried to outdo him and succeeded only in making a fool of himself.

Mistaken with his balding head for the dull Governor-General Sir Herbert Gladstone, Ned alternately clowned and pontificated. He lectured the South Africans, Botha and Smuts, on how they should build in their own country, and he irritated Hugh Lane by playing the fool at gallery committee meetings. The talk of projects became giddier – a town plan, a university, a cathedral; his mind outran his pen, and letters home dissolved into incoherent scrawl. The jokes never ceased. The Bishop of Cape Town came to tea wearing an amethyst ring 'as big as the tea cup he offered me. Of course I tried to take the ring and he nearly spilt the tea.' Mr and Mrs Pim, whom he met at dinner, were embarrassed to be asked 'if there were any pimples'.[16]

Ned wrote to Baker on Boxing Day from the train on the journey home, thanking him for his 'unwavering hospitality. Not a carping or ungenerous word to me, who must by my very nature have tried you sorely.' He had indeed. So sorely that Herbert Baker never forgave him.

Baker had himself suggested that Lutyens should design the Rand Regiments' Memorial, and he supported Lutyens's claim for the art gallery, though both jobs were 'to my obvious disadvantage'. He helped overcome opposition from South Africans, who objected to appointing an architect from overseas. But Lutyens seemed totally unaware of his debt to Baker. On the contrary, on his return to England, he behaved (Baker related) 'with such a ruthless want of consideration for the wishes and instructions of his friends and clients that I wrote to him that his methods would make it difficult for me ever to collaborate with him'.[17]

Ned wrote to Baker on 20 January 1911, lecturing him on classical architecture, boasting of Heathcote and criticizing Baker's work, apparently oblivious to the fact that Baker had designed public buildings in Pretoria which were far more prestigious than anything Lutyens had yet been called upon to design.[18] No wonder Baker was annoyed; the younger man must have seemed cocky, conceited and condescending.

At least Ned succeeded in clinching the deal with Mrs Lionel Phillips who, pushed by Hugh Lane, agreed to his elegant art gallery design. (As he told Baker: 'You say New Country, therefore Rough. I say New Country, therefore Slick.') The only additional commission that materialized was the classical design for the Rand Regiments' Memorial.

There was something slightly desperate about Ned's clowning. Being a balding forty-two-year-old who refused to grow up wasn't easy. Never Never Land was not a comfortable place to live, as his friend J. M. Barrie had discovered.

Unable to repeat the critical success of his early plays, Barrie was tortured by insomnia. Ned sometimes gave him dinner at 2 a.m., and he watched as first Barrie's marriage disintegrated and then Mrs Llewellyn Davis, 'that pretty graceful woman' whom Barrie loved, died cruelly of breast cancer. Emily thought Barrie 'very man-like' and indifferent to his wife's feelings. Neither Emily nor Ned knew of Barrie's sexual impotence, the guilty secret at the heart of his tragedies. Still less did they admit the failure of their own sex life. Ned's instinctive reaction to such difficult issues was to play the fool, but his evasion only made Emily all the more determined to seek fulfilment elsewhere, as Ned was well aware. He wrote to her anxiously from on board ship: 'You are not advancing by great leaps and bounds along your new road and leaving me behind; are you? Don't leave me, darling – at least not very far behind – behind you I always shall be but don't let the space between us get too long and wide.'[19]

Somewhere off the coast of Africa Ned's letter crossed with a letter written by Emily from a smog-bound London. 'Shall we ever pick up the strings of this time,' she wrote. 'I feel as if I were growing at such a pace – I can hardly keep up with myself.' She was like a woman in love, glowing with the excitement of her new life. She celebrated New Year 1911 by staying at a suffragette health farm, sleeping in a wooden hut, doing exercises and taking air baths in the January chill, wearing only a skimpy flowered muslin chemise and sandals. Accompanied by a broken-down suffragette and an elderly depressive who never spoke, Emily found it 'such a rest having no one to think of but myself', and emerged 7½ lbs lighter and feeling ten years younger.[20]

At Queen Anne's Gate, the Lutyens office was growing as the business boomed. In January 1911 the young New Zealander W. H. Gummer joined and Lutyens set him to work on Drogo, the biggest job in the office. 'Mr Lutyens is a real gentleman to work for and the staff are equally pleasant so that as regards environment I am lucky,' wrote Gummer. In spite of being given the hardest job, Gummer enjoyed himself. Next day he wrote: 'Am more at home in Mr L's office. Ripping work. RA in evening.'[21]

For Lutyens's biographer, Christopher Hussey, the early months of 1911 were Lutyens's flood tide, when his career and powers reached their peak. Little knowing that the age of humanism was doomed, Lutyens was its last protagonist, pouring out a flood of designs while modernist barbarians massed at the gates. April 1911 was an iconic moment: grand projects materialized. Lutyens sent off designs for Drogo revisions, a Trafalgar Square Memorial for Edward VII (abortive) and the Rand Regiments' Memorial, while the Rome authorities agreed to make his exhibition pavilion the permanent building that became the British School at Rome.

The grand climacteric was, in fact, clouded by anxiety. It was not Ned but Emily who was triumphant. Ned memorialized the dead with pure, humanist design, but his heart wasn't in it. 'I must go on and stick to my work,' he wrote on 19 April, 'and yet I feel I don't work hard enough somehow. It seems a mere slavery unless you are by and near me.' Writing despairingly on interminable train journeys, he implored Emily to come home from her theosophical lectures, which took her to Bath. '*Do* be very careful what you do there on account of my King [Edward's] Memorial,' he wrote. Bath was so very near to the Horners at Mells, where he was staying, and he worried about gossip.[22]

Emily had no intention of surrendering her new-found freedom. Staying with the Horners at Mells would be torture to her, she explained, while a theosophical congress in Bath was 'a great lark'.

'Society touting and planning' was unworthy of them both, and 'you would not really love me if I was the kind of wife you sometimes imagine I ought to be'. 'I know I am odd and perhaps growing odder,' she wrote, but escaping from society made her feel like a flower transplanted from a cold clay soil into sunshine. 'I now feel daily as if I was opening out and growing and stretching glad petals to the sun.'[23]

Ned could hardly complain at her happiness, even if she was a 'wallflower not a peony', but theosophy frightened him. True, architecture took him away from her, but not into 'vasty mists' as theosophy did. 'Architecture is divine and spirit-making in its best sense, but it never separates from the world – it brings divine essence to the world – I am frightened of the Buddha that sits on *her* haunches and star gazes and lives in a world away from the surface of this [world].'

Emily was unrepentant. She couldn't follow him into the mysteries of architecture, but theosophy came naturally to her. 'I seem to have embarked on a shoreless sea of wonder and beauty and gladness – only it does make most things seem a little empty and wearisome by comparison.' At least Ned had an intuitive understanding of the mystical imagination, which the still faithful Arthur Chapman utterly lacked. 'Darling, thank God I have married you not Chippy,' she wrote, only now admitting the intimacy that once existed between them.[24]

Architecture kept Ned sane. Bringing loveliness into *this* world provided an escape from Emily's star-gazing. Consols, which had floated the Surrey houses a decade earlier, were still depressed – down from a 1903 average of $90\frac{3}{4}$ to a 1911 average of $79\frac{7}{8}$ – but money was being made in the City, and this brought new clients – bankers and financiers. Emulating Norman Shaw thirty years earlier, he became architect to the partners of Barings Bank, now recovered from the crash of 1890 to become a cautious, traditionalist trading house. For Cecil Baring he restored 26A Bryanston Square, letting in the sun with south-facing bay windows, and he altered 28 Portman Square for Alfred Mildmay. Barings also brought Lutyens the patronage of Gaspard Farrer, a partner in the bank; kindly and cultured, Farrer was a genius with figures but (according to his friends) 'essentially Aristocratic socially and economically'. For the bachelor Gaspard and his solicitor brother Henry of the family firm of Farrer & Co., Lincoln's Inn, Lutyens smartened up the interior of a large house at 7 St James's Square.

The Farrer brothers commissioned one of Lutyens's last pre-war country houses: The Salutation, near Sandwich. A bachelor pleasure house built next to a gasworks which was supposedly good for Gaspard's asthma, The Salutation is a superb paradox. It is a brick box modelled on an eighteenth-century town house so when Henry Farrer went to the country for the weekend it seemed as if he went to work. But at The Salutation Lutyens subtly undermined the eighteenth-century programme. The plan is not simple and axial but complex and circulating. No eighteenth-century house was ever designed like this. A huge central staircase, which occupies one-third of the volume, is lit by a section cut from the side of the house. Instead of an eighteenth-century pediment the house has a very un-eighteenth-century hipped roof, which nevertheless contrives to imply a pediment.[25]

Not all Lutyens's work was slick, social and symmetrical. He could still evoke the English dream, the old deep country life, as he did at Great Dixter, near Northiam (Kent), a fifteenth-century house he restored for Nathaniel Lloyd. Lloyd was typical of Lutyens's clients of a decade earlier; having made a fortune from colour printing, he retired at the age of forty-two to devote himself to family life in Kent. In 1910 he bought Dixter, a tumbledown farmhouse which had been on the market for ten years, and invited both Lutyens and Ernest George to propose schemes. Lloyd rejected George's scheme for a brutalist Edwardian remodelling in favour of Lutyens's historically sensitive restoration. Ned thought it 'cruel and callous the way our preservation destroys the work of our fathers', and at Dixter he lovingly reconstructed the original builder's intentions.

The great hall had been partitioned in the Tudor period when it was sliced horizontally into three storeys reached by ladders. Gutting the Tudor interiors revealed the fifteenth-century hammer-beamed shell, which Lutyens enveloped in a steep, sweeping roof. Nathaniel Lloyd, who became an authority on traditional building, wrote that 'nothing has been done without authority, nothing has been done from imagination; there has been no forgery'. It is as if one craftsman was speaking to another across five centuries, though today's conservationists might frown at Lutyens for transplanting thither a ruined Benenden yeoman's house named The Old House at Home. Bought for £75, the building was carefully numbered, photographed, dismantled and re-erected at Dixter, where it was incorporated into the house.[26]

In May 1911 Mrs Besant arrived at Charing Cross Station from India, bringing with her the two Indian boys, Krishnamurti and his younger brother Nitya. Emily was among the waiting crowd of theosophists.

She had eyes, she remembered, only for Krishna, an odd figure in a Norfolk jacket with enormous, dark, vacant eyes. One woman in the crowd almost fainted, so overcome was she by Krishna's aura.

At first Emily's feelings towards the fifteen-year-old Indian boy were strongly maternal. Krishna appealed to her protective instincts in a way that her own son, Robert, now eleven, did not. Robert was difficult, small for his age, backward at school and had no friends. His bad reports from Miss Motto's school for girls produced regular end-of-term anguish, when Emily scolded Ned for taking no interest. But it was Krishna not Robert whom she longed to hug. Her heart bled when she saw him shivering at a cold May garden party in Oxford or suffering tortures of indigestion from the alien Western diet of milk and eggs enforced by Leadbeater, allegedly acting on the orders of the Master KH.[27]

Emily's rejection of Robert left scars which never really healed. In his unpublished autobiography he mentioned neither Krishna nor theosophy, but wrote bitterly of his mother, accusing her of 'an aggression that was not the least vigorous for being concealed under a manner of almost total loving kindness'. Emily could be ruthless, but Robert was too harsh. Her unhappy childhood made it hard for her to warm to her own children, but it left her with a deep-seated need for heroes. 'I am one of those people to whom hero-worship is the greatest joy in life. I want to be always at someone's feet.' Deprived of love as a child, she needed constantly to validate herself by adulating genius – brilliant and creative, like Ned, or spiritual and god-like as Krishna was. Of course, the genius could never live up to expectation; he must always turn out to have feet of clay, as poor Ned was discovering. Perhaps she could only be set free if the genius himself renounced his destiny, as eventually Krishna did, but that was to take two decades and almost destroy her family in the process.[28]

Emily's growing obsession with Krishna drove her into emotional dependence on Annie Besant. A skilled manipulator, Mrs Besant controlled her weird and unruly flock of fanatical middle-aged women, defrocked priests and paedophiles like a Marxist party leader, by multiplying organizations. Like Lenin or Rosa Luxemburg, she was the guardian of the shrine of doctrinal purity. With her privileged access to the Masters only she and Leadbeater were able to interpret the Masters' wishes with regard to promotions to the Esoteric Section or the still more exclusive Order of the Star in the East (OSE), formed to prepare for the coming of the World Teacher. Emily was speedily promoted to both and, like a good Brownie, rewarded with a five-pointed gold star. She was never happier than when travelling third class as a humble member of the entourage (Mrs Besant of course went first class), while Mrs Besant lectured to packed halls. 'How funny it seems for me to be writing to you from an hotel in the North, the tables are quite reversed!' she wrote gleefully to Ned from Bradford.

Unlike the Marxists, who could never be sure of delivering the socialist revolution on cue, Mrs Besant had already picked her messiah and, with the second coming scheduled for 1929, when Krishna would be thirty-two, theosophy was on a roll. As numbers swelled (13,000 in 1907, 16,000 in 1911) and money poured in, Mrs Besant presided over the education of the World Teacher. Krishna, she decided, should be educated at Oxford; the boys were put down for Balliol and New College and, though excused Latin, they received coaching in Shakespeare and arithmetic. Mrs Besant did her best to westernize and gentrify them. They dressed in suits made in Savile Row, exercised in Sandow's fashionable gym and took riding lessons in Rotten Row. This cut them off from their Indian roots but didn't make them English. When Emily took them to watch the Coronation of George V from Admiralty House, they walked home through the crowded streets. Krishna suffered agonies from his narrow, tender feet, encased in expensive but excruciatingly painful shoe leather, and he was taunted by voices from the crowd shouting 'Get yer 'air cut'.[29]

Emily and her children spent the summer at Varengeville. They rented a farmhouse, and Robert remembered 1911 as the hottest and loveliest summer ever. He and Barbie squabbled constantly, and Emily, who had convinced herself that Robert was so dense at school that he must be an artistic genius, arranged for him to have painting lessons. Jacques Emile Blanche, the 'Sargent of France', painted his portrait, while poor Barbie was shipped back to England in disgrace. Nothing was allowed to interrupt Emily's theosophical idyll. Wearing loose, flowing silk gowns (and, of course, the five-pointed star) Emily meditated beneath the clear azure skies amongst the pink and powder-blue hydrangeas that had once inspired Claude Monet. Sheltering from the fierce sun in the cool, convent-like rooms Ned had built at Le Bois des Moutiers, she whispered theosophy with Madame Mallet.

When Ned proposed to interrupt the idyll she was indignant. There was no bed, no meat, no wine. He must stay with the Mallets. 'Please bring your chequebook as I shall need some money,' she added tartly.[30]

Of course it was a disaster. When Ned tried to kiss her she flinched and pushed him away, complaining that he smelled of pipe smoke. As for sex, the very thought nauseated her. Ned was hurt and angry. Emily cried and he walked away.

Once Ned had left, Emily felt nothing but relief at having said what had been unsayable for so long. She wanted to lay her head on his shoulder, she told him, not lip kisses. Unfairly, she raked over the fiasco of their honeymoon love-making. 'I was left in constant pain and disappointment, and you never left me alone.'[31]

Ned needed her more than ever. Their rare sexual encounters, he ruefully admitted, found his 'body self rampant, aggressive, horrid'.[32] In an era of cynical marriages and sexual hypocrisy it apparently never occurred to him to take a mistress, and divorce was too scandalous to contemplate. Angry and unhappy, but never resentful or violent, he could see no alternative but to accept the role Emily had written for him.

Back in London in August 1911, as the temperature soared to 97°F and the House of Lords hammed up the constitutional pantomime over the Parliament Bill, Ned was irritable, sleepless and short-tempered. He snapped at the men in his office and worried that his temper was affecting his work. Approached by Mrs Besant to build a London headquarters for the Theosophical Society, Ned feared that her psychic powers enabled her to see into his eyes, which were red from lack of sleep and crying, but Emily was delighted. 'I shall begin to take an interest in your work at last,' she wrote.[33]

It wasn't an easy commission. Ned had no clear idea what Mrs Besant wanted, perhaps because she didn't either. 'I am working out a scheme for Mrs Besant in the train,' he wrote. 'What the drawings will look like I can't imagine.' Cost was a worry too. Mrs Besant chose an expensive site in Tavistock Square and planned to spend £50,000. 'How she is going to raise the money I don't know,' wrote Ned. Emily replied ordering him to waive his fee, a hefty £2,500 which he could ill afford to give away. Being christened Vishvakarman (architect to the gods) by Annie and given honorary membership of the society was scant consolation.

Annie knew very well where the money was to come from: Miss Mabel Dodge, the American heiress, whom Emily had helped to convert (she had once taken Ned on a Baltic cruise). No wonder Emily climbed so quickly up the spiritual ladder. Emily thought Miss Dodge 'the most nobly generous woman I have ever met'. Her millions provided salaries all round and allowances for Krishna and Nitya, funding a theosophical gravy train. Crippled by arthritis and confined to a wheelchair, Miss Dodge was 'a dear', Ned thought, with a deep gruff voice; she lived in St James's Place and West Side House, Wimbledon with her companion, the smartly dressed Lady De La Warr, who resembled a small wire-haired terrier.[34]

Strong-minded women everywhere were flocking to theosophy, which cut a swathe through Ned's clients. At Wittersham, Alfred Lyttelton's widow DD meditated in the sitting room Ned had made for her. Down the road at Moon Green lived Violet Markham, feminist and heiress, also afflicted by theosophy. Lutyens made alterations to a round-roomed oast house for her, adding a miniature white-banistered Wittersham staircase. He sat talking until 1 a.m., finding her cruelly disappointed at missing marriage (she was thirty) and being childless. 'Her life she says is a penance for some previous existence. £6,000 a year is a fair assuager, though she does give away some £4,000 of it.'[35]

Things seemed to be falling apart. He thirsted for Emily – 'My poor old body is just aching for you. I feel ashamed to tell you but there it is – I just burst.'[36]

Railway strikes and dock strikes paralysed the economy. Walter Hoare sat up all night trying to get his drays out from the Old Basing brickworks. Everywhere there was violence beneath the façade of civilization. 'Manners seem skin deep and a thin crust that blisters and cracks easily and shows the cad rampant and triumphant.' Travelling on delayed, strike-bound trains Ned found it 'awfully difficult' to design a memorial for Edward VII, whose death had brought an end to the order Ned understood.[37]

Ned's response to the cracking of the old certainties was not modernism, nor (to his credit) a crusty toryism. Neither fascist nor theosophist, hating violence and distrusting quack religion, he escaped into a world of his own: a world of pure art. It was his good fortune to find a patron in the government of India; few other artists except perhaps Christopher Wren have found an institutional patron of such enduring generosity.

Chapter Eleven
India
1912–1913

Ned to Emily, 16 September 1913: 'Getting on with Government House and beginning to see my way... Chattris are stupid useless things.'

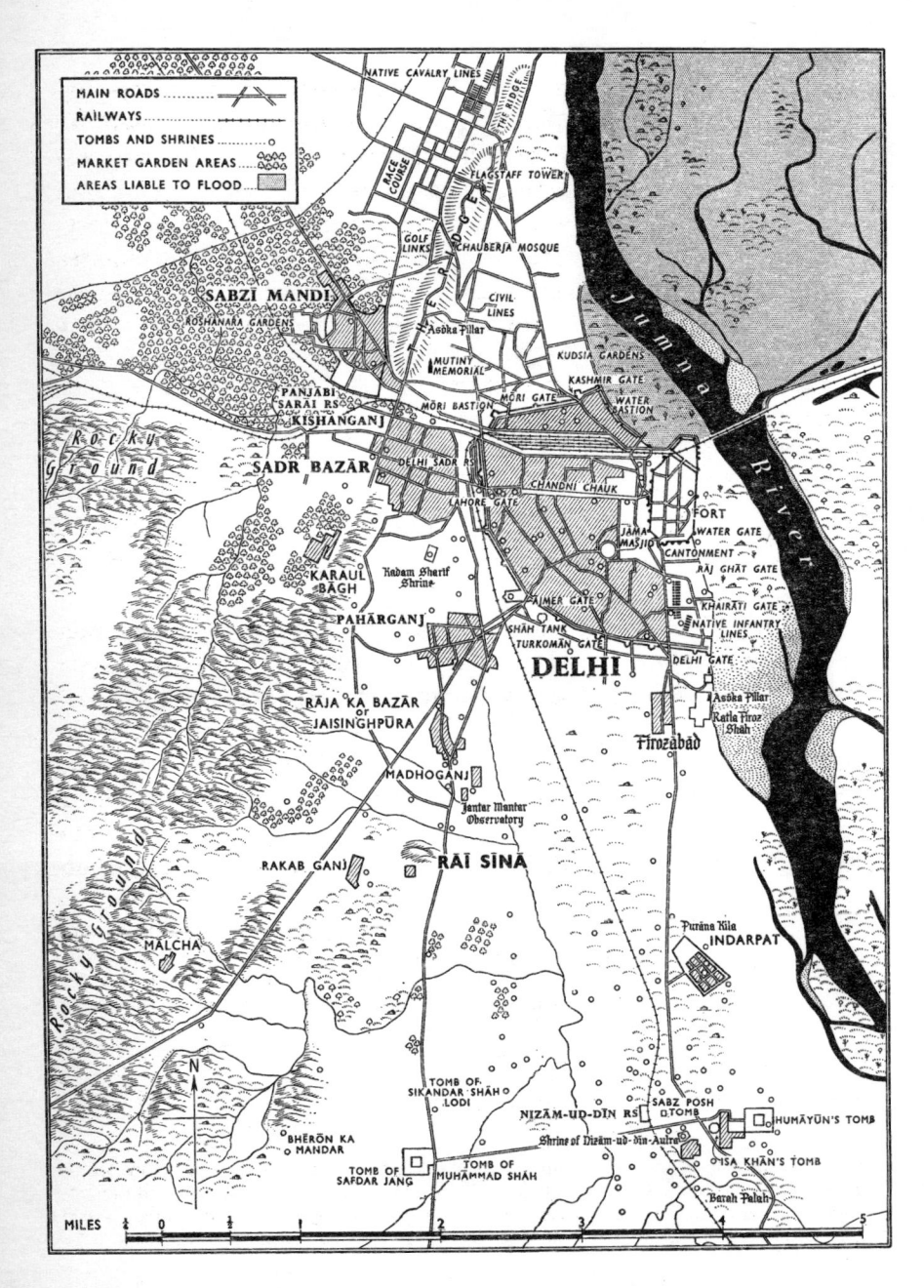

Map of Delhi and its environs at the time of the Delhi Planning Committee.

Lutyens's appointment to India is still something of a mystery. According to his biographer Christopher Hussey, who based his account on what Lutyens told him, it was (unlike most of his jobs) unsolicited and unsought-after. The story as Lutyens recalled it began when Sir Richmond Ritchie, Permanent Secretary at the India Office, summoned him early in 1912 and invited him to serve on a committee charged with finding a site for the new city of Delhi. Lutyens agreed and, ever hopeful, asked to design the principal buildings. They lunched afterwards at the Garrick Club and Lutyens gave his address in the visitors' book as Delhi.*

This anecdote is probably apocryphal. The Garrick Club visitors' book has no record of Lutyens lunching as a guest in 1912.[1] But the story underlines the importance of this new beginning; the beginning of the rest of his life. No longer the artist-architect of dream houses, Lutyens now became the establishment lackey, architect to governments, kings and empires.†

Lutyens believed that he owed his appointment to a chance meeting at a country-house party at Buckhurst with the Viceroy, Lord Hardinge, but official papers reveal an involved bureaucratic process. Hardinge wanted to get 'from home the very best architect procurable with town-planning experience', and Lord Crewe, the Indian Secretary, who knew Lutyens's work at Hampstead, where he had laid a foundation stone, consulted the Local Government Board and the RIBA. Reginald Blomfield, President of the RIBA, wanted the job

---

*In 1938 Lutyens was asked to write the history of the designing and building of New Delhi from 1912. 'It will begin,' he wrote, 'with my first interview with Richmond Ritchie.' The book was never written, but Lutyens collected a mass of documents about Delhi. He told his version of the story to Christopher Hussey, who had access to his papers. These seem to have since disappeared, but they form the basis of Hussey's account, which is the closest we have to the story as Lutyens would have written it.

†Lutyens's career as a country-house architect can be traced in society memoirs where he features as an elusive presence, often referred to merely as 'the architect'. After 1912 I follow him through the files of the India Office, now housed in the new British Library. Computerized, catalogued and little explored, this massive archive holds untold secrets about Britain's paper-obsessed Indian empire. Like someone rowing across a vast ocean with a bucket, I dip my computerized catalogue choices into the deep, and come up with random gold: minutes of the committees that Lutyens entertained and infuriated, typed correspondence of Indian civil servants, politicians' diaries and mandarins' letters home.

himself, but suggested Lutyens, an act of generosity he was later to regret. The other name to emerge was that of H. V. Lanchester, planner of Cardiff, who was already in India courting the Viceroy. Hampstead Garden Suburb clinched the decision in Lutyens's favour, and Crewe telegraphed his appointment to a sceptical Hardinge, who knew nothing of his work. 'I believe I am fixed up for Delhi,' Lutyens wrote jubilantly to Herbert Baker on 29 February 1912. 'As regards the building, who does it, they won't commit themselves. There will be more than one man can do . . . Oh what fun if we could come together on it.'[2]

Before he left on 28 March it was 'rush, rush, work, work, all thrilling and exciting' as he struggled to get on top of a cluster of projects: the British School at Rome, the Shakespeare's England Exhibition at Earls Court, Mrs Besant's Theosophical Headquarters and the King Edward Memorial. In between, there was lunch with Lord Crewe and an audience with the King. Emily warned him not to be flippant. When George V said, 'You are going to design the new buildings,' Ned replied, 'Yes, sir.'

Emily was in Amsterdam, acting as unofficial lady-in-waiting to Mrs Besant on a lecture tour, and she was unable to help him pack. Alone with Nannie, Ned struggled with hat boxes and solar topis, boot bags and bedding, filling shiny new black tin boxes with the elaborate formal wardrobe which etiquette dictated for Europeans in India. Emily was unrepentant. 'I don't regret having come because I have really been able to help Mrs Besant a little,' she wrote.

Emily and the children came to see him off at Victoria Station. Ned was close to tears. 'If we do a fine thing and get our chance it will be the most wonderful thing that ever happened,' he wrote from the train.[3] It was his forty-third birthday.

Paid for by the government, he travelled first class, crossing France by train and embarking at Marseilles. On board the P & O liner were the two other members of the Delhi Planning Committee. J. A. Brodie, the borough engineer of Liverpool, was a 'dear, broad matter of fact Midland middle-class thing'. Captain George Swinton, Chairman of the London County Council, 'a very pleasant fellow', was a dilettante with an irritating habit of talking as if making an election address, telling everyone that he, Swinton, was the envy of all men, having to design New Delhi.

Past Aden it grew hotter, and by Bombay Ned was 'in a perpetual bath of sweat', in spite of a thinner suit and new topi. At Bombay three

Indian bearers were presented to them. Swinton chose the best looking, Brodie the next and Ned was left with 'an old scallywag dressed in an uncouth dhoti'. His name was Persotum. Swinton's bearer stole his possessions and Brodie's was arrested for murder, but Persotum, who excelled at cleaning Ned's pipes ('I always have two clean ones going'), became Ned's closest Indian friend.

Bombay was Ned's first glimpse of British India and its hybrid, bombastic architecture, pointed arches and onion domes stuck on to a gothic substructure. He thought the buildings not worth seeing, but he warmed to the old club with 'its fine simple upstanding rooms full of ghosts of choleric old Indian Bob Webbs who lived and died and growled with their hearts in England'. India, he wrote, like Africa, 'makes one very Tory and pre-Tory feudal'. Sitting in the red-hot train for Delhi he felt an affinity too with the landscape. 'Hampshire is the mother of many scenes.'[4]

'The Delhi experts', as Lutyens, Brodie and Swinton were called, spent a month in Delhi, staying in pampered luxury in the Maiden's Hotel. The PWD (Public Works Department) provided a bungalow for their office, equipping them with a room each (Lutyens brought out his assistant Hall); they had secretaries, a typewriter and PWD engineers. Getting up at 5 a.m. to avoid the heat – the temperature rose to 105°F – they first examined the obvious site: the Ridge to the north of Delhi, scene of fighting during the Mutiny, drenched with history and the blood of Englishmen. This was where George V had laid foundation stones for the new city, but the experts swiftly decided that sentiment should not overrule practicality; the Ridge gave height but it was too narrow, confined and inaccessible for the development they envisaged, and they turned instead to the south of the old city.

The country here was a wilderness of ruins and scrubby undergrowth, impassable by motor car or cart. The experts conducted their survey from the back of an elephant, sweltering in waistcoats and stiff collars and ties as they lurched perilously down steep nullahs and stony ravines or along the narrow banks of overgrown canals brushed by overhanging trees. After a week the experts had settled on a site of flat land at Malcha to the south-west of the old city. It was, wrote Lutyens, 'a beautiful site – aspects, altitudes, water, health, virgin soil etc right and views across old Delhi and that wilderness of ruined tombs that form the remains of the seven older Delhis'.[5]

The Viceroy appeared a few days later. The man who was to play Pope Julius II to Lutyens's Michelangelo was a career diplomat who, at fifty-two, had achieved his life's glittering ambition. Tall, moustachioed and imperious, Charles, Lord Hardinge of Penshurst held sway like an oriental despot over Indian maharajahs, signalling disapproval or alliance by snubs or smiles. He filled albums with snapshots of the tigers he shot, lined out in rows like fish on a slab. A private press printed his correspondence and special timetables were issued when he travelled by train.

He stood at the pinnacle of a system of government closer to the autocracy of tsarist Russia than Edwardian Britain. Omnipotent in theory, he was impotent in practice. It was a government renowned for its leaks and tittle-tattle. 'All business is discussed at tea or at meals,' complained Edwin Montagu, the Indian Under-Secretary. 'Every member of the Government has his own crony in the India Office . . .' All on the make, all quarrelling, all with their own spies, agents and lady friends; this was government by gossip and dinner party.

Hardinge's letters show him anxiously scanning the Indian press, both native and European. Though an autocrat by nature, he was peculiarly thin-skinned. 'He has been so successful all his life,' wrote one observer, 'that he can't stand criticism easily.'[6] His decision to transfer the capital to Delhi made him acutely unpopular in Calcutta, and he was savaged in the English Calcutta press. This made him all the more determined to push through the change of capital, which became his special project.

When the Viceroy departed for the cool of Simla to prepare 'Tin Delhi', the temporary capital housed on the northern site, the experts remained behind. Brodie and Swinton quarrelled. Swinton was a 'map bumping illogical jumper' who irritated the methodical Brodie, a 'brow-furrowed slow-pacer'. Ned kept clear of disputes and tried to go his own way. He had decided on a site, but not how to treat it, and he needed to evolve a scheme before he next saw the Viceroy at Simla. He looked at hardly any mosques or temples, but inspected native houses in Delhi ('I must find out exactly how they live'). It was his first exposure to the real India, the world beyond the Raj, and the experience came as a shock. The 'mad-child' taste, the 'chromo prints of smirking women covered with a sort of small pox of lustre sequins', appalled him, as did the squalor, the smells and the strange and frightening food. He knew that the Viceroy was 'fixed on an Oriental style of architecture', and before leaving Delhi he went to the Red Fort and requisitioned the fountains to play 'so as to see the effect of water – sight and sound – down the carved cascades'.

Simla was cold, infested by monkeys ('I have an irrational dislike of our cousins') and an architectural nightmare. 'If one was told the monkeys had built it one would have said what wonderful monkeys they must be shot in case they do it again.' Between incessant luncheon parties, dinners and balls (he had forgotten to pack a stiff shirt, which was embarrassing, especially as people kept mistaking him for Hardinge: why had the Viceroy taken to attending state balls in a soft shirt, they asked), he worked on the sketches for Government House. We know what these were from a letter he sent to Baker in June[7] – the sketches are already similar in outline to the final result, except for the portico and dome. It is remarkable how quickly the scheme evolved, and also how little Lutyens had seen of Indian architecture when he conceived it. Many of the ideas had been stored in his head ever since he drew the Castle in the Air sketchbook for Barbara Webb back in 1893–6; he added a dome from St Paul's and a Palladian portico.

In Simla Lutyens made friends with Harcourt Butler, father of Rab, the cleverest man in India, but also (according to Edwin Montagu) a smooth and accomplished liar who was always waiting for the cat to jump. Butler guided Lutyens through the machiavellian intrigue of the viceregal court, telling him that 'Hardinge has Crewe [Indian Secretary] in his pocket, and Lady Hardinge has Hardinge, which I am to keep secret as he Butler alone knows it'. Lutyens acted accordingly. He joked with Lady Hardinge and showed his sketches to her husband. Hardinge he found 'delightful to work with, wide viewed, non-fussy and autocratic'. Soon he could report to Emily: 'I think I have got their ear and talked to Hardinge as himself and not the Viceroy.' Sure enough, Hardinge was converted, and he wrote to Crewe proposing Lutyens's appointment.[8]

The next step was to hook Lord Crewe. '*A great deal depends on Lord Crewe*: everything,' Ned told Emily. Back in London, Emily galvanized her cousin Lionel Earle, one-time private secretary to Crewe, now Permanent Secretary at the Office of Works. His influence was critical in getting Lutyens public work, though he was too good at covering his tracks to leave many traces. 'He is working splendidly for your interests with Lord Crewe, who seems much struck,' she reported. According to his memoirs, Lionel Earle told Crewe that 'Mr Lutyens had a greater capacity of absorbing the atmosphere of a foreign country than any architect I knew, but ... I should not recommend him to carry out the buildings did I not know that the Indian government were able to chain him between elephants as regards finance.' (The tenders for the

British School in Rome had come out twice as high as Lutyens's estimate.)⁹

In India, however, Lutyens showed no signs whatsoever of absorbing the architectural atmosphere. 'Personally,' he told Emily, 'I do not believe there is any real Indian architecture at all, or any great tradition. There are just spurts by various mushroom dynasties with as much intellect in them as any other art nouveau.' It was, he thought, the building style of children; architecture without intellect, at best veneered joinery in stone. When Emily asked if he was 'glamoured' of India, he was scornful. 'The very low intellects of the natives spoil much and I do not think it is possible for the Indians and whites to mix freely,' he wrote.

Nor did Lutyens keep his views to himself. His cultural chauvinism and his dismissive attitude towards Indian architecture raised eyebrows even among the English. Harcourt Butler, who thought him 'excellent company' and 'one of the most amusing creatures I have seen', reported that 'He is full of paradox and can see nothing in the Mogul architecture. Bad materials and good decoration. By bad materials he means rubble faced with stone or marble, which is what the buildings including the Taj are. Good enough for me, none the less.' It wasn't good enough for Lutyens though. The Taj, he wrote, 'is wonderful but it is not architecture and its beauty begins where architecture ceases to be'.*

Back in Delhi, Ned worked on his drawings while Brodie and Swinton thrashed out the wording of the report. He returned home in July 1912 confident that he had got all he wanted – 'my site, my layout etc, so I am pleased,' he wrote, mentally estimating his Government House buildings at £1 million.¹⁰

In India Ned had heard ominous rumours about Mrs Besant and Alcyone. Emily dismissed the rumours as spiteful gossip, but the intelligence officers of the India Civil Service kept files on Mrs Besant.† The rumours concerned Krishna's father Naraniah who demanded Krishna's complete separation from Leadbeater and threatened a

---

*In 1923 Lutyens, by now more mellow, took Cecil Baring and his daughter Daphne round the Taj Mahal. 'He said it only looked right when seen from the front,' Daphne remembered. 'When viewed from anywhere else it became, he said, "untidy".'
†The intelligence officer Francis Younghusband dismissed theosophy as adapted only to 'neurotic and partially educated ladies', but feared that Mrs Besant did real harm by making Hindus believe themselves superior to Europeans.

lawsuit depriving Annie of custody of the boys. Naraniah was inspired and financed by Mrs Besant's enemies among the orthodox Hindus, who wanted to expel her from the Central Hindu College at Benares which she had founded. She smuggled Krishna and Nitya out of India, where they had returned the previous winter, and sent them secretly to Taormina in Sicily, where Leadbeater presided over Krishna's crucial second Initiation which, conveniently enough, he judged to be imminent. From now on, Krishna and Nitya lived as fugitives, moving from one secret place to another, hiding from their enemies in India, whom Mrs Besant feared planned to kidnap them.

Deprived of Krishna as well as Ned, Emily was bored and listless. Her life, she wrote, could be summed up in four words – children, servants, friends, meetings. Not even her involvement with the Temple of the Rosy Cross, a new theosophical sect founded by James Wedgwood, could distract her. Wearing a long white satin gown trimmed with crimson and gold and a Knight Templar's headdress and carrying a sword, Emily lit a ritual candle for each World Teacher, leaving the last unlit for Krishna. 'I worked myself into a state of spiritual ecstasy at every meeting,' she wrote, 'always picturing to myself the day when Krishna's "divine hand" would light that unlit candle.'[11]

At Bloomsbury Square the telephone never ceased ringing, and she was obliged to employ a secretary at 10 shillings a week. The children succumbed to whooping cough, and Emily herself to colitis, which necessitated daily enemas. Her doctor told her that if she accompanied Ned to Indian she would get dysentery and die. Then her sister Con suffered a severe stroke which left her a permanent invalid. Emily brought Con from her flat to Bloomsbury Square where, installed in the drawing room with two nurses in attendance, Con made a slow, partial recovery.[12]

On 19 July 1912 Ned returned home from India. A few days later Emily departed with the children for the summer to a rented house at East Runton in Norfolk.

Alone in London, Ned had no time to miss Emily. 'I am very busy – early and late – working hard at Delhi.' He needed to produce drawings of Viceroy's House to show the King at Balmoral in September, and he worried that the King would insist on the Mogul style. 'Fancy Shakespeare being asked by Elizabeth to write an ode in Chaucerian metre,' he wrote, thinking perhaps of the half-timbering replica he had designed for the Earls Court exhibition of Shakespeare's England that summer. Meanwhile, 'the town planning of Delhi must wait (it does not affect the designs for Government House I think) until all the reports etc come in'.[13]

Waiting for the town planning was a mistake. While Lutyens lobbied to gain his palace, the Viceroy was busy unpicking all that the Delhi Planning Committee had done. Lanchester, whom Hardinge had originally favoured, came out to Delhi as the experts went home, and made a far better impression, doing more work in one month than the experts had done in three. 'I have not a high opinion of the business capacity of the Delhi experts,' wrote Hardinge on 27 August, 'and the moment it came to my seeing their proposals actually on the spot at Delhi, where I went at the end of July, I was convinced of their impracticability and lack of common sense.' In his memoirs he described how he visited the Malcha site, asked to be left alone for a quarter of an hour and then pronounced the site impossible. Mounting his horse he galloped over the plain to a hill named Raisina and announced, 'This is the site for Government House.'[14]

But, as it happened, instead of pressing the case for Raisina, Hardinge turned back to the original northern Ridge site, acting on the advice of PWD engineers who warned that the Malcha site would entail clearing a suburb of 35,000 people. Inspired by Lanchester, he criticized Lutyens's town layout – the avenues were too long and too wide – and demanded an oriental style. 'Can you not imagine how splendid a white Government House with red tiles and a gilt dome would look?' he asked Lutyens.

Lanchester's manoeuvres infuriated Lutyens. The man looked 'like a Labour member', he told Swinton, and the Catherine wheel plan he sent was commonplace and boring, 'just a carpet pattern, and no sense of skyline and realities'. As for the Viceroy, Lutyens attempted to trump him by 'playing the King card'. At Balmoral (9 September) he found the King sympathetic although Crewe the cautious Indian Secretary had warned him not to commit himself. The impression you get, Ned told Emily, is 'two blue eyes and very large moustachios carefully groomed. A kilt and sporran complete.' George V thought the drawings 'beautiful'. So did the Queen, who remembered Ned from Holy Island, where the cobbles had hurt her feet.

In his report to Hardinge, Lutyens stressed the King's approval, explaining 'how natural and Indian a western motif can look, treated for the Indian sun *with* Indian methods applied *without* throwing away the English tradition and clinging too much to the curiosities of a less intellectual style'.[15] This was to be the guiding principle of the synthesis he achieved at Government House.

As for the site, Lutyens reported that the King was 'very strongly' against the northern Ridge – 'He preferred our original site'. (Curiously enough, the King always agreed with Ned in their architectural conversations.) Swinton, who personally favoured the northern site, and who was bombarded by weekly missives from Hardinge, felt acutely uncomfortable, squeezed between the King and the Viceroy. The question of the site really turned on who was to be appointed architect, he told the King's private secretary. 'If Lutyens is to be responsible for Government House I feel ... that we must defer to his views as to the management of sites.' If, on the other hand, there was to be a competition, the position would be quite different.[16]

'I am very sorry for your worries about India, but I suppose they are inevitable,' wrote Emily somewhat snappishly. Spending the summer with Arthur Chapman and the children in a leaking, fungus-infested house in Norfolk, she felt neglected and unloved, 'lost and deserted' as Ned hurried importantly between Balmoral, Ireland and Lindisfarne, rarely answering her letters or telling her of his whereabouts.

When Leadbeater, whom she had not yet met, invited her to stay with Robert and Barbie in Genoa, she jumped at the chance. Ned was unwilling; he worried that the children were too much under the influence of theosophy, especially Robert, whose chief friend was Krishna. 'I think Robert must have intimacies and friendships with English boys and not be so influenced by the darkie ones,' wrote Ned. He joked that Robert was John the Baptist to Krishna's Jesus, but he worried that Leadbeater would cast evil spells and sexually abuse his son. 'If Robert does go bad or mad or worse will no responsibility rest on us?' But he knew that he couldn't stop Emily, merely imploring her not to tell the children how he felt. 'I hold their affection by necessarily so slight a thread – a word from you might cut it.' Emily responded by begging him to give more time to the children, 'that is, if you want in any way to influence them ... It is difficult to put you much into our lives when you are never there.'

To Emily's request that Robert, who was making little progress at King Alfred's School in Hampstead and wanted to be a painter, should be given art lessons, Ned replied that he should learn geometry and sciagraphy – the art of drawing shadows. 'To know what shapes a shadow could be ... It is no use starting off painting pictures – I don't mean to discourage it – for the fun of it! but it is not serious unless it teaches observation.'[17] Shadows were crucial to Ned's work in India, where wide cornices threw bold horizontals against bright sunlight, but sciagraphy was little use to a twelve-year-old boy. Nor was Ned's eccentric childhood a good model for his son, especially as Ned was always lamenting his own lack of education. Where his own children were concerned Ned was too self-absorbed to afford them time or imagination. His own family was too difficult, too threatening, too resentful; it was far easier to enchant the children of other people, who made no demands upon him. His daughter Mary remembered her burning shame at Knebworth Christmases, when Ned tipped extravagantly merely in order to keep face with the rich Lytton cousins.

Emily's visit to Genoa left mixed feelings. Leadbeater was exactly the type of man she longed to worship – big, bearded, barefooted, masterful and intuitive. In spite of a mincing walk and a drawling parson's voice, he was overpoweringly physical. 'He is a mixture of Wilfrid Blunt, Bernard Shaw and his Rev [Elwin] rolled into one,' wrote Emily in a letter that surely sent shock waves down Ned's spine. That Leadbeater hated women, had an obsession with Dracula and believed in vampires only made him the more fascinating. He charmed the children, especially admiring Barbie, for whom he magnetized an aspirin to cure a headache; she had the dubious honour of being the only girl he ever liked. While Robert irritated Leadbeater by aimlessly strumming on the piano for hours on end, Emily and Barbie spent days in the villa contentedly copying his genealogical charts showing the past lives of Alcyone – a compilation of gobbledygook that the strongminded Emily accepted uncritically.

But Leadbeater also made Emily feel small and rather silly. He ridiculed her idea for a new badge in the shape of a star with wings, and he mocked the Temple of the Rosy Cross with its ritual and dressing-up. Emily was shocked by his harsh words on the subject of Mrs Besant, whom she saw as a quasi-divine figure beyond criticism. Genoa left her deflated and disillusioned. Little wonder she felt 'a revulsion in favour of family life'.[18]

If this was a plea for Ned, he was too busy to heed it. Of course he worshipped Emily, comparing her to the feeling his best buildings gave – 'Still, level-eyed, clear and a brave quiet outlook as passive as a Holbein portrait'. But his mind was taken up with India, and when he thought of Genoa he remembered the 'shape of the blue sky seen above the cornices of the narrow streets' – an effect he realized at Delhi, where he designed a staircase court with coving open to the sky.

Back in England, Emily returned to her theosophical speaking tours, staying in cold houses where, horror of horrors, she was expected to wash in the family bathroom instead of having water brought to her room. She was lecturing in Cardiff when Ned left for his second visit to India at the end of November 1912. 'No distance can really separate us for we are one in our great love for each other,' she wrote. He wrote in his turn: 'I go to India full of courage and high endeavour in the likeness of that poor little knight that swore fealty to you some sixteen years ago.'[19]

By 29 November 1912, when the men working in his office stood on the steps of Queen Anne's Gate to cheer his departure, Ned knew that his appointment was more or less certain, though nothing had yet been formally agreed.

In the end it was Herbert Baker who was the deciding factor. Worried about the charge of cronyism if he appointed Lutyens, Hardinge pressed for a competition; Lanchester drew up the terms. Lutyens, after the humiliation of his failure at County Hall, dreaded this more than anything. But the work in Delhi was too great for one man, and to forestall a competition he suggested a partnership with Baker, who would design the Secretariats – the two massive blocks accommodating the Indian civil service, which Lutyens had planned flanking the approach to Government House. Whenever the threat of Lanchester or a competition loomed, Lutyens dashed off a friendly letter to Baker – the greater the threat the more extravagant the letter. Lutyens later claimed that he had secured the job for Baker, which was only partly true; Ned needed Baker just as much as Baker needed him.

Baker believed that he was appointed by the Indian civil servant Sir Thomas Meston to keep a check on Lutyens. Without consulting Lutyens, he wrote eloquently to *The Times* (3 October 1912) on the question of New Delhi's architectural style, very publicly joining the debate as well as infuriating Lutyens, who felt that Baker was stealing his glory. On 26 October Lutyens saw Sir Thomas Holderness, Permanent Under-Secretary at the India Office, who asked whether he was willing to collaborate with Baker, if only to strengthen Crewe's hand in dealing with criticism. Lutyens telegraphed Baker immediately. 'Willingly co-operate,' wired Baker in reply, though he did have doubts which he explained by letter. 'I shall find it rather difficult to collaborate with you. You rather heartless in ignoring the human side of clients, I too tender-hearted perhaps.' He was still smarting from the ruthlessness that Lutyens had revealed in South Africa.

Waiting in the hall of the India Office before accepting his appointment, Baker looked up at a portrait of Warren Hastings. Any doubts he had about Lutyens were removed by the thought of the infinitely greater difficulties Hastings had faced in collaborating with his colleagues in India. Baker believed he was a man of destiny. When Emily saw him in London in December, she thought he looked 'older and not too well'.[20]

Nothing could be announced until Hardinge, as Viceroy, had made the final decision. Meanwhile 'kind Mr Barratt', a painter and friend of Hardinge, acted as intermediary and kept Emily informed. 'It would indeed be the perfect arrangement and what I have always wanted,' she wrote – 'that you and Baker should come into partnership'.

When Ned sailed into Bombay on SS *Osiris* on 13 December he was met by Persotum, his faithful bearer, and by a wire from Hardinge telling him to visit three Mogul cities, Mandu, Indore and Lucknow. Hardinge had apparently gone 'clean mad on Indo-Saracenic' again, but Ned was reassured by letters from Lady Hardinge and Valentine Chirol, *The Times* Indian expert, explaining Hardinge's political agenda – this was a gesture to the Indian princes who wanted an Indian style. The trouble with Hardinge, confided Ned's gossipy friend Harcourt Butler, was 'the way he changes his mind and plays to the native gallery etc'.[21]

There was pressure from England for an Indian style too. A storm had blown up over the architecture of the new city: a Battle of the Styles of the kind that made Ned uneasy, lacking as he did Baker's journalistic skill in penning articles for *The Times*. The novelist Mrs Belloc Lowndes attended a lunch party that January and wrote in her diary: 'There was a great deal of talk about the New Delhi and the way in which Mr Edwin Lutyens would do the work . . . they all thought it would have been better to employ Indian architects.'

The Battle of the Styles for New Delhi was essentially a political battle, with Hardinge urging an oriental style for political, not aesthetic reasons. 'I say,' responded Lutyens, 'what on earth can an Indian Rajah know about architecture and its ethics.' Even if Lutyens had a point, which was questionable, he failed to understand that, for men like Hardinge, architecture had to be a coded political language. The pointed arch, which Hardinge urged, was the functional equivalent of the Morley–Minto reform of 1909, which admitted Indians to provincial councils; it signalled an aspiration towards partnership between the British and the Indians.

The architectural language for this political programme was the style known as Indo-Saracenic, a hybrid of Victorian gothic and Islamic, which made much use of pointed arches and plaster decoration. One of its chief practitioners was the veteran Anglo-Indian* architect Sir Swinton Jacob, whose work (Daly College, Indore) Lutyens thought 'Very elaborate, cheap and oh! Absolutely in want of all that Haldane has described as clear thinking'.

'They want me to do Hindu. Hindon't I say,' punned Ned, and nothing he saw in Central India made him change his mind. The Durbar Hall at Mandu which Hardinge had admired was a room 25 feet wide requiring a wall 40 feet thick to support it. He found stone treated like timber and everywhere a 'wonderful made picturesqueness but no intellect'. 'I cannot allow the superiority of the Eastern over the Western mind,' he thundered, damning himself in the eyes of posterity as a chauvinist and a racist.[22]

Lutyens was cheated of his plan to 'have it out' with the Viceroy by a terrorist outrage. On 23 December, as Hardinge made his ceremonial entry into Delhi in a gorgeous howdah perched upon an elephant, he was horribly wounded by a bomb. The incident gave Lutyens a vivid insight into the vulnerability of the British. The 'sly slime of the Eastern mind' repelled and frightened him, and he foresaw nothing but disaster for a system of Indian self-government. 'I am not sure but that the only gentlemanlike thing we can do is to leave India,' he wrote. 'Poor India, she will have some iron-shod foot across her throat.'

Emily scolded him for taking 'such an extremely Anglo-Indian point of view when you really have had no possible opportunity of judging Indians fairly from their own standpoint'. Surely it was wrong, she urged, to condemn a whole nation as liars, 'when you only take that opinion second hand?' Her criticism makes Ned's racism even less forgivable; he was well aware that there was another point of view.

His contempt for Indian culture and his racist jibes can be excused only partly as the unthinking prejudice of his age and class. In him it went deeper; its subtext was fear. India and its culture were identified in his mind with theosophy, with the dangerous and immoral antics of

---

*Anglo-Indian in this context is a term for the British in India, not for those of mixed parentage.

Mrs Besant, with the depraved sodomy of Leadbeater and, above all, with Emily's weird relationship with Krishna. Indian sexuality terrified him. He thought 'the crime that Leadbeater has been libelled about is *so* prevalent in this country amongst the natives that I do not see how you can recognise it in a court of law without condemning and prosecuting thousands, millions of Indians',[23] while mixed marriage was 'filthy, beastly and they ought to get the sanitary officer to interfere'. India was a metaphor for everything that threatened his own family; the embodiment of fear and the dangers of the unknown.

Yet Lutyens was not really an imperialist. Certainly, he was no more imperialistic than the advocates of an oriental style. The Indo-Saracenic party had a political purpose, an agenda of control, which they believed could best be achieved by adopting Indian motifs. For all his insistence on the superiority of the Western architectural intellect, Lutyens was making an aesthetic judgement. He believed that art began where words left off; it was an end in itself. He wanted, quite simply, to build beautiful buildings.

Lutyens's appointment was officially confirmed by Hardinge soon after the bomb attack, but Lutyens found the Viceroy a changed man. Hardinge had lost his old self-confidence, and become petulant, indecisive and even more morbidly sensitive to criticism. 'The Viceroy changes his mind every time I see him,' complained Lutyens. On Crewe's orders, Hardinge dropped everything but Delhi, which was his special toy. 'He is mad keen about this and talks the wildest stuff about architecture,' wrote Harcourt Butler. 'But every Viceroy must have a hobby. Why not this one Delhi? His name will be associated with it and he will get all the praise and the blame.' He added: 'Personally I think that everything concerned with it is in a mess.'

Lutyens was trapped. No Hardinge, no Delhi; yet Hardinge was unfit and impossible to deal with. Ned tried to gain the Viceroy's ear by wooing Lady Hardinge, who now did much of her husband's work. He found her 'awfully plucky and intelligent but naturally fearsome of decisions which might be wrong unless [Hardinge] is a party to them'. Ned thought he knew where he was with her; this was the old, happy architect-client relationship, and soon he was joking, a sure sign that he felt in control. 'I will wash your feet with my tears and dry them with my hair,' he told her. 'True, I have very little hair, but then you have very little feet.' What he did not know was that his unguarded remarks were passed directly to the Viceroy, and the arch, flirtatious letters he wrote to the Vicereine were printed by the Viceroy's private press and as official documents circulated among sniggering ICS* officials.²⁴

In January 1913 Hardinge suddenly ordered a change of site back to the northern Ridge. This stunned the Delhi experts, who had drafted a report proposing the southern site at Raisina, and who now found their year's work wasted.† Edwin Montagu explained the reasons for Hardinge's volte-face in the diary he kept of his official trip to India. 'The viceroy is extraordinarily sensitive to press criticism and India is so much governed by dinner-table conversation that anything which focuses gossip is marvellous in its effect,' he wrote. The mischief had started with a letter in the *Pioneer* newspaper written by a lady novelist, Mrs Everard Cotes. Her letter caused a stampede. Lady Hardinge was warned that an 'ambitious city which was a failure would become known as "Hardinge's Folly" and she shuddered'. She told the sick Viceroy that all opinion favoured the northern site; His Excellency spent a sleepless night, was worse in the morning, sent for the experts and ordered a change back to the north.

Lutyens, Swinton and Brodie set wearily to work to prove conclusively that the northern site wouldn't do; it was too small and too restricted. Hardinge, who had by this time lost all confidence in the experts, questioned Lutyens's plan to provide a city of 6 square miles for 57,000 Europeans when, according to his figures, the Government of India numbered only 5,630 men. Lutyens was jeered for allowing four-acre compounds and planning streets wider than the Champs-Elysées. 'If we allow the Town planners to have their own way they will make our city ridiculous,' wrote Hardinge.²⁵

'I am inclined to think the political argument unanswerable,' wrote Montagu, who played a key part in persuading Hardinge that a decision to build a small city on the northern site would be seen as weakness, a change of policy prompted by the bomb. Having made the case for a large imperial city, the government must stick to it, especially when 'you have powerful enemies ... who object to you building Delhi at all'.

Chief among these enemies was Lord Curzon, who campaigned furiously against moving the capital to Delhi. By partitioning Bengal – one of the most disastrous blunders ever committed by the British – Curzon had provoked the unrest which triggered the decision to move

---

*Indian Civil Service.

†In June 1912 the Delhi experts favoured the flat southern site at Malcha, but they abandoned this in December 1912, when they turned to the Raisina site.

from Calcutta to a new site, and this made him all the more determined to oppose New Delhi. Curzon's correspondence with Hardinge's enemies verged on the treasonable but, as the Indian civil servant Fleetwood Wilson pointed out, 'the fact remains that the Tory party are making a party question out of the move to Delhi'.[26]

Party politics played into Lutyens's hands, as the Liberal government were forced to stick to Delhi for the sake of 'consistency'; but they also tied themselves to totally unrealistic estimates. Curzon had estimated, rightly in Lutyens's view, that the new city would cost £12 million, but Hardinge insisted on an arbitrary and unrealistic figure of £4.5 million – a figure apparently plucked out of the air by a PWD official in a railway carriage, and one which assumed a building estimate of 4d per cubic foot, for which, Lutyens told Montagu, 'you could not build a gardener's cottage in England'.

In Delhi in the winter of 1912–13 Montagu found Lutyens

> posing as usual, cheerful and dangerous as ever. He draws beautiful watercolour sketches of enormous Government Houses of white marble with tiny figures moving in them and deep blue skies. He refuses to look at anything about him, he hates Indian architecture as much as ever, he likes straight, final roads and wants everything levelled. Rocks and pine trees are hateful to him. He has absorbed nothing of the country. The word 'picturesque' he finds beastly. He has, I fully believe, great genius; but, uncontrolled, he will produce a building or buildings intended to insult the aspirations of everything Indian.[27]

Little wonder that Hardinge and his hard-boiled officials despaired; Lutyens must have seemed almost wilfully perverse, deliberately and obtusely talking himself out of a job he desperately wanted.

Baker arrived in February, and Lutyens travelled to Bombay to meet him. He found him 'so gentle and wise – a good fellow', adding ominously, 'I don't think he takes architecture as seriously as I do.' Ned took Baker to Agra. They saw the Taj Mahal and Akbar's ruined city of Fatepuhr Sikri, and Ned was scathing as ever: 'it is all pattern – just the same as on any carpet hung up, on ceilings, wall, inside or outside. The buildings are tents in stone and little more.'

Baker insisted on one major change to the city plan: the Secretariats, which he was to design, should be raised to the same great platform as Government House. His arguments were political and symbolic; placing the Secretariats, which housed the Indian Civil Service, on the acropolis with the Viceroy's Government House meant that the buildings would form a single composition, 'expressing unity in the instrument of government', as he put it. Lutyens was perhaps too preoccupied with the struggle against the southern site to examine the implications of raising the Secretariats – did he stop to consider the possibility that it might block the vista to Government House? – and he signed a joint report with Baker agreeing to the proposal.[28]

Baker was used to working with governments, and officials found him far easier to deal with than Lutyens. Fleetwood Wilson, who stood in for Hardinge, thought Baker 'by far the best of the bunch. Quiet, businesslike and resourceful.' 'I had no trouble with Baker,' Hardinge wrote pointedly in his memoirs. Soon he was using Baker to control the wayward Lutyens.

Before he left India in March 1913 Lutyens heard from his friend Harcourt Butler that the Viceroy had finally decided on the southern site. 'I am glad – any other decision would have been fatal – extraordinary how one distrusts any opinion but one's own in times of crisis,' he wrote.

The architects' fees were settled too. He and Baker were each to receive £35,000 over seven years with £8,000 in advance for the first year, reducing by £1,000 a year to £2,000 in year seven.

The voyage home was harmonious. Baker and Ned worked peacefully on their sketches high up on the captain's deck, alone, quiet and out of sight. 'Like being on a very large yacht by oneself.'[29]

Before leaving India Lutyens had heard that he had been elected to the Royal Academy, something that he apparently had hardly dared to hope for while the painter Edmund Poynter was President (1896–1918). His sponsor was Aston Webb, whom he had adopted as an unofficial patron in the profession. Many thought that Lutyens should have been elected years before.* Perhaps he was blocked by professional jealousy, or possibly his name was tarnished by stories of his eccentric painter father's feud with the Academy over the Venetian Secret. Old Charles was among the first to congratulate him.

Back in London, rushing between Ireland, Castle Drogo and Derbyshire, Ned cursed awkward clients including Mrs Norman, for whom he built The Corner House in Cowley Street, Westminster. 'She is so difficult and wants impossibilities and never does a thing I say. She

---

*Emily heard in May 1912 that he had missed being elected by three votes. 'They did not elect an architect or you would certainly have got it. This is good I think and I expect you are certain for next election of an architect.'

buys rubbish in Italy and wants it fitted in and expects me to design the noses [sic] of putti cherubs in places where cherubs should never go. Makes rooms larger than the site will hold and then wants to pack in anyhow essentials.' Barrow-in-Furness, where he designed an 'entertainment' house for Vickers Maxim, found him irritated and depressed. What use was it to build at all, he wondered gloomily, after seeing Furness Abbey, when great buildings in a very few hundred years were in ruins?[30]

Big schemes came to nothing. Part of the problem was that Ned had made no proper arrangements for supervising the office when he was away in India. A. J. Thomas, whom he had left in charge, was (thought Emily) not a gentleman, and 'not fit for such a post of responsibility'.

Emily urged Ned to 'get someone over Thomas or give up your work here', and Ned made an arrangement with the architect Curtis Green, whom he bumped into at a dinner party. Next day, he invited Green to call. 'Hullo Green! I like your work. Do you like mine?' Green thought it doubtful Ned had ever seen any of his work. 'Will you look in here and keep an eye on the boys while I am away? I go to Delhi tomorrow.' Green looked in most mornings, but it was still Thomas who ran the office. Thomas cost little to employ, since part of the arrangement was that he could take his own work, and Ned trusted him in spite of complaints that he was incompetent and, later, dishonest: in any case, Ned could never bear confrontation.

Hubert Worthington, who joined the office in 1912, remembered a busy, thriving practice. In the office, 'Lut' was king; he could do no wrong. 'We revelled in the flashing wit of the man, his creative flair, his unfailing imagination. He could memorize everything, and his capacity for work was terrific.' He told Worthington that he even designed in the bath, using the children's slates as drawing boards.[31]

One of the schemes Worthington worked on was the Dublin Art Gallery, the brainchild of Ned's friend, the Irishman Sir Hugh Lane. He planned to present the city of Dublin with a collection of thirty-nine continental paintings, mainly Impressionist works, by Manet, Mancini, Monet and Degas. Lane's gift was conditional on the Corporation providing a permanent gallery to house the collection, but his enemies in Dublin resisted all his attempts to find a site. Asked by Lane to design a gallery, Lutyens suggested an ingenuous solution to the Battle of the Sites: two galleries linked by a public bridge across the Liffey. William Walcot's perspective drawings captivated artistic Dublin. Yeats was enraptured by Ned's 'beautiful' classical design. 'Two buildings linked

(*Left*) Ned as boy, about twelve. Painted by his father Charles.

(*Below*) Sketch of The Hut inscribed 'Abandoned Oct 9th/1982/Restored to favour July 16th 93'. The Hut was the first Surrey cottage which Ned built for Gertrude Jekyll.

(*Below*) Sketch of Plazzoh, the fantasy house that Ned drew for Miss Jekyll in 1893. Later, he built her Munstead Wood, which was a modified version of Plazzoh.

(*Left*) Barbara Webb, Ned's friend and patron who introduced him to Emily.

(*Below*) *Castle in the Air*, c. 1894. Architectural fantasy, which Ned drew to amuse Barbara when she was dying of cancer. Note the sheep; Ned called her 'Baa-Lamb' and his cipher in all his sketches for her was a lamb.

(*Left*) Le Bois des Moutiers, Varengeville. Art nouveau 'dream house' in France, for Guillaume and Marie Mallet who introduced Emily to Theosophy. (*Right*) Tigbourne Court, for Surrey businessman Edgar Horne. Elaborate 'Surrey style' finishing made this commission expensive. (*Below*) Deanery Garden, the first of the houses Ned built for Edward Hudson, founder of *Country Life*.

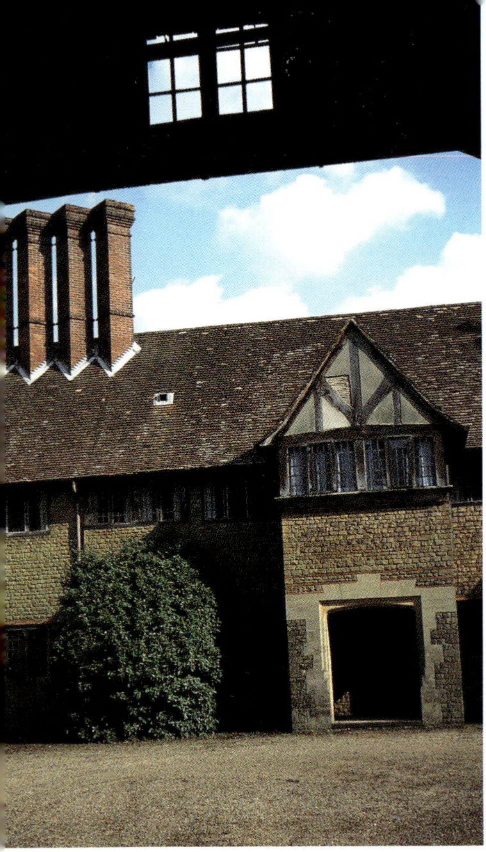
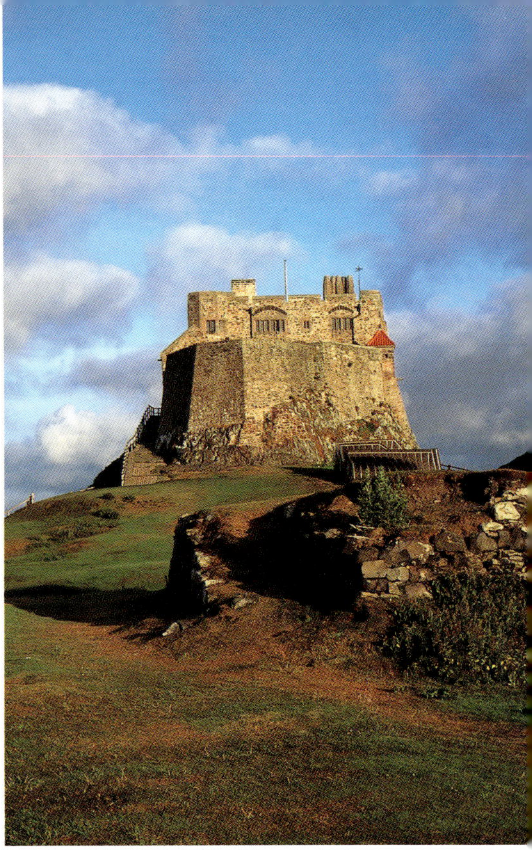
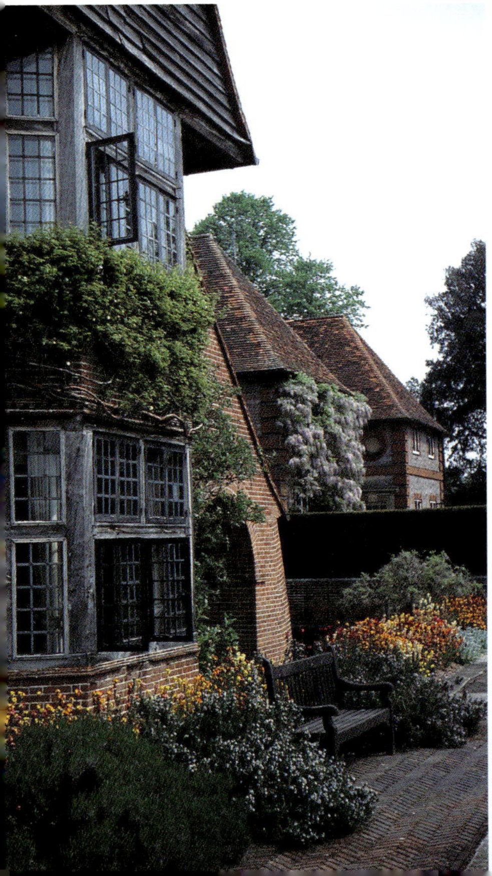
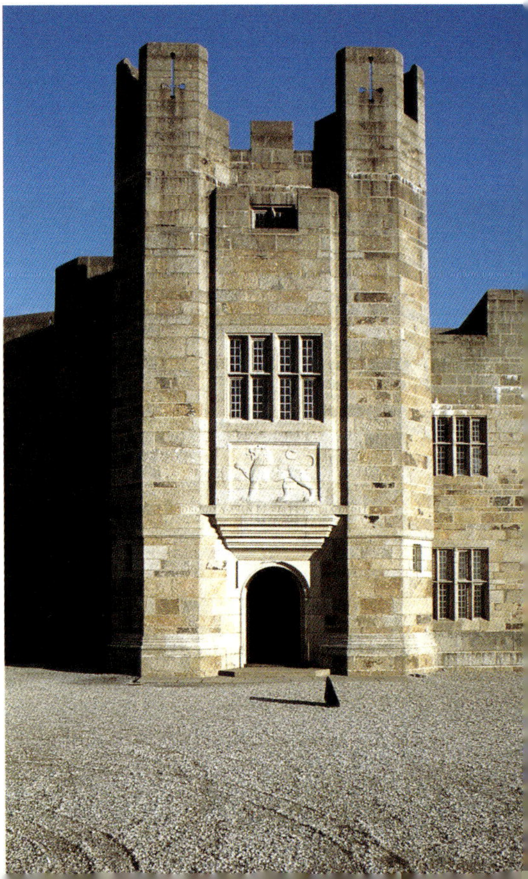

Marsh Court. Built of 'clunch' or chalk for Herbert Johnson with a Lutyens-Jekyll garden. This giant house is the closest Ned came to realising the design for the Little White House which he gave to Emily as an engagement present.

FACING PAGE

(*Above left*) The entrance to Orchards, which Ned built for William and Julia Chance, after they sacked their architect Halsey Ricardo. The window in the gatehouse roof lights only the open roof beams: a Lutyens joke. (*Above right*) Lindisfarne, the 'dream' castle which Ned built for Hudson. Ned's batteries grow out of the shell of a Tudor fort. The cobbled ramp frightened George V and hurt Queen Mary's feet.
(*Below left*) Folly Farm, which Ned and Emily borrowed from Mrs Merton ('Mertoni') for the summer of 1916. Ned designed the 'cowsheds' in the centre and the part in the foreground, which he added onto a house he had built a decade earlier.
(*Below right*) Castle Drogo, for Julius Drewe. Only one-third of the original design was actually built, but Drogo is still one of the finest fairy tale buildings of the twentieth century.

Cartoon Bust of 'Lut', made by the staff of his Delhi office (1917). The dome-like sola-topi is made up of pieces of the architectural models for Viceroy's House. Lutyens put this bust over the front door of his house in Mansfield Street.

FACING PAGE
(*Above*) Viceroy's House. View from the gates with the Jaipur Column in the foreground.
(*Below*) Viceroy's House. Front portico and dome surrounded by Buddhist *stupa*.

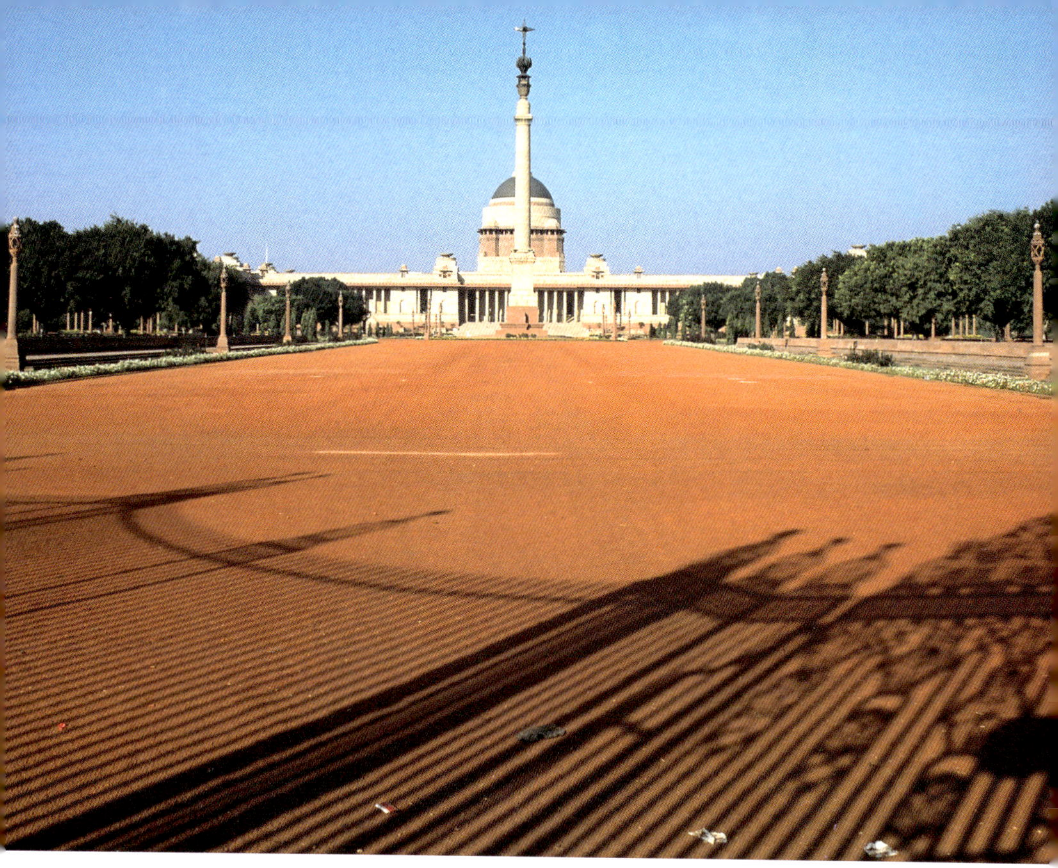

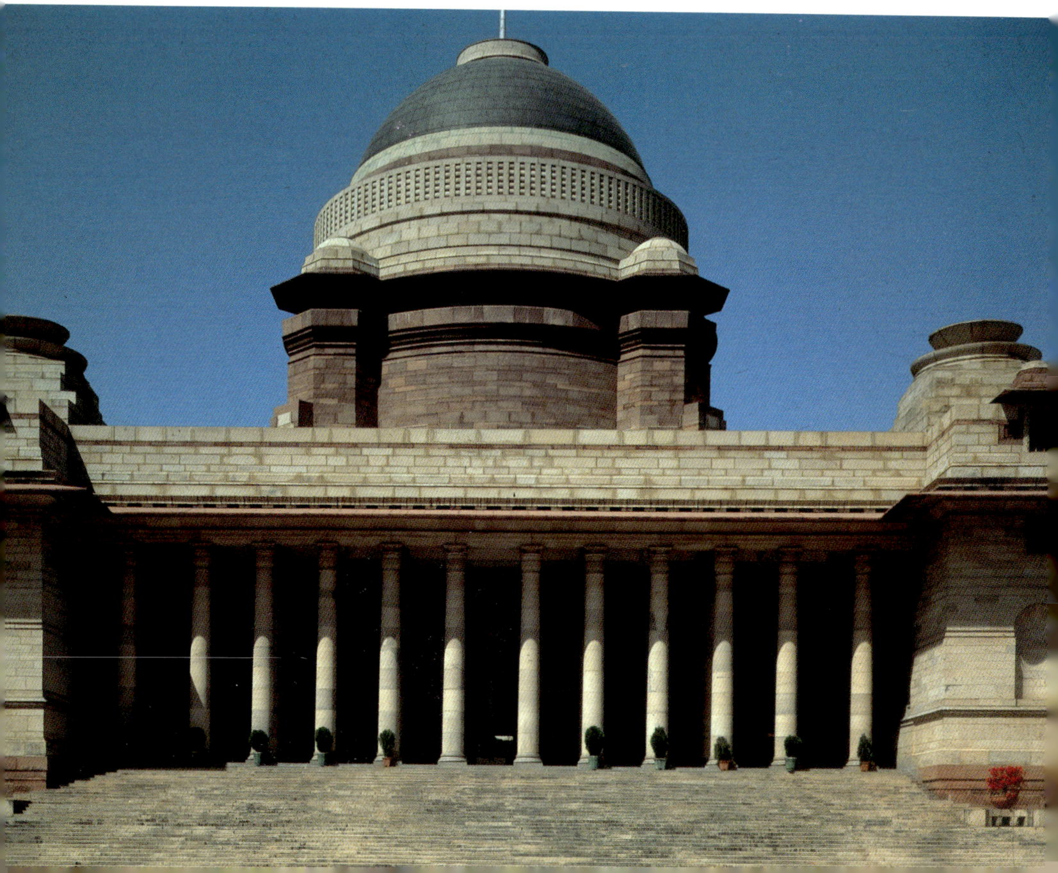

(*Above*) Garden front of Viceroy's House showing the butterfly garden as it is today. Lutyens designed the planting so that, on one or two days a year, the colour in the garden would be supplied by clouds of butterflies. (*Below left*) Indian motifs disciplined by western geometry in the *chujjah* or projecting cornice of Viceroy's House. Full size drawings, showing the exact angles to use in taking the pipal leaf design round a corner, exist in the Delhi archives. (*Below right*) Portrait of Lutyens as Master of the Art Workers Guild in 1933, by Meredith Frampton. Ned smoked almost more matches than he did tobacco. Bryant & May matchboxes were his favourite toys.

by a row of columns, it is meant to show sunset through the columns, there are to be statues on top.'

Hugh Lane was so entranced that he insisted upon the adoption of Ned's design as the condition of his gift. Ned estimated the cost at £45,000; the Corporation undertook to pay half, and the remainder was to be raised by private gifts. Although Lane's energetic aunt, Lady Gregory, confounded the pessimists and raised thousands in America, the Corporation still grumbled. They took particular exception to the choice of architect. Despite having an Irish mother, Lutyens was perceived as an English architect; he was probably also resented as Lane's nominee. Lane's remark that the beauty of Lutyens's bridge-gallery 'would set a standard for Irish architects to look up to' can't have helped. In September 1913 the Corporation voted to reject Lutyens's design, resolving that 'the selection of the site and the nomination of the architect must be left to its own decision'. The Corporation was still prepared to find half the cost, but it wouldn't accept Lutyens. 'No Lutyens, no gallery, no pictures,' was Lane's response; he promptly withdrew his paintings.[32]

Lutyens thought it 'all very Irish and very involved', but he seems to have lost little sleep over it. Staying at Lambay in August, he was more excited over Cecil Baring's building projects ('They are in love with the place again. They drink buttermilk. The rheas thrive') than depressed by the loss of the Dublin scheme. Lane, on the other hand, pretended to be mortified. He changed his will, leaving his money to the Irish National Gallery and his paintings to London, and he blamed Lutyens for his eccentric choice of site. His plan was to postpone the founding of an Irish gallery until the Home Rule Bill had been passed and Ireland had a parliament, and meanwhile to found a great international gallery in London.[33]

Over the Dublin fiasco, Lutyens displayed the same wilfulness as he did in South Africa and in India. If he cared less about the Dublin fiasco, it still spelled a lesson: namely, that classical architecture, however 'beautiful', projected an imperialist message and acted as an irritant to edgy, insecure nationalist politicians.

Hugh Lane was not an easy man to deal with. He suffered from 'advanced neurasthenia', a term which means little today, but nervous symptoms clouded his judgement. No man who ordered envelopes in a shade of azure blue specially chosen to match the pink of the penny stamp could be called easy. Ned sympathized with Lane's urge to rearrange every mantelpiece that he saw, and he sensed that beneath his fastidiousness and Philip II black beard Lane was an outsider like himself, educated at home, insecure and uncomfortable in the company of his peers. Lane paid him in paintings, among them two portraits of old ladies, whom Ned joked were his ancestors. He offered to design Lane a room with twelve panels containing twelve portraits of his ideal wife as visualized by his favourite artists, including Sargent, Orpen, Steer, Augustus John – the joke being that Lane was not remotely interested in women. Ned's jokes touched dangerously near sensitive points. With Lane he got away with it – a sign that he was sure of his ground. Lane was notoriously mean about small things like food, and he gave Lutyens dinner at his favourite Chelsea restaurant for a mere eighteen pence. 'Wonderful,' said Lutyens, 'let's have it over again.'

In August 1913 Lane motored Lutyens down to Sussex to see a moated, timber-framed Elizabethan house. He wanted Lutyens to restore it and hang it with Holbeins, 'to show England a perfect Elizabethan house in perfect order'.[34] The house was Plumpton Place, but Lane's English dream was never realized. He was killed in the wreck of the *Lusitania* in 1915, leaving a last unwitnessed codicil to his will, which bequeathed his pictures once more to Dublin, and gave rise to a generation of legal wrangling. In 1913, however, Lutyens was preoccupied with Delhi. Not until 1927 did he turn back to Plumpton Place, which Hudson bought, and which Ned made into a hauntingly beautiful place.

Emily and the children spent the summer of 1913 at Varengeville. 'You must think,' she told Ned, 'that I am with *your* – *our* – children and so doing the greatest thing for *you*, darling.' It is hard to know whom she was deceiving most, Ned, the children or herself.

Emily installed the children, Nannie and nursery maid in a couple of primitive farmhouses, within easy walking distance of Les Communes, Ned's dream house, which was occupied by Krishna and Nitya. They had been smuggled in by Mrs Besant while she prepared to appeal against their father's victory in the courts. Life at Varengeville was simple, wholesome and teetotal. Emily read Shakespeare to the children, held theosophical meetings with Krishna several times a day and played energetic games of rounders after tea. The chief excitement was Mary's fifth birthday, when she was crowned with a wreath of white roses. 'She was shy and very solemn and never uttered – but just ate solemnly and winked.'[35]

Mary was Krishna's special pet, and she already loved Nitya, or so she later claimed. But it was Emily who lingered after rounders to walk alone with Krishna, convincing herself that Krishna's attraction was purely spiritual. She logged her theosophical life in a special diary. The transforming experience or spiritual awakening came on the night of 11 August. She wrote in her diary: 'I woke with a feeling of intense peace and happiness and a remembrance of being with Krishna. The following afternoon Krishna told me that I had been with him the night before and asked me if I remembered anything, and I felt happy.' (Emily felt it needless to add that all these encounters occurred on the astral plane.) Cables whirred across the world to Mrs Besant in India, who sent spiritual cables to the Master in Tibet, and Emily was placed on spiritual probation.

Emily was radiant, but she told none of this to Ned, who suspected nothing, though he worried that they were drifting apart and that Emily thought of him as 'a railway accident'. Nonsense, said Emily, they had never been together in their minds: 'Your work always meant more to you that anything else . . . and I was always looking for what I have now found.'

Ned worried about Robert, especially when well-meaning friends such as Maude Baring frightened him with stories about Leadbeater's treatment of Krishna. But Ned was barking up the wrong tree. The truth – which Emily couldn't yet admit to herself, let alone to Ned – was that it was she who was obsessed with Krishna. The migraines which had always plagued her now became worse. She spent whole days in darkened rooms, eau de Cologne pressed to her head. Nothing could relieve the pain, not even the faith healer (produced by Miss Dodge), who dressed her in white silk pyjamas and expertly rubbed her as she lay in a darkened room in Park Lane. She was living a lie. As she later wrote, 'I was never really happy away from Krishna. My husband, my home, my children faded into the background; Krishna became my entire life, and for the next ten years I suffered all the difficulties of trying to sublimate a human love.'[36]

Chapter Twelve
East and West
1913–1914

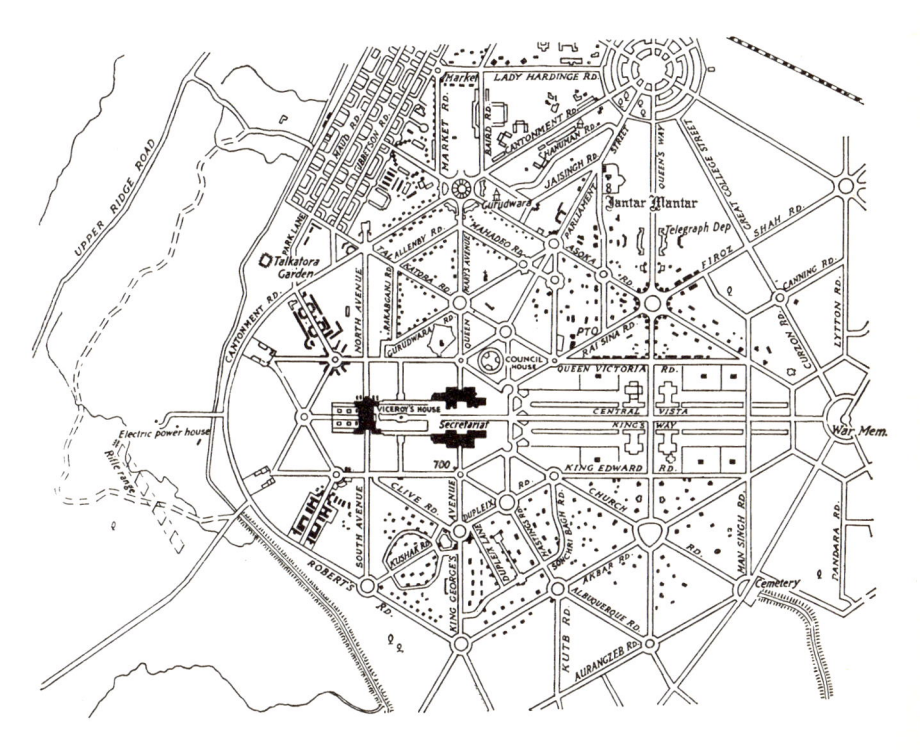

Town plan of New Delhi.

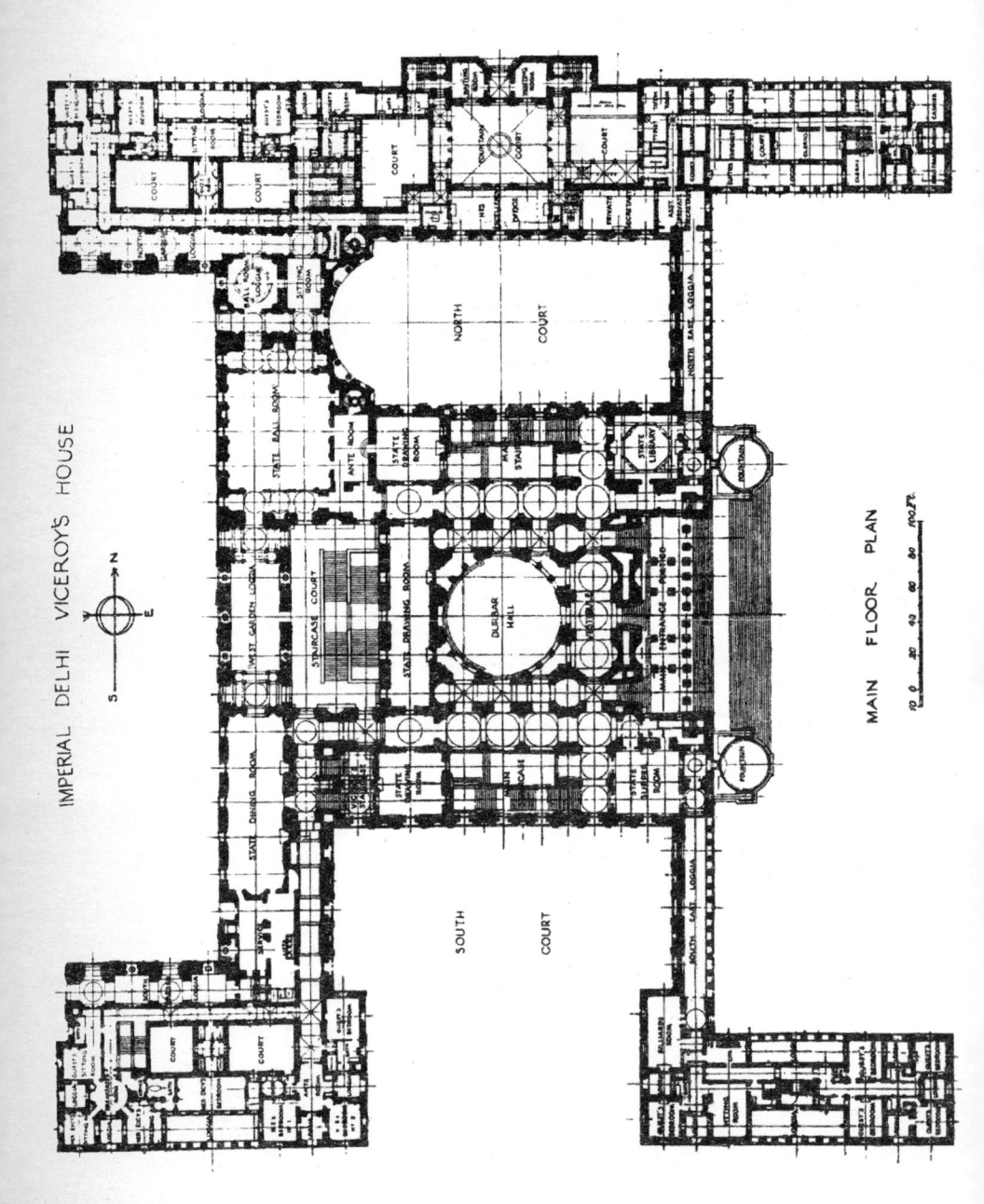

Main floor plan of Viceroy's House.

At the very moment that Emily was crossing continents and creeds to approach Krishna on the astral plane, Ned was struggling to achieve a synthesis of east and west in art. Unaware of her transcendental experiences at Varengeville, he spent long smoke-filled nights at Bloomsbury Square wrestling with the problems of classical geometry. 'My comfort,' wrote Emily, 'is that you love your work and it is really more to you than wife or child.'

Gaspard Farrer lent him the mews house at 7 Apple Tree Yard, behind St James's Square, for his Indian office. Ned thought it 'A1 – far better than Queen Anne's Gate. More room on a floor and larger rooms and v. well lighted'.[1]

Lord Hardinge bombarded him with letters demanding the use of the pointed arch, to which Lutyens retorted, 'I should like to ask him to what country the Rainbow belongs! One cannot tinker with the round arch. God did not make the Eastern rainbow pointed to show His wide sympathies.' This kind of remark, as Baker pointed out, was calculated to enrage the Viceroy. Then Sir Swinton Jacob, appointed as 'a sort of walking dictionary on Indo-Saracenic art', decided to resign. 'I have a strong suspicion that he is disgusted with the unreasonable attitude of Lutyens,' grumbled the Viceroy. To control the loose cannon Hardinge turned to Baker, whose job it now became to persuade Ned that he 'must recognize the political standpoint in a political capital'. Not realizing that Baker had been 'got at' to act as his minder, Ned raged against Hardinge for allowing politics and sentiment to spoil art.* Only one set of drawings survives to show that he did (briefly) attempt to obey his masters and design pointed arches and onion domes.[2]

---

*Part of the problem for Lutyens was that he had no language to describe what he was trying to do. He constantly bewailed his inarticulacy, which he ascribed to his lack of a public-school education. But the problem was only partly one of education; the fact was that there was no language to convey his meaning. Apart from Ruskin, who was impossibly verbose (and anyway wrong-headed, in Lutyens's view), no one had invented a satisfactory way of describing architecture. Not until the 1930s did Robert Byron and Christopher Hussey develop a rhetorical language of architectural criticism, which derived from Geoffrey Scott's *Architecture of Humanism* (1914). Lutyens didn't even attempt to put his meaning into words: 'I think an art begins where words fail it. An art has to be something which it alone can express in its own medium.' Frustrated by his lack of a grammar he could only make puns and outrageous remarks and draw what he thought on paper. Little wonder the Viceroy thought him unreasonable.

'Getting on with Govt House and begin to see my way. It is the mass of internal planning etc that takes so much time in puzzling out,' Ned told Emily in September, 'Chattris are stupid useless things.' But now *chattris*, the miniature roof pavilions which perch on the rooftops of Muslim palaces, marched boldly across Ned's drawings. Using *chattris* taken from the fort at Agra and from Fatepuhr Sikri – Akbar's ruined city which he had scorned so witheringly a few months before – and the sweeping, blade-like *chujjah* or cornice of Muslim architecture, Ned translated his designs of 1912 into an Indian architectural language of his own devising.[3]* At Apple Tree Yard in the summer of 1913 he evolved his synthesis of east and west. Abandoning the Palladian portico, he added a long, low colonnade, stressing horizontals in Islamic fashion.

Ned left London for his third passage to India in November 1913. The journey started as badly as could be with a quarrel with Baker; it was about money.

Among his papers Baker preserved a sheaf of foolscap pages torn from his diary for 1913–14. This bald record of engagements shows that he was very busy in the weeks before they sailed for India negotiating an agreement about the division of the Delhi fees with his solicitor Balfour, with the India Office, with Lutyens and Lutyens's solicitor Francis Smith. The architects signed the agreement a couple of days before they were due to depart, and Baker retired contentedly to his home in Kent to pack. Next day at 4.30 p.m., on the eve of departure, he received a wire from his solicitor saying (according to his diary) that 'Smith insisted on a 2 to 1 limit on E.L.L.'s expenses'. Baker wrote a memorandum in 1921 in which he claimed that Lutyens was 'going back on his promise' embodied in the agreement by insisting on a clause which 'would have tied me hand and foot to him financially'.[4]

The point at issue was how to divide the architects' expenses or 'pool' account. The architects were to receive a commission of 5 per cent, to be divided equally, from which they were to deduct their office expenses. Baker insisted that all expenses should be divided 50:50, and this was the gist of the agreement signed on 11 November. But Baker's expenses were higher than Lutyens's, swollen by his South African office, and by his policy of paying higher wages (wages in Lutyens's

---

*He later told Daphne Baring that he admired Fatepuhr Sikri as the cream of Indian architecture; its austere grandeur was the source of much of his inspiration for Delhi.

office were notoriously low). A 50:50 split effectively meant that Lutyens was bearing part of Baker's costs. Lutyens, who was absorbed in last-minute revision of his plans, paid little attention to the negotiations and only realized what he had committed himself to after the agreement was signed. Hence the wire suggesting a 2 to 1 limit on his expenses, which could potentially leave Baker with a smaller residue from his half of the commission.

On the boat train at Victoria Station next morning Lutyens found Baker 'awfully hurt and bruised', saying 'something about happy days being over'. Baker had taken an early train to London and had spent two hours closeted with his lawyer. Lutyens thought the quarrel absurd, 'as it is only a money question and a lawyer safeguard in the interests of my family', but Baker's sulks stiffened him. After five days of not speaking they spent a whole day discussing the agreement. Baker agreed that his expenses should be fixed at 60 per cent and Lutyens's at 40 per cent of the 'pool' account. If either exceeded this ratio, their expenses would be deducted from their share of the profit. Lutyens drafted a letter in mock legal language, 'whereas-to-before-why-not', which was sent home to the solicitors Francis Smith and Balfour to write into an agreement.[5]

Lutyens had won, but it was a pyrrhic victory as it left Baker feeling sore and angry and convinced that the clause would hit him unfairly.* Lutyens had gone back on his word at the last minute, breaking the gentleman's code and confirming Baker's worst fears. Jealous and resentful of Lutyens's social and artistic success, Baker now saw him as an arrogant bounder: no longer a colleague but an enemy.

The Viceroy liked Ned's drawings, which was something. No more was heard about the pointed arch, though Hardinge disliked the dome, which he threatened to eliminate. 'But that I don't mind,' wrote Lutyens – his dome was still Wren, and he needed to translate it into Indian idiom. 'He likes Baker's elephants up upon his domes! I think them awful!' But Hardinge, who stubbornly clung to the £4 million estimate for the entire city, insisted that Lutyens's design was too expensive and ordered him to reduce it to £500,000.

*In fact, as Baker noted in a memorandum written in 1931, the clause worked not against him but against Lutyens, 'owing to the long delay over Government House during the last few years of the prolonged contract'. However, 'the advantage which should thus have accrued to me, I renounced in the final settlement made in the end of 1930, thus reverting to my original proposal of mutual equality.'

On 13 December Lutyens wrote a memorandum spelling out the implications of Hardinge's orders. The Delhi Committee had stipulated a maximum for the building of 8 million cubic feet. In order to accommodate Hardinge's demands for ceremonial and public space, the main floor alone came out at 8,838,503 cubic feet, and this in turn determined the massive basements beneath. The plan exceeded 8 million cubic feet by an additional 6,711,686 cubic feet – in other words, it was almost twice as big as the Committee had suggested. The structure alone would cost £536,000 to build. The choices were stark. Either the house could be built as a carcass, Lutyens suggested, which 'if well built, might be mighty fine in effect', or the plan reduced by ratio, 'without altering the arrangement of the plan, which would bring it nearer to or within the prescribed cost'. But this would throw Government House out of alignment with the Secretariats, which would need to be correspondingly reduced.[6]

The sheer scale of Lutyens's conception is staggering. This was partly a matter of politics. As Harcourt Butler urged, 'I think it of utmost Imperial importance that the thing should be done on a big scale; something which will impress Indians with our determination to stay out here and govern the country on Imperial lines.' That Lutyens could in all seriousness propose building an empty carcass nearly twice as large as the massive structure that was finally built shows how important mass was to his conception.

Hardinge dismissed Lutyens's 'carcass option' and insisted on reductions to the plan. 'I am afraid I shall have to cut down Govt House – a great blow,' wrote Ned on 17 December. By then he was ill with dysentery. 'I passed a good deal of blood, about a port wine glass full this morning,' he reported. Lady Hardinge visited him in bed, telling him not to worry about the estimates as it was bound to come out right. Lulled by her bedside reassurances and dulled by the emetic drug ipecacuanha ('it made me feel very odd'), Ned failed to realize that Hardinge was working against him. While he lay in bed, tortured by the dysentery he called his 'small but bloody master', writhing and vomiting, Baker and Hardinge discussed cuts to Government House. As the politically attuned Baker was well aware, the Viceroy now considered that the greater importance of the ICS justified giving the Secretariats a higher symbolic eminence on Raisina Hill than the Viceroy's House. Unknown to Ned, the programme and rationale of his palace was already being undermined.[7]

Ned was sufficiently recovered to make a brief Christmas tour with

Baker and Harcourt Butler. Butler's mother sent out a Christmas pudding from England, which they ate in a railway carriage. They saw Lucknow, where Harcourt Butler reported the architects 'contemptuous of the buildings old and new, but warm in appreciation of the gardens etc.' At Benares, where Ned talked with Mrs Besant, he was shocked and repelled by the deformities, the beggars and fakirs, the dirt, filth and stench – 'barbarism in terms of evil smelling slime'. Emily agreed, regretting only that 'you have no opportunity of seeing what lies behind, the *real* India – It is impossible among official surroundings but perhaps it will come some day.' Architecturally speaking, however, 'the real India' was coming already.

From Benares they motored out to Sarnath, where Buddha first preached. Here they saw the famous lion capital of the Asoka pillar, which Harcourt Butler thought 'the best thing in India, but the architects were disappointed thinking to find Greek perfection'. Lutyens, however, admired 'the remains of a fine stupa and many interesting fragments of Hindu sculpture'. The Buddhist *stupa*, or dome surrounded by carved stone rails, provided the inspiration he needed to translate his dome from Wren, which Hardinge disliked, into something more Indian, at the same time giving it a greater height than it had in the earlier sketches.

Next day, at Bodhgaya, where Buddha attained his Buddha-hood, Lutyens saw Asoka rails, a stone fence seven or eight feet high, 'which I admire most of all India's work'. He used these at Delhi, throwing them around the perimeter of the Great Place at the foot of Raisina Hill. The general form of Hindu temples and Buddhist shrines, he wrote, was 'an elongated pyramid going up in steps and flanked with ever-diminishing pinnacles like a cactus or child's toy tree'.[8] There's an echo of this at Viceroy's House which is constructed on a pyramidal principle, an effect created by steeply battered basements and subtly sloping walls.

At Bodhgaya Ned picked a leaf from the pipal tree beneath which the Buddha sat, and sent it home to Emily. The pipal leaf reappears at Delhi too. The bold cream pattern on a reddish ground which runs beneath the *chujjah* (cornice), like the lining of a Mogul tent, is in fact a pipal leaf. Among the archive of 8,500 drawings by Lutyens and Baker, carefully preserved in the basement of the Delhi Public Works Department, there exists a full-size measured drawing, showing exactly what angles to use in taking the pipal leaf design around a corner. That drawing is a diagram of Lutyens's synthesis at Viceroy's

House. The grammar is western, geometrical and classical, but the language is Indian – though Indian distilled and digested to its stylized essence.[9]*

That brief Christmas tour crystallized Lutyens's Indian style. Back in Delhi, he set to work to make the reductions commanded by the Viceroy. 'I have been very busy on what are practically new plans,' he wrote. Baker later recorded how 'I watched silently and with admiration his tenacity in the fight with the Viceroy and the Government; a difficult position of conflicting loyalties, as I probably alone knew how the immense mass of building in relation to floor area contributed to the expense of his plan'.

Baker was being disingenuous. If there was a conflict of loyalties, there was no doubt where Baker's sympathies lay. His diaries show him frequently discussing Government House with Hardinge, while remaining stonily indifferent to Lutyens's appeals for support. Lutyens complained that Baker was so 'used to cheap work and getting over difficulties in a slovenly way he is no real help', and he despaired of ever making the reduced Government House fit into alignment with Baker's Secretariats. ('I cannot get Baker to alter his drawings to fit mine.')[10]

Embattled and depressed, and worn out by working until midnight each night, Ned nearly broke down. He contemplated resigning. Eventually he wrote a pessimistic letter to Lady Hardinge, warning that the only way to meet the costs was to leave out the dome altogether and build the upper part of the house in plaster. The effect was electric. Lady Hardinge, whom Ned had noticed looking 'awfully tired', raddled by the cancer, as yet undiagnosed, that was soon to kill her, rushed down to the architects' office miserable at Ned's 'black letter'. But Baker helped persuade her that Ned exaggerated the problems. Ned complained that Baker 'won't face difficulties just slurs them and does something muddy which I cannot bear doing without a fight'.

By March the reductions were at last achieved and the estimates had

---

*The historian Tom Metcalf suggested in 1989 that Lutyens deliberately used Buddhist motifs in order to evade the political tangle of Muslim and Hindu. There were no Buddhists in British India, so Buddhist architecture, unlike Hindu and Muslim forms, would not proclaim the mastery of the Raj. Not only was Lutyens's use of Buddhist forms a confession of Britain's inability to resolve India's communal conflicts, but there was (says Metcalf) 'no place in his architecture for the English-educated Indian'. Certainly, the Indian middle class was a closed book to him; he spent most of his time in India in the official bungalow which he shared with Baker, and when he did travel it was in the isolated splendour of an official railway carriage. But what Lutyens was trying to do was to devise an architecture that satisfied the demand for an Indian style but moved beyond what he saw as the aesthetic nightmare of Indo-Saracenic.

come out near to budget, but the Secretariats were too big for the reduced Government House and Baker refused to modify them. Having made the reductions in his plans required by the government, speedily effected with the help of his South Africa partner F. L. H. Fleming, Baker was reluctant to alter them further. 'He wants to get on and build. I say work on until it all fits and make a competent scheme. A few months won't matter in 50 years time.' By now, however, Ned was desperate to get home. He started passing blood again, which frightened him, though the doctor diagnosed nothing worse than an internal pile.[11] Six months' stressful, lonely and acrimonious work on Delhi had burned him out.

On 9 March 1914 Hardinge at last approved the plans. He was anxious to start work. Blasting to flatten the crest of Raisina Hill was begun. On 17 March Lutyens and Baker signed an agreement guaranteeing that there would be no further alterations to the plans.[12] Appended to this was a document concerning the gradient of the approach to the Secretariats and Viceroy's House. The gradient was set at 22½. Lutyens didn't pay much attention to the matter at the time, but by signing that minute he committed himself to a gradient which would ensure that the portico and dome of Viceroy's House were obscured at some point on the approach.

Lutyens had assumed that Viceroy's House would be visible along the entire length of the vista, as shown in the perspectives which had been drawn by William Walcot according to Baker's sketches in September 1913. Baker did nothing to enlighten him, remaining as cold and unfriendly as he had been ever since the November quarrel over money. Baker's silence on this point was extraordinary. If he knew that Lutyens was signing away his vista – and it seems likely that he did know; certainly he never denied it – he was being little short of dishonourable.

But Lutyens ought to have seen it for himself. Frightened about his health, obsessively revising his plans, working under immense pressure, he had paid insufficient attention to the layout. His conception of a Great Court between the Secretariats and Viceroy's House had been initially developed for the flat Malcha site. When in February 1913 Baker insisted on the Secretariats being moved to Raisina Hill, Lutyens did not object. He failed to realize that there was insufficient room on the acropolis for all the central buildings.

Lutyens was a perfectionist and obsessive. He couldn't accept any failure that prevented him from realizing his conception in full. His later bitterness about the gradient caused him to obscure the far more important victory of 1914. He came back to England having reduced his plan for Government House and persuaded the Viceroy to accept it. That was his achievement. In gaining it, however, he had almost exhausted his creative energy.

In January 1914, tired out by family Christmas in London, including the annual ritual of shopping with Hudson ('This is always a nightmare to me. Five children to steer through the crowded shops and I never know what price he wants to give for anything'), Emily had run away for a month. Without telling anyone where she was going, she had left her children with Nannie and joined Krishna and Nitya, who were in hiding in Taormina, Sicily.*

She found the boys staying in the Via Naumachia, a steep, narrow street in the town, with overhanging balconies and street stalls, near a Roman reservoir surrounded by lemon orchards. The Hotel Naumachia (which no longer exists) was a modest hotel, classified by Baedeker as respectable, clean and reasonably priced. Krishna and Nitya were chaperoned by two grey-haired spinsters, Dr Mary Rocke and Miss Arundale, and a tutor, George Arundale, who was Miss Arundale's nephew. They occupied the entire top floor of the hotel and spent their days working themselves up into a fever of occult anticipation, hoping that someone would 'bring through' on the astral plain at night. Emily agonized over her feelings for Krishna, and was too engrossed to realize that she was ousting Arundale in his affections. Arundale, who was joint editor with Emily of the *Herald of the Star in the East*, became watchfully resentful. He reported Emily to Mrs Besant, who wrote her a stern letter, upbraiding her for leaving her children, who were her responsibility, to look after Krishna, who was not. Emily had disgraced herself, earning penalty points or *karma*, which set back her spiritual promotion on the Path for many years.

At about the same time, Ned wrote to Emily from India: 'I feel some things very strongly indeed. The colour question is one, and there is no compromise . . . Don't darling go so far as to blast our happiness.' Emily pretended not to understand what he meant. 'I am not wanting Barbie to marry an Indian if that is what your fear is,' she wrote.

---

*The lawyers had advised them to go into hiding before the Privy Council hearing of the case brought by their father (27 January 1914), in case his friends should kidnap them.

But Ned's outburst was provoked by the 'surprise' that Emily had prepared for his homecoming. 'I want you to understand just how I feel,' she wrote. Krishna's mother had died when he was nine, and Mrs Besant was far away. 'So we have gradually come to feel for each other as mother and son. I know your feeling for Indians makes this hard for you to understand, but try to remember that I have no such feeling and they seem to me like my own boys.'[13]

Emily validated her feelings for Krishna by persuading the theosophists to recognize her as his mother. In May even Mrs Besant was persuaded to go along with this. In an odd little ceremony, she told Emily it was a very peculiar relationship but she didn't object. 'Then Krishna came in and knelt beside [Mrs Besant] and she gave us her blessing and we were very happy.'[14] Emily might have been describing a marriage; her mother–son relationship with Krishna was profoundly incestuous. He wrote her letters, which she later destroyed, pouring out his adolescent love for her. She later admitted that if it had not been for her love for Krishna, she would have tired of theosophy.

Mrs Besant won her appeal for custody of the boys in the Privy Council in May, and ordered Krishna and Nitya to prepare for the Oxford entrance examinations. Supported by a £500 allowance from Miss Dodge, Krishna was condemned to a twilight existence in gloomy villas in the Isle of Wight or Cornwall, taking golf lessons and being coached by tutors, his solitary life ruled by occasional cables from Mrs Besant in India.

In London, Emily became increasingly distanced from reality. Totally preoccupied by theosophy, she saw less of her children. Mary, her youngest child, remembered being brought up entirely by Nannie. Emily only appeared in the nursery after tea, when she would read Dickens, Bulwer or Jane Austen, all of which she knew by heart, knitting as she read and invariably dropping a stitch at the exciting parts. Oddly, Mary felt no resentment: 'we always used to say how beautiful she looked, and she was like a princess to me'. Highly strung Betty was not so placid or docile. Incapable of sitting still, allegedly because of growing pains in her legs, she hated being read to. She didn't like Nannie Sleath, she screamed, she ruined all her clothes, and she was only really happy hiding in the cistern cupboard of the downstairs lavatory. 'Poor Betty is a great trial to herself and others,' wrote Emily. 'She is very naughty over her lessons and refuses some days to do anything, and she is very rude and self-willed.'[15]

Ned returned from India in March 1914 to find his country-house practice celebrated and boomed by the *Country Life* writer Lawrence Weaver. His lavishly illustrated *Houses and Gardens by E. L. Lutyens* was published by *Country Life* in December 1913. Emily reported on 17 December that 870 copies had already been sold, and Hudson thought it 'a splendid tribute to your genius'. Ned had helped Weaver with the book (he went to Lambay with him, and grew irritated with Mrs Weaver's harp-playing), but he thought it 'rather vulgar and the whole thing makes me hot'. He refused to read the proofs. 'It is just a catalogue of mistakes and failures,' he groaned.

It seemed in March 1914 that the whole of aristocratic London was at his feet. Hubert Worthington, who was a pupil, remembered a constant stream of clients. Three carriages queued in the street outside and two or three peers a day left their cards. The boys in the office crowed at the jealousy of the Aston Webb office next door.[16]

But theosophy dogged his work. The Theosophical Society's headquarters in Tavistock Square was a bottomless source of trouble. The estimates came to £110,000, twice as high as the £40,000 or £50,000 Ned had originally predicted to Mrs Besant. Emily attacked him as 'dreadfully dishonest', but Ned blamed Mrs Besant for enlarging the building and the site. He had been too trusting, hypnotized by her tiger-brown eyes, allowing her to 'add, add, add, admiring her courage without questioning her banking and business arrangements'. Ned had drawn three sets of plans for her, each larger than the last. Mrs Besant turned out to be an impossible client, mixing socialist politics with building. Having once campaigned for trade unions, she now insisted on doing without a builder, rejecting the advantageous terms Ned had obtained from Cubitts and trying an experiment in direct labour.

Building operations were supervised by the socialist theosophist Dr Haden Guest, who promptly sacked Lutyens's clerk of works, Mr Green. Lutyens was furious and complained that the theosophists had sent spies into his office to ransack Green's desk, searching for evidence that he was working on other jobs. Haden Guest then produced a list of serious charges against Green. 'If true,' wrote Ned, 'which they must be for the most part, it is serious and I shall have to confront Green – oh the worry of it – and probably sack him ... All these years I have been educating Green in his craft are wasted.'[17]

Emboldened by the sacking of Green, Haden Guest next produced two thick folios of allegations against A. J. Thomas, the Lutyens office manager, including incriminating letters from builders' firms. Lutyens was very angry with Haden Guest. 'If he had not been a friend of my wife's I would have kicked him out of the house,' he told Mrs Besant. But the charges against Thomas were too serious to be ignored, and Ned suspended him from the office, pending an inquiry by an independent arbitrator named Mr Watkin. Most galling was Emily's indifference. 'I know you are against me here and I have not even your sympathy,' wrote Ned.

'The whole question turns on Thomas – is he honest or is he not?' wrote Emily. 'Remember you were very angry with me for doubting Badcock and I was quite right.'[18] But Thomas was saved by the outbreak of the First World War. Work was abandoned on the half-finished building as theosophical funds ran low, and Haden Guest departed for France to establish a military hospital. Thomas, whom Ned thought a slow and faithful servant, was reinstated. He was too useful to sack. 'I cannot let Thomas go while I am in India,' wrote Ned. He was relieved when Thomas won a competition to build St Pancras Town Hall in January 1915 – 'this will set him on his feet'. Haden Guest's allegations, his spying and interference in the office, rankled with Ned for many years. Ned refused to allow him in the house. Because Haden Guest had behaved with such 'dastardly cruelty' to Thomas, Ned came to believe that Thomas was an innocent scapegoat, the victim of a socialist plot, and the charges against him were never fully investigated – though Emily remained convinced of his guilt.[19]

The war changed everything. Ned watched helplessly as his practice melted away in the stock market panic that followed the diplomatic crisis of July 1914. Arthur Grenfell went spectacularly bankrupt in the falling market, forfeiting a commission of £1,400 he owed Ned on Roehampton House. Herbert Johnson telephoned to stop building at Marshcourt (a ballroom) on account of the war and falling stock prices. Player stopped his tobacco factory and Sir George Sitwell abandoned a club house he had commissioned.

Cecil Baring, Frank Mildmay and Gaspard Farrer all cancelled work on the same morning, and Ned panicked that Barings were in trouble and he would receive no payment. Worried by Betty Balfour, who told him that both Gerald and Arthur Balfour had been refused loans and that she feared Barings was going bankrupt, Ned saw Cecil Baring and repeated Betty's story. This got back to Arthur Balfour, who scolded poor Betty for being indiscreet, while Gerald cut Ned in public, behaving to him as Baker had done on the platform at Victoria Station. Fortunately Barings was strong (they had few German debts), and Ned received his money, but the incident was a painful reminder of his status as an outsider, and of his ignorance of the gentleman's code, which he blamed (as usual) on his lack of a public-school education.[20]

When Chippy's speculations in American stocks crashed, Ned, whom he approached, refused to lend him money. Crooksbury was sold for £11,000 to people named Briggs ('They are common but seem pleasant as such and rich,' wrote Ned), and to please Chippy Ned unwillingly added bay windows and roughcast the brickwork for the new clients, which he thought spoiled the house. 'It is like digging up Mrs Chapman in her grave.' He later said that these additions were the worst architectural crime he had ever committed.

Once war was declared on 4 August Ned could do nothing but watch and wait. He found it very hard to work. Twelve men in his office joined up within a week. On the hall wall of Queen Anne's Gate he painted a list of the names of those who had enlisted. Fishing for work was no longer any use. He lunched with Mrs Jack Tennant 'with a view to talking business with her', but she ran away to her Red Cross work, 'so I wasted my time, but I do waste my time at this crisis'. At Munstead, he found Bumps and Aggie Jekyll making shirts and kitbags, stuffing bags with exquisitely rolled bandages and everything imaginable from hairbrushes to soap.[21]

Ned, who was used to being so busy and highly valued, had no role. He talked vaguely about volunteering, but at forty-five could not contemplate joining up. Yet there was no place for an architect in wartime. He walked down the Mall with Colonel Sefton Brancker of the Royal Flying Corps, 'with a view to disguising London by falsifying the directions of streets by rearrangement of lamps'; but that was all. Each evening he called in at the Athenaeum Club; as the British seemed incapable of stopping the German advance towards Calais, the club drones predicted that 'this week will absolutely wipe out our army to a man'. Still more depressing was dinner with his brother Frank to meet his new wife, whom he found dreadfully vulgar and Frank 'very cocksure and fat (I feel all I am saying fits me) and very irritating'.[22]

Emily was on holiday in Bude when the war broke out, and she was euphoric. She scolded Ned for his pessimism – 'I wish you belonged to a more cheerful club than the Athenaeum' – and declared that she had never before so much wanted to be a man so that she might fight. 'I am so proud of England.' The war, she thought, was like a dream – 'in less than a fortnight that political parties should be embracing, militancy abandoned and prisoners released. Emmy in a war fever and writing friendly letters to McKenna! Neville showing a patriotic spirit! Hudson praising the government!'

Emily's war fever did not mean that she felt the need to do anything, least of all return from Bude to London. Krishna and Nitya were staying nearby, and naturally theosophy took precedence over other considerations. She was having far too nice a time, riding in the sidecar while Krishna drove his shiny new motorbike. He was a frighteningly erratic driver, so she was glad for the divine protection he gave her. Krishna was eligible for war service but he did not enlist. 'He is not a fighting type, any more than you are,' Emily told Ned.[23] In any case, Mrs Besant forbade it, not because she disapproved of killing, but on the rather curious grounds that he might be forced to pollute his body by eating meat.

In August Emily had been fully expecting to be accepted by the Masters, as this was the anniversary of her probation at Varengeville, but nothing happened and she was deeply disappointed. A month later she wrote to Ned:

> The thing I want to say is what has been growing upon me for a long time and that is that if our love is to continue it can only be on my side by a severance of our *physical* relationship . . . I have suffered *intensely physically* during all my married life. There were compensations when I wanted the children and had them. But now we are both entering upon middle age. I have done my duty to you and my country as regards children and I could never face another. With that incentive gone your coming to me has been increasingly difficult for me to bear.
> I believe and hold firmly that a woman has the right over her own body. Where she gives it willingly the relationship is beautiful – where she gives it because she *must* it becomes prostitution whether in or out of marriage and is a degradation.[24]

Emily talked the language of Sylvia Pankhurst and the suffragettes, but her purpose was theosophical. Only by controlling and transcending her lower, physical nature could she attain Acceptance, which would bring her close to Krishna. She didn't admit to herself that she loved Krishna so intensely that she could no longer bear to sleep with her husband.

For years Emily had made plain her dislike of sex, and Ned was hardly surprised by this ultimatum. 'I had expected this,' he wrote, 'but it seems hard somehow, but your feelings about it all make it impossible to contemplate.' Emily always found it easier to write than say things, and by now they saw each other so little and talked so rarely that their daily letters had virtually *become* their marriage. Henceforth it was to be a marriage consummated in ink, a long, long conversation scrawled on paper for over thirty years.

Ned mourned the death of his romantic ideals. 'As faith wills so fate fulfils was a very empty boast,' he wrote wryly.[25] In a symbolic act, he ceased wearing his mother's Claddah ring, and returned it to the casket. How he regretted being so faithful to Emily, who now condemned him to a lifetime of celibacy. She was merciless, refusing to relent in spite of his misery and self-pity. 'The whole thing is so mysterious to me,' she wrote. 'How could you ever have found pleasure in what you knew I hated.' To which Ned responded angrily, 'How could you darling be intimate and petting with the Krishnaji party ... How I have hated the large photographs, the constant chuckle at my discomfiture when what I hated was introduced into my house and home.'[26]

Emily's defection emasculated Ned, plunging him into depression. 'Whatever I say makes you sad now,' she wrote. It was so sudden and hard to understand, coming on top of the war, the quarrel with Baker, the troubles with Thomas and the disintegration of his country-house practice. He later said he was like an old elephant in the rutting season, who went 'must', driven by sexual frustration to a state of frenzy. He blamed Mrs Besant. He could never fully accept that the real cause of Emily's defection was Krishna. That thought was inconceivable to him.

Chapter Thirteen
31 Bedford Square
1914–1916

Ned to Emily, 27 January 1916: 'I am having difficulty with Baker. I find he has designed his levels so that you will never see Government House at all!! from the Great Place. You will just see the top of the dome!'

They talked of leaving each other but not of divorce; instead they moved into a new house in Bloomsbury, 31 Bedford Square.

The lease of 29 Bloomsbury Square had expired, the house was due to be demolished, and Emily chose the new house, which was close by, while Ned was in India. Leaving Bloomsbury Square was almost more of a wrench to him than the loss of his conjugal rights. 'I believe the chief cause of your unhappiness is the wrecking of your beautiful and much-loved house. You feel it is the break up of so much you have loved,' wrote Emily. 'Yes,' wrote Ned, 'I am very *very* sad leaving Bloomsbury Square, and so much else came along with it, a sea of surf and sorrow.'[1]

Everyone hated Bedford Square. It still stands today (now Number 29), a big, plain Georgian house facing east. The only sunny room in the house was the nursery, occupied by Mary and Nannie. Ned papered the hall in metallic silver and painted the upstairs drawing room black like Bloomsbury Square. He opened out the dark, mean staircase by building classical arches at the half-landings; the lower one led to a sitting room for Barbie, the upper to a meditation room for Emily, fitted with a picture-rail, his pet hate, from which she hung huge photographs of goggle-eyed Madame Blavatsky and Krishna.

Emily thought the house was haunted and had it exorcized, but it was still creepy. Her headaches grew worse.*

Ned made feverish calculations about money. With building at a standstill, economies became urgent – in 1913–14 he had spent £3,000 on living expenses while the office cost £3,400. He expected his income from building to fall to £2,715 in 1914–15 and, in spite of the money he would earn in India, he proposed cutting living expenses to £2,500 and reducing Emily's allowance. But even this was too much for Emily. 'Don't think I am not doing my best to economize in every way,' she wrote, having sacked the French cook who used 180 eggs a week. 'After this term stop all education if you wish – sell or let Bedford Square – make any arrangements you think wise – only don't ask me to live in a

---

*The legation of the Turkish Republic of Northern Cyprus, who occupied the house when I saw it in 2000, complained of depression, giddiness and headaches. Mushrooms grew on the downstairs walls and no one liked being alone there after dark.

big house and pig it like Onslow Square.' The squalor of Ned's childhood home could only be avoided, she reckoned, by employing at least seven servants in Bedford Square.

Emily offered to go away right out of Ned's life. 'I can offer myself to the Front in some capacity,' she wrote vaguely.[2] But when Dr Haden Guest told her of his hospital in France and the muddle and carnage he found at the Front, Emily's jingoism faded. Convinced that German atrocities were wildly exaggerated by the propagandist British press, she became anxious to go and see for herself. This Ned was determined to prevent; Emily would be bound to draw attention to herself; if anyone was to leave, it must be him.

But not to the war. In spite of his anguish at the casualty lists and his admiration for the courage of 'those evil-smelling bad-tobacco-smoking genial Tommies', he felt no need to help. He could think of little but his own pain. Not even his work mattered much now. He was distraught at Emily's rejection, complaining to her mother Edith Lytton that she wouldn't let him 'come to her'. Edith told Emily that she 'ought to bear everything', but when Emily explained how she felt, Edith 'was very kind and nice'. Ned dreamed that he was in India and found Emily in a procession and 'the natives adulate you before your face and laugh behind your back and lead you on to a temple and on the temple is a horrid word written and you do not or will not understand, and I cannot get near you'. Emily tried to comfort Ned by telling him that 'you can pour both your love and your pain into your work and make it bigger than ever before'. She was right, but it was not until 1919 that he was able to project his own pain into the monument of the Cenotaph.[3]

Ned escaped to India. Emily cried a good deal at the station when he left in December 1914. She loved him more than ever before, she said, somewhat unconvincingly, now that the damoclean sword of sex no longer hung over her. India, once hated as a land of exile – Bedlampore, he called it – offered Ned a retreat from the scolding and failure of Bedford Square and the worries of war. It also provided a much-needed salary of £2,500.

This time Ned brought with him the painter William Nicholson, for whom he had secured a commission to paint an official portrait of the Viceroy, Lord Hardinge. Nicholson became a friend – perhaps the only real male friend Ned had had except Baker, with whom he had been on good terms only when the whole of Africa lay between them. Nicholson was small and fastidious and a natty dresser; he wore spotless white ducks and spotted bowties. Ned thought him bohemian – he and his artist wife Prydie (sister of the painter James Pryde) lived in a studio with a dog, two cats and a parrot, a crowded space very different from the unfriendly roominess of Bedford Square. But Nicholson, in fact, recoiled from artistic squalor; he valued order and neatness, a clean kitchen and linen napkins.

On that wartime voyage to India, a new Ned Lutyens began to emerge. He no longer shut himself in his cabin, doggedly working for hours on end. Instead he played chess 'fast and furious' all day as the ship rolled, and he made an unending stream of puns and jokes which, thought Nicholson, were like an architect's commission – only $7\frac{1}{2}$ per cent were good. The ship was packed with soldiers, sailors and shells, and Ned struck up a friendship with three unsoldierly soldiers, Auberon Herbert ('mad!'), George Lloyd ('a tory demagogue – his mannishness tempered by a life long friendship with Herbert') and the archaeologist Leonard Woolley. Auberon Herbert thought Lutyens 'a divine imp, sillier than anything I have ever dreamed of, quite futile and occasionally brilliant'. Lutyens sat all day writing nonsense verses

> From a stomach over laden
> Mr Woolley died at Aden
> Captain Lloyd has died at Malta
> Perished on his honour's altar
> Shed no bitter tears of salt, ha
> He might have perished at Gibraltar

which he illustrated with blasphemous and indecent caricatures. His method of playing chess infuriated the pompous George Lloyd. When Lloyd made a wrong move, Lutyens produced a match, lit it and stuck it in the hole of the chessboard where the piece should have been put.[4]

Baker was also on the ship, and Ned complained about his idleness and refusal to discuss work – Baker insisted that he was having a moratorium ('I call it a tomorrowtorium').

Near Port Said, Ned wrote to Emily reminding her of their engagement. 'Do you remember the river – we were to rush together, the two streams joined, and on and out to the open sea? It is now the open sea and we seem separate, and I have no oar or rudder and seem helpless, drifting, God knows where.' He was too hurt and full of self-pity to see that Emily's ultimatum had in fact released him, forcing him to look outwards rather than clinging to the wreckage of a marriage that existed only in his imagination. It was Emily, not Ned, who was the loser, for, as he saw, all her strength of character was thrown away on a narrowing, doctrinaire creed – 'a mucous of spirituality that seems to have made a *chemise glissante* that slips to disaster'.[5]

Each day he wrote to Emily, long, rambling diary letters, which he scrawled very fast on thin shiny paper, posting the sheets in the weekly mail. All his woes, his resentment and bitterness about Haden Guest and the Theosophical Society, his misery and anger at Emily's defection, his worry at Robert's dilettantism and lack of discipline (Robert was fourteen), his own lack of education and of moral courage – all were poured out in barely legible, repetitive late-night confessions. He had never written to Emily like that before, never said such angry, cruel, hard things. But there was a time lag, and Emily received them a month after they were written, which somehow weakened their impact. This was less conversation than therapy; not communication but a writing cure.

In India Ned found Lord Hardinge devastated by the recent death of his son from war wounds. Lady Hardinge had died in a London nursing home the previous July, killed by a botched operation for cancer of the uterus. Ned mourned the loss of a very good friend. 'She had a wonderful knack of being at every corner to help a body round it.' Working on the Viceroy's wing of the house always reminded him of her; it was like a country house of which she was the patron.

In Delhi he settled to a comfortable routine, working productively and contentedly all day on detail drawings which showed Viceroy's House up to 15 feet above ground, and meeting the Commissioner for Delhi, Malcolm Hailey, and the Delhi Committee twice a week. 'It is much better fun and the time goes quick,' he wrote.[6] Puns flowed non-stop. The Canon from the Cambridge Mission visited, bringing his colleague, a young Mr Weston: 'I asked if he was related to the "Great Western", and oh dear it took a long time to explain my joke!'*

'I am very relaxed here,' he told Emily. Too relaxed perhaps; or perhaps made irritable by chronic indigestion from Indian food ('name for a racehorse: Indigestion Bi Carbonate out of Soda'). Certainly, relations with Baker were worse than ever. Ned resented Baker's verbal

---

*This is an example of what Ned called a 'Drop Jaw' – an outrageous remark which was intended to break the ice, often causing acute embarrassment to younger, more vulnerable members of the party.

fluency and complained constantly of the sloppiness of his work, accusing him of serving Mammon not art. Baker flared up. 'He said I was rude, perhaps I was. But I returned his rudeness to me at Victoria that day over our agreement. He said after my behaviour that day it was the wish of a Christian to want to work with me at all.'

Professor Patrick Geddes, an authority on Indian town planning, criticized the monumental baroque geometry of New Delhi's town plan. Geddes, who believed in organic planning, proposed putting the city's roads into winding nullahs or watercourses. This, said Ned, was the most idiotically amusing affair, as the nullahs would flood in the rains – 'He seems to talk rot in an insulting way'; but humiliating the hot-tempered Scot with his flowing professorial beard was probably a mistake as Geddes later savaged Lutyen's work.[7]*

The Viceroy was prickly as usual, if anything made more so by William Nicholson's portrait. Nicholson would later say that it was the trickiest portrait he ever had to tackle. He found the Indian light very hard to paint. He produced two or three versions, each more facetious than the last. Hardinge was not best pleased by the version in which spectacular Sikhs in red and gold tunics, huge black beards and white turbans occupied the foreground, while the Viceroy could be seen as a tiny, insignificant figure standing on top of a staircase at the back. Nor was he amused when after six months of sitting and only four days before Nicholson was due to leave, he found a clean canvas. The final version, which still hangs today in the Marble Hall of Viceroy's House, a graveyard of viceregal portraits, shows a small and insignificant full-length Hardinge, cheekily positioned beneath a Lutyens rounded arch. Hardinge commented acidly: 'The picture was said to be like me but in my opinion was not good.'[8]

War made little difference at first to Emily's life at Bedford Square. A Belgian refugee couple named Delville occupied two rooms on the ground floor. They got on Emily's nerves, and she did her best to avoid them, but they complained that she was unkind and that Ned made jokes about them. No room in the house was warm, not even when fires burned all day. Damp patches and mushrooms sprouted on the walls.

---

*Geddes, who was a friend of Lewis Mumford and a leading influence on the inter-war town-planning movement, later dismissed Lutyens as the architectural equivalent of a Rolls-Royce, a rich man's plaything with no relevance to the modern world. Of the abortive plan for Lucknow University, which Lutyens made in 1922, he was scathing: 'super-extravagant monuments to himself in coldest refinement of Georgian architectural indifference to Indian and European alike, and of fabulous expense'.

Emily sat for hours in the gloom of her meditation room, cross-legged and wearing a yellow robe, burning incense in front of a statue of Buddha. Each morning Betty and Mary came and recited a prayer: 'I am a link in a golden chain of love which stretches round the world and I promise to keep my link bright and strong.'9

Theosophy for Emily naturally took precedence over the war effort, and Krishna occupied most of her thoughts. For his sake, she wrote and edited the *Herald of the Star,* the society's monthly newsletter, and endured dreary, gruelling speaking tours, travelling on crowded wartime trains. At Cardiff she addressed 150 people and made several weep. 'I saw the handkerchiefs come out.' Her theosophical connections brought links with Labour, and she addressed a meeting at George Lansbury's Bow constituency, speaking after Sylvia Pankhurst. But she badly misjudged the mood, only discovering too late that her working-class audience was violently anti-war, and she was booed for cheering the war effort.

She tortured Ned with her talk of her 'higher' – that is, sexless – love. 'I think and think about our relations,' she told him. 'I know I cannot give in about your coming to me – it has got to be so impossible for me. I think your long absences made me feel how glad I was to sleep alone.' She could not go back on her position, so he must choose: 'will you keep me as I am or send me away and take another wife. No one will blame you if you did and I would never trouble you.' But that neatly put the decision back to Ned, as she knew very well: 'perhaps I am sure of your answer or I could not ask it'.10 Had Ned put his foot down and insisted that she break with theosophy, she would doubtless have left him.

Krishna's existence was far more remote from the war than Emily's. Living a lonely life at Bude, a seaside resort in Cornwall, he was neglected by Mrs Besant who, having won the legal battle for his custody in May 1914, lost interest both in him and theosophy. Instead, she returned to India to rebuild her political position and when the war came was well poised to launch her campaign for Indian Home Rule. Alone at Bude with his minders, Miss Arundale and her nephew George (Nitya was studying in Oxford), Krishna's self-obsession deepened. Though Mrs Besant was determined that he should go to Oxford, the private tutoring he received made little impression on him; he didn't really understand his lessons, but the adulation he received as World Teacher in exile gave him an abnormal confidence in the importance of his own feelings. Childlike in his naivety, he could be intuitively perceptive. From Bude he wrote long, rambling letters to Mrs Besant (Mother) and Leadbeater, pouring out his feelings about Emily, whom he loved besottedly, his emotions distorted and exaggerated by his lonely exile.

Both Emily and Krishna worked hard at making their love less 'selfish'. Warned by Mrs Besant, they tried not to show their feelings openly. In the autumn of 1914 they agreed a trial separation in order that Emily could become more self-reliant. In February 1915 she visited Bude for a weekend, bringing with her a white Siberian dog for Krishna, and he wrote to Leadbeater: 'I love her *very, very* purely and I am glad that I am not like normal people in that respect. I am *not* that way and *never* shall be.' That Krishna was not and could never be 'that way' was part of his attraction for Emily, but though he called her 'Mummy' she was deceiving herself if she thought her affection for him was part of a pure mother–son relationship; her love was shot through with possessiveness and sexual jealousy. As for Krishna, for all his talk of purity, he was infatuated with Emily, as his brother Nitya perceived – an infatuation potentially more damaging to theosophy than the old charges of sodomy against Leadbeater.[11]

In March 1915 Mrs Besant wrote Emily one of her stern letters, reproaching her for throwing Krishna's exquisite nature 'out of tune'. Krishna had not been able to 'get through' on the astral plane for too long, she wrote. 'An effort to affect the lower consciousness is again being made, and there is a little more response. His health cannot be good when his real life cannot reach the body and he is in a whirl of passion for which his delicately poised frame is wholly unfit.'

Emily, after all her efforts to be less 'selfish', was mortified. Whether Mrs Besant was right to accuse her of trying to invade Krishna's lower consciousness is unproven: the secrets lie buried in Emily's 'lost' theosophical diaries. But her obsession with Krishna was making trouble with her own children. Lacking any real contact with Ned, who was rarely there, and when he was at home was despised as a lowly meat-eater, the children were excessively dependent on Emily. To earn her approval, Barbie and Robert joined her in the theosophical life, becoming friends with Krishna and Nitya. When Barbie grew up to became a strikingly pretty sixteen-year-old, this caused merry havoc. First Nitya fell in love with her and then George Arundale wanted to marry her, which made Nitya miserable though Barbie didn't like Arundale at all.

Increasingly jealous of Emily's infatuation with Krishna, Barbie revolted against theosophy altogether. She scorned Emily's weird friends and nun-like lifestyle – the bare oak boards, and pestle and mortar and lumps of cheese on the table. 'She wants white table cloths and silver salt cellars and says she can't invite her friends to *such* a house,' wailed Emily. Ned's resentment of Krishna ('he is an anglo-Indian and you can understand that,' explained Krishna) was one thing; but the rebellion of her children was something over which Emily had far less control.[12]

Dreading Ned's return, Emily advised him to stay in India where at least he was paid; there was no work in England, and Muntzer the upholsterer had told her that the architect Voysey was in despair and Ned's ex-pupil Paul Phipps had joined the army. But Ned came home in April 1915, and slept in Emily's dressing room, an arrangement that he found unbearable. He lacked energy and complained that he had lost interest in work. Accustomed to easy success, he was frightened by the drying-up of his creative power. Even the war failed to move him. Burned out, stale and depressed, he blamed everything on Emily and her withdrawal of confidence. His life, dedicated for so long to a romantic ideal of service, now seemed to have little meaning.

His father died in May aged eighty-six, but this was nothing beside Emily's defection. (Old Charles left Ned a handsome £2,000, which caused trouble with his envious and impecunious brothers; he tried to keep the legacy secret.)

Ned could see no way to make things better with Emily. 'I hate being away from you. I suffer when with you. So there it is – a long grey twilight.' He sketched a bleak future for their marriage in a parody of Kipling's 'If':

> If I take no interest or care in what you do or how
> If I expect you to take none in me
> If I give up smoke and drink and meat
> If I can make enough money to free you
> From all worldly care now and in the future
> Believe as you believe and change my faith as yours may
>   change . . .[13]

Emily was touched and worried by his misery but felt powerless to help. She couldn't see that her rejection of him had triggered a psychological crisis.

Emily spent June and July working with Dr Haden Guest to convert the Endsleigh Palace Hotel into a war hospital. Krishna and Nitya were staying at Wimbledon in a 'hideous' rented villa, and they came up by underground to Bloomsbury each day to help. Emily scraped meat grease from the gas stoves, which she found a particularly unpleasant task for a vegetarian, especially as she had never in her life cleaned a stove. All this she did willingly for Krishna, while stubbornly resisting Ned's pleas to economize at Bedford Square, which cost as much to run, Ned scolded, as Frances Horner's country house, Mells.

Emily worked for a few months as a VAD in the hospital, but Krishna was not allowed to work with the patients; it was thought that they would object to his colour. Mrs Besant had other ideas for him. The World Teacher must be transformed into an English gentleman. Harold Baillie-Weaver, his new 'keeper', taught him how to dress as an English peacock, wearing suits from Meyer & Mortimer (he later changed his tailor to Huntsman), shirts from Beale & Inman and shoes made by Lobb, which Baillie-Weaver taught him to polish to an acme of shininess. Emily, who never bothered much about clothes, smartened her wardrobe to please Krishna, but he was banished once more to a crammer in Kent to prepare for his Oxford entrance examination.

Ned spent very little time in London that summer. Escaping both the war and Bedford Square, he went to Rome, where the British School was in difficulties. Ned blamed the building committees – there were two in London as well as one in Rome – and especially the chairman, Lord Esher ('rude and brusque and ignorant'), who had appointed a nice but futile clerk of works, Mr Squire. The committees of course blamed Ned for being in India, and Thomas, whom he left in charge, was little help – he was 'tactless as usual and puts everyone in the wrong'. Ned gave up his fee, a hefty £1,500, but his quixotic generosity failed to mollify the committee and certainly failed to solve the problems.*

Back in London in September he complained that the scullery girl wouldn't cut the rind off his breakfast bacon, there was not a single chair to sit on and he had a rotten life. 'Work, work, work – rush, rush, rush and no sympathy and no help . . . A wife who is not a wife and whose every friend seems to count more than a husband – so you see darling I feel sometimes that I must break away and smash up.'[14]

---

*Only the front range of Lutyens's design for the British School was built; the quadrangle was finished in 1938 by another architect. Lutyens was criticized for insisting on using a British contractor and for importing British materials at huge expense in wartime; a consignment of radiators was torpedoed.

He left for India early. He stayed first in Paris, calling on Etienne Mallet, Guillaume's brother, whom he found living in a hotel with a drawing room like an untidy office, littered with parcels and boxes of cigarettes. This brush with reality reminded him of Bedford Square. Like him, Etienne Mallet complained that he didn't have a comfortable chair to sit on, and had to put up with nagging from a wife who was living on her nerves, waiting to hear if any of her sons had been killed. Ned travelled thankfully to Spain, where a commission for the Duke of Peneranda transported him happily into the realms of the never-never.

Peneranda was the younger brother of the Duke of Alba, whom Ned had met with Ivor Guest at Ashby St Ledgers. Fabulously rich owner of the Liria Palace, Alba was a grandee of Spain thirteen times over with the silky charm of an English aristocrat; descended from a son of James II and Arabella Churchill, he was 10th Duke of Berwick and called Winston Churchill 'cousin'. Ned found Peneranda delightful – 'very young and simple in the nice way, full of fun and life'. At last Ned was able to return to the pre-war game of artist and patron. Staying in Madrid in ducal luxury in the Liria Palace, he studied the Escorial and the age of Philip II. 'Grand conceptions but weak in architectural technique and when they leave the doric order – which by the way they run to death – they come awful croppers.'

With an English chauffeur at the wheel of Peneranda's Rolls-Royce, they purred over dog-infested dirt tracks through the poverty-stricken plains of the river Tagus. At Ventosilla they stayed with the Duke of Santona, Alba's brother-in-law, who wanted a new house. The duchess, Alba's sister, whose money paid for everything, was 'very small – always in breeches and gaiters – more like a boy to look at than a woman. Has no nerves and rides astride, though in the evening she appeared gowned like a Byzantine queen.' Ned empathized at once with the chaotic jumble of children, priests and Irish nannies. 'They are keen only on country life,' he wrote. 'They are independent of everything and everybody. Their own farm, bakery, they breed mules, pigs, preserve their game, make their own electric light and power for their farm machinery. A Lambay in a sea of Spain.'[15] So it was; but a Lambay of feudal privilege surrounded by a sea of angry peasant Spain that was soon to erupt into civil war.

For the Duke of Santona, Ned designed a courtyard house and chapel at Ventosilla, a Spanish version of Orchards. Half a day's drive, this time in a Mercedes, took him on to El Gordo, where Peneranda wanted to build. The estate was impassable by car and Ned crossed the steep ravines and nullahs jolting in a mule cart behind Peneranda and his sister, who rode horses. They found a site overlooking the Tagus, and Lutyens made designs for a house arranged around an arcaded courtyard. Perspectives of this were exhibited at the Academy in 1917. But the site turned out to be a prehistoric burial ground, and a new site had to be found at El Guadalperal two miles away.

The construction of El Guadalperal was overtaken by the Spanish Civil War, and the house was never built, though Lutyens's red-tiled, white-washed farm buildings still survive.[16] Ned's Spanish castles really *were* castles in the air, an escape into a doomed, unreal world of baroque patronage. Wanting so badly to believe in the fairy tale, Ned shut his eyes to the reality. Less a reactionary than a dreamer, he allowed his artist's imagination to respond to the drama of an old order poised, as British India also was, on the brink of collapse and implosion.

At Gibraltar Ned was joined by Baker. En route to India they spent a week sightseeing in Egypt, studying the Pyramids. Ned refused to be impressed. 'Great God-fearing children playing with huge toy bricks and then telling their stories in picture words with no adjectives.' He was far more impressed by Lady Anne Blunt, whom he visited at Sheykh Obeyd; she looked wonderful in Bedouin clothes, and the house she had designed he admired more than any pyramid. 'I don't think she realizes what a very able designer she is and how she achieves the obvious and simple and that with grace.'

On the boat to India Ned noticed Baker absorbed in a large tome by an Italian on religion in art. 'Judging by the selection of illustrations the connection cannot be proven,' was Ned's caustic comment. When he saw Baker designing emblems and inscriptions for his Secretariats, Ned couldn't resist giving a lecture. An architect, he told Baker, should design in three dimensions rather than merely decorating his structures.[17]

In January 1916, as construction began on the inclined way up Raisina Hill, Lutyens realized for the first time that the approved gradient of 22½ was so steep that it partially blocked the vista. By drawing his own sections he discovered to his horror that Government House disappeared altogether from view at certain points along the Processional Way. He instantly fired off a typed letter of complaint to Baker. 'This is not a satisfactory collaboration!' he fumed. Baker wrote notes on Ned's letter: the gradient was agreed last year 'and you did not object then ... It is silly writing formal letters to me. I have explained my point of view so often.'[18] Thus began one of the most notorious quarrels in architectural history, documented in files bulging with the letters typed on flimsy copy paper that flew between Lutyens, Baker, Malcolm Hailey and Lord Hardinge.

Lutyens freely admitted that he had blundered in signing the guarantee but demanded that the gradient be flattened, creating a longer, lower slope to restore the vista. Baker insisted that the steep incline was essential to his design. It enabled him to create a level platform, known as Government Court, linking the two Secretariats on either side. Flattening the gradient as Lutyens demanded would create a deep 'railway cutting' between the two blocks of Secretariats, preventing intercommunication. The steep gradient was the inevitable consequence of the decision to raise the Secretariats on to Raisina Hill, which Baker had demanded and Lutyens agreed to back in 1913.

Though Baker may have known all along that the gradient would have this result, and was perhaps guilty of bad faith in not discussing it, the point was so basic that Lutyens should have seen for himself. Only now did he realize that the perspectives drawn by William Walcot at Baker's instruction in 1913 gave a misleading impression of an uninterrupted vista to Government House; they were 'as much value as regards truth as a seaside resort council's station advertisement to show the amenities of the place'. Ned raged against Baker's attempt to emulate 'the shop window effect of a South African Kopje', but the fact was that he had failed to check the figures for himself.

Lutyens and Baker both addressed formal letters stating their case to the Delhi Committee. On 18 February the Committee, chaired by Malcolm Hailey, decided in favour of Baker, as they were almost bound to do on the legalistic grounds that Lutyens had already signed an agreement, as well as on grounds of cost. Lutyens then appealed to the Viceroy.

Lutyens lunched with Hardinge on 10 March. 'I feel rather nervous about the interview,' he wrote. Hardinge was preparing to leave India in April, and the previous day had been awarded the Order of the Garter. This must have come as a relief to Hardinge whose career was in serious jeopardy as a result of his misjudgement in agreeing to the disastrous Mesopotamian campaign, when Indian troops had been routed at Kut by the Turks. Lutyens found him in a most unpleasant mood, steely, hard and determined to say no. Refusing to go into the merits of the case, Hardinge insisted that Lutyens was bound by his agreement and he offered only one chink of hope – Lutyens could raise the matter with the incoming Viceroy, Lord Chelmsford.[19]

A few days later Hardinge lunched alone with Baker. He told him he was 'very angry' with Lutyens for reopening the issue. Lutyens had been 'a thorn in his side from the beginning'; his estimates could never be trusted and his wild and conceited talk irritated him. Hardinge laughed as he told Baker that Lutyens had said, 'You know I am accustomed to have my opinion always taken.' Lutyens was indeed used to having his way with personal clients, Baker said. 'Yes,' Hardinge responded, 'the spoilt child.' Hardinge then asked Baker, as a sensible man, to persuade Lutyens on the voyage home to change his ways. 'His whole attitude of grousing and disloyalty and wild talk when he does not get his way in everything is doing everyone harm and more especially himself.'

Baker wrote a record of this extraordinary outburst, thinking that it might one day protect his reputation. 'I told the VR,' he wrote rather smugly, 'that the more I worked with Lutyens, the more I wondered at his extraordinary talents but the difficulty was that these were so uncontrolled of human consideration and feeling for other people's point of view.' To his wife Baker wrote rather differently. 'Oh dear! Two weeks more of Lutyens. He is such an awful brute to work with ... I have got to despise him so – such arrogance and egotism.'[20]

It is clear from Baker's account that – for him and Hardinge – the real issue was not so much the artistic merit of the gradient as Lutyens's personality and behaviour. Lutyens did not play the game according to the rules; he behaved like an artist, not a government servant. For Ned, however, the issue was wholly aesthetic. 'It is not right or fine that the central object of a vista should disappear and reappear. An avenue stops at its first break and the stop should have a designed termination, not an ever varying one.' As for Hardinge and Baker's insistence that to flatten the gradient would create a 'railway cutting' between the Secretariats, he wearily explained that the slopes could be used to good effect for steps, as in an Italian garden. 'I have done *so* many gardens.'[21]

'Ought I to resign?' Ned asked Emily. He talked so freely of resigning that the Delhi Committee almost began to believe him. Claude Hill of the Delhi Committee asked Baker if he thought Ned was serious. 'I said *no* emphatically,' wrote Baker in his diary.

Lutyens and Baker sailed home together at the end of March. Barely on speaking terms, the two architects avoided each other. Baker did try once to have it out with Lutyens but, hardly surprisingly, he found him impossible to deal with. 'I told him I would not talk unless he kept temperate.' Baker then delivered a homily on disloyalty and seeing the good in others which, inevitably, went down badly. Lutyens refused to stick to the point and threatened to refer the matter to the King. Baker pleaded with him to have a sense of humour with regard to himself sometimes, 'but I never got a smile'.[22]

'I own I do not see where the joke comes in,' wrote Ned.

For six years he fought to persuade the Government of India to reverse their decision. The gradient – his Bakerloo, as he called it – became an obsession, much as Emily's ending of sex had been. The anger he felt towards Emily was transferred to Baker, whom he never ceased to vilify. His shameless propaganda certainly undermined Baker's reputation and probably destroyed his confidence too.

The avalanche of hurt, angry letters from India continued to rain down upon Emily. 'I know I have lost you and no interest of mine is of interest to you and we can but write just the daily journal and there is little behind it and other shadows lie across my way and you are ever on the other side.'

He returned to England in April 1916 full of the woes of middle age. A chronic hydrocele, or swelling in the scrotum, had been a source of dragging pain for months. Dr Fripp reassured him that it was 'just a mechanical fault, nothing sexual or harmful or ill-mannered or malignant', but draining did no good; it continued to swell, and Ned had to undergo a painful but effective operation. Somehow the condition seemed to symbolize the failure of his sex life. 'I don't think you can possibly come to the hospital when I am there,' he told Emily. In hospital, however, he played cheerful host to old friends, who visited in droves while Emily stayed away – William Nicholson, Lady Horner of Mells, Cecil and Maud Baring.

Instead of sleeping in Emily's dressing room at Bedford Square, he now slept downstairs in Barbie's old sitting room, 'further away from the worry and failure of it all'. He told Emily: 'I cannot go through this year what I went through last.' Emily was unrepentant. 'I know I cannot perhaps understand a man – a man's point of view and his difficulties. But perhaps you do not on your side quite understand the woman's point of view.'

Have you no heart? wailed Ned. 'Is it to be Krishna-Jill to Krishna-Jack when Mrs Besant nods her head?'[23]

But not even Mrs Besant nodded her head at Emily's next venture. Since January 1915 Emily had been planning a political initiative, a Home Rule for India League in London, to support the nationalist movement which Mrs Besant had launched in India as leader of the Congress Party. 'Don't be alarmed darling I don't think you will mind this one!' she wrote to Ned, explaining that her new movement was quite distinct from theosophy. Self-government for India, argued Emily, was the only way Britain could hope to reward India's loyalty in wartime, and retain the support of the English-educated Indian middle classes, schooled to believe in the virtues of parliamentary government. That she was promoting disaffection and division in wartime did not occur to her as she canvassed the support of London's progressive intelligentsia.

Ned watched with growing dismay as his wife organized a movement intended to undermine the Indian empire which had commissioned his life's work. 'If you come to India on a *political* mission,' he wrote, 'I suppose I shall have to chuck Delhi and leave it to Baker! Which will spell ruin for us.' By now Emily was so estranged that whatever he said made her determined to do the opposite. 'Don't think me unmindful of your wishes but remember you always wanted to squash everything I ever wished to do from the first . . . I must go ahead with what I believe to be right.'

In June 1916 when Ned was safely out of the country, visiting Peneranda in Spain,* Emily launched her league in the drawing room at Bedford Square. *The Times* promptly condemned it as a mischievous movement. 'Cranky people . . . do many mad things but surely the maddest is to encourage a "Home Rule" movement in India at a moment when we are just entering upon the greatest crisis of the war' (19 June 1916). Emily replied next day, making it plain that she was indeed the cranky person. Mrs Besant wrote telling her to 'keep out of this as it will irritate my dear Vishvakarman' (her name for Ned). Edward Hudson annoyed Emily even more by telling her that Ned was a genius in her care and it was her duty to look after him.[24]

On 24 June, the week after Emily launched her league, Ned went to the opera (Verdi's *Otello*) as a guest of Maud Cunard. The party in her box included Arthur Balfour and Ezra Pound, and a woman he had never met: Lady Sackville. She gave him a lift home in her Rolls-Royce.

---

*Ned took Robert, and they travelled via Paris, where the sight of the Champs-Elysées made them 'boil at the chance lost at Delhi by the narrow ineptitude of colonialism and bureaucracy'.

If Lutyens's life had been a novel, her entrance could hardly have been better timed. Lady Sackville was rich, with a beautiful complexion, great warmth, a French accent and 'a general ambience of deliciously scented opulence'. She always wore hats and sables, 'the softness of the fur emphasizing the softness of everything else about her (except her will)'. To Ned, she must have seemed an ideal client; an aristocratic Edwardian hostess who talked seriously about building in wartime. Older than he (she was fifty-four to his forty-seven), she was instantly attracted. 'He is charming,' she wrote in her diary after the opera. More worldly and more sexually experienced than naive, romantic Ned, Lady Sackville had the power to release him from the bitterness and recrimination that was souring his marriage. She knew it, too.

On 29 June she lunched at Bedford Square. 'He is amusing; she is dull,' she wrote. Lutyens came back to see her house at Hill Street. 'He is inclined . . .' she wrote; and the page was later torn off.[25]

Victoria Sackville was the illegitimate daughter of one Lord Sackville by a Spanish dancer, Pepita, and the wife of another, her first cousin Lionel Sackville. She had inherited a fortune from her admirer of ten years, Sir John Murray Scott, an immensely fat and rich bachelor who had inherited *his* fortune from Sir Richard Wallace, whose secretary he had been. But the publicity of the law case about the will (1913), which she won, made her notorious, humiliated Lionel and wrecked her marriage. By 1916 Lionel Sackville was seriously estranged, having an affair with a mistress named Olive Rubens, and Lady Sackville was planning to build herself a bolt-hole, a house by the sea to which she could escape.

Meanwhile, her home was the magnificent palace at Knole, a house as big as a medieval town. Ned visited her there on 27 July. Guns boomed from France all day and the windows rattled as together they explored the vast complex of buildings, even the roof. Ned begged her to let him build her the house she wanted by the sea at Hove. 'His ideas agree with mine thoroughly,' she wrote, 'and I am tempted, as it would add great value to the house later on.'

In the summer of 1916 Ned and Emily borrowed Folly Farm from Mrs Merton. It was the only summer they ever spent together in one of his houses. Ned had designed extensions to Folly Farm for Mrs Merton's husband Zackery in 1913–14. To the neat, careful brick William and Mary box he had designed for H. Cochrane in 1906, he persuaded

Zackery Merton to add what he called cowsheds – an exuberant barn-like structure with steep tiled roofs sweeping down to a lily tank surrounded by chunky pillars. It seems unbelievable that this was designed in the same year as classical New Delhi.

Antonia Merton, now widowed, was rich, kind and plain with a strong German accent and good grooming from a French maid. Ned persuaded her to decorate the hall at Folly Farm, painting the walls black with a red wooden balcony and commissioning murals from William Nicholson. To Ned she was another mother figure – he called her Mere-Toni or The Mert – but she soon became intimate with Emily. After Zackery died she had confided in Emily, who comforted her; she was later converted to theosophy and became a generous benefactor.[26]

The Lutyens children remembered the summer of 1916 as an idyll. William Nicholson was there, painting a *trompe l'œil* of birdcages, bell pulls and red lacquer windows in the dining room, where the giant fireplace reached to the ceiling. He spent a lot of time painting a portrait of Ursula; she sat in the billiard room with its strange black marble pillars and the alphabet painted in red in an arc above the chimney piece (capital A for Antonia at the beginning, capital Z at the end and capital M in the middle for Zackery Merton). The portrait went through seven versions but remained stubbornly unfinished: he eventually painted her wearing a bearskin. Ursula laughed at 'Nick's' clowning with the playwright Edward Knoblock as giant to his dwarf, and was flattered by his admiration for her, but Mary disliked him. She thought he was like a mischievous monkey with a sharp clever tongue, but she adored his wife Prydie, who played the pianola for hours in the gallery.

Mary liked Folly Farm for its luxury, the rich satin eiderdown on her bed and the sense of order and harmony that she later recognized at Munstead Wood. But for Emily and Ned the truce was an uneasy one. 'I know what you feel and the hopelessness of my position,' wrote Ned on 4 August. 'I expect no change but what you do not know there is no good reason to tell you.'[27] Was he thinking of Lady Sackville? He had told Emily six months before that he thought she should release him from his vows, and now he had the opportunity.

Lady Sackville visited Folly Farm on 10 August and stayed a night. She had bought a plot at Hove, and she wanted to talk about her house. 'I like him very much and I think I shall make him amenable to what I want.'

Back in London they began in earnest to play the game of architect and client. He drew plans for a house which was 'delightful' but too expensive, with a grand double cube hall (measuring 60′ × 30′ × 30′), she noted on 10 October. Next day they visited Hampton Court, where she noticed a back staircase with a big sweep which she wanted to copy. Ned introduced her to Roger Fry, 'an ugly, dirty-looking individual', whom Ned asked mockingly if he was searching for inspiration. 'Oh certainly not,' snapped Fry.

On 18 October Ned stayed the night at Knole, bringing with him a third and a fourth plan. She gave him his favourite *filet de bœuf* and noticed that he was afraid of the dark. 'He wears extremely well, and I like him and his work more and more.' A week later he was again at Knole, confiding his anxieties about Emily. 'He told me about the Monk, and the refusal of the Mother Superior,' she wrote, referring presumably to Krishna and Mrs Besant. Emily had failed to break with Krishna and theosophy, and Ned's unhappiness brought him closer to B.M. (Bonne Mère), as Lady Sackville was known. On 2 November: 'He looks so tired and does too much.'

'We seem to hit it off like he did with Miss Jekyll,' Lady Sackville wrote.[28] The Hove house, they both knew, was a fiction, as no building could begin until the war was over. But Lady Sackville promised to promote Ned's career in England. She also planned to smooth his path in India by persuading Hardinge, who had once been an admirer of hers, to soften towards him.

In May Ned had received a telegram: 'GOVERNMENT INDIA HAVE ISSUED OFFICIAL ORDERS DIRECTION COMMITTEE TO RETAIN INCLINED PLANE AT GRADIENT ONE IN TWENTY TWO ALREADY DECIDED ON.' This was followed by a letter from Claude Hill of the Delhi Committee telling him to treat the matter of the gradient as closed and to collaborate with Baker.[29]

Naturally, Ned did the opposite. He appealed to the highest authority he knew: Queen Mary. In August the ramrod-backed, gimlet-eyed Queen paid a visit to Apple Tree Yard to inspect the Delhi drawings. 'She was rather prim and sticky and horribly shocked to find Govt Ho had been cut down,' wrote Ned, who afterwards regretted abstaining from making jokes.

Next he saw the Indian Secretary Austen Chamberlain, who was polite but showed little interest in Delhi. On 4 November Ned brought his plans to Buckingham Palace, spreading them out on the dining-room table to explain the gradient to the King. Ned wrote a memorandum, putting his own words into the King's mouth – the King, he said, had deplored the gradient and agreed, of course, that Government House should be given priority over everything else. ('I'm not much of a fisherman,' Ned quipped afterwards, 'but if I had caught him, I should have let him go.')[30]

Ned thought he had a trump card, but it turned out to be a joker. When he circulated his memorandum of the interview with the King, it provoked a damaging counter-attack. Austen Chamberlain told Stamfordham, the King's Private Secretary, that Lutyens was 'an artist with no regard for money and little aptitude for business'. Hardinge, who had managed neatly to sidestep the mess he had made of the Mesopotamia campaign, emerging unscathed as Permanent Secretary at the Foreign Office, was poisonous, in spite of Lady Sackville's honeyed words, or perhaps because of them. 'It is so like Lutyens to try in a spiteful way to stir up mud,' he told Malcolm Hailey, 'but happily in this instance he has failed entirely.' He arranged for Baker to see the Queen, and soon she was reproaching Hardinge for having appointed Lutyens in the first place.

Unknown to Lutyens, the very existence of New Delhi was in jeopardy and Hardinge was fighting to stop the whole project from being shelved. Austen Chamberlain was, like many Unionists, convinced that the Liberal government's decision to move the capital to Delhi was a mistake. In 1916 he drafted a dispatch to Chelmsford, the new Viceroy, urging reconsideration of the Delhi project in view of the altered financial conditions caused by the war. He withheld this on receiving an intemperate memorandum from Curzon, demanding the 'peaceful extinction' of the Raisina scheme, on the grounds that it was an unpardonable extravagance, likely to cost £18 million, a financial incubus which was indefensible in wartime. When a copy of this was leaked to Hardinge at the Foreign Office, he acted swiftly to block it. Hardinge saw himself as the founder of New Delhi, in which he had invested much personal vanity, and he warned Chamberlain that abandoning the capital now would be read as evidence of British irresolution, signalling the impermanence of British rule. He alerted the palace too. George V was 'perfectly furious' when he heard of Curzon's memorandum and insisted on the completion of the original design. Chelmsford was commanded by the King to ensure that the original design was carried out, even if the war meant that it took twenty years.[31]

Lutyens seems to have known nothing of this secret manoeuvring. His obsession with Baker and the gradient, coupled with his political naivety, blinded him to the real danger that Delhi might be shelved, not only for the duration of the war, but for all time. To Hardinge, who was in the midst of this battle, Lutyens's demands for yet more money and his 'disloyalty' over the gradient were surely exasperating.

Ned left for India in November 1916 in better spirits, encouraged by 'loving words' from Emily (she was always nice to him when seeing him off). He felt happier than he had for years, he told her: 'when I am older I shall be able to hold you without fear and we shall be a very happy and contented Darby and Joan with lots of grandchildren'. The same day he told Lady Sackville that Emily had been very hard and uncompromising and that it made him wretched.[32]

It was an adventurous journey. First he visited Peneranda in Spain, where he was nearly killed twice by accidents to the ferry and the Rolls-Royce. After working like a slave to peg out both the Santona house and El Guadalperal, he spent a day with King Alfonso, who came to Alba's shooting party. Ned stood beside the King as he shot with two loaders and three guns. 'I know a king and like the feeling of it,' he told Emily. 'So very different to ours!'

Ned had his next brush with death just past Marseilles. As he was shaving one morning the ship's guns fired. He struggled into his inflatable Gieves waistcoat, which fortunately he had with him.* Bowing to Emily's photograph ('I hope you only remembered that I loved you and not how I have hurt you,' she wrote), he marched up on deck to find the ship being torpedoed by two submarines firing shells which splashed into the water behind it. After a sharp gun battle lasting an hour and forty minutes, which the passengers watched while breakfasting on deck, the submarines disappeared. It was 'very nerve destroying': Ned spent the rest of the voyage in a state of anxiety, never daring to undress or bath.[33]

He had hopes of enlisting the sympathy of the new Viceroy. But the schoolmasterly forty-seven-year-old Chelmsford was a disappointment: his previous appointment had been as a Captain in the Dorset territorials guarding a wireless station near Simla. Ned was embarrassingly late for his first viceregal dinner – his car broke down

---

*The year before, having wired the children, 'Pa sails from Ma sails', he had sent the Gieves home with a message, 'If anything should happen to me you have only to take out the cork and listen to father's last breath.'

and by the time he arrived at Government House, pudding was already being eaten. Chelmsford listened to him with apparent sympathy but he did nothing to intervene. 'Lord Chelmsford leaves everything to the government,' complained Ned, 'and takes little personal interest, and that is of a non-interfering sort.' Chelmsford did exactly what his civil servants wanted, and left all decisions to Malcolm Hailey and the Delhi Committee, which naturally, or so Ned thought, being in Baker's pocket and anxious to avoid more expense, saw no reason to reopen the gradient question. What Ned failed to realize was that Chelmsford and Hailey were both wholly engaged in maintaining work on Delhi and resisting pressures to abandon the new capital.

Ned spent a lonely Christmas at Delhi and buried himself in work. By 24 January 1917 he had covered 25 yards of tracing paper; on 1 February the tally was 40 yards. He worked from 9 a.m. until 11 or 12 at night, never went out in the day, took almost no exercise and allowed himself only the briefest of intervals for meals. This was perhaps a classic case of sublimation; certainly, the enforced celibacy of India made it easy for him to work, removing the sense of failure that Emily's presence inevitably brought. He covered many yards of paper with detailed drawings for the Government House estimates and more with plans for the gardens, 'my *pièce de résistance*'.[34] This was the Mogul garden occupying ten acres of barren ground on the west front of Government House. As building operations slowed to a standstill on the house, the contractors' teams of hundreds of men turned to work on the garden, creating a hospitable terrain for Ned's dream of carpet-like Mogul patterns, fountains, canals and red sandstone lily leaves.

Cheered by an additional £130,000 to spend on Government House, Ned continued to design feverishly, even though the stop on building meant that no more detailed drawings were required. He was paid £5 5s. a day, and he devoted every spare moment to designing 'something that may or may not be' – the Ethnological Museum, the Record Office and a possible cathedral ('I find myself singing Te Deums all day and doing diasporas ?? in my bath'). In the evenings after dinner he worked on jobs back in England until lights went out at midnight. Each day he designed a different mantelpiece for Lady Sackville, as proof that 'the house of the future is not forgotten'. That winter he sent home £2,000. 'I look to Delhi to provide a fortune for you all after I have made my exit,' he told Emily. 'It seems about all I can do for my family now.'

By 1917 Government House was reaching upper basement level, and a pattern of catacombs and piers could be clearly discerned on Raisina

Hill. The building site swarmed with labourers and bristled with wooden scaffolding poles; it was criss-crossed with trolley lines for the trucks conveying the brilliant pink sandstone cut from the quarries of Dholphur. As the walls rose, Ned gleefully watched Baker sink into 'the furrowed clay of his own despondency'. Already it was apparent that Ned's buildings were better than Baker's. Edwin Montagu, Ned's old adversary, newly appointed Indian Secretary, visited Delhi in the winter of 1917 and was greatly impressed by Lutyens's superiority over Baker. 'Lutyens shows distinction of architecture and novelty of idea which is very refreshing and is obvious, although the basement storey and lay-out is practically all that has been done.'[35]

Chapter Fourteen
MacSack
1916–1920

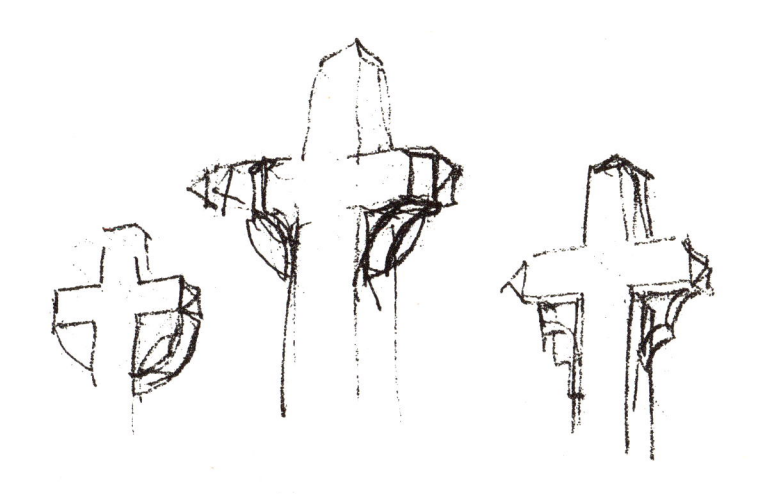

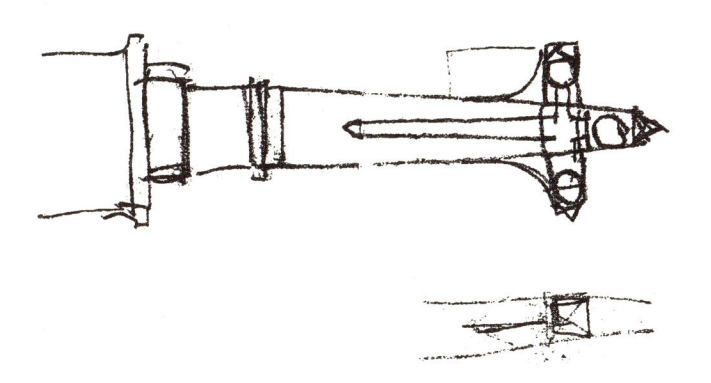

Ned's sketches of the War Cross, doodled on the back of a letter from Emily.

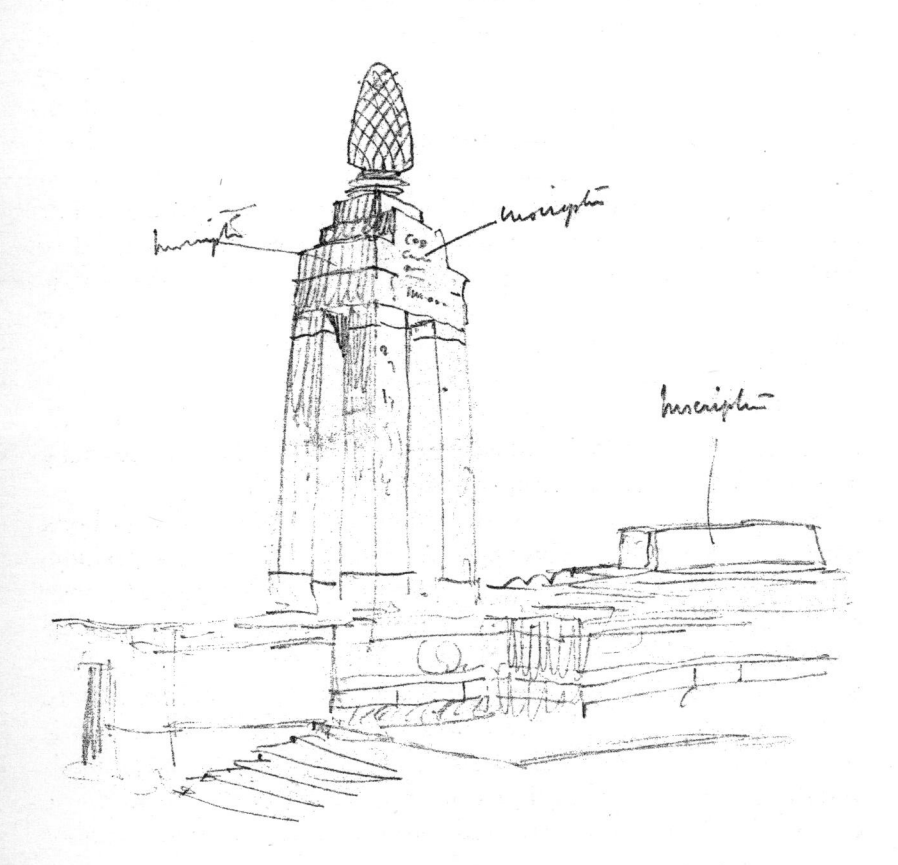

Sketches by Ned of the Hyde Park War Shrine (August 1918). The design was not executed. No one liked the pylons and fir cones.

For Emily, the winter of 1916–17 was the worst winter of the war. Coal shortages and arctic winds made 31 Bedford Square colder than ever. The servants' rooms were so damp that their clothes were wet in the morning. Emily retreated to bed whenever she could, but even with several hot-water bottles and a dog and a child for company it was too cold to sleep. 'Words will never describe to you the awful coldness of this house,' she told Ned.

Both Barbie and Robert were now in revolt against theosophy and their mother. Robert dressed eccentrically in long yellow socks and stocks, chain-smoked cigarettes and fancied himself as a Byron or a Bulwer Lytton. He wanted to be a writer and go to Cambridge, but he knew no Latin or Greek, for which he blamed Emily and the progressive education she had given him at King Alfred's. Emily dispatched him to a series of clergyman tutors in the country, who regularly expelled him for smoking cigarettes. Barbie was more conventional and more focussed. Socially ambitious, she determined to remove herself from her mother's weird life by making a fashionable marriage. Emily did none of the chaperoning and party-giving that was expected of upper-middle-class mothers; it never occurred to her that she should. Barbie went to dances every night of the week and worked as a telephonist in Pamela Lytton's hospital by day. Emily scolded her for leading a life of idle pleasure-seeking and extravagance in wartime. To which Barbie replied frankly that she couldn't feel the war, or its call, or any national need – she wished she could. At least she kept the young men from more harmful occupations and companions.[1]

Money was a worry. Ned would not allow Emily a chequebook when he was in India, nor give her a statement of his financial position; rather than trust his wife, he gave Thomas, the office manager, power of attorney and Emily drew money from Thomas. She was appalled when Thomas announced that Ned was £600 overdrawn and the bank would lend no more. 'It is not right that I should be kept in ignorance of our position. I had no idea it was so bad.' She introduced drastic economies. The French cook was sacked, along with two housemaids and the parlourmaid. She told Barbie to stop going out at night to save on taxis. This was not well received. 'She is far too selfish and luxurious at present,' was Emily's comment. Emily made do with one housemaid, shut up the big rooms and made her own bed. Christmas was grim. No turkey, for economy, but a sham chicken made out of pounded haricot beans; Barbie and Robert were glum and rude and irritable with the younger children. 'Life is too horrible for any words at this moment, nothing but tragedy, cold and gloom.'

The one bright spot was the fall of the Tsar. Emily cheered the Russian Revolution of March 1917 in the theosophical *Herald*, annoying Mrs Besant who believed in the divine right of kings. Influenced by George Lansbury, Emily championed Labour and urged pacifism, of which the Masters disapproved. 'Oh Nedi! It is really an awful time and one's little personal worries and troubles seem swallowed up in the vast unhappiness of the world.' That cruel winter taught her that 'the old world is gone, and we have laboriously to build a new world out of the ruins'.[2]

It was a lesson that Ned did not want to learn. He returned from India that May to greater financial uncertainty than ever. Delhi was now shelved for the duration of the war, eliminating his sole reliable source of income. The London office staff had shrunk to two, which meant that he found himself working as hard as ever.

Ostrich-like, he buried his head in the sand and played games of make-believe with Lady Sackville. The prototypical Edwardian, as defined by her daughter Vita (in *The Edwardians*), Lady Sackville made him feel safe.

At first it seemed as if Ned might tire of Lady Sackville, and that Emily would take her up, as had happened with Arthur Chapman, Marie Mallet and Mrs Merton – all clients whom Emily had befriended once Ned had ceased to build and had no further use for them. In May Lady Sackville asked herself to lunch with Emily: 'I know you will collar Lady S and her spare cash for the TS,' wrote Ned to Emily.

But Lady Sackville had no intention of becoming another Mère-Toni, nor was she remotely interested in theosophy – on the contrary, she was faintly shocked at Emily receiving such low-caste Indians as Krishna and Nitya in her house.[3] Lady Sackville wanted Ned for herself.

They were already calling each other by private names – he was McNed to her MacSack.*

MacSack kept a diary which charts their relationship; her terse,

---

*When Barbara Jekyll married Francis McLaren, her sister Pamela having married Reginald McKenna, Ned had joked that to be loved by a Jekyll you must be a Mac.

matter-of-fact entries fill out the gaps and silences left by Ned in his increasingly illegible and disjointed jottings to Emily. His letters to MacSack are even less informative, often written in the form of baby language ('velly velly, Bleth you'), puns and cryptic one-liners.

Patron, older woman and *grande dame*, MacSack played Lady Ashburton to Ned's Thomas Carlyle, introducing him to the glitzy, plutocratic society of Maud Cunard, the Astors and Diana Cooper while Emily, like Jane Carlyle, stayed at home. Ned was lionized as a genius and celebrated for his wit; but in becoming a professional socialite and diner-out he lost the intensity, the emotional involvement and puritanical simplicity that had fired his early work.

By the spring of 1917 MacSack's marriage was beyond repair. In March Lionel Sackville had returned from the war, and she complained of his coldness and indifference. His mistress Olive Rubens was now installed in the laundry at Knole, and he admitted his feelings to his wife, telling her that he would understand if she loved someone else. Ned came to Knole every weekend. Although the building plot in Hove was abandoned in the face of planning difficulties with the council, MacSack and McNed played the game of patron and artist with increasing intensity. Taken to visit her daughter Vita and Vita's husband Harold Nicolson at Long Barn, Ned advised about alterations to their staircase and garden (they became the MacVitas). MacSack and McNed busied themselves with rearranging Knole and buying a site in Mayfair, while MacSack continued to angle for a house in Brighton ('I ought to have one, as I feel miserable at times at Knole!'). They visited Chevening and stayed with the Astors at Hever, where Ned proposed a butterfly garden growing everything that butterflies liked.*

In June, so MacSack recorded in her diary, Ned told her 'how he had never, never loved another woman or touched anybody but his wife and she refuses him now'.[4]

In July 1917 Lutyens was invited by the Imperial War Graves Commission to advise on military cemeteries in France and their memorials. He was surprised, honoured and (according to MacSack) 'very emotional' about it.

Lutyens was joined on the project by the ubiquitous Baker and by Charles Aitken, director of the Tate Gallery ('oh such a namby pamby ass', according to Ned). On the boat he bumped into J. M. Barrie,

---

*He built a fully-functioning butterfly garden at New Delhi.

coming out to look for the grave of 'his boy', George Llewellyn Davies, and Barrie joined the party. Billeted in a comfortable chateau near Montreuil, they were not allowed to see the front, but took long motor drives among the sites of past slaughters and temporary cemeteries. Ned joked so much that they called him the War Baby, and he sparred with Baker, who contradicted everything he said. Under the clowning, Ned was deeply stirred. The cemeteries, he told Emily, 'are pathetic . . . What humanity can endure and suffer is beyond belief. The battlefields – the obliteration of all human endeavour and achievement and the human achievement of destruction is bettered by the poppies and wild flowers that are as friendly to an exploded shell as they are to the leg of a garden seat in Surrey.'

From the poppies of northern France his mind went back to a Surrey garden; to Bumps and a vision of pastoral. Conventional monuments – crosses, lych-gates – seemed to him utterly inadequate beside the mass deaths and suffering of war. He wrote:

> Ribbons of little crosses each touching each other across a cemetery, set in a wilderness of annuals and where one sort of flower is grown the effect is charming, easy and oh so pathetic. One thinks for the moment no other monument is needed . . . But the only monument can be one where the endeavour is sincere to make such monument permanent – a solid ball of bronze![5]

Very soon the idea of the great ball of bronze evolved into something equally permanent: the Great War Stone.

Baker and Charles Aitken both urged a cross – Baker suggested five points, one for each colony. Others wanted a lych-gate to recreate the homeliness of an English churchyard. Ned, on the other hand, wanted to give the war cemeteries an altar. On a platform of three steps ('the upper and lower steps of a width twice that of the centre step to give due dignity'), he proposed to place a stone 12 feet long, facing the men who lay buried looking east towards the enemy. But the stone was also a segment of a vast circle: all its horizontals were parts of parallel spheres 1,801 feet 8 inches in diameter, and its verticals met 1,801 feet 8 inches above the centres of the spheres. Not just a block of stone, the great stone had a secret geometrical meaning. It was barely visible to the naked eye and easily weathered by erosion (the rise on the centre of the bottom step was only one inch) but the spherical surface was a symbol of hope. For Lutyens the symbol of happiness had always been a circle.

Ned was greatly helped with his idea for the stone by Barrie, who saw at once that the cross was too conventional. 'What appeals to the English church party does not appeal to all,' he wrote, urging that the war cemeteries 'seem to call for something special to themselves'. When Ned suggested calling his stone an altar, Barrie objected that it was too 'churchey' and would offend the Scots. He told General Fabian Ware, the Director of the War Graves Commission: 'I think there is something rather grand in its simplicity about this proposal ... Lutyens's is one of the most imaginative minds I have ever known, and I'd like to see some practical development of this idea from him.' Asked by Barrie to supply a name for his stone, Ned wrote out a 'stoneology': 'Altar – the Stone – the war stone – the great stone – the Great War Stone ...' Fabian Ware, an ex-editor of the *Morning Post*, was immediately sympathetic to Ned's concept of the great war stone, in spite of the fact that Ned wrote jokey letters addressing him as Mon General and signing himself Votre Toujours.

Back in London, Ned immediately began canvassing support for his stone. 'I have seen many people,' he told Ware on 3 August, 'and they one and all like the idea of the big stone to the East, the flanking pyramid oaks and the sky ... forming the vault to them all'.[6] Artistically, he explained, in a country of poplars like France, you want building lines to be horizontal, not vertical like Baker's cross. Arthur Balfour was '*most* sympathetic'. And at the Atheneaum Ned bearded Randall Davidson, Archbishop of Canterbury, who seemed impressed by Ned's talk of permanency and non-denominationalism but was otherwise non-committal.*

Ned enlisted Bumps as well. MacSack drove him down to Munstead in the Rolls with Vita. Ned was shocked by how much older Bumps looked; she was worried about money and talked about giving up Munstead. 'Too funny Bumps and Lady S together!' wrote Emily. MacSack's diary: 'She is 74, very ugly in her features, but has a very fresh and clear skin, charming voice and *timbre de voix*, and a very kind smile.' They had a conversation in French and agreed to make an exchange of *foie gras* and *pot-pourri*. 'She is such a *grande dame*,' wrote MacSack, who observed her closely, mindful of her own self-appointed role as a latter-day Bumps. Vita was less impressed. 'Miss Jekyll rather fat and grumbly; garden not at its best, but can see it must have been lovely,' she wrote in her diary.[7]

---

*Eventually Randall Davidson decided for the cross, as he was bound to do.

Bumps wrote out the war stone idea for Ned. Together they drafted a memorandum, proposing to put a Great War Stone in every war cemetery, suggesting the thought of memorial chapels in one vast cathedral whose vault was the sky. The cemeteries, which would be appropriate for Jews, Hindus and Muslims as well as Christians, must not be sad or gloomy. 'Good use should be made of the best and most beautiful flowering plants and shrubs . . .'*

Even Emily was enthusiastic about the stone. 'It appeals to *my* side of life – as houses don't and I see so much true symbolism in it.' She agreed that Ned should not charge a fee; it must be his war work, he must give his services for free, even if it meant living on savings. 'I shall have lots to do directly the war is over,' wrote Ned. 'When? How long? I don't think I could last two years. It would take *all* my savings.'[8]

Ned spent August 1917 in London, living in an empty house and dining in an empty club. From a dark room at the Athenaeum he wrote gloomily to Emily about 'the second best in all things aimed at and a mild third achieved'. Growling to Emily had become a habit. In fact, jobs were beginning to come. He had persuaded Barrie to let him start work on his Adelphi flat, building a giant inglenook for the diminutive author to shelter in. Mark Fenwick wanted him to build again at Abbotswood, where Mrs Fenwick, who had been crippled by a hunting accident, had begun to recover her old twinkle. 'She reminds me very much of Mrs Barbara Webb,' wrote Ned; always an auspicious sign for a client.

Above all, there was MacSack. Their plans and schemes were now in a feverish state of architectural foreplay. Elaborate plans were made for joining two houses in Upper Brook Street, Mayfair. 'Have settled at last,' he wrote on 13 August, 'she gets her bedroom where she wants it.' Days later, MacSack lost her nerve about the expense and cancelled, McNed accused her of wasting his time, and they quarrelled. On 9 September, according to her diary:

> Took pity on poor McNed and let him come this evening. I have never seen him under better colours than he was when he explained he was so sorry to have annoyed me over the house. I saw him under quite another aspect – so patient and persuasive and obedient and willing to be shown the right way with me. I must get my friends moulded in my way or else I can't get on with them.

*The plantings by Bumps, far from being evanescent, were to give the cemeteries the restful sense of an English garden, which has endured just as long and appealed more widely than the secret abstract geometry of Ned's war stone.

A new Mayfair site was picked, and the game began over again, giving Ned the excuse to come often to Knole. On 22 September Emily came too. 'She is so deaf, so grey, so joyless and such a contrast to McNed who tries to be so nice to her.' Diana Cooper stayed on 7 October. 'She was brilliant and very amusing with McNed during dinner.'⁹

Harold Nicolson asked himself to dinner at Bedford Square on 19 October, expecting to find Ned alone, but Emily was at home too with a theosophist friend. 'Emmie is a devil,' Harold told Vita. 'She nags and sniffs and sighs at MacNed as if he were a naughty schoolgirl, and the poor man is snubbed before that little swine of a Theosophist, who is not worthy to tie his bootlaces. There were only a few rissoles, and the rest, veg. Poor, poor MacNed. She *is* a gloom. I do understand why BM cheers him up.'

MacSack commissioned Augustus John to paint Ned's portrait, but the result was disappointing. 'The finished portrait is horrible and makes him look like a sickly Japanese instead of his pink and jolly face.' The sketch was a better likeness, and she bought it for £100 and gave it to him. Ned told her 'how miserable he was at home, always excusing E who does not know better, and is a saint but treats him like a dog'. On 21 December MacSack and McNed quarrelled about another house he wanted to build her. 'I was annoyed and firm for 1½ hours, but I had to give way during the last ten minutes and so we are good friends again. I simply find that I can't quarrel with him or shake him. He wants me to be his best friend, and would eat the humblest of humble pies to remain in my good graces.'¹⁰

In this relationship, bizarrely caricaturing the relationship of architect and patron, there was little need for sex; building was its functional equivalent. Ned wooed her with plans which she accepted and then ditched, blowing hot and cold; they quarrelled, made up, quarrelled again. But it was MacSack who was dominant, as the patron must always be.

Lutyens was somewhere in France, travelling to Spain and suffering from a heavy cold, when his reward for the war graves work was announced: a knighthood in the New Year's Honours List for 1918. Sentimental thoughts about the knight who set out to woo his lady twenty-one years ago were tartly checked by Emily, who made clear that she thought honours were vulgar. 'I wish somehow you could have refused it,' she wrote, pointedly asking whether Baker, who was not on the list, had refused. 'I hate recrimination,' wrote Ned, 'but we are getting darling very wide apart and I don't see any bridge. If I didn't love you darling and at heart admire you – your courage, your sincerity and truthfulness – it might be easier.'

Out of range of Emily's disapproval, Ned's jokes were irrepressible. Staying in Paris at the Hotel Bristol, 'nature having forsaken me for two whole days, I asked the waiter for a *"verre de selles Epsom"*. He brought me an *oeuf à la coque*! I humbly ate it and, wonderful to relate, nature suddenly returned to me immediately – such is the action of God, who cares for people who are as children.' Not even sitting for thirty-two hours in a train snowed up on a Spanish mountain top without fuel, light or food could check his puns. 'I feel thoroughly beknighted. It snows and snows and snows, I with a fearful cold in my snose – it was all s'nose as my mouchoir s'knows too well!' From the Liria Palace he set out for El Guadalperal by train and mule carriage to supervise a temporary house for Peneranda. The Santona house was cancelled but, according to MacSack, Ned took this 'very philosophically'.[11]

The winter of 1917–18 was the first Ned had spent at home since 1911. He felt, he said, 'like a boat scraped of its winkles' but he sidestepped most of the war's discomforts. As London braced itself for the bombing raids, which made this the most dangerous winter of the war on the home front, the hated house in Bedford Square was shut up, Betty was sent to boarding school and Ursula and Mary were evacuated to the country. Church Stretton, where they went with Nannie and nursery maid Annie and a cook, was an idyllic Shropshire moorland valley, chosen by Emily because of the scenery. Emily hired cheap lodgings in a 'vulgar' villa, crammed with ornaments and hangings. For the children it was paradise to exchange London gloves and hats for breeches and boots; while Ursula learned to ride, Mary lived an imaginary life, acting out the adventure stories of her books. Emily visited every few months; Ned came only once and stayed for two days.

Emily took a 'funny little house', Number 9 Montagu Street near Marble Arch, a Georgian terraced house which pleased Barbie, who refused to live in unfashionable dreariness at Bedford Square. Ned played chaperon when young men such as Ivo Grenfell stayed until 2 a.m., but he complained to Emily: 'I feel you have planted me here to keep me quiet and caged!'[12]

At Knole MacSack alternately spoiled and scolded him. She criticized his old clothes and his puns, which bored people, among them possible clients, such as Sybil Rocksavage. They quarrelled repeatedly about the three houses which she bought in Brighton (Numbers 39, 40, 40a Sussex Square). On 24 March, 'we almost fought at his stupid remarks about the "grammar" of the house'. On 27 May, 'he found fault with every moulding and cornice, and could not bear my doing anything permanently as he seems to wish to rebuild the house inside . . . He says I don't really like him as I won't give him the one chance of making for me the perfect house.' They were becoming like a married couple. From a safe distance, Emily predicted that 'she will be a bad enemy when she ceases to be a friend'.[13]

At least MacSack built *something*. Most of Lutyens's house-building projects commissioned in 1917–18 came to nothing.*

Ned soft-pencilled designs for war crosses on the back of Emily's letters and tried to anaesthetize himself to the slaughter. The only way to survive was to carry on and discount everyone in France as killed, and 'so make the joy of welcoming them that do come home more vivid'. For the sons that did not come home, heirs to the country houses he had built, he designed memorials. For Harold Tennant, son of Mrs Jack Tennant, a memorial in the church at Great Maytham: the parson objected to his design, which meant a visit – 'awful waste of time and the Parson is acknowledged to be crass'. For Billy Congreve, Hudson's adopted heir to Lindisfarne, a simple tablet at Chartley; for Marc Noble, son of Saxton Noble, a monument at Wretham in Norfolk. For his nephew Derek Lutyens he designed a simple cross in Thursley churchyard. At Mells for Edward Horner a deceptively simple pedestal supported the statue by Munnings of a young cavalry officer, riding out of the dark of the medieval church towards the light of a Virgin and Child in a stained-glass window.

Ned had a smaller staff in the office than he had had since 1897. At Apple Tree Yard (Queen Anne's Gate was let) he had only two draughtsmen, William Wands and Clare Nauheim, the first woman in the office, whom he thought 'little use'.† Hall continued to work on Delhi, but neither he nor the office manager A. J. Thomas really had

---

*Edwin Montagu built additions to Breccles, the house which Detmar Blow had designed for him in Norfolk. But the massive Marsh Court-like additions costing £100,000 that Sir John Ramsden commissioned at Muncaster Castle, Ravenglass, were not executed. Nor was the ideal communal village and church that the millionaire Morrison commissioned at Basildon (Ned built only two cottages before the scheme was dropped).
†According to Robert, she was later responsible for the 'banal' covered approach to Folly Farm, which 'merely robs it of homogeneity'. Lutyens later employed one other woman as an assistant, Elisabeth Benjamin.

enough to do. No money was coming in, as Ned found himself 'doing so much more for nothing than ever I did, and all these small monuments'.

'I get very tired by 6 o'clock and find relaxation means a man to dinner or some such excitement.'[14] He no longer worked late at night, there was no work to do. Next door at 11 Apple Tree Yard lived William Nicholson, for whom Lutyens converted a mews stable into a studio, adding a tall window. With Nicholson, Ned would dine with Barrie, watching the sky scarred red by Zeppelins from the roof of the Adelphi. He often dined also at the Garrick Club, to which he was elected in 1916, proposed by the sculptor George Frampton and seconded by the playwright Alfred Sutro.

'Waring has been in – wants me to do the War Shrine in Hyde Park,' Ned told Emily on 21 August. The temporary war shrine which had been erected in Hyde Park to mark the fourth anniversary of the war was visited by thousands who laid flowers on it, and Waring (of the department store Waring and Gillow) wanted to sponsor a more permanent structure. Ned produced a design in a flurry of excitement. Robert, who had joined up under age as a private soldier in June, came home on leave, and Ned was emotional, with tears very near the surface.

Waring 'mightily approved' of his design for a plaster structure of the great war stone flanked by monolithic watching pavilions or glorified sentry boxes carrying fir cones, the emblem of eternity. Sir Alfred Mond at the Office of Works approved it also. Emily liked it too, and helped compose an inscription – the eventual choice was a single word AMEN inscribed on the altar. The public was not so sure. Critical letters appeared in the papers. 'Heaven keep one from plaster pylons and cones symbolical of eternity,' growled one letter to *The Times*. Sir Martin Conway, a friend of MacSack who wanted Ned to build a National War Memorial Museum, wrote a friendly article in *Country Life*. But the shrine was not built; the King did not approve. Not only was he annoyed at not being consulted as Ranger of the Royal Parks, but he disliked the design. The Duke of Connaught expressed himself 'horrified' by it. The King's private secretary Lord Stamfordham wrote to Mond, tactfully suggesting that 'Sir Edwin Lutyens's genius will produce something which though not on strictly theoretical artistic lines, may be more acceptable to the perhaps debased taste of the man in the street'. Mond instructed Lutyens to produce a simplified design, scrapping the pylons and fir cones, but nothing was built; the war shrine was overtaken by events as the armistice intervened.[15]

That autumn at Montagu Street Emily and Ned shared a bedroom. A scribbled note survives among her letters: 'I missed you so much last night. I do love being near you and our midnight sleepy conversations ... I suppose no hope of your coming home tomorrow night?' Did she want him back? In 1918 Krishna was twenty-four and a pathetic figure. Rejected by both Oxford and Cambridge in 1917,* he repeatedly failed the matriculation examinations for London University. Mrs Besant condemned him to cram with a tutor named Mr Sanger in Kent, endlessly resitting examinations he had no hope of passing.

In May 1918 Emily was dismissed as editor of the *Herald*. 'Another bitter blow for me, another failure,' she wrote in her diary, imagining that she had offended the Lord Maitreya. In fact Leadbeater disapproved of her pacifism, which she shared with Krishna. Nevertheless she continued to do most of the work, as her successor E. Wodehouse, brother of P. G., was able but exceedingly lazy.

Any hope Emily might have had of reconciliation with Ned that armistice autumn was quickly crushed. Soon she was writing that if they were to start a new life in London together, 'it must be by my mutual *in*clusiveness not *ex*clusiveness'. She couldn't break into the MacSack–McNed duet.[16]

In September MacSack moved into one of her Brighton houses in Sussex Square. McNed approved of MacSack's decoration, though he never liked other people's taste. 'He is much too correct – afraid of boldness in furniture and colouring,' wrote MacSack in her diary. He told her on 21 September that 'he has kept a secret diary in which I am very much mixed up, because I have been such a help to him and made him put up with Emmie'. MacSack was fifty-six, 'and I am still malade which pleases me rather as I am cracking the record, I think'. McNed wanted to make her a white room with white peacocks on the walls, and a Chinese garden composed entirely of very wide steps. On 1 December he remodelled the three Brighton houses, which they now called the Chester, for her in half an hour. 'I must admit his genius; it never struck me more forcibly than today, which was fairylike and as if he had touched the houses with a wand and transformed them.' Still

---

*In Mary Lutyens's view it was not surprising that Oxford and Cambridge refused to have an Indian boy 'who had not only been proclaimed as the coming Messiah but had been accused of homosexuality by his own father' – she was referring to the allegations by Naraniah, Krishna's father, that Krishna had been sexually abused by Leadbeater.

they quarrelled. 'He hurts me so often, unwittingly, and he is so tactless!' Four days later she relented:

> McNed was so unhappy about so much of his work falling through, and my chucking today the hall to be painted by William Nicholson, that I have seriously considered letting him do the Chester as he thinks it ought to be done. He says it will be such a tremendous help to him if I am a confrere; he says he can't work when I am cross with him. So I have decided to be what Harold calls a 'patriotic worm' and let McNed do his best at the Chester.

McNed's best was not a success at the Chester. He created a windowless cavern in the basement for her grandchildren to have as a playroom (they never used it) and a barn-like dining room, capable of seating one hundred people, though MacSack never had more that two guests and preferred eating her meals out of doors wearing furs in the loggia. He installed a lift and central heating, which was never used because it consumed more than a ton of coal a day. Sussex Square was yet another Lutyens folly, a bottomless pit absorbing at least £50,000 of MacSack's fortune.[17]

With so little to do at home, Ned travelled, first to Spain and then in March 1919 to South Africa, to assess the designs for Cape Town University by J. M. Solomon, a disciple of Baker who had once worked in Ned's office. 'It is such a triumph for McNed,' purred MacSack, 'as generally it is Herbert Baker who is employed there', and she offered to pay for the journey as he was to be paid a mere £1,000.

The *Balmoral Castle* was a dry ship ('I feel nettled at the deep pleasure it will give you,' he told Emily) but in spite of nothing to drink but tea and ginger ale, Ned enjoyed himself. The young Herbert Ward accompanied him as secretary. Ned shocked the captain's table with stories about an American lady who ate so many clams that her stomach rose and fell with the tide, and a wife who petitioned her chain-smoking husband for divorce on the grounds that he used her open mouth as an ashtray in bed. Ward squirmed when Ned told the ladies that he took two little animals to bed each night – 'two little calves'. 'Madeira, my God to Thee!' he cried out as they approached, punning on the evangelical hymns of his childhood. 'How sweet the sound of cheeses / Sounds in the vegetarian's ear.' He told Ward that he had been crippled by shyness when young, but now he behaved like a puppy rolling on its back. 'I now say whatever comes into my head and hope that no one will kick my soft round tummy.' At Cape Town he was asked to address the exclusive Owl Club. He began with a pun. 'Gentlemen, I cannot claim to have t'wit t'woo you.' He was so nervous and spoke so inaudibly that no one heard, and the joke was greeted by an appalled silence.

Ned and Ward stayed in Cape Town with Solomon in a house called The Woolsack which Rhodes had commissioned Baker to build for Rudyard Kipling. 'A nice little house,' wrote Ned, 'but full of schoolboy error. Sort of early me! and I am glad I didn't do it!' Ned liked Solomon and his red-headed actress wife, and heartily approved of his plans. He wrote a long favourable report, suggesting only that the plans were unduly conscious of economy. (The South African government threatened to cut them because they exceeded the estimates.) 'It is not always the cheapest that is the most economical ... these buildings will be standing long after the anxieties of accountancy will be forgotten.' Unfortunately, Lutyens's support was not enough to stop Solomon from shooting himself eighteen months later.[18]

MacSack met Ned on his return on 25 April and took him home, where she found Emmie, Barbie and Ursula 'barely nice to him. How sorry I felt for him,' she wrote, little guessing that she might be part of the reason.

But if MacSack was Ned's 'bit of blue sky in the background when everything was black and stormy at home', MacSack's home life was even stormier. On 17 May she wrote in her diary that she had decided to leave Knole. She could no longer stand Lionel's indifference. Not only had he installed his mistress Olive, but he had also invited her complaisant husband Walter Rubens to stay though Walter was still infectious with TB.

Ned was at Knole the weekend that she left. He asked Vita what was the matter, and she replied, 'Mother has legitimate cause to feel very unhappy.' Ned drove up to London with MacSack, who didn't tell him that she was leaving for good. 'But he sees that I cannot stay at Knole any longer. He was so nice and friendly about it all. He proposed all sorts of charming plans to distract my attention, about the Chester and making a little guest-house like Lord Battersea's. I shall let him do exactly as he wants ...' She now needed him more than ever, and she was dangerously available, though Ned was aware that Lionel might cite him as a co-respondent if he wanted a divorce.[19]

Money was an insoluble problem. 'All costs go up and up and nothing comes in. It is weary work,' Ned told Emily. Draughtsmen now cost

£300 a year (before the war the wage was £2 or £3 a week). Thomas sent out exorbitant bills ('They do know how to charge in McNed's office,' wrote MacSack) but, with the exception of MacSack herself and the Farrer brothers, very few clients actually paid. Thomas told MacSack that he dreaded the Horners rebuilding Mells Park House, which had been burned down, 'as they will never pay'. McNed was oblivious to the accounts. 'He is hopeless about money.' Thomas threatened to leave if Ned didn't make him a partner and he told MacSack that he hated Emily and Barbie who were always asking him for more money. 'And poor MacNed hasn't got any as he is owed such a lot.'[20]

Lutyens's first break after the fiasco of the Hyde Park war shrine was the temporary Cenotaph in Whitehall. Sometime in early July 1919 the prime minister Lloyd George summoned Lutyens to Downing Street and asked him to build a catafalque for the victory parade and peacetime celebrations on 19 July. Lutyens agreed to build a non-denominational structure, but said it should be called not a catafalque, which was French, but a cenotaph – a word he had first heard twenty-five years before in Bumps's garden, where she had a garden seat which she dubbed the cenotaph of Sigismunda.

Later the same afternoon Sir Frank Baines of the Office of Works called at Apple Tree Yard, and in a couple of minutes Ned sketched a design for an empty tomb uplifted on a high pedestal. At dinner that evening he sketched it for Lady Sackville. Next morning the finished drawings were handed to Frank Baines.

The Cenotaph was architectural journalism, but it wasn't dashed off quite as instantaneously as the anecdote suggests. There exists a drawing of the Cenotaph dated 4 June, which suggests that Lutyens had been thinking about it several weeks before, possibly tipped off by Lionel Earle at the Office of Works. In July his War Memorial at Southampton was unveiled – also a high pedestal but topped by an anonymous recumbent figure, reminiscent of the tomb of the Unknown Warrior in Westminster Abbey.

At the Office of Works Sir Frank Baines's staff worked day and night for five days to construct the temporary cenotaph out of wood and plaster.[21] It was only one of many events along the processional way, but it caught the public mood and made an immediate impact. The night before the parade piles of flowers were laid on it, and fresh bunches appeared every day. The press raved. 'Simple, grave and beautiful' (*The Times*); 'a light was shining in the daylight like a light in an altar' (*Manchester Guardian*); 'near the memorial there were moments of silence when the dead seemed very near, when one almost heard the passage of countless wings' (*Morning Post*). Men doffed their hats as they rode past on London buses. It was the people's shrine.

Ned was first puzzled, then thrilled by his success. Emily told him that praise was bad for any mortal and accused him of having a swollen head, but MacSack found him 'very excited' about it; he took her in a taxi to see it at twilight. Thomas reported that Ned could think of nothing else as the newspaper cuttings poured into the office. The Cenotaph had made him famous; he became at once an architectural celebrity with an international reputation.

On 29 July Lutyens wrote to Sir Alfred Mond proposing a permanent Cenotaph in Whitehall. His letter was read out in Cabinet, and on 30 July the Cabinet agreed to erect a permanent monument on its present site in Whitehall. This was opposed by Lionel Earle, whom Lutyens now suspected of being a snake in the grass. The church party wanted a cross, and their case was put by Lord Selborne, who proposed 'a great granite cross with the Union Jack proudly prominent in the design'. To a bishop who worried that there was no cross on the design, Lutyens replied that there were at least twenty-two crosses on it or associated with the flags which guarded it. The campaigning of the churchmen infuriated Ned, who thought every cross erected by the church to commemorate the war was 'a faggot to her pyre'. He claimed that the Cenotaph was what the people wanted, and he urged Emily to write to her friend George Lansbury. 'Of course if Labour said so they would do it.' But Emily refused, quibbling that she was not prepared to 'make influence for a personal matter'.[22]

The design for the permanent Cenotaph differed subtly from the temporary structure. 'The difference is almost imperceptible,' Ned told Mond, 'yet sufficient to give it a sculpturesque quality and a life, that cannot pertain to rectangular blocks of stone.' Like the Great War Stone, its horizontals were arcs of a circle whose centre was 900 feet below ground; its verticals were radials of a circle whose centre was 1,000 feet above ground. Ned told Vita Sackville-West that the fiendishly detailed mathematical calculations filled a book of 33 pages, and templates were cut for every surface.[23]

Lionel Earle approached Lutyens and suggested that he should forgo all fees for the Cenotaph. Ned agreed: 'I don't mind as an undertaker being an architect, but as an architect I don't want to be an undertaker,' he told Earle. 'And I am too jolly grateful not to be whitening in France myself.'[24]

The Cenotaph was designed around the same time that Lutyens found a new house, 13 Mansfield Street, a large Adam house behind Portland Place which belonged to the Tory MP William Bridgeman (the landlord was the Howard de Walden estate). Ned loved it as much as he hated Bedford Square, but it was far bigger and grander than he could afford. The move was financed by MacSack. 'I saw Mr Thomas about the Mansfield Street mortgage and gave him £7,800 in case I died,' she wrote on 26 June. During the months it took to reorganize and remodel the new house, MacSack lent the Lutyens family her house in Hill Street. Emily worried that MacSack didn't want her there, but MacSack was less jealous of Emily than sorry for her, watching her return exhausted after long days she spent working with Mrs Besant. When Annie Besant returned to England in June, so MacSack noted, Emily was 'ready to follow her and leave McNed and her child, if she only holds up her hand'.

Emily seemed more and more strange. That summer she rented a house at Thorpeness in Suffolk, a plain whitewashed wooden hut with one long room for meals. It was primitive and uncomfortable, but Emily loved it, though she knew Ned would hate it and of course he didn't come. To Emily's dismay, Barbie filled the house with party after party of her smart friends – Patsy Ward and George Curzon's daughters, Irene, Cimmie and Baba (Alexandra), who brought suitcases bulging with fashionable clothes. The gramophone played non-stop, tunes such as 'On the Level You're a Little Devil' and 'Till the Clouds Roll By'. Emily worried that Barbie and her friends thought her weird and eccentric. 'I feel she does not want me and is rather ashamed of me before her friends. She keeps them all away and has never wanted me to share in a thing they do.' Ned warned her not to walk about with her hair down; 'it used to make me shy'.[25]

Emily never questioned her financial dependence on Ned, but it was a constant cause of friction, especially when he was earning so little. She was obliged to ask for another £50 a month, increasing her allowance to £150; 'it is rather awful when you are away to feel always short and overdrawn and have to finally appeal to Thomas,' she wrote. Yet she did none of the looking after her husband that wives were supposed to do. Ned had no collars, no handkerchiefs, no ties; everything needed mending; but (according to MacSack) 'Emmie instead of attending to him goes and saves souls'. Ned complained that he had nothing but rags 'and my behind views the world through shreds of cloth as I go bathward'.[26]

The millionaire Lord Leverhulme commissioned a hotel on the island of Lewis. For Ned, the journey to the island with the retinue of sycophants and the two deaf Miss Levers with snow-white hair and deaf boxes was torture, a rough twelve-hour crossing. 'Old 'ulme' was bored and deaf. He told Ned that 'he had never met an architect who was so quick to realize and understand his ideas', but Ned disliked him and refused to toady like the other guests, who queued for ten-minute interviews with the old autocrat. 'McNed left highly disgusted,' wrote MacSack; and Lutyens refused the commission. He was still in debt and nothing seemed to pay. 'Big things hung up and little things cost more in time and effort than they bring in. However, I struggle with my theory of money unconsciousness and spend as little as possible.'[27]

When Ned left on his sixth visit to India in November 1919, the Adam staircase at Mansfield Street was covered in scaffolding, new brown marble Ionic columns were going up in the hall and the drawing-room walls were being painted trademark black with an emerald green floor which, said Pamela Lytton, made her eyes green and her heart black with envy. Later, the 'awful' tiles in the hall were replaced by smart black and white marble, given as a present by Cecil Baring. Betty made a home for herself in the cistern cupboard above the gents' lavatory, and even Barbie condescended to approve and entertained her friends to smart dinner parties. Emily, who naturally was not asked to Barbie's gatherings, would creep up to bed, tiptoeing through the hall like a madwoman on the way to her attic, hoping no one saw her.

Ned dreaded going to India like going to prison, and the *S.S. Caledonia*, which was still arranged as a wartime hospital ship, was noisy, cramped and crowded. He was able to work two hours each morning in his poky cabin; at 12 he drank a cocktail; then followed lunch 'at which I greatly overeat', a sleep and 'the rest of the time I walk till I am ready to drop'. Tilak, the Indian nationalist leader, was on board ('a funny little wizen, ill-dressed and rather difficult to understand') and a raving soldier, who had been shot in the head and went mad in the Red Sea; he believed himself to be engaged to Princess Mary, to whom he repeatedly sent telegrams. 'The only idea I had was to put my arms round him and comfort him nannie-wise, but it might have been misunderstood.' Of the 507 passengers Ned knew precisely three: young Delhi architects, Walter George ('Baker's grievancing assistant'), C. G. Blomfield and Henry Medd, who had once worked in his office. When Medd was describing an old house Lutyens suddenly turned to him and said, 'Are you keen?' Keenness, thought Medd, was for Lutyens the criterion of a person's worth.

On arrival in India, Lutyens stayed with George Lloyd, who was now Governor of Bombay. Lloyd's brother-in-law Tommy Lascelles thought Ned buffoonishly amusing, but 'a little of him goes a long way. He makes a facetious curtsey to Blanche [Lady Lloyd] when he meets her in Bombay – that's his *genre* of humour.'[28]

Back in Delhi, Ned was installed once more in the long low bungalow which the architects called Raisina Mill. Ned had been provided with an additional drawing office, but he still slept in one wing and Baker in the other. After their spat over the Great War Stone, relations with Baker were as bad as ever. Ned complained of Baker's 'odious pecksniff manner and sentimental attitude'. His work, according to Ned, was even worse – slovenly and capricious, especially the bungalows (bungle – ohs). 'A little more of the T square and a little less of the Round Table.' The Cenotaph had brought Ned fame, while Baker's stock had fallen, and the younger architects all turned to Ned for guidance. Ned was generous with his encouragement; he told the young men in his office, John Brandon, Russell, Blomfield and Greaves, that their villas were far better than Baker's slapdash bungle-ohs. 'I may have influence to help them as the younger men are charming to me and listen! Do you despise me for this?' he asked Emily.[29]

The dispute over the gradient was frozen, pending the appointment of a new viceroy, so they quarrelled instead about the new legislative chamber. The Montagu–Chelmsford Reform of 1919, granting limited Indian self-government, created a legislative assembly, an upper house of notables and a chamber of princes. As a result, the Council Chamber which Lutyens had designed inside Government House, intended to hold sixty, was totally inadequate. A separate Council Chamber holding six hundred was urgently needed.*

Baker was given the Council Chamber to design, and he proposed a triangular plan, one wing for each chamber (democratic, senate, princes), joined by a dome symbolic of the overarching authority of the

---

*Lutyens has been criticized for failing to provide for Indian democracy, but to his credit both he and Montagu had implored Hardinge to build a separate Council Chamber back in 1913. Hardinge the autocrat had refused: 'No – I as Governor General with my council (of six) govern India, so it must be in my house!' he told Ned.

Raj. This, thought Lutyens, was full of 'obvious childish faults'; it was over-fussy and not properly related to the site and vistas. He demanded instead a circular plan which was eventually agreed, largely because Baker's ambitious and expensive design didn't fit the site. 'I have got the building where I want it and the shape I want it,' crowed Lutyens; but Baker's Chamber is one of the least satisfactory of the New Delhi buildings. Its site below the acropolis and to one side of the central vista suggests its unimportance as an afterthought. Baker placed three semicircular chambers inside a circular coliseum, at 120-degree intervals like three giant spokes of a merry-go-round. His design, which contained half a mile of passages, was said to be reminiscent of elephants dancing; one wit dubbed it a 'dreary-go-round', another suggested installing a tramway.[30]

Lutyens spent Christmas alone in the bungalow with a pet kitten and the servants, headed by the faithful Persotum. For ten days he had nothing to do but work; he never left the bungalow but worked right through the day, 'from bed to bed, which I like', though he slept badly. He had much designing to do. The buildings at Point B of the town plan, the Record Office, Ethnological Museum, Medical Research Building and War Museum, all gained approval from the Delhi Committee, though all except the Record Office were later abandoned on grounds of expense. The massive All-India War Memorial Arch, however, still dominates the Delhi vista. Seventy-five feet high, as big as the Arc de Triomphe, Delhi Gate is the first instance of Lutyens's post-war monumental geometry. Its proportions all derive from multiples and fractions of a 30-foot unit, the width of the main arch. The names of 13,516 missing Indian and British soldiers who fell on the North-West Frontier are inscribed on its walls, and pine cones, vetoed at Hyde Park, stand in urns beneath the smaller arches.

Puns and buffoonery gave a diversion from the intellectual rigours of monumental geometry; the more mathematically demanding the work, the sillier the jokes. E. V. Lucas, the prolific *Punch* humorist and Garrick Club man of letters, stayed at Delhi and they embarked on a week's dissipation, visiting Lucknow where they went tiger shooting with Lord Goschen. Lutyens, who was always sickened by the killing of animals, rode an elephant but had no gun. At first he was frightened by the wounded tigress, then excited and then sorry for the dying beast.

'I am much happier about Delhi this year,' Ned told Emily. At last he had succeeded in achieving an ascendancy over Baker. When Baker tried to upset the decision about the Council Chamber site, they quarrelled, but 'I kept my head and gave him what for . . . When he is particularly uncomfortable he sings at the top of his voice! To show he don't mind!' Baker admitted that he had no architectural objection to the reduction of the inclined way. Ned told him that unless he agreed to reopen the gradient, he would refuse to collaborate with him.[31]

At Raisina Mill the two architects ate lunch at a long table, Baker at one end, Ned at another, and Ned kept open house. Whoever came into the office, the governor of a province or a stonemason or foreman, was asked to stay to lunch. Inarticulate with humanity at large, Ned found it easier to be on good terms with the individuals with whom he worked on a daily basis; his racism was generalized, not specific. Like the young architects, the Indians laughed at his jokes. He invited students of the Bombay School of Art to dinner; though their masters wanted them to sit at a separate table, Ned insisted that he had only one table – 'anyone who sits with me dines at my table. The God of Art was above creeds and castes.'

'There is an enormous amount of building going to be done all through India – specially under the Reform. Is it our swan-song? I only hope it may be a good tune well sung to our and India's dignity,' wrote Ned. He had no illusions about the permanence of British rule. He thought the Amritsar Massacre of July 1919 'all wrong', but he sympathized, as he always did, with the maharajahs. He warmed to princely Indian clients, such as the Gaekwar of Baroda, who like the French nobility at Versailles wanted him to build palaces in New Delhi. Lutyens criss-crossed India by train, making plans for improvements and new buildings in Bombay and Madras, and a university in Lucknow. Everywhere he went, Mrs Besant had been before him, campaigning for Home Rule. The Governor of Madras, Lord Willingdon, 'adores naughty Annie', Ned told Emily.[32]

Only two of Lutyens's palaces for Indian maharajahs were built, those for the Gaekwar of Baroda and the Nizam of Hyderabad. It was Mrs Besant, leader of Indian nationalism, who made the more lasting impact.

At Mansfield Street most afternoons after school Mary would find lying on the hall table the grey Homburg hats and gold-headed canes belonging to Krishna and Nitya. Emily had given up much of her theosophical lecturing and committee work, but she hadn't given up Krishna, who spent long hours with her in the back drawing room.

Krishna had just discovered the novels of P. G. Wodehouse, and he would stand leaning against the bookcase (he never seemed to sit), laughing aloud. Soon he began to speak in a Wodehousian way, his Indian lilt peppered with 'By Jove'. Emily kept her relations with Krishna secret from Ned, nor did she tell much about her new political work, campaigning for the Labour Party. 'We shall never agree about politics,' she wrote. In spite of taking Nannie with her to meetings to protect her in case of rowdiness, she was invited to stand as Labour candidate for Luton, but she declined because financial backing was required. 'Besides I might get in which would be too horrible.'

In January 1920 Krishna was sent to Paris to learn French, Mrs Besant having at last given up hope of London University. Krishna wrote Emily long, intimate letters full of longing. 'You must tell me *everything, everything* you do, you think, you buy . . .'

Emily suddenly developed an urgent desire for French travel, telling Ned in India that she was desperate to escape, as the responsibilities of family life (the children had measles) had driven her close to breakdown. She stayed at Grasse, in the house Ned had built, with the Mallets. Guillaume, who was absorbed in his garden, she found 'the same as ever only more cross and rude if possible and intensely royalist and national'. He was passionately anti-German, 'so I have to be careful'. Marie looked much older, 'terribly serious and no sense of humour'. Most of the time Emily was seeing Krishna in Paris, where she stayed with a family of theosophists, the Manziarlys. There was a visit to a Belgian medium who claimed to be the mouthpiece of the Great Being and insisted on her entourage wearing slippers – Emily thought her 'rather common and not over clever'.[33]

Emily was in France and Ned in Colombo (he designed the war memorial there) when Barbie became engaged. Euan Wallace was tall and dark with a black moustache; he resembled his friend Tom Mosley, who married Barbie's friend Cimmie Curzon the day after Barbie married Euan. Euan had been married before, and had two sons in his care.* Neither Emily nor Ned much minded that Euan was divorced; he was very rich with an estate in Sotland and he was 'just what Barbie needed'. He was not Emily's type – 'I neither feel frightfully attracted to him physically or mentally' – but she thought him '*nice* through and through'. Barbie was on the rebound from an unhappy love affair with

---

*His first wife was Idina, daughter – somewhat improbably – of the theosophist Lady de la Warr. A compulsive bolter, Idina married Lord Errol and became queen of scandalous orgies in Kenya's Happy Valley.

a married man which, said Emily, 'has been the deepest thing in her life'; Barbie had broken it off, behaving 'with a wisdom and courage which were quite extraordinary but she suffered fearfully'.

Ned returned from India just in time for Barbie's marriage in the Savoy Chapel on 10 May. MacSack was there to welcome him. 'I was so glad to see him, and evidently his delight at seeing me was very great. I *am* his great friend.' The game of patron and artist began once more. They quarrelled about the terrace at Sussex Square, and MacSack gave in – 'He generally *is* right, and I am so horrid to him and he is so patient' (20 May). Ned made plans for the dining room. 'He was so miserable because I said I did not like them, that he almost cried and got so white. I thought afterwards that it was rather a shame not to let him do that room according to his Grammar and his perfect measurements.'[34]

In 1920 Lutyens was elected a full Royal Academician, and in June he gave an address to the Architectural Association. He spoke with a 'rapid, significant and rather deprecating voice', making jokes which were largely inaudible and, in spite of fibbing about his early life, conveyed the personality of 'a superbly entrenched artist thinking in terms of Leonardo and inevitably indifferent to our world'. Someone asked him, 'What is proportion?' Lutyens replied: 'God.' That was impressive.

Emily had written to Ned in India that she had never wanted or missed him more ('this must not rouse hopes in you of what I *don't* want'), but soon after the return of 'the superbly entrenched artist' they quarrelled. Vita dined in July and, according to MacSack, 'saw that Emmie was a shocking hostess and had absurd little vegetarian dishes brought specially for her and looked so bored and McNed anxious and fussed'.[35] The quarrel between them was about Robert.

After the war Robert had returned to Cambridge. He did very little work and spent too much money, and Emily worried that he was drinking and becoming unhealthily sex-obsessed. He had socialist friends and was reading about psychoanalysis, and he shocked her by telling her that he was a degenerate and super-sexed. He annoyed her even more by telling her that she lived in ostentatious luxury while denying him a proper allowance.

No one was surprised when Robert was sent down after failing his Cambridge exams in June. Ned persuaded Hudson to employ him as a sub-editor at *Country Life*. Ned grudged paying Robert an allowance, constantly reminding him of the 'nine dreadful years' when he had worked himself to the bone to make his career. Robert twitted Ned for drinking champagne and made scenes in the office which embarrassed Ned, who paid such low wages that members of his staff were on the verge of a strike. Ned taunted Robert with being a dilettante and lacking perseverance, and he raged at his lack of respect for authority, for which he blamed Emily; torrents of angry words rained down on her, justifying his refusal to give Robert more money and niggling at the worry that 'there must be something wrong or unhealthy' with Robert.

If Ned thought Robert was homosexual he was mistaken. What was 'wrong' with Robert was that he wanted to marry. He was only just nineteen, but he was besotted by Eva Lubryjinska, a Polish Jew who was seven years older than he. Eva was not so much pretty as sexy. 'She had a strong Polish accent, walked like a foreigner, slightly swaying her behind, and wore high-heeled black patent leather shoes in the country.' She had a chemistry degree from Manchester University. Emily was immediately attracted to her, influenced perhaps by the fact that she was a niece of Chaim Weizmann, friend and protégé of the Zionist Balfours. She thought Eva highly intelligent, with immense charm and a fine character. If Robert had searched the world over he couldn't have found a better woman, she told Ned. The only thing that puzzled her was what this paragon could see in Robert, unless it was the possibility of making him the vehicle for her ambition.[36]

Emily begged Ned to bless the marriage. 'I do not think she is your type at all,' she conceded, but 'You must trust my judgement here'. Ned took an instant dislike to Eva. Her long fingernails, which she painted red, reminded him of a vulture's claws dipped in blood. He refused to give his consent to the engagement despite Emily's pleading. Emily insisted that he had no right to control another person's life. In November, a few days after the unveiling of the permanent Cenotaph, Ned made Robert a ward of court, prohibiting him from marrying without parental consent until he became twenty-one. Robert was sacked by Hudson, and in November he ran away with Eva to Scotland. Emily knew where they were but refused to say, so Ned instructed the solicitor Sir George Lewis, for whom he was redecorating Rottingdean, to trace him. Private detectives were engaged and everyone at Mansfield Street was interrogated.

In one sense Ned had a point. Robert was young and emotionally confused. But Ned's refusal to let him marry was strongly coloured by anti-Semitism, a fact which escaped neither Emily nor Eva's uncle Chaim Weizmann. The real quarrel was not between Ned and Robert, however, but between Emily and Ned. Emily refused to help him trace Robert and Ned, so MacSack recorded, 'has had such words with Emily that he feels like leaving home'.

Ned tried to take refuge with MacSack, but here, too, there were storms. MacSack complained that Sussex Square had been *'vilely'* finished, that Thomas supervised nothing properly because he had taken on so much of his own work that he neglected Ned's. In October Thomas sent in estimates that were £7,000 higher than he had originally quoted, and MacSack stopped all work. Worse, Ned built a portico on to her house at Ebury Street without first asking the permission of the landowners, the Grosvenor estate, which insisted that it was pulled down. Ned threatened to sell Mansfield Street to pay her back.*

Ned told MacSack that he was more unhappy when he had a row with her than when he quarrelled with Robert. 'What is home life without another to share it?' he murmured, holding her hand.[37] Meanwhile, he escaped from all the rows and from worrying about money – his overdraft now topped £25,000 – by immersing himself in design.

---

*I can't help believing she has large reserves of money, but nothing would make her so angry as me saying it,' Ned told Emily.

Chapter Fifteen
The Dolls' House
1920–1924

Memorial to the Missing, Thiepval, France.

Early idea for Gledstone sketched on one of Emily's letters.

'Robert is to marry today,' Ned told MacSack on 4 December 1920. 'Have I stopped him? I doubt it.' Of course he hadn't. On the contrary, by making him a ward of court and sending Sir George Lewis's private detectives after him, he had forced his son to flee to Scotland and marry earlier than Robert and Eva had planned. Immediately after the wedding Robert succumbed to mumps.

Without speaking to Robert or making his peace with Emily, Ned escaped to India. Even MacSack was growing weary of him. 'I do hope I shall see much less of him when he comes back from India. He has been a great darling, but an immense worry too, and with Thomas's help, has made me waste an immense amount of money.'

Cocooned by *S.S. Caledonia* from the pain and disorderliness of real life, Ned read Gibbon's *Decline and Fall* and worked on plans for Gledstone in Yorkshire, the symmetrical and rather French country house commissioned by the cotton spinner Sir Amos Nelson, who was also on the ship.* He spent a lot of time playing patience or chess, protected from the other passengers by his two satellites, Herbert Ward, who acted as a kind of aide-de-camp, and A. G. Shoosmith, who had come out to take charge of the Delhi office. For Emily he had no Christmas present. 'The best present I can give you is my absence!?'[1]

Even in Delhi, he was shielded on this visit from difficulty. Raisina Mill, shared jointly with Baker, was still the architects' office, and mealtimes still crackled with tension, with Baker squirming defenceless against Lut's cruel puns and leg pulls from the far end of the table. But this year Lutyens was allocated for his own use the Military Secretary's bungalow, with seven bedrooms. Persotum, who looked more than ever like a beggar, ran the household with unexpected efficiency, and Ned gave semi-official dinners ('very tiring and expensive') for Indian representatives whom he entertained round the circular blackboard table he had designed. When the vegetarian 'naughty Annie' Besant came to lunch, Ned drew a cabbage on the blackboard beside her place.

---

*The earliest sketches for the house are pencilled on the back of a letter from Emily, imploring him to give his consent to Robert's marriage – 'Let your big generous heart speak and silence every other less worthy thought'.

301

Even though the war was over, progress on New Delhi was painfully slow. Budget cuts brought building almost to a standstill and Ned worried that he would be £12,000 out of pocket. The Government of India now proposed to save money by finishing the central buildings in plaster which, Ned pointed out, would mean at least a year's work making an entirely new set of drawings. Blithely disregarding the political pressure to abandon Delhi altogether, Ned ordered his staff to make exhaustively detailed drawings in accordance with constantly adjusted measurements and ratios.[2]

Herbert Ward, who had worked briefly in the London Delhi office at Apple Tree Yard before coming to India, remembered that Lutyens had rarely visited, which was perhaps just as well, for when he did he stood over the drawings puffing hot ash from his pipe on to the paper. Ward had been told to revise a plan of the Delhi Record Office, the measurements of which had been altered and rubbed out so often that the discoloured paper was known as the mezzotint. Ned was proud of the Record Office elevation: a huge block of wall with 161 windows which he planned to relieve by recording the names of the Indians killed in the war. 'It gets me out of a great difficulty as the windows will be mere spots among the names.' This was little consolation to Ward, who was reunited with the mezzotint in Delhi, where the prospect of grappling with its hated erasures, and especially the vacuities of the so-called Upper Part of Clerks, filled him with 'nausea'.

Eadred Lutyens, Ned's nephew, joined the Apple Tree Yard office in 1920. He spent the entire two years he was there working on the south-west wing of Government House. He remembered an irascible and frightening Lutyens.

> One assistant had been drawing out the India Memorial Arch for several weeks, and finally went into Sir Edwin's room with a bundle of drawings under his arm. There was a few moments silence and then an explosion with a rending tearing sound, and out came the assistant, purple in the face, and holding a tattered remnant of the bundle.

Even Walter George, the head of Lutyens's office in Delhi, who was a committed architect, sometimes wondered 'Is it worth it?' when calculating the hugely complex modular figures for Viceroy's House. His answer was Yes, but there must have been times in the 1920s when it seemed otherwise. Meticulous detailing absorbed a disproportionate amount of Lutyens's earnings, eating away at his margin of profit on the Delhi project.[3]

Back in London in March 1921, Ned received a cool welcome from MacSack. 'Lunched with McNed,' she wrote on 23 March, 'I was horrid to him. I want to break our friendship and be more independent. He takes too much of my time.'

She saw little of him that spring, when Ned was absorbed in a new exercise in architectural fantasy. Rather than design model working men's cottages in response to the new post-war housing legislation – homes fit for heroes, rewarding the sacrifices made for King and Country – Lutyens designed an outrageously expensive toy for the Queen: Queen Mary's Dolls' House.

The idea for the dolls' house was supposed to have originated at a dinner given by Sir Herbert Morgan in 1920, when someone suggested presenting the Queen with an exact replica of a gentleman's house of 1920. Princess Marie Louise,* a first cousin of George V, who was a guest at the dinner, agreed to approach the Queen. Lutyens's first reference to a dolls' house occurs in 1916, when he met MacSack and told her that he would build her a bungalow at Hove, to be called 'the Dolls' House, as Doll will build it'.[4]

Like an architectural model, the Queen's Dolls' House was designed on a scale of one inch to one foot; a square Wrennaissance box, it was raised by an electrical mechanism to reveal the rooms within.† Being designed by Lutyens, it soon turned into a miniature royal palace, with a grand entrance hall and staircase, barrel-vaulted corridors and magnificent royal apartments. Sixty artists were involved in the decoration, many of whom were friends of Lutyens. William Nicholson painted the staircase mural of Adam and Eve being expelled from the Garden of Eden watched by their pets, the entire animal kingdom. George Plank painted a *trompe l'œil* in the Queen's bedroom, Orpen painted state portraits of the King and Queen, and Jagger added miniature busts of Haig and Beattie. The garden was designed by Bumps, Muntzer was the upholsterer and A. J. Thomas the engineer. The Library (45 inches long, 21 wide and $15\frac{1}{2}$ high) contained 350 miniature leather-bound books hand-written by leading authors. Purdey supplied the King's miniature shotguns, which were 4 inches long.

---

*Marie Louise was the daughter of Queen Victoria's ninth child, Princess Helena of Schleswig-Holstein.
†Writing in 1937, Sir John Summerson judged the Dolls' House 'one of the few really dull things Lutyens has done'.

The wooden shell of the dolls' house was first erected at Apple Tree Yard, where it grew so wide (it measures 102 inches × 58½) that a wall had to be pulled down to get it out. The 250 craftsmen were co-ordinated by Ned, who designed the furniture and decoration, commissioned the makers, and then sent the bills to sponsors, many of whom were clients. Nothing was cheap. The silk patterns for the royal bedrooms cost £80 each to weave, the hand-carved frames for the state portraits were £50 each. Ned laid out £11,000 of his own money paying the artists, and then had the gall to approach sponsors to carry the cost – even though all they received in return was a mention in the roll-call of 500 donors in the *Book of the Queen's Dolls' House*. It was a curiously involved and expensive way to make plain his respect for the Queen.

MacSack scolded him for spending so much time on the dolls' house; it had become an obsession. By flattering the Queen, Ned hoped to enlist her support over the Delhi gradient, but she saw through his guile. When he visited her on 1 June to discuss the dolls' house, 'she was very guarded and would not talk about Delhi'.

Queen Mary's 'stunt', so Ned reported, was mimicking him describing the beauties of Delhi. 'I did not think she had the personality to do it,' he wrote; but his facetious jokes left her like a 'frightened mare'. With Princess Marie Louise, whom he called Mary Louse, he tried to engage in socialistic talk, but 'she don't really like it, and is all for "her order"'. With Queen Mary he could never resist punning about Lazy Majesty (drawing of king and queen in bed) or Lays Majesty (picture of a hen laying a crowned egg). But what intrigued and delighted him was the idea of the Queen playing with the dolls. The Queen, he told Emily, had asked to be able to open the dolls' house herself, without the help of servants. 'Can't you see the Queen? Going hush hush to play with the dolls?'[5]

With the dolls' house Ned could escape from the disappointments of the real world, creating a world in miniature where he was in complete control. That the make-believe world was shared with a real-life queen made it all the more compelling.

Ned's daughter, Mary Lutyens, then aged thirteen, recognized much of the dolls' house furniture. The St Ursula beds in the Princess Royal's room were models of the two beds Ned had designed for Ursula and Barbara, inspired by the Carpaccio paintings of the legend about St Ursula. The nursery chandelier was like the one Ned had designed for Barbie; the kitchen cupboards came from Mansfield Street. 'I realized that this was the house we would have lived in if father had been rich enough to build it for himself. It was his own dream-house.'⁶

Ned found his own family far harder to control than the Queen and her dolls. He still could not accept Robert's marriage. Marrying at nineteen was 'an indulgence' which, said Ned, would alienate professional men; it was also a threat to Ned's own manliness. That Emily should deny him 'the one essential and personal intimacy that can only belong to those married and beyond the pale of friends' while encouraging Robert to enjoy that intimacy although under age seemed doubly cruel. Robert's seeming fecklessness frightened him too, awakening his own fear of failure and bitter memories of old Charles. 'I saw father's profession fail him and fortune vanish at the same time. A woman may weep, but a man bleeds.'

Prompted by Emily, who begged him to avoid recrimination and bitterness, Ned had written to Eva, stiffly holding out the olive branch. But by then the damage was done. Parental opposition blights a marriage like nothing else. Emily did all she could to make it work. She befriended Eva's Polish mother, entertained uncle Chaim Weizmann, became an enthusiastic Zionist and persuaded Ned to rent a Mayfair house off Park Lane in South Street for Robert and Eva. She even gave a dinner party, something she had never done for Ned, inviting Hudson, who had taken Robert back on to the staff of *Country Life*. He told Emily that Robert was much improved and working well. Emily reported ominously, however, that Eva needed 'a little operation'. 'They could not manage their marriage successfully and Robert was very unhappy thinking he was stupid and not wanting to hurt her', but the doctor declared that 'it could never happen in the normal way as she was too small and she [the doctor] must operate'.⁷

At least MacSack thawed towards Ned. She entered with zest into the dolls' house project, showering Ned with miniature treasures made by Fabergé which she listed in her diary: 'Tiny red lacquer round Chinese table, 3 pots with roses and tulips and tomatoes, the smallest stone cat Fabergé ever did especially for me; 5 Sevres and Wedgwood plaques . . . tiny jade book mounted in gold . . . very good diamond miniature frame . . . 2 crystal bottles'. She also commissioned Stanley Gibbons to make an album of miniature stamps for the stamp-collecting King.

At last Ned was making money again. For Lucknow University he received £6,000 (the scheme was cancelled two years later) and this, together with £2,000 from Delhi, allowed him to pay off his overdraft of £6,000, though he still complained to MacSack that Emily spent too freely. The Cenotaph brought recognition in the shape of the Royal Gold Medal for Architecture. 'It does not make up for the OM which you ought to have had,' wrote Emily. When he received the gold medal Ned was overcome by tears and unable to make his speech.

Post-war recovery and speculation brought new work in the City. Ned had hoped for the new Bank of England.* The night he heard that Baker had got the job he could eat no dinner. 'I have seldom seen him so upset and white,' MacSack reported, 'and yet he was very brave and we hardly talked about it.'[8]

Anglo-Persian Oil (later British Petroleum) commissioned Britannic House, Lutyens's first City palace. Ned's brother Frank, an embarrassing figure in large check trousers, claimed to have been instrumental in getting him the commission, but, according to MacSack, 'the Cenotaph was the cause of this job being offered to him'. Anglo-Persian Oil, booming with Britain's post-war mandate over Iran, proposed to spend at least half a million pounds and pay a commission of 4½ per cent. Lutyens's first design for the curving site in Finsbury Circus was a 'mighty fine tower' 221 feet high, capped with exuberant classical orders on the eighth floor. 'I hope it goes through the LCC alright,' wrote Ned doubtfully (the Building Acts prohibited the construction of buildings over 100 feet). When the LCC duly rejected his tower he produced an abbreviated version, retaining the Corinthian *piano nobile* far above street level on the fifth floor.[9]

'There is no excuse,' wrote Pevsner sourly, 'for the wretched American vice of breaking out into grand columniation on the top floors.' Modernists dislike the building because Lutyens covered a steel frame in thousands of tons of Portland stone, creating classical elevations which are not truthful to the structure. Small windows pierce the mezzanine floor, contrasting with the great windows of the *piano nobile*, but the rooms behind are the same height, 11 feet 6 inches throughout the building. 'You have only to look at Baker's Bank of England to see how good Lutyens's building is,' said the critic Furneaux Jordan in 1959, 'but if you want to know how bad it is look at the Palazzo Farnese. It is the same height as Britannic House but whereas

---

*Ned told MacSack that the Bank had been promised to him by the Governor, Lord Cunliffe, who unfortunately died, and Montagu Norman, his successor, was a friend of Baker. According to another story, the governors of the Bank were put off by Lutyens's jokes, deciding that they wanted an architect and not a court jester.

the *piano nobile* in Britannic House is about 12 feet 6 inches, in the Palazzo Farnese it is 35 feet 6 inches. That is real baroque.'

The contradiction between the building's steel interior and its baroque exterior, argued Furneaux Jordan, reflected the contradiction between Lutyens's approach to design and the era in which he was living. No artist, he thought, can live out of his time. 'It may to Lutyens ... have been a beastly time, but you cannot deny its essence without some architectural loss.' Denying the essence of the time was, however, precisely what the Edwardian generation was about; as Vita Sackville-West perceived, the whole effort of the Edwardians was spent on maintaining outward appearances in spite of crumbling inner certainties. Christopher Hussey got it right when he described Britannic House as 'that Edwardian cynosure, "a raging beauty", decked, though with a new look, in all the armoury of classical opera'.[10]

Ned liked that sort of woman. Dame Nellie Melba, the Australian prima donna, lived next door at Great Cumberland Place, where he briefly hired a house in 1919. They first met at dinner with Sybil Colefax. Ned leaned across the table. 'And what do you do?' he asked, knowing perfectly well. A pause. She finished her fish, sipped her wine, then burst into Mimi's song, snapping 'That's what I do!' They went to plays together ('she provides the box, I the dinner'), sometimes asked each other to breakfast. 'I've just cabled to have him put a lift in my house,' Dame Nellie said. 'I don't know how he's going to do it, but he will.'*

Younger feminist women alarmed him. His daughter Ursula, who was clever and drew well, wanted to work in his office, but he discouraged her, in spite of pressure from MacSack and Emily, who both tried to persuade him to give her a chance. Asked about the future of women in architecture, he quipped, 'It depends upon which architect she marries.' It wasn't a joke; he meant it.[11]

Emily accompanied Ned to India for the first time in the winter of 1921-2. Ned was apprehensive. 'If you came and played a *wife's* part it might help *me* very much, but if the political element came in it would make my work HELL instead of ELL.' Emily agreed not to play politics, but she had little intention of playing wife. She came to India to follow Krishna who, after nearly two years in Paris, was suddenly summoned to India by Mrs Besant in October 1921.

---

*Lutyens later designed Melba's tombstone in Melbourne.

During Krishna's time in Paris his relationship with Emily had subtly but significantly changed. At first he missed her dreadfully, writing aching lovesick letters every day. In February 1920 he wrote: 'Oh mother mine how I do want you but I can never have you. It is a very depressing thought and I had better drop it.' And drop it he did.*

He still confided in Emily and wrote her letters, assuring her that 'My love for you is as pure and lasting as snow on Mont Blanc!' But the letters grew briefer and more perfunctory; Krishna no longer needed Emily; he no longer felt a failure, nor was he depressed as he had been in England. He shared Emily's horror of sex and he was of course sexually inexperienced – virginity and celibacy were part of his job description – but he was obsessed by sex. He wrote to Emily about his 'bad' dreams, which he thought 'beastly'. Women frightened him, but his exquisite looks and film-star aura turned women's heads. In Paris he flirted with the Manziarly girls, whom he found far more lively than the Lutyens sisters, and he 'fell in love' with an American girl named Helen Knothe. 'I hope you are not jealous, dear old Mum?'[12]

The less he needed her, the more Emily craved him. She had a new hold over him now. In May 1921 Nitya, who was recovering from a bad attack of chicken pox in London, coughed blood after visiting the cinema with Emily. The search for a cure for Nitya's TB gave Emily a new mission.

When Emily learned of Krishna's summons to India, she told him that she felt like a man about to be hanged. She was rescued from the noose by Ned, who agreed to bring her to New Delhi.

At Bombay, Krishna and Nitya were there to meet her, looking gorgeous in their Indian clothes. For Emily, who hadn't seen India since she was nine months old, when her father was Viceroy, it felt like coming home. Not that she liked the Raj one bit. In spite of being a viceroy's daughter, she thought British colonialism a relic of barbarism, utterly out of touch with Indian life. 'I suppose there is nowhere else left now in the world where little nobodies can play at being kings and queens,' she wrote. After the suffocating stuffiness of staying with the George Lloyds at Government House in Bombay (even unforgiving Emily would have sympathized with Ned's facetious curtseys to Lady Blanche) she found the railway journey to the theosophist convention at Benares a liberation. Breaking with convention, she insisted that her ayah, an elderly lady with a gold stud in her nose, share her carriage for

---

* From that point, in the opinion of Mary Lutyens, Emily ceased to have an influence on Krishna's life.

the night, instead of squashing into the servants' squalid third-class carriage. (What the ayah thought is not known.) Once, when her train was three hours late, she unrolled her bedding on the platform and slept there – behaviour then unheard of in the middle-aged daughter of a Victorian viceroy. The primitive simplicity of life in Benares delighted her. She didn't even demur at her bathroom, a stone floor with a drain in the middle and an earthenware pitcher of water. She removed her shoes indoors, ate in the Indian fashion with her left hand, and wondered, like E. M. Forster, why the English persisted in eating their own disgusting version of English food when Indian food was so delicious.

Back in Delhi, Emily entertained more for Ned than she had ever done in England, inviting Indians whenever she could. She even dined alone with the Viceroy to meet Lord Northcliffe, with whom she played Happy Families in the hopes that he would further Robert's career on the *Daily Mail*, where the young man now worked.*

To MacSack Ned reported that he really liked having Emily with him in India, though the thorny issue of marital sex was still unsettling. 'You don't know how it hurts me to hurt you and yet I see no way out,' wrote Emily. 'I know it must seem so hard for you – and yet I cannot make you understand that I am not cold or hard. I would give you everything but one thing, and I cannot give you that without such physical repulsion that it would kill everything else.' Ned was by now sufficiently relaxed to joke. 'May peace and happiness beflower your path to your next incarnation which will probably be a passionate man linked to a cool woman!'[13]

Emily, the passionate woman, escaped Delhi to visit Krishna her cool guru in February, fleeing the official visit of the Prince of Wales, whose presence in India was causing the new Viceroy, Lord Reading, much anxiety.

In Delhi the Prince of Wales made an official tour of the new buildings. He looked very bored. When Ned showed him the model which he had had made (to Baker's fury) to illustrate the gradient, the Prince looked through the periscope, but all he said was 'Good God'. To Baker he said, 'This building ought to be stopped, it is costing too much money.' Ned noticed him playing to the people, hitting on the legs with his cane a policeman who was shoving back a crowd of

---

*Northcliffe promised that he would promote Robert to work directly under him, but Robert was fired a year later.

masons. 'The masons gleed [*sic*] at the rebuff to the hated policeman. I was sorry for the policeman too.' Not that the Prince was any less 'colour-conscious' than his contemporaries. When Mountbatten reported that Mrs Besant, who believed in the divine right of kings, thought he was a reincarnation of Akbar, he was annoyed at having been a 'black man' in a previous life.[14]

The Prince's visit sparked a newspaper controversy about 'Delhi's Costly Glories – Historic Monument or Folly?' Ned could hardly have chosen a worse moment to reopen the issue of the gradient, but the appointment of the new Viceroy offered his final chance to reverse the earlier decision and restore the inclined way.

Ned's optimism merely showed how naive he was. Lord Reading doubted the wisdom of moving the capital to Delhi, and 'shook his head sadly at the constant stream of money poured into the building of a great new site at a moment when the country's financial position was imposing drastic economies upon every other field of public expenditure'. Spending so freely on a new imperial capital while Gandhi set the country alight for independence was politically unfortunate. For Ned to ask for even more money to correct an aesthetic blemish was crying for the moon. The real question in 1922 was whether New Delhi should be built at all.

How Ned must have wished that Victor Lytton, who had been in the running for Viceroy, had got the job. Ned's only real friend in the government was Edwin Montagu, but he was sacked in March 1922. The final blow was cost. In March 1922 the government engineer reported to the Delhi Committee that flattening and reconstructing the inclined way would cost £166,650, nearly half as much as the Government House estimates. (The figure quoted in 1916 had been £8,000.)

Reading still had to give his verdict, but Ned knew the game was up. He made up his mind to resign. 'I have few years left and I must cut myself off from such a fiasco as this.' Emily, who was in Adyar, wrote him the kind of letter that only she could write.

> I think it would be *absolutely fatal* to your whole professional career if you resigned and on that point. It would be the biggest triumph of Baker's life and give every enemy a handle to blaspheme. You have made one big blunder and you *must* pay for it. Be a man and stand up to your own mistake . . . Register your opinion and your protest in such a way that future generations will know and exonerate you from blame and then go ahead.[15]

It was what he wanted to hear. He must accept his Bakerloo. After 1922 he wasted no more time trying to reverse the gradient. He concentrated instead on revenging himself against Baker.

Lord Reading officially decided against flattening the gradient in June 1922. By then Lutyens was back in England, and he had moved on. He worried about his failure to secure the commission for the RAF memorial, which Lord Hugh Cecil blocked on the grounds that Lutyens had no religion. (The Cecil family of churchmen had not forgotten his campaign against the cross in 1918.)*

Fortunately for Lutyens, Fabian Ware of the Imperial War Graves Commission was no churchman. As consulting architect to the War Graves Commission Lutyens was paid an annual salary of £600 during the 1920s, for which he supervised the design and layout of a total of 126 cemeteries in France and Belgium, accounting for over 130,000 British and empire dead. Lutyens suggested a design which he called a green church, composed of his War Stone and Baker's Cross of Sacrifice surrounded by trees. The detailed design for each cemetery was carried out to his instructions by the assistant architects working in France. Lutyens visited France to inspect cemeteries each summer, supervising the creation of order and clinical neatness out of the ugly chaos of haphazard wooden crosses scattered at random over the cratered battlefields. Rows of regimented white headstones now stood forever to attention, men facing east towards the enemy. The exact area of each burial was precisely calculated, along with its unit cost: at Barlin, for example, each of the 1,190 burials was allowed 3.07 square metres and the average cost per grave was £8 6s. 2d.

The massive war cemetery at Etaples, which contained nearly 11,000 dead, brought Ned often to France in the summer of 1922. He designed two classical temples bearing cenotaphs, flanked at each corner by flags of plain stone.†

In Paris Ned stayed with Miss Elsie de Woolfe, later Lady Mendl, at her villa in Versailles. It was his first encounter with rich Americans

---

*One of Ned's few clergymen allies was the Reverend Basil Bourchier, vicar of St Jude's in Hampstead, who had supported the Great War Stone against the cross. When Lutyens walked into St Jude's one day to say hello, Bourchier exclaimed, 'Hush! The sacrament is exposed.' 'I thought he meant my buttons were undone.'

†Lutyens had wanted painted stone flags at the Cenotaph, but the Cabinet vetoed them, much to his distress, as he feared, wrongly as it turned out, that the silk flags would become tattered and old. The painted stone flags which he designed at Rochdale and Leicester make one feel today that the Cabinet had been right.

abroad. His particular favourite in the party was a dear old lady, exquisitely dressed, who wore a necklace of black pearls and diamonds which Ned admired. She asked him if he would like a pearl; he replied that he would rather have her face. She gave a great squeal of delight, and 'we got off'. She refused to believe that ivy hurts trees, so Ned wrapped his arms round her elegant form and gave her a death squeeze to show how it was done. Only then did he realize that this was the formidable Anne Vanderbilt, queen of New York. Miss de Woolfe, though sixty years of age, gave a nimble exhibition of her 'drill' to the gramophone, wearing tights and an India rubber corset, standing on her head and waving an amazingly youthful pair of legs. Ned's visit was not wasted. Among the guests was Elsa Maxwell, who pledged herself to find £15,000 for the 300 dolls needed for the Dolls' House, which each cost £50. As for Elsie de Woolfe, she seems to have become somewhat enamoured of Ned; MacSack noted darkly, 'he admitted he was flattered but that was all'.[16]

Emily took a house near Hemel Hempstead for the children in the summer of 1922, and Ned visited for four days. As a silver wedding present he gave Emily some pearls which, MacSack noted, cost £300.

With Emily safely out of the way in Hemel Hempstead, Ned seems to have more or less moved in with MacSack. 'Dear McNed dined for the last time [at her house in Ebury Street], as he is returning to Mansfield Street,' she wrote on 12 September. The following day: 'McNed is gone, very shy; simply shook me scantily by the hand . . . No man can do without the little kind attentions I surrounded him with, and he is so neglected chez lui, poor little fluffy Ned.'[17]

Before leaving for India in October 1922 Ned stayed at Balmoral. He boasted to MacSack that he was received by Queen Mary lying in her dressing gown on a sofa in her dressing room; he walked five miles with her talking all the time about the dolls' house. But he still made facetious jokes.

In Delhi, Baker asked Ned if he was going to cut him. 'I said I had nothing to say to him.' He said, 'Still proud?' 'Go and look at the job,' growled Lutyens. Lord Reading privately admitted to Ned that he agreed about the gradient but money made it impossible, which (whether or not it was true) comforted Ned. In spite of Baker's victory, he felt easier. All the same, he was dismayed when Baker was elected ARA. 'I did hope he would not get it.'[18]

While Ned was in India Emily visited the Mallets at Varengeville. She was positively feisty. She argued with Marie Mallet about the position of women: 'I did get quite angry when she made the surprising and foolish statement that all women and girls who worked in factories were immoral!' She quarrelled with Guillaume about the Jews and the right-wing movement Action Française; she found it hard, she said, to discuss things with people 'who live in a tight little closed circle and refuse to believe in the existence of anything outside it'. In London, MacSack came to lunch with Emily in November. Emily preached Labour politics and told her that children should be brought up by letting them do exactly as they liked. 'She is quite mad,' MacSack wrote in her diary.

Ned returned from Delhi in January 1923. He confided in MacSack that Emily had been recklessly extravagant: 'she told him that she had never cared for him so much since she had become a Sister to him. He told me how grateful she was to me for my friendship for them all, especially to him, and he said it had made all the difference to his life. I know it has.' When MacSack dined at Mansfield Street in April, she was appalled by Emily's 'Bolshie' views. '[She] was ridiculous about the New Birth of the World, coming from the War. Her gestures were those of a mad woman. I felt so sorry for McNed, whom she humiliated at every turn.'[19]

Emily's manic state was partly related to the menopause, which she welcomed because it brought relief from the torture of migraine headaches. She no longer saw MacSack as a threat; she was now reconciled to Ned's relationship with her, and even prepared to encourage it. Meanwhile, her euphoria was intimately linked to weird developments in California. As usual, Krishna was at the bottom of it.

After leaving Adyar in March 1922 Krishna and Nitya had sailed to Sydney for a Theosophical Society convention. Here they found C. W. Leadbeater installed in full regalia as a bishop of the Old Catholic Church and surrounded by beautiful boys. Leadbeater had been made a bishop by James Wedgwood, who discovered in the Old Catholic Church of breakaway Catholics opposed to papal infallibility the perfect opportunity for indulging his passions for ritual, dressing up and control. Being a bishop gave Leadbeater new power, as he could now create priests. While Krishna was in Australia the old scandals surrounding Leadbeater revived, and the newspapers screamed about 'Swish Bish for Boys' and 'Dandy Coloured Coons'.

Krishna was bruised and anxious about Nitya's health. X-rays now showed worrying patches on both lungs. The brothers retreated to

California, borrowing a cottage at Ojai high up in the mountains among orange groves and apricot orchards. Each sent a drop of his blood to a Los Angeles follower of Dr Abrams (they distrusted ordinary doctors) and he diagnosed TB in Nitya, and prescribed the 'Abrams machine'. Nitya sat for many hours each day strapped into plates wired up to a box which ticked; the treatment, which was supposed to send electrical waves into the affected parts, was painless and very boring. But he was cared for by a nineteen-year-old American girl named Rosalind Williams who was pretty with blue eyes like a Siamese cat.

While Nitya's condition see-sawed alarmingly, Krishna meditated for hours each day. After about five days he noticed acute pain in his neck and spine. He tossed and moaned, trembled and shivered, and complained of great heat. Only the nubile Rosalind was allowed near to soothe him. He grew semi-conscious, he raved as if delirious about his long-dead mother, and at last seemed to leave his physical body. This happened every day for several weeks. Krishna's mysterious 'process', as they called it, seems to have been a life-changing mental illness of the kind which gurus sometimes experience. The strange, isolated adolescence, the long war years of depression and failure, the traumatic crisis over Nitya's health – all the chaos and meaninglessness of his life was suddenly, magically resolved in illness followed by a blinding moment of revelation. His 'process' gave him a new authority and a magnetism. He prohibited his followers from working for themselves, ordering them instead to perform pointless tasks, ostensibly to promote their spiritual improvement but rather as a way of exercising power. In spite of his horror of sex, he surrounded himself with pretty young women like Rosalind and could only achieve his 'process' with the assistance of one of his *gopis*.

Emily was one of the first whom Krishna told of his experiences in September 1922. She was in raptures. 'At last it has come,' she thought. She was thrilled, too, that after her long years of disgrace, she had at length achieved acceptance from the Masters. Leadbeater had relented; presumably he no longer saw her as a sexual threat to Krishna's lower consciousness.

Emily went to meet Krishna on his return to England in June 1923. She worried that she might feel shy at his new spiritual stature, but 'to my unspeakable joy I found him exactly the same'. He seemed more beautiful than ever, and she was conscious of 'a controlled but immense concentrated power flowing from him'. When she started to talk about his experience, he went into a dead faint.

The brothers stayed with Miss Dodge in Wimbledon, and Mary, now fifteen, who knew nothing about the 'process', noticed the seductive atmosphere of glamour and enchantment that surrounded them. 'Krishna and Nitya might well have been princes, with their air of aristocracy, their delicious fragrance, the best of everything surrounding them, their closely guarded privacy and the sense of privilege one had at being with them at all, let alone on terms of joking intimacy.'[20]

Emily's closeness to the messiah made her more contemptuous than ever of the mortal Ned. Snubbed and despised at home, Ned spent more and more time with MacSack. By now the fortune she had inherited from Sir John Murray Scott had dwindled, much of it spent for her by McNed. As well as the £50,000 (at least) she spent on Sussex Square in Brighton, she calculated that she had spent £40,000 on her London house in Hill Street, where she installed three lifts and five bathrooms. She planned to sell Sussex Square but could not find a buyer, and she held a sale of the contents, most of which went for giveaway prices. For the first time Ned realized that she was not as rich as he thought. Her financial troubles reduced her to a state of nervous anxiety, and he no longer worried her with schemes for a perfect house and criticisms of her architectural 'grammar'. She bought a house on the cliff at Roedean named White Lodge, 'but I simply can't afford much building by darling McNed, who always begins with a low estimate and generally doubles it before the work is finished, thanks mostly to that A. J. Thomas, who manages all McNed's money affairs'. But Ned was unusually submissive, admired her alterations, 'and says he will do anything I like with the house'. To ease her financial position he paid off the £4,500 still owing on Mansfield Street. Emily was delighted. 'That debt rather weighed on my mind,' she wrote. 'I hated to be under such an obligation to her.' Not all Ned's obligations to MacSack were cancelled, however. In January 1923 she had given him a Rolls-Royce with a chauffeur named James, so that he could say 'Home, James,' and nothing was said about repaying the cost of that.[21]

Between 1923 and 1926, McNed and MacSack were again close. McNed's daughter, Mary, thought their relationship was 'certainly close enough to be called a love affair', though she was uncertain whether they were lovers in the physical sense. MacSack's daughter, Vita, who was close to her mother, thought they *were* lovers; she destroyed some of Ned's letters after BM's death.* Ned's letters to MacSack after about 1923 were written in a private language of lisping baby talk: 'yeth' and 'bleth you', 'vely velummy' (he could not pronounce his 'r's'). 'Ooroose' is 'our house.' Endlessly punning, his meaning often dissolved into incoherence. Sometimes instead of writing out a word he drew a symbol. Snatches such as '8 years does tie [picture of bowtie] my tie' suggest a shared intimacy – it was eight years ago that they had met, back in 1916. But the letters are fluffy and evasive, deliberately so perhaps, in order to avoid the danger of Lionel Sackville using them in a divorce case.

The strongest evidence of their affair is a letter written by Emily twenty years later. She told Ursula: 'I am sure that he lived with MacSack, though purely as a physical outlet'. It is significant that Emily was referring to a book by her son, Robert Lutyens: a brief study of his father which claimed that Lutyens was essentially childlike and asexual, lacking deep emotions such as love and hate. This Emily strongly denied; 'I think he feels intensely both love and hate but cannot express them'. The fact that Lutyens and MacSack were lovers was important to her because it showed that behind the smokescreen of puns and buffoonery he was capable of adult emotions. In an odd way, she was thankful. Having a grown-up relationship was what she wanted him to do.

George Plank, American artist friend of MacSack, remembered her hints about the relationship as being 'more than broad'. Driving down to White Lodge one day Ned put his arm on Plank's: 'Dear Plankino, I have not one single secret kept from you only I cannot talk.'[22]

MacSack was his muse. With her Ned could pun and smoke, play interminable patience, draw rude pictures and eat good food. Wrapped in her comfort, warmed by her sun, he could escape into the intellectual world that mattered to him: the world of pure geometry and proportion.

In June 1923 Lutyens designed a memorial for 60,000 missing soldiers at St Quentin. The Imperial War Graves Commission wished to commemorate the half million 'missing' war dead by putting their names on memorials. Rather than build a wall of names, Lutyens proposed to inscribe the name of each missing man on a monumental

---

*Other letters Vita Sackville-West returned to Ned's daughter Ursula, who tried to investigate the affair, hoping to prove that her father's sex life had not ended for ever when Emily expelled him from her bed at the age of forty-five.

arch, as he had on the Memorial Arch at Delhi. Creating sufficient surface area was itself a geometrical puzzle. The St Quentin design was an exercise in elemental geometry, inspired by the Roman triumphal arch, piling arches upon arches.

The detailed drawings were produced at the Queen Anne's Gate office, which had reopened in 1919. Ned, so he reported to MacSack, had eighty-two jobs in August 1923; he was making money again.

'Lut', as the office called him, would arrive punctually at 10 each morning. Tripping out of the taxi with his quick, dancing steps, he called for Tribe the caretaker to pay the taxi. After brief words with Thomas he would slip into his rooms, escaping the assistants who queued to see him. 'It was,' wrote Christopher Hussey, 'a repellently barren place, his room. He had torn out its chimney-piece and was content with the large open wound and generous fire which was left.' An untidy sea of drawings lay stacked against the bare dirty white walls. Lutyens worked with his back to the fire at an old board, to the right of which lay six small pipes which Tribe arranged each morning together with a fresh box of matches.

He never used ink now but worked in soft pencil on squared paper which he smudged and rubbed out with his fingers. He smoked continuously, furiously lighting matches as he concentrated and the pipes went out. His fingernails were permanently blackened with tobacco and pencil lead – the expensive nailbrushes which MacSack supplied made little impression. Working absorbedly in a slough of loose tobacco, ash, dead matches and India rubber, he blocked out designs or corrected or altered drawings using nine-inch rolls of tracing paper specially prepared by Tribe and resembling Bronco lavatory paper.

The rough sketches that emanated from Lutyens's Dickensian room were given to his assistants to draw out, using Batty Langley's 1750 template, *The City and Country Builder's and Workman's Treasury of Designs*. Elementary rules applied throughout a building. All window panes were identical in proportion, generally that of a square to its diagonal in height. All mouldings were set at an angle of 54.43 degrees to the horizontal. This, the 'secret angle' of Lutyens's work, the angle formed by the relation of a square to its diagonal, was the angle of his roofs, rarely departed from in the last thirty years (in the early houses he had used the angle of the pyramid, 51.5 degrees). He worked entirely by relation of parts, his assistant W. A. S. Lloyd recalled, which involved extraordinary fractions. Approximations were not tolerated.* 'About! I don't know what you mean by 'about'!'

'God sees it,' Lut would say to the unhappy assistant who fudged a roof or hidden window. But as Lloyd and another pupil A. S. G. Butler testified, he was concerned primarily with surfaces. 'Lutyens was not interested in what held the building up or composed the core, heated or drained it.' It was Thomas or the collaborating architects who made the building stand up, put in the steel, bonded the thin bricks. No wonder Thomas was so important to him. 'Lutyens's neck', as Thomas was known in the office, was a miniature version of Lut, smaller, rounder, pinker and Welsh. He smoked similar pipes and wore similar clothes.[23] Emily was annoyed by his familiarity as he puffed smoke into her face in imitation of Ned, and MacSack complained about his inefficiency, sloppiness and carelessness with money, but by now Thomas had made himself indispensable. It was he who allowed Lutyens to work as an artist, protecting him from the men in his office and shielding him from unpleasantness. But it may well have been Thomas who was partly to blame for the disintegration of Lutyens's domestic practice.

Emily, Mary and Betty spent the summer of 1923 in Austria. With Krishna and Nitya and the travelling circus of theosophical hangers-on (Rajagopal, Mar de Manziarly, Isabelle Mallet) they stayed in chalets at Ehrwald in the Austrian Tyrol. They spent their days walking in pine forests, taking hip baths in ice-cold mountain streams and sunbathing naked, which was prescribed by an elderly Austrian theosophical naturist named Cordes. Each evening at 7 Betty and Mary were banished to their separate chalet. Betty remembered an atmosphere heavy with mystical import. She was made to feel privileged to know Krishna; he and his life were all that had meaning. 'It was as if the curtain was about to go up on a world-shattering miracle play.' Torn between adolescent rebellion and a desperate desire to earn her mother's approval, Betty swallowed her scepticism and embraced the new religion.

Emily spent her evenings with Krishna. She watched him sob and groan, lose consciousness and leave his body, reappearing as a little

---

*Bertram Carter, who was a pupil of Lut's from 1919 to 1922, was shocked to discover when he entered the offices of Yates, Cook and Darbyshire, 'then in the process of destroying Regent Street', that fewer drawings were done for a whole job than Lutyens would devote to a dormer window.

child. He insisted on having beside him Helen Knothe, a Dutch-American girl he had fallen for in 1921. When Emily tried to help him he told her that her being married made it undesirable; 'when in this state he is very particular that everything round him should be of the purest'. She thought it odd that he needed to have young girls close to him, but never questioned it. 'I try to be Mother to them all,' she told Mrs Besant, 'and fit in when I am wanted. With so many girls an older woman is rather necessary.'

Emily returned to London elated and totally convinced of Krishna's divine powers, feeling privileged to be so close to him – 'I only pray to be worthy of it all'.[24] She found it hard to come down to earth; in fact she was determined not to return to normal life. Ned, writing to MacSack nearly every day, complained that he had no home life. MacSack wrote in her diary (5 November 1923):

> He told me that Emmie is more than ever mad about her Indians and the idea of the new Redeemer soon coming to alter the world. I simply can't bear to go again to Mansfield Street and hear her ranting against the upper classes and the wickedness of the world and the rights of the Bolshies. It is too painful and she treats McNed shamefully and humiliates and nags him for not being a vegetarian, and she says he likes eating carcases. He is so loyal to her and the children, who also treat him with such levity.

The Dolls' House had been moved into Mansfield Street, where it occupied the entire drawing room, making Ned's dream life seem to reproach the emptiness of his real life. The landlord, Howard de Walden estates, complained that the house was being used for purposes other than a private residence, contrary to the lease. Ned was very busy and dined out most nights – the McKennas, the Astors, Robert's friend Brendan Bracken, Elsa Maxwell, Curzon – and he would bring late-night visitors home to see the dolls. The Queen herself often came; once she stayed four hours and demanded to be left alone to play with the dolls. When asked why the pillowcases in the Queen's bedroom were embroidered MG and GM, Ned explained that it stood for *May George?* and *George May*.[25]

No sooner was Emily back in London than she was travelling again. Since she could not be with Krishna, who had returned to Ojai where his 'process' had resumed, she went to India, where she felt closer to him. She took the fifteen-year-old Mary out of school because she was unhappy at Queen's College, Harley Street, thus earning the disapproval of Mrs Besant who believed strongly in women's education. Ned followed them in January 1924, leaving Betty in London, alone in the huge house with Nannie and eight servants, studying music and conscientiously looking for auras that might guide her to the Path.

In Bombay Emily's spirits lifted. 'Oh! I am so happy,' she told Ned. 'I am just revelling in every moment and bless you for making it possible.' Mary wrote in her diary: 'Mummy is too funny – I have never seen her so happy before.' Both Emily and Mary became enthusiasts for Gandhi and Swaraj, his campaign for Indian self-government. Emily put away her knitting needles and started spinning cotton. She gave lectures and press interviews and lunched with the Governor of Bombay – 'a very commonplace middle-class couple with I should think very little brains'.

At Adyar Emily took off her shoes indoors and sat cross-legged on the floor at meals; Mary could barely restrain her from wearing a sari, which she plainly itched to do. Mary had never before spent so long with her mother; it was a revelation when Emily held her head and sponged her face when she was sick in the train. She wrote in her diary: 'I think I love her more than anyone else in the world. She is wonderful and beautiful inside. I am very proud of her and, I think, everyone adores her although they make fun of her. She certainly has the strength of her own opinions, which is a quality I admire immensely.' These were exactly the qualities Ned admired in Emily. She could still enslave people. Even though she deserted her family, ruined her home and abandoned her responsibilities, her children adored her. As Betty wrote: 'There was something in Mother so loveable and innocent that everyone wished to spoil her – and spoilt she was – and protect her, as a rare and beautiful object, from the harshness of a life which she had never experienced.'[26]

Emily and Mary stayed with Victor Lytton, newly appointed Governor of Bengal, in Calcutta where they were joined by Ned and Ursula. Mary wrote in her diary: 'Father isn't the tiniest bit pleased to see me and I know he doesn't like me a scrap which makes me a little miserable, as I am very fond of him indeed.' Victor was an extravagant and pompous governor, insisting on his guards being mounted (bad for the horses) and flying flags and taking bodyguards everywhere he went, but he shared Emily's pro-Indian sympathies. Emily dreamed of using Victor and Mrs Besant to build a bridge between the British and Gandhi's Swaraj.

They travelled back to Delhi by train, Ned going first class and Emily and five girls crowding into a second-class carriage. Fearing an accident, Ned refused to take his socks off at night; 'he said he could not possibly walk along the cold railway lines in bare feet'.

Installed in their bungalow at Number 1 Viceregal Estate (now 2 Willingdon Crescent), the first house Ned built in New Delhi, the family bickered and squabbled. Ned (according to Mary) was happy because Ursula, his favourite and the only child who was never influenced by theosophy, was there. He thought it a waste of time if no one came to dinner, so every evening Ned hosted a dinner party followed by the same routine. Ursula and her friend Patsy Ward sang to their ukuleles, 'I Am Weary of the Ballroom Sang the Girl,'; Mary, who found these evenings excruciating, sang a Victorian song, 'Little Tottie Went to Ma', and as a grand finale Ned sang, 'Ta-ra-ra Boom De-ay', gracefully kicking his legs high in the air. 'Topi or not topi,' Ned would say each morning as he picked up his solar topi. Persotum grinned and Emily snubbed, 'Oh Nedi, *not* that one again.' Emily spent her days in the Legislative Assembly, listening to debates. Mary reflected that the bungalow was not *real* India at all but 'a horrible little piece of usurping England', set down in the country where she and Emily thought they had been born in past incarnations.[27]

Ned's jokes cheered poor Lady Reading who, like Lady Hardinge before her, was dying of cancer. He sent drawings into her sickroom via the Sister. 'Baby's Weak in the Jungle' showed the aides as wild animals and all that could be seen of HE and HER was one natty pair of shoes and one pair of rough shooting boots hanging from a branch. She thought him 'mad as a hatter' but very amusing. He also charmed the Nizam of Hyderabad, for whom he built a palace in Delhi with rooms for twenty-four ladies, two queens and a grandmother.

In March 1924 Ned returned to London and Emily went back to Adyar. Mary dreaded the journey with Ned and Ursula, 'those two adoring each other, Father disliking me'. Ned wrote to Emily regretting the 'widening waters between us', but Emily was so happy at her freedom that she felt only thankful. 'It is very wonderful of you to go on loving me when I am such an unsatisfactory wife. I often wonder why you do! But I am very glad of it.'[28]

As soon as he was back in London Ned telephoned MacSack. 'He is tiresome and upsets all my plans again,' she wrote in her diary, annoyed by his revisions at White Lodge. 'I never get from him what I really want on account of that everlasting grammar, and his fear of being criticized if he does the slightest thing wrong architecturally. Enfin! He is such a friend and such a genius that I must lump it, and he clings fiercely to me, however horrid I am. It is very touching.'

Soon they were back in the old routine, quarrelling and making up; their fights had become a source of energy, necessary to both of them; a travesty of the artist–client relationship. They quarrelled about a flat roof at White Lodge: McNed was 'very naughty and we parted very cross with each other and I shall punish him, as he kicks against doing what I want to do.' Ned wrote nine letters and MacSack relented. 'I let him come and dine and I have never seen him more penitent. He had had a brainwave, by which he will light up the house by making a long west window . . . He is so supremely devoted to me that he said that if I had refused to let him come to dinner, he would have gone without any dinner and walked about the streets all night.' It was always Ned who was the 'naughty' one, penitent for his sins and begging forgiveness from the all-powerful MacSack.[29]

In April the Queen's Dolls' House was moved to Wembley for the British Empire exhibition. Press photographs show a startled and dishevelled Lutyens standing beside a furiously glaring Queen Mary. Lutyens had received no invitation to the opening. Princess Marie Louise loyally wrote to the Queen, complaining about the snub to 'one of England's most distinguished men', and he was asked at the last minute.

Like the Cenotaph, the Dolls' House was a hit. It became the main attraction of the exhibition; crowds queued to see it. No doubt it says something about post-war Britain that a miniature exhibition of social snobbery, backward-looking nostalgia and royal voyeurism should have pulled such crowds, but Ned showed himself once again in touch with the people's mood.

At Mansfield Street the room where the Dolls' House had stood was cleaned and the back drawing room converted into a bed-sitting room for Emily. Here she had a *chowki*, a low Indian couch on which she slept and sat cross-legged. A communicating door linked her back drawing-room door to Ned's first-floor bedroom. To Mary the communicating door signified that her parents had reached a modus vivendi. If they had, there is little evidence of it in their letters. Ned grumbled vigorously. 'I must get someone to look after and help me . . . I work damn hard and have an absolutely rotten home.' He squabbled with Nannie who, being no longer needed by her charges, now became an altered woman; she dressed in fashionable clothes, wore an engagement ring and had her nails polished.[30]

MacSack's Ebury Street was second home to Ned. In the summer of 1924 he saw Emily only twice a week; other nights he dined and slept at Ebury Street. This was living dangerously, as Lionel Sackville now wanted a divorce in order to marry Olive.

With MacSack, Ned went to lunch with Bumps at Munstead. MacSack brought a chicken pie and twelve eclairs. Bumps gave them a 'horrid smelly' beefsteak pie and didn't offer any of her chicken. As MacSack described it: 'I asked for some and she gave me half a wing, having a whole chicken to herself. She looks like a pig, as her eyes, which are very small, are sinking in her cheeks, and she grunted like a satisfied pig. McNed and I left starving.' Ned told MacSack of the places he had visited long ago with Bumps in her pony cart, 'and we were in our big Rolls-Royce', she wrote, conscious of the irony. 'He told me he was ashamed of his early work.'

As a surprise, Ned dumped heaps of the finest white Portland stone at White Lodge to make a Georgian entrance. MacSack was furious, protesting that it would be 'absolutely wrong' on her Queen Anne house. McNed showed no temper or resentment but gave her a great hug and explained that a Georgian porch would have been like the child of the William and Mary house, sadly saying that 'he dreaded American architects seeing White Lodge now as it wasn't good enough'.* Naturally the porch was built.

There was a world of difference between the early Surrey houses and the work he did now, from MacSack's Georgian porch to Tyringham Park in Buckinghamshire. This was a severe house by Soane where he designed a swimming pool, built of concrete, and two temples – one a bathing pavilion, the other a Temple of Music – for the Konig family of Silesian bankers who had converted to theosophy. Mrs Konig, who was musical, was 'a pretty, tiny, plump little figure who wore extremely high heels even while playing the organ'.[31] The Temple is a perfectly proportioned humanist shrine; Tyringham translates into landscape garden the humanist traditions which Lutyens developed for the War Graves Commission and at Delhi.

---

*Lutyens had a following among American architects. In 1922 Eadred Lutyens introduced an American architect, Mr 'J', to Lutyens. '"You will be glad to know, Mr Lutyens, that in our country your book [by Lawrence Weaver] is our bible. Hardly a house goes up which has not got your doors, your windows, your chimneys or your roofs." There was a pause, and then Sir Edwin said rapidly and quietly: "Why don't you think it out for yourself?" I have never seen anyone so crushed as Mr "J" . . .'

Chapter Sixteen
Emily's Great Adventure
1924–1925

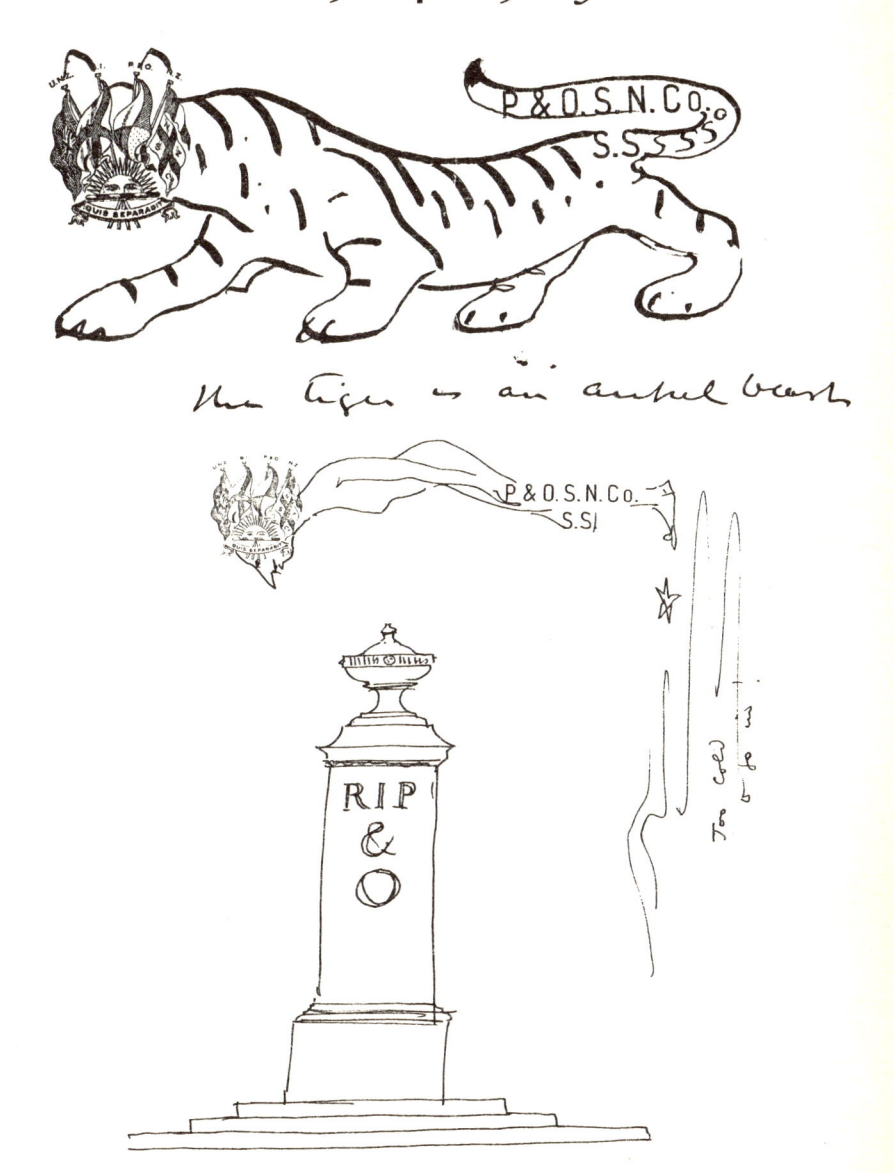

'The tiger is an awful beast.'
Puns and doodles *(above and overleaf)* made by Ned on P & O writing paper on the journeys by sea to and from India.

"The Camp fire"

P & O. S. N. Co.
S.S.

On the twenty-seventh anniversary of their wedding, in August 1924, Emily wrote Ned a letter thanking him for being 'endlessly good to me, patient and loving and long-suffering . . . I have hurt you far more than you have hurt me . . . We have not succeeded in building a joint life or making a home together such as you would have liked. This is sadder for you than me because I have exactly the life I want and the home I want.' True, Ned could never accept her theosophy, and 'this makes for apparent separation for a time. At the end we shall reach the same goal and rejoice to find ourselves together.' Emily had reached her apotheosis. There was no arguing with a saint, even though she had deserted her family, ruined her children and spent most of her husband's money.

'Money is all that is left for me to serve you with,' Ned wrote. As a knighted architect, acting as consultant on big London projects, he was making more than ever before. In 1923 he spent only £3,000, saving £20,000. In 1924 they spent £5,000, and he still planned to save £12,000. His capital had suddenly grown to £44,000. Where all this money had come from is something of a mystery to historians, as it was perhaps to him. There is no doubt, however, that his big city projects yielded more than the country houses which he designed less and less.

In 1924 the British Medical Association, which had bought the shell of Lutyens's unfinished Theosophical Society building in Tavistock Square, asked him to complete it; they planned to spend £50,000 on finishing and decorating.* Ned found the work done by the theosophists' building committee 'very bad'; 'I can put it right now and I am glad I have been saved the ignominy of other people seeing it.' He was pleased with his results. 'The big hall designed for Mrs Besant looks very well', and the flat he designed for her was flooded with light.[1]

When Lutyens addressed the Architectural Association in 1920 he had insisted on using the word patron, not client. 'The distinction is an obvious one, a patron employs you because he admires your work, and a client for what he can get out of you.' Reginald McKenna, the Liberal politician who had married Pamela Jekyll and commissioned a sober

---

*The history of this building is complicated. The front range of buildings on Tavistock Square was built by C. Wonter Smith in the 1920s.

square brick house at 36 Smith Square in 1910, belonged most definitely to the patron class. An Asquith Liberal, of conservative social views, as Home Secretary he was arch-enemy of the suffragettes; a sore point with Emily.

In 1919 McKenna became Chairman of the Midland Bank, and Ned was showered with commissions. In 1923 McKenna commissioned him to rebuild Mells Park House. The original house near Mells Manor, where Frances Horner lived, was torched during the war. In 1918 Ned had sketched for her a design for a stone-roofed French house, but she could not afford to build, and Ned's Mells design was transposed to Gledstone, which also has a stone roof of Cotswold stone. The McKennas came to Mells because Pamela McKenna was Frances Horner's niece. For them, Lutyens designed a different house, a plain square box. It seems to have been a case of what Lutyens called umbrella architecture, acting under the client's strict supervision; McKenna held strong views and (as Christopher Hussey wrote) 'Lutyens was not given a free hand, and the result is not especially notable'.

Cautious too was the Midland Bank in Piccadilly, which Lutyens designed in 1922: a gemlike red-brick box which (according to John Summerson) 'pokes perpetual fun at the dreary Wren church alongside' (St James's, Piccadilly).[2]

In 1924 Lutyens got his reward for pleasing his patron: the Midland Bank headquarters at Poultry in the City. 'We all aim at getting something that is a credit to the City,' said McKenna, justifying his choice of architect. 'We are anxious not to disfigure the City of London by putting up buildings that are unworthy of the positions that they are to occupy.' The bank's position was crucial. One face of the building gives on to the narrow thoroughfare of Poultry, the other on to Princes Street, where it fronts the grim rusticated screen wall which Soane threw round his Bank of England.[3]*

At the Midland Bank, Lutyens's façade echoes Soane's banded wall, which Ruskin once likened to the pages of a ledger. Lutyens clothed the

---

*Inside that wall, as Lutyens knew only too well, Baker was demolishing Soane's masterpiece – vandalism that was the more bitter because Lutyens had wanted the job so badly for himself. He feared that Baker's sermonizing had hoodwinked his clients, and that 'we will all be dead before he is found out'; but Baker was not so lucky. Baker was still alive, an old man of eighty-three, when John Summerson waspishly wrote that he was 'antipathetic to his predecessor [Soane] in such a degree that whatever respect has been intended the result has been a grotesque insult'. As Gavin Stamp pointed out, the top-lit dome in the kitchen at Castle Drogo, which Lutyens designed about this time, is taken from Soane's banking halls.

six-storey steel-framed building erected by Lawrence Gotch in a façade of Portland stone; Christopher Hussey described it as his 'most *learned* work'. Lutyens solved the problem of making a building in a narrow street look tall from ground level by playing tricks with perspective. At Poultry he created a building that is the embodiment of his favourite worm's-eye view. The entire building is rusticated. The rustication bands are each one-eighth of an inch less than the one beneath, and at intervals the vertical plane is stepped back an inch, giving an extraordinary impression of recession and height. The mathematics this involved for his unfortunate draughtsmen was fiendish; the rustication blocks progressively diminished by the amount .273 recurring of an inch. The use of precise mathematical fractions and geometry to evoke perspective recalls the Cenotaph, but here Lutyens played with the most basic building form of all, the wall, making it stand on tiptoe.

Posterity has approved Lutyens's architectural sculpture. No one, wrote Pevsner, could deny the opulent splendour of the banking halls: 'very tall, and broader than anything previously seen in a City bank, with a forest of square Corinthian columns in green African verdite, off-set against white marble walls'. Some contemporaries were less impressed by the elevations. The *Builder* commented sourly that the severely architectural model exhibited at the Royal Academy, which was probably the largest ever shown, occupied too much space. The upper storeys would be invisible from the street, 'and this has apparently been in the architects' minds, for the upper recessed portion has little or no concern with the lower part of the building'.[4]

There was no place for Emily in the world of the knighted architect. MacSack's diaries are missing for this year, and without her commentary Lutyens, dining out every night and lunching at his club, becomes almost unknowable. Out of duty and habit he and Emily still corresponded, but they revealed little of each other in their letters. These were in many ways the most important years of Emily's life, the climax of her theosophical career. She wrote about them at length in her autobiography, *Candles in the Sun*. How much this was ghosted by Mary is impossible to say, but the detached voice of her narrative contrasts oddly with the bizarre events and the messianic fervour she describes.

In the summer of 1924 Emily took Betty and Mary to the Star camp at Ommen in Holland. Ommen was near Castle Eerde, the estate presented to the Theosophical Society by a wealthy Dutch aristocrat,

Baron Pallandt. This was the first Star camp, and 250 theosophists slept under canvas. At night they sat round the campfire, listening to Krishna's talks; he spoke impromptu as the spirit moved him, urging compassion, sincerity, and the need for everyone to find their own way to enlightenment. His teachings conflicted with the doctrine of the society, which emphasized hierarchy and the Path, but his audience were so mesmerized by his charismatic presence and physical beauty that no one seemed to care. In any case, it was noticeable afterwards that no one could agree exactly what he had said; like all great actors perhaps, Krishna was in a sense the creation of his audience, reflecting back to his hearers what they wanted to believe.

Krishna, Nitya and the travelling circus of hangers-on and *gopis*, together with Emily, Mary and Betty, next pitched tent at Pergine near Milan. Here they stayed in a hotel in a medieval castle overlooking the Dolomites, and in the evenings Krishna's 'process' returned. 'Never had it been easier for me to sublimate my love for him than in those never-to-be-forgotten evenings in the square tower,' wrote Emily. In the afternoons Krishna had little talks with each of them, preparing them for promotion along the Path. He told Mary (who kept a diary) that she was 'too damn calculating and like an iceberg', that she must change for his sake. Girls could not have marriage and serve the Master too. Mary wrote in her diary: 'I'll work for his sake as Mummy has always worked. I won't add to his suffering. I will strive my utmost to relieve it.' Mary, who was his favourite, escaped relatively lightly. Krishna's home truths could be devastating. His psychological cruelty had already begun to make Betty ill, and he often reduced Emily to tears; but this made her all the more devoted.[5]

Alone in London, Ned growled about money. He went to see his lawyer Francis Smith and shocked him by saying that he needed to make provision for another woman should he marry again. Emily thought this an excellent idea ('I know I am a rotten wife'), and she encouraged him to bring another woman into his life. 'Another woman doubtless alluring,' replied Ned, 'but how can I afford it?' 'Well we must make every economy so that you *can*,' came the reply. Mansfield Street was a white elephant and too expensive, so Emily proposed to take it over and run it as a community. Her sister Betty Balfour wrote reproaching her for deserting her home and responsibilities, and Emily tried to explain that no one really needed her.

That summer season in London Ursula had triumphed, with her curls, her ukulele and a Cossack dance she did with folded arms and red boots, clicking her heels horizontally in the air. (Mary sourly commented that she always knew when Ursula was going to a dance because of the smell of hair-removing cream.) Ursy became engaged to Matt Ridley. Young, rich and a viscount, he was the nephew of Ned's client, Ivor Guest of Ashby St Ledgers. Ursy and Matt were embarrassingly in love, holding hands all through meals.

Emily conveniently ignored poor Betty. Left alone in London the previous winter, Betty had written desperate pleas for help, but all Emily could say was 'Forget yourself and think of others'.[6]

The last straw for Ned was a letter from Emily breezily announcing that Eva was pregnant and that the baby would be born at Mansfield Street. Ned replied that he was 'deeply hurt and shocked' at Eva wanting to turn him out of his home. Emily responded with a lengthy account of Eva's gynaecological problems, but Eva miscarried.

'How badly his children treat him,' wrote MacSack in October 1924, 'but he accepts it serenely saying he is an old man (at 55 only) and says that young people hate old ones.'[7]

At fifty-five Ned already thought of himself as old. His hair, the little that remained, was now white (he cut it himself, twisting each strand into a rope and chopping it off with nail scissors). Rather than attempting to connect with his children, he remained indifferent and remote, lacking the insight to realize how vulnerable Emily's defection made them.

That summer Ned was invited as a Distinguished Guest of the newly established Irish nation to the Taillteann Games in Dublin, a revival of an ancient Celtic festival. Forgetting his irritation at Dublin's behaviour over the Art Gallery in 1913, he went with Cecil Baring. Oliver St John Gogarty, who commanded the social operations, gave Augustus John champagne for lunch. 'He soon got blind to the world and it was amusing it *was*! whilst we were all hurried to get away to see John relinquishing the bottles with reluctance.' Ned had never much liked John: when he dined at John's London haunt, the Eiffel Tower restaurant, he told MacSack that he hated the 'sex talk and Augustus John and his drunken little lady called Zaharoff and a Mrs Wallace, very fat and who made tremendous advances to everybody'; but when Gogarty brought a party to Lambay for the day, Ned danced a minuet with John on the terrace. What struck Ned most about Dublin was the way they all lived without servants. Yeats had only one servant who was 'fey and almost felt one as the door was opened by inches with nerveless hands', while O'Brien had no servants at all and Mrs O'Brien did the cooking herself. This was what Labour would bring them to in England, thought Ned, vowing yet again to sell Mansfield Street.[8]

Ned hated most things about modern middle-class life. His dislikes included: long-stemmed glasses, fish knives, cut flowers, silk lampshades, pile carpets, the seaside, the placing of furniture diagonally, painted nails. Yet he still could not bring himself to vote Conservative. He annoyed MacSack at the December 1923 election by telling her that he intended either not to vote at all or to vote Labour. 'My excuse is that I have paired with you,' he told Emily, who once more threatened to stand as a Labour MP.[9]

Emily returned from Italy a fortnight before Ursula's wedding in October 1924. She did little to organize the grand society wedding in St Margaret's, Westminster; Ursula might have been thankful, for Emily usually served Marmite sandwiches at her teetotal parties. The wedding was organized by Barbie.

Emily was preoccupied with higher things: Krishna had told her to visit Leadbeater in Australia, in order to bring Mary and Betty promotion on the Path. Ned was not pleased but there was nothing he could do to stop it, as Miss Dodge had offered to pay their fares. Emily even arranged for him to have 'another woman'. She saw MacSack and asked her to care for Ned while she was away. 'She was perfectly charming,' wrote MacSack, 'and very friendly and wants me to be the one person to look after poor neglected McNed.'

Emily left London on 28 October. She wrote in her diary: 'Off on the great adventure. Where will it end?'[10] For Mary the long sea voyage was a taste of paradise. Nitya told her he loved her, reciprocating the calf love which (she believed) she had secretly felt for him since the age of six. Her rapture was clouded only by the realization that she had lost her faith in the Masters. Two days before they reached Bombay Nitya coughed blood again. Mary's idyll was doomed.

At Adyar, Krishna was god, surrounded by adoring middle-aged European women decked unbecomingly in saris and sitting cross-legged, 'bunioned foot over bunioned foot', their eyes half-closed as they floated on the astral plain. Mary, Betty and the *gopis*, Helen and Ruth, spent their days on Krishna's veranda within range of his aura, addressing Theosophical Society envelopes and typing with one finger. Krishna already manifested the guru's authoritarian need to control his followers. His little talks with Betty made her feel that she was being played with like a cat with a mouse. His repeated insistence that everyone liked Mary best gnawed into her already fragile self-confidence; painfully conscious of her long nose and acne, she was the most vulnerable of the Lutyens children. She longed to retaliate and answer back. It was not so long ago that she had chanted 'Cowardy, cowardy custard, your face is the colour of mustard', when Krishna entered the nursery, but answering back was now against the rules. When Krishna criticized her for being untidy, rude, bourgeois (this because of her interest in 'all that sex stuff') she was obliged to submit. He left her feeling 'a freak – not normal'.

To Emily Krishna was ruthless too. He told her that she must rid herself of her childishness, be more considerate and not talk for the sake of talking. Always a glutton for chastisement, Emily lapped it up; she could never have enough of Krishna's teaching. Meanwhile, Nitya grew steadily weaker as his TB spread. He knew that he needed to return to Europe for treatment, but he refused to let his illness interfere with Krishna's plans to travel to Australia. Krishna's ascendancy encouraged a complacency among the groupies that was frightening. The Masters, they believed, would take care of everything.[11]

Ned arrived in India in January 1925. He was 'fearfully busy', and 'everyone wants to see Government House which is beginning to have a success'.

Ned's masterpiece was beginning to rise at last. When New Delhi was shelved in 1917 because of the war, Government House had reached upper basement level. Building began again in 1919, but there was little progress on the house. By 1921 it was only one-third finished (the Secretariats were two-fifths built). Nothing could be done until the report of a committee chaired by Lord Inchcape, whom the Viceroy, Lord Reading, had appointed to recommend cuts in Indian expenditure. Ned called it the Axe Committee. Inchcape published in early 1923; far from cutting, he left Government House alone and proposed increased spending on quarrying.

The rhubarb-red and creamy buff sandstone that Ned used at Government House came from the quarries of Dholphur and Bhartpur, which had supplied the stone for Fatepuhr Sikri and Agra over four centuries before. The stone was quarried and dressed using labour-intensive methods which had barely changed since Akbar's time. Before 1914, when work was at its height, an army of 29,000 men worked on the Delhi project.

By 1922, one-third of the required stone – one million cubic feet – had been conveyed along 115 miles of railway line from Dholphur to Delhi. Here, in the biggest stone yard in the world, 3,000 masons (*sangtarash*) squatted on their haunches, dressing stone and carving it in the fashion of Shah Jihan. Many of these *sangtarash* were descended from the stone carvers of Fatepurh Sikri. All day long the workers chanted monotonously, 'Haisa, haisa', and the 'put-put' of the mechanical stone saws could be heard through the night.

Increased spending after 1923 brought more stone from Dholphur, and the building site at Delhi swarmed with labourers – *bagris* from Rajasthan and *bandhanis* from the Punjab. There were no cranes or mechanical weight-lifting equipment, and the bamboo scaffolding was tied together with string. Harcourt Butler's daughter Iris remembered 'little wizened people' who scrambled up rickety bamboo ladders with hods of bricks or bags of cement on their heads (for each load they received a cowrie token).[12]

Ned spent long, weary days on the site. Watching his minutely controlled building rise out of this sprawling chaos of rubble and humanity was more like commanding a medieval battle than supervising a site. It is a miracle that his intricate classical geometry – the precise angles cut to a fraction of an inch, the exact entasis of a column or the subtle batter of a wall – should have been followed to the letter by illiterate peasants and craftsmen using medieval technology. Little wonder he had insisted on his Delhi draughtsmen drawing everything out in meticulous, wearisome detail, producing thousands of drawings for Government House alone.

As well as Mary and Betty, Emily brought Mrs Besant with her to stay with Ned in New Delhi. Mrs Besant had enlisted Emily in her campaign for independence for India, hoping that Emily could influence her brother Victor, the Governor of Bengal. Emily was confident of Victor's support, telling Ned not to judge by Pamela's silly remarks, 'as she really knows nothing of the political situation and hates all Indians'. Mrs Besant brought a 'church all day' feeling which Ned found unbearable, and young men who came to dinner would dread being placed on the solemn vegetarian side of the table. Mrs Besant was not amused by Ned's facetious jokes. He drew a sketch of her on a camel with a caption, 'Have you seen Mysore?' Tom and Cimmie Mosley stayed, and Ned made them 'roar' with his motto for India: 'India expects every man to do his dhoti'; but Mrs Besant just looked sad.

Mindful perhaps of Krishna's injunction that she talked too much, Emily was even more neglectful of her guests than usual, bleakly offering cheese or wine 'if we have any', and producing a tepid bottle of sweet Graves. Betty was so embarrassed that she took over the housekeeping herself. Mary, thinking to start a conversation with her father, plucked up courage to ask him how he became an architect without going to school. Without looking up from his patience cards or taking his pipe out of his mouth Ned replied grumpily: 'All you've got to know is that water runs downhill and any fool knows that.' She felt snubbed and frightened of boring him. Later, she reflected how unhappy he must have felt at seeing his daughters being ruined by theosophy while he was powerless to enforce his authority. Perhaps. Or perhaps the long years of separation and snubs had made him genuinely indifferent to his two youngest children.

In February 1925 Emily returned to Krishna at Adyar. Mary wrote in her diary: 'Poor Father was so upset when Mummy went. I pity him and, in a way, admire him from the bottom of my heart. He works and slaves from dawn till dark and we spend his money on the things he loathes. And to make matters worse, Delhi, his life's work, is already crumbling before his eyes.' Betty was miserably unhappy at Adyar. 'O God, please give me wet fields and greyness; take away the tiredness of this glare, this sun ... The breakdown, and no hand to help ...'[13]

Back in England in March 1925 Ned found an angry MacSack. She blamed him for bungling the work at White Lodge; irritation turned to jealous anger when she heard rumours that he had flirted with the Duchess of Sutherland in Paris. Soothed by Vita, who told her 'it was a national duty on my part to be nice to McNed', she eventually relented, softened by McNed's offer to pay all the builders' bills. She thrived on adulation but, according to her grandson, Nigel Nicolson, in middle age she was repelled by physical lust. Ned clung tenaciously, writing her daily letters, thirsting for her company, but she disliked it when he became what she called 'lully', a private word coined after a visit to Lullingstone, back in 1917, where 'something' happened. 'McNed was not lully today – thank God,' she would write in her diary. Vita, still emotionally dependent on her mother, whom she described as a 'great warm sun irradiating all my days', confided in her diary: 'I do understand McNed's feeling so well.' Lionel Sackville was now talking seriously of naming Ned in a divorce case.[14]

'Lionel Earle tells me – but it is *private* – that they want me to design the new Embassy at Washington,' Ned told Emily. 'That would be fun and glory of my sort!' The Institute of American Architects had awarded him their gold medal, and Ned, who had hesitated about travelling to the ceremony, now promptly accepted. The prospect of speechmaking and the unknown filled him with nerves. Before leaving in April 1925 he wrote MacSack a love letter in plain English. 'My own darling BM, I cannot bear even to say au revoir to you.'[15]

At New York he was formally received by a deputation of architects, led by Harvey Corbett. 'Ah,' said Ned to a serious-looking architect as they strolled through the docks, 'so this is McKim's great railway station!' As the architects earnestly explained that the docks were not in fact Pennsylvania Station, designed by McKim, Meade and White, Ned replied, 'I think I have your goat!' Only then did they realize that he was pulling their leg, and roars of laughter ensued. Ned was unimpressed by McKim's Pennsylvania Station when he eventually saw it. 'A colossal hall modelled on the baths of Caracalla – 150 feet high. Of no use.' But he liked the scale of New York and the skyscrapers, 'growing from monstrosities to erections of real beauty'.

He travelled first to Washington for the real business of his visit: the new Embassy. The Union Station he dismissed as 'a great pompous building built in the spirit of advertisement', and L'Enfant's city plan, thought by some to be an inspiration for Delhi, was 'not as good as Delhi or as fine', though the buildings were far better. 'The public patronage is alive whereas at Delhi it is nil.' He stayed with the British ambassador Esmé Howard in the residence on Connecticut Avenue, the house where, as a girl in the 1880s, MacSack had entertained for her father, then British Minister. With its balconies, bow windows and sunblinds it resembled a villa in Newport; trams thundered past the windows of the ambassador's study. Britain's dependence on America, underlined by the First World War and the Washington Conference of 1921–2, called for something grander.

Esmé Howard showed him the possible site and introduced him to F. H. Brooke, the collaborating architect. After dinner he 'talked Embassy' into the small hours with Sir Esmé, travelling back next morning to New York. Here the horrors began. He was presented to the Architectural Convention one evening and the Town Planning Convention the next. He shirked speeches to both on the plea that, having been only a few days in the country, he couldn't speak American (Harvey Corbett spoke on his behalf), but there was no escaping the final, dreaded ceremony at the Metropolitan Museum in New York.

After an hour of hand-shaking in a packed hall the President, surrounded by architects wearing robes, spoke a eulogy praising the Cenotaph – 'all very upsetting' – and Ned made his speech. 'I found myself trembling, but could steady myself by pulling the paper I was reading from hard. Then I was frightened that if I pulled as hard as I was pulling, the paper would burst.' It was ten minutes of torture, but 'no one could hear me, which was something'.[16]

Ned sketched designs for the Embassy on the ship home, and back in England he moved fast to secure the job. He stayed with Vita and Harold Nicolson in May at Long Barn, where Vita wanted him to design a Dutch garden. He needed to 'talk Embassy' with Harold, 'and get his view as to how it should work etc from a very possible future ambassador'. Later that summer, Ned tracked Esmé Howard on the house party circuit. He managed to enlist his support for key points of the design: 'The lantern lit kitchen etc. The courts in the roof for the bedints [servants] and exactly how he wanted his secretary's room arranged a. in relation to the staff, b. in relation to a colleague of distinction, both operating a. and b. from opposite directions.'

Lionel Earle went to Washington in September and he and Esmé Howard finally decided on a scrub-covered site high up on Massachusetts Avenue.* Lionel Earle secured Lutyens's appointment, using the incontrovertible argument that 'he was the only British architect ... who had been awarded the gold medal for architecture by America, and that, in consequence they could not pay a greater tribute to Washington than by selecting the architect that they themselves had honoured'.

With his design for the awkward sloping P-shaped site, Ned paid homage to American colonial architecture. He had spent an afternoon at George Washington's Mount Vernon, where he grasped the pathos of the settlers' unspoiled world ('so charming ... so pathetic and all so small'). But the American influence most plainly to be read at Washington is that of early eighteenth-century Williamsburg (itself influenced by Wren), which is especially marked on the entrance front on Massachusetts Avenue. Here Ned solved the problem of restricted street frontage by placing the Chancery offices in front of the Embassy house, giving access to the two entrances by designing a courtyard entrance to the Chancery and making cars carrying the ambassador's guests drive round behind the Chancery and through a tunnel, where

---

*Esmé Howard liked the site because the first time he saw it he put up a covey of quail.

they could deposit their guests and drive out again. Like Delhi, the plan depends on the circulation of motor cars. He solved the problem of the sloping site by placing the Chancery on the lower level, linking it to the Embassy on the higher level by placing the ambassador's study over the *porte cochère*; he punched a magnificent wide corridor right through the Embassy, and then set a giant portico at right angles to it, facing on to the garden.*

Lutyens's Washington designs brim with jokes. Giant doors open on to shallow cupboards, and small hidden doors give on to a grand circular staircase that leads to the bedroom floor.† A spy window on the staircase is mirror on the outside so that children can see who is coming upstairs without being seen. There are capitals without columns. The roof has no guttering (the gutter is a slit cut into the roof, which leaks), so the roof is flush with the cornice below rather than projecting. Christopher Hussey thought that this gave the building an expression of alertness, as of 'a face with wide open eyes and brows raised'; a self-portrait of Lutyens himself. The Washington Embassy is slick, elegant and light-heartedly subversive, like a Noël Coward lyric, where the architect plays the conjuror, pulling rabbits out of classical hats. Perhaps the inspiration for this jokey classicism was those slightly wicked visits Lutyens made to Paris, where he stayed (much to MacSack's disapproval) with the American Elsie de Woolfe, met Elsa Maxwell, and flirted late into the night with Anne Vanderbilt and the Duchess of Sutherland.

No one could call the Washington Embassy a folly; on the contrary, the Anglo-American relationship expanded to fill it. Treasury cheese-paring and short-sightedness jeopardized the project. The Treasury was hostile to Lutyens's appointment. 'I believe his reputation is that of an extremely extravagant architect who doesn't care what he lets his clients in for,' one Treasury servant complained to Lionel Earle, 'but perhaps I do him an injustice. The British taxpayer is paying a pretty tall sum to U.S.A. as it is, and I don't suppose international relations will really be improved by Lutyens's employment.' Lutyens was forced

---

*The portico has been read as Wren (Chelsea Hospital), though a portico fronting a garden also recalls a southern plantation house; but perhaps the real template was the portico on the entrance front at Gledstone, which seems in many ways the prototype design for Lutyens's post-war country houses.

†Lutyens played a similar joke in one of the staff houses in Delhi, which has a central space with eight doors, some of which lead into housemaid's cupboards. The seventeen-year-old Iris Portal remembered him saying: 'I thought it would be terribly funny that if people had too much to drink at a big party, they'd come home and they wouldn't know which was their door. They'd all end up in the cupboards.'

to produce four schemes, scaling down his design by 10 per cent, before the Treasury eventually agreed in 1927 to authorize £193,000. The Chancery buildings were pitiably cramped, and Lutyens was asked at the last minute to add an extra storey to the pavilions fronting the street.[17]

In March 1925, as Ned prepared to sail to America, Emily had steamed out of Colombo bound for Australia. Instead of sending Betty and Mary to Paris to be 'finished', she took them to C. W. Leadbeater, to be 'brought on' along the Path, undeterred by new scandals alleging that he was a fake and a paedophile. At Colombo she saw Ned's war memorial. 'It looked like the eye of a needle, and I did not like it very much. I understand it is meant for a flame but without the light it looks odd.'[18] Krishna and Nitya were on the same boat, but the ailing Nitya was kept in isolation; Mary spent most of the voyage peeping at him through a porthole.

At Sydney Leadbeater came to meet them, prancing down the wharf like a lion on the arm of a beautiful blond fifteen-year-old boy. His flowing mane of white hair and repulsive fang-like teeth were only less conspicuous than his bishop's costume – purple cloak, red cassock, great amethyst cross and amethyst ring. Bishop or Brother, as he liked to be called, lived at Mosman, a Sydney suburb, where he ruled despotically over a community of fifty or so initiates, most of whom were exceptionally good-looking. His house, the Manor, was lined with walls of beaten copper, hammered into hideous shapes, which Brother had magnetized.

'Oh darling,' Emily told Ned, 'never come to Australia. You would go mad over the ugliness of everything... I don't think they know what taste or beauty is. It is like living at Margate.' Emily shared a room with Betty and Mary, something she had never done before. They were expected to tidy their own room and wash the bath, tasks which they found very hard and time-consuming. 'Australia sounds too awful,' wrote Ned. 'Poor darling, having to do your own washing.'

Emily and the two girls spent their days at the Manor hanging about on the veranda waiting for Brother to emerge from his room: to miss him was disgrace. Betty recalled waiting like an inactive Stock Exchange for messages to come through on the astral ticker tape. At meals, which they all ate together, no one spoke, for Brother could not abide noise. It was like 'being blind and deaf inside a power station'. For weeks before the occult festival of Wesak, when Brother made spiritual advancements, the community throbbed with expectant tension as the initiates crammed for discipleship. Emily contributed lavishly to expenses, cabling Ned for money which he always sent, and gained her reward – her First Initiation. She described in her diary how that night she felt 'a wonderful realization of a tremendous and resistless power which was yet so calm and like a great ocean, and I had a feeling there was nothing in the world I could not accomplish and I dedicated that new power to the service of the world'. Mary and Betty, who had both been baptized and confirmed into the Liberal Catholic Church, were placed on Probation. Emily now developed ambitions to start her own order, a World League of Motherhood, visualizing her future as an abbess of the order, dressed in a habit which would relieve her of ever needing to worry about clothes again.[19]

In June Emily reluctantly detached herself from the esoteric power station. She had wanted to stay behind with Krishna, who was caring for Nitya in the hills; but even Krishna was impatient with her exaltation. Leaving Betty and Mary with Leadbeater in Sydney, Emily travelled home to be with Mrs Besant and also with Ursula, who was expecting her first baby.

No sooner was Emily back in London than she was off again. Leaving Ursula and the baby, not yet born, she travelled with Mrs Besant to Holland, where far more exciting things were happening.

Emily's autobiography is the only source for this episode, and the goings-on seem fantastical to the point of madness. At Huizen near Amsterdam she and Mrs Besant found George Arundale and James Wedgwood in an atmosphere of near-hysterical excitement. George Arundale had gone into psychic overdrive. He took his third and fourth initiations, and then announced that he and Mrs Besant, Leadbeater, Wedgwood and Krishna had all achieved their fifth and final initiations. Emily gained her second initiation, and her name was also among the list of twelve apostles which George Arundale 'brought through'. Among the celestial telegrams was an injunction that priests of the society must always wear silk underclothes and that Mrs Besant, George Arundale and Wedgwood must not eat eggs.

Never had Emily seen Mrs Besant so excited. Now seventy-eight, she was tired, frail and credulous. Eager for apotheosis in her lifetime, she announced all Wedgwood and Arundale's psychic promotions, in spite of angry telegrams from Leadbeater refusing to give confirmation. Emily was still in thrall to Mrs Besant, though she noted that on the night of her second initiation she felt no sense of peace as she had on her first, but lay awake fighting with a bat in her room. She must have known, too, that Wedgwood was a drug addict who had been caught smuggling cocaine in his crozier. He also had a string of convictions for sodomy.

Comedy spiralled into farce when Mrs Besant, George Arundale and Wedgwood set off on a secret journey to visit the theosophical Master the Count in his castle in Hungary. Emily, who was by now back in England, was cabled by Mrs Besant, asking her to join the party. Emily dutifully obtained a visa, cashed a large cheque and told her family that she was going into retreat. Three days later (20 August) came another cable: 'Postpone journey until further advice. All well. Besant. George.' Emily heard no more for three weeks. On 12 September Mrs Besant and the others returned to London, looking woebegone. Mrs Besant was very stern. Nothing was said about Hungary, but next day Mrs Besant referred to the Black Forces, which had been too strong for them. That was all that was ever said. In fact they had got no further than Innsbruck. George's power-crazed fantasy had turned out to be a hallucination, dissolving like snow in the sun. Theosophy was spinning out of control, as the rival gurus battled for leadership of the movement and the near-senile Mrs Besant lost her grip.

Krishna watched George's antics from Ojai where he had gone to nurse Nitya, whose illness worsened alarmingly. As George insinuated himself into Mrs Besant's favour, persuading her to appoint him as her heir apparent, Krishna hastened to England to pitch his claim to the succession. To Emily's surprise Krishna poured blistering scorn on the goings-on at Huizen: 'Although I myself was by this time a little sceptical of some of the revelations, I trusted Mrs Besant implicitly and did not see she could have been deceived.' When Krishna tried to tackle Mrs Besant, however, she seemed not to take it in; it was as if she had been hypnotized by George.

Emily went to India in November, travelling to the Theosophical Society convention at Adyar with Krishna, Rajagopal, Mrs Besant, Arundale and Wedgwood. They stopped in Rome, staying at the Hotel Bristol. George Arundale and James Wedgewood pranced through the streets, flaunting their purple cassocks and pectoral crosses while Emily wondered about Mussolini – 'the Italians are a rotten people I think, and perhaps a dictatorship was the only way for them, but liberty is dead'.

At Port Said arrived an ominous telegram from Nitya. 'Flu rather more serious. Pray for me.' Next day came the news that Nitya had died.

George Arundale immediately started 'bringing through' messages from Nitya but they were obviously faked. None of them had believed that the Masters would allow Nitya to die, and the theosophical pantomime now turned from farce to tragedy. Krishna was devastated; though outwardly acting as if nothing had happened, he was profoundly changed. It was as if Nitya was '*in* him now in some indefinable way'.[20] He had *become* Nitya. Nitya was not allowed to die; Krishna didn't mourn him, but absorbed his being. When Krishna arrived at Madras Emily thought his face was radiant, but it was a strangely inhuman happiness.

Leadbeater arrived from Australia, bringing a boatload of pilgrims, including Betty and Mary, both of whom had been accepted by the Masters. (Neither had slept a wink during the night of their Acceptance, which made them somewhat sceptical.) Among the pilgrims was poor Mrs Merton, Mertoni of Folly Farm. Once plump and well groomed she was now haggard and dowdy, despised by Mary and Betty because of her lowly status along the Path.

Theosophy was now more popular than ever, its heady mix of universal brotherhood, vegetarianism and psychic thrills appealing to the idealistic youth culture of the 1920s. The 1925 Congress was written up in the Indian and American press and over 3,000 attended. However, it was an organizational disaster. The monsoon deluged Adyar, and the crowds shivered in a sea of mud. Mrs Merton squatted miserably in a wet hut, trying not to think of the luxury of Folly Farm.

Behind the scenes the leaders quarrelled. Leadbeater disputed Arundale's psychic revelations in Holland, and Arundale countered by claiming that Leadbeater was a prisoner of the 'blacks' or evil forces. Then Krishna dramatically changed the agenda. As he talked one day about the Lord, who comes to those who want, suddenly his voice rang out: 'And *I* come for those who want . . .' This was the moment Emily had been waiting for. She knew instantly, or thought she did, and so did Leadbeater and Mrs Besant, that Krishna was speaking with the voice of the Lord.

Not everyone heard. Arundale and Wedgwood both denied noticing any difference. And Krishna's manifestation was all too convenient. As Emily's sister, Betty Balfour, wrote, 'no other Messiah had had the stage so carefully set for him, trained from babyhood to believe that Christ *would* inhabit him, and then his manifestation made at a carefully organized public meeting'.[21]

Whether or not Krishna was a fake was not an issue for Emily. Emily was utterly convinced of his authenticity; and for her Krishna's manifestation was a welcome release. It allowed her quietly to put the Theosophical Society and its mumbo-jumbo behind her, and to devote herself solely to following Krishna.

Chapter Seventeen
The Elemental Mode
1926–1931

Electroliers for the nursery: Chicken lays a lightbulb as an egg.

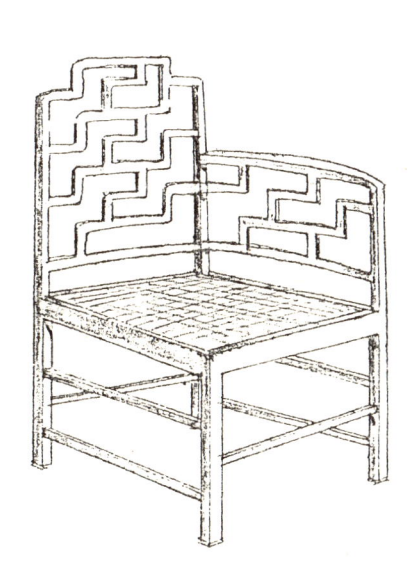

Arm chair

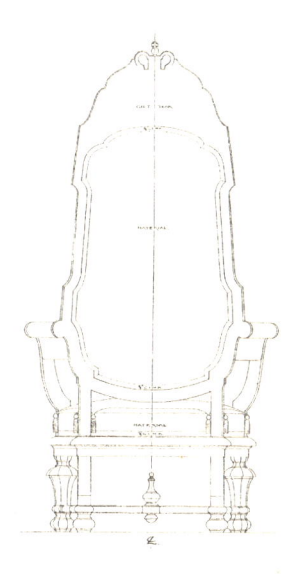

Scale drawing for the Viceroy's throne in the Durbar Hall: the epicentre of imperial Delhi.

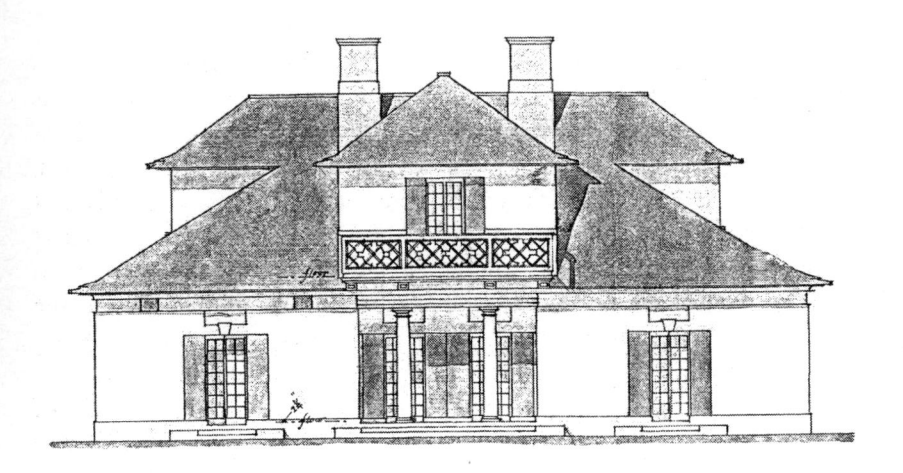

Bungalow designs for New Delhi.

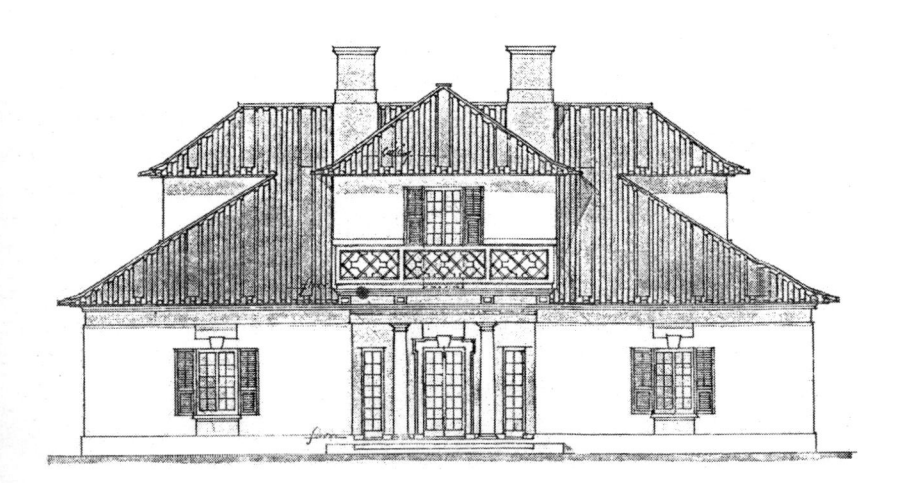

Ned was ill a lot over the years 1926-7. He had gastritis and then a duodenal ulcer; he was laid up with an ulcer on his leg, which was swollen and purple from knee to ankle. MacSack nursed him at Mansfield Street, bringing caviar and Evian water, but she was even more ill than he. She was going blind, she had colitis, diabetes and heart trouble; but still Ned depended on her. He designed a garden for her at White Lodge, composed of squares made of pebbles or flowers, and a path with stone rings filled with slates. He would motor down in the 'little car', the Rolls she had given him and for which he was beginning to repay her. They spent the General Strike (3-12 May 1926) discussing plans for a sunken summer house she wanted him to build of coal or chalk approached by a tunnel. Appearing at White Lodge after important lunches with McKenna or Fabian Ware of the Imperial War Graves Commission, Lutyens was in the habit of going straight to bed or playing endless games of patience. 'Cela me porte sur les nerfs,' MacSack wrote irritably. She was weak and tearful and very quarrelsome.[1]

She accused A. J. Thomas of stealing £2,000 back in 1919, which she needed now to pay for a new Rolls-Royce. Ned at first appeared to side with Thomas, which 'hurt me so deeply [that] I really intended to break off our friendship,' MacSack wrote, 'but he lunched with MacVita and said he really adored me and would do anything to get me back'. Ned spent a Sunday in bed reading her diaries ('very amusing ... and every other sentence opened paths to endless byways'), trying to unravel her tangled dealings with Thomas. To mollify her he now appeared to agree with her. 'McNed now says he only pretended to believe AJT to prevent a scandal,' she wrote. Unfortunately for MacSack, Lutyens had already told Emily about the row. 'I suppose I ought to be glad that Lady MacSack has made it up with you but I greatly fear you are only paving the way to fresh troubles as she is so very unreliable,' wrote Emily. She was right. Ned's office found £1,500 to pay back to MacSack, but then MacSack discovered that she had in fact sold the bonds she accused Thomas of stealing. She magnanimously 'forgave' him his alleged theft of cash, but Thomas once more threatened to resign.

MacSack wrote in her diary that Ned looked forward unhappily to a lonely old age:

> McNed is terrified of getting blind and being a pauper when he is old and I am dead. He knows that his wife and his children would forget him and neglect him. I must say that he never cadges from me, but generally he is frightened of the future. I have told him that I would never fail him, but of course I may die soon.[2]

Ned's troubles were everywhere. He was embroiled in a damaging row with the architect Reginald Blomfield. 'You are a werry nice man, but a werry, werry bad architect,' Ned had told Blomfield once; but now 'Bloomy' no longer seemed even nice.

In 1925 Ned had been invited by the London County Council to advise on the artistic effect of widening Rennie's engineering masterpiece, Waterloo Bridge. His report, published in November, considered the effect of two schemes: throwing a gigantic single-arch road bridge above Rennie's bridge, or alternatively heightening the bridge in order to widen it. 'I cannot but believe,' he wrote, 'that, no matter what the council's decision may be, the bridge, to be maintained, must eventually be rebuilt.' To his regret, he could find no way of widening Waterloo Bridge which did not 'mar its brave appearance'; his report didn't make clear what he did want, but he certainly didn't urge preserving the existing bridge.

Reginald Blomfield responded with a furious letter to *The Times*, insisting that the bridge should be kept as it was, underpinned and repaired and not in any way altered. Blomfield was right; Rennie's Waterloo Bridge was a work of genius which deserved to be preserved. The counterblast wrong-footed Lutyens – though he later claimed that he had wanted to preserve Rennie's original bridge. If he had hopes of getting the job of rebuilding Waterloo Bridge himself, he was disappointed, as the LCC wanted an experienced engineer ('alas for McNed,' wrote MacSack).[3]

Blomfield intrigued against Lutyens on the Royal Fine Art Commission.* Ned proposed to place a Mercantile Marine Monument on the Thames embankment. 'I yet hope you will be able to convince the Office of Works that the Fine Art Commission's advice is bosh,' Ned told Fabian Ware, but to no avail; the Commission's objections

---

*The Royal Fine Art Commission had been found in 1924 to review public building projects. Lord Crawford, the Tory politician, was chairman, and both Lutyens and Blomfield were founder members.

prevailed, and the monument was built on Tower Hill. Another design vetoed by the Fine Art Commission was Ned's bridge in St James's Park ('I am very low about it').[4]

Increasingly an outsider in his own profession, Lutyens came to rely on journalists. To Edward Hudson was now added the dubious Brendan Bracken.

When Robert was fired by Northcliffe from the *Daily Mail* in 1924 he became assistant to the twenty-three-year-old Bracken, who had founded a magazine named *English Life*. Bracken, a red-headed adventurer rumoured to be Winston Churchill's son, moved into the attic of Robert's house in South Audley Street and soon became a regular visitor at Mansfield Street. He persuaded Lutyens to contribute to his magazine, a snobbish rival to *Country Life*. Bracken was a genius at playing both ends against the middle, and confidential information that *English Life* had commissioned a special article from the great architect undoubtedly helped loosen the chequebooks of the quality advertisers who financed the magazine.

With Bracken it was hard to see where using people turned to genuine affection. Mary believed that he was in love with her, but then she thought lots of people were in love with her. Robert always maintained that Bracken had made a pass at him, and Betty thought that Bracken, a repressed homosexual, was in love with Robert. One evening at Mansfield Street, Bracken suddenly leaned over from an armchair and rumpled Ned's hair. To the amazement of his children Ned said nothing; he appeared not to disapprove or even to notice.

In 1926 Bracken persuaded his publisher Crossthwaite Eyre to back his project for a new magazine, the *Banker*. This was far more successful than the loss-making *English Life*, which folded shortly afterwards, and it gave Bracken the power to repay his debt to Lutyens. The new magazine gave him access to City potentates including Rankin of the Midland Bank, whose backing was crucial to Lutyens in obtaining Midland Bank buildings at Leadenhall Street (1928) and Manchester (1929) – 'an awful struggle to get the work,' Ned wrote. Bracken also commissioned Professor Charles Reilly of the Liverpool School of Architecture to write a monthly *Banker* article on bank architecture, and Reilly duly praised Lutyens's work at the Midland Bank.*

*Reilly asked Lutyens to speak at his Liverpool school; he can't have enjoyed Lutyens's address on 'Gas', which turned into an attack on art schools for producing 'men who, failing in the world's arena, return to the schools as masters to earn a modest wage under Government auspices and attempt to teach what they themselves have been unable to acquire'.

In spite of Bracken's charm, Ned was suspicious. Emily, who thought Bracken 'intolerable' and heading for a breakdown, was irritated by his climber's habit of knowing her family better than she did herself, and she worried about his influence on Robert. In 1926 Bracken wrote an unctuous appreciation in the *Banker* of Edith Lytton on her eighty-fifth birthday.

By 1927 Bracken had quarrelled with Robert, and Ned dismissed him as 'a cad to all beholden to him' and a 'sponge to those who have any influence he needs'; yet Bracken continued to promote Ned's interests when he could, defending him in the House of Commons when he became an MP.[5]

Lutyens's most lucrative client was a private patron: Bendor, Duke of Westminster. Bendor's Grosvenor Estate was a fabulously rich private fief, as yet unregulated by public overlordship and planning regulations. In 1916 Ned had found his old friend the architect Detmar Blow acting as 'bailiff and Maitre d'Hotel' to Bendor, his practice having melted away during the war. The duke preferred life as playboy to the task of managing his West End estate, and Blow assumed charge of the estate, shaping policy at a time when Mayfair's aristocratic town houses were being transformed into private flats.

In June 1926 Lutyens was summoned to a meeting with Detmar Blow to discuss the Grosvenor House site on Park Lane. This plum site, once the duke's town house, had been leased by a Yorkshire developer, A. O. Edwards, who commissioned an architect named Guthrie to design two linked blocks of flats and a hotel. Blow persuaded the duke to appoint Lutyens consultant architect to approve Guthrie's design. At their first meeting Edwards told Lutyens that he wanted a building 'as tall as the LCC would allow'. 'What fun we are going to have,' said Lutyens, producing five small pipes from his pocket.

The elevations which Lutyens drew transformed Guthrie's boring blocks by stressing the horizontals, adding four tall rooftop pavilions, joining the blocks with a spectacular high-level bridge, and dressing the lower shop stories with classical colonnades. These changes exasperated Edwards, who got his solicitors to write to Ned (11 November 1926): 'We are astonished to hear from our client that their architect yesterday afternoon received from Sir Edwin Lutyens a fresh set of what he is pleased to term a tentative set of drawings. This really must come to an end.' Lutyens's brief, they wrote, was not to prepare plans but to approve plans submitted by Guthrie. On 13 November

MacSack recorded in her diary that McNed was very worried about Grosvenor House, 'as he can't approve of what is proposed to be done there. He is *so* conscientious about his buildings. I have only seen him once almost as dejected: the day the Bank of England was given to Baker.'

The duke approved Lutyens's elevations, but the result was a compromise. The high-level bridge was omitted, and Lutyens was denied the 'upward recession in mass' that he had achieved in buildings such as the Midland Bank in Poultry. Clough Williams-Ellis in the *Observer* praised Grosvenor House as 'a fine forthright cliff of brick, a little dressed up for its fashionable position in elegant white spats and a grey top hat from designs by Sir Edwin Lutyens'; but most critics were hostile, deploring the commercialization of Park Lane by uncontrolled private developers. Grosvenor House, said *The Times*, 'is not designed as a big building. It is an overgrown small building, stretching a familiar and endearing style of domestic architecture beyond its capacity to please.'[6]

At least Grosvenor House pleased the duke, and Lutyens received more work.* At the Millbank Housing Development (1928), he designed a block of startling chequerboard flats on land rented by the Grosvenor Estate to Westminster Council at a pepper-corn rent for working-class housing. Here at least he could improvise. 'Nobody else,' wrote Butler in the *Memorial Volumes* in 1950, 'would have had the imagination or courage to do anything so odd yet so successful.'

For Grosvenor House alone Lutyens received at least £9,000 in 1927–9 (he may have been paid more: his commission was 1.1 per cent on a building that cost at least £1¼ million). Blow's arrangements with the estate were notoriously elastic, and it was rumoured at the time that both Blow and Lutyens were helping themselves too generously at the duke's expense. These rumours have never been substantiated.[7] But the gossip cast a shadow over Lutyens's financial integrity, and his artistic reputation suffered too. He had been lavishly paid to approve and give his name to designs that he could not control.

Ned's work for the Imperial War Graves Commission ran into difficulties too. In June 1926 the Commission reported gloomily that the Memorials to the Missing at St Quentin and Arras were both in

---

*At Hereford House in Oxford Street the building was erected by Gamages Store (later C & A), but to the 'satisfaction of Sir Edwin Lutyens and Mr Blow as . . . Estate Architects'. Lutyens designed the elevation with its roof-level pavilions.

THE ELEMENTAL MODE

abeyance owing to the obstruction of the French. At Arras Lutyens's design for a tall thin arch which the Commission had accepted 'after some demur' (having rejected earlier designs) was rejected by the French Beaux-Arts Commission. 'The design in consequence will more or less fall to the ground and will require to be entirely reconsidered,' minuted the Commission. The 1923 St Quentin design for the Missing of the Somme had been accepted by the Commission 'with acclamation' but the French again objected. Erecting a monument 55 metres high was considered 'unreasonably intrusive'. Lutyens's arches were taller than the Arc de Triomphe. Crewe, the British ambassador in Paris, was unhelpful to Lutyens, as he had been in Delhi. 'You know how strongly I feel that expensive and ostentatious Memorials are out of place in this country,' he told Fabian Ware.[8]

Worried about the sensitivities of the French, Fabian Ware tried to avoid making the issue a formal matter between Foreign Ministers by arranging a compromise. In July he sent Lutyens to France. In August Lutyens met Potremoli, the French Director of Works, who approved the design, in spite of its size, provided it was erected on a new site: the bare ridge at Thiepval. Potremoli and Lutyens inspected the site together in October, and (according to the records of the Commission) Potremoli 'entered into the question as to the exact position the Monument should occupy on the ridge with Sir Edwin with a great deal of enthusiasm'. In November a formal meeting took place on the site, and Lutyens 'entered into the suggestions made to him by the French architects in a very friendly spirit'. Kipling wrote congratulating Ware on 'the successful issue of your intrigue with the French *and* Lutyens. It isn't an embassy that *I* would care to have chaperoned!'[9]

At Thiepval Ned used the design he had made for the monument at St Quentin in 1922. Instead of punching holes through a slab of masonry – the basic design of the Arc de Triomphe – he piled massive arches one on the other, carrying the hierarchy along two axes and in two dimensions. The height to width ratio of the arches is $2\frac{1}{2}$ to 1, and the mass is set back first on one plane and then on the other. The result is a vast architectural sculpture, a pyramid-like cliff of Portland stone and small pink French bricks, pierced by catacombs of criss-crossing tunnels.

Christopher Hussey described this as Lutyens's elemental mode, where it was axiomatic 'that the motivations of heart and eye must be subordinate to and disciplined by the mind . . . combined in some ratio or series that it is for the architect to ascertain'. Yet Thiepval succeeds precisely *because* it appeals to the heart and eye; a great arch with no traffic through it, standing gaunt and alone on the bare ridge, it is a massive monument to the loss and waste of war. The roll-call of the 73,357 missing men of the Somme is inscribed on the walls of Portland stone, like footnotes reaching to the sky.* 'The magnitude of that host of boys that lie fearfully still, quickens the senses of unspeakable desolation,' Ned had written in 1925; and at Thiepval he brilliantly evoked that sense.[10]

While Ned memorialized the tragedy of the Somme, Emily was transported to an enchanted world, a Kingdom of Happiness, where she lived in beautiful esoteric unity with Krishna. At the Ommen summer camp in 1926 Krishna spoke again with the voice of the Lord Maitreya, and she was 'carried to heights of experience which I think must change life completely for us all. I never thought such happiness was possible on Earth.' Unfortunately, not everyone, even in the Theosophical Society, shared her joy. Wedgwood insisted that Krishna was in the grip of a black magician, and the rifts within the society deepened.

By now Ned was seriously worried about Mary and Betty, and for once he put his foot down, refusing to allow Betty to return alone to Leadbeater in Australia that autumn. Emily waited until Ned was safely embarked for his winter in India before producing yet another bombshell: she and Mary were summoned to California, invited by Krishna to spend the winter at Ojai. 'My only consolation for hurting you,' wrote Emily, 'is that I believe it may be the saving of Mary's life.' Since Nitya's death Mary had lost weight alarmingly; her periods had ceased, and doctors diagnosed incipient TB. 'Why take her to the very place Nitya died in?' asked Ned, reasonably enough.[11]

Mary stayed with Emily at Ojai for five months. She spent several hours each day strapped to the Abrams machine, which discharged electric currents into her body. Ned thought it a 'dull twilighty life for the young', but Krishna's filmstar charisma generated an atmosphere pulsating with sexual intrigue. Since Nitya's death, when Krishna had seemed to absorb Nitya's being, Mary had found that her love for Nitya was transposed to Krishna. Mary and Rosalind Williams, who was also at Ojai, competed to act as *gopis*, to hold and nurse him

---

*Fabian Ware worried that all individuality would be lost in a lengthy list of names, and 'the Joneses of the South Wales Borderers will be more painfully numerous than ever'. But the list of names adds to the dignity of Thiepval, which is an extraordinarily powerful memorial.

during his out-of-body experiences, the strange trance-like states he entered each afternoon. In the mornings Krishna assumed a different persona, giving Mary thrillingly frightening driving lessons in his fashionable pale blue Lincoln.

To the end of her life Mary believed that Emily knew nothing of her passion for Krishna, but this is hard to credit. Emily confessed that her own feelings for Krishna occasionally got the better of her at Ojai, and she found it hard to stay 'on a sublime level'. Krishna frequently reduced her to tears by his harsh words, criticizing her for being too possessive as though she had a special claim on him. She began to hope that Mary would marry Krishna. If she couldn't possess him herself, at least she could be his mother-in-law; the ultimate act of sublimation.

Emily dreamed of making a new life in California. The simple ways gave a refreshing sense of self-respect, she thought, and she dreaded the return to the dark, dirty, fog-bound house in Mansfield Street with its ten essential servants. She planned to earn money by giving lectures in Hollywood.

Ned spent the winter of 1926–7 in India, returning to London in February. 'He arrived like a hurricane,' wrote MacSack, 'but he soon told me that he was in great pain, having had a chill and a fever.' She summoned a doctor who gave an awful account of him; his heart was out of place and missing beats and his liver was enlarged. The doctor told MacSack's secretary, Mr Bull, that 'unless he took care, McNed would not live 10 years.' Emily's antics, in MacSack's opinion, didn't help his recovery. 'Elle voudrait que Mary épouse Krishnamurty!' she wrote.[12]

Back in Mansfield Street, Ned found a 'lonesome' Betty; she had stayed behind to study at the Royal College of Music while Mary and her mother went to California. For once she was able to connect (or so she thought) with Ned. 'He's been so sweet and friendly, nicer than he's ever been, and brings home queer friends.'* Ned enjoyed talking about the links between music and architecture, and Betty, in retrospect, exaggerated these few weeks into a real closeness. What was remarkable was that it happened at all. Father and daughter were very different, though perhaps each found comfort in rigorous intellectual discipline, whether it was the mathematics of elemental architecture or

---

*Betty remembered dinners with Nicholson, Munnings, Orpen and Yeats; the latter barely spoke but dribbled gluttonously over the *homard à l'américaine*.

Stravinsky's idea of music as 'achieved order' which was increasingly to dominate Betty's composing. Ned wrote Betty a letter on her twenty-first birthday in July. 'I am not much of a father in a fatherway, but you make it up by being a perfect daughter in a daughterly way as I think you aughterly should do.' Yet Betty was not Ned's kind of girl; she had no ambitions to make a conventional marriage like Ursie or Barbie. She was violent in her affections too. Once she greeted him with an enthusiastic hug that knocked him over. 'Did he fall absolutely flat?' asked her cousin Eve Balfour. 'Don't be absurd – how could Father fall flat, you know what shape he is.'[13]

Ned had never paid much attention to Betty before, and now he began to take an interest in Mary, who had always thought that her father disliked her. In April 1927 he visited the Embassy at Washington and, avoiding California, travelled back from America to England with Emily and Mary.

By now Mary's infatuation with Krishna was becoming obvious. In July, while Emily and Mary were at the Ommen summer camp, Ned received a telegram from Lord Riddell's Central News Agency stating that Mary was engaged to marry Krishnamurti. Ned stopped publication on the grounds that it was libellous and both he and the Theosophical Society threatened to take immediate action. At the same time, he begged Emily to bring Mary home at once. Emily dismissed the rumour as groundless – Krishna would never marry a white woman; she was more concerned about the effect the rumour might have on Krishna than Ned or Mary, even though Betty, who was at Mansfield Street, wrote telling her that Ned was 'in a dead panic lest it be true'. 'Poor Father, he has such incredible family pride which none of us have inherited. It's very funny but we daren't laugh here.'[14]

Emily got her way, as she usually did. Mary stayed on at Ommen for the duration of the summer camps; but after this crisis her devotion to Krishna began to waver. Always to be left behind while he cruised from one glamorous part of the world to another was indeed a twilight life of waiting. She spent most of her time reading and rereading his letters; 'he wrote beautiful love letters'. She forced herself to eat meat, symbolically repudiating theosophy.

One day Ned telephoned Mary at Mansfield Street and summoned her to lunch at Claridge's, something he had never done before. He wanted her to meet the writer Enid Bagnold, the wife of his client Sir Roderick Jones, who was interested in Mary's own writing. Jones, who was chairman of Reuters, was a neighbour of Ned's client Sir George

Lewis at Rottingdean, and Ned was decorating his London house, 29 Hyde Park Gate.[15]*

That lunch, Mary believed, changed her life. Roderick Jones began a flirtation with her. He took her on early morning walks in Regent's Park, he took her dancing at the Embassy Club, he delivered a daily letter to her by Reuters messenger. They were an odd couple. Roderick, who was fifty, was short and dapper, a bad-tempered, self-important martinet who rather resembled a wasp. Mary could see herself in the mirror draped over him when they danced at nightclubs. His wife Enid Bagnold was having an affair with a handsome Reuters correspondent named Neil, but she was more threatened by her husband's infatuation than Mary realized or wanted to admit. Nonetheless Enid Bagnold befriended her, encouraged her writing and introduced her to her literary friends – H. G. Wells, Logan Pearsall Smith, Desmond MacCarthy.

Though Mary was only nineteen, Ned was unperturbed. He understood that kind of relationship – it was not so different from his own friendship with Barbara Webb. The truth was that Ned had succeeded in extricating both Betty and Mary from theosophy. He had freed them to live their own lives, though neither lived as he wished his daughters to live, by making socially ambitious marriages. Betty became a composer, bravely fighting losing battles with money, divorce and drink; but in the end she won recognition for her music. Mary became a writer, creating fictional narratives which mirrored the story of her life, crossing and blurring the boundaries between life and fiction. Perhaps neither Betty nor Mary would have had the independence to fashion their own future without the unconventional theosophical upbringing Emily gave them. But theosophy itself was a prison, and Ned released them from it – no small achievement for an egotist who had taken very little interest in his children's problems.

In October 1927 Lady MacSack wrote a long entry in her diary. She wrote in French, into which she lapsed at times of stress. She complained that she could no longer bear to spend time with Ned. His visits made her illnesses worse. She couldn't stand the perpetual pipe-smoking, patience and puzzles. Even worse was his obsession with his lewd drawings.

---

*It had a dramatic square drawing room at garden level. 'To enter guests had first to come down a magnificent wide oak staircase with a rope handrail. At the top of the stairs, one looked over and down at the other guests below before disappearing behind the wall of the staircase to reappear at the bottom.'

Lutyens in 1920 photographed
by Walter Stoneman.

Emily in 1915.

Heathcote House, Ilkley: Ned's 'high game' of classicism in the suburbs of Leeds.

(*Above right*) Betty, Ursula and Mary in 1915.

(*Right*) Lady Sackville, dining al fresco in the loggia at White Lodge, Roedean, Sussex. Early 1930s.

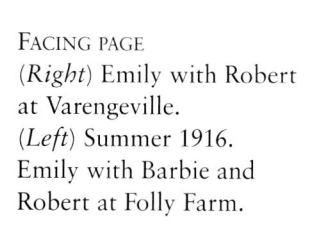

FACING PAGE
(*Right*) Emily with Robert at Varengeville.
(*Left*) Summer 1916. Emily with Barbie and Robert at Folly Farm.

Queen Mary's Dolls' House being packed up in the drawing room
at 13 Mansfield Street.

FACING PAGE
(*Above left*) Bare interior of 13 Mansfield Street with table designed by Ned.
(*Above right*) Krishnamurti speaking to his disciples under the apple tree at Pergine in 1924.
(*Below left*) The Midland Bank in Piccadilly.
(*Below right*) Lutyens at the temporary Cenotaph in 1919. He was hurt not to receive an
invitation to the official march past.

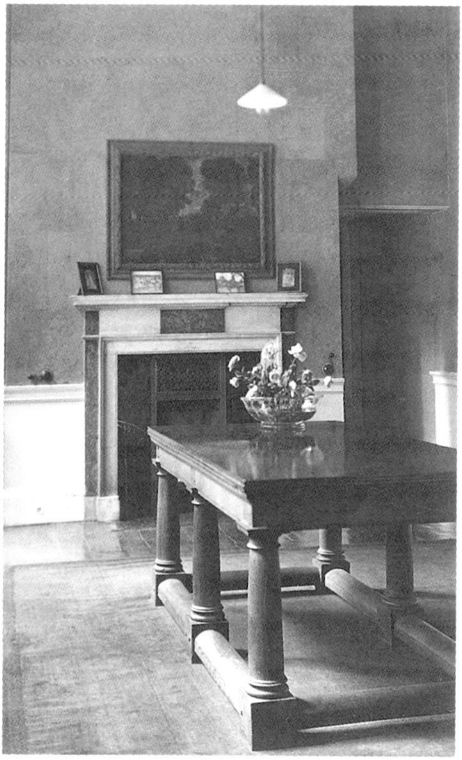

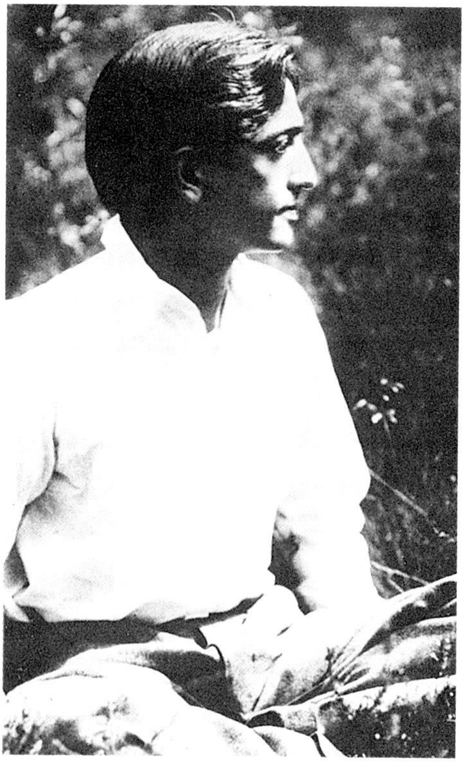

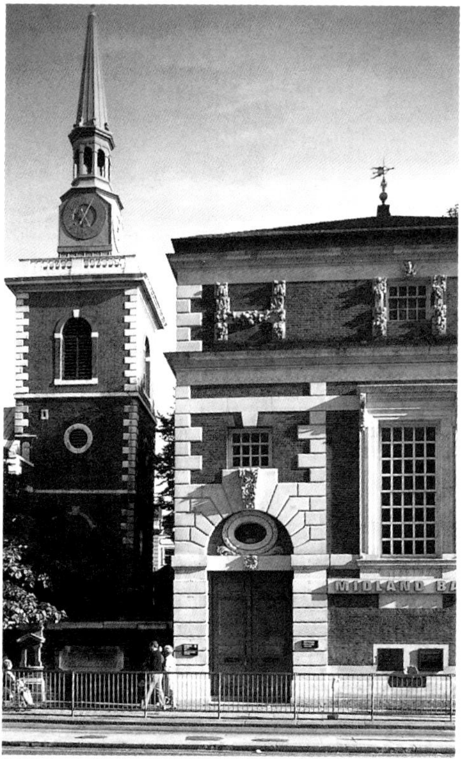
MIDLAND BA

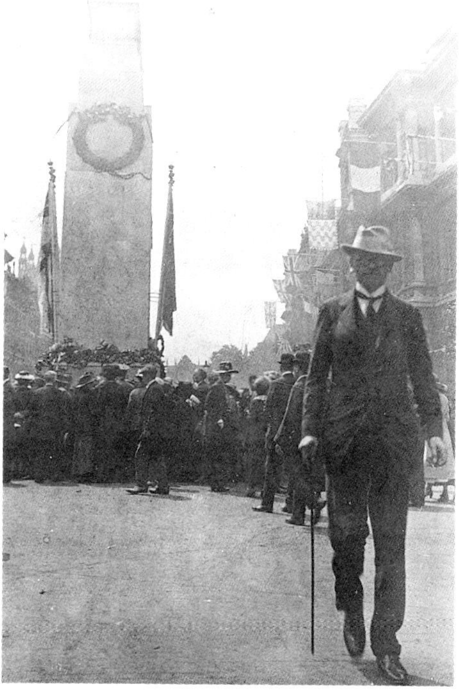

Lord Hardinge, Viceroy of India, and eight dead tigers.

Herbert Baker in India, 1913.

The Delhi Town Planning Committee, surveying from the back of an elephant. *Left to right*: Swinton, Lutyens, Baker.

(*Above*) Garden front of Viceroy's House, 1931.
(*Below*) Stone pergola at Viceroy's House.

Ned snapped by Ursy at the Parthenon.

Ned loved entertaining children with his drawings and jokes.

Emily on her 80th birthday with her five children: Ursula, Robert, Barbie, Betty and Mary.

Je trouve ses dessins trop indécents, quoique cela le laisse très froid. Il me dit que ces dessins viennent de son 'mind' et nullement de ses sens. Quelle curieuse mentalité! Mais ses jeux continuels sont très durs pour moi, car il est impossible d'avoir la moindre conversation soutenue. Quand il me demande quel dessin je voudrais, je demande toujours un croquis des grandes maisons qu'il bâtit actuellement. Mais cela l'amuse moins que de faire des grotesques caricatures de Dieu ou des choses indécentes et incompréhensibles pour moi, car c'est un homme d'une décence extrême. Il déteste la moindre conversation sur la question de Sexe.

Doodling indecent drawings yet hating to talk about sex; designing in a pure abstracted classicism when his mind teemed with lewd pictures: Lutyens's austere elemental mode perhaps failed to fill his emotional needs in the way his sensuous country houses had done, when each commission was almost a love affair. It was as if he was drifting into emotional autism, a self-enclosed world of mathematical ratio and proportion which released him from the need to register the world outside. MacSack complained that he never spoke to her:

Et cependant, il peut parler si bien de tout, mais il ne parle jamais; il joue ces jeux et tâche de répondre quand je lui fais la moindre de question. Mais je le fais rarement, car je vois l'effort mental. Il dit que jouer ces cartes et ces puzzles lui repose son mind fatigué. Mais comme il adore que je suis près de lui dans la même pièce, avec les fenêtres fermées, l'électricité illuminée, et les sept petites pipes allumées sans cesse, tour à tour – je trouve le temps long.[16]

That was the last entry she made in her diary.

Robert Heal, a student from Professor Reilly's Liverpool School of Architecture, joined Lutyens's Delhi office at 17 Bolton Street in 1927. The office was like a private house. When he rang the bell he thought he had gone to the wrong address: Mrs Boyce the housekeeper opened the door wearing a white apron. Heal was one of the five draughtsmen who worked upstairs in the master bedroom. Acting the 'little gentleman', like characters from a P. G. Wodehouse novel, they carried wash-leather gloves and carefully furled umbrellas and played chess in the tea break. There was a quiet club-like atmosphere and very little to do.

Lutyens came to the Bolton Street office most afternoons but he never entered the drawing office and never spoke to the draughtsmen. He went straight to his office in the first-floor drawing room, where his drawings were laid out on a large table. In the centre stood a large jar of tobacco which Hall, the office manager, was instructed to keep full. Lutyens would produce one pipe after another from the pockets of his baggy jacket, smoke it and put it down as he looked at a drawing. When he was satisfied with the drawing, he called for Heal, the chief draughtsman, who sent it to be drawn out by the young gentlemen in the office. Everything, down to the smallest detail of bedroom decoration, was controlled by Lutyens. He accepted no suggestions, never discussed anything, barely spoke. 'One had the sort of feeling one had to be a bit careful not to upset him.' It became a kind of game in the office to persuade Lutyens to accept an idea: Heal succeeded only once.

Once there was an office party at Mansfield Street. Heal remembered menu cards and rows of cylindrical glasses, all the same diameter, ranging in height from a tumbler to a flat dish for liqueur. Someone filled Lut's tumbler with liqueur and he became very merry, and they trooped off to the music room, raided the kitchens for partners ('there were about 30 or 40 of us and there seemed to be as many kitchen staff') and held an impromptu dance. Lutyens gave an imitation of the Russian ballet: 'it was surprising how light he was on his feet'.

Heal soon began to feel that he was wasting his time, stranded in an Edwardian backwater at Bolton Street designing a palace. The English translation of Corbusier's book, *Vers une Architecture*, had just come out. Beside Corbusier's streamlined modernism, Lutyens's classicism seemed outdated and old-fashioned.[17]

Lutyens positioned himself towards Corbusier in 1927-8. Professor Reilly, who taught French Beaux-Arts classicism in his school at Liverpool, accompanied him to India and on the boat helped him compose a review of *Towards a New Architecture* for the *Observer*. Lutyens disputed Corbusier's idea of the house as a 'machine for living' – a simple box built of reinforced concrete, with strong horizontals, free façades, free plan. This, thought Lutyens, was inhuman. People 'would lose the pleasure of thick soft walls, dumb to noise, when compelled to live in stark noisy little boxes, where skilled plumbers take the place of house-proud maids ... To be a home the house cannot be a machine.'

Yet Ned was wearily aware that Corbusier was the future. When Emily's Indian friends suggested a competition between Lutyens and Corbusier to design a new Indian city, Ned refused to consider it. The two sets of plans would be 'so vastly different' that you couldn't compare them; and if he won, the shade of Corbusier would crop up at every difficulty. 'With Corbusier I think your friends would be far happier and his flow of language would carry them all.' Ned knew that the tree-lined spaces of his own New Delhi were far better suited to India's needs than Corbusier's 'chassis built architecture with concrete (hot and noisy) bodies'. He saw too that Corbusier's labour-saving machinery was irrelevant to Indian needs. 'In India you want intelligent labour-creating hours to give self-pride and self-reliance and possession.'[18] Not until 1951 did Corbusier design the Indian city of Chandigar, to commemorate India's independence, but twenty years before Lutyens already anticipated its critics.

Professor Reilly had agreed to come out to India with Lutyens in 1928 because Brendan Bracken, who paid his fare, had commissioned him to write a book jointly with Victor Lytton about New Delhi. Already Ned was seeking revenge on Baker by manipulating publicity at home. Reilly was 'terribly impressed' by Viceroy's House, though disappointed to discover that it was not yet sufficiently finished to write up, which meant that the book fell through. But he enjoyed Lutyens's healthy (and unprintable) Rabelaisian wit.

The walls of Viceroy's House had reached *chujjah* level, the roofs were being built and the wings were almost complete, but the dome was not yet up, and it seemed impossible that the house would be ready for the Viceroy to move in as scheduled in 1929. Ned had warmed immediately to Irwin when he succeeded Reading as Viceroy in 1926. Reading, in Ned's view, was pompous and unpleasant. He treated his aides-de-camp like flunkies, and after dinner sat in his chair arrogantly puffing his cigarette as he waited for the gentlemen to be brought to his left and right. Irwin, Ned noticed, was modest and waited for his guests to sit down first. Ned found the Irwins 'simple, interested and deferential and one can say anything and one is or seems to be understood'.[19]

But even Irwin could not make the creaking Indian official machine work more efficiently. The vast palace was without furniture, as English antiques cracked in the heat. For thirteen years Ned had pressed the Government of India to establish a Delhi school of design, and now Gandhi's campaign for self-government in India made the furnishing of the palace a political issue. Indian newspapers campaigned against the use of European fabrics. Ned's response was to engage the art historian Kennedy North to scour the villages of India for traditional crafts; he insisted that home-spun Indian cotton or *kaddah* was to be the fabric for Viceroy's House, 'not because it's Indian, but because it's the best – silk and cotton, Paris and Manchester can't touch it'.*

By the time of Ned's next visit (January–March 1929) the big dome was going up and the house nearly complete. Each morning he breakfasted with W. R. Mustoe of the Horticultural Department, the plantsman who had transformed the Mogul garden from a debris-strewn desert to a Persian carpet planted with brightly coloured English roses. 'The tanks run and refill and ripple and my rainbow in the deep fountain has come off – a vivid rainbow and children *can* find its start!' With Mustoe Ned created the butterfly garden he had once suggested to MacSack. Indian visitors flocked to the Viceroy's gardens, which they called 'God's own Heavens'.

The King decreed that Government House was to be called Viceroy's House, 'and no other house in India is like the Viceroy's house ... I do think it is a gentleman's house, though original in that it is built in India for India – Indian.'[20] Each day Ned walked at least once over the entire house, which took two hours and wore him out. He still designed unceasingly. For the nurseries he invented electroliers in the form of chickens which laid light bulbs as eggs. 'But this is a very lightsome mood, for the rest is solemn furniture.' No two mantelpieces were alike. The timber-drying plant had not arrived in time to allow the wood a year's drying time, and much of the furniture fell to pieces.

Hari Sing, the Maharajah of Kashmir, asked Lutyens to design his own house in New Delhi and then changed his mind so often that Ned wrote withdrawing his name and handing it over to his assistant Walter George. 'They don't understand that they [can't] do anything and alter anything and yet call it a Lutyens house.' Indian craftsmen, Ned said, were incurably careless, breaking 50 per cent of what they mended. One day he came across a man walking though the house with a pickaxe on his shoulders, 'right, left, bang, bang, corners of finished corridors and rooms being chopped off. They ought to be reduced to slavery ... and beaten like brute beasts and shot like man eaters.' But in the same breath Ned could write of meeting Gandhi's friend, Pandit Nehru, most aggressive of the Swarajists, who told Ned that Gandhi deplored the waste of money on architectural piles. 'I said it was all

---

*The carpets for Government House were based on traditional Persian designs. Five hundred weavers worked for two years to weave 7,000 miles of wool for the carpets of the state rooms.

Indian work and much better to do than spin kaddah! That India where once she led in the fine arts is now deplorably behind times and peoples, and the only live thing in India was half-baked statesmanship and agitation.' Ned succeeded in convincing Nehru that the building was an education for the Indian craftsmen. He liked the whisky-drinking Nehru, who wore a black coat and jodhpurs, 'on which I drew buttons so that he looked exactly like an English bishop'.[21]

As Ned's work in India at last neared completion, Emily's commitment to theosophy faded. According to Krishna's new preaching all the ritual and doctrine lovingly developed by the Theosophical Society was needless. The years they had all spent struggling to advance along the Path had been so much waste of time. In a manner typical of gurus, Krishna poised himself to dissolve his church. To her credit, Mrs Besant supported him, in spite of George Arundale's accusations that he was a fake. At Krishna's behest, Mrs Besant dissolved the Esoteric Section in 1928, and in 1929 Krishna dissolved the Order of the Star. Still bewitched by Krishna, Emily followed the old theosophical routine, spending summers at Castle Eerde and camp at Ommen, and holidaying with Krishna in the Swiss Alps. Theosophy, however, was losing its meaning for her.

Mary remembered dull, silent meals at Mansfield Street. Ned would take the *Times* crossword into the dining room while Emily read her novel, usually a wild western, all through the meal. Robert and Eva were difficult and unhappy. Desperate to have a child although doctors had warned her that she could never conceive, Eva worried about her gynaecologists and pestered Ned to buy them a house. Robert, who had taken to designing furniture since he lost his job at *English Life*, was drinking heavily. Emily dreaded the evenings when he came back night after night completely 'out'. Ned never ceased to nag him, which only made matters worse, as Emily always rushed to Robert's defence. In February 1928 Emily went on holiday to Corsica with Robert and Ursula, whose marriage was collapsing. Ursy cried all day and all night for three days solid while Robert drank. 'I was in agony,' Emily wrote later. 'I thought it was all my fault, my weakness and ignorance as a mother. I remember writing such a bitter article on the mother of Judas.'[22] At last Emily was beginning to realize how Robert and Ursy, both vulnerable, had been damaged by her commitment to theosophy.

It was partly in order to escape life at Mansfield Street that Mary became engaged in March 1929. Anthony Sewell was everything that

Krishna wasn't: red-blooded, worldly, meat-eating and a stockbroker. They met at one of Emily's charity functions, where there was nothing to drink. Mary fell in love with Anthony immediately because 'he said what fun this is, and it was awful, and he was so nice about it, that, you know, he won me immediately, because of the way he took this ghastly party'. His father was a partner of Somerset Maugham's father, which gave him a literary cachet, but he had no money. Roderick Jones pretended not to mind; he told Mary that he had been training her to be a wife, but that she ought to have married an ambassador and not a penniless city clerk. When he returned Mary's letters, she discovered that he had corrected them in red ink.

Ned saw less of MacSack, who was now more of a burden than a mistress. Lionel Sackville's sudden death in 1928 had unhinged her, and she quarrelled violently with Vita, making a terrible scene at the lawyers, Pemberton's, about Vita's jewellery which ended with Vita cutting twelve pearls from her necklace. MacSack became increasingly unstable and paranoid. She couldn't keep her servants and complained when they objected to her throwing things at them. 'If only they knew how much it relieved her in all her worries.' But Ned was still loyal to her, and when she bought a house in Streatham, she expected him to design it for her.

MacSack's insanity brought Ned no closer to Emily. He wrote to her from America in October 1928 describing a dream which probably came all too close to his real feelings:

> So much divorce is talked of here that I dreamed last night that you wanted to divorce me – you sobbed a great deal and there was a great deal of anger and I was very angry as you had troops and hundreds of Theosophists walking over miles of priceless carpets – my carpets!

Emily saw their marriage rather differently. She wrote Ned a letter on their wedding anniversary in 1929:

> Do you know any other couple so loving and so *free* after thirty-two years. I have been such a trying and unsatisfactory wife and yet you love me! I too have been very *patient*!! But how I love you . . . How wise I was to recognize your great genius 32 years ago! You see I can't praise you without praising myself!! I may be covered with the mantle of your glory but I had the foresight to take shelter there![23]

'Ever so much love and gratitude for your sweet darling wedding letter,' Ned replied, ignoring the fact that she had used her freedom to cover herself in Krishna's mantle too, and that her freedom had robbed him of the cosy domesticity he yearned for.

Ned's uneasy truce with Emily coincided with a revival of creativity. In 1929 Ned gained the commission he wanted as a climax to his career: to build a cathedral that was bigger than St Paul's.

Ned liked to say that he met Dr Downey, the Roman Catholic Archbishop of Liverpool, dining with the playwright Alfred Sutro at the Garrick Club. 'What fun for you,' said Ned when Downey told him of his plan to build a new cathedral. Downey remarked that as Liverpool's new Anglican cathedral was being built by a Roman Catholic, Giles Gilbert Scott, *his* architect should be an Anglican.

Later, Dr Downey invited Ned to Liverpool. 'I was shown into a large dull-gloomed room, and waited, feeling nervous and rather shy, till in came His Grace – a red biretta on his head and a voluminous sash around his ample waist.* He held out a friendly hand. His pectoral Cross swung towards me, and the first words he said were "Will you have a cocktail?"'

Like the legend of the Garrick Club lunch that launched New Delhi, the Dr Downey stories are probably partly apocryphal. Brendan Bracken claimed that it was he who persuaded Downey to appoint Lutyens by promising £10,000 for the building fund. Bracken probably couldn't afford £10,000, and some suspected that he was acting as a front man for Lutyens. Certainly Bracken promoted Lutyens whenever he could, acclaiming him in parliament as 'the greatest architect alive . . . who has done more to increase the loveliness of this country than any architect of our time'. Lutyens no doubt learned of the Liverpool Cathedral project from Reilly, but Reilly wanted a competition for the design and he was annoyed when the autocratic Dr Downey appointed Lutyens without one.[24]

The story goes that the cathedral project was kept a closely guarded secret until the site was bought in 1930, but in fact Dr Downey announced Lutyens's appointment on 6 July 1929. By 31 July a considerable sum towards the £200,000 needed had been raised. Lutyens told *The Times* that 'a design of the type required would take a long time to evolve, perhaps several years. Though he had some ideas in his mind, these had not yet crystallized into a definite plan.'

In truth the design was already taking shape in the racquets court at

---

*Later the Archbishop was to reduce his weight by 8 stone, no mean achievement.

Mansfield Street and on the backs of Emily's letters. When rain leaked into the racquet court and sopped his drawing, Ned wrote, 'Is it heaven blessing my work?' 'I hate to leave it,' he wrote, dreading the interruption to his late-night work made by a visit to Washington in September. 'But in a week or so before I go to America I shall have completed my first of what may be a series of Cathedrals.'[25]

Archbishop Downey publicly declared that the cathedral should express the spirit of the twentieth century, but that it would be 'calamitous' if his search for a modern interpretation of Christianity was achieved by 'something Epsteinish'. Epstein, the pugnacious sculptor, responded by asking in a newspaper interview: 'Does Sir Edwin Lutyens mean to turn to the traditional ecclesiastical sculptor who has filled our churches with dull, expressionless works which don't evoke the faintest response or flicker of feeling in the spectator?'*
In a letter to the *Evening Standard* Epstein claimed that the Catholic Church had employed great artists of the day such as Michelangelo: 'Whom else can they turn to today but the Jew Epstein?' Ned thought the letter 'horrid' but Downey blundered in, publicly attacking Epstein. From its inception Liverpool Cathedral was a battleground between modernism and classicism. Reilly hailed it with rave reviews in the *Observer* and the architectural press, but soon after he became a convert to modernism, and in his memoirs he deplored the conservatism of Lutyens's Roman baroque design.[26]

But Lutyens's design was not really baroque. On the contrary, it was a massive sculpture, 'a vast building thought out from the beginning in solid geometrical relationships', the supreme expression of his elemental classicism. Developing the theme of Thiepval, he piled arches on arches, criss-crossing tunnels with tunnels. He used a ratio of one to three in order to give a loftier effect than Thiepval's tunnels ($1:2\frac{1}{2}$), making Liverpool taller and narrower than most gothic cathedrals. The plan is a Latin cross, its arms wider than usual, and at their crossing is a huge central space under a dome, 'its diameter the biggest in the world, 168 ft,' as he explained. 'There are five vaulted aisles, the nave being 46 ft wide and 160 ft high, so that, in spite of being wider than that of St Paul's, its predominant impression will be of height.'

He described the principle underlying the design in 1932 as 'a progression of vaults carrying greater vaults at right angles to their direction'.

---

*Lutyens did not admire Epstein's work. 'I feel as though I have been modelled by Epstein,' he quipped after paying an especially big tax bill in 1924.

Vaults 15 feet in diameter springing at a level of 37 feet 6 inches running North–South carry vaults 22 feet in diameter springing at 55 feet running West and East. These carry vaults 32 feet in diameter springing at 80 feet, forming the Chapels, running North–South, and these carry the Main Nave vault 46 feet in diameter springing at a level of 115 feet running West and East. It sounds simple enough, but complications grow, and to keep an even scale of diminution as the building grows in size, gives an ever-increasing acreage for thought and invention.

Manipulating the intersecting arches in mathematical ratio was like playing a fiendish game of architectural patience. Like Thiepval, Liverpool has two 'triumphal' arches set at right angles to one another. As at Thiepval, the arcades consist of two major arches alternating with two minor arches, but the design is far bigger and more complex. The two arcades follow different 'rhythms'.* The arches are really tunnels, but the tunnels themselves are pierced by the aisles, which shoot through them at right angles.

Over the central crossing Ned placed his massive dome, which paid homage to his hero Wren at St Paul's. The dome posed the classic architectural puzzle which had baffled Wren: how to reconcile the circular central space beneath the dome with the square formed by the crossing of nave and aisles which support it. Ned achieved an elegant solution; nave and aisles were reconciled harmoniously with the central space. That great circle beneath the dome was the chief space of his cathedral, as the piers of the tunnel-arches were so bulky that relatively little room was left within the nave.[27]†

Did Liverpool succeed, as Thiepval did, in transcending mathematical virtuosity and expressing an emotion? Back in 1910, Ned had written to Herbert Baker: 'You may laugh at me a bit, but *au fond* somewhere, I am horribly religious, but cannot speak it, and this saves my work.'

Hussey speculated that Lutyens's cathedral was inspired by a buried atavistic religious sense which was reawakened in 1926 when he attended the garrison church in Gibraltar. Listening to the hymn 'From Greenland's Icy Mountains' revived old memories of his mother's evangelical singing, he told Emily. 'But it is all beyond my reach –

---

*The rhythm of the arches on the west–east series is: small a, small a, large A, small a, small a. On the north–south series the arches go: small b, large B, small b, large B, small b.

†In spite of its huge size, Liverpool is relatively wasteful of space. The estimated capacity is about 5,000 people. The nave is short by comparison with other cathedral plans (it is broader than it is long). The concentration of space beneath the circular dome rather than in the nave posed problems for the Catholic liturgy.

whether too high or too low – I only know it's a level I shall reach again.' Did this prefigure Liverpool's religious inspiration? Or did he really mean to write *'never* reach again', as his daughters Mary and Ursy thought? Ned was notorious for his anti-church feeling; he had annoyed the Anglican establishment by insisting on the Great War Stone rather than the cross, and there is no real evidence that he changed his mind. On the contrary, the 'aesthetic science' of elemental architecture had *become* his religion, as he explained in 1932: 'the intricacies of proportions and recurring ratios are without end and admit some fourth dimension which cannot be expressed. As in the Hindu Faith where the Name of God may not be mentioned, save perhaps under the mystic monosyllable of "OOM".'[28]

Archbishop Downey signed his letters to Ned with an archbishop's double cross. Lutyens responded by signing with a symbol which combined an architect's T-square and a triangular set square. The T-square was the secret motif at Liverpool; it was his signature, hidden like a child's puzzle in keystones and crypt doorways.* But it was also remarkably similar to a cross. Perhaps the elision of T-square and cross was the closest Lutyens came to an admission of the convergence of his elemental mode of architecture with the Christian faith.

'Charing Cross bridge may be mine,' Ned told Emily in August 1929. 'I shall know this week.' But his appointment as architect to the London County Council over the scheme for the redevelopment of Charing Cross and London's South Bank brought nothing but trouble.† Late-night games of architectural patience puzzling over the intricacies of Liverpool's geometry must have seemed bliss by contrast with the endless, pointless rows stirred by the vengeful Blomfield.

Lutyens's appointment as consulting architect had been intended to silence opposition, but it had the opposite effect. Charing Cross raised important questions about the powers of local authorities to embark on major schemes of redevelopment without consulting architectural

---

*He had played the same game with crosses on the Cenotaph, where at least twenty-two crosses are concealed in the design, many made by the flags.
†The LCC and the Southern Railway proposed to move Charing Cross Station from the north side of the Thames to the south or Surrey side, close to Waterloo, building a new high-level bridge at Charing Cross and driving a new road through to Trafalgar Square. This drastic scheme had been drawn up by the LCC in secret without consultation with the RIBA, with the public or with the Royal Commission on Cross River Traffic. It ignored the alternative proposals for keeping the station where it was on the north side, and it left undecided the fate of Rennie's Waterloo Bridge, which was already a sore point of public controversy.

opinion, and Lutyens seemed to be conniving. Did he support high-handedness at the LCC by giving the Charing Cross scheme his blessing and thereby undermining the RIBA? His role in the affair was hotly debated in the national and architectural press. Some blamed him for the entire design, others suggested that he was hired to give cosmetic gloss and aesthetic approval to a design worked out by the engineers.[29]*

When the scheme was made public in December 1929 it was greeted by a storm of angry letters in *The Times* and savaged in the architectural press. By then Ned was safely out of the country, unable to reply and on board a P & O liner bound for India. This did not escape the attention of Reginald Blomfield, who wrote to *The Times* demanding that Lutyens return to answer the architects' objections to the scheme. From Delhi Ned watched. 'The various letters in *The Times* don't frighten me a bit,' he wrote. 'They mostly, if not all, are too misunderstanding and silly for words.'[30]

In Delhi in the winter of 1929–30 Shoosmith, who was supervising Viceroy's House, found Lutyens edgy, irritable and easily upset. 'I was apt to get my *ears boxed* for something that had nothing to do with me at all.' The house was being frantically furnished and decorated and cleaned in preparation for the Irwins to move in at Christmas. Three thousand panes of glass were smashed, five hundred keys were stolen, seventeen miles of garden hedges cut. It took Ned three or four hours to go round the house, supervising men placing furniture or cutting stone to get fountains to flow or hanging pictures of viceroys.

Exhausted by his twice-daily round of the house, suffering from a heavy cold and exasperated by unsupervised sloppy work, Ned exploded and threatened to sack Shoosmith who blithely announced that he was taking a Christmas holiday. 'Sir Edwin do you want me to go?' asked Shoosmith. 'Don't be a bloody fool,' replied Ned. 'If I want you to go I shall tell you so ... I don't mean it. I always say rude things to people I like; I dare not say them to the others.' And he put

---

*As the *Architects' Journal* put it, the LCC 'contend that in employing Sir Edwin Lutyens to advise them they have completely fulfilled their artistic obligations and have done full justice to the architectural aspects of the Charing Cross Bridge problem. But we should like to be informed as to the amount of liberty which was given to Sir Edwin to modify the scheme which was agreed upon between the engineers of the London County Council and the Southern Railway.' The architect D. S. MacColl wrote to *The Times* denying that Lutyens was responsible for the scheme. 'Actually he was called in (under outside pressure) to make the best of a bad job. For initial and radical defects he cannot be held responsible.'

his arm round Shoosmith's shoulder and they walked down the garden.

On 23 December 1929 Ned got up at 7 a.m. and donned a tailcoat and top hat. It was a wet morning, but as the sun peered through the fog at 8 a.m. the Irwins arrived in an official car with a guard of honour. In spite of an attempted terrorist bomb attack on the official train, Irwin was unfuffled. He walked up the stairs to the great portico, Ned was formally presented, the doors were opened and Irwin and his wife walked into the house, 'and we left them alone and for the first time in seventeen years the house closed on me'.[31]

Viceroy's House was not officially opened until 1931, but his departure left Ned feeling emotionally bereft and somehow older. 'I have no one who cares to listen to me save strangers who treat me . . . with super respect. It makes me feel very lonely.' Among these respectful strangers was Robert Byron, a twenty-four-year-old writer whom Ned showed round the house with Penelope Chetwode, bluestocking daughter of Sir Philip, Indian Commander-in-Chief, on Boxing Day 1929. Byron, had made a study of Indian architecture, had been commissioned to write an article on New Delhi for the *Architectural Review*. Ned told him: 'I feel as if the Viceroy's House were a newly married daughter. It seems extraordinary not to be able to wander about it whenever I want to any more.' On New Year's Eve Ned heard that he had been made a Knight Commander of the Indian Empire in the Honours List. 'Now that's a surprise!' he told Emily. 'I suppose, but don't know, that I can wear a ribbon and star.' He couldn't have known that Byron's article was to transform his reputation far more effectively.[32]

Ned returned from India in time for Mary's wedding to Anthony Sewell on 18 February 1930. It was a bitterly cold day, and Ned wore his overcoat buttoned up over his morning clothes as he walked up the aisle to give her away. It wasn't a happy occasion. To supplement Anthony's meagre earnings of £10 a week, Mary demanded £500 a year, which she thought was what Ned had given Ursula and Barbie (in fact they received £250), and the rows about money revived Ned's old fears about dying a pauper. Ned thought that Anthony shouldn't marry Mary if he couldn't afford it; what he didn't know was that Mary by now had changed her mind too.

During the engagement she had become friends with Anthony's brother Percy. Fifteen years older than Anthony, Percy was a war hero who had survived four years in the Royal Flying Corps, a gambler who worked as a journalist on the *Daily Express*. Percy and Mary went skating together and lunched afterwards, and 'of course what happened was that he and I fell in love. And this was awful because . . . I had made all this fuss about getting married, and it was very awkward being in the family.' Percy told her, 'It won't happen, your marriage won't happen. Don't worry, I know it won't.' She believed him. But as Anthony knew nothing and Mary did nothing, the preparations were made, the invitations sent out, the pages dressed in pale blue velvet, and in a surreal way getting married became inevitable. On the wedding day she fully expected Percy to shout out and then elope with her from the church. But nothing happened. Like someone in a dream, she realized with a shock by the time she reached Paris for her honeymoon that she was now married to Anthony.*

The Charing Cross bill had its second reading in Parliament the day after Mary's wedding (19 February 1930). Shortly before the debate, Ned handed Herbert Morrison, the Transport Minister, a letter addressed to him by the RIBA's Arthur Keen, chairman of the Thames Bridges Conference, asking him to publish a letter denying responsibility for the Charing Cross layout. This, said Blomfield, who no doubt had something to do with it, was a perfectly innocent letter intended as a friendly suggestion to a colleague. Morrison read the letter aloud in Parliament, quoting it as typical of RIBA dirty tricks: Lutyens had in fact spent considerable time designing a detailed layout on the basis of the engineers' plans; the drawings survive to prove it. As the *Architects' Journal* commented, 'when the obscuring clouds had rolled away . . . Sir Edwin Lutyens was with the gods in earnest consultation . . . What need have we to fear?'[33]

Shortly afterwards, Ned resigned from the RIBA.

Ned's relations with Blomfield had been bad ever since the row about Waterloo Bridge in 1924. Lord Crawford, who chaired the Royal Fine Art Commission on which they both sat, complained that they quarrelled incessantly, making the commission almost unworkable. Lutyens, who never stopped chattering irrelevancies, agreed with Blomfield on one thing only, namely the ghastliness of Baker's design for South Africa House in Trafalgar Square. (Crawford was shocked by the violence of Lutyens's hostility towards Baker. 'Professional jealousy

---

*Percy Sewell committed suicide in December 1931. Mary found him in a hotel room in Monte Carlo with an empty glass of veronal beside his bed. 'He looked very happy, and he was lying in bed in a dressing gown. I felt rather cross with him.'

I have encountered . . . but never anything quite so cynical or uncompromising.')³⁴

The Charing Cross scheme was thrown out by a select committee and Blomfield had his way, but resigning from the RIBA was the best thing Ned could have done. It distanced him from the stuffy architectural establishment, from the older generation of pompous Edwardian architects.

During July and August 1930 Ned was absorbed in his plans for Liverpool Cathedral, working until 12.30 each night in the racquets court, 'with the result of swollen legs and a bad head'. He found it curiously comforting to be working alone in the big empty house on a big project once more, like those long lonely summers he had spent in London working on Delhi.³⁵ The plans ballooned as all his great projects did. Liverpool promised to be an even greater folly than Delhi or Drogo. Bigger (naturally) than Giles Gilbert Scott's Anglican Liverpool Cathedral (area 100,000 square feet), bigger than St Paul's (59,700 square feet), Liverpool's area of 216,500 square feet was second only to St Peter's in Rome (227,069 square feet).

Lutyens presented provisional plans and elevations to Archbishop Downey and the bishops of his grand diocese at a luncheon in Liverpool in September 1930. Reilly was there. Going into the dining room behind the Bishop of Leeds he heard Lutyens murmur, 'Leeds kindly light in Liverpool's encircling gloom.' After lunch Lutyens prepared to display the plans. It was a solemn moment. Seeing that the Archbishop needed a light for his cigar, Lutyens produced a box of Bryant and May's safety matches.* When His Grace picked it up, it buzzed and shook with a loud internal noise. It was a Woolworth toy. Laughter all round. Next Lutyens pointed to the apse at the end of the central vista. 'That is where your Grace is to be buried. My Lord of Leeds, that is where you are to be,' pointing to another place. 'My Lord of Middleton, that is your spot.' Reilly noted how skilfully he had interested each of the bishops in the plan and given them a freehold precluding alteration. Pointing to the great narthex at the west end, as big as an ordinary cathedral, he said he wanted it always open night and day with lavatories sunk into its great piers. 'My Lords, I want the poor of Liverpool to come there at any time of the day or night, to sleep

---

*Lutyens's favourite joke involved a matchbox into which he stuck two matches which he invited someone to hold, telling them he was about to demonstrate an electric current. 'Can't you feel anything? Now do you feel your leg being pulled?'

there if they have nowhere else to go, but if so to wake up always in sight of a distant altar'.* The bishops by now were eating out of his hand, calling him the best Catholic of all.³⁶

Lutyens had succeeded in selling a scheme that was as grandiose as it was impractical. In Dr Downey and the Catholic Church he found a patron who, unlike the Government of India or Julius Drewe of Castle Drogo, imposed neither cuts nor spending limits. No estimate was ever made for Liverpool Cathedral. Instead, the project became a giant fantasy, spinning uncontrollably into unreality. It was unbuildable; but it was the greatest building never built.

---

*The cathedral was on Brownlow Hill, on the site of the hated Victorian workhouse, where evangelical Poor Law officers had cruelly treated Liverpool's Irish Catholic poor. The Cathedral was intended to make atonement, a point underlined by the brick of the crypt, which evoked the brick of the workhouse.

Chapter Eighteen
The Torch of Humanism
1931–1937

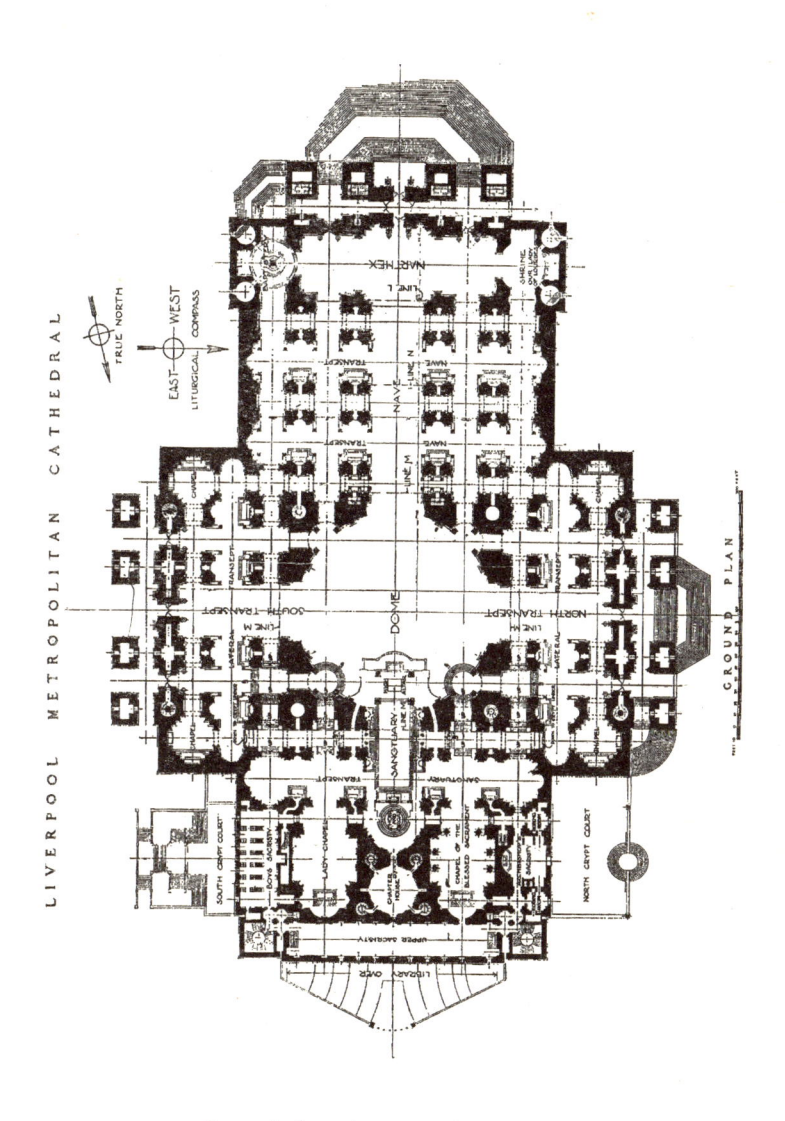

Ground plan of Liverpool Cathedral.

Emily was delighted by Ned's Liverpool Cathedral but disgusted too at 'all that mumbo jumbo, robes etc and the poor people starving'.

> I love to think of your great building but I do wish it had been model dwellings and not a church! If you had been going to build a Cathedral when we were first married I should have been thrilled but now I could weep . . . It saddens me that men should still be perpetuating priestcraft when I long to set them free from such things.

Emily had broken with the 'priestcraft' in her own life. In 1930, following Krishna's example, she resigned from the Theosophical Society. She went to the Ommen camp that summer and found the movement in ruins. Mrs Besant had aged (Wedgwood said she was senile) and was dismayed at her inability to bridge the splits in the society and troubled by Krishna's sweeping declarations. Leadbeater, who had turned against Krishna, was 'very bored and quite uncomprehending'.[1]

Leaving the Society made a hole in Emily's life. For twenty years theosophy had been her work – speaking, writing, organizing. Now it all seemed futile. She still wanted to be Krishna's disciple, but he didn't want disciples. He had cut the ground from beneath her feet, 'and I felt I was dropping into nothingness'.

It was in this state of depression that Emily accompanied Ned to India in January 1931, to see the official opening of Viceroy's House. She felt ill and very unhappy, longed to be at Adyar (Krishna was at Castle Eerde) and became convinced she would die before returning to England. India's politics dismayed her. 'They have got practically everything they asked for but I doubt how far any of them are going to settle down to the constructive task of framing a constitution.' The Indians, she felt, hated the British, and she vowed never to come to India again.

But even Emily succumbed to the charm of the Irwins, declaring that she had never felt so easy staying anywhere before. She was awed by Ned's achievement. She deplored Baker's 'great crime' in the shape of 'the silly slope'. Hardinge, who came out too, was euphoric. In spite of all the years of confrontation, he never ceased to praise. As for

Edward Hudson, who also came (*Country Life* ran a feature on the opening), he was so moved by Viceroy's House that he was close to tears. 'Poor old Christopher Wren could never have done this,' he told Emily.[2]

'My everlasting prayer is for the genius and help of a Wren or Newton,' Ned had written back in 1912; but 'if Wren had built in India, it would have been something so different to anything we know of his that we cannot name it'. That is the key to Lutyens's entire conception at Viceroy's House. It is Wren, but Wren translated into an Indian language so skilfully and subtly that few can read it. 'I do think it's a gentleman's house,' said Ned in 1929, 'though original in that it is built in India for India, Indian.'*

A. S. G. Butler analysed the complex geometry of Lutyens's plan in the *Memorial Volumes*.

> The entire design, which comprises a central square block and four wings projecting at each corner, can be contained within a short rectangle. Its sides are in the relation of 5 to 4.75. Where its diagonals cross in the exact centre is the centre of the dome. The dome itself is the centre of a square, which is against the west wall of the Durbar Hall, and this overlap of 40 feet dictates the depth of the Portico, the west State rooms . . .[3]

Butler's architect's preoccupation with proportion is tediously technical, but it underscores a key point: the planning of Viceroy's House was ruthlessly, rigorously western and logical. Starting by pencilling blocks on squared paper, Lutyens achieved a design that depended on repeated areas and proportions.

The programme was simple: to design a palace that was also a working centre of executive government. Lucky Ned; designing such a palace was the opportunity for which architectural students had trained and readied themselves in vain for generations. The house must be the processional climax, the ceremonial apex of the British Raj. It must contain the Viceroy's secretariat, his aides-de-camp, his private printing press, the tents which accommodated his party on tour, his massive wine cellar. There must be room for the monarch and his

---

*Ned told the Architectural Association in 1932: 'There are two ways of building in India, one to parade your building in fancy dress as at a Fancy Ball, mixing dates and styles, so that the creation becomes something really funny; or to build as an Englishman dressed for the climate, conscious only that your tailor is of Agra or Benares, and not of Savile Row or Petticoat Lane.' The first, fancy-dress method was Baker's; the second was Ned's. 'Take your own ratios, use them, and adopt them to the necessity of the climate.'

entourage – this despite the fact that the monarch or Prince of Wales visited India only three times during the entire history of the Raj. There must be room for the Viceroy's domestic apartments, which really formed a country house on their own, the home Ned had designed for Lady Hardinge. Clerks must be separated from the Indian Civil Service, European servants segregated from Indian servants, aides-de-camp separated from housekeepers.

The building ballooned. In spite of the savage cuts to scale which Hardinge forced Ned to make in 1913–14, Viceroy's House is massive; it occupies four and a half acres, which is an area of 210,430 square feet. This makes it larger than Versailles (198,300 square feet), though still smaller than the Palace of Westminster (247,200 square feet).

In retrospect, perhaps, Viceroy's House seems an architectural dinosaur, its gigantism a denial of reality, reflecting Britain's loss of imperial certainty. The American historian Tom Metcalf perceived Lutyens's monumental classicism as 'a device to mask a growing insecurity by shouting forth an assertive magnificence. Sheer size, so this mammoth palace seems to say, could help obscure, if not deny altogether, the waning of Britain's authority over its premier dependency.' But the monumental is constantly undercut by irony. It is as if Ned were designing a fairy-tale palace, an oriental fantasy. In spite of its vast size, it is neither pompous nor overbearing.

The plan depends upon circulation, centring upon the circular Durbar Hall beneath the dome, the void at the core of the cubic mass. Circulation occurs over several levels, starting from the lower basement, which grips the flanks of Raisina Hill and contains kitchens and stores and servants' quarters. The composition is pure mass, punched by openings – by tunnels and by courtyards and fountains which allow cooling air to circulate.[4]

At upper basement level, motor cars enter to one side of the portico, circulate around a fountain, enter a tunnel, drop their guests and drive out again by a different court. From the muffled dark of the vaulted tunnel, visitors climb into the bright light of the staircase court. Above the curving marble staircase, which cascades like the masonry in one of Ned's gardens, the coved cornice is capped by blue – the violent blue of the Indian sky.

The Durbar Hall is the climax. The circular domed hall nods homage to the Pantheon at Rome; hints of the design appear as early as the sketches Ned drew for Barbara Webb. In darkness it is reminiscent of the cool, cave-like circular burial chamber at the heart of a Mogul tomb, such as Humayun's tomb in Delhi. Open the high door facing the throne, and a shaft of dazzling light stabs the gloom, linking the Viceroy's throne to the pink, sun-blasted vista which leads straight down towards the Jaipur Column, the processional way and the All-India Arch. This is the theatre of empire. Here is the symbolic, dramatic centre of the Raj, the epicentre of power, where all bucks stop and all axes terminate – just as all the avenues of Versailles were supposed to meet on the pillow of *Le Roi Soleil*, but only (Ned noted) when in bed alone.

Lutyens designed his own order for Delhi. The stone bells of the 'Delhi order' can never ring to announce the end of a dynasty – a joke in stone, but also a denial of the reality of British imperial decline. Delhi has four different fronts. 'Versailles seems both naïve and boring by comparison.'*

Everything – from staircases to furniture – was individually designed by Lutyens himself. Little wonder that he lost money on the project. As Robert Lutyens explained: 'with much of the laborious finishing detail – and in particular the furnishing – the contract price of any one item at Indian wage rates was often less than the cost of the drawings involved, which might even be as much as 50 times greater than the fee'.

Ned hung the walls with portraits of all the viceroys since Warren Hastings – 'Hardinge and Reading are the biggest, Chelmsford one of the smallest'.[5] Today they have all been banished from the walls. The only Englishman who remains is Ned himself. His bust by Reid Dick stands at the foot of the staircase court. India is grateful for her palace.

Robert Byron's review of Viceroy's House appeared in the *Architectural Review* in 1931 while Ned and Emily were in Delhi. At the distant sight of New Delhi's domes, 'the traveller looses a breath ... With a shiver of impatience he shakes off contemporary standards and makes ready to evoke those of Greece, the Renascence and the Moguls.' Byron understood Indian architecture, and he could gauge Ned's debt to India; Ned may also have briefed him. He saw (or perhaps Ned told him) that the *chattris* or roof-top pavilions derived from Agra, the sweeping blade-like cornice or *chujjah* from Fatepuhr Sikri. He saw too

---

*At Viceroy's House the orders do not dictate the proportions of the building, as in conventional classicism. As Gavin Stamp has written: 'Viceroy's House has an extraordinary dynamic quality, governed by strong and continuous horizontals which, at lower levels, are extruded to form retaining walls. This dynamism is achieved by a series of layers, with each thick wall built on a slope, or batter.'

that Ned had learned from Indian building how to manipulate light and shade, using the black shadow cast by the deep *chujjah* to give a unity to the massive structure. Lutyens, claimed Byron, had not merely decorated his buildings with Indian motifs, but achieved a real synthesis of east and west, a fusion of humanist principles of solid form and exact proportion with Mogul colour, mass and horizontality.

Byron hailed Viceroy's House as modern architecture, constructed on a 'pyramidical principle' with its battered walls producing a feeling of 'movement in mass', which was dynamic and 'expressive of growth and union with the earth'. It was astonishing, he wrote, that its design should have been completed twenty years before.

Tipped off by Ned, Byron poured eloquent scorn on the fancy-dress style of Baker's buildings. The fretted stone panels of his Council Chamber, wrote Byron, resembled underwear hanging on a clothes line ('Here are not only pants, but petticoats, camisoles, night-dresses, and even tea gowns'), and the Secretariats were decorated with domes like toreadors' hats and gaggles of elephants' heads and arches hung with underwear, this time upside down and red. 'As the years pass these apartments will bear silent witness to the discord between England and India that marked the time of their building, just as, in the Viceroy's House, may be read a contrary faith in some ultimate and far-distant harmony between the two countries.'[6]

Emily agreed. 'Every word that Byron says of Baker is true, though not strong enough.' She deplored the lack of construction in the Secretariats, the patterns and copybook mottoes.* As for the Council Chamber, 'it is just like a gasworks outside, and inside it is indescribably bad – heavy, ugly, misshapen ornament'. If few people were able to see the difference between Baker's work and Lutyens's, at least Byron's articles now alerted them to the difference.

Nor had Ned yet finished with Baker. In *Country Life* Byron challenged Baker to give a public explanation for the gradient, which deliberately and selfishly spoiled the greatest architectural effort since Versailles. 'Either Sir Herbert Baker must prove that the decision was not his, or he must admit his mistake and expound the sincerity of his misapprehension. If he does neither his record in the archives of posterity will not be an enviable one.' Baker's reputation has never

---

*LIBERTY WILL NOT DESCEND TO A PEOPLE; A PEOPLE MUST RAISE THEMSELVES TO LIBERTY; IT IS A BLESSING WHICH MUST BE EARNED BEFORE IT CAN BE ENJOYED was the motto Baker had inscribed over the doorway of the Secretariats. Lord Irwin thought this 'rather pointed', but the motto still remains today.

really recovered. Ned was merciless. The *Country Life* criticism, he wrote, 'won't help to make Baker amend his ways. In Africa when I was there he drew criticism from me and appeared grateful and willing to learn. He came to Delhi, and he was just obstinate and did everything I had warned him not to do.'[7]

Lutyens's obsessiveness about the gradient was exaggerated. For every one who takes Lutyens's side, there are others who say that the existing gradient in fact creates an element of drama and surprise. Baker and Hardinge both justified it as a picturesque interlude in a classical design. Even Robert Byron thought that an asphalt gradient leading to the sky riveted the eye to the axis of the design. Most people today taking the unforgettable taxi ride along Kings Way's red asphalt would agree. For Lutyens this was scant consolation. The effect, after all, had not been *intended*. He had lost his artist's control; and the iron ate into his soul.

Viceroy's House is a palace at the centre of a city of radiating axes. Baker's Secretariat buildings are a fortress on a cliff, towering above the people below. The two ideas can never be reconciled, and the gradient is where they clash, the point where Lutyens's avenue meets Baker's steep cliff.

Lutyens designed New Delhi as a garden city for motor cars. His city plan superimposes a complex design of hexagons upon grand symmetrical axes.* There are traces here of Washington, of Canberra and of Wren's plan for London; another source is Hampstead, where Ned had designed a hill-top centre for a garden city. New Delhi, with its wide tree-lined avenues, its dusty, leafy spaces bisected by dry canals, is Hampstead enlarged on a giant scale and transposed to Asia: a green lung or oasis, giving respite from the noisy, grilling heat of the old Indian city.†

Leaving Viceroy's House in 1931 for what he thought was the last time after the celebrations were over, Ned had not the nerve to say goodbye to Irwin. 'I just walked out and kissed a wall of the house.' Ned and Emily sailed home on the P & O with the Bakers, which, said Emily, 'will be most uncomfortable'.[8]

---

*S. J. Perelman wrote in 1947: 'Driving through the tremendous hexagonal parks and plazas that crisscross New Delhi, one has to admit that New Delhi is certainly crisscrossed with tremendous hexagonal parks and plazas.'
†The total cost of New Delhi (including land purchase) was £10,625,000, of which Viceroy's House cost £1,253,000. The whole of the new city cost twice as much as London's County Hall, according to Ned.

Emily returned from India in 1931 feeling ill and depressed. She was tormented by noises in her head. A doctor diagnosed anaemia and prescribed a diet of liver extract and raw beef sandwiches. It seemed a cruelly ironic reward for all her years of vegetarianism. 'Even you could not wish for more,' she told Ned. 'The idea of the raw beef makes me feel quite sick.' More disheartening still was her encounter with Krishna at the Ommen camp in September, when she was overcome with a sense of the emptiness and inadequacy of his teaching. He now rejected all systems of belief, dismissing personal love as corrupt, and when Emily confided in him he urged her to detach herself from her family and become a nun, aspiring to a universal love for all. Even Emily jibbed at this. 'There was a cold aridity, a dullness about the idea which repelled me.' Bitterly disillusioned, she felt that he had taken everything away from her and given nothing. 'My eyes were suddenly opened to the fact that my absorption in Theosophy and Krishna had largely separated me from a very wonderful human love.'[9] She turned to Ned, and found shelter and forgiveness, she later said, but not the need to serve that validated her sense of self. That she now found in her children, whose problems overflowed to fill the unaccustomed emptiness of her life.

The completion of Delhi left an emptiness at the heart of Ned's life too. Developing a public role as a scourge of modern architecture, he became President of the Incorporated Association of Architects and Surveyors, a breakaway group from the RIBA. In 1933 he was elected Master of the Art Workers' Guild, aligning himself with the survivors of Arts and Crafts. In articles and addresses he attacked the influence of foreign fashions on architectural education and deplored the passing of the craftsmen of his youth – the illiterate hedge carpenter who kept his accounts on a tallystick and selected oaks by tasting the sweetness of the acorn, or the waller who taught him his craft as a boy. 'The textbook has a knack of killing sap.' Addressing the Architectural Association in 1932 he showed little enthusiasm for steel construction. 'I crave for soft thick noiseless walls of hand-made brick and lime, the deep light reflecting reveals, the double floors, easy stairways and doorways never less than 1 foot 6 inches away from a corner.'[10]

Echoing Baldwin's Conservatism, Ned evoked a vanishing village England of tinkling smithies and burly craftsmen – source of the myth that his boyhood was spent in builders' yards. Overlooking the training Ernest George had given him, Ned reinvented himself as the Surrey wild child who had learned to draw buildings with a piece of sharpened soap on a framed pane of glass. (He resurrected that contraption and took it with him on a tour of the Mediterranean in 1932.) That the rigorous mathematical ratios and classical discipline of his Delhi could indeed be taught in architectural school was conveniently forgotten. Nor did Surrey repay the compliment and acclaim its famous child: when the Surrey County Council proposed paying Lutyens a fee of 200 guineas for the bridge he designed over the Pilgrim's Way, someone suggested that one-tenth of that figure would be sufficient.

At least Ned was tolerant and witty, sympathizing with younger men who wanted to do something different. John Summerson remembered a dinner at the Whitefriars Club where Ned was guest of honour. Summerson made a 'clumsy' speech arguing the case for modernism. 'Afterwards I apologized for my performance. "Never mind," he said, "you were *thinking* all the time." At the end of the evening he took a soft hat off a hat stand, put it on upside down like a biretta and gave me a mock-episcopal blessing.'[11]

Ned by now had his Boswell: Christopher Hussey, a protégé of Hudson's on *Country Life*, was already accumulating material for what was to become, when published twenty years later, the greatest architectural biography ever written. In August 1931 Hussey motored Lutyens down to Somerset in his open-topped Austin Six. First they called on the gardener Norah Lindsey at Sutton Courtenay on the Thames. Ned described the garden she had made in a long rambling letter to Emily: 'Great trees, level waters and a soil that grows abundantly ancient yews and wonderful flowers and plants. The beds all too wide, too wide for what is called practical purposes – unmanned and the dead and dying things mixed with the living in a riot of mysterious beauty.' Like him, Norah Lindsey was a survivor from the Edwardian era, and Ned noted how short of money she was. The house itself was admirable and old but a dirty mixture of squalid odds and ends; after dinner they had to turn off the fountains by torchlight to allow water for baths in the morning.

They drove on to Mells and asked themselves to lunch with Frances Horner, who commissioned a muniment room (which was built) and Ned showed Hussey the monument he had designed for Edward Horner's statue in the church. Next they drove to Cothay, the medieval manor house belonging to Reggie Cooper, amateur architect and air force DSO. He 'fell desperately in love' with Ned's plan for a 'green house' for Saxton Noble, who wanted a large house which he couldn't afford, so Ned had drawn plans for a house bigger than Viceroy's House whose rooms were yew hedges and waterways with two great ruined staircases forming rockeries: the ultimate integration of house and garden. They motored on to Hestercombe, 'and I felt I must be 190 years old at least to have planted so hoary and old a place'. At Andover they telephoned 'Johnnie' (Herbert Johnson) – 'I couldn't pass Marsh Court' – stayed the night and talked of old times. Johnnie now sported an unbecoming glass eye, and he had lost a lot of money in the slump. Ned discovered him telling the footman to lay the table without light to save electricity. (Marsh Court, which cost £150,000 to build, was sold the following year for £60,000.) Driving back to London next morning Ned told Hussey of his youth in the cottage at Thursley, of Randolph Caldecott's visits and drawings, of his excitement at discovering Philip Webb's buildings, of how the Cenotaph originated in the garden at Munstead. The myth of the romantic architect was born.[12]

Recherche du temps perdu was one escape from the present. Liverpool Cathedral was another. By now the design had grown bigger than that of St Peter's, though this was denied in the press, as the Archbishop was coy about publishing his ambition to rival the pope. No estimates had been made. The construction was of thin Roman-shaped brick with granite dressings, and Ned avoided using iron for support, even in the dome. 'There can be no real permanence in a building of iron and brick,' he told the AA. Ned's cathedral sparkled with jokes. Confessional boxes and lavatories were embedded in the piers, there were forty-four altars, running holy water in the stoups (this was a tease for grand Catholics such as the Duchess of Norfolk) and a sunken organ. Inside it was bare of all decoration apart from the altar clothes and brightly coloured vestments which Ned himself designed.[13]

In 1934 the Roman Catholic hierarchy stipulated changes to the design, to conform to the needs of the liturgy; the sunken altar was moved and the running holy water (alas) eliminated. A model of the final version was exhibited at the Royal Academy in 1934.

In Hussey's view, so immersed was Lutyens in his Cathedral that he became in his last years something of an architectural mystic. Not that he converted to Catholicism. 'It is rum,' Ned told Emily, 'that our only source of income will be from a faith we neither hold nor have.' He took a perverse pleasure in twitting Archbishop Downey, who fortunately enjoyed having his leg pulled; but Ned sympathized with the Archbishop's Catholic politics. He told Dean Inge, whom he met at Mells, that the Anglican church would break up through lack of discipline, leaving the Catholics alone to stem the tide of Communism and atheism. When Inge said that all Irishmen should be turned out of the country, Ned quipped, 'Like Hitler and the Jews?'

Work began on the Cathedral site in 1931, and the foundation stone was laid in June 1933. As the brick catacombs of the crypt slowly rose, Ned worried that he wouldn't live to see the project's completion. He saw a doctor, who dismissed his fears of cancer and told him his blood pressure was wonderful. 'So that's all right. I may see a big bit of my Cathedral.'

The wooden model of the Cathedral 17 feet long and 11 feet high filled the drawing room at Mansfield Street. Walking back one night about midnight with the architect Andy Butler, Lutyens invited him to see the model. Butler found this 'an extraordinarily moving experience, because for once at least he was deadly serious, and kept asking me whether I liked this and that, with an enchanting humility'.[14]

MacSack was nearly blind, ill with a weak heart, and growing weak and very paranoid. She wrote to Emily asking for £1 for a fund she was making for Liverpool Cathedral in the name of her Catholic butler. Emily refused. Ned avoided MacSack, hating the odd, irregular meals at White Lodge which she insisted on eating either outside in the loggia or in the bathroom because it was the warmest room in the house. Once when he visited she insisted on getting out of bed to show him her leg – 'how wonderful it was for 70 (far thinner than I expected and quite white)'. When he ignored her she bombarded him with wild letters demanding money. She threatened to write to Francis Smith and Lord Revelstoke (Cecil Baring), and she sent a 'killing' letter asking for £500.

She wired Lutyens's office: 'The cesspool has gone over the cliff.'[15] When Ned didn't answer, she scrawled crazy letters to Sir Giles Gilbert Scott, President of the RIBA, vilifying him. 'Beware of Sir E L. No more false and dishonest man has ever existed. I have had a terrible awakening. He may go to prison some day.' She told Sir Giles that Ned had stolen furniture she had lent him, pretending that he had paid for it. He had unhooked a Charles II silver looking glass with the Sackville arms hanging at the foot of her stairs, and 'rushed up to his motor with it as my weak heart stopped me rushing after him . . . I could go on for ever,' she told Gilbert Scott, 'but you can judge how that clever man can be a horrid and dishonest CAD'. 'I cannot tell you what he has got out of me helped by his queer wife who is as bad a cadger as he is.' Ned had altered a house for MacSack in Streatham in 1929 for £11,000 and she had sold at a loss for £6,000 in 1932, but Ned continued to send her builders' bills.

MacSack's ravings were too confused and crazed to be really damaging, but they no doubt helped to discredit Ned and make him ridiculous in the eyes of his architectural colleagues. And MacSack did have the pleasure of fighting Ned in court. She brought a libel case in 1933, claiming £2,000, and persuading her doctor to testify that the worry of quarrelling with Ned had affected her blood pressure. Unfortunately for her, she argued with the judge, who threatened to turn her out of court, and the jury found against her and brought in malice, ordering her to pay £150. 'I hope this will help her to forget me!' wrote Ned.[16]

In 1934 Emily and Ursy played planchette and received a message from MacSack who said that she had died the night before and 'made somewhat scandalous confessions of her past relationship with you!' But MacSack lingered on until 1936.

Vita commemorated her mother in *Pepita* (1937), and Ned wrote congratulating her on her novel: 'I wish I had had more patience at the end! It failed me! . . . The w.c. seats were all screwed down – "she could never ask any man to the house"! . . . It was all too much for me and then the troubles began. Oh dear!'[17]

As the slump kicked in, Ned's work dried up. Commissions were cancelled or went to younger men – London University, costing £3 million, for which Lutyens made drawings, went to Charles Holden, 'a great disappointment'. After Detmar Blow was disgraced and ignominiously sacked by the Duke of Westminster in 1932, no more work came Ned's way from the Grosvenor estate, even though, according to Loelia Westminster, who engineered Blow's dismissal, there was never any suspicion that Lutyens had cheated. 'I am depressed at yet another job stopped – so my income this year will be less than last year's taxes,' he told Emily in 1932.

He received no fee for the Cathedral. Instead of taking a portion of the £30,000 which was his due, he made an arrangement to avoid taxes which meant that nothing was payable until his death, and even then a mere £10,000 was paid. Besides, 'if I took all the money I am entitled to there would probably be no Cathedral'. Handing on the torch of humanism was an expensive business.[18]

Not that all his work was cancelled. At Magdelane College, Cambridge, he built Benson court; it was so dark that when the undergraduate Roualeyn Cumming-Bruce was introduced to Lutyens and asked how he liked it, he replied that it was a pity the studies were so designed as to make it impossible to work without artificial light on a bright summer's day. There were lodges at Runnymede and a bridge at Hampton Court, but big commercial buildings eluded him.

In 1932 Ned paid a tax bill of £5,800 on Delhi. Tax vobiscum, he punned. 'I feel as thin as a moulted sparrow in a snowstorm.' Emily scolded him for getting into such a bad position financially in spite of the enormous jobs he had had. She blamed his advisers. 'Thomas may be splendid over some things but he is not a businessman, Francis Smith is old and not much use.' Instead of planning for tax and putting money on deposit, Lutyens gave his money to Cecil Baring to invest and, because of the slump, he was forced to sell out at a loss. For this he blamed Hall, 'trying to save money without telling me'.[19] Ned had as usual neglected his business interests and been badly caught out. His costs were too high. The meticulous detail of his drawings absorbed an unprofitably high proportion of profit.

In 1931 the Delhi office in Bolton Street was closed down, Queen Anne's Gate given up and the work of both combined in a new office housed in a large house at 5 Eaton Gate, off Eaton Square. The Delhi office was on the top floor, the Cathedral room on the first floor. There was never enough work to fill the big rooms, Thomas and Hall spent their time quarrelling, and the Lutyens office remained notorious for paying the lowest wages in London.

Mansfield Street was also too big, and Emily once again urged Ned to sell it, but he couldn't bear to. Instead the kitchen was moved from the basement on to the ground floor, allowing Emily to cut down on servants, though she still insisted that the house could not be run for less than £3,500 a year. Photographs show a house that had become a museum. With its black walls, it resembled a mausoleum. It was lifeless, empty and depressingly tidy, and the bare floorboards and high ceilings made it glacially cold. Very little of the furniture was actually allowed to be used, and pewter plates and precious rugs were hung on the walls like exhibits.

Into Mansfield Street's 'wicked basement' moved Betty, the most rebellious of the children. She liked to believe that she and Ned, as the two creative members of the family, were especially close, but this was wishful thinking. In fact, as Emily coolly wrote in 1929, Betty had been badly scarred by theosophy; even so, she still clung desperately to Emily. 'She adores me and yet hates everything about me. She is bitterly resentful of Theosophy . . . There is a very good reason. She plunged into it all too deeply and strained herself and got ill and now it frightens her to look back on.'

Betty took refuge from the emotionalism of theosophy in composing music deliberately lacking in emotional content, a precision instrument which took its source from the musical material available rather than exploring and expressing her feelings and personality. In this perhaps she was similar to Ned, who found in the intellectual discipline of classicism an escape from the mystic woolliness of theosophy. He liked to discuss the parallels between music and architecture: 'Proportion in Architecture is what time and key are to music.' But Betty was a modernist, following the influence of Schoenberg and Stravinsky to achieve the conceptual breakthrough that her father condemned among the younger generation of Corbusier-influenced architects. Ned found her music tuneless (as did many of the less musical members of her family). 'Publish it not,' he told Emily, 'her playing on the piano was very irksome. Noise and no music for me sense at all, and her finger nails clicked and clicked.'[20]

Nor did Ned take Betty seriously as a composer. For Ned, as Betty knew, marriage and babies were his daughters' true vocations; he wanted them to marry well 'as a justification for his achieved position in the world'. This Betty could never do. She was untidy, warm-hearted and foul-mouthed, her conversation peppered with bugger-*orfs*. Cigarette perpetually in hand, she was a bohemian, a gregarious heavy drinker and compulsive talker whose desire to shock masked a touching vulnerability. Ned took her to lunch at the Berkeley Grill, and she talked (he told Emily) 'a good deal of you, me and herself. The latter was rather terrifying . . . That all experience is the right of the young to indulge in – how could she believe that? When I was young I was not as practically inquisitive as she purports to be herself.'

While Ned lived upstairs in Mansfield Street's frozen spaces, Betty converted the basement kitchen into a music room, knocked down rabbit-warren partitions to reveal an Adam pillar, painted the floor red and wall black, and threw wild and noisy parties which Ned called Dartmoor because you never knew whom you might meet. In 1933 Betty married the singer Ian Glennie: at twenty-six she was the only unmarried sister and she urgently wanted children. Ian had no money but they lived rent free at Mansfield Street. When her first child was born in 1934 Betty heard herself roar at the astonished woman doctor: 'And I still want to write music, fuck you!'[21]

In August 1932 Ned crossed to France for the official war graves ceremonies at Arras and Thiepval. He cracked jokes unceasingly, which Lord Crawford found somewhat tiring. 'To have to laugh at every remark he makes (and they are all witty) – to have to do so incessantly (for he never stops talking for a moment) is the most fatiguing experience I know! One can't remember anything he says, and yet his conversation is brilliant – often wise, always vivacious; none the less his good spirits depress everybody – and one sees people getting quietly out of his way, simply because the effort of sympathetic laughter is overwhelming.'

Ned had become the sad comedian, hiding his unhappiness behind a mask of forced hilarity. In spite of photographers clustering round the Prince of Wales 'like flies round something nasty and oversweet', he found the war graves ceremonies intensely moving and wept a good deal. At Thiepval he was glad to find that when he mounted the steps to the great stone under the great arch the wide battle area was framed by the series of arches, but he was saddened by what seemed to be the end of an era: 'the graves work is closed as with Delhi, Spain, America – all seem to close together – and what now will a new era bring?'[22]

That autumn Lutyens made a Mediterranean tour, visiting the Parthenon with Ursula, his favourite daughter. Outwardly Ursy's life was enviably rich and privileged. She had good looks, charm, wit, social success; she dressed in beautiful, expensive clothes and was married to a handsome viscount, Matthew Ridley, with a large country house at Blagdon in Northumberland. But she was tormented by unhappiness and depression and, in 1932, having suffered several miscarriages, she was constantly in tears, distraught at the repeated unfaithfulness of her adulterous husband. Ursula at twenty-eight lived entirely on her emotions, confiding in Emily, who thrived in her role as the still point amid her daughters' emotional turmoil.

Ursy was rather doubtful about the Mediterranean tour. The fact that she was not intimate with her father, and unable to talk over her feelings with him, would be good for her, she thought. In the event, father and daughter became closer than before. Long letters home chart their impressions, which were nothing if not opinionated. Pompei was a vulgar seaside resort – 'a horrible atmosphere of decadence, bad taste and unintelligence'. Athens their next call, was 'an ugly, squalid, uninteresting, jerry-built bungaloid growth'. The Parthenon itself was heartbreaking, showing to Ned's mind 'the utter valuelessness of all human endeavour'. Ned was disappointed that it was so badly sited, lacking the Romans' sense of drama. But the design itself was a perfect unit, full of cunning and requiring months of patient labour with accurate instruments to analyse. 'The podium and the cornice are on curves, the columns vary in length and the whole combination of vertical and horizontal lines runs, labours conforming, to make the whole, one. Destroyed for its beauty by man, as God surely destroyed Pompei for its bestiality.'

Ned had travelled to the source of his inspiration and found it imperfect. Always critical of other men's work, he made no allowances for the ancient Greeks. At least Ursy could comfort him in his disillusion. She was, he said, 'my great and greatest solace, patient, cheerful and translates the humanities with thoughtful humour'.[23]

Ned's brother Lionel died in the summer of 1932, the sixth Lutyens brother to die, 'so now there are five'. 'I hate not to go and hate to go,' Ned wrote of the funeral, dreading being asked by the widow for financial help that he felt unable to afford.

In October 1932 Herbert Jekyll died. The funeral was 'very Munsteady'. Crimson damask cloaked the coffin, which was flanked by Italian candlesticks, and Ned found it all 'horribly moving'. Bumps, now eighty-nine, was very feeble but self-possessed and missing Herbert dreadfully. Her hands had shrunk and her face was a dark brownish colour. It was his last glimpse of her. She died a few weeks later.

Ned commemorated Herbert and Bumps with a monument in Busbridge churchyard. Bumps, Herbert and Aggie Jekyll lie cosily together in a generous tomb like a family bed, enclosed by Buddhist railings. A small piece of New Delhi, it could hardly be more unlike the vernacular of Bumps's Surrey style.* Her tombstone proclaims: ARTIST GARDENER CRAFTSWOMAN. Bumps's nephew, the tactless, difficult Francis (Timmy) Jekyll, wrote her life. Ned contributed a foreword, but he thought the book 'deadish somehow'. Emily considered it 'very dull and gives no picture at all of her personality'.[24]

In 1933 Mary published a collection of short stories entitled *Forthcoming Marriages*. It contains a thinly veiled portrait of her father as the self-made connoisseur Sir Terence Maloney-Lee, who has 'an

---

*Perhaps a better memorial was the portrait by William Nicholson which Ned had commissioned in 1920. Not wanting to waste precious daylight Bumps would only sit to Nicholson after dusk, so Nicholson spent the daytime painting her gardening boots. The painting of the boots hung at Mansfield Street, but Ned gave the portrait to the Tate, and in 1940 he pulled strings to move it to the National Portrait Gallery.

exceptionally distorted and contradictory view on life'. Being married to the poorly paid stockbroker Anthony Sewell made Mary acutely aware of how differently Ned treated his wealthy sons-in-law Euan Wallace and the millionaire Matt Ridley. Mary's fiction was sharply critical, too, of Ned's treatment of her brother Robert. Maintaining that all young men should start at the bottom as he had done, Sir Terence (Lutyens) refuses to help his son to get on in the world, but encourages him to earn a humiliating £5 a week as a newspaper reporter. The son is justifiably bitter. 'What is the point of making a fortune, he asked, unless it is to help one's own children?'

Ned recognized himself in the book, and was shocked by the 'sex galore', but he had no answer to Mary's charge that his snobbery and meanness with money had blighted her marriage and wrecked Robert's career, if indeed he recognized the charge at all.[25] Responsibility for his children was not something he was inclined to feel. Wreathed in pipe smoke, cocooned by routine and jokes, he avoided all confrontation and unpleasantness. He was the most childlike and least responsible of men.

Yet the lives of his grown-up children were seriously troubled. Mary's marriage to Anthony Sewell had been a mistake. Unhappy, dangerously discontented and eaten up with jealousy of her sister Ursy, and believing, probably wrongly, that Ursy was looking elsewhere, Mary began an ill-judged affair with Ursy's husband Matt Ridley. This wrecked Ursy's marriage, drove Ursy to the edge of breakdown and left Mary frighteningly alone. Unable to see any way out, Mary attempted suicide in the summer of 1933. In *Forthcoming Marriages* Mary had described Emily as a cripple who is rarely at home, but goes about the country in a bath chair lecturing on anti-vivisection and birth control among the lower classes. Mary's attempted suicide jolted Emily out of this fictitious role, and she threw herself into the task of bringing Mary back from the grave. She carried her off to Italy, to Stresa, and there she nursed her back to strength. Weeks of peaceful monotony made Mary feel 'more of this world and less like a balloon tied to a thin string'.

Forthcoming Marriages was a success, and that autumn Mary began a new novel while staying with Emily at Munstead Wood, which Ned had rented. Emily was sufficiently recovered from her depression after Krishna to embark on writing her memoirs, the candid account of her relationship with theosophy and Krishna that she published as *Candles in the Sun*. Happy at Munstead, Emily pressed Ned to buy it ('I feel you would be happy there') but Ned refused, pleading as his excuse the garden, which had already collapsed without its eleven 'essential' gardeners. But perhaps the real reason was that Bumps's presence was too strong. Her clothes still hung in the bedroom cupboard, her gardening boots stood by the back door and the drawers of her workroom were filled with her meticulously neat collections of shells and coral.[26]

No sooner had Mary recovered than Emily was drawn into a new crisis with Ursula. Every twist in the saga of Ursy's marriage brought Emily closer to her. Irritated by Ursy's nagging and tearfulness, Matt spent little time at Blagdon, avoiding Ursy's scenes and painful attempts to have things out. Left alone at Blagdon, Ursy engaged a tutor for her son Nicholas, a good-looking Oxford graduate named Rex Whistler. He was succeeded by Lawrence Whistler, whose interest in Vanbrugh's architecture took them on drives together in search of Seaton Delavel and Lumley Castle. For Ursy's birthday Whistler engraved a sonnet on her bedroom window, his first attempt at the glass engraving that was to bring him fame. As her relationship with Whistler deepened, Ursy wrote letters to Emily from bed each morning, agonising about whether to divorce Matt, or live platonically with Matt and have Lawrence's baby, or live monogamously with Matt and have *his* child. She wrote with the urgency of a woman desperate for a child, and soon she was pregnant by Lawrence Whistler. It was a dangerous pregnancy, and she spent the winter of 1935 desperately ill and lying horizontal in a vain attempt to save the baby.

Ursy gave birth to a stillborn daughter at Christmas 1935. Emily, who nursed her through the crisis, was mightily relieved that she was still alive. Determined that Ursy should never put her health at risk by becoming pregnant again, Emily hastened to an orphanage and collected six baby girls in a taxi, one of which Ursy selected to adopt. Emily bombarded Ursy with letters of brisk, astringent advice, urging her to seek a modus vivendi with Matt, however alien she found his world of fast cars, bridge-playing and shooting. 'You know,' she wrote, 'I think that Matt is awfully like Father as you are like me.'

> Father is a pure artist but completely inarticulate as regards his work and something of a bore about other things. Matt . . . is inarticulate about the things that are very real and deep in him . . . But neither he nor Father are speculative or subjective. Now you and I and Robert are just the opposite. We are desperately striving, groping, striving . . . We all three can shine – can be brilliant and amusing and a roaring success in a milieu that draws us out, but in a milieu like Barbie's which crushes us we take our revenge by despising them because they really make us discontented with ourselves.

Looking back on the years she had spent in thrall to Krishna, Emily believed that she had done nothing with her life, but at least she had attained 'an indefinable power and strength which means I have not failed utterly'. Her closeness to Ursy allowed her to relive her own past. Seeing Ursy's misery showed Emily how needlessly unhappy she had made Ned, and she was torn by remorse. 'I now realize as I never realized at the time how fearfully cruel I was to Father turning him out of my bed at a moment's notice and quite ruthlessly. I had suffered so much from his attentions that I had no pity for him.'[27] Yet despite her new-found contrition, Emily was no closer to speaking the same language as Ned. In Mansfield Street's arctic rooms she and Ned still lived separate lives. All they had in common was *The Times* crossword, the 1930s craze to which they were both addicted, and which neither could complete without the other.

Outside his own family, Ned was worshipped by his admirers. To the younger generation of architectural writers, men like Robert Byron or John Betjeman at the *Architectural Review*, Lutyens was the only Edwardian classical architect whom they could respect. Betjeman rediscovered Lutyens's early Arts and Crafts houses, hailing him as a pioneer of the Modern Movement which it was the policy of the *Architectural Review* to promote. 'We all knew, of course,' wrote Betjeman, 'that the [Arts and Crafts] movement was laughably out of touch with the great machine age into which we were emerging, but we realized that it was at least "sincere" and not copying Greek and Roman details. And anyhow Lutyens was a rebel. Hadn't he had a row with the RIBA?' When Betjeman called on him, he was captivated: Lut was 'as welcoming as he was fascinating', showing him how to draw a living curve with a pencil and a penny.

In 1937 John Summerson, editor of the *Architect and Building News*, wrote an unsigned profile of Lutyens in *Night and Day*. 'He is rather a big man with a phenomenally round, bald head fixed with wonderful precision on his shoulders. He has small, very blue, provocatively innocent eyes, curiously set . . .' Lut, wrote Summerson, was a 'character'. Bores all over the empire hoarded his doodles and retold his stories at fifteenth hand. 'You rarely see him but in the company of a pack of fans, sniggering at his cracks and wondering what the great Lut will do or say next.' Summerson, who certainly did not class himself as belonging to the category of the bore, thought him 'one of the cleverest people alive': 'he has the capacity, fantastically rare, for taking architecture seriously'. Especially to be admired, he thought, was Lutyens's Italianate fantasy at Britannic House. 'It is about as relevant to modern office design or to Persian oil as this article is to the Nicene Creed; but anybody with half an eye for architectural values knows that for invention and sheer ornamental eloquence it has never been surpassed.'[28]

In the mid-1930s Lutyens's London work and his Wrenaissance enjoyed a vogue, coinciding with the Georgian revival and a new scholarly nostalgia for the eighteenth century and for Wren. This was part reaction against the quaint Olde Englishness of the Arts and Crafts movement, part nostalgia for the landed values of the eighteenth century shown by the newly dispossessed élite, many of whom found themselves living in London and now commissioned Lutyens and his followers to decorate their houses. Bright Young Things, among them Evelyn Waugh, admired his work, and Ned in turn charmed them. Waugh was flattered when Lutyens asked him the first time they met to call him Ned – 'True he had his arm round my neck at the time,' Waugh told Mary. Rex Whistler, artist brother of Lawrence, was charmed too, and Ned gave him work, painting murals on a staircase at 36 Hill Street for Mrs Porcelli.[29]*

Summerson thought Lut's humour was surreal. Ned always saw the 'backward logic' of a situation. Someone asked Ned what he would do with the Crystal Palace. Answer: 'Put it under a glass case.' Kenneth Clark, socialite director of the Tate Gallery, announced at a lunch given by Lady Cunard that his wife had just had twins. 'Boys or girls?' asked Lutyens. 'A boy and a girl.' 'Always means two fathers,' said Lut. On Christmas morning he joked: 'Have you heard the news? It's a boy.' Staying with Sir George and Lady Ida Sitwell, Ned couldn't resist the pun: 'Is Lady Ida down?' Lord Inchcape was not amused when Lutyens proposed an inscription on his tomb: 'R I P & O'. Nor did Lord Birkenhead (F. E. Smith) appreciate Lutyens's quip when he asked for a memorial: a rolling stone.[30] Lutyens nonetheless designed his grave at Charlton in 1931.

Lutyens's key commissions still came from old patrons. For Reginald McKenna there was yet another house, Halnaker Hall near Goodwood, superficially a reversion to 'roofy, whitewashed Randolph Caldecott', but in fact a house which passed A. S. G. Butler's test of

---

*Unfortunately, Mrs Porcelli refused to pay her bills. Rex Whistler complained that 'She (the old cat Porcelli) keeps thinking up new things for me to do and alter'.

symmetry in design, where nothing was left to chance. For Mary's old admirer Sir Roderick Jones there was the Reuters building in Fleet Street, a last exercise in restrained Portland Stone classicism encasing a steel frame which, said Pevsner, with its 'ornamented base, plain middle and eyecatching top suggests a skyscraper *in parvo* rather than Lutyens's commercial palaces of the 1920s with their lovingly differentiated storeys'.[31]

Frances Horner, still loyal after thirty-seven years, brought another Catholic commission: Campion Hall, the Jesuit house at Oxford. The moving spirit behind Campion Hall was Father D'Arcy, the live-wire Jesuit at the heart of inter-war Catholicism, that world epitomized by Evelyn Waugh in *Brideshead Revisited*. Waugh characterized him in *Vile Bodies* (1930) as Father Rothschild S.J., whose happy knack it was 'to remember everything that could possibly be learned about everyone who could possibly be of any importance'. D'Arcy had commissioned a Birmingham architect to enlarge the Jesuit house in St Giles's, and on Frances Horner's advice he asked Lutyens to give an opinion. Lutyens dismissed the design as 'Queen Anne in front, Mary Anne behind', and suggested another site in St Aldates. When D'Arcy asked him to recommend another architect, Ned replied 'Why not me?' 'But you are far too expensive,' said D'Arcy. Somewhat doubtfully D'Arcy accepted Lutyens's offer, feeling glad 'that I had Lady Horner to check extravagances... She had given him the chance as a young man and so could control him.' Lutyens had poached the job from another architect, but he got away with it. Built of rubble with a secret entrance off a sidestreet and an austere windowless wall fronting the street, Campion Hall is oddly reminiscent of Ned's very earliest work at Munstead Wood, which was once thought to resemble 'a monastery at the time of the Heptarchy'. But there is no sentimental looseness about this late romanticism, ordered (as Hussey wrote) by 'the scale and rhythm of the aesthetic science'.[32]

Another charge of poaching was levelled against Lut over the Australian National War Memorial at Villers Bretonneux, designed in 1935. The original architect was the Australian William Lucas, whose 1927 design for a look-out tower was approved by Gilbert Scott, President of the RIBA, but cancelled by the Australian government, allegedly because it allowed insufficient wall space for the 11,000 names of the Australian missing. Lutyens was asked to design something cheaper and simpler, but the Australian government still insisted on a central tower which he reluctantly provided, provoking furious protests from Lucas, who bombarded Gilbert Scott with letters complaining about Lutyens.[33]

By 1937 even his old friend Professor Reilly was wearying of Lutyens's methods of getting work. When it emerged that Lutyens had been appointed to design the National Theatre on a Cromwell Road site without a competition (Victor Lytton was Chairman of the National Theatre Committee, so the job was sewn up), Reilly urged an open competition. To his credit, Lutyens bore no grudge. Next time he met Reilly he merely remarked, 'Really, Reilly, you must not think by advocating this modern stuff it is the torch you are handing on. It is the kerosene tin.'

In 1935 Lutyens was appointed consultant architect to Sir Charles Bressey in the preparation of the Highway Development Survey (Greater London) which reported in 1938. For the first time in his life he flew, anxiously committing his 14 stone to a bumping, roaring plane. The bridge he had designed at Hampton Court looked better than any other. 'Why? I know but shan't write it . . . you know at once whether a good architect or a bad has been at work. Very refreshing knowing one was looking at things from what one might call God's point of view.'[34]

The Bressey–Lutyens report on Greater London traffic was largely academic, as it had no power to implement its proposals. Lutyens's role was to advise on the architectural aspects. Bressey recommended making London the focus for a national system of motorways, driving straight roads through and under the capital and eliminating London's rural pockets and winding lanes. Ned, who predicted so accurately the follies of modern architecture, welcomed the imperatives of the motor car with uncritical enthusiasm. By improving communications and bringing more traffic and therefore more building, the Bressey report sought, as Betjeman pointed out in a review, to destroy what little countryside remained near London.[35] Yet this was the country – Surrey, Berkshire, Kent – where Ned had built his early houses. By a cruel irony he was architect to the report which proposed the obliteration of Bumps's Surrey dream, ripping apart the fragile countryside with motorways and suburban development.

At Cockington near Torquay the wealthy Indian Behar family asked Ned to develop the village and design an inn. 'They have 7,000 acres and most lovely country and oh my they are laying it with rows and rows of up and down little miserable houses. *They will be the slums of the future and as bad.*' (This prediction was wrong.) Ned was asked to advise on the village and site and design a hotel, the Drum Inn. The village, with its remarkable trees, was 'lovely – a rough and tumble thatch village', and he sought to capture this in his cottagey thatched Drum Inn.

Robert joined him over the Cockington scheme, where he designed the village layout. It was their first real collaboration. Emily had been pushing Ned for years to work with Robert, who made a somewhat aimless living, designing sybaritic bathrooms and cocktail bars and furniture which Ned thought dreadfully overpriced. Ned's objections that Robert was untrained and feckless were eventually overcome by vanity; he desperately needed a successor for the Cathedral, which would take at least thirty years to build. Robert, who had never passed an exam in his life, was given a crash course on the great masters and, aged thirty-three, joined his father as architect to the Cathedral. Not only would this provide Robert with a much-needed income for life, but for Ned it was 'a chance of influencing the coming generation, a torch to keep our 2000-year tradition – just – alive'.

Ned was flattered too when Mrs Marks (of Marks and Spencer), who was a client of Robert's, rang and asked Ned to build her a house. Miss Webb the secretary answered the telephone, 'It's Mr Robert you want.' 'No, it's the great artist I WANT.'[36]

The office at Eaton Gate was emptier than ever. For years, Hall of the Delhi office had had very little to do, and Ned resented paying his salary and wished he would resign. Hall retaliated by accusing Thomas of taking more work on his own account than he was allowed. At last Ned nerved himself to confront Thomas. 'I asked him straight out, "Thomas, are you cheating me?" He said, "No, Sir Edwin." What more can a man say?' According to the story Thomas told his family, Ned had a bad leg and he was too lame to climb the stairs to Thomas's first-floor office to check Hall's allegations. In the end, both Thomas and Hall were sacked.

Into the empty rooms at Eaton Gate, in 1936, moved Robert and his architectural partner Harold Greenwood. The office was now run by Miss Webb, Ned's secretary since 1922, who managed the business and acted as agent, paymaster, financial adviser and confidante to the entire family. The collaboration between father and son was never easy. Ned criticized much of Robert's work – he thought Robert had made mistakes at Cockington which had cost the Behars a great deal of money.[37] Robert slavishly worshipped Ned's genius, but he worried about his father's unbusinesslike methods and his vagueness about money, and complained of him to Emily.

Their most important collaboration was Middleton Park near Bicester, for the Earl of Jersey. This, Lutyens's last country house, was in a way his most conventional: a grand country seat for an aristocratic landowner with an expensive American wife – Virginia Cherrill, the second Lady Jersey, was a film star who had been briefly married to Cary Grant. Far more luxurious than the houses Ned designed before 1914, Middleton was built to hold forty people at weekends. Ned was too infirm to travel regularly to the site; Robert supervised the work and flirted with Virginia Jersey. He understood her need for luxury far better than Ned did. Robert provided twelve visitors' bathrooms, lavishly designed in pink onyx and white marble, and a Hollywood-style cocktail bar. Visiting valets, maids and chauffeurs were accommodated outside the house, in four little boxlike houses. Ned encased all this opulence in steeply tapered, rather French-like elevations which stand proudly aloof from the surrounding countryside; the entrance front is blank and unfriendly, protected from the outside world by a windowless ground floor. It is as introverted as Ned himself had become. He had no time for Lady Jersey, whom he thought 'a common little woman without brain'. She had 'no idea of what an Englishman's house should be', and filled it with American luxuries and 'foreign, cheap bric-à-brac'. It is not easy to build well for clients whom you despise. Middleton Park was perhaps the greatest of all Lutyens's follies. 'Grandy' Jersey spent only two nights there before war was declared; he didn't move back afterwards and the house was subsequently sold.[38]

Ned was now finding fault with all his clients. Lesley Hore Belisha, for example, ebullient self-publicizing Minister of Transport, for whom Ned designed a London house (16 Stafford Place), was 'full of fuss and delays, altering, altering and has no sense of money cum labour – he is pernickety without reason and no taste'. Arriving late for a meeting with Lutyens, his contractor and several others, Hore Belisha cheerily remarked, 'Ah! Quite a Cabinet meeting.' 'But much more intelligent,' was Ned's acid reply.[39]

Chapter Nineteen
Lord Cough of Cough
1937–1944

29, Bloomsbury Square.
17, Queen Anne's Gate.
7, Apple Tree Yard.
17, Bolton Street.
5, Eaton Gate.

24-2-1939.
Café Royal,
London, W.1

Menu of dinner at Café Royal given to Lutyens by his assistants and pupils in honour of his becoming President of the Royal Academy.

Menu for dinner to Lutyens at the Arts Club.

Ned, sixty-eight in 1937, was already old. He no longer had the energy to visit his commissions. He designed a canal and a new garden for Ursula at Blagdon, and Matt Ridley grumbled about the endless delays. One autumn day Ned visited the site with the contractor and his accountant, two elderly gentlemen in bowler hats and overcoats. Lawrence Whistler emerged from the house and (Ursula wrote)

> in the most whimsical Barrie manner proceeded to try and catch the falling leaves, saying it was extremely lucky to catch twelve before they reached the ground. Before long all the old men were trying to do the same, and I've never laughed so much as at the sight of these elderly respectably dressed gentlemen springing about after the leaves like goats on the mountains! It was just like a Rackham drawing of a Barrie story!

In 1938 a client named Black brought an action for negligence, alleging contractual delay and complaining that the chimneys in his house smoked – to which Ned's response was 'Like hell they do'. Emily thought that Thomas was at the root of the trouble; he had taken 'a rake off'. Ned lost £800 in fees owing from Mr Black, and was ordered to pay £700 costs, but at least Miss Webb managed to ensure that the case was settled privately, avoiding damaging publicity. Ned could ill afford £1,500, and Robert told Emily that he was 'very worried about Father's financial position generally unless some very big jobs came in'. Worse still was the blow to Ned's professional pride. His confidence was so shaken that he worried that Ursy would blame him for negligence at Blagdon.[1]

There was so little work coming in now that Robert contemplated selling Mansfield Street to enable his father to live on the capital, but no one dared discuss money and schemes of this kind with Ned. Emily and Robert both confided their worries in Miss Webb. Ned spoke very little when he was at home. He would sit playing patience or absorbed over a jigsaw puzzle. No one knew what he was thinking. As Robert observed: 'He is invariably silent: not formidable – he is never that; but turned inwards and vaguely unhappy ... perplexed by the incontinent demands of a restless and dissatisfied age.'[2]

*

One piece of unfinished business remained: Lady Willingdon's 'improvements' in New Delhi. Lady Willingdon was a battleaxe with a passion for interior decoration and during her rule as Vicereine (1931–6) her husband allowed her to indulge her taste on Viceroy's House. In her defence, it should be said that Viceroy's House was not an easy or a comfortable house to live in. Lady Willingdon's favourite colour was mauve, which she painted wherever she could on Lutyens's white walls. 'Mauvey sujet,' punned Ned, but he couldn't bear to speak to her when he heard that she had filled the eye of the Durbar Hall with a chandelier and glassed in the sides of the loggias. Nothing was safe from Lady Willingdon. She redid the gardens, planted cypresses ('in Villa d'Este, yes, but in India detestable'), moved Jagger's elephants from the gate piers into the garden as ornaments, and cut down the blue gums to make a soldiers' football pitch. Her crowning crime, in 1935, was to paint the Durbar Hall.

In 1937 Robert travelled to India by aeroplane to inspect the damage. He was awestruck. 'Why did Father have to build his greatest work out here?' he wailed. Viceroy's House was, he thought, 'the greatest single masterpiece of European architecture', an astounding one-off. Not even Ned could repeat a work of such consummate imagination. 'It is too concentrated; it is too original; it is too sensuous; and too intellectual to permit repetition.' Robert was unperturbed by Lady Willingdon's vandalism. No one, he thought, could do real harm to Ned's masterpiece. The glazing of the colonnades, the furnishing and carpets were as bad as they could be, but 'none of it matters a rap'. Some alteration was necessary; 'it is only stupid and arrogant of Lady Willingdon not to have consulted the architect, who would have found, as usual, an ingenious solution. No one suffers, ultimately, but Lady Willingdon.'[3]

Ned didn't share Robert's philosophic attitude; he was intensely protective of the house, which he cared about almost more than he did his own children. In October 1938 he travelled to India at the invitation of the Viceroy Lord Linlithgow to report on the restoration of Viceroy's House to its pre-Willingdon state. It was his eighteenth journey to India, he was nearly seventy and becoming frail. He travelled out on the same boat as the Linlithgows, but was not invited to sit at the Viceroy's table, a snub which upset him. No Persotum was there to meet him at Bombay and he had difficulties with customs. Thinking he said *plants*, an official seized his plans and threatened to fumigate them.

No one was there to help him on the night train from Bombay to Jaipur. After the heat of Bombay it was a cold night, he couldn't shut the window or turn off the fans, a roaring draught blew off his bedclothes and at dawn he was a shivering wreck. By the time he reached Jaipur he was delirious. From the hospital a telegram was sent to Robert: 'Regret inform you Sir Edwin is suffering from patch pneumonia.'

After eight seemingly endless days in the hospital at Jaipur he was well enough to travel to Delhi, accompanied by two nurses. It was an emotional visit. 'My thrill to be here gives me a choke and, perhaps being a little on the weak side, tears are very near the surface.' He found the place on the wall he had kissed on leaving the house in 1931, and rubbed it very gently with his handkerchief. He told Lady Linlithgow that if she had not been a queen he would like to kiss her. 'She at once put her arms round my neck and kissed me.'

He was given a stenographer and went round the house, dictating comments and criticisms. Mustoe the horticulturist arrived, and together they inspected the garden trees. He managed, with great effort to compile a report, but what joy it was to be busy again with three tables overflowing with papers and plans. 'I think they will do everything and put the house back as I left it.' Unlike Baker's gradient, Lady Willingdon's sins were easily reversible. Ned made rude drawings about her. His design for a fountain featuring two legs in the air and a bottom producing wind and water caused, he said, much mirth.

Before leaving Delhi he received a distressed letter Emily had written when she heard that he was ill and thought he might die. 'I have it in writing,' he wrote. At Bombay, he met Persotum, now very old and feeble.[4]

Ned was never really the same after his visit to India. Soon after his return in December 1938 he was elected President of the Royal Academy. Baker wrote to say that he was voting for him. 'I should like to vote for you for the sake of our old friendship which I enjoyed so much, and forget all the soreness and harm – as one must in the assurance and peace of old age.' Thanks to Baker's vote, Ned defeated Sydney Lee on the second ballot by twenty to eighteen votes.[5]

For the summers of 1938 and 1939 Barbie's husband Euan Wallace lent Emily an old rectory named Beechwood, near Petworth in Sussex, which had once been Cardinal Manning's, near to the Wallaces' new house at Lavington. Euan was Minister of Transport in Chamberlain's government, and a supporter of appeasement, to which Barbie was furiously opposed. She and Emily agreed that Munich (October 1938) gave Europe over to Hitler's domination – 'all this Barbie expressed vividly and I – I am afraid – more violently, as is my way, and Euan got so hurt and angry he was almost in tears'. In spite of siding for once with Barbie, Emily still could not get close to her. 'Something went wrong with our relationship somewhere in the early days and I am sure it was my fault. In some way Nannie took my place,' she wrote. Ned on the other hand agreed with Euan Wallace. In January 1939, along with Vaughan Williams, G. M. Trevelyan and Masefield, he was persuaded by Halifax to sign a manifesto from men of goodwill, appealing for co-operation with Germany, which rather embarrassingly was broadcast in Germany before it was released in England. But Ned wasn't really an appeaser, just an old man anxious to avoid another war.[6]

If anything, the threat of war brought Ned and Emily closer together. 'My darling,' wrote the sixty-five-year-old Emily skittishly from Beechwood in the summer of 1939, 'it is such fun when I come up to you, like an improper adventure with a strange man in a strange flat!' And when war seemed inevitable she wrote: 'If the end of all things is on us, I want you to know I have had a wonderful life, and love you more now I think than when we were married.' Not that this meant that she felt any need to be with Ned in London. Quite the contrary, she was adamant that her place was at Beechwood, where she filled the house with grandchildren, and spent her days merrily sawing wood for fuel, digging the garden for vegetables and knitting jerseys.

The grandchildren, evacuated from London, were the casualties of her children's broken marriages. Mary's daughter Amanda arrived after Mary separated from Anthony Sewell, and Betty's children, Sebastian and the twins Rose and Tess, came when Betty split with her husband Ian Glennie to live with the musical impresario Edward Clarke. The Glennie children were held hostage by Emily while Ian and Betty quarrelled painfully about custody. Ian was slow and heavy and Ned found his 'predatory ichthosaurus' attitude to life very trying and never understood how Betty could stand it. He grudged giving Ian whisky and soda, he refused to allow him to stay at Mansfield Street, yet one can't help thinking that he would have happily welcomed Ian if he had been one of the rich sons-in-law. Betty had married Ian for his singing voice, and she was shocked to discover that he had lost his baritone voice and was now training to become a tenor. 'What a mess

Betty has made of her first thirty years,' wrote Ned. 'What will she do twenty years on?'⁷

In London during the blackout Ned found it impossible to work. Interrupted by wailing air-raid warnings and distracted by constant wireless news bulletins, he could think only of Emily. He showered her with love letters. 'I have always loved you, a rosebud perhaps in my button hole, but now you have opened to a glorious flower, the best I have ever seen.' They had always got on best when they were apart, but that first winter of the Second World War brought a sense of time running out, of things needing to be said that couldn't be said later. 'I have fallen in love again – it's a warming and exhilarating experience. She is such a darling,' he wrote. 'Have you guessed, who it is I *really* love?' But this late flowering was etched by fear. 'The New Year is full of terror,' he wrote on 31 December 1939. 'I am in the dark and my hand will be out. Will God find it?'⁸

Eaton Gate had been sold in May 1939 and the office moved to Mansfield Street, a return to the old arrangement at Bloomsbury Square soon after their marriage, with Ned and Emily now living in a converted flat on the bedroom floor. When war broke out most of the staff joined up except for a draughtsman named George Stewart and the redoubtable Miss Webb. 'I shall go on – something may turn up for me to do,' Ned wrote. 'Money outlook looks bad, as nobody pays, all work stops.' Miss Webb harried clients for cheques, 'which by the way is very bad for one's credit', and Ned wrote gloomy balance sheets, setting his shrinking income against the costs of maintaining not only Mansfield Street but also Betty, who now had yet another penniless man, Edward Clarke, on her hands.⁹* Like the pencil-smudged boy of sixty years before, Ned escaped from real life into the never-never world of his drawing board. He could lose himself for hours in problems of his own initiative, solving puzzles of the Cathedral and designing an Indian Federal Court, another project that was destined never to be.

His position as President of the Royal Academy gave him an occupation and an excuse to stay in London. Walter Lamb the secretary was indispensable. Addressing the Academy Banquet in April 1939 after his election, Ned declared, 'The Lamb is my shepherd, I shall not want.' He would whisper to Lamb during meetings: 'Am I doing all right?'

---

*Ned cut the allowances he paid to the other children at the beginning of the war, partly in order to pay for the education of two Austrian Jewish boys named Heller whom Emily adopted.

Under Ned's predecessor William Llewellyn, the Academy's reputation for stuffy conservatism had grown; there had been quarrels with Stanley Spencer, Sickert and Augustus John, all three of whom resigned. Ned did little to push the Academy towards embracing the modern world – the office had no typewriter until 1951, and Lamb wrote all his correspondence by hand – but at least Ned ensured the re-election of Augustus John. When Llewellyn objected that re-election was against the rules, Ned secretly enlisted the support of the King, quoting the precedent of Sir Joshua Reynolds, whose re-election had been sponsored by George IV. This made Llewellyn 'perfectly jibberty furious', but Ned's 'wheeze' was nearly thwarted when John, who half disapproved of the Academy and half longed to be accepted by it, refused to reapply. Fortunately, John wrote a letter rescinding his refusal at the last minute, and Llewellyn made himself ridiculous by opposing it.[10]

Something did turn up for Lutyens to do, too: the Royal Academy plan for the rebuilding of London. In January 1940 Austen Hall, a conservative ex-pupil and admirer of Lut, seeing that 'for the first time in his life [Lutyens] had nothing to do', suggested that he should chair a committee to plan the rebuilding of London, now that bombing made the reconstruction sketchily envisaged in the Bressey–Lutyens report on traffic a practical possibility. With Austen Hall acting as secretary, Lutyens formed a committee of academicians and ageing architects including Curtis Green, Professor Richardson, Giles Gilbert Scott and Edward Maufe, as well as Lord Esher. Austen Hall called at Mansfield Street three or four times a week, and Lutyens found his time taken up with meetings which Hall thought were the breath of life to him, lonely and depressed as he was at Mansfield Street.

An interim report was published by *Country Life* in October 1942. *London Replanned* was a crude exercise in straight-line planning, perhaps, as Gavin Stamp wrote, 'the most disappointing project Lutyens ever got involved with: all roundabouts and symmetrical axes and no subtlety or romance at all'. The idea of creating megaroundabouts at Oxford Circus, Piccadilly Circus and Tottenham Court Road originated, it is true, with Alker Tripp, the Assistant Commissioner of Police responsible for London traffic. But *London Replanned* proposed to demolish the asymmetrical approach to St Paul's up Ludgate Hill, driving a wide symmetrical axis which destroyed the cathedral's picturesque setting; the old streets in front of the British Museum were to be bulldozed to give a vista from Holborn, and the winding streets around Westminster were also to be blitzed. In order to create broad vistas exposing London's classical monuments, the report proposed to destroy everything that intervened.

The *Architectural Review* damned it as a reactionary absurdity, and Osbert Lancaster skewered it in the *Observer*, remarking that the new London 'will be not unlike what the new Nuremberg might have been had the Führer enjoyed the inestimable advantage of the advice and guidance of the late Sir Aston Webb'.[11] Lutyens's plan to bulldoze London did real damage to his reputation, branding him as an architectural dead-beat. Austen Hall's well-meaning attempts to cheer him did him no favours, but the real trouble was Ned's refusal to retire and stop work. He didn't know it, but he was dying.

In April 1940 he had another bout of pneumonia followed by a stroke. Emily was ill in the next-door room with German measles, fretting because the doctors wouldn't allow her to see him just when he needed her most. The stroke affected his speech, which became inaudible, and his writing, never legible, was now totally indecipherable. He found it very hard to work, and even drawing was an effort, 'lacking the inspiration of things that may be'. The doctor thought he made a good recovery, however, and he was dissuaded from resigning from the Royal Academy. He continued to work on the London plan; it was as if the crude straight lines of city planning short-circuited the subtle communications his brain could no longer supply. Hussey would meet him lunching in the Garrick Club, where he was 'serene and jocular as ever', discussing façades and vistas over a glass of port, scribbling skylines on a 'virgin' (sketchpad) while the sirens whined and German bombers roared overhead.

The London plan gave him an excuse to stay in London, much to Emily's annoyance. Even the onset of the Blitz in September 1940 failed to shake him. He slept in the basement; as the house shivered and each bomb seemed to be coming straight to his bed, he took comfort in the thought that at three score years and ten it made very little difference whether he was killed or not, and in any case he would be unconscious of a hit. Emily found him 'perfectly serene' on 10 September, happily occupied with jigsaw puzzles, content while the office remained open and he didn't feel he was running away. On 17 September Robert tried to persuade him to spend the night at the Langham Hotel, where he was staying, as was Robert Byron. Ned refused, only to be woken in the night by a furious ringing of the door bell: Robert had been evacuated from the Langham, which had been hit by an unexploded bomb.[12]

On 20 September Robert persuaded him to leave Mansfield Street and stay at Knebworth. Pamela Lytton thought him a good deal changed: 'he cannot remember any of the funny pictures he used to draw', and he longed only for Emily. Touched by his devotion, Emily felt she must devote herself to nursing him. Their first, unlikely plan was to live in a caravan at Knebworth. It was Ned's idea, not Emily's, but she thought it an inspiration. Confident as ever, she told Ursula, 'I can make fun for him.'[13] The caravan was hired but they never slept in it. Instead they rented a house at Ockham Mill in Surrey from Lady Stokes, mother of the painter Adrian Stokes, and Ned commuted up and down to London three days a week, entertaining the Royal Academy Council at the Garrick to wartime lunches of oysters and grilled salmon. Words escaped his memory like naughty children hiding, and at meetings he was less audible than ever.

Driving up to London one day with Robert, the car ran into a stationary vehicle. The windscreen was smashed, Ned swallowed glass and suffered bad bruising around the throat. He wasn't seriously hurt, but that night, Emily recalled, he began to cough violently and expectorate streams of mucus. He lost weight alarmingly, complained of giddiness and sweated profusely at night.

In September 1941 he visited Ursula, now running a wartime babies' hospital at Blagdon. Betty was nearby at Ponteland where she had gone to live with Edward Clarke, while waiting for a divorce from Ian Glennie. By now she and Edward had a new baby, Conrad, born in August 1941, but Ned failed to visit Betty in the semi-detached modern villa with stained glass over the door. She was hurt and snubbed, believing that her father shrank from witnessing her slide into bad taste and poverty. He wrote humbly: 'I was sorry and somewhat ashamed of missing the chance of seeing you ... Ursy offered me a car, but I funked my emotions ... If I didn't love you I could have done. But I love you. Please forgive your ever-loving father, Father.' Perhaps it was just as well he funked his emotions. As Emily wrote, 'I felt it would in the end have hurt more had he gone and been critical about everything as he was bound to be.'[14]

In October Ned began to cough blood. He saw a doctor who took an X-ray and reassured him it was nothing serious, only adhesions left over from his pneumonia. Emily worried as his cough became worse, he suffered from a constant fever and he was always tired. 'He is so pathetic,' wrote Emily, 'it wrings my heart. He has grown so thin – his clothes look much too big for him.'

But he couldn't, wouldn't stop work. Suddenly, he was given the go-ahead on Liverpool Cathedral, which had been hanging fire for years as relations with the Catholic authorities soured over the project's cost. In December 1941 Father Turner, the Treasurer of Liverpool Cathedral, lunched at Mansfield Street and, warmed by a scarce wartime pheasant from Blagdon and a bottle of port, he agreed to the proposal Ned put to him: Liverpool should pay £5,000 which they owed him and £2,500 a year to cover the costs of completing the Cathedral drawings. Ned was jubilant at the prospect of four years' steady work, and he and Emily prepared to give up Ockham Mill and move back full-time to Mansfield Street.

A few days later Emily saw Dr Fleischmann. He told her that Ned's X-ray had shown cancer in the right lung. Emily's worst fears were confirmed. Ned, Fleischmann told her, had only months to live. Doctors did not yet link smoking with lung cancer,* and Emily blamed the motor accident. Perhaps she had been negligent, perhaps she should have consulted a specialist. Ursula's doctor Jimmy Spence reassured her that the cancer had been there for years and was the cause of his pneumonia and thrombosis; no one seems to have realized the probability that Ned had been slowly killing himself for decades with his five little pipes.

Deeply depressed, Emily cursed the short-sightedness of the Liverpool Catholics. 'It wrings my heart when I know there won't be four years and I think what fools these people have been wasting precious years when he could have been happy and busy on *their* work.' It was now a race against time to complete the plans.[15]

A few days later Ned heard that he had received the Order of Merit.† When they read the letter he and Emily both burst into tears and wept and hugged each other for ten minutes. 'It is the crown of his life, the one honour he coveted and he is so proud and happy.' He was the first architect to receive it; and he was 'still happier at the thought of how furious Blomfield will be! Apparently he of all the RAs wrote to Lamb that it was time they had a new President!'[16]

Ned didn't know, as Emily did, that the OM had come just in the nick of time. He never even asked the result of the X-ray, merely grudged its expense. It was Emily who carried the burden of knowing; Ned was content to be told that he was suffering from chronic

---

*Sir Richard Doll published his statistical correlations between lung cancer and smoking in 1951.
†Lord Crawford had been pressing for this since 1939.

bronchitis. An elaborate charade was now played out, concealing the truth, maintaining the pretence of normality.

Emily dedicated herself entirely to nursing Ned. Sitting alone in the dreary spaces of Mansfield Street, made colder than ever by wartime fuel shortages, with its bare, wooden floors and high Adam ceilings, with nothing to do but knit, had seemed unbearable before. 'Now I am thankful and regard it as a refuge. I don't want to see anyone or talk to anyone, but just be quiet with Father,' she told Ursy.

She became convinced that she too was dying of cancer, in her case cancer of the uterus. Listening to the wireless, which was their chief evening occupation, they heard a play about lung cancer and, like an electric shock, she felt Ned thinking, 'That is what I have got', but they neither of them spoke. She thought to herself, 'Here is Father thinking he has cancer of the lungs, and I thinking I have the same thing elsewhere, but we neither of us can talk of it.' It was as if they were once again on the beach at Scheveningen where they had spent their honeymoon sitting side by side not speaking but holding hands.

Upstairs in the icy bedroom, they slept in Ned's hard, narrow St Ursula beds which were arranged head to head along the wall.

Anne Balfour, Emily's seventeen-year-old great-niece, who was recovering from a fractured skull, came to Mansfield Street to rest in the afternoons after her morning lessons. Ned was always delightful and welcoming. Aunt Emily frightened her. Emily was sharp-tongued and waspish with a knack of saying the thing that hurt, of touching the sensitive spot.[17]

Throughout the winter and spring of 1941–2 Ned toiled on the Liverpool Cathedral plans in the office downstairs, expectorating profusely into a basin as he drew. Archbishop Downey told him the plans were beautiful, and they were exhibited at the Academy, but there was no money available to pay him. 'God Wills and the Pope Fulfils,' wrote Ned, punning on his youthful motto, 'As Faith wills, / So Fate fulfils'.

In July 1942, Ned made the exhausting journey to Liverpool, old, ill, alone and confused. No one turned up at the committee meeting, everyone was 'too busy' to look at his plans. Miss Webb boiled with rage at their rudeness, but it was plain at least that the Liverpool Catholics had lost interest in the Cathedral and had no intention of paying. None of Ned's letters was answered; Archbishop Downey, once so genial, was now always 'away'. 'It seems tragic that all the lovely creations in his head cannot be recorded because no one will pay his expenses,' wrote Emily.

Emily talked bravely about giving up Mansfield Street and closing the office – 'one must face old age like death' – but Robert insisted that Ned should live his last year at Mansfield Street. It would mean selling another block of shares (the house cost between £3,000 and £4,000 to run) but the house and its contents were anyway unsaleable in wartime. Ned was owed money by Lord Wimborne, the Behars and Mrs Porcelli, but his solicitor Francis Smith advised that as President of the Royal Academy he was unable to sue.

Ned had nothing in his life but work. For him to retire and close the office was *really* to die. So the pretence was maintained; Miss Webb and George Stewart stayed on downstairs, and Ned remained PRA. He still lunched at the Garrick, though when Emily came too she was enraged by his cronies like 'that tiresome old Saxton Noble', whose conversation was 'only regrets for that nice comfortable world in which they have always lived'. Meetings were increasingly an ordeal for him, as he couldn't speak or carry any weight. 'He can't get words and coughs all the time.'[18] At the Academy, Blomfield, whom Ned had left out of the London planning committee, complained that Ned was inaudible, and that he ought to resign as he never spoke at meetings but let the RA secretary Walter Lamb do all the talking. Ned laid Blomfield's letter before the Council, which supported him to a man; quarrelling with Bloomy was oxygen to him.

Clough Williams-Ellis visited Lutyens at Mansfield Street that autumn. He wanted to pick Ned's brains on Wren, about whom he was composing a broadcast for the BBC. They sat by the fire drinking tea and eating buttered buns. Williams-Ellis found Ned 'cordiality itself', but maddeningly perverse and whimsical. He deliberately avoided talking about Wren, but talked at length about Inigo Jones, which was interesting but not what Williams-Ellis had come to hear.

Erno Goldfinger, the Hungarian modern architect, organized an exhibition of Soviet Russia in November 1942, which brought him into contact with Lutyens as PRA. 'I was surprised how nice he was . . . He was a charming person, and funny. He didn't take himself very seriously.'[19]

Emily's cancer scare was a false alarm, but watching Ned try pathetically to carry on made her frantically depressed. 'It suddenly swept over me with such a wave of misery that he is going downhill fast and there is nothing but continuous decline of all his powers in front of him and how I wish he could slip away and I too "fade upon the midnight with no pain" – I just felt it was the end and I wished it would come quick for us both.' Ned fretted that he had no work. Emily encouraged him to draw picture letters for his grandchildren – the Flower Hunt, with drawings of Fox-glove, Dog-rose, My Peony and the pack. He struggled to write an article about London, the Ideal City – 'I wish he wouldn't as it worries him so much and writing is not his mode of expression and it won't be good and it is only a peg on which to hang an attack on modern architecture, which is bad policy'.

Robert published his short appreciation of Ned in 1942. It contained a technical discussion of Ned's theory of architecture (the armature of planes, Robert called it) which Ned said he didn't understand – 'but then,' as Emily wrote, 'he never does understand anything put into *words* which is why, I think, he is incapable of passing on his knowledge either by writing or speaking'. Robert was uncomfortably aware of how dated and unfashionable his father seemed. He defended him as a genius, a man born out of his time, the last of the humanists: whatever he was, he wasn't a man of 1942. What bothered Emily was Robert's statement that Ned's childlike nature made him incapable of deep emotions.

For her war work, Emily worked in a WVS shop, sorting refuse in Marylebone. Often as she sat alone at Mansfield Street, in the dark and gloomy office, sifting through old letters, she went back to writing her autobiography. Reading her girlish letters to His Rev, she felt so detached from her old self that 'it is like another incarnation'. She thought her letters were 'an extraordinarily frank and truthful record of emotion and expression'. Her whole life, she realized, was complete in letters, which she had written every day, pouring out her feelings. After His Rev came a complete correspondence with Judith Blunt, then a lifetime of letters to Ned, and now she was pouring herself out once more to Ursula. 'Of course my love for Judith was really because she was Blunt's daughter and my friendship with her kept me in touch with him. My feeling for Blunt went on for years and varied between my showing him how much I cared and then drawing back.'[20]

In the spring of 1943 Ned's condition seemed to have stabilized. Dr Fleischmann pronounced that the patch on his lung had spread a little but that he was better than could have been expected. Emily now began to wonder whether she had been too hasty in accepting the doctors' verdict of terminal cancer. The Cathedral still absorbed him, and he took on a new job – the town plan for Hull with Sir Patrick Abercrombie. 'He will never give up or retire,' wrote Emily.

But the cancer was only in remission. In May Ned travelled to Oxford for a dinner at Campion Hall. Evelyn Waugh thought him 'very gaga, making his old puns and obscenities but without gusto or relevance'. Joe Links, a friend of Robert's who became Mary's second husband, saw him about this time. 'The one time I met him, I found him absolutely terrifying,' he recalled. 'He was one of those people who are frightened of people and are frightening as a result. He was shy.'[21]

A few weeks later Ned suddenly grew worse. He still dragged himself downstairs to the office but he could do nothing and slumped there feeling ill and miserable or sleeping in his chair. The doctor ordered him to bed, prescribed morphia and advised him to stop work, 'as Father himself said his work was no good'.

But he couldn't stop working. Even if he had wanted to, Miss Webb would not allow it. She refused to accept that he was seriously ill and still talked of him serving another two years as PRA. She thought his weakness was due to staying in bed, and told Emily that he was being lazy and giving in. Emily dreaded Miss Webb bustling in each morning with the day's letters and told her to lie and pretend there were none when the post brought difficult correspondence about Hull. Sitting beside him as he slept, breathing fast and heavily, she noticed how his face had fallen in – 'oh if only he could slip into the next world without pain or struggle, how happy I should be'.

Miss Webb continued to harry him, nagging him to come down to the office and get on with the National Theatre designs.* He was pursued on his deathbed by the vengeful Thomas, who claimed Ned owed him money from nine years' back. How ironic it now seemed, reflected Emily, that Ned should have given Thomas power of attorney for all those years, without ever trusting Emily with a joint account. 'Of course, Chippy [Arthur Chapman] always said Thomas was not paid enough to keep him honest, and Miss Webb says his office has always been the worst paid in London. He has been a fool about the people he trusted. But it was partly laziness – he would not face facts and none of his men could speak to him because he always pushed them on to Thomas.'[22]

Throughout December 1943 the farce dragged on. Ned attended a Royal Academy meeting on 7 December, and offered himself for re-election for a final year as president (seventy-five was the retirement

---

*These were new National Theatre designs, as the project had been transferred from South Kensington to the South Bank in 1942.

age). George Stewart the draughtsman was driven demented about the house over which he was collaborating with Ned, 'as nothing he does is right by Father and yet Father cannot put it right or concentrate – his creative power even for his work has really gone'. Lutyens could never do Hull, thought Miss Webb. But he continued to hold meetings about the planning of Hull with Patrick Abercrombie, though this meant a terrible exertion, crawling out of bed and gasping for breath through the coughing fits as he struggled to shave and dress. After an hour's meeting he was carried upstairs, unable to go to bed because he was too tired to undress. He merely sat with his head in his hands saying, 'I feel rotten.'

Emily was exhausted by the everlasting tug between work and illness. 'He is *not* well enough to get about, or dress or be left alone, and so he drags himself down and all the paraphernalia of papers, night light, basin etc is carried up and down so that he may play patience in the office, and drag up exhausted in the evening. However, there is no alternative, so it will go on till someone collapses, and I don't think it will be Father!' Ned wrote to Ursula on 13 December: 'It is awful being in bed. I am missing a great deal. I long for warmer weather to give my cough a chance. If I was raised to the peerage I should call myself Lord Cough of Cough. I am tired of bed, yet Mother won't let me get up.'

He had a day and a night nurse now, and his hands, always so blackened and grimy with pencil dust and tobacco, lay unnaturally white and thin on the counterpane. Betty visited often that winter, bringing whisky which she bought with money she hadn't got. He told her, 'It is werry, werry hard to die.' Miss Webb was asked to bring the cathedral drawings to his room, and they were arranged around his bed.

At Christmas he drank a little hock. Emily had flu and was banished to another room. She sent a note to his room: 'My darling, thanks to you I am having flu in great luxury with your nurses to attend to my needs . . . Have a good night and meet me in dreamland.'

Robert sat with Ned all night on New Year's Eve, watching him sleep his life away, drugged with morphine, the silence broken by his struggle to breathe or feebly cough fluid from his lungs. Ned was not at peace. He was more unreachable than ever. Robert watched the transparent, emaciated hands close and unclose aimlessly, 'revealing surely a distress of mind which drugged stupor cannot banish'.[23]

*

Early in the morning of New Year's Day 1944 the telephone rang to tell Mary that her father had died. She was working as a barmaid at the Churchill Club, a services club sponsored by Winston Churchill which Barbie managed. Numbed by the death of a lover and by the losses of war, Mary felt little emotion when she heard the news. She took a Number 88 bus to Mansfield Street, and as she passed the Cenotaph, she felt a surge of love and sadness. 'The aloof, lonely beauty of its perfection pierced me.' When she reached Mansfield Street, she tried to find something that had belonged to her father. Going into the bathroom, she took his razor, an ordinary old Gillette. It reminded her of how he used to shave in the bath without a mirror. She remembered how Ned used to smell – a mixture of pipe tobacco and pencil dust.

The funeral at Westminster Abbey was solemn and grand but impersonal; Robert noted that the cost was one hundred and twenty guineas. Emily panicked on the way and arrived a few minutes late. By the time she reached her seat, the abbey was full, Beethoven's seventh symphony had begun and the funeral procession was advancing up the aisle. She was bitterly hurt and upset that the service had begun without her. Herbert Baker, by now half-paralysed from a stroke, shuffled up behind the coffin. At least he could pay his debts in Lutyens's wake. The lesson was a chapter of Ecclesiasticus chosen by Emily: 'all their desire is in the work of their craft'.

After the service, muffled bells pealed from the abbey as the coffin speeded in an undertaker's limousine to the West Finchley crematorium. A theatre organ piped a shrill crescendo while the thin coffin slid into the wall. Emily cried; Robert felt too sick to giggle.

'The piece of cod that passeth all understanding,' Ned had once punned, peering at the fish on his plate. He had spent a lifetime poking fun at religion but, as he once admitted, he was at heart deeply religious. Emily believed that they were both, in their very different ways, striving after truth. The difference, she wrote, was that 'I talk, but you act. What I preach, you live.' But Ned had talked and written and punned for nearly fifty years of marriage. And though Emily had preached, she could hardly deny that she had acted over theosophy.

Reflecting on her marriage, Emily considered that the thing of real value she had given Ned was complete freedom – the freedom from domestic ties that he needed to pursue his art. She had taken her own freedom too; Ned had never hindered her attempts, however misguided, to realise her ideal.

Their marriage had not always been easy, but when Emily talked about freedom she didn't mean indifference; far from it. True, neither had lived up to the ideal they formed for the other. Emily rebelled against the domestic role that Ned expected the architect's wife to play, and Ned turned out not to be the hero that Emily felt such a burning need to worship. Both sought and found their ideals outside marriage. Ned built countless little white houses for other women, and Emily discovered a hero in Krishna. But in the end perhaps they learned to love one another as they were. The Architect and his Wife had reached a kind of acceptance; an understanding that went beyond words and ran far, far deeper than their youthful romanticism.

'Sir Edwin Lutyens has died,' wrote James Lees-Milne in his diary. 'He was leonine, breezy, untidy, flamboyant and inspired.' Ned was barely cold before Baker wrote to *The Times*, negotiating his reputation with history. He rationalised their quarrel as an expression of the dualism between abstract and intellectual values (Lutyens) and human and national sentiment (Baker).

The obituaries tried to forecast the verdict of history. Undoubtedly, they agreed, Lutyens was the greatest architect of his generation. John Summerson, writing his obituary in the *Architect and Building News*, conceded that Lutyens had long since ceased to be a leader of his profession. Nevertheless, the magazine brought out a black-edged edition as if the sovereign had died. He was Lutyens the magnificent, the aging monarch of a vanished era. In *Country Life* Hussey claimed that Lutyens was not only the last of the Romans, but one of the immortals.[25]

Lutyens was magnificently memorialised in print. His pupil A. S. G. Butler published three folio Memorial Volumes in 1950, and Christopher Hussey immortalised him in a classic biography. But even they could not stop the collapse of his reputation. Lutyens left no school of followers to carry the torch of humanism as he perhaps had hoped. The Liverpool Cathedral project lingered on, but no more than the crypt was built; Lutyens's design was eventually cancelled in 1953.

But the houses remain.* Miraculously, Lutyens's work at New Delhi survived the new thinking and strife associated with Indian independence. Ned's great gift was his power to translate his patrons' dreams into houses whose sculpted space and geometric proportions make them a constant source of aesthetic pleasure. His good luck was to live at a time when he could build for a leisured élite without

---

*The only significant house by Lutyens to have been destroyed is Papillon Hall, demolished in 1950. It was badly haunted.

compromising either his artistic or his financial integrity. He fought the greatest battle of his career in a vain attempt to undo an aesthetic blemish, the gradient at New Delhi. Design was what he lived for; as his motto proclaimed, *Mitiendo vivendum*, by measure we must live. As much an artist as an architect, the buildings he designed were often monuments or follies: giant sculptures which expressed essential truths about their time.

'I get such an aching longing for father,' Emily wrote a few months after he died. She lived on for twenty years, remaining the emotional reference at the centre of her children's lives. The Lutyens family reminded Joe Links of a country dance – always one out, one in and Emily in the middle.

Two years before she died, an old lady of eighty-seven and suffering from Alzheimer's, she was taken by Betty on a motoring tour of Ned's Surrey houses. They stopped at Thursley, but Emily had not the slightest idea where they were. When Betty explained, she asked in bewilderment, 'Have I ever been married?'[26]

Ursula, whom Emily thought had inherited both Lutyens genius (though undeveloped) and Lytton melancholy, committed suicide in 1967. 'I always feel that Father and I battle in you more than in any of the others,' Emily had written, thirty years before. 'As soon as you are becoming happily absorbed in the Lutyens side of you the Lytton rears up and destroys it and *vice versa*.'[27]

Barbie, whom Emily thought had completely eliminated the Lytton element and 'developed all Father's qualities except his artistic genius', suffered atrociously during the war. Euan Wallace died of cancer. Three of his sons were killed in the war, another died during a minor operation. She married a second husband, Herbert Agar, and committed suicide in 1981 shortly after the death of her only surviving son Billy Wallace.

Robert ('far more Lytton than Lutyens which makes him often unhappy, but gives him also an inner kernel of content') divorced Eva; their brilliant, odd son David was a schizophrenic. Robert married three times. He died in 1972.

Betty ('more of a Lutyens') was inspired by her father's death to earn her living through music. Shunning the easy money she made from copying, she took to composing with renewed professionalism, eventually achieving recognition as a composer and – in her sixties –

fame. Betty in old age was still appearing in pink trouser suits, roundly cursing and perpetually smoking.

Mary ('more of a Lytton') married Joe Links shortly after Ned died. Joe 'made her nice', and she lived to achieve both recognition as a writer and happiness. She died aged ninety in 1999.

'The Flower Hunt': Ned's drawings for Mary's daughter Amanda, October 1942.

NOTES

Abbreviations Used in the Notes

The letters of Ned and Emily Lutyens form the chief source for this book. Four thousand four hundred and sixty-eight of their letters now belong to the RIBA. Some of these were printed in *The Letters of Edwin Lutyens to his Wife Lady Emily* ed. Clayre Percy and Jane Ridley (Collins, 1985). Where possible, I have cited the printed source.

N[ed] and E[mily]	Edwin (Ned) Lutyens and Emily Lutyens
LuE/20/49/29 etc	Letters by Edwin Lutyens and Emily Lutyens held by the RIBA
Letters	*The Letters of Edwin Lutyens to his Wife Lady Emily* ed. Clayre Percy and Jane Ridley
Hussey, *Lutyens*	Christopher Hussey, *The Life of Sir Edwin Lutyens* (Country Life, 1950)
Blessed Girl	Lady Emily Lutyens, *A Blessed Girl* (Rupert Hart-Davis, 1954)
Candles	Lady Emily Lutyens, *Candles in the Sun* (Rupert Hart-Davis, 1957)
Lutyens Family Papers	Papers in the possession of Charles Lutyens
Lady Sackville Diary	Transcript of diary in the possession of Nigel Nicolson
Baker Papers	Papers of Herbert Baker in the RIBA
Knebworth Archive	Lytton family papers at Knebworth Estates
Ursula Ridley Papers	Letters in the possession of Clayre Percy
P R O	Public Record Office

CHAPTER ONE 16 ONSLOW SQUARE 1869–1876
Notes to pages 1–20

1 N to E, 20 February 1940, LuE/20/14/29. Lutyens Family Papers, Wangenheim Family Bible.
2 ELL Baptism Certificate, 11 June 1869, Greater London Record Office. Lady Sackville Diary, 17 September 1919. PRO, Will of Miss Landseer (d. 29 August 1880), leaves bequest to Edwin Lutyens, 'godson of my late brother Sir Edwin Landseer'. Mrs George Wemyss, *Things We Thought Of* (Constable, 1911), 23.
3 Wemyss, *Things We Thought Of*, 17, 30–1. Mrs George Wemyss, *All About All of Us* (Constable, 1911), 17, 18.
4 *Survey of London*, ed. F. H. W. Sheppard, vol. 41 (Athlone Press, 1983), 110–13.
5 Wemyss, *Things We Thought Of*, 42.
6 N to E, 9 August 1907, LuE/9/1/5. N to E, 28 November 1926, *Letters*, 407.
7 N to E, 24 January 1915, LuE/14/9/7.
8 Eadred Lutyens, 'The Lutyens Family 1700–1950' (typescript), Lutyens Family Papers. Note by Charles Lutyens [1897], Knebworth Archive. PRO, Will of Martha Lutyens (d. October 1858).
9 Lees Knowles, *Letters of Captain Englebert Lutyens* (Bodley Head, 1915). Mary Lutyens, *Edwin Lutyens* (John Murray, 1980), 2.
10 Lutyens Family Papers, Note by Francis Lutyens, 24 November 1925; letter by Edith Holding, 21 April 1926.
11 PRO, Wills of Charles Lutyens (d. 1849), Frances Jane Lutyens (d. 1850). N to E, 31 August 1906, LuE/8/4/10.
12 Pedigree of the Kerry Branch of the Gallwey Family, Lutyens Family Papers. Mary Lutyens, *Lutyens*, 6.
13 He appears in the 1881 Census as an artist living at 21 Gordon Place, Kensington.
14 Raymond Watkinson, *Catalogue* of Charles Lutyens Exhibition (Eastbourne 1971), 5.
15 *Survey of London*, vol. 41, 110.
16 PRO, Will of Samuel Lutyens (d. October 1865).

NOTES

17 Charles Lutyens, *The Venetian Secret* (Digby, Long, 1893).
18 Francis and Fred appear in the *Westminster School Register* (Macmillan, 1892). Arthur and Lionel are in the Cheltenham College lists.
19 N to E, 16 January 1903, LuE/6/3/8.
20 Osbert Sitwell, *The Scarlet Tree* (Macmillan, 1946), 236.
21 N to E, 2 August 1905, LuE/7/8/1.
22 N to E, 27 August 1902, LuE/5/9/11. N to E, 26 September 1906, LuE/8/6/1. Wemyss, *All About All of Us*, 50–1.
23 Wemyss, *All About All of Us*, 12, 26–29, 36–40.
24 N to E, 26 September 1906, LuE/8/6/1.

CHAPTER TWO   SURREY   1876–1887
Notes to pages 21–42

1 Wemyss, *All About All of Us*, 4. *Victoria History . . . Berkshire*, vol. III (St Catherine Press, 1924), 468.
2 Gertrude Jekyll, *Old West Surrey* (Longmans, Green, 1904), 291. 'I Remember, I Remember', *Thursley Parish Magazine* (1960), Godalming Library.
3 M. B. Huish, *Happy England* (A. & C. Black, 1903), 69.
4 Georgiana Burne-Jones, *Memorials of Edward Burne-Jones* (Macmillan, 1904), vol. II, 95.
5 Wemyss, *All About All of Us*, 2–3, 5–6, 12–13, 35–9.
6 Lady Emily Lutyens, *A Blessed Girl* (Rupert Hart-Davis, 1953), 294.
7 N to Mary Lutyens, 17 January 1878, Author Collection.
8 N to Mary Lutyens, 17 October 1879. N to Mary Lutyens, 31 October 1879, Author Collection.
9 Wemyss, *All About All of Us*, 61–2.
10 Caroline Dakers, *Clouds: The Biography of a Country House* (Yale, 1993), 69. Margaret Richardson, *Sketches by Edwin Lutyens* (Academy Editions, 1994), 11. Charles Lutyens, *Venetian Secret*, 7, 19, 119–25.
11 *Victoria History . . . Surrey*, vol. II (Constable, 1905), 489–90. Gertrude Jekyll, *Old West Surrey*, 25–9.
12 Lutyens Family Papers, Frank to Eadred Lutyens, 6 December 1926.
13 Lutyens was eventually tracked down for me at Sutherland House

NOTES

in the 1881 Census by Patric Dickinson; I am grateful.
14 N to Mary Lutyens, 14 November 1881, Author Collection.
15 Robert Lutyens, *Sir Edwin Lutyens: An Appreciation in Perspective* (Country Life, 1942), 21.
16 Eadred Lutyens, 'The Lutyens Family', 24–5. A. M. and J. Ferguson, *Ceylon Directory* (Colombo: Observer Press, 1875). J. Ferguson, *The Ceylon Handbook and Directory* (Colombo: A. M. and J. Ferguson, 1901), 3–57. N to E, 9 July 1927, LuE/19/8/9.
17 PRO, Will of Miss Jesse Landseer (d. 29 August 1880).
18 Mary Lutyens, *Lutyens*, 11.
19 N to E, 25 January 1908, *Letters*, 150.
20 Mary Lutyens, *Lutyens*, 7. Charles Lutyens, *The Venetian Secret*, 19, 48, 118–9.
21 Hussey, *Lutyens*, 5. Robert Lutyens, *Sir Edwin Lutyens*, 20.
22 N to E, 24 August 1902, LuE/5/9/7.
23 N to E, 20 April 1911, LuE/12/1/13.
24 N to E, 24 August 1902, LuE/5/9/7.
25 N to E, 20 April 1911, LuE/12/1/13.
26 Richardson, *Sketches*, 11. Walter Crane, *An Artist's Reminiscences* (Methuen, 1907), 183.
27 Paul Thompson, *William Butterfield* (Cambridge, Mass.: MIT, 1971), 15. Burne-Jones, *Memorials*, vol. 1, 145.
28 A. Saint, *Richard Norman Shaw* (Yale, 1976), 35.
29 M. Huish, *Happy England*, 128.
30 George Sturt, *The Wheelwrights Shop* (Cambridge University Press, 1993), 19.
31 Christopher Frayling, *The Royal College of Art* (Barrie & Jenkins, 1987). Stuart MacDonald, *The History and Philosophy of Art Education* (University of London, 1970). V & A, National Art Library, *33rd Report of Science and Art Department* (1886), 389.
32 National Art Library, *33rd Report of Science and Art Department* (1886), Report by Roger Smith. *35th Report of Science and Art Department* (1888), Report by Roger Smith.
33 *35th Report*, Report by Roger Smith, xxii–xxiii.
34 *Recollections of T. G. Jackson*, ed. Basil Jackson (Oxford University Press, 1950), 260. *33rd Report of Science and Art Department*, 391.
35 Richardson, *Sketches*, 22.
36 *Lutyens*, ed. Colin Amery and Margaret Richardson, (Arts Council, 1981), Hayward Gallery Exhibition Catalogue, 59.

37 Reginald Blomfield, *Memoirs of an Architect* (Macmillan, 1932), 44–7. Roger Smith, 'Mistakes in Architecture', *Builder*, 6 October 1888, 246.
38 Crane, *Artist's Reminiscences*, 436–7.
39 N to E, 10 September 1910, LuE/11/6/8.

CHAPTER THREE
ERNEST GEORGE VERSUS GERTRUDE JEKYLL 1887–1892
Notes to pages 43–60

1 Violet Stuart-Wortley, *Grow Old Along with Me* (Secker & Warburg, 1952), 30–2.
2 Saint, *Norman Shaw*, 326–30.
3 N to E, 21 September 1897, LuE/3/1/6.
4 Blomfield, *Memoirs*, 41. H. S. Goodhart-Rendel, *English Architecture since the Regency* (Constable, 1953), 146.
5 Blomfield, *Memoirs*, 55–6. See Reginald Blomfield, *Richard Norman Shaw* (Batsford, 1940), 87–99. Margaret Richardson, *Architects of the Arts and Crafts Movement* (Trefoil, 1983).
6 Saint, *Norman Shaw*, 274.
7 Hilary Grainger, 'The Office of Sir Ernest George', Leeds University, PhD thesis (1985), vol. 1, 376–7.
8 Darcy Braddell, 'Architectural Reminiscences', *Builder*, 12 January 1945, 27.
9 Braddell, 'Reminiscences', 27.
10 Herbert Baker, *Architecture and Personalities* (Country Life, 1944), 15.
11 *Survey of London: Volume 42, South Kensington*, ed. Hermione Hobhouse (Athlone Press, 1986) 184–95. Mark Girouard, *Sweetness and Light: The 'Queen Anne' Movement 1860–1900* (Oxford: Clarendon Press, 1977), 224.
12 Hussey, *Lutyens*, 17. Mary Lutyens, *Lutyens*, 20.
13 N to E, 24 May 1897, LuE/2/2/7. N to E, 6 July 1897, LuE/2/5/7.
14 Richardson, *Sketches*, 13, 23.
15 Speech by Ernest George, *The Architect*, 26 June 1896.
16 H. Muthesius, *The English House* (Crosby Lockwood Staples, 1979), 37–9. James Lees-Milne, *Prophesying Peace* (Chatto, 1977), 40.
17 *Architectural Association Journal*, 36 (1920), 55.

18 Information supplied by A. W. Potter of the Royal Academy, 4 April 1996. Blomfield, *Memoirs*, 38–42.
19 *Letters*, 145.
20 Grainger, 'Ernest George', vol. I, 400. 'I Remember, I Remember', *Thursley Magazine* (1960). Douglas Watson, 'The Young Lutyens and his Thursley Houses', typescript, n.d.
21 Hussey, *Lutyens*, 18. Jane Brown, *Lutyens and the Edwardians* (Viking, 1996), 15–17. N to Mary Lutyens, 14 November 1881, Author Collection. Charles Lutyens's Painting Book lists the portrait of Mrs Chapman: he was paid £25 in 1882.
22 N to Molly Lutyens, n.d., Author Collection. E to N, 9 March 1900, LuE/23/3/7.
23 Grainger, 'Ernest George', vol. I. 400–1. Roderick Gradidge, *The Surrey Style* (Surrey Historic Buildings Trust, 1991), 72.
24 Ian Nairn and Nikolaus Pevsner, *The Buildings of England: Surrey* (Penguin, 1971 edn), 175. N to E, 26 September 1906, LuE/8/6/1.
25 Brown, *Lutyens*, 46–8. Letter by Ross Mangles, *Country Life*, 1 July 1976. Richardson, *Sketches*, 26–7.
26 Foreword by Lutyens to Francis Jekyll, *Gertrude Jekyll: A Memoir* (Jonathan Cape, 1934), 7–8. Stuart-Wortley, *Grow Old Along with Me*, 34.
27 *Blessed Girl*, 297.
28 Michael Tooley in *Gertrude Jekyll: Essays on the Life of a Working Amateur*, ed. Michael Tooley and Primrose Arnander (Witton-le-Wear: Michaelmas Books, 1995), 124.
29 Judith B. Tankard and Martin A. Wood, *Gertrude Jekyll at Munstead Wood* (Sutton Publishing, 1996), 40–56.
30 Godalming Library, Microfilm of Gertrude Jekyll Photo Albums, Album 4. Judith B. Tankard, 'Annotated Catalog of Gertrude Jekyll's six Photo-Albums at College of Environmental Design Documents Collection, University of California, Berkeley' (1990), items 1017, 1023–27, 1044, 1049, 1051. Tankard and Wood, *Gertrude Jekyll*, 72–4. Hoe Farm and Park Hatch lodges were illustrated in the *Builder*, 15 November 1890 and 30 May 1891.
31 Foreword by Lutyens to Francis Jekyll, *Gertrude Jekyll*.
32 Herbert Baker, *Architecture and Personalities*, 16.
33 N to E, 11 April 1897, *Letters*, 40. Herbert Baker Sketchbook No. 1, RIBA Drawings Collection. Baker, *Architecture and Personalities*, 17. Grainger, 'Ernest George', Vol. I, 401. Augustus Hare, *The Story of My Life* (George Allen, 1900), vol. V, 459.

34 *Builder*, 15 November 1890.
35 E. L. Lutyens, 'The Work of the Late Philip Webb', *Country Life*, 8 May 1915, 618. Fiona Macarthy, *William Morris: A Life For Our Time* (Faber, 1994), 105. Michael Drury, *Wandering Architects* (Stamford: Shaun Tyas, 2000), 20.
36 Microfilm of Jekyll Photo Albums, Album 4. Tankard, 'Catalog', item 1091. Tankard and Wood, *Gertrude Jekyll*, 72–3. Gradidge, *Surrey Style*, 37–42.
37 N to E, 5 February 1897, *Letters*, 24. N to E, 4 March 1920, LuE/17/10/1.

CHAPTER FOUR
MUNSTEAD WOOD AND BARBARA WEBB   1892–1896
Notes to pages 61–78

1 *Survey of London*, vol. 42, 166–7.
2 N to E, 24 August 1906, *Letters*, 105–6. Drury, *Wandering Architects*, 22, 28, 37.
3 *Baily's Magazine*, June 1885, 215.
4 E to N, 12 May 1898, LuE/22/4/2. *Blessed Girl*, 314.
5 Neville Lytton, *The English Country Gentleman* (Hurst & Blackett, 1925), 82–3.
6 E to N, 13 September 1899, LuE/23/2/15. E to N, 20 September 1899, *Letters*, 81–2.
7 N to E, 25 September 1899, LuE/4/1/5. N to E, 27 September 1899, LuE/4/1/18.
8 *Blessed Girl*, 314.
9 Eadred Lutyens, 'The Lutyens Family', 32–3. N to E, 27 September 1899, LuE/4/1/18. Letters to author from Susan Rands, 6 June 1999, 6 July 1999. *Letters of John Cowper Powys to Louis Wilkinson* (Macdonald, 1958), 112, 319. Herbert Williams, *John Cowper Powys* (Seren, 1997).
10 Annabel Freyberg in *Gertrude Jekyll*, ed. Tooley and Arnander, 33. Foreword by Lutyens to Francis Jekyll, *Gertrude Jekyll*, 8.
11 Violet Stuart-Wortley, *Grow Old Along With Me*, 34. Francis Jekyll, *Gertrude Jekyll*, 120.
12 Foreword by Lutyens to Francis Jekyll, *Gertrude Jekyll*, 9. N to E, 11 April 1899, LuE/3/8/11.
13 *Blessed Girl*, 297. Gertrude Jekyll, *Home and Garden* (Longmans,

Green, 1900), 121.
14 Jekyll, 'How the House was Built', in *Home and Garden*, 16.
15 David Ottewill, *The Edwardian Garden* (Yale, 1989), ch. 1. Lawrence Weaver, *Houses and Gardens by Sir Edwin Lutyens* (Country Life, 1925 edn), 7–11. Walburga, Lady Paget, *In My Tower* (Hutchinson, 1924), vol. II, 503, 508–9.
16 N to E, 11 January 1908, *Letters*, 145. PRO, Will of Miss Landseer (d. 29 August 1880).
17 H. S. Goodhart-Rendel, 'Sir Edwin Lutyens', *RIBA Journal*, January 1944. Jane Brown, *Lutyens and the Edwardians*, 50–3.
18 Stuart-Wortley, *Grow Old Along with Me*, 36. Lady Sackville Diary, 20 November 1916.
19 Jekyll, *Home and Garden*, 17.
20 Jekyll, *Home and Garden*, 15.
21 John Rollo, '*Metiendo Vivendum:* "By Measure We Must Live"', *Architectural Research Quarterly*, 3 (1999).
22 Jekyll, *Home and Garden*, 7. Gertrude Jekyll to Mrs Hammond, 27 August 1905, Godalming Library, 1222A.
23 *Letters of Mary Sybilla Holland*, ed. Bernard Holland (Edward Arnold, 1907), 105–6. N to E, 14 July 1897, *Letters*, 50. N to E, 26 August 1899, *Letters*, 77.
24 *Blessed Girl*, 293–4.
25 Barbara Webb to Lady Lytton, n.d [1896], Author Collection. N to E, 31 August 1906, LuE/8/4/10. Clive Dewey, *The Passing of Barchester* (Hambledon Press, 1991), 118.
26 N to E, 9 August 1907, LuE/9/1/5.
27 N to E, 15 April 1897, *Letters*, 43–4.
28 Pevsner gives the date of Red House as 1897–9 (*Surrey*, 259) and so do Gavin Stamp and André Goulancourt, *The English House 1860–1914* (Faber, 1986), 100. Francis Jekyll gives 1896 (*Gertrude Jekyll*, 211). Margaret Richardson gives 1897 (*Catalogue*, 197).
29 Christopher Hussey, 'An Early Lutyens Castle in the Air', *Country Life*, 22 January 1959, 148–9. Hussey in 'Reminiscences on Sir Edwin Lutyens', *Architectural Association Journal*, 74 (1959), 229–30.
30 *Blessed Girl*, 294.

NOTES

CHAPTER FIVE EMILY AND THE LYTTONS 1896
Notes to pages 79–98

1. Hare, *Story of My Life*, vol. V, 415–16. *Blessed Girl*, 10–11.
2. Leslie Ward, *Forty Years of 'Spy'* (Chatto & Windus, 1917), 250.
3. John Lowe Duthie, 'Lord Lytton and the 2nd Afghan War: A Psychohistorical Study', *Victorian Studies* (1984), 467.
4. Lady Betty Balfour, *Personal and Literary Letters of Robert, First Earl of Lytton* (Longmans, Green, 1906), vol. I, 188–9, vol. II, 224–5. Ward, *Forty Years of 'Spy'*, 249–50.
5. Bulwer to Robert Lytton, 20 January 1853, Betty Balfour, *Lytton*, vol. I, 40. Victoria Glendinning, *Trollope* (Hutchinson, 1992), 207–8.
6. Betty Balfour, *Lytton*, vol. II, 424.
7. Aurelia Brooks Harlan, *Owen Meredith* (Columbia University Press, 1946), 178. Lytton Strachey, *Characters and Commentaries* (Chatto & Windus, 1933), 118.
8. Lady Emily Lutyens, *The Birth of Rowland* (Rupert Hart-Davis, 1956), 81, 114–15.
9. Elizabeth Longford, *A Pilgrimage of Passion: The Life of Wilfrid Scawen Blunt* (Weidenfeld & Nicolson, 1979), 46–8.
10. Robert Blake, *Disraeli* (Eyre & Spottiswode, 1966), 658. Mary Lutyens, *The Lyttons in India* (John Murray, 1979).
11. Michael Holroyd, *Lytton Strachey* (Vintage, 1994), 22, 709.
12. *The Diaries of Edward Henry Stanley, 15th Earl of Derby* ed. John Vincent (Royal Historical Society, 1994), 443.
13. *Blessed Girl*, 8.
14. *Blessed Girl*, 20–1.
15. Mary Lutyens, *Lyttons in India*, 99, 186. Betty Balfour, *Lytton*, vol. II, 332–6. *The Later Derby Diaries*, ed. John Vincent (University of Bristol, privately published, 1981), 72.
16. *Blessed Girl*, 53, 68.
17. Owen Meredith, *Marah* (Longmans, Green 1892), 81, 92–3. *Blessed Girl*, 107.
18. 'Lord Lytton's Last Poem', *Marah*, 194. Mary Lutyens, *Lyttons in India*, 186. *Blessed Girl*, 76.
19. Walburga Paget, *In My Tower*, vol. I, 107, 164.
20. Neville Lytton, *English Country Gentleman*, 258. E to N, 5 April 1897, LuE/21/11/4. E to N, 7 April 1897, LuE/21/11/7.
21. *Blessed Girl*, 238.

22 *Blessed Girl*, 115, 182.
23 *Blessed Girl*, 217–23.
24 Longford, *Blunt*, 305.
25 Fitzwilliam Museum, Scawen Blunt MSS, 536/1976, Emily Lytton to Wilfrid Blunt, 5 September 1893.
26 *Blessed Girl*, 281–2.
27 Longford, *Blunt*, 319. *Blessed Girl*, 261.
28 *Blessed Girl*, 276.
29 Blunt MSS, 568/1976, Emily Lytton to Blunt, 27 August 1895.
30 Blunt MSS, 568/1976, Emily Lytton to Blunt, 23 August 1895; 574/1976, Emily Lytton to Blunt, 4 November 1895.
31 Blunt MSS, Autograph Diaries, 350/1976, 22 April 1896.
32 Blunt MSS, Autograph Diaries, 350/1976, 20, 26 May 1896.
33 E to L, 14 April 1897, LuE/21/11/19.
34 N to E, 13 April 1897, LuE/1/5/22.
35 Blunt MSS, Autograph Diaries, 350/1976, 14 May 1896.
36 *Blessed Girl*, 199.
37 *Blessed Girl*, 295–6. Virginia Woolf, *Moments of Being* (Sussex University Press, 1976), 100.
38 N to E, 22 April 1897, LuE/1/6/18. *Blessed Girl*, 294.
39 *Blessed Girl*, 296–7.
40 N to E, 22 April 1897, LuE/1/6/18.
41 E to N, 19 April 1897, LuE/21/11/26.
42 E to N, 21 April 1897, LuE/21/11/29.
43 N to E, 22 April 1897, LuE/1/6/16.
44 N to E, 17 October 1896, *Letters*, 17–18.
45 Hussey, *Lutyens*, 39.
46 *Letters*, 15–17.

CHAPTER SIX ENGAGEMENT 1896–1897
Notes to pages 99–116

1 N to E, 19 October 1896, *Blessed Girl*, 300. Hussey, *Lutyens*, 46.
2 Lutyens to Mrs Streatfeild, 21 October 1896, Jane Brown, *Fulbrook* ed., (Marlborough: Libanus Press, 1992, Limited edition), vol. I. N to E, 23 March 1897, LuE/1/4/21.
3 N to E, 26 March 1897, LuE/1/4/24. Gavin Stamp, *Edwin Lutyens: Country Houses* (Aurum Press, 2001), 61.

4 E to N, 9 April 1897, LuE/21/11/12. E to N, 11 April 1897, LuE/21/11/15.
5 Constance Battersea, *Reminiscences* (Macmillan, 1922), 167–73, 264. Lucy Cohen, *Lady de Rothschild and her Daughters* (John Murray, 1935), 221–2. Girouard, *Sweetness and Light*, 181–91. Roderick Gradidge, *Architect Laureate* (George Allen & Unwin, 1981), 17–18.
6 N to E, 3 August 1904, LuE/7/1/4. N to E, n.d., LuE/7/11/1. N to E, 9 September 1905, LuE/7/9/9.
7 Barbara Webb to Lady Lytton, n.d. Author Collection.
8 *Blessed Girl*, 300–5. N to E, 29 August 1903, *Letters*, 106.
9 *Blessed Girl*, 308–10.
10 Lord Loch to Lady Lytton, 3 December 1896, Author Collection. Emily to Lady Lytton, 14 December 1896; Ned to Lady Lytton, 15 January 1897, Hussey, *Lutyens*, 55–7.
11 Lord Loch to Lady Lytton, 22 January 1897, 29 January 1897, Knebworth Archive. Hussey, *Lutyens*, 49.
12 N to E, 29 January 1897, LuE/1/2/1. E to N, 29 January 1897, LuE/21/9/1. N to E, 16 February 1897, LuE/1/3/17.
13 Barbara Webb to Betty Balfour, n.d., Author Collection. N to E, 15 February 1897, LuE/1/3/16. Jane Brown, *Fulbrook*, vol. I, 37. E to N, 9 February 1897, LuE/21/9/8. *Lady Lytton's Court Diary*, ed. Mary Lutyens (Rupert Hart-Davis, 1961), 93.
14 E to N, 16 February 1897, LuE/21/9/13. E to N, 23 February 1897, LuE/21/9/18. E to N, 2 March 1897, LuE/21/9/24.
15 N to E, 11 February 1897, LuE/1/3/12. E to N, 25 February 1897, LuE/21/9/21. N to E, 22 March 1897, LuE/1/4/18. E to N, 23 March 1897, LuE/21/10/7.
16 E to N, 23 March 1897, LuE/21/10/8. E to N, 9 April 1897, LuE/21/11/11.
17 E to N, 16 February 1897, LuE/21/9/14. E to N, 2 March 1897, LuE/21/9/24. *Letters*, 44.
18 E to N, 5 February 1897, LuE/21/9/4. E to N, 8 March 1897, LuE/21/9/27. N to E, 16 February 1897, *Letters*, 30.
19 E to N, 9 February 1897, LuE/21/9/8. E to N, 19 February 1897, LuE/21/9/16. E to N, 6 April 1897, LuE/21/11/5.
20 *Blessed Girl*, 314. N to E, 12 February 1897, *Letters*, 27. N to E, 2 March 1897, *Letters*, 34.
21 N to E, 9 April 1897, *Letters*, 37.
22 N to E, 8 February 1897, LuE/1/3/5. N to E, 8 February 1897,

LuE/1/3/6. N to E, 22 April 1897, LuE/1/6/16.
23 N to E, 19 April 1897, LuE/1/6/10. N to E, 27 April 1897, LuE/1/6/22. E to N, 28 May 1897, LuE/22/1/27.
24 N to E, 5 February 1897, LuE/1/3/2. N to E, 16 February 1897, LuE/1/3/19. N to E, 18 February 1897, LuE/1/3/22. N to E, 1 April 1897, LuE/1/5/2.
25 Rollo, 'Metiendo Vivendum', 4. N to E, 29 September 1896, Letters, 17.
26 Elizabeth Longford, Darling Loosy: Letters to Princess Louise (Weidenfeld & Nicolson, 1991), 35, 57–63.
27 N to E, 11 February 1897, LuE/1/3/12. N to E, 1 April 1897, LuE/1/5/1. N to E, 5 April 1897, LuE/1/5/5. N to E, 12 April 1897, LuE/1/5/19.
28 E to N, 11 February 1897, LuE/21/9/10. N to E, 14 April 1897, Letters, 42.
29 N to E, 17 June 1897, Letters, 49–50.
30 N to E, 16 February 1897, Letters, 30. N to E, 22 April 1897, LuE/1/6/17. N to E, 4 May 1897, LuE/2/1/2.
31 E to N, 5 May 1897, LuE/22/1/5. N to E, 5 May 1897, LuE/2/1/4. Letters, 45–7.
32 N to E, 27 May 1897, Letters, 47–9. Mary Stocks, My Commonplace Book (Peter Davies, 1970), 13–16. Jane Brown, Lutyens and the Edwardians, 32.
33 Letters, 49. E to N, 5 July 1897, LuE/22/3/4. N to E, 5 July 1897, LuE/2/5/4. E to N, 20 July 1897, LuE/22/3/13.
34 N to E, 27 May 1897, Letters, 47. E to N, 28 May 1897, LuE/22/1/27. N to E, 2 June 1897, LuE/2/3/3. N to E, 2 June 1897, LuE/2/3/4. N to E, 29 June 1897, LuE/2/4/15.
35 Nairn and Pevsner, Surrey, 379.
36 N to E, 15 June 1897, LuE/2/4/1.
37 E to N, 9 June 1897, LuE/22/2/10. N to E, 30 April 1897, LuE/1/6/24. N to E, 3 May 1897, LuE/2/1/1. E to N, 19 May 1897, LuE/22/1/2.
38 E to N, 6 July 1897, LuE/22/3/5. N to E, 6 July 1897, LuE/2/5/7.
39 E to N, 7 July 1897, LuE/22/3/7. E to N, 8 July 1897, LuE/22/3/9.

NOTES

CHAPTER SEVEN 29 BLOOMSBURY SQUARE 1897–1900
Notes to pages 117–134

1 N to E, 2 August 1897, LuE/3/1/1.
2 Knebworth Archive, Emily to Lady Lytton, 8 August 1897; Emily to Lady Lytton, 19 August 1897; Ned to Lady Lytton, 22 August 1897.
3 N to E, 20 September 1897, LuE/3/1/4. N to E, 21 September 1897, LuE/3/1/6.
4 N to E, 14 July 1897, *Letters*, 50–1.
5 N to E, 14 July 1897, *Letters*, 53. N to E, 20 September 1897, LuE/3/1/4.
6 N to E, 5 December 1899, LuE/4/2/8. N to E, 25 September 1897, LuE/3/1/8. Horace Farquharson in 'Reminiscences on Lutyens', *Architectural Association Journal* (1959).
7 E to N, 16 September 1898, LuE/22/4/12. Richardson, *Sketches*, 15. Jane Brown, *Fulbrook*, vol. I, 42, 71.
8 E to N, 14 November 1898, LuE/22/5/14. E to N, 15 November 1898, LuE/22/5/15.
9 N to E, 29 September 1899, LuE/4/1/20. Hussey, *Lutyens*, 143. Lorimer quoted by Margaret Richardson in *Lutyens Catalogue*, 74.
10 Roderick Gradidge, *Dream Houses* (Constable, 1980), 141. Stamp, *Lutyens*, 22–3.
11 N to E, n.d. [March 1898], LuE/3/3/1.
12 N to E, 20 April 1897, LuE/1/6/12.
13 N to E, 13 May 1898, LuE/3/3/5. Emmanuel Ducamp, *Le Bois des Moutiers* (Paris: La Maison Rustique/Flammarion, 1998).
14 N to E, 7 June 1898, LuE/3/4/7.
15 E to N, 11 May 1898, LuE/22/4/1. N to E, 31 May 1898, LuE/3/3/6. N to E, 1 August 1898, *Letters*, 58.
16 Jane Brown, *Fulbrook*, vol. I, 65.
17 E to N, 26 September 1898, LuE/22/4/17. N to E, 27 September 1898, *Letters*, 62.
18 Blunt MSS, Autograph Diaries, 361/1975, 25 December 1898.
19 E to N, 5 October 1898, LuE/22/5/2. E to N, 12 October 1898, LuE/22/5/5. Gradidge, *Dream Houses*, 145–6. *Survey of London*, vol. 41, 14–17.
20 N to E, 29 September 1899, LuE/4/1/20. E to N, 29 December 1898, LuE/22/5/21.

21 E to N, 29 December 1898, LuE/22/5/21. E to N, 30 March 1900, LuE/23/3/9.
22 N to E, 23 February 1899, LuE/3/8/9. E to N, 30 January 1899, LuE/23/1/6.
23 N to E, 10 February 1899, *Letters*, 68. Brian Edwards, *Goddards* (Phaidon, 1996), 9. Stamp, *Lutyens*, 73–6.
24 E to N, 11 April 99, *Letters*, 69. N to E, 17 August 1899, LuE/3/10/15.
25 N to E, 7 August 1899, LuE/3/10/5. E to N, 25 August 1899, LuE/23/2/3. N to E, 26 August 1899, LuE/3/10/20.
26 N to E, 11 October 1898, LuE/3/6/7. N to E, 22 December 1900, LuE/4/7/7. N to E, 19 September 1899, *Letters*, 80.
27 E to N, 12 May 1898, LuE/22/4/2. E to N, 22 September 1899, LuE/23/2/20. N to E, 20 September 1899, *Letters*, 82.
28 Knebworth Archive, Emily to Edith Lytton, 28 October 1899.
29 N to E, 9 December 1899, LuE/4/2/9. E to N, 8 June 1900, LuE/23/3/23.
30 N to E, 3 February 1900, *Letters*, 84. E to N, 8 June 1900, LuE/23/3/23.
31 N to E, 29 December 1899, LuE/4/2/16. N to E, 8 March 1900, LuE/4/4/11.
32 E to N, 31 March 1900, LuE/23/3/11. N to E, 31 March 1900, LuE/4/4/15. N to E, 7 March 1900, LuE/4/4/10. N to E, 25 July 1901, LuE/5/1/3.
33 E to N, 27 August 1900, LuE/24/4/18. E to N, 30 March 1900, LuE/23/3/9.
34 N to E, 8 August 1900, LuE/4/6/6. E to N, 12 August 1900, LuE/23/4/9.
35 N to E, 8 August 1900, LuE/4/6/5. E to N, 12 August 1900, LuE/23/4/9. E to N, 15 August 1900, LuE/22/4/11.
36 N to E, 2 January 1899, LuE/3/8/1. E to N, 28 August 1900, LuE/24/4/20. N to E, 27 August 1900, LuE/4/6/17.

CHAPTER EIGHT *COUNTRY LIFE* 1901–1905
Notes to pages 135–160

1 N to E, 24 April 1901, LuE/4/10/11. Knebworth Archive, Neville Lytton to Lady Lytton, 11 February 1902.
2 E to N, 23 March 1901, LuE/23/5/15.

3 N to E, 27 March 1901, *Letters*, 87. N to E, 12 April 1901, *Letters*, 88.
4 Baker Papers, Lutyens to Herbert Baker, 30 November 1901, BaH/1/1/1.
5 Edith Lyttelton, *Alfred Lyttelton: An Account of his Life* (Longmans, Green, 1917), 228. N to E, 11 April 1899, *Letters*, 70. N to E, 29 August 1899, LuE/3/10/24. N to E, 11 August 1900, LuE/4/6/8. N to E, 12 April 1901, LuE/4/10/7.
6 N to E, 2 January 1902, *Letters*, 96. Churchill College, Cambridge, Lyttelton Papers, Lutyens to Edith Lyttelton, 17 November 1899; Lutyens to Edith Lyttelton, 29 December 1901, CHAN 5/12.
7 Knebworth Archive, Neville Lytton to Lady Lytton, 11 February 1902. E to N, 21 May 1900, LuE/23/3/18. N to E, 13 August 1900, LuE/4/6/11. E to N, 3 February 1905.
8 N to E, 29 August 1905, LuE/7/8/11. Author interview with Anne Fraser (23 January 1998).
9 Knebworth Archive, Lutyens to Constance Lytton, 7 August 1900. N to E, 1 August 1901, LuE/5/2/2. N to E, 16 March 1904, LuE/6/8/2. E to N, 4 September 1904, LuE/25/2/36. Author interviews with Samantha Pollock-Hill (4 July 1995) and Mary Lutyens (16 July 1995). Peter Inskip, *Edwin Lutyens* (Academy Editions, 1979), 29.
10 N to E, 22 September 1899, LuE/4/1/14. Holroyd, *Strachey*, 435. Pamela Maude, 'Portrait of a Perfectionist', *Country Life*, 12 January 1967.
11 N to E, 25 July 1901, LuE/5/1/3. Inskip, *Lutyens*, 22. Robert Williams, 'Edwin Lutyens and the Formal Garden in England', *Die Gartenkunst*, February 1995.
12 N to E, 11 August 1901, LuE/5/12/13. N to E, 28 August 1901, LuE/5/3/22. John Cornforth, *The Search for a Style: Country Life and Architecture 1897–1935* (André Deutsch, 1988), 41–2.
13 E to N, 28 March 1901, LuE/23/5/15. E to N, 30 March 1901, LuE/23/5/18. N to E, 29 March 1901, LuE/4/9/14.
14 N to E, 28 July 1901, LuE/5/1/5. Baker Papers, Lutyens to Baker, 30 November 1901, BaH/1/1/1. Lutyens to Baker, 26 December 1904, BaH/1/1/4.
15 E to N, 28 July 1901, LuE/24/1/4. N to E, 23 April 1901, *Letters*, 89.
16 N to E, 12 August 1900, LuE/4/6/10. N to E, 25 May 1901, LuE/4/10/14. N to E, 21 September 1905, LuE/7/9/16.

17 N to E, 2 August 1901, LuE/5/2/3.
18 N to E, 29 March 1901, LuE/5/3/6. N to E, 18 August 1901, LuE/5/3/6. N to E, 20 August 1901, LuE/5/3/10. Hussey, *Lutyens*, 100–1.
19 N to E, 12 April 1901, LuE/4/10/7. N to E, 20 August 1901, LuE/5/3/10.
20 N to E, 24 July 1904, *Letters*, 111.
21 E to N, 6 August 1901, LuE/24/1/5.
22 E to N, 25 August 1901, LuE/24/1/31. N to E, 21 September 1901, *Letters*, 96.
23 N to E, 23 August 1901, LuE/5/3/14. E to N, 18 September 1901, LuE/24/2/8. E to N, 28 September 1901, LuE/24/2/14. E to N, 2 January 1902, LuE/24/3/2. Author interview with Mary Lutyens (16 July 1995).
24 N to E, 31 December 1901, LuE/5/4/16. Typescript note by Lutyens, 1932, Author Collection
25 N to E, 2 January 1902, *Letters*, 96.
26 Holroyd, *Strachey*, 435.
27 'Reminiscences on Lutyens', *Architectural Association Journal*, 74 (1959), 232–3. Joyce Grenfell, *Joyce Grenfell Requests the Pleasure* (Macmillan, 1976), 36.
28 N to E, 9 August 1902, LuE/5/8/6. N to E, 11 August 1902, LuE/5/8/11. N to E, 23 August 1902, LuE/5/9/6. *Building News*, 8 August 1902, 204; 22 August 1902, 243–4; 29 August 1902, 311. 'Reminiscences on Lutyens', *Architectural Association Journal*, 74 (1959), 232. Richardson, *Sketches*, 51.
29 N to E, 27 August 1902, LuE/5/9/11. N to E, 5 September 1902, LuE/6/1/7. N to E, 23 September 1902, LuE/6/1/22. Baker Papers, Lutyens to Baker, 26 December 1904, BaH/1/1/4.
30 N to E, 15 March 1902, *Letters*, 97–8. N to E, 9 August 1902, *Letters*, 99–102. Jekyll, *Home and Garden*, 15.
31 Lutyens to Barrie, 18 September 1902, LuE/6/1/18. Mary Lutyens, *Lutyens*, 66. Alan Powers, *Apollo*, December 1992, 389.
32 N to E, 9 August 1902, LuE/5/8/6. E to N, 2 August 1903, LuE/24/5/10. E to N, 13 August 1903, LuE/24/5/21.
33 N to E, 6 August 1903, LuE/6/4/10. N to E, 14 August 1903, LuE/6/4/16. N to E, 4 February 1905, *Letters*, 117.
34 N to E, 16 August 1903, LuE/6/5/1. N to E, 23 April 1904, *Letters*, 110. Ottewill, *Edwardian Garden*, 89–90. Williams, 'Lutyens and the Formal Garden', 206–8.

35 E to N, 15 August 1903, LuE/24/5/23. N to E, 18 August 1903, LuE/6/5/6. N to E, 27 August 1903, LuE/6/5/16. N to E, 28 August 1903, LuE/6/5/18.
36 N to E, 28 August 1903, LuE/6/5/18. N to E, 9 October 1903, LuE/6/6/15.
37 N to E, 17 September 1903, LuE/6/6/8. N to E, 29 August 1903, LuE/6/5/20.
38 N to E, 9 February 1903, LuE/7/5/13. Herman Muthesius, *The English House* (Crosby Lockwood Staples, 1979), 129.
39 Baker Papers, Lutyens to Baker, 15 February 1903, BaH/1/1/2.
40 N to E, 24 July 1904, *Letters*, 111. N to E, 31 July 1904, *Letters*, 112–15.
41 Baker Papers, Lutyens to Baker, 26 December 1904, BaH/1/1/4. N to E, 24 August 1904, LuE/6/8/28. N to E, 4 August 1904, *Letters*, 115.
42 Baker Papers, Lutyens to Baker, 26 December 1904, BaH/1/1/4. E to N, 21 July 1905, *Letters*, 120–2. N to E, 13 September 1905, LuE/7/9/13.
43 N to E, 1 August 1901, LuE/5/2/2. N to E, 9 August 1904, LuE/7/1/12. N to E, 14 August 1904, LuE/7/2/4. N to E, 15 August 1904, LuE/7/2/6. N to E, 29 August 1905, LuE/7/8/13. E to N 1 July 1905, Author Collection.

CHAPTER NINE THE TURN TO CLASSICISM 1906–1910
Notes to pages 161–186

1 N to E, 1 January 1906, LuE/8/1/1. N to E, 2 January 1906, LuE/8/1/2. E to N, 5 January 1906, LuE/25/6/3. N to E, 26 September 1906, LuE/8/6/1. N to E, 28 September 1906, LuE/8/6/3. N to E, 9 August 1907, LuE/9/1/5. N to E, 16 August 1907, LuE/9/1/14.
2 N to E, 26 April 1906, LuE/8/1/25. N to E, 29 April 1908, LuE/9/6/21. N to E, 4 May 1906, LuE/8/2/5. N to E, 4 May 1906, *Letters*, 129. N to E, 31 August 1906, *Letters*, 134.
3 Lutyens to Baker, 29 January 1911, Hussey, *Lutyens*, 133. Michael W. Brooks, *John Ruskin and Victorian Architecture* (Thames & Hudson, 1989), 328.
4 'Reminiscences on Lutyens', *Architectural Association Journal*, 74, (1959).
5 E to N, 6 September 1906, *Letters*, 134–5. N to E, 2 January 1907,

LuE/8/7/3. *Builder*, 15 February 1908, 94.

6   N to E, 29 March 1907, LuE/8/8/1. N to E, 31 March 1907, LuE/8/8/2. N to E, 12 August 1907, LuE/9/1/7. N to E, 21 August 1907, LuE/9/2/7.
7   N to E, 27 August 1907, LuE/9/2/12. N to E, 23 October 1907, LuE/9/4/3. N to E, 5 December 1907, LuE/9/4/4. Lutyens to Baker, 10 May 1908, Hussey, *Lutyens*, 141.
8   N to E, 9 October 1907, LuE/9/4/1. E to N, 25 January 1908, LuE/26/4/3. E to N, 6 April 1908, LuE/26/4/10.
9   N to E, 4 May 1906, 6 May 1906, *Letters*, 130–1. E to N, 3 January 1907, LuE/8/7/4. E to N, 9 January 1907, LuE/8/7/8. N to E, 9 January 1907, LuE/8/7/8. N to E, 9 October 1907, LuE/9/4/1.
10 E to N, 11 September 1907, *Letters*, 144. N to E, 23 August 1907, LuE/9/2/9. E to N, 6 September 1907, LuE/26/3/31.
11 Robert Lutyens, 'Fragments of Autobiography' (typescript, 1942), 30.
12 N to E, 29 July 1907, LuE/8/9/15. E to N, 18 August 1907, LuE/26/3/17. E to N, 8 April 1908, LuE/26/4/12.
13 N to E, 12 August 1907, LuE/9/1/7. N to E, 13 August 1907, LuE/9/1/9. N to E, 14 August 1907, LuE/9/1/10. E to N, 10 August 1907, LuE/26/3/10. E to N, 13 August 1907, LuE/26/3/13.
14 N to E, 9 August 1907, LuE/9/1/6. E to N, 16 August 1907, LuE/26/3/16. N to E, 10 September 1907, LuE/9/3/5. E to N, 22 August 1907, *Letters*, 141–2.
15 N to E, 16 August 1907, LuE/9/1/14. E to N, 29 August 1907, LuE/26/3/27. E to N, 5 May 1908, LuE/26/4/32.
16 Robert Lutyens, 'Fragments of Autobiography', 15. N to E, 27 August 1906, LuE/8/4/6. E to N, 13 April 1908, LuE/26/4/16. E to N, 16 September 1908, LuE/27/1/14.
17 Knebworth Archive, Lutyens to Victor Lytton, 1 January 1904. N to E, 6 April 1906, LuE/8/1/7. E to N, 1 January 1907, LuE/26/2/1. E to N, 12 September 1908, LuE/27/1/8. E to N, 30 September 1908, LuE/27/1/20. N to E, 2 October 1908, LuE/10/2/2.
18 Daphne Pollen, *I Remember, I Remember* (privately printed, 1983), 58, 69–70. N to E, 2 October 1906, *Letters*, 135.
19 Lutyens to Gertrude Jekyll, 6 September 1907, copy at Lambay. N to E, 9 April 1908, LuE/9/6/6.
20 Inskip, *Lutyens*, 21.
21 Daphne Pollen, *I Remember*, 62–86.
22 N to E, 2 August 1907, LuE/9/1/1. N to E, 21 August 1907, LuE/9/2/7.

23 N to E, 21 September 1905, LuE/7/9/17. N to E, 27 September 1906, LuE/8/6/2. N to E, 17 August 1907, LuE/9/2/2. N to E, 4 August 1909, LuE/10/5/3.
24 N to E, 7 April 1906, LuE/8/1/8. N to E, 31 August 1906, LuE/8/4/10.
25 N to E, 8 August 1907, LuE/9/1/3. N to E, 16 August 1907, LuE/9/1/14. N to E, 9 April 1908, LuE/9/6/7.
26 See Mervyn Miller and A. Stuart Gray, *Hampstead Garden Suburb* (Chichester, Sussex: Phillimore, 1992). N to E, 9 April 1908, LuE/9/6/7. N to E, 14 April 1908, LuE/9/6/11. N to E, 3 July 1908, *Letters*, 153–6. Sketches on E to N, 4 July 1908, LuE/26/4/37. E to N, 12 September 1908, LuE/27/1/12.
27 Lutyens to Baker, 15 July 1909, Hussey, *Lutyens*, 190. N to E, 7 April 1909, *Letters*, 168. N to E, 12 October 1909, *Letters*, 182.
28 N to E, 26 April 1906, LuE/8/1/25. N to E, 20 April 1907, LuE/8/8/15.
29 N to E, 10 September 1907, *Letters*, 143.
30 Inskip, *Lutyens*, 24–5. N to E, 14 April 1911, *Letters*, 213.
31 N to E, 25 January 1908, *Letters*, 151. N to E, 4 February 1905, *Letters*, 116. N to E, 10 February 1905, LuE/7/5/16.
32 N to E, 5 August 1908, LuE/9/8/2. E to N, 1 September 1908, LuE/27/1/2. E to N, 2 September 1908, LuE/27/1/3. E to N, 17 September 1908, LuE/27/1/6.
33 N to E, 3 July 1908, *Letters*, 153–6. E to N, 12 September 1908, LuE/27/1/12. N to E, 6 October 1908, LuE/10/2/6. N to E, 24 October 1908, *Letters*, 163–4. Inskip, *Lutyens*, 16, 86.
34 N to E, 17 September 1908, *Letters*, 157–9. N to E, 12 October 1908, LuE/10/2/11. N to E, 13 October 1908, LuE/10/2/12.
35 E to N, 15 October 1908, *Letters*, 163. E to N, 26 April 1909, LuE/27/2/10. *Letters of Constance Lytton*, ed. Betty Balfour (William Heinemann, 1925), 155.
36 E to N, 15 October 1908, *Letters*, 163. E to N, 24 February 1909, *Letters*, 167–8. Con to Aunt T, 25 March 1909; Emily to Aunt T, 26 March 1909, *Letters of Constance Lytton*, 159–60.
37 N to E, 31 July 1909, LuE/27/3/2. E to N, 5 August 1909, LuE/27/3/6. E to N, 9 August 1909, *Letters*, 173. E to N, 10 August 1909, LuE/27/3/11. N to E, 13 August 1909, LuE/10/6/1.
38 N to E, 8 August 1908, LuE/10/5/7. N to E, 9 August 1909, *Letters*, 173–5.
39 E to N, 3 August 1909, LuE/27/3/4. E to N, 16 August 1909,

LuE/27/3/17.
40 E to N, 21 September 1909, *Letters*, 181. *Letters of Constance Lytton*, 182.
41 N to E, 29 October [1907 or 1908], LuE/21/6/2. N to E, 25 April 1909, LuE/10/3/16. N to E, 16 August 1909, *Letters*, 177–8. N to E, n.d. [14 October 1909], LuE/11/2/2.
42 N to E, n.d. [October 1909], LuE/11/2/8. N to E, 18 October 1909, *Letters*, 184–7. N to E, [18 October 1909], LuE/11/2/7. N to E, 21 October 1909, *Letters*, 187–8.
43 Hussey, *Lutyens*, 200.
44 *Letters of Constance Lytton*, 187–209. E to N, 23 August 1910, LuE/27/5/2. E to N, 24 August 1910, LuE/27/5/22.

CHAPTER TEN 'THE SHORELESS SEA' 1910–1911
Notes to pages 187–208

1 E to N, 17 August 1911, LuE/27/6/37. Lady Emily Lutyens, *Candles in the Sun*, (Rupert Hart-Davis, 1954), 13.
2 Author interview with Marie Mallet (17 July 1999). Ducamp, *Le Bois des Moutiers*, 25–9. N to E, 30 April 1911, LuE/12/1/28.
3 *Candles*, 14–19.
4 Arthur H. Nethercot, *The Last Four Lives of Annie Besant* (Rupert Hart-Davis, 1963), 166–8. Peter Washington, *Madame Blavatsky's Baboon* (Secker & Warburg, 1993), 35–7, 94–9. E to N, 27 April 1911, LuE/27/6/19. E to N, 2 April 1912, LuE/28/1/10.
5 *Candles*, 23. Washington, *Madame Blavatsky's Baboon*, 122–31. Mary Lutyens, *Krishnamurti: The Years of Awakening* (John Murray, 1975), 15–19.
6 E to N, 5 August 1910, LuE/27/5/11. E to N, 11 August 1910, LuE/27/5/14. E to N, 17 September 1910, LuE/27/5/34.
7 Mrs Earle, *Letters to Young and Old* (Smith, Elder, 1906), 252. N to E, 24 August 1910, LuE/11/5/7. *Candles*, 15, 36.
8 N to E, 6 May 1910, *Letters*, 195. N to E, 6 July 1910, LuE/11/3/10. N to E, 17 August 1910, LuE/11/5/3. N to E, 30 August 1910, LuE/11/5/8. N to E, 31 August 1910, LuE/11/5/9. E to N, 1 September 1910, LuE/27/5/25. N to E, 1 September 1910, LuE/11/6/1.
9 E to N, 3 August 1910, *Letters*, 198. N to E, 3 August 1910, *Letters*, 198–9.

10 Peter Inskip, 'The Compromise of Castle Drogo', *Architectural Review*, vol. 165 (1979), 220–1. Stamp, *Lutyens*, 20.

11 N to E, 6 August 1910, *Letters*, 200–1. N to E, 9 September 1910, *Letters*, 205. *Castle Drogo* (National Trust, 1996), 6.

12 Hussey, *Lutyens*, 225. Nikolaus Pevsner, 'Building with Wit: The Architecture of Sir Edwin Lutyens', *Architectural Review*, vol. 101 (1951), 217–25. Inskip, 'Compromise of Castle Drogo', 225. Stamp, *Lutyens*, 141–9.

13 Lady Gregory, *Sir Hugh Lane: His Life and Legacy* (Gerrards Cross: Colin Smythe, 1973), 122–3, 137. Jane Brown, *Lutyens and the Edwardians*, 146–50.

14 Lady Gregory, *Hugh Lane*, 14–15, 138–9. David Kynaston, *The City of London: Volume II, Golden Years 1890–1914* (Pimlico, 1996), 507–8. Weaver, *Lutyens*, xxxix.

15 N to E, 19 November 1910, LuE/11/7/1. N to E, 19–22 November 1910, LuE/11/7/4. N to E, 23 November–5 December 1910, LuE/11/7/6. E to N, 5 December 1910, LuE/27/5/37. Hussey, *Lutyens*, 204.

16 N to E, 7 December 1910, LuE/11/8/3. N to E, 13 December 1910, *Letters*, 208. N to E, 1 April 1917, LuE/16/3/5. Lady Gregory, *Hugh Lane*, 113. Hussey, *Lutyens*, 215.

17 Baker Papers, Baker's 'Memorandum of My Relations with Lutyens', March 1931, BaH/2/2/53. Hussey, *Lutyens*, 216.

18 Hussey, *Lutyens*, 128–35, 209.

19 N to E, 4 January 1909, LuE/10/3/2. N to E, 7 January 1910, LuE/11/3/3. N to E, 30 August 1910, LuE/11/5/8. E to N, 1 September 1910, LuE/27/5/25. N to E, 5 December 1910, LuE/11/8/1.

20 E to N, 30 December 1910, *Letters*, 210–11. E to N, 5 December 1910, LuE/27/5/37.

21 Extracts from Diary of W. H. Gummer (19, 20 January 1911), courtesy of Barbree Gummer.

22 Hussey, *Lutyens*, 216–17. N to E, 18 April 1911, *Letters*, 216. N to E, 19 April 1911, LuE/12/1/11.

23 E to N, 16 April 1911, *Letters*, 215. E to N, 20 April 1911, *Letters*, 216.

24 N to E, 26 April 1911, LuE/12/1/23. N to E, 27 April 1911, LuE/12/1/25. E to N, 27 April 1911, LuE/27/6/19. E to N, 30 April 1911, LuE/27/6/23.

25 Kynaston, *City of London: Volume II*, 540–1. Philip Ziegler, *The*

NOTES

Sixth Great Power: Barings 1762–1929 (Collins, 1988), 272. Inskip, *Lutyens*, 12, 16, 94.

26 N to E, 27 May 1911, LuE/12/2/7. Christopher Lloyd and Charles Hind, *A Guide to Great Dixter* (Romney Marsh, Angel Design, 1995).

27 *Candles*, 30–2. E to N, 18 April 1911, LuE/27/5/11. N to E, 20 April 1911, LuE/12/1/13. N to E, 20 April 1911, *Letters*, 217.

28 Robert Lutyens, 'Fragments of Autobiography', 165. E to N, 10 August 1911, *Letters*, 221.

29 E to N, 21 July 1911, LuE/27/6/25. Washington, *Madame Blavatsky's Baboon*, 138–9. *Candles*, 33. Mary Lutyens, *Krishnamurti*, 49–51.

30 Robert Lutyens, 'Fragments of Autobiography', 175–6. E to N, 2 August 1911, LuE/27/6/28. E to N, 3 August 1911, LuE/27/6/29. E to N, 19 August 1911, LuE/27/6/40.

31 N to E, 8 August 1911, *Letters*, 220. E to N, 10 August 1911, *Letters*, 221. E to N, 17 August 1911, *Letters*, 223.

32 N to E, 14 August 1911, *Letters*, 222.

33 N to E, 8 August 1911, *Letters*, 221. N to E, 9 August 1911, LuE/12/3/6. N to E, 10 August 1911, LuE/12/3/7. E to N, 21 August 1911, LuE/27/6/41.

34 N to E, 12 August 1911, LuE/12/3/10. N to E, 23 August 1911, *Letters*, 224–5. *Candles*, 33–4. Washington, *Madame Blavatsky's Baboon*, 136–7.

35 N to E, 17 August 1911, LuE/12/4/2. Moon Green, Wittersham, is not listed as a Lutyens house. Lutyens probably knew Violet Markham through her friend Mrs Tennant, wife of Jack Tennant, for whom he built Great Maytham. Violet Markham came to his office in September 1910 (N to E, 5 September 1910, LuE/11/6/4), and he went to see her and the Lytteltons at Maytham on 12 September (N to E, 12 September 1910, LuE/11/6/10). Moon Green has features and workmanship in common with Wittersham.

36 N to E, 17 August 1911, LuE/12/4/2.

37 N to E, 11 August 1911, LuE/12/3/8. N to E, 14 August 1911, LuE/12/3/12. N to E, 16 August 1911, LuE/12/4/1.

CHAPTER ELEVEN   INDIA   1912–1913
Notes to pages 209–232

1 Hussey, *Lutyens*, 245. Information from Enid Forster, Garrick Club Librarian, March 2000.
2 Robert Grant Irving, *Indian Summer: Lutyens, Baker, and Imperial Delhi* (Yale University Press, 1981), 39–41. India Office, Harcourt Butler Collection, MSS Eur. F/116/69, Lord Hardinge, 'Laying Out the New Delhi', 26 December 1911. Hussey, *Lutyens*, 246.
3 N to E, 21 March 1912, LuE/12/6/7. E to N, 22 March 1912, LuE/28/1/9. N to E, 28 March 1912, LuE/12/7/1. Hussey, *Lutyens*, 247.
4 N to E, 1 April 1912, LuE/12/7/4. N to E, 14 April 1912, *Letters*, 230–1. N to E, 15 April 1912, LuE/12/8/3.
5 N to E, 23 April 1912, *Letters*, 235. N to E, 9 June 1912, *Letters*, 253.
6 Hussey, *Lutyens*, 243. Lord Hardinge of Penshurst, *My Indian Years 1910–1916* (John Murray, 1948). Martin Gilbert, *Servant of India* (Longmans, 1966), 2–5. Mark Bence-Jones, *The Viceroys of India* (Constable, 1982), 211–17. India Office, Edwin Montagu Papers, Indian Diary, vol. III, 18 January–18 March 1913, ff. 9–10, MSS Eur. D/523/40.
7 N to E, 29 April 1912, *Letters*, 236–7. N to E, 9 May 1912, *Letters*, 239. N to E, 12 May 1912, *Letters*, 242. N to E, 16 May 1912, *Letters*, 243. N to E, 22 May 1912, *Letters*, 245. Hussey, *Lutyens*, 258–9.
8 India Office, Edwin Montagu Indian Diary, vol. III, 1913, f. 9, MSS Eur. D/523/40. N to E, 3 June 1912, *Letters*, 249. N to E, 9 June 1912, *Letters*, 252. N to E, 18 June 1912, LuE/12/11/6.
9 N to E, 9 June 1912, *Letters*, 252. E to N, 27 June 1912, LuE/28/1/20. Sir Lionel Earle, *Turn Over the Page* (Hutchinson, 1935), 87. Hussey, *Lutyens*, 272.
10 N to E, 26 May 1912, *Letters*, 247. N to E, 4 June 1912, *Letters*, 251. N to E, 18 June 1912, *Letters*, 254. E to N, 11 July 1912, LuE/28/1/21. N to E, 16 February 1913, *Letters*, 280. India Office, Harcourt Butler Collection, Harcourt Butler to his Mother, 13 May 1912, MSS Eur. F/116/8.
11 Mary Lutyens, *Krishnamurti*, 56–9. E to N, 30 May 1912, LuE/28/1/17. *Candles*, 39–40.
12 E to N, 27 June 1912, LuE/28/1/20. E to N, 11 July 1912,

LuE/28/1/21.
13 N to E, 19 August 1912, LuE/12/12/4. N to E, 28 August 1912, LuE/12/12/7. N to E, 30 August 1912, *Letters*, 259.
14 India Office, Fleetwood Wilson Collection, Hardinge to Fleetwood Wilson, 27 August 1912, MSS Eur. E/224/5. Hardinge, *My Indian Years*, 72. See Irving, *Indian Summer*, Appendix, 367, and Hussey, *Lutyens*, 273.
15 Swinton Papers, Lutyens to Swinton, 15 August 1912. N to E, 8 September 1912, *Letters*, 261. Hussey, *Lutyens*, 268.
16 Swinton Papers, Lutyens to Swinton, 9 September 1912, 11 September 1912; Swinton to Lutyens, 14 September 1912; Swinton to Stamfordham, 14 September 1912.
17 E to N, 28 August 1912, LuE/28/1/32. N to E, 29 August 1912, LuE/12/12/8. E to N, 1 September 1912, LuE/28/1/35. N to E, 5 September 1912, LuE/13/1/3. E to N, 10 September 1912, LuE/28/1/42.
18 E to N, 19 September 1912, LuE/28/1/45. E to N, 20 September 1912, *Letters*, 267. *Candles*, 45–52.
19 N to E, 16 September 1912, *Letters*, 265. N to E, 28 November 1912, LuE/13/3/5. E to N, 29 November 1912, LuE/28/1/55.
20 Hussey, *Lutyens*, 243–4. Irving, *Indian Summer*, 95–6. Baker Papers, Baker's 'Memorandum of my Relations with Lutyens', March 1931, BaH/2/2/53. E to N, 25 December 1912, LuE/28/1/58. Hussey, *Lutyens*, 271–2. Irving, *Indian Summer*, 97.
21 E to N, 11 December 1912, LuE/28/1/56. N to E, 19 December 1912, LuE/13/4/7. N to E, 16 December 1912, *Letters*, 268. N to E, 26 December 1912, *Letters*, 273.
22 *Diaries and Letters of Marie Belloc Lowndes 1911–1947*, ed. Susan Lowndes (Chatto & Windus, 1971), 42. N to E, 16 September 1912, *Letters*, 265. N to E, 16 December 1912, *Letters*, 268. N to E, 17 December 1912, *Letters*, 270.
23 N to E, 26 December 1912, *Letters*, 273. N to E, 13 January 1913, LuE/13/5/4. N to E, 16 January 1913, *Letters*, 276–7. N to E, 26 January 1913, LuE/13/5/8. E to N, 25 February 1913, LuE/28/2/7. See Jane Ridley, 'Edwin Lutyens, New Delhi and the Architecture of Imperialism', *Journal of Imperial and Commonwealth History*, 26 (1998), 67–83.
24 Harcourt Butler Collection, Harcourt Butler to his Mother, 17 January 1913, MSS Eur. F/116/8. N to E, 7 January 1913, *Letters*, 276. N to E, 8 February 1913, LuE/13/6/6. Mary Lutyens, *Lutyens*,

106. India Office, Hailey Collection, MSS Eur. E 220/1A, Hardinge to Hailey, 12 February 1913; Hardinge to Hailey, 13 August 1913; Lutyens to Lady Hardinge, 25 July 1913 (printed copy).

25 India Office, Edwin Montagu Indian Diary, vol. III, ff. 27–8, MSS Eur. E/224/5. Hailey Collection, Hardinge to Hailey, 12 February 1913; Hardinge to Hailey, 28 July 1913, MSS Eur. E/220/1A. Fleetwood Wilson Collection, Hardinge to Fleetwood Wilson, 27 August 1912, Hardinge to Fleetwood Wilson, 2 February 1913, MSS Eur. E/224/5–6.

26 Edwin Montagu Indian Diary, vol. III, f. 30, MSS Eur. E 224/5. Fleetwood Wilson Collection, Fleetwood Wilson to Hardinge, 1 September 1912, MSS Eur. E/224/5; Fleetwood Wilson to Lady Hardinge, 25 June 1912, MSS Eur. E/224/7.

27 Edwin Montagu Indian Diary, vol. III, ff. 32–4, MSS Eur. E/224/5.

28 N to E, 8 February 1913, LuE/13/6/6. N to E, 18 February 1913, *Letters*, 280. Baker Papers, Baker's 'Memorandum of My Relations with Lutyens', March 1931, BaH/2/2/53.

29 Fleetwood Wilson Collection, Fleetwood Wilson to Hardinge, 17 February 1913, MSS Eur. E/224/6. Hardinge, *My Indian Years*, 96. N to E, 8 February 1913, LuE/13/6/6. N to E, 18 February 1913, *Letters*, 280. N to E, 9 March 1913, *Letters*, 283. N to E, 9 March 1913, LuE/13/7/2. N to E, 25 March 1913, LuE/13/7/3.

30 Hussey, *Lutyens*, 290–3. N to E, 18 April 1913, *Letters*, 283–4.

31 'Reminiscences on Lutyens', *Architectural Association Journal*, 74 (1959), 233.

32 Lady Gregory, *Hugh Lane*, 90. Thomas Bodkin, *Hugh Lane and his Pictures* (Dublin: Stationery Office and Arts Council, 1956), 27–36.

33 Roy Foster, *W. B. Yeats: A Life. I: The Apprentice Mage* (Oxford University Press, 1997), 493–8. N to E, 27 August 1913, LuE/13/9/9.

34 Bodkin, *Hugh Lane*, 70–1, 76. Mary Lutyens, *Lutyens*, 136. Hussey, *Lutyens*, 232.

35 E to N, 9 July 1913, LuE/28/2/11. E to N, 1 August 1913, LuE/28/2/18.

36 *Candles*, 57, 60. E to N, 17 September 1913, Author Collection.

NOTES

CHAPTER TWELVE EAST AND WEST 1913–1914
Notes to pages 233–248

1. E to N, 6 August 1913, LuE/28/2/22. N to E, 8 September 1913, LuE/13/10/4.
2. Hussey, *Lutyens*, 296. N to E, 26 December 1912, *Letters*, 274. India Office, Hailey Collection, Hardinge to Hailey, 12 February 1913, MSS Eur. E/220/1A.
3. N to E, 29 November 1913, *Letters*, 282. Daphne Pollen, *I Remember*, 187.
4. Baker Papers, Diary, 30 October–12 November 1913. Baker's Memo, March 1921, BaH/2/2/30.
5. N to E, 13 November 1913, LuE/13/11/1. N to E, 14 November 1913, LuE/13/11/2. Hussey, *Lutyens*, 308–10. Diary, 13, 18 November 1913. Baker Papers, Baker's Memorandum, March 1921, BaH/2/2/30.
6. N to E, 9 December 1913, *Letters*, 289. Hussey, *Lutyens*, 318–20.
7. Harcourt Butler Collection, Harcourt Butler to Sir William Meyer, 17 February 1914, MSS Eur. F/116/69. N to E, 15–17 December 1913, LuE/13/11/11. N to E, 22 December 1913, LuE/13/11/13. Hussey, *Lutyens*, 312.
8. Harcourt Butler Collection, Harcourt Butler to his Mother, 28 December 1913, MSS Eur. F/116/8. N to E, 28 December 1913, *Letters*, 290–2. N to E, 28 December 1913, LuE/13/11/15. E to N, 22 January 1914, LuE/28/3/4.
9. Thomas R. Metcalf, *An Imperial Vision: Indian Architecture and Britain's Raj* (Faber, 1989), 238.
10. Baker Papers, Baker's 'Memorandum of My Relations with Lutyens', March 1931, BaH/2/2/53; Diary, 1, 18 January 1914. N to E, 1 January 1914, *Letters*, 292. N to E, 21 January 1914, LuE/14/1/6. N to E, 27 January 1914, LuE/14/1/8.
11. Baker Papers, Diary, 10 February 1914. N to E, 4 February 1914, LuE/14/2/2. N to E, 10 February 1914, LuE/14/2/3. N to E, 2 March 1914, LuE/14/3/1. N to E, 4 March 1914, LuE/14/3/2.
12. Hussey, *Lutyens*, 323. Baker Papers, Diary, 17 March 1914.
13. E to N, 19 February 1914, LuE/28/3/9. Meirion and Susie Harries, *A Pilgrim Soul: The Life and Work of Elisabeth Lutyens* (Michael Joseph, 1989), 23–5.
14. N to E, 10 March 1914, LuE/14/3/5. E to N, 28 March 1914, LuE/28/3/15.

15 E to N, 20 December 1913, Author Collection. *Candles*, 62–9. Mary Lutyens, *Krishnamurti*, 80–3.
16 N to E, 4 February 1914, LuE/14/2/2. E to N, 17 December 1913, Author Collection. 'Reminiscences on Lutyens', *Architectural Association Journal*, 74 (1959), 233.
17 E to N, 20 November 1913, LuE/28/2/48. N to E, 21 July 1914, LuE/14/4/2. N to E, 28 July 1914, LuE/14/4/8.
18 N to Mrs Besant [copy, n.d., July 1914], LuE/14/4/13. N to E, n.d., LuE/14/4/14. E to N, 5 September 1914, LuE/28/3/45. E to N, 6 September 1914, LuE/28/3/46.
19 N to E, 17 January 1915, LuE/14/9/6.
20 N to E, 22 July 1914, LuE/14/4/4. N to E, 28 July 1914, LuE/14/4/7. N to E, 29 July 1914, LuE/14/4/10. N to E, n.d., LuE/14/4/14. Ziegler, *The Sixth Great Power*, 320–2, 48–51.
21 N to E, 11 August 1914, LuE/14/5/8. N to E, 22 August 1911, LuE/14/5/12. N to E, 24 August 1914, LuE/14/5/14.
22 N to E, 27 August 1914, LuE/14/5/18. N to E, 30 August 1914, LuE/14/5/21.
23 E to N, 18 August 1914, LuE/28/3/29. E to N, 29 August 1914, LuE/28/3/37. E to N, 1 September 1914, LuE/28/3/40. E to N, 3 September 1914, LuE/28/3/42.
24 E to N, 11 September 1914, *Letters*, 302. *Candles*, 70.
25 N to E, 13 September 1913, LuE/14/6/14. N to E, 20 July 1915, LuE/15/2/5.
26 E to N, 18 September 1914, LuE/28/3/53. N to E, 19 September 1914, *Letters*, 303–4.

CHAPTER THIRTEEN   31 BEDFORD SQUARE   1914–1916
Notes to pages 249–272

1 E to N, 7 September 1914, LuE/28/3/47. N to E, 29 September 1914, LuE/14/7/15.
2 E to N, 5 September 1914, LuE/28/3/45. E to N, 6 September 1914, LuE/28/3/46.
3 N to E, 24 September 1914, LuE/14/7/7. N to E, 30 September 1914, LuE/14/7/16. E to N, 4 November 1914, LuE/28/3/73. E to N, 5 December 1914, LuE/28/3/75.
4 N to E, 17 December 1914, LuE/14/8/14. N to E, 22 December 1914, LuE/14/8/16. Margaret Fitzherbert, *The Man Who was*

NOTES

Greenmantle (John Murray, 1983), 145.

5 N to E, 10 December 1914, LuE/14/8/9. N to E, 17 December 1914, LuE/14/8/15.
6 Knebworth Archive, Lutyens to Lady Lytton, 14 July 1914, N to E, 14 January 1915, LuE/14/9/3. N to E, 4 February 1916, *Letters*, 331.
7 N to E, 3 January 1915, *Letters*, 307-8. N to E, 17 March 1915, LuE/15/1/4. *Lewis Mumford and Patrick Geddes: The Correspondence*, ed. Frank G. Novak (Routledge, 1995), 140, 343.
8 Elisabeth Lutyens, *A Goldfish Bowl* (Cassell, 1972), 42. Hardinge, *My Indian Years*, 129. Marguerite Steen, *William Nicholson* (Collins, 1943), 121.
9 Mary Lutyens, *To Be Young* (Rupert Hart-Davis, 1959), 16.
10 E to N, 31 December 1914, LuE/28/3/79.
11 Mary Lutyens, *Krishnamurti*, 90, 96.
12 E to N, 13 February 1915, *Letters*, 310. Mary Lutyens, *Krishnamurti*, 90-2.
13 N to E, 2 July 1915, *Letters*, 312-13. N to E, 3 August 1915, LuE/15/2/7.
14 N to E, 2 July 1915, *Letters*, 312. N to E, 18 September 1915, LuE/15/3/7.
15 N to E, 21 October 1915, LuE/15/4/2. N to E, 5 December 1915, LuE/15/6/2. N to E, 27 October 1915, *Letters*, 316-18.
16 Gavin Stamp and Margaret Richardson, 'Lutyens Spain', *A. A. Files* 3 (1983), 51-9.
17 N to E, 16 November 1915, *Letters*, 321. N to E, 19 November 1915, *Letters*, 322. N to E, 30 November 1915, LuE/15/5/12.
18 Baker Papers, Lutyens to Baker, 27 January 1916, BaH/2/1/19. Irving, *Indian Summer*, 150.
19 N to E, 4 February 1916, *Letters*, 331. N to E, 17 February 1916, *Letters*, 332-4.
20 Baker Papers, Herbert Baker to Florence Baker, 1 March 1915; Herbert Baker to Florence Baker, 15 March 1915.
21 Lutyens, *Hussey*, 357. Baker Papers, Note by Lutyens on Hardinge's letter to Hailey, BaH/2/1/9.
22 N to E, 24 February 1916, *Letters*, 335. Baker Papers, Baker Diary, 17 March 1916, 26 March 1916. Irving, *Indian Summer*, 154.
23 N to E, 21 July 1915, LuE/15/2/6. N to E, 20 December 1915, LuE/15/6/4. N to E, 28 December 1915, LuE/15/6/6. E to N, 18 March 1916, LuE/28/5/3.
24 E to N, 9 March 1915, Author Collection. *Candles*, 79-80.

25 Mary Lutyens, *Lutyens*, 130. Lady Sackville Diary, 24 June 1916, 29 June 1916.
26 Mary Lutyens, *Lutyens*, 130. E to N, 28 July 1914, LuE/28/3/17. E to N, 28 December 1914, LuE/28/3/77.
27 N to E, 4 August 1916, LuE/15/10/2. *William Nicholson: Painter*, ed. Andrew Nicholson (Giles de la Mare, 1996), 142–7. Mary Lutyens, *To Be Young*, 41–2.
28 Lady Sackville Diary, 10 August 1916, 10 October 1916, 11 October 1916, 18 October 1916, 24 October 1916, 1 November 1916, 2 November 1916.
29 Baker Papers, Telegram to Herbert Baker, 13 May 1916, BaH/2/1/22; Claude Hill to Lutyens, 18 May 1916, BaH/2/1/24.
30 N to E, 8 August 1916, *Letters*, 336–7. Cynthia Asquith, *Diaries 1915–1918*, (Hutchinson, 1968), 231.
31 Irving, *Indian Summer*, 119–20, 156.
32 N to E, 8 November 1916, LuE/15/11/1. N to E, 8 November 1916, LuE/15/11/2. Lady Sackville Diary, 8 November 1916.
33 N to E, 17 November 1916, *Letters*, 337–9. N to E, 9 December 1916, LuE/15/12/4. E to N, 8 January 1917, LuE/28/6/1.
34 N to E, 5 January 1917, LuE/16/1/2. N to E, 16 January 1917, LuE/16/1/4. N to E, 24 January 1917, LuE/16/1/5. N to E, 1 February 1917, LuE/16/2/1.
35 N to E, 2 March 1917, LuE/16/3/1. N to E, 4 March 1917, LuE/16/3/2. N to E, 1 April 1917, LuE/16/3/5. Lady Sackville Diary, 1 December 1916. Edwin Montagu, *An Indian Diary* (William Heinemann, 1930), 31.

CHAPTER FOURTEEN   MACSACK   1916–1920
Notes to pages 273–298

1 E to N, 17 January 1917, LuE/28/6/2. E to N, 22 February 1917, LuE/28/6/5. E to N, 27 February 1917, LuE/28/6/6. E to N, 4 March 1917, LuE/28/6/7. Lady Sackville Diary, 29 July 1917.
2 E to N, 19 December 1916, LuE/28/5/22. E to N, 4 March 1917, LuE/28/6/7.
3 N to E, 19 May 1917, *Letters*, 349. Lady Sackville Diary, 5 January 1917.
4 Lady Sackville Diary, 10 June 1917, 25 June 1917, 4 November 1917.

5 N to E, 12 July 1917, *Letters*, 349–51. Lady Sackville Diary, 8 July 1917, 22 July 1917, 15 December 1917.

6 Hussey, *Lutyens*, 376. Commonwealth War Graves Archive, Barrie to Fabian Ware, 25 July 1917; Lutyens to Fabian Ware, 27 July 1917; Lutyens to Ware, 3 August 1917.

7 N to E, 28 August 1917, *Letters*, 354. E to N, 29 August 1917, *Letters*, 355. Lady Sackville Diary, 25 August 1917, 28 August 1917. Victoria Glendinning, *Vita: The Life of Vita Sackville-West* (Penguin, 1984), 85.

8 Commonwealth War Graves Archive, Lutyens's Memorandum, 'Graveyards on the Battlefields', 28 August 1917. E to N, 5 September 1917, *Letters*, 355. N to E, 14 September 1917, LuE/16/6/9.

9 N to E, 13 August 1917, LuE/16/5/3. N to E, 24 August 1917, *Letters*, 352–3. Lady Sackville Diary, 9 September 1917, 22 September 1917, 7 October 1917.

10 Harold Nicolson to Vita, 19 October 1917, *Vita and Harold: The Letters of Vita Sackville-West and Harold Nicolson*, ed. Nigel Nicolson (Weidenfeld & Nicolson, 1992), 59–60. Lady Sackville Diary, 4 November 1917, 15 November 1917.

11 E to N, 1 January 1918, *Letters*, 356–7. N to E, 1 January 1918, *Letters*, 357. Hussey, *Lutyens*, 385. Lady Sackville Diary, 18 January 1918.

12 N to E, 5 April 1918, LuE/16/9/3. N to E, 13 January 1919, LuE/17/1/1.

13 Lady Sackville Diary, 24 March 1918, 27 May 1918. E to N, 16 April 1918, LuE/29/1/15.

14 N to E, 4 September 1917, LuE/16/6/2. N to E, 5 September 1917, LuE/16/6/3. N to E, 20 April 1918, LuE/16/9/10. N to E, 30 October 1918, LuE/16/13/5.

15 Public Record Office, WORK/16-26/8, Philip Ashworth (Secretary to the Duke of Connaught) to Lionel Earle; Stamfordham to Alfred Mond, 30 September 1918; Mond to Stamfordham, 2 October 1918. N to E, 21 August 1918, LuE/16/12/3. N to E, 24 August 1918, LuE/16/12/7. N to E, 29 August 1918, LuE/16/12/10. Sir Martin Conway, 'The Proposed Temporary War Shrine on Hyde Park', *Country Life*, 21 September 1918. Alex King, *Memorials of the Great War in Britain* (Berg, 1998), 56–7.

16 E to N, 26 October 1918, LuE/29/1/65. E to N, 3 December 1918, LuE/29/1/69.

NOTES

17 Vita Sackville-West, *Pepita* (Hogarth Press, 1937), 259. Lady Sackville Diary, 10 September 1918, 21 September 1918, 23 September 1918, 1 December 1918, 5 December 1918.
18 Lady Sackville Diary, 10 January 1919, 27 February 1919. N to E, 4 March 1919, LuE/17/2/2. N to E, 20 March 1919, LuE/17/2/3. Rev. Hebert Ward, *An Erratic Odyssey* (Odyssey Books, 1988), 66. Lutyens's Memorandum to Registrar of University of Cape Town, 28 March 1919, Gavin Stamp Collection.
19 Lady Sackville Diary, 25 April 1919, 17 April 1919, 19 May 1919.
20 N to E, 24 May 1919, LuE/17/3/1. Lady Sackville Diary, 4 January 1919, 7 March 1919.
21 PRO/WORK/21/74, 'Peace Celebrations', July 1919. King, *Memorials of the Great War*, 139–40. Hussey, *Lutyens*, 392.
22 Lady Sackville Diary, 27 July 1919, 28 July 1919, 1 August 1919. N to E, n.d., LuE/17/4/6. N to E, 25 September 1919, LuE/17/5/7. Lutyens, 'The Story of the Cenotaph', *Journal of Remembrance*, PRO/WORK/20/139.
23 Alan Greenberg, 'Lutyens's Cenotaph', *Journal of the Society of Architectural Historians*, 148 (1989), 5–23. Andrew Crompton, 'The Secret of the Cenotaph', *A. A. Files*, 34 (1997). King, *Memorials of the Great War*, 141–50. Hussey, *Lutyens*, 391–5.
24 Lutyens to Lionel Earle, 19 September 1919, PRO/WORK/20/139.
25 Lady Sackville Diary, 13 June 1919, 26 June 1919. N to E, 1 August 1919, LuE/17/4/1. E to N, 3 August 1919, LuE/29/2/14. Mary Lutyens, *To Be Young*, 57.
26 E to N, 8 September 1919, LuE/29/2/22. Lady Sackville Diary, 12 September 1919. N to E, 25 September 1919, LuE/17/5/7.
27 N to E, 27 August 1919, LuE/17/4/9. N to E, 12 September 1919, LuE/17/5/3. Lady Sackville Diary, 18 September 1919, 25 September 1919.
28 E to N, 18 November 1919, LuE/29/2/29. N to E, 9 November 1919, LuE/17/6/2. N to E, 18 November 1919, LuE/17/6/3. Henry Medd in 'Reminiscences on Sir Edwin Lutyens', *Architectural Association Journal* (1959), 235. *End of an Era: Letters and Journals of Sir Alan Lascelles 1887–1920*, ed. Duff Hart-Davis (Hamish Hamilton, 1988), 299.
29 N to E, 11 December 1919, LuE/17/7/2. N to E, 17 December 1919, LuE/17/7/3. N to E, 21 December 1919, LuE/17/7/4. N to E, 13 January 1920, *Letters*, 378.
30 Irving, *Indian Summer*, 295–302. Metcalf, *Imperial Vision*, 241.

N to E, 17 December 1919, LuE/17/7/3. N to E, 8 February 1920, LuE/17/9/3. Baker Papers, Bakers's 'Memorandum of My Relations with Lutyens', March 1931, BaH/2/2/53.

31 N to E, 28 December 1919, LuE/17/7/5. N to E, 13 January 1920, LuE/17/8/2. N to E, 25 February 1920, LuE/17/9/7. N to E, 20 March 1920, LuE/17/10/4. Hussey, *Lutyens*, 417.

32 N to E, 13 January 1920, LuE/17/8/2. N to E, 21 January 1921, *Letters*, 379–80. N to E, 4 April 1920, *Letters*, 383–4. N to E, 8 April 1920, *Letters*, 386–9.

33 E to N, 27 January 1920, LuE/29/3/4. E to N, 16 March 1920, LuE/29/3/11. E to N, 22 April 1922, LuE/29/3/15. Mary Lutyens, *Krishnamurti*, 110.

34 E to N, 22 April 1920, LuE/29/3/15. Lady Sackville Diary, 11 May 1920, 20 May 1920, 10 July 1920.

35 'Reminiscences on Lutyens,' *Architectural Association Journal* (1959), 230. E to N, 22 April 1920, LuE/29/3/15. Lady Sackville Diary, 14 July 1920.

36 N to E, 19 August 1920, LuE/17/12/11. E to N, 3 August 1920, LuE/29/3/17. E to N, 7 September 1920, LuE/29/3/29. Mary Lutyens, *Lutyens*, 202.

37 Lady Sackville Diary, 9 November 1920, 11 November 1920. *Letters of Chaim Weizmann*, ed. Meyer W. Weisgal, vol. 10 (Israel Universities Press, 1977), 109. E to N, 20 September 1920, LuE/17/13/10.

CHAPTER FIFTEEN   THE DOLLS' HOUSE   1920–1924
Notes to pages 299–324

1 Lady Sackville Diary, 4 December 1920. E to N, 19 September 1920, LuE/29/3/34. E to N, 16 December 1920, LuE/29/3/36. N to E, 14 December 1920, LuE/17/14/3. N to E, 19 December 1920, LuE/17/14/4.

2 Ward, *Erratic Odyssey*, 82. N to E, 7 January 1921, LuE/18/1/1. N to E, 17 January 1921, LuE/18/1/2. N to E, 24 February 1921, LuE/18/1/4. Diary of Lady Sackville, 15 February 1921.

3 Ward, *Erratic Odyssey*, 79, 86. N to E, 1 August 1920, LuE/17/12/3. Eadred Lutyens, 'The Lutyens Family' (typescript). 'Reminiscences on Lutyens', *Architectural Association Journal* (1959), 230.

4   Lady Sackville Diary, 15 September 1916, 23 March 1921.
5   N to E, 14 October 1917, *Letters*, 355. N to E, 1 August 1920, LuE/17/12/3. N to E, 17 August 1921, *Letters*, 397. Lady Sackville Diary, 1 June 1921, 11 June 1921, 29 November 1921.
6   Mary Lutyens, *To Be Young*, 81. *The Book of the Queen's Dolls' House*, ed. A. C. Benson and Sir Lawrence Weaver (Methuen, 1924). Mary Stewart-Wilson, *Queen Mary's Dolls' House* (Bodley Head, 1988).
7   N to E, 17 January 1921, LuE/18/1/2. E to N, 5 January 1921, LuE/29/4/1. E to N, 9 February 1921, LuE/29/4/6.
8   Lady Sackville Diary, 11 June 1921, 22 June 1921, 26 June 1921, 7 July 1921, 28 September 1921. E to N, 2 February 1921, LuE/29/4/5.
9   E to N, 16 December 1920, LuE/29/3/36. N to E, 17 August 1921, LuE/18/3/2. Lady Sackville Diary, 28 September 1921, 29 January 1922.
10 'Reminiscences on Lutyens,' *Architectural Association Journal* (1959), 231. Hussey, *Lutyens*, 469. Colin Amery, *Britannic House: A Palace Upon a Cliff* (1991).
11 Hussey, *Lutyens*, 438, 440. Commonwealth War Graves Archive, WG 462, Box 2003, Cutting from *Adelaide Register*, 22 January 1925. N to E, 4 August 1923, LuE/18/10/2. E to N, 26 September 1921, LuE/29/4/22. Lady Sackville Diary, 9 October 1921.
12 *Candles*, 91. Mary Lutyens, *Krishnamurti*, 114, 131–2.
13 N to E, 21 February 1922, LuE/18/5/4. E to N, 17 January 1922, LuE/29/5/2. E to N, 27 February 1922, LuE/29/5/4. Lady Sackville Diary, 15 April 1922. *Candles*, 92. Mary Lutyens, *Krishnamurti*, 131.
14 N to E, 20 February 1922, *Letters*, 398. Lady Sackville Diary, 12 March 1922. Philip Ziegler, *King Edward VIII* (Fontana, 1991), 136.
15 N to E, 4 March 1922, *Letters*, 398. E to N, 9 March 1922, *Letters*, 399. Hussey, *Lutyens*, 408. *Rufus Isaacs, Marquess of Reading* by his Son (Hutchinson, 1945), vol. II, 178.
16 N to E, 3 July 1922, LuE/18/6/1. Lady Sackville Diary, 7 August 1922, 12 September 1922, 13 September 1922.
17 Lady Sackville Diary, 7 August 1922, 12 September 1922, 13 September 1922.
18 N to E, 22 October 1922, LuE/18/7/7. N to E, 13 November 1922, LuE/18/8/1. N to E, 18 November 1922, LuE/18/8/2. N to E, 5

December 1922, LuE/18/8/4. Lady Sackville Diary, 26 October 1922.
19 E to N, 17 October 1922, LuE/29/5/34. Lady Sackville Diary, 19 November 1922, 20 January 1923, 21 April 1923.
20 *Candles*, 102–3. Mary Lutyens, *Krishnamurti*, 172. See Anthony Storr, *Feet of Clay: A Study of Gurus* (HarperCollins, 1996).
21 Lady Sackville Diary, 18 January 1923, 25 June 1923, 29 June 1923, 20 July 1923, 22 August 1923, 4 September 1923. N to E, 10 September 1923, LuE/18/11/1. N to E, 19 September 1923, LuE/18/11a/3. E to N, 14 September 1923, LuE/29/6/21.
22 Mary Lutyens, *Lutyens*, 196–9. Victoria Glendinning, *Vita*, 133. Ursula Ridley Papers, Emily to Ursula, 19 December 1942.
23 Author interview with Tim Drewitt (May 2000). Lady Sackville Diary, 6 August 1923. Hussey, *Lutyens*, 485–94.
24 Mary Lutyens, *Krishnamurti*, 130, 174–5. Elisabeth Lutyens, *Goldfish Bowl*, 25.
25 Howard de Walden Estate Archive, Edward Blount to Lutyens, 29 November 1923. (I am indebted to Sir Nigel Mobbs for this letter.) N to E, 13 December 1923, LuE/18/11a/5. Hussey, *Lutyens*, 451–2. Lady Sackville Diary, 5 November 1923.
26 *Candles*, 105. E to N, 20 December 1923, LuE/29/6/35. Mary Lutyens, *To Be Young*, 96, 102. Elisabeth Lutyens, *Goldfish Bowl*, 30.
27 N to E, 13 November 1922, LuE/18/8/1. N to E, 22 December 1922, LuE/18/8/6. Mary Lutyens, *To Be Young*, 102–4. Mary Lutyens, *Lutyens*, 206–7.
28 Iris Butler, *The Viceroy's Wife: Letters of Alice, Countess of Reading from India* (Hodder & Stoughton, 1969), 160. Lady Sackville Diary, 4 February 1924. Mary Lutyens, *To Be Young*, 104. *Candles*, 106. E to N, 3 March 1924, LuE/29/7/4.
29 Lady Sackville Diary, 15 March 1924, 30 April 1924, 2 May 1924.
30 N to E, 17 April 1924, LuE/18/13/2. N to E, 24 April 1924, LuE/18/13/3. Mary Lutyens, *Lutyens*, 208–9.
31 Elisabeth Lutyens, *Goldfish Bowl*, 41. Lady Sackville Diary, 10 July 1924, 28 July 1924, 30 July 1924. Eadred Lutyens, 'The Lutyens Family' (typescript).

CHAPTER SIXTEEN
EMILY'S GREAT ADVENTURE 1924–1925
Notes to pages 325–344

1 E to N, 3 August 1924, LuE/29/7/11. N to E, 22 August 1924, LuE/18/13/8. N to E, 29 August 1924, LuE/18/13/10. N to E, 17 September 1924, LuE/18/14/4. N to E, 25 March 1925, LuE/18/15/9.
2 *Architectural Association Journal*, 36 (1920), 56. Hussey, *Lutyens*, 464. John Summerson 'Daniel' (in the Lion's Den), 'Architect Laureate', *Night and Day*, 28 October 1937.
3 John Summerson, *Georgian London* (Penguin, 1962), 158. David Kynaston, *The City of London, volume III: Illusions of Gold 1914–45* (Chatto & Windus, 1999), 265–7. Stamp, *Lutyens*, 146.
4 John Booker, *Temples of Mammon: The Architecture of Banking* (Edinburgh University Press, 1990), 234–5. Hussey, *Lutyens*, 469–71, 491. Edwin Green, *Buildings for Bankers: Sir Edwin Lutyens and the Midland Bank* (1980). Jane Ridley, 'Architect for the Metropolis', *City Journal*, Spring 1998. Simon Bradley and Nikolaus Pevsner, *London I: The City of London* (Penguin, 1997), 580. *Builder*, 6 May 1927, 714.
5 *Candles*, 112. Mary Lutyens, *To Be Young*, 116–17. Washington, *Madame Blavatsky's Baboon*, 215.
6 N to E, 22 August 1924, LuE/18/13/8. N to E, 29 August 1924, LuE/18/13/10. E to N, 26 August 1924, LuE/29/7/14. E to N, 29 August 1924, LuE/29/7/15. E to N, 3 September 1924. LuE/29/7/17. Daphne Pollen, *I Remember*, 187. Meirion and Susie Harries, *A Pilgrim Soul*, 43–4.
7 Mary Lutyens, *Lutyens*, 214. N to E, 17 August 1924, LuE/18/13/7. E to N, 16 August 1924, LuE/29/7/15. E to N, 21 August 1924, LuE/29/7/13.
8 N to E, 4 August 1924, LuE/18/13/6. N to E, 17 August 1924, LuE/18/13/7. Lady Sackville Diary, 29 July 1921. Michael Holroyd, *Augustus John: The New Biography* (Vintage, 1997), 485. Daphne Pollen, *I Remember*, 210.
9 Mary Lutyens, *To Be Young*, 141. Lady Sackville Diary, 1 December 1923. N to E, 29 October 1924, LuE/18/14/6.
10 Mary Lutyens, *Lutyens*, 214. *Candles*, 113.
11 Mary Lutyens, *To Be Young*, 132. Meirion and Susie Harries, *A Pilgrim Soul*, 46.

12 Irving, *Indian Summer*, 135–6. N to E, 12 January 1925, LuE/18/15/1. Iris Portal interviewed in William Dalrymple, *City of Djinns* (Flamingo, 1994), 79–80.
13 E to N, 29 August 1924, LuE/29/7/15. N to E, 25 December 1924, LuE/29/7/24. Mary Lutyens, *Lutyens*, 215–6. Mary Lutyens, *To Be Young*, 141–3. Elisabeth Lutyens, *Goldfish Bowl*, 34–5.
14 Nigel Nicolson, *Portrait of a Marriage* (Weidenfeld & Nicolson, 1973), 61. Susan Mary Alsop, *Lady Sackville* (Weidenfeld & Nicolson, 1978), 221, 224. Victoria Glendinning, *Vita*, 145.
15 N to E, 25 March 1925, LuE/18/15/9. Mary Lutyens, *Lutyens*, 218.
16 N to E, 28 April 1925, *Letters*, 403–6. Hussey, *Lutyens*, 459.
17 Cumbria County Record Office, Lord Howard of Penrith Papers, Lutyens to Sir Esmé Howard, 8 July 1925, DHW8/23. Earle, *Turn Over the Page*, 192. Esmé Howard, Lord Howard of Penrith, *Theatre of Life* (Hodder & Stoughton, 1936), vol. II, 560. Gavin Stamp, 'Lutyens in Washington', forthcoming.
18 E to N, 19 March 1925, LuE/29/8/8.
19 N to E, 21 May 1925, LuE/19/1/1. Mary Lutyens, *To Be Young*, 158. *Candles*, 124.
20 *Candles*, 135–9.
21 *Candles*, 140–2. Mary Lutyens, *Krishnamurti*, 221–3.

CHAPTER SEVENTEEN
THE ELEMENTAL MODE   1926–1931
Notes to pages 345–372

1 Lady Sackville Diary, 17 June 1926, 18 June 1926, 21 June 1926, 21 August 1926.
2 Lady Sackville Diary, 16 October 1926, 23 October 1926. N to E, 5 October 1926, LuE/19/5/3. E to N, 6 October 1926, LuE/30/1/18.
3 Elisabeth Lutyens, *Goldfish Bowl*, 45. *Builder*, 13 November 1925, 698. *Journal of RIBA*, 33 (November 1925), 53–5. *Architectural Association Journal*, 48 (August 1932), 67. N to E, 5 December 1925, LuE/19/2/1. Lady Sackville Diary, 5 April 1926.
4 Commonwealth War Graves Archive, H. C. Bradshaw to Lionel Earle, 8 June 1926; Lutyens to Fabian Ware, 28 June 1926. N to E, 5 October 1926, LuE/19/5/3.
5 N to E, 5 December 1925, LuE/19/2/1. N to E, 6 March 1927,

LuE/19/8/1. *Builder*, (October 1926), 701–2. Andrew Boyle, *Poor Dear Brendan: The Quest for Brendan Bracken* (Hutchinson, 1974), 132–5, 345. Charles Lysaght, *Brendan Bracken* (Allen Lane, 1979), 76–86. C. H. Reilly, *Scaffolding in the Sky* (Routledge, 1938), 260. Mary Lutyens, *Lutyens*, 230.

6 Lady Sackville Diary, 13 November 1926. City of Westminster Archive, Grosvenor Estate Archive, 1049/9/78, Duke's Instruction Book, 16 June 1926, 18 June 1926; 1049/10/38, Grosvenor Estate to Lutyens, 21 June 1926; 1049/10/38, Enever (Edwards's solicitors) to Boodle Hatfield (Duke's solicitors), 11 November 1926. *Survey of London, Volume 39: The Grosvenor Estate in Mayfair, Part I*, ed. F. H. W. Sheppard (Athlone Press, 1977), 73–8, 164–5. *Survey of London, Volume 40: The Grosvenor Estate in Mayfair, Part II*, ed. F. H. W. Sheppard (Athlone Press, 1980), 270–3. *Observer*, 29 January 1928.

7 *Survey of London*, vol. 40, 272. *Survey of London*, vol. 39, 76–7. Hussey, *Lutyens*, 482.

8 Commonwealth War Graves Archive, ACON 56, Box 2054, Colonel Ingpen to Fabian Ware, 28 April 1926; Fabian Ware to Ingpen, 4 May 1926; Memo by H. Robinson, 5 July 1926; Crewe to Fabian Ware, 9 July 1926; H. Robinson to Fabian Ware, 26 October 1926.

9 CWGA, ACON 56, Box 2054, Fabian Ware to Ingpen, 4 May 1926; Fabian Ware to General Macready, 23 June 1926; Memo by H. Robinson, 12 October 1926; Fabian Ware to Kipling, 22 November 1926; Kipling to Fabian Ware, 23 November 1926.

10 Hussey, *Lutyens*, 275. Cumbria County Record Office, Lord Howard of Penrith Papers, Lutyens to Esmé Howard, 8 July 1925, DHW8/28.

11 *Candles*,149, 156. N to E, 4 February 1927, LuE/19/7/5.

12 E to N, 4 February 1927, *Letters*, 408. *Candles*, 157. Lady Sackville Diary, 13 February 1927, 15 February 1927, 19 February 1927.

13 Meirion and Susie Harries, *Pilgrim Soul*, 57.

14 N to E, 14 July 1927, LuE/19/8/10. Mary Lutyens, *Lutyens*, 230–1.

15 Anne Sebba, *Enid Bagnold* (Weidenfeld & Nicolson, 1986), 96–7.

16 Lady Sackville Diary, 30 October 1927.

17 Author interview with Robert Heal (June 1998).

18 Lutyens's *Observer* review is in Mary Lutyens, *Lutyens*, 285–7. N to E, 4 January 1928, LuE/19/9/1. N to E, 31 July 1928, LuE/19/10/6.

19 Reilly, *Scaffolding in the Sky*, 266–7. N to E, 23 December 1926,

LuE/19/6/3. N to E, 4 February 1927, LuE/19/7/5.

20 N to E, 5 February 1926, LuE/19/3/2. N to E, 17 January 1929, LuE/19/12/3. N to E, 24 January 1929, LuE/19/12/4.

21 N to E, 24 January 1929, *Letters*, 416–17. N to E, 14 February 1929, LuE/19/12/7. N to E, 27 February 1929, *Letters*, 419.

22 Mary Lutyens, *Lutyens*, 240. Ursula Ridley Papers, Emily to Ursula, 25 June 1942.

23 N to E, 22 October 1928, LuE/19/11/3. E to N, 2 August 1929, LuE/30/4/4. N to E, 5 August 1929, LuE/19/13/4.

24 Hussey, *Lutyens*, 527. Boyle, *Poor Dead Brendan*, 165. Lysaght, *Brendan Bracken*, 86. Hansard, *House of Commons Debates*, vol. 251, col. 525. Reilly, *Scaffolding in the Sky*, 257–8.

25 *The Times*, 6 July 1929, 31 July 1929. N to E, 31 July 1929, LuE/19/13/2. N to E, 24 August 1929, LuE/19/13/5.

26 Stephen Gardiner, *Epstein* (Michael Joseph, 1992), 306. *Evening Standard*, 31 July 1929. N to E, 31 July 1929, LuE/19/13/2. *Architect and Building News*, 9 January 1931, 61–5. *Builder*, 20 June 1930. Reilly, *Scaffolding in the Sky*, 265.

27 *Architectural Association Journal* (1932), 63. 'Reminiscences on Lutyens', *Architectural Association Journal* (1959), 236. John Summerson, 'Arches of Triumph: The Design for Liverpool Cathedral', *Lutyens Catalogue*, 53. Hussey, *Lutyens*, 533. Lecture by David Crellin, 4 October 2001.

28 Hussey, *Lutyens*, 190, 528. N to E, 28 November 1926, *Letters*, 407. *Architectural Association Journal* (1932), 65.

29 N to E, 5 August 1929, LuE/19/13/4. *Architects' Journal*, 11 December 1929; 5 March 1930; 19 March 1930. *Builder*, 6 December 1939; 13 December 1929. Reginald Blomfield, *Memoirs of an Architect*, 239. *The Times*, 7 December 1929.

30 *The Times*, 6 December 1929. N to E, 31 December 1929, LuE/19/14/8.

31 N to E, 18 December 1929, LuE/19/14/5. N to E, 25 December 1929, *Letters*, 420. 'Reminiscences on Lutyens', *Architectural Association Journal* (1959), 234.

32 N to E, 31 December 1929, LuE/19/14/8. Hussey, *Lutyens*, 521. *Architectural Review*, 69 (1931), 12.

33 *Architects' Journal*, 13 March 1929. *Builder*, 28 February 1930. Blomfield, *Memoirs of an Architect*, 240.

34 *Crawford Papers*, ed. John Vincent (Manchester University Press, 1984), 497, 533.

35 N to E, 4 August 1930, LuE/19/15/6. N to E, 9 August 1930, LuE/19/15/7.
36 Reilly, *Scaffolding in the Sky*, 262–3.

CHAPTER EIGHTEEN
THE TORCH OF HUMANISM 1931–1937
Notes to pages 373–398

1 E to N, 7 August 1930, LuE/30/5/14. E to N, 6 September 1930, LuE/30/5/18.
2 Ursula Ridley Papers, Emily to Ursula, 1 February 1931.
3 *Letters*, 257. Butler, *The Architecture of Sir Edwin Lutyens*, vol. II, 30.
4 Tom Metcalf, *Imperial Vision*, 236. Stamp, *Lutyens*, 185.
5 Mary Lutyens, *Lutyens*, 287. Stamp, *Lutyens*, 185. Robert Lutyens, *Sir Edwin Lutyens:* 81. N to E, 18 December 1929, LuE/19/14/5.
6 Robert Byron, 'New Delhi', *Architectural Review*, vol. 69 (January 1931). Robert Byron, 'The Architecture of the Viceroy's House', *Country Life*, 6 June 1931. Robert Byron, 'The Architecture of Sir Herbert Baker', *Country Life*, 4 July 1931.
7 Ursula Ridley Papers, Emily to Ursula, 1 February 1931; Emily to Ursula, 9 February 1931. N to E, 3 July 1931, LuE/19/16/5. Robert Byron, 'The Setting of the Viceroy's House', *Country Life*, 27 June 1931. Irving, *Indian Summer*, 290.
8 N to E, 18 November 1938, *Letters*, 443. Ursula Ridley Papers, Emily to Ursula, 9 February 1931.
9 E to N, 2 July 1931, LuE/30/6/7. N to E, 3 July 1931, LuE/19/16/5. *Candles*, 186.
10 *Architectural Association Journal* (1932). Lutyens, 'How and Why?', *Architectural Review*, 71 (1931), 123–4. Lutyens, 'What I Think of Modern Architecture', *Country Life*, 20 June 1931. Hussey, *Lutyens*, 546. Robert Lutyens, *Sir Edwin Lutyens*, 27.
11 John Summerson to Gavin Stamp, 25 June 1981, Gavin Stamp Collection. *Builder*, (1931), 733.
12 N to E, 31 August 1931, LuE/19/17/8. N to E, 13 July 1932, LuE/20/1/10. Hussey, *Lutyens*, 570–1.
13 Robert Lutyens, *Sir Edwin Lutyens*, 51. N to E, 3 July 1931, LuE/19/16/5. N to E, 8 May 1932, LuE/20/1/7. *Crawford Papers*, 538–9.

14 Hussey, *Lutyens*, 537–8. N to E, 26 May 1931, LuE/19/16/1. N to E, 24 March 1932, LuE/20/1/4. N to E, 15 August 1934, LuE/20/6/4. 'Reminiscences on Sir Edwin Lutyens,' *Architectural Association Journal*, 74 (1959), 236.
15 N to E, 7 August 1931, LuE/19/7/1. N to E, 28 September 1931, LuE/19/18/2. N to E, 13 July 1932, LuE/20/1/10.
16 Richard Gilbert Scott Collection, Lady Sackville to Sir Giles Gilbert Scott, 3 June 1932, 30 September 1932, 18 October 1932, 9 December 1932. I am grateful to Gavin Stamp for these references. N to E, 19 July 1933, LuE/20/3/8.
17 Victoria Glendinning, *Vita*, 289–90. E to N, 7 September 1934, LuE/30/9/20.
18 N to E, 31 May 1931, LuE/19/16/2. N to E, 6 July 1931, LuE/19/16/7. N to E, 29 January 1932, LuE/20/1/2. Mary Lutyens, *Lutyens*, 252–3.
19 N to E, 24 March 1932, LuE/20/1/4. E to N, 26 March 1932, LuE/30/7/2. Obituary of Roualeyn Cumming-Bruce, *Daily Telegraph*, 14 June 2000.
20 N to E, 28 September 1931, LuE/19/18/2. N to E, 29 January 1932, LuE/20/1/2. *Architectural Association Journal* (1932). Meirion and Susie Harries, *Pilgrim Soul*, 52.
21 N to E, 24 January 1932, LuE/20/1/1. Meirion and Susie Harries, *Pilgrim Soul*, 58–60. Elisabeth Lutyens, *Goldfish Bowl*, 72.
22 N to E, 2 August 1932, LuE/20/2/2. *Crawford Papers*, 546.
23 N to E, 22 August 1932, *Letters*, 426–8. Mary Lutyens, *Lutyens*, 256–60.
24 N to E, 16 May 1932, LuE/20/1/11. N to E, 18 May 1932, LuE/20/1/13. N to E, 4 October 1932, *Letters*, 428. E to N, 3 October 1933, LuE/30/8/22. N to E, 8 August 1933, *Letters*, 430. N to E, 9 January 1940, LuE/20/14/4. N to E, 10 January 1940, LuE/20/14/5.
25 Mary Lutyens, *Forthcoming Marriages* (John Murray, 1933), 304–5. N to E, 8 August 1933, *Letters*, 430.
26 E to N, 12 July 1933, LuE/30/8/7. E to N, 12 August 1934, LuE/30/9/13. Mary Lutyens, *Lutyens*, 26–7.
27 Ursula Ridley Papers, Ursula to Emily, 4 December 1934; Emily to Ursula, 10 December 1934.
28 [Summerson], 'Architect Laureate', *Night and Day*, 28 October 1937. Bevis Hillier, *Young Betjeman* (John Murray, 1982), 263.
29 Laurence Whistler, *The Laughter and the Urn* (Weidenfeld & Nicolson, 1985), 203. Mary Lutyens, *Lutyens*, 191. Peter Mandler,

The Fall and Rise of the Stately Home (Yale University Press, 1997), 278–84.

30 E to N, 20 August 1928, *Letters*, 411. Robert Lutyens, *Sir Edwin Lutyens*, 75. Kenneth Clarke, *Another Part of the Wood* (John Murray, 1974), 201.
31 Bradley and Pevsner, *London*, 498.
32 Hussey, *Lutyens*, 544. Jane Brown, *Lutyens and the Edwardians*, 223–6. Evelyn Waugh, *Vile Bodies* (Penguin, 1938), 9.
33 Commonwealth War Graves Archive, WG 855/3/2/2, Recollection of letter dictated by Lutyens to Lucas on 26 June 1935; Lutyens to Fabian Ware, 10 October 1935. *Builder*, 5 April 1935.
34 N to E, 3 September 1935, *Letters*, 435–6. Reilly, *Scaffolding in the Sky*, 266.
35 John Betjeman, 'The Bressey Report', *Criterion*, 18 (October 1938), 1–12.
36 N to E, 6 July 1931, LuE/19/16/7. E to N, 7 July 1931, LuE/30/6/10. N to E, 8 September 1931, LuE/19/18/1. N to E, 19 July 1933, LuE/20/3/8. N to E, 1 August 1933, LuE/20/4/1.
37 N to E, 1 March 1942, LuE/21/4/11. Author interview with Tim Drewitt (23 May 2000). Mary Lutyens, *Lutyens*, 269.
38 N to E, 12 June 1939, LuE/20/12/1. Hussey, *Lutyens*, 547. James Lees-Milne, *Ancestral Voices* (Chatto & Windus, 1975), 179. Stamp, *Lutyens*, 175–6.
39 N to E, 6 January 1940, LuE/20/14/3. Hussey, *Lutyens*, 492.

CHAPTER NINETEEN
LORD COUGH OF COUGH 1937–1944
Notes to pages 399–418

1 Ursula Ridley Papers, Ursula to Emily, n.d. [autumn 1937]; Emily to Ursula, 11 May 1938; Emily to Ursula, 12 May 1938; Emily to Ursula, 15 May 1938.
2 Robert Lutyens, *Sir Edwin Lutyens*, 77.
3 Robert Lutyens, 'Air Passage to India', typescript (1937), 57–9, 61, 65.
4 Hussey, *Lutyens*, 555–6. N to E, 18 November 1938, *Letters*, 442–3.
5 Hussey, *Lutyens*, 560. Sidney C. Hutchinson, *History of the Royal Academy* (Robert Boyce, 1986), 164.

6 Ursula Ridley Papers, Emily to Ursula, 1 October 1938; Emily to Ursula, 26 April 1943. *Crawford Papers*, 493. *The Times*, 28 January 1939.

7 E to N, 8 June 1939, LuE/31/2/5. E to N, 21 August 1939, LuE/31/2/11. N to E, 18 October 1939, LuE/20/13/7. N to E, 28 December 1939, LuE/20/13/33.

8 N to E, 17 October 1939, LuE/20/13/6. N to E, 18 October 1939, LuE/20/13/7. N to E, 31 December 1939, LuE/20/13/35.

9 N to E, 3 September 1939, LuE/20/12/5. N to E, 6 September 1939, LuE/20/12/7. N to E, 8 September 1939, LuE/20/12/8. N to E, 18 October 1939, LuE/20/13/8.

10 N to E, 26 January 1940, LuE/20/14/18. N to E, 30 January 1940, LuE/20/14/19. N to E, 31 January 1940, LuE/20/14/20. N to E, 2 February 1940, LuE/20/14/22. N to E, 14 February 1940, LuE/20/14/24. N to E, 15 February 1940, LuE/20/14/25. N to E, 17 February 1940, LuE/20/14/27. Mary Lutyens, *Lutyens*, 272.

11 'Reminiscences on Sir Edwin Lutyens', *Architectural Association Journal*, 74 (1959), 235. Author e-mail from Gavin Stamp, 11 September 2000. *Architects' Journal*, 22 October 1941, 261.

12 N to E, 17 September 1940, LuE/21/1/12. N to E, 21 September 1940, LuE/21/1/15. Hussey, *Lutyens*, 569. Ursula Ridley Papers, Emily to Ursula, 10 September 1940.

13 E to N, 24 September 1940, LuE/Uncat. Ursula Ridley Papers, Emily to Ursula, 27 September 1940.

14 Ursula Ridley Papers, Emily to Ursula, 26 September 1941.

15 Ursula Ridley Papers, Emily to Ursula, 25 October 1941; Emily to Ursula, 12 November 1941; Emily to Ursula, 6 December 1941; Emily to Ursula, 10 December 1941; Emily to Ursula, 23 December 1941.

16 Ursula Ridley Papers, Emily to Ursula, 19 December 1941. *Crawford Papers*, 491.

17 Author interview with Anne Fraser (23 January 1998). Ursula Ridley Papers, Emily to Ursula, 31 December 1941; Emily to Ursula, 2 February 1942.

18 Ursula Ridley Papers, Emily to Ursula, 9 April 1942; Emily to Ursula, 10 April 1942; Emily to Ursula, 2 July 1942; Emily to Ursula, 4 July 1942; Emily to Ursula, 10 July 1942; Emily to Ursula, 27 July 1942; Emily to Ursula, 29 July 1942; Emily to Ursula, 23 August 1942.

19 N to E, 7 August 1942, LuE/21/4/13. Clough Williams-Ellis, *Architect Errant* (Golden Dragon Books, 1980), 239–41. Erno

Goldfinger interview, Gavin Stamp Collection.
20 Ursula Ridley Papers, Emily to Ursula, 19 October 1941; Emily to Ursula, 10 July 1942; Emily to Ursula, 1 October 1942; Emily to Ursula, 22 April 1943.
21 Author interview with Joe Links (3 December 1994). Ursula Ridley Papers, Emily to Ursula, 24 March 1943; Emily to Ursula, 26 April 1943. *Diaries of Evelyn Waugh*, ed. Michael Davie (Weidenfeld & Nicolson, 1976), 538.
22 Ursula Ridley Papers, Emily to Ursula, 7 June 1943; Emily to Ursula, 13 July 1943; Emily to Ursula, 4 October 1943; Emily to Ursula, 1 December 1943.
23 Ursula Ridley Papers, Emily to Ursula, 10 December 1943. Hussey, *Lutyens*, 579-80. Elisabeth Lutyens, *Goldfish Bowl*, 146. Mary Lutyens, *Lutyens*, 282-3.
24 Mary Lutyens, *Lutyens*, 283-4. Robert Lutyens, 'Fragments of Autobiography, 97-8. Knebworth Archive, order of service at the funeral of Sir Edwin Lutyens.
25 James Lees-Milne, *Prophesying Peace* (Chatto & Windus, 1977), 3. *The Times*, 4 January 1944. Christopher Hussey, 'Sir Edwin Lutyens', *Country Life*, 14 January 1944. Gavin Stamp, 'The Rise and Fall and Rise of Edwin Lutyens', *Architectural Review*, 170 (1981).
26 Elisabeth Lutyens, *Goldfish Bowl*, 284.
27 Ursula Ridley Papers, Emily to Ursula, 22 August 1938.

Author's Acknowledgements

I owe a great debt to the late Mary Lutyens and Joe Links. For permission to quote from Mary Lutyens's writings and reproduce photographs, I am grateful to Adam Pallant. Thanks also to Amanda Pallant. Charles and Issy Lutyens made researching the Lutyens family history a pleasure. Candia Lutyens and Paul Peterson were generous with Robert Lutyens's material and photographs.

I should like to acknowledge the Royal Institute of British Architects for permission to quote from the letters between Edwin and Emily Lutyens and to reproduce illustrations from the letters and sketch books. The RIBA has been generous with the copyrighted material it controls.

I am indebted to the owners who have allowed me to explore their Lutyens houses, especially Wing Commander Douglas Watson, Tony and Shula Laws, Lady Adam Gordon, Johanna Walker, Geoffrey Robinson, Samantha Pollock-Hill, Douglas Moller, Barry Reuter, Charlotte Atkins, Timmy and Penny Norton, Sir Robert and Lady Clarke and the late Hugh and Mrs Astor. I have learned much from the excellent study days organised by the Lutyens Trust. The National Trust was helpful at Lindisfarne and Castle Drogo. I owe a special debt to Margaret and Patrick Kelly for an unforgettable visit to Lambay. At Le Bois des Moutiers I was warmly welcomed by Madame Marie Mallet and Emmanuel Ducamp.

I am indebted to the following for information: Anne Balfour Fraser, Martin Lutyens, Major-General Sir John Swinton, Jane Brown, Andrew Saint, the late Roderick Gradidge, Colin Amery, Alan Powers, David Crellin, John Rollo, Alan Greenberg, Hilary Grainger, Susan Rands, Patric Dickinson, Virginia Surtees, Cressida Inglewood, Helena Francis, Judith Tankard, Annabel Freyberg, Stuart Martin, Tom Duncan, Angela Brown, Michael Edwards, Roland Quinault, Clyde Binfield. For memories of the Lutyens office, I am grateful to Robert Heal, Tim Drewitt and the late Sir Martyn Beckett. Patricia Reed helped unravel the relationship with William Nicholson.

My visit to Delhi was made possible by a grant from the Authors' Foundation. I am grateful to Professor Mansinh Rana, Kushwant

Singh, Patwant Singh, Shri Duggal, Charles and Marko Lutyens. My trip to Washington was organised by Lauree Feldman and Constance Collins of the Royal Oak Foundation. My thanks to Sir Christopher and Lady Meyer, Amanda Downes, Lucy and Berkeley Tittman and Richard Wendorff. Andrew Hopkins and Gavin Stamp organised a conference at the British School at Rome in 1999; a very early version of Chapter 11 was published in *Lutyens Abroad*.

I am grateful to Nigel Nicolson for permisson to quote from Lady Sackville's diary. Letters in the Knebworth Archive are quoted by courtesy of www.knebworthhouse.com; my thanks also to archivist Clare Fleck. For permission to quote from the Herbert Baker Papers in the RIBA, I am grateful to Michael Baker. For permission to quote from the Giles Gilbert Scott papers my thanks to Richard Gilbert Scott. I should like to thank the staff at the following institutions: Godalming Library, Commonwealth War Graves Archive, India Office Library, University of Buckingham Library. Much of this book was written in the London Library, where members of the staff were efficient and friendly as ever.

I am grateful to Margaret Richardson for her expertise and encouragement. Gavin Stamp read the manuscript, gave unstintingly of his expertise, was generous with his photographs and answered my endless email questions. Caroline Dawnay's enthusiasm sustained both me and the book through thick and thin: no one could have a better agent. Nor could I hope for a better editor than Penelope Hoare at Chatto. I am also grateful to Alex Butler and Ali Reynolds.

My mother Clayre Percy scoured record offices, read the manuscript, compiled the index and gave moral support. My sons Toby and Humphrey willingly put up with spending more time than they might have liked in search of their great great-grandparents. My husband Stephen has cheerfully shared his life with the Architect and his Wife.

Index

Abreviations: ELL = Edwin Landseer Lutyens
EL = Emily Lutyens

Abbey House, Barrow, 228
Abbotswood, 138, 145, 280
Abercrombie, Sir Patrick, 413, 414
Agar, Barbara, see Lutyens, Barbara
Aitken, Charles, 277, 278
Alba, Duke of, 260
Alfonso, King, 270
Allendale, Viscountess, see Beaumont
Allingham, Helen, 23, 34, 35
Anderson, Mary, 87
Arbuthnot, Elinor, (Guthrie), 45, 54, 69
Arbuthnot, Foster, 45
Architectural Association, 52, 172, visit Marsh Court 177, ELL's addresses to 296, 327, 381, on Viceroy's House 376n
Architectural Review, R. Byron on Viceroy's House 378–380; 392
Armstrong, Thomas, 36
Art Workers' Guild, 48, 63, ELL Master of 381
Arundale, George, tutor to K & Nitya 242, 256, 257, at Huizen 340, 341, claims to be Mrs Besant's heir 341, quarrels 342
Arundale, Miss, (George's Aunt), 242, 356
Ashby St. Legers, 158
Asquith, Raymond, 198
Astor, Viscount, 277
Athenaeum Club, 177, 246

Badcock, E. Baynes, of Badcock & Maxey, partner, awkwardness at Fulbrook 123, rows with ELL, joke tombstone 138, 144, 245
Baillie Scott, M.H., 137
Baillie-Weaver, Harold, 259
Baines, Sir Frank, 288
Baker, Sir Herbert, 49, walking tour with ELL 58, 59; 133. In S. Africa: ELL writes to 156–7, 158, 164, 174, tires of S. Africa 179, fails to stop ELL coming 198, Pretoria Union Building criticised by ELL 199, never forgives ELL for clowning 199–200, helps ELL get Art Gallery & Memorial 199. New Delhi & the gradient: partnership over New Delhi suggested by ELL 212, appointed 221–2, gets Secretariats 221, alters plans: Secretariats moved up to level of Viceroy's House 226–7, does not warn ELL of effect 241, used by Hardinge to control ELL 227, quarrel over division of fees 236–237, works against ELL 238, row over gradient 261–264, mealtimes at Raisina Mill 301, gets Council Chamber 292–293, ELL's hostility towards 370, Robert Byron's opinion of Baker's work 379. Advisor to Imperial War Graves Commission 277, wants five point cross 278, gets Bank of England 306 & n, & S.Africa House 370, at ELL's funeral 415
Balfour, Arthur, 92, 129, 245, 265, 279
Balfour, Lady Betty, 85, 86, 88, beautiful & a Soul 89; 90, 94, 104, 111, 120, 129, & Fishers Hill 141; 181, 245, & Krishna 342

465

INDEX

Balfour, Eustace, 111–112, 129
Balfour, Lady Frances, 112, 141
Balfour, Gerald, 89, 94, 140, 141, 245
Balfour Fraser, Anne, 141, 410
Baring, Cecil, & Lambay 171–3, 229, 245, ELL restores 26A Bryanston Square for 202, visits ELL in hospital 264, gives marble for floor in Mansfield St, 291, in Dublin with ELL 331, loses ELL's money in slump 386
Baring, Maude (Lorillard), her life at Lambay 172–3, 'socialistic' 194; 231, 264
Baring's Bank, 245–6
Barnett, Henrietta, & Hampstead Garden Suburb 174–7 philistine 176; 183
Baroda, Gaekwar of, 294
Barrie, James M, 24, 97, *Quality Street* & *Peter Pan* 153; Great War Stone 278–9, Adelphi flat 280, 284
Batsford Park, 49, 50
Battersea, Constance de Rothschild Lady, hates Overstrand 102, bazaar with EL 168
Battersea, Cyril Flower, Lord, & The Pleasaunce at Overstrand 102, 114, 124, & Nonconformist Chapel 130
Batty Langley, *The City & Country Builder's & Workman's Treasury of Designs*, 317
Beaumont, Hon Mrs Wentworth, 153, as Viscountess Allendale 173
Bedford, Duchess of, 69
31 Bedford Square, 251
Behar, family, & Cockington 395–7
Belcher, John, 151
Belloc Lowndes, Mrs, 222
Berniers, Mr & Mrs, ELL's godparents, 3
Berrydown, 127
Besant, Mrs Annie, as theosophical leader: *London Lectures* 189, meets EL 190, 191, her generalship 204, on tour with EL 205, 212, at camps 330, 346. And Krishna: adopts Krishna & Nitya 192, arrives with them in London 203–4, plans their future 204, rumours re boys & Leadbeater in India 216, Naraniah (father) threatens lawsuit 216, smuggles boys to Sicily 217, 243, wins appeal for custody 243, disapproves of Krishna – EL relationship 257, & Krishna's education 259, 285 & n, 295, 307. And Theosophical Society HQ: suggests ELL to build 206, impossible client 244. And Indian politics: interest switches to Home Rule 256, Leader of Congress Party 265, against EL's Home Rule for India in London League 265, 'naughtie Annie' in India 294, 301, 334. Loses control: farcical journey to find 'Master the Count' in Hungary 341, dissolves Esoteric Section 361, out of control 375
Betjeman, John, *Architectural Review* 392
Birch, Mr, (schoolmaster) 28
Birkenhead, Earl of, 393
Black, Mr, brings action for negligence 401
Blackburn, Ernest, 150–1
Blagden, Isa, 83
Blagdon, 388, 391, delays with canal & garden 401, ELL stays 408
Blanche, Emile Jacques, portrait painter, 205
Blavatsky, Mme, 190, 191, 251, 267
Blomfield, C.G., 291–2
Blomfield, Reginald, 41, 47, 48, 69, President of RIBA, consulted re ELL & India 211, & Waterloo Bridge 348, rows with ELL over Charing Cross Bridge 360, 367, 369; & Royal Fine Art Commission 370, & RA 409, 411

INDEX

29 Bloomsbury Square, 48, 121–2, 137, 251
Blow, Detmar, 42, 63 & n, 283n & Grosvenor Estate 350–1, 385
Blumenthal, M. & Mme Jacques, 76, 94
Blunt, Lady Anne, 89, in Egypt 261
Blunt, Judith, 89, 90, & EL 92–5 & 116, & Victor 128, marriage 128; 170, 412
Blunt, Wilfrid Scawen, 84, & EL 89–94, 97, 120, opinion of ELL 127, & EL in retrospect 412
Bodichon, Barbara, 56
Bodley, G.F., 47
Boehm, Joseph, 14, 111
Le Bois des Moutiers, 'dream house' 125–6; 138, the locked cupboard 190; 205
Bond, Dr, Henry, 174 & n
Bracken, Brendan, 319, & *English Life* & *The Banker* 349–50; 363
Bradell, Darcy, 50
Bradlaugh, Charles, 191, 192
Brancker, Colonel Sefton, 246
Brandon, John, (in New Delhi office) 292
Breccles, 283n
Bressey, Sir Charles, appoints ELL consultant Architect to Highway Development Survey (Greater London) 395, 406
Britannic House, 306–307, John Summerson on 393
British Pavilion, International Exhibition in Paris 1900, 125, 132, 138
British School at Rome, 184, 201, 212, 216, problems ELL visits 259 & n
Broadmead, W., of Enmore Castle, tiresome & doesn't build 173
Brodie, J.A., Borough Engineer of Liverpool, on Delhi Planning Committee 212, quarrels with Swinton 214, works on report 216, 225
Brooke, F.H., 336
Browning, Elizabeth, 83
Broxbourne, nr Watford, Lutyens family home 6
26A Bryanston Square, restored for Cecil Baring, 202
Buckhurst Park, 196, 211
Buckley, Mr, 173
The Builder, 54, 329
Burne-Jones, Edward, 12, 26, 41, 108, 137
Butler, A.S.G. (Andy), 318, *Memorial Volumes* 351, analyses Viceroy's House 376, with ELL & model of Liverpool Cathedral 384, & Halnaker Hall 393
Butler, Harcourt, clever 215, amused by ELL 216, criticizes Harding 222, 227, on scale of New Delhi buildings 238
Butterfield, William, 34
Byron, Robert, shown Viceroy's House by ELL, his writing's effect on ELL's reputation 368, praises ELL & criticizes Baker in *Architectural Review* & *Country Life* 378–80, in Blitz 407

Caldecott, Randolph, 17, 24, 33, 36, 97, 383, 393
Campion Hall, commissioned by Father Darcy 394; 413
Canterbury, Archbishop of, & war stone 279 & n
Carpenter, Edward, *Love's Coming of Age* & contraception 167–8
Cecil, Lord Hugh, 311
The Cenotaph, temporary catafalque of wood in Processional Way 288, named 288, design 289, permanent monument 292, 311, 366, 383
Chamberlain, Austen, 268, 269
Chance, Julia & William,

467

commissioning of Orchards 114; 149
Chapman, Agnes, nee Mangles, & Crooksbury 53–55, kind to ELL as student 54
Chapman, Arthur (Chippy) MP, & Crooksbury 53–55, as widower with EL at seaside 169, 219, companion 181–2, no interest in theosophy 193, 202, sells Crooksbury 246, 276, 413
Chelmsford, Viscount, Viceroy 263, ordered by George V to support New Delhi 249, character 270, & Delhi Committee 271
Chetwode, Penelope, 368
Chinthurst Hill, described, & Goodhart-Rendel on 69–70; 72, 75, 196
Chirol, Valentine, of *The Times* 222
Churchill, Winston, 171, 260
Clarke, Conrad, 408
Clarke, Edward, 404, 405
Clutterbuck, G., 178
Cobden-Sanderson, 48
Cochrane, H., 266
Cockerell, Sidney, 42, 59n
Cockington scheme near Torquay, 395–7
Colefax, Sybil, 307
Collie, Arthur, 63, 147
Combe, Richard, 101
Connaught, Duke of, 284
Conway, Sir Martin, 284
Cooper, Lady Diana, 277, 281
Cooper, Reggie, 382
Corbett, Harvey, 336
Corbusier, Le, *Towards a New Architecture* 358, & Chandigar 359
The Corner, Thursley, 53
Cotes, Mrs Everard, 225
Country Life, 112n, 124n, 143, Hudson promoting ELL in 129, 142, 151, photographs 144, *Houses and Gardens by ELL* published by 244, on opening of Viceroy's House 376, criticizes Baker 379–80, & Christopher Hussey 382, obituary of ELL 416, and Robert Lutyens 296, 297, 305
Country Life Building, 174
County Hall, 165, enters competition & fails 165–6, 199, 221
Cowper, Countess of, 93
Crane, Walter, 33, 36, 37, 48
Cranston, Miss, of the tea-room, 112, 137n
Crawford, Earl of, Chairman Fine Art Commission, 348n, 369–70, 387–8
Crewe, Marquess of, Indian Secretary, Suggests ELL for Delhi Planning Committee 211–2, apppoints him 212, lobbied 215, as Ambassador in Paris unhelpful re Thiepval 352
Crooksbury, 52–5, 144, 163, later alterations 246
Cumming-Bruce, Roualeyn, 385
Cunard, Maud, 265, 277, 393
Curzon, George, Marquess of, against building New Delhi 225–6, hostile memo 269; 319
Curzon, Marchioness of, 113
Curzon, Irene, Cimmie, Baba 290, Cimmie marries Tom Mosley 295

Dalton, secretary, 122, 139
Dance, George, 152
Daneshill, 138, 145
D'Arcy, Father, 394
Dawber E. Guy, 49
Deanery Garden, 138, *Country Life* photographs 143–4
Debenham, Ernest, 114
De la Warr, Lady, 207, 295n
Delhi Planning Committee: 'Delhi experts' 212–3, survey site on elephant 213, decide on Malcha SW of city 213, 216, Hardinge reverses decision 225, south site chosen 227
Delville, M. & Mme, 255

INDEX

Derby, Earl of, 35, 85, 86
Disraeli, Benjamin, 82, 84
Dodge, Miss Mabel, heiress 206, to pay for Theosophical H.Q. 206, pays for Krishna & Nitya 207, 231, 243, in Wimbledon 315, pays EL's fares to Australia 332
Dolgorouki, Princess, 157, 180
Dorking, *St. Martin's Church*, Pixham, 155
Downey, Dr, Archbishop of Liverpool, meets ELL 363, appoints ELL 363, rejects Epstein 364; 366, sees plans 370, teased by ELL 383, no money 410
Dream Houses, 124 & n
Drewe, Julius, & Home & Colonial Stores 194, chooses site for Castle Drogo 195, cuts down size 196, son killed 196
Drogo, Castle, 195–7
Drum Inn, Cockington, 395–6
Dublin Art Gallery, 228–9, 331
Duckworth, Gerald, & EL 95, 96, 107, 121
Duckworth, Stella, 95
Dutch House, Holmwood, 169

Earle, Lionel, cousin of EL 120, 125, Permanent Sec. at Office of Works, influences Lord Crewe 215, warns about ELL's overspending 215–6, & Cenotaph 288–9, & Washington Embassy 335, 337
Earle, Teresa (Aunt T), 107–8, *Pot Pourri from a Surrey Garden* 109, friend of Marie Grunelius & vegetarian 125, 189; 140
Edward VII, King, coronation 152–3, King Edward Memorial 212
Edward VIII, Prince of Wales, 309–10, 388
Elcho, Mary Lady, 92
Elphinstone, Sir Graeme, 16, 29
Elwin, The Rev Whitwell, editor of *Quarterly Review* 86, & EL 86–7, 89, disapproves of her relationship with Blunt 91–2, 104, & marriage to ELL 127
Elwin, Mrs, 86
Epstein, Jacob, 364
Esher, Lord, Chairman of British School in Rome Building Committee 259

Fargie (boatman at Lambay), 172
Farrand, Barbara, 57n
Farrer, Gaspar & Henry, & 7 St. James's Square 202, commission Salutation 203, lend ELL 7 Apple Tree Yard 235, work cancelled due to war 245
Fatepuhr Sikri, 236
Fenwick, Mark & Mrs, 145, 280
Ferry Inn, Rosneath, 111, 112 & n
Fishers Hill, 138, 139, 140–141
Fleischmann, Dr, 409, 412
Flower, Wickham, 59
Folly Farm, 266, enlarged, ELL & EL holiday at 267; 342
Fosberry, Mr, 53
Fowke, Captain Francis, 36
Fowler, Henry, MP, 133
Frampton, George, 284
Franklyn, Mrs, 178n
Freake, Charles, 14
Fripp, Dr, 264
Fry, Roger, 268
Fulbrook, expensive 101, opposite opinions of 102n; 109, 114, 115, awkwardness involving Badcock 123

Gallwey, Bridget (Biddy) nee Blood grandmother, 9
Gallwey, Christopher, 9
Gallwey, General John (grandfather), 9
Gallwey, John de Bourge, 9
Gallwey, Peter, 10
Gallwey, General Thomas (uncle), 9, 15

469

INDEX

Gandhi & Swaraj (campaign for self-government), 320, 359, 360
Gardner, Starkie, 51, 70, 147
Garner, Thomas, 131
Garrick Club, 211, visitor's book 211, ELL elected to 284, meets Dr Downey lunching at 363, with Hussey at 407, 408, 411
Geddes, Professor Patrick, critical of New Delhi plan 255 & n
George V, King, as Prince of Wales at Lindisfarne 179, coronation 205, & Delhi foundation stone 213, shown drawings 218, & the gradient 269, supports completion of original design 269, dislikes War Shrine in Hyde Park 284
George, Ernest, 45, 46, 48, office 49, as architect 50–2, influence on ELL 53–5, 68, praises Paris Pavilion 132, plan for Great Dixter rejected 203
George, Walter, 291, 302
Gladstone, Herbert, 180, Governor General of S. Africa 199
Glasgow School, 108, 124, 137n
Gledstone, 301, 328, 338n
Glennie, Ian, 387, 404
Glennie, Sebastian (Bill), 404
Goddards, 128–9, 138
Godman, Joseph, 59 & n
Godwin, E.W., 26
Goldfinger, Erno, 411
Goodhart-Rendel, H.S., 70, 112n
Goschen, Lord, 293
Gosse, Edmund, 31
Gotch, Lawrence, 329
Gradidge, Roderick, 102n, 124n
Great Dixter, 203
Great Maytham, 174, 178
Green, Curtis, 228
Green, Mr, clerk of works for Theosophical HQ, 244
Greenwood, Harold, Robert Lutyens's partner, 396
Gregory, Lady, 197, & Dublin Art Gallery 229
Grenfell, Arthur, 198, 245
Grenfell, Ettie (Lady Desborough), 93
Grey Walls, 129, 138, windows 139–40; 149
Grogarty, Oliver St.John, 331
Grosvenor House, 350, criticism of 351
Grove, Archibald & Mrs, 124, 127, 133, 153
Grunelius, Marie, 125, 189
El Guadalperal, farm buildings, 261, 270, 282
Guest, Ivor, see Wimborne
Gummer, W.H., 201
Guthrie, Sir James, 108
Guthrie, Maggie, 69,70
Guthrie, Violet, 46

Haden–Guest, Dr, & Theosophical Society HQ 244–245; 252, 258
Hagreen, Mr, teacher of architecture, 38
Hailey, Malcolm, Commissioner for Delhi, 254, & gradient 262, 269, & Chelmsford 271
Haldane, Lord, 174, 223
Halifax, Earl of, see Irwin
Hall, Austen, 406, 407
Hall, E.E., assistant to ELL, 199, 213, 283, 358, 386, 396
Halnaker Hall, 393–4
Hampstead Garden Suburb, 174–177, St. Jude's 175, influence on appointment to New Delhi 211–2
Hampton Court Bridge, 395
Hannen, Nicholas, 150
Hardinge, Charles, Lord, of Penshurst, Viceroy, meets ELL 211, told of ELL's appointment to Planning Committee 212, autocrat 214, proposes ELL's appointment as architect to Crewe 215, & the site 218, 225, 227, presses for competition 221, wounded by

terrorist 223, appoints ELL officially 224, wants pointed arch 235, reduces size of Viceroy's house 238, son dies of war wounds 254, dislikes W. Nicholson's portrait 255, Order of the Garter 262, & gradient 262–3, fights for New Delhi 269, at opening of Viceroy's House 375

Hardinge, Lady, influential 215, reassuring 222, stands in for sick Viceroy 224, & ELL's jokes 224–5, dies of cancer 254

Hatchard Smith, 151–2

Hay-Boyd, Major, 9

Heal, Robert, 357, 358

Heathcote, 163–4, 178, 200

Heaton, Aldham, 121, 122

Hemingway, John Thomas, 163-4

Herbert, Auberon, 253

Hestercombe, 154–5 & n, 383

Hewitt, Samuel, 48

Hill, Sir Claude, 263, 268

Hillingdon, Lord & Lady, 130, 133

Hoare, Walter, 145, brickworks 174; 207

Hobson, Mr, 173

Holderness, Sir Thomas, Permanent Sec. at India Office, 221

Home, Earl of, 40

Homewood, 139, 141–2

Hore Belisha, Leslie, Minister of Transport, 397

Horne, Edgar, 131, 138 & n

Horner, Frances Lady, 89, 93, 96, 167, 201, 264, 288, 328, commissions muniment room 382, & Father D'Arcy 394

Horsley, Gerald, 48

Howard, Esmé, Ambassador in Washington, 336–7

Hudson, Edward, owner of *Country Life* 129, description 142–3, & Deanery Garden 143–4, & photographs 144, partisan & publicist 145, 151, Lindisfarne Castle 149, & Prince & Princess of Wales 179, ELL stays with in London 194, shops for Lutyens children 242; annoys EL 265, & Robert 296, 297, 305

Hull, town plan for, 413

Hussey, Christopher, 23, 97, 120, 124n 137, 146, 197, 'Flood Tide' 201, & ELL's appointment to India 211 & n, & Britannic House 307, & Queen Anne's Gate Office 317, Thiepval & ELL's Elemental Mode 352, speculates on ELL's religious sense 365, Boswell to ELL: greatest architectural biography 382, at Garrick Club, ELL's obituary 416

The Hut, 68, 73, 75, 96

Hydrabad Nizam of, palace built for 294, 321

Hylton, Lord, 145

Imperial War Graves Commission, ELL architectural advisor to 277, sees battlefields in France 278, Great War Stone 278–280, 284, designs for war graves 311, St. Quentin 316–7, & French obstruction 351

Incorporated Association of Architects & Surveyors, ELL President 381

Irwin, Lord, Viceroy, 359, charm 375, as Halifax 404

Jackson, T.A., 47

Jacob, Sir Swinton, his architecture 223, resigns 235

Jagger, C.S., 303

James, Willie, 152

James, Mrs Willie, 147, 152n, 157

Jekyll, Aggie, Lady, 96n, 163, 246

Jekyll, Francis (Timmy), biography of Gertrude Jekyll 389

Jekyll, Gertrude, meets ELL 56. Architectural education of ELL: explores Surrey with 57 & n, 58,

Philip Webb & Arts & Crafts 59, 65, *Old West Surrey* 58, 71, 129, as Bumps 67, Plazzoh design discarded 68, The Hut 68, Munstead Wood 71. Her influence with clients: 69, Chances 113–114; 123–4, Mirrielees 128, and Hudson 142. Meets EL 96, 97, 'The Lament of the Neglected' 110, stays with ELL & EL 169, lifestyle 182, war-work 246, meets Lady Sackville 279, & Great War Stone 279, planting of war graves 280 & n, & Queen Mary's Dolls' House 303, aged 389, her tomb 389 & n

Jekyll, Sir Herbert, 71, 73, Commissioner for British Section of International Exhibition in Paris 125, ELL gets commission for British Pavilion 125, 163, funeral 389

Jekyll, Julia, 71

Jersey, Earl & Countess of, 397

Johannesburg Art Gallery, 199, 200

John, Augustus, portrait of ELL 281; 331, 406

Johnson, Herbert, & Marsh Court 145–6, 245; 383

Jones, Lady (Enid Bagnold) 355

Jones, Sir Roderick, 355, 362, 394

Jordan, Furneaux, & Britannic House 306–307

Keen, Arthur, Chairman of Thames Bridges Conference, 369

Kerr, Lord Mark, 9

Kipling, Rudyard, 24, 29, 'If' 258, 352

Knebworth, 81, 85, 87, 119, 171, *golf club houses* 174

Knoblock, Edward, 267

Knothe, Helen, 308, 319, 332

Knott, Ralph, wins County Hall Competition, 166

Krishnamurti, as Alcyone in the *Theosophist* 191. Boyhood: discovered by Leadbeater & adopted by Mrs Besant 192, arrival in London 204, mothered by EL 204, future planned by Mrs Besant 205, Miss Dodge pays allowance 207, father demands separation from Leadbeater 216, friends with Robert 219, at Varengeville 230–1, motorbike 247, Mrs Besant wins custody 243, smart clothes 259. Education: George Arundale tutor 242, fails for Oxford, Cambridge & London universities 285 & n, in Paris to learn French 295, 308. Theosophist conventions & camps: Benares 308, Sydney 313, Ommen, Holland 330, 355, Adyar 332–3, 341–2. At Ojai 314, 341, 353–4. Relations with EL: 231, infatuated with 257, 295, 308, in Taormina 242, mother & son ceremony 243, rebukes EL & Mary 330, 332–3, rumoured engagement to Mary 353–5. Mystical experiences: the 'process' 314, 318, 330, at Nitya's death 342, speaks as Christ 342, dissolves Order of Star 361, nihilism 381

Lamb, Walter, secretary of RA 405–6, 411

Lambay, 171–3, 229, 244, 260

Lancaster, Osbert, 49, & *Observer* 407

Landseer, Sir Edwin, 3, 4, 13

Landseer, Jessie, 30, 69

Lane, Hugh, & Lindsey House 197–8, & Johannesburg Art Gallery 199, & Dublin Art Gallery 228–30, & Plumpton Place 230, drowned 230

Lansbury, George, 256, 276, 289

Lascelles, Sir Allen, 292

Lascombe, 122

Latham, Charles, 144

Lawless, Emily, 114
Leadbeater, C.W., finds Krishna & Nitya in India 192, father demands boys' separation from 216, in Genoa with EL, Barbie & Robert 219–20, character 220, 223, homosexual 224, 257, & EL 285, 314, in Sidney as Bishop of Old Catholic Church 313, his community with Betty & Mary 339–40, Theosophical Congress at Adyar 342, quarrels with Arundale 342, turns against Krishna 375
Lees–Milne, James, 174n, 416
Les Communes, 189 & n, 196, 230
Lethaby, William R., 48
Leverhulme, Lord, 291
Lewis, Sir George, 130, 297, 301
Lindisfarne Castle, 149–50, & Prince & Princess of Wales 179
Lindsey House, Cheyne Walk, 197
Lindsey, Norah, 382
Links, Joe, 413, 418
Linlithgow, Marquess of, Viceroy, 402–3
Little Thakeham, 150-2 & n, 178
Little White House, 110, 155
Liverpool Cathedral, Dr Downey appoints ELL to build 363, classicism v. modernism 364, description & comparison with *Thiepval* & St. Pauls 365 & n, presents plans 370, no estimate 371, crypt 371n, model at 13 Mansfield St 384, go ahead 409, model exhibited at RA 410
Llewellyn, William, 406
Lloyd, George, Lord, 253, Governor of Bombay 292, 308
Lloyd George, David, 182, 288
Lloyd, Nathaniel, 203
Lloyd, W.A.S., 317–8
Loch, Lord, 104, 114
Locker–Lampson, Frederick & Jane, 92, 102, 130, 133

Lorimer, Robert, 5, 124
Lorne, Earl of, 111
Louise, Princess, 111-3, 124, 139
Lowe, Sir Hudson, 7
Lucas, E.V., 293
Lucas, William, 394
Lucknow University, 255n, 305
Lutkens, Bartold (Bartholomew), 6
Lutkens, Martha, 6
Lutkens, Nicholas, 6
Lutyens, Aileen (sister), 5, 16, 63, 64, 65
Lutyens, Anna, 7
Lutyens, Arthur (brother), 16, 30, 40, 63, 156
Lutyens, Augustus Wilhelm, 7
Lutyens, Barbara (Barbie), birth 126–127, & Jekyll 128; 148, 154, 170, 179, 182, 191, in Genoa with Leadbeater 219–212, & Nitya 257, reacts against Theosophy 258, social ambitions 275, 290, 291, engaged to Euan Wallace, 295, married in Savoy Chapel 296, anti-appeasement 404, tragic war 417
Lutyens, Beatrice Airey, wife of Charles, brother, 28
Lutyens, Betty see Lutyens, Elisabeth
Lutyens, General Charles (grandfather), 7, 8
Lutyens, Captain Charles (father), 3, 7, 8, soldier 9, 11, marriage 10. His painting: becomes a painter 11, 12, his paintings 13, of horses 14, & presentation pictures of hunts 15, later painting 64, Venetian Secret 31, 64, 130. Move to Thursley 23, 25, 26, love of hunting 27, short of money 29–30, 63, eccentric 32, 45, sight fails 65, economies 65, 66, 108, 116, & EL 130, 137, 163, dies 258
Lutyens, Charles (Charlie), brother, 16, 17, 28, 29, 63, 106
Lutyens, Charlotte nee Wangenheim, 7

473

Lutyens, David, 417
Lutyens, Eadred, 302, 323n
Lutyens, Sir Edwin Landseer, birth 3, baptised 4, childhood 4-7, 10, 11. Boyhood: 16-17, rheumatic fever 17, close to mother 17, 19, 40, Claddah ring & mother's death 163, & brothers 25, school 27-8, Surrey boyhood & pane of glass 32-3, & Caldecott 34. Student: Kensington School of Art 36-40, describes St. Bartholomew's 38-40, Normandy 41-2. Young architect: Ernest George's office 45, 49-52, meets Norman Shaw 46, first commissions 52, 53, walking tour in Wales with H. Baker 58, 59. And Gertrude Jekyll: meets 56, explores Surrey with 57 & n, 58, introduced to Philip Webb & Arts & Crafts 59, 65, Bumps 67, builds for 68-9, Plazzoh design discarded 68, The Hut 68, ELL & Jekyll partnership 69, 147, her influence with clients 69, ELL's architectural education & Munstead Wood 71-2. And Barbara Webb: Milford House 74, tutoring 74-5, *Chateau d'Ease en Air sur Fleuve des Reves* sketchbook 76, her influence on engagement 95, love for her 109, illness & death 76, 109, 116. Engagement: obstacles to 103-4, insures his life 104, engaged 105, feelings of inferiority 107, incompatability 108-9, ideal interior 108, little white house 110-111. Marriage: 119, honeymoon 119-20, love-making 126-7, approval-seeking & fears 156, growing apart 167, sex 168, worries 200, 206, 207, no more sex 247-8, depression 258, 264, war brings EL closer 405. Homes: 29 Bloomsbury Sq 121-2, redecorated 137; 31 Bedford Sq 251, 255, 275;

9 Montagu St 282; 13 Mansfield St 290, decorated 291, Dolls' house at 304, 319, 322, office party at 358, too big 386, Betty in basement flat 386-7, ELL & EL in flat on bedroom floor 405, in the Blitz 407, dies there 414. Health: rheumatic fever 17, dysentry 238, operation for chronic hydrocele 264; 347, 354, pneumonia 403, stroke 407, motor smash 408, lung cancer 409, last illness & death 414. Relations with his children: with Robert 219-220, makes him ward of court 297, forbids his marriage to Eva 297-8, 301, 305, 361, collaborates with Robert 396; family holiday at Folly Farm 266, Barbie's wedding 296; with Mary 335, 353, 355-6, 368, 389-90; with Betty 354, 408, 414; Mediterranean cruise with Ursula 388-9; picture letters 412. Income: 104, 327, expenses 121, overdraft 275, office bills 287, commissions cancelled 385, financial difficulties 386, 405. Lady Sackville: 265-6, plans her house 267-8, confides his problems 268, McNed & MacSack 276-7, she commissions Augustus John to paint ELL 281, Sussex Sq, Brighton a failure 286, game of patron & artist 296, 298, 301, 303, 305, Rolls Royce 315, possible physical relations 312, 315-6, 322, private language 316, stays with 323, to Jekyll with 323, money 347, MacSack angry 335, 347, 357, avoids her 384-5. Jokes: 46, 50, 180, 224, 253-4, 282, 286, 292, 301, 304, 307, 319, 321, 334, 336, 338, 370 & n, 382, 383, 386, 388, 393, 402, 405. Politics: 182, 194, hatred of modern middle class life 332. Honours: Knighthood 281, RA

474

227, Royal Gold Medal for Architecture 306, Institute of American Architects gold medal 336, Knight Commander of the Indian Empire 368, resigns from RIBA 369–70, President of Incorporated Institute of Architects and Surveyors 381, Master of Art Workers' Guild 381, elected President Royal Academy 403, meetings 405–6, 414, O.M. 409, funeral in Westminster Abbey 414. Offices: 6 Gray's Inn Sq 101, at 29 Bloomsbury Sq 122, & Badcock 123; 150, 17 Queen Anne's Gate, pipes & Paget 194, 201, office life 228, 311, queues of clients 244, practice melts with war 245–6, Queen Ann's Gate let 276, 283, re-opens 317, ELL at work 317–8, closes 386, Apple Tree Yard New Delhi Office 235, 283, 302, 17 Bolton St routine 357–8, closes 386; worst paid draftsmen 413, 5 Eaton Gate 386, sold 405, moves to ground floor of 13 Mansfield St 405. Architecture: Influence of Ernest George 51–2, Surrey style 54, influence of Jekyll 57–8, and Philip Webb 59, 68, and proportion 72, and art nouveau 102 & n, 112 & n, 124–5, and little white house 110, architectural wit 141–2, geometry 143, Wren 157, Palladio & High Game 158, 'Wrennaissance' 174, classicism 164, 178, 184 & n, 'flood tide' 201, escape to world of pure art 207, dislike of Anglo–Indian & Mogul 213, 216, 217, 218–9, Taj Mahal 216 & n, battle of styles 222, Mandu damned 223, pointed arch 235, ELL's synthisis of East & West 235–6, 239–40, entasis on Great War Stone 278, Cenotaph 289, elemental geometry 317, 329, on American architecture 336, 'elemental mode' 352, & at Liverpool Cathedral 364, on Corbusier & Chandigar 358–9, and modern architecture 381–2; Parthenon disappoints 388–9. Country houses described: *Chinthurst Hill* 70, *Munstead Wood* 71–2, *The Pleasaunce* 102, *Rosneath* 112n, *Orchards* 115, dream houses 124, 127, *Bois des Moutiers* 125–6, *Goddards* 128–9, *Tigbourne* 131, *Grey Walls* 139, *Homewood* 142, *Hudson & Deanery Garden* 143–4, *Marsh Court* 145–6, *Lindisfarne* 149–50, *Little Thakeham* 152 & n, *Hestercombe* 154–5, Princess Dolgorouki & *Nashdom* costs 158, *Ashby St. Legers* 158, *Heathcote* 163–4, *Lambay* & *Barings* 171–3, Julus Drewe & *Castle Drogo* 195–7, Farrer Bros & *Salutation* 203, N. Lloyd & *Great Dixter* 203, *Folly Farm* 266–7, *Middleton Park* 397; see *Country Life*. Government commissions: British Pavilion at Paris Expo 1900 125, gold medal for 132, consulting architect to Royal Commission responsible for exhibitions in Italy 183, in Genoa 183, commissioned to design British entry 183–4, exhibition building later British School in Rome 259, & St. Pauls 184; works for County Hall competition 165, fails 166; *Hampstead Garden Suburb* 174–7; *British Embassy in Washington* 336–8, vists USA 336–7, Waterloo Bridge 348. Charing Cross Bridge: ELL & LCC v. RIBA row 367 & n; consultant architect to Highway Development Survey for Greater London 395, first flight in aeroplane 395, London plan damages reputation 406–7; plans for Hull 413–4. Institutions & Financial Houses: *Theosophical Society HQ* 206, *Midland Bank* 328–9, *Britannic House* 306–7, *Grosvenor House* 350. South Africa: 198–200, plays the fool 199, criticises & infuriates Baker 199–200. New Delhi: appointment to Delhi Planning Committee 211 & n, 212, leaves for India 212, surveys site on elephant 212, estimate 216, argument with Hardinge re site 218–9, King & Queen shown drawings 218, Baker appointed partner 221, arrives 226, fees 227; quarrel with Baker re fees 236–7, tour of India with Baker & Harcourt Butler 239–40, to India with W. Nicholson 253, fears EL's Indian Home Rule politics 265, New Delhi in the balance 269, 271, life on board ship 270, 292, life at Raisina Mill 292, 294, Montagu-Chelmsford Reform 292, Council Chamber 292, Delhi Gate 293 & 302n, *Record Office* 302. *Viceroy's House*: first sketches 215, synthesis of East & West evolved 236, Baker changes city plan: secretariat on level with Viceroy's House, ELL doesn't notice implication 226, notices 241, ELL to reduce costs 237–8, reduces plans & Hardinge approves 241, relations with Baker deteriorate 255, row over gradients 261–4, gradient alteration closed 268, 310, ELL appeals to King & Queen 268–9, political naivety 270, EL advises him not to resign 310, Bakerloo 311, the garden 271, building 272, 334, furnishing 360, 367, doors close on ELL 368, Robert Byron 368, 378–80, official opening 375, description 375–8, Lady Willingdon's alterations 402, stays with Viceroy, Lord Linlithgow 402–3, makes report on alterations 403, Architectural Adviser to War Graves Commission 277, 311, visits battlefields in France 278, designs memorials 283, Great War Stone 278–80, War Shrine 284, see *Cenotaph, Thiepval, Liverpool Cathedral, Queen Mary's Dolls' House*

Lutyens, Elisabeth, (Betty later known as Liz), 169, 179, 182, difficult 243, 'chain of love' 256, at boarding school 282, alone at 13 Mansfield St 291, 320, 331, with ELL 354–5, moves into Mansfield St basement 386, parties 386. Theosophy: at Adyar 332, & Krishna 332–3, hating Leadbeater's community in Sydney 339–40, resentful of Theosophy 386. Music: Royal College of Music 354, composer 356, 386–7, 418. Marries Ian Glennie 387, children 404, marries Edward Clarke 405, 408, ELL shirks visiting 408

Lutyens, Lady Emily, forbears & family 81–5, unhappy childhood 85–6, Rev Whitwell Elwin 86–7, Wilfrid Blunt 89–94, Judith 90, 93–4, meets ELL 94, meets Jekyll 96, obstacles to engagement 103–4, engaged 105, ambition for ELL 107, tastes differ 108, marriage 119, honeymoon 119–20, 29 Bloomsbury Sq 121, spartan 122, love-making 126, 127, Thursley 130–1, EL's relations as clients 139, problems with marriage 159, 167, 168, & Arthur Chapman 169, 181, collects Con from prison 184, vegetarian 122, 193, at suffragette health farm 201, no more sex 206, 247, 309, servants 251, VAD 259, economises 275–6, left-wing politics 276, 313, money 290, as hostess 296, Zionist 305, with ELL in New Delhi 309, 334, advises ELL not to resign over gradient 310, menopause 313, on ELL's relationship with Lady Sackville 316, on her marriage 362, at opening of Viceroy's House 375–6, her remorse re ELL 392, anti-appeasement 404, nurses ELL at 13 Mansfield St 409–10, his death 415, *A Blessed Girl* 417. Children: birth of Barbara 126, of Robert 148, of Ursula 159, of Betty 169, of Mary 178, seaside life 154, 179, 181–2, 219, their education 170, 179, relations with Robert 204, at Varengeville 205, 275, & Barbie 275–6, 290, & Robert & Eva 297–301, & Eva's relations 305; guilt regarding Robert 361, central to their lives 386–92, & grandchildren 404. Public life: campaigns for Moral Education League 168, joins Women's Social & Political Union 169, sells *Votes for Women* 181, resigns from WSPU 182, launches Home Rule for India in London League 265. Theosophy: introduced to by Mme Mallet 189–90, meets Mrs Besant 190, new life in theosophy 193, 201–2, promoted to Esoteric Section 204, Order of Star of the East 205, on lecture tours with Mrs Besant 205, 212, Genoa with Leadbeater 219–20, edits *Herald of the Star in the East* 242, 256, 276, Benares 308–9, accepted by 'The Masters' 314, Ehrwald 318, Adyar 320, 332, Star Camp Ommen, Holland 329–30, Sidney with Leadbeater 340, Huizen with Mrs Besant 340, rejects theosophy & follows Krishna 342–3, resigns from Theosophical Society 375. Krishnamurti: arrival 204, obsessed by 204, 231, 235, 247, 257–8, 295, 308, 330, in Taormina 242, mother & son ceremony 243, & his 'process' 314, 318, *Candles in the Sun* 329, 390, 417, rebuked by 330, depressed by his nihilism 381

Lutyens, Eva Lubryjinska, description 297, ELL won't accept 297, operation 305, marries Robert 307, miscarries 331, at 13 Mansfield St. 361, divorce 417

Lutyens, Frances Jane nee Fludger, grandmother, 7, 8

Lutyens, Francis (Frank), brother, 8, 16, 27, 40, 246

Lutyens, Frederick, brother, 16, 17, 30, 33, *Mr Spinks and his Hounds* 65

Lutyens, Graeme, brother, 16, 17–18, 28

Lutyens, John, brother, 16, 29

Lutyens, Lionel, brother, 16, 389

Lutyens, Louisa, aunt, 8

Lutyens, Margaret, sister, 16, 63

Lutyens, Mary nee Gallwey, mother, confinements 3, 4, childhood in Ireland & marriage 9–10, 12, ELL favourite child 17–19, 25, absorbed in religion 32, 54, 55, 65, ELL writes to 38–40, & EL 106, 116, 130–1, death 163

Lutyens, Mary, aunt, 8, 9

Lutyens, Mary, daughter, 10, 66, 153, born 178–9, 220, at Varengeville 231, loves Nitya 231, 339, brought up by Nannie 243, "chain of love" 256, at Folly Farm 267, evacuated to Church Stretton 282, finds Krishna & Nitya glamorous 315, at Adyar 320–1, stays with Victor Lytton in Calcutta 320, at Star Camp 330, & ELL 335, 356, in

INDEX

Leadbeater's community in Sydney 340, on Abram's Box at Ojai, California 353, & Krishna 353–4, & Sir Roderick Jones 355–6, & Enid Bagnold 356, writer 356, engaged to Anthony Sewell 361–2, marriage 368, *Forthcoming Marriages* 389, & Ursula 390, & death of ELL 415, & Joe Links 418

Lutyens, Robert, 8, birth 148; 154, 170, 191, & anger with EL 204, at Miss Motto's School for girls 204, painting lessons 205, portrait by E.J. Blanche 205, King Alfred's School Hampstead 219, 275, ELL on his education 219–20, Genoa with Leadbeater 220, dilettante 254, clothes 275, joins up under age as private 284, sent down from Cambridge 296, gets job at *Country Life* 296, 297, 305; wants to marry Eva Lubryjinska 297, ELL disapproves & makes Robert ward of court 297, marries in Scotland 301, flat in Mayfair 305, marriage difficulties 305, on *Daily Mail* 309 & n, & Brendan Bracken 349, & Eva at 13 Mansfield St 361, in *Forthcoming Marriages* 390, collaborates with ELL on Cockington Scheme 396, designs Baker St office for M & S 396, to succeed ELL as architect for Liverpool Cathedral 396, awestruck by Viceroy's House 402, in Blitz 407, refuses to sell 13 Mansfield St 411, publishes appreciation of ELL 412, at ELL's deathbed 414, marriages & death 417–8

Lutyens, Ursula, born 159, 170, 179, portrait by W. Nicholson 267, Church Stretton 282, wants to work in ELL's office 307, with Victor Lytton in Calcutta 320, stays with ELL in New Dellhi 321, ukelele 321, social success 331, engaged to Ridley 331, wedding 332, depression 361, 388, Corsica 361, Mediterranean cruise with ELL 388–9, & Lawrence Whistler 391, ELL stays with 409

Lutyens, Samuel, 13–4

Lutyens, William, brother, 5, 16, 66 & n 119, 131, 154

Lutyens & Ripley bill brokers, 6, 14

Lyall, Sir Alfred, 73, 116

Lyttleton, Alfred, 129, 139, 140 & n, 149, 174, 176

Lyttleton, DD, 129, 139, 140 & n, 207

Lytton, Bulwer 1st Baron, EL's grandfather, 81, 82, 83, 88, occult novels *Zanoni* & *A Strange Story* key texts for Theosophists 191

Lytton, Con (Constance), 82, 85, described 88–89, 92, 109, & Homewood 141–2, militant suffragette 180, arrested & Holloway 181, arrested in Newcastle 182, speech in Queen's Hall 183, in prison as Jane Warton & forcibly fed 184–5, health 185, stroke 217

Lytton, Edith Countess nee Villiers, 84, 86, widow 88, impoverished becomes Lady in Waiting to Queen Victoria 91, 113; opposes EL's engagement 103–4, 105, relents 106, portrait by Burne-Jones 137, & Homewood, 139, 142, upset by Con as suffragette 180–1, 183

Lytton, Neville, 3rd Earl, 85, 88, 125, marriage to Judith 128, 137, 140, 170

Lytton, Pamela Countess, 167, 170, transforms Knebworth with ELL 171, 181, 184, 291, 334, 408

Lytton, Rosina Lady nee Wheeler, 82, 168

Lytton, Robert, 1st Earl (Owen

INDEX

Meredith), 81, character 82-3, as poet 83, as diplomat 84, Viceroy 84-5, Ambassador in Paris 85-6, death 87, 88, 103

Lytton, Victor 2nd Earl, 85, 88, 116, 119, 128, 142, fishing with ELL in Norway 159; 170, 171, 179, Chairman of Royal Commission for Exhibitions in Italy 183, commissions ELL to design British Pavilion in Rome 184, 310, Governor of Bengal 320, ELL, EL & Mary stay with in Calcutta 320, 359, Chairman of National Theatre Committee 395

Macartney, Mervyn, 48
McKenna, Reginald & Pamela nee Jekyll, 276n, 319, patrons 327-8, Midland Bank 328, Halnaker Hall 393
Mackintosh, Charles Rennie, 112, 137
Mackmurdo, A.H., 127
Magdalene College, Cambridge, *Benson Court*, 385
Malet, Etienne, 260
Mallet, Guillaume, 125, 189, 193, 295
Mallet, Isabelle, 318
Mallet, Marie-Adelaide, 125, & Theosophy 189, 205, 276, 295
Mangles, Harry, 54, 55, 56, 70
Manziarlys (Theosophists in Paris) 295, 308, 318
Marie Louise, Princess, 303, 304, 322
Markham, Violet, 207
Marks, Mrs of M & S, 396
Marochetti, Baron Carlo, sculptor, 12, 13
Marsh Court, 110n, 138, 145-6 & n, 150, 155, 177, 383
Mary, Queen, 179, visits Apple Tree yard 268, & Doll's House 303, 312, plays with dolls 319, 322
Maxwell, Elsa, 312, 319
Medd, Henry, 291

Melba, Dame Nellie, 307 & n
Mells Park House, 288, 328, Muniment Room 382
Mendl, Lady see de Wolfe, Elsie
Merriman, Dr, 3
Merton, Zackery & Antonia, & Folly Farm 266, 267, 276, at Adyar 342
Messman, David & Mary, 6
Meston, Sir Thomas, 221
Metcalf, Tom, 377
Middlefield, 174 & n
Middleton Park, collaboration with Robert 397
Midland Bank Piccadilly 328, *Poultry* 328-9, model shown at RA 329
Milbank Housing Development, 351
Mildmay, Alfred, 194, 202
Mildmay, Frank, 245
Milford House, 73, 95, 101, 109, 116, 121
Miller, William, 14
Milne, Oswald, 150, 151
Mirrielees, Frederick, 128, 195
Molyneux, Rev. Capel, 4
Mond, Sir Alfred, 284
Monkton, 152
Montagu, Edwin, Indian Under Secretary, 214-5, 225-6, Indian Secretary 272, Breccles 283n, sacked 310
Moore, Tom, 10
Morgan, Sir Herbert, 303
Morris, William, 34, & S.P.A.B. 35, 37, 41, 47, 76, 97
Morrison, Herbert, 369
Mothecombe, 194
Munstead Wood, 68, & building with Jekyll 71-3, cost 75; 113, 114, 115, Lorimer on 124; 124, 143, 144, 383, ELL rents 390
Muntzer, George, upholsterer, 147, 258, 303
Murray Scott, Sir John, 266, 315
Mustoe, W.R., Head of Horticultural Dept., Delhi, 360, 403

479

INDEX

Muthesius, Herman, *Das Englisch Haus* 156

Nairn, Ian, 115, 132n, 152n
Nannie, Priscilla, 4, 5, 18, 65,165
Nannie, Alice Louisa Sleath, 126, 127, 128, 148, 170, 181-2, 212, importance 243; 322, 404
Narianiah, 192, demands sons' seperation from Leadbeater 216
Nashdom, 157
The National Theatre, plans for 395, 413
Nauheim, Clare, draughtsman, 283 & n
Nehru, Pandit, 361
Nelson, Sir Amos, 301
Nevill, Ralph, 54
New Delhi, the site: George V's foundation stone on north ridge 213, ELL & 'experts' chose SW site at Malcha 213, Hardinge reverts to north ridge 218, ELL takes plans to King 218, southern site agreed 227. Plan: criticised by Lanchester 218, 380. Style of Architecture: Indian or Western? 214-218, Battle of the Styles political 222, Indo Saracenic 223. Costs: estimates unrealistic 226, 271, architects' fees 227. Politics: New Delhi in the balance 269, 271, 310, ELL unaware 271, Montagu – Chelmsford Reform necessitates Council Chamber 292. Building starts 271-2, Delhi Gate 293, Record Office 302, 29,000 men on site 333, re-starts after war 333, quarrying 333-4, timber-drying 360
New Place, Botley 178n
Newton, Ernest, 48
Nicholson, William, 152, 153 & n, with ELL in India 251-3, portrait of Hardinge 255, visits ELL in hospital 264, portrait of Ursula 267, at Folly Farm 267, at 11 Apple Tree Yard 284, & Queen Mary's Dolls' House 303, Jekyll's boots 389
Nicolson, Harold & Vita, Macvitas, & Long Barn 277, 279, 287, on ELL–Lady Sackville relationship 315-6, on EL 281
Nicolson, Nigel, 335
Nitya, 192, education 207, in Taormina 242, & Barbie 257, at 13 Mansfield St 294, TB 308, 313, at Ojai, California 314, & Abrams Box 314, & Mary 332, 339, illness & death 341
Noble, Saxton, 382, 411
Norman, Florence Lady, 228
Northcliffe, Lord, 309

Olcott, Colonel, 190
16 Onslow Square, 3, description 4; 12, 14, 49, 63
Orchards, 114-5, 144, 149, 150
Overstrand Chapel, 130, 138
Overstrand Hall, 130

Pagenstecher of Wiesbaden, Dr, 66
Paget, Mr & Mrs, 194
Paget, Walburga, 69, 88, 131
Palladio, 157, 158
Pallandt, Baron, 329
Pallant, Amanda, 404
Pankhurst, Emily, 180
Pankhurst, Sylvia, 256
Peneranda, Duke of, in Spain 260, 265, 270, 282
Penfold, J.W., 35
Penrose, Mr, schoolmaster, 28
Persotum, bearer & friend, 213, 222, 293, 301, 403
Peterborough, Carr Glynn, Bishop of, 111, 115
Pethick Lawrence, Mrs, recruits EL 169, 180, sells *Votes for Women* 181
Peto, Harold, 49

Pevsner, Nikolaus, 196-7, & *Britannic House* 306, & *Midland Bank, Poultry* 329, & *Reuter's* 394
Phillips, Mrs Lionel, & Johannesburg Art Gallery 198
Phipps, Paul, 258
Plank, George, & Queen Mary's Dolls' House 303, ELL confides in 316
The Pleasaunce, 102, 130
Plowden, Mrs, 85 & n, 170
Plumpton Place, 230
Plymouth, Earl of, 131
Ponsonby, Arthur, 88, 141, 142
Porcelli, Mrs, 393 & n, 411
Portman, The Hon E.W. & Mrs 154
28 Portman Square, 202
Pound, Ezra, 265
Poynter, Edmund, 227
Prior, Edward, 48
32 Queen Anne's Gate, 173

Queen Mary's Dolls' House, scale & description 303-4, cost to ELL 303, *The Book of the Queen's Dolls' House* 304, dream-house 304-5, & Lady Sackville 305, at 13 Mansfield St 319, Queen Mary plays with 319, at British Empire Exhibition 322, success 322

Railton, William, 13
Rajagopal, 318, 341
Rand Regiments Memorial, 199, 200
Rashtrapati Bhavan see Viceroy's House under Lutyens, Sir Edwin
Read, Mr, 91
Record Office, New Delhi, 302
Reading, Lord, Viceroy, 309, 310, disliked by ELL 359
Reading, Lady, 321
The Red House, 75, 76 & n, 196
Reid Dick, Sir William, bust of ELL 378

Reilly, Professor Charles, 349, 358, 359, & Liverpool Cathedral 363-4, 370, & National Theatre 395
Renishaw, 180
Reuter's, 394
Ricardo, Halsey, 114
Riddell, George, 143, 144
RIBA, 48, 151 & n, 152, 211, 367, 369-70
Ridley, Ursula, Viscountess see Lutyens, Ursula
Ridley, Matt, Viscount, 331, 388, 390, 391
Riley, W.E., 165
Ritchie, Sir Richard, Permament Secretary at India Office 211
Robinson, William, 56, 69, 107
Rodd, Sir Rennell, 183
Roehampton House, 198, 245
Rowton, Lord, 88
The Royal Academy, & Venetian Secret 31, schools 52, ELL elected to 227, President of 403, meetings 404-5, *London Replanned* 406-7, Royal Academy Council 407, model of Midland Bank, Poultry, exhibited at 329, model of Liverpool Cathedral 410
Royal Fine Art Commission, & Mercantile Marine Monument 348 & n, vetoes bridge in St James's Park 349, Charing Cross Bridge 369
Rubens, Olive, 266, 277, 287
Rubens, Walter, 287
Ruskin, John, 37, 41, 42, 164, 235n

Sackville, Victoria, Lady, 67n, meets ELL 265, perfect client 266, Knole 266, ELL confides in re EL 268, 270, & EL 276, 281, MacSacs 276 & n, marriage to Lionel ends 277, meets Jekyll 279, commissions John portrait 281, leaves Knole 287, pays for move to Mansfield St. 290, & ELL 312, ELL repays 315, relations

with ELL physical? 315–6, Rolls
Royce 315, 321–2, 335, 336, 347,
health 347, 351, 354, 356–7,
quarrelsome 362, paranoid 384,
libel case fails 385. Her houses:
wants to build 267, plans 268,
drawings 271, 280, buys 39–40a
Sussex Square, Brighton 282–3,
decorates 285–6, a costly folly 286,
& A.J. Thomas 288, 298, 315, 347,
alterations to 39 Sussex Sq 296,
problems with estimates 298, &
Ebury St 298, White Lodge Roedean
315, 321–2, Georgian porch for
323, bungled 335, garden 347;
Streatham 362, 384
Sackville, Lionel, Lord, 265, 277, 287,
362
Salisbury, Marquess of, 89
Salisbury, Marchioness of, 106
Salutation, 203
Sanger, Mr, 285
Santona, Duke & Duchess of, 260,
270, 282
Schultz, Robert Weir, 124, 133, 152
Scott, Sir Gilbert, 34, 46, 47
Scott, Sir Giles Gilbert, President of
RIBA, 370, 384, 394, 406
Selborne, Earl of, 289
Sewell, Anthony, 361, 368–9, 390,
404
Sewell, Percy, 369
Shakespeare's England Exhibition at
Earl's Court, 212, 217
Shaw, Bernard, 191
Sharpe, Miss, secretary of
Theosophical Society, 190, 191
Shaw, Richard Norman, 34, 38, 45,
46, 47, 49, 51, 52, 70, 101, 121,
145, 156, 157, 158, 165, 202
Shoosmith, A.G., 301, 367–8
Singh, Hari, Maharajah of Kashmir,
360
Sitwell, Sir George & Lady Ida, 180,
245, 393

Smith, Mrs Eustace, 179
Smith, Francis, (ELL's solicitor), 236,
330, 384, 411
Smith, Professor Roger, 37, 41
36 Smith Square, 328
Soane, Sir John, 115, 328, 323
South Kensington School of Art, 36,
38, 42
Solomon, J.M., 286, 287
SPAB, 35
Spence, Sir James, 409
Spencer, Colonel, 122
7 St. James's Square, 202
St. Peter's Home, 154
16 Stafford Place, 397
Stamfordham, Lord, 269, 284
Stamp, Gavin, 130n, 328n, 378n, 406
Stephen, Leslie, 95
Stephen, Vanessa, 95
Stephen, Virginia, 95
Stokes, Lady, 408
Strachey, Colonel, 149
Strachey, Lytton, 83, 85, 114, 142,
150
Strachey, Sir Richard & Lady, 85
Streatfield, Mrs Gerard, 101, 106,
109, 114, 123, 126
Street, G.E., 34, 41, 46, 48, 51
Summerson, John, 382, profile of ELL
in *Night & Day* 392, obituary in
Architect & Building News 415
39–40a Sussex Sq, Brighton (see
Sackville, Victoria, Lady)
Sutherland, Duchess of, 335, 338
Sutro, Alfred, 284, 363
Swinton, Captain George, Chairman
of LCC, on Delhi Planning
Committee, 212, 213, 214, works
on report 216, & the site 218, 225

Taj Mahal, 216
Tennant, H.J., 174, 178
Tennant, Mrs Jack, 246
Theosophical Society Headquarters,
190, 192, 212, estimate doubles

244, the Society in ruins 375
Thiepval, commissioned as St Quentin memorial to 60,000 missing 316–7, problems with French re height 352, site moved to Thiepval 352, design 352–3, ceremony at 387
Thomas, A.J., Head of ELL's office, 150, 198, in charge while ELL in India 228, dishonest? 228, 244, 248, has power of attorney 275, 413, does little work 283, sends out exorbitant bills 287, & EL 288, 290, & Lady Sackville 298, 301, 347, & Dolls' House 303, importance to ELL 317–8, sacked 396, 413
Thursley Cottage, 23, 24, 25, 30, 32, 55, squalid 65, 417
Tickner, George, 35
Tigbourne Court, 131–2, 137, 138 & n
Tribe, caretaker, 317
Turner, Father, 409
Tweed, John, 63, 130
Tyringham, *Temple* at, 323

Underwood, Thomas, 115
Unwin, Raymond, 175

Vandebilt, Anne, 312, 338
Verney, Captain E.H., RN, godfather, 3
de Vesci, Lord & Lady, 168
Victoria, Queen, 46, 106
Vincent, Lady Helen, 154
Viceroy's House see Lutyens, Sir Edwin
Vitelleschi, Madame, 95
Voysey, C.F.A., 127, 164, 258

Walcot, William, draws Dublin Art Gallery 229, Viceroy's House 241, & the gradient 262
Wallace, Barbara, see Lutyens, Barbara

Wallace, Euan, engaged to Barbara Lutyens 295 & n, marriage 296; 390, Minister of Transoport 403–4, death 417
Wallace, William 'Billy', 417
Wallace, Sir Richard, 266
Walton Heath Golf Club House, 174
Wands, William, draughtsman, 283
War Memorials: for Harold Tennant, Billy Congreve, Mark Noble & Derek Lutyens & pedestal for statue to Edward Horner 283, War Shrine in Hyde Park 284, Catafalque for Victory Parade 288, War Memorial in Colombo 339, Mercantile Marine Monument 348, Australian National War Memorial 394 (see also Cenotaph & Thiepval)
Ward, Herbert, (secretary to ELL), 286, 287, 301, 302
Ward, Lady Patricia, Patsy, 290, 321
Ware, General Fabian, Director of War Graves Commission 279, & Great War Stone 279; 348, & French objections to monuments 352
Waring, S.J., & War Shrine in Hyde Park 284
Warren Lodge, 95, 119
Warren, Margaret, 5
Washington Embassy, 335, 336
Watts, G.F., 13
Waugh, Evelyn, 393, 394, 413
Weaver, Lawrence, *Houses & Gardens by E.L. Lutyens* 124n, 244
Weaver, Mrs, 244
Webb, Aston, 39, 145, 165, sponsors ELL for RA 227, 244, 407
Webb, Barbara, 52, 53, 73, influences ELL 74–6, cancer 76; 81, in India 85, & Betty Balfour 89, 104, & EL 95, discourages engagement 97, illness & ELL's involvement 109–110, EL not ELL at deathbed 116; 126, 156

Webb, Bob, 73, 95, 114, 116, 119
Webb, Miss E., secretary & confidant to family, 396, 401, 405, 411, 413
Webb, Philip, 47, 51, 59, 383
Webb–Peploe, Rev. Hanmer, 5, 19, 39
Webbe, Mrs A.G. (Pussy), feminist influence on EL 155, 169, & modern marriage 168, & de Vesci scandal 168, sells *Votes for Women* with EL 181, 184, & Mrs Besant 190, 193
Wedgwood, James, 217, 313, 340, 341
Weizmann, Chaim, 297, 396
Wemyss, Earl of, 149
Wemyss, George, 63
Wemyss, Mrs George (Molly), ELL's favourite sister 16, her children's book 18, 24, 37; 45, 63
Westminster, Duke of, 64, 112
Westminster, Bendor, Duke of, 171, & Grosvenor House 350-1, & Detmar Blow 385
Westminster, Loelia Duchess, 385
Whalton Manor, 179
Wheeler, Anna, 82, 89
Wheeler, Francis, 82

Whistler, J.M., 26
Whistler, Lawrence, 391, 401
Whistler, Rex, 391, 393 & n
White Lodge, Roedean (see Sackville, Victoria, Lady)
Wilde, Oscar, 87
Williams, Rosalind, 314, 353
Williams–Ellis, Clough, 351, 411
Willingdon, Marquess of, 294
Willingdon, Marchioness of, 402
Wilson, Fleetwood, 226, 227
Wimborne, Lord, as Ivor Guest 158 & n, 260, 331; 411
Wittersham, 174, 207
Wodhouse, E., 285
WSPU (Women's Social & Political Union), 169, 181, 185
de Woolfe, Elsie, later Lady Mendl, 311, 312, 338
Woolley, Leonard, 253
Worthington, Hubert, 228, 244
Wright, Whitaker, 109
Wyndham, Percy, 26

Yeats, W.B., 228-9, 331, 354n
Younghusband, Francis, & theosophy 216n